VISUAL BASIC 5
CLIENT/SERVER
HOW-TO

Noel Jerke

George Szabo

David Jung

Don Kiely

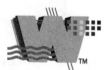

Waite Group Press™
A Division of
Sams Publishing
Corte Madera, CA

Publisher: Mitchell Waite
Associate Publisher: Charles Drucker

Acquisitions Manager: Susan Walton

Editorial Director: John Crudo
Project Editor: Laura E. Brown
Developmental Editor: Harry Henderson
Technical Editors: Chris Stone, Wei Li
Copy Editor: Ann Longknife/Creative Solutions

Production Director: Julianne Ososke
Production Manager: Cecile Kaufman
Senior Designer: Sestina Quarequio
Designer: Karen Johnston
Production Editor: K.D. Sullivan/Creative Solutions
Production: Jenaffer Brandt, Laura Delfeld, Polly Lavrick, Paula Lowell, Kevin Fulcher, Lisa Pletka
Illustrations: Steve Adams, Clint Lahnen, Casey Price, Marvin Van Tiem
Cover Illustration: ©Javier Romero/Image Bank

© 1997 by The Waite Group, Inc.®
Published by Waite Group Press™, 200 Tamal Plaza, Corte Madera, CA 94925.

Waite Group Press™ is a division of Sams Publishing.

Printed in the United States of America
97 98 99 • 10 9 8 7 6 5 4 3 2

Library of Congress Cataloging in Publication Data
Visual Basic 5 client/server how-to / Noel Jerke ... [et al.].
    p.   cm.
    Includes index.
    ISBN 1-57169-078-6
    1. Client/server computing. 2. Microsoft Visual BASIC.
I. Jerke, Noel.
QA76.9.C55V58 1997
005.2'768--dc21
                                   97-5116
                                    CIP

DEDICATION

I would like to dedicate this book to our extended family at Fellowship Bible Church. God has truly blessed us with your friendship and fellowship.

—Noel Jerke

I would like to dedicate my work on this book to my mother. Over the years she has never wavered in her love and support for me, regardless of what I do.

—George Szabo

To my Mom and Dad, Sylvia and Chester Jung.

—David Jung

To Julia and Tom, who helped me find what I'm supposed to be doing.

—Don Kiely

ABOUT THE AUTHORS

Noel Jerke is an Internet enthusiast and currently works in the printing industry at Judd's, Inc. in Strasburg, VA. There he manages the company's online services department, assisting publishers of all types to move to the Internet. His background includes receiving a B.S. degree in Computer Science and Economics from Trinity University, San Antonio, developing banking applications, and being the manager of research and development for a graphics company. Noel is an experienced programmer familiar with C, BASIC, Visual Basic, and VBScript. Currently his interests include writing about Internet programming and building Web sites. Noel has also authored Waite Group Press's *Visual Basic Multimedia How-To, Visual Basic API How-To,* and *VBScript Interactive Course.* He is married with no children (yet), but is kept busy with an energetic dog and freelance writing. His other interests include basketball, politics, and church activities. Noel's Web site can be seen at `http://www.ActivePubs.com`. You can e-mail Noel at `NoelJ@JUDDS.com`.

George Szabo oversees the development and implementation of Intranet Technologies for the Universal Music Group. He was involved with the technical beta of the Visual Basic 4 Enterprise Edition and has been working with Visual Basic since its original release in 1989. A graduate of Loyola Marymount University, George specializes in the development of enterprise-wide information systems and infrastructure.

David Jung is a software engineer for Moss Micro, LLC. He specializes in cross-platform client/server and distributed database solutions using Visual Basic, Access, SQL Server, Oracle, and Internet components. A graduate of California State Polytechnic University, Pomona, David has a degree in computer information systems. He is a member of the Pasadena IBM Users Group's technical staff and leads its Visual Basic Special Interest Group. He is a frequent speaker at seminars and users groups showing how Visual Basic and the Internet can solve business problems. He is a Windows 95/NT associate sysop on *PC World's* PC Tech Forum on CompuServe. David is also co-author of Waite Group Press's *Visual Basic 4 Objects and Classes SuperBible* and *Visual Basic 4 OLE, Database, and Controls SuperBible.*

Don Kiely is a techno dweeb from way back, who lives and breathes Visual Basic. He writes about it, both in books and in numerous trade journals, programs with it in subzero temperatures, and teaches it at Ilisagvik College in Barrow, Alaska. In his spare time he works as development manager at the Arctic Development Council, an economic development agency in the North Slope Borough, where he works with small companies and large government agencies and their computing needs. In the rest of his spare time, which comes only occasionally, he wanders the Arctic tundra frolicking with snowy owls, Arctic foxes, and polar bears. He is the luckiest person on the face of the earth, and lives in the most pristine and beautiful place on earth.

TABLE OF CONTENTS

CONTENTS

ACKNOWLEDGMENTS

First, I would like to thank Waite Group Press and Mitch Waite for providing me the opportunity to write this book. The proven How-To series format provides an excellent method of delivering programming know-how and techniques. Waite Group Press continues to be a pioneer in the field of publishing. As I have mentioned in every book dedication, I could not have done it without the support of my wife. She continues to be supportive of my interest in writing. Thank you, darling! I would like to thank Laura Brown for enduring with us through this long project. I would also like to thank the many editors who reviewed the chapters and code. Microsoft also deserves credit for continuing to improve what has been a revolutionary programming tool. I am sure we will soon be taking a look at early previews of Visual Basic 6.0. Last, but certainly not least, I thank the Lord for providing me with the skills and capabilities to write this book. Thank you for the many blessings you have provided my family.

—Noel Jerke

Thanks to Mitchell Waite for the opportunity to write this book, and to Laura Brown for her perseverance in assembling the mountain of writing material. Thanks also to the other editors, including K.D. Sullivan, Harry Henderson, Wei Li, and Chris Stone; they help keep our work honest. I would personally like to thank Ken Moss, Terry McVay, John Coffey, Erik Klitzner, and Ryan Reid of Moss Micro, LLC, for giving the technical support and work schedule I needed to make this writing possible; my friends and family for their support and encouragement; my wife, Joanne, for always understanding when I was "one or two days" behind schedule, and my parents for getting me my first computer and always supporting me on whatever crazy venture I embarked on.

—David Jung

A book project requires a lot of work and support from a lot of people. I can't say how much I appreciate that the folks at Waite Group Press put up with me and supported me in my book projects. In particular, Laura Brown is a tough taskmaster, just what such a project needs, and sends some of the wackiest e-mail of anyone I know. My colleagues at the Arctic Development Council in Barrow, Alaska, are a constant source of support under every kind of circumstance.

—Don Kiely

INTRODUCTION

Visual Basic 5 Client/Server How-To is a practical step-by-step guide to implementing three-tiered distributed client/server solutions using the tools provided in Visual Basic 5. This book addresses the needs of programmers looking for answers to real-world questions and assures them that what they create really works. It also helps to simplify the client/server development process by providing a framework for solution development.

Question and Answer Format

The How-To format of this book seeks to clearly define the question or "task" that will be tackled in each section. Every How-To includes an overview of how the task will be accomplished, followed by an explanation of the project code, and finalized by a thorough demonstration of the techniques used. At the end of each How-To, comments are provided on how to accomplish additional variations on the task performed.

Expected Level of the Reader

This book is designed to be used by all levels of readers. However, basic knowledge of Visual Basic programming is assumed. Each How-To is given a complexity rating at the beginning of the discussion. The three levels are Beginning, Intermediate, and Advanced. The How-To's with a Beginning rating are straightforward for an entry-level Visual Basic programmer. The Intermediate How-To's go more in depth while the Advanced How-To's employ more difficult techniques and are intended for experienced Visual Basic programmers.

How This Book Is Organized

Visual Basic 5 Client/Server How-To is divided into 11 chapters as follows:

Chapter 1: Client/Server Basics

This chapter provides an introduction to client/server basics and is especially helpful in explaining client/server development. It also gives a general overview of Visual Basic 5's strategic role in the client/server model.

Chapter 2: Getting Connected

The How-To's in this chapter demonstrate the various ways you can make a connection to a database. Since the Enterprise Edition's remote data objects are based on ODBC, the examples here discuss the different ways to make a connection with connect strings, the ODBC API, and other ODBC techniques. The final How-To discusses ways to determine the best connection for your particular application given the existing hardware, software, and network setup.

Chapter 3: Remote Data Objects

In this chapter you will explore basic RDO methods, along with more advanced topics such as stored procedures, resultset management, and asynchronous queries.

Chapter 4: User Interface Design

The How-To's in this chapter demonstrate the standard user interface design for your client-tier applications. Each How-To builds on the last to produce a fully integrated and feature-rich application interface. The sample application used throughout the chapter is a simple image-tracking database. This program will allow you to categorize and track all bitmap (BMP) and icon (ICO) format files on your system.

Chapter 5: Presenting Data to the User

The rate at which data is displayed to the user, especially large amounts, is an important factor in developing most client/server applications. Through the use of business components, optimizing your applications can become much easier. This chapter's How-To's demonstrate different data-displaying methods for a fictitious hotel chain.

Chapter 6: Object-Oriented Application Development

This chapter provides an introduction to the basic fundamentals of object-oriented analysis and design and, most importantly, how to apply these techniques to your client/server programs. You will discover how to implement an object model and build a simple three-tier application utilizing ActiveX components.

Chapter 7: Business Objects

The toughest part of building business objects is knowing where to start. This chapter shows how to set up an ActiveX project that you can use as the starting point for all your business objects.

Chapter 8: Reporting and Data Connection Support

This chapter provides a series of How-To's for the decision support aspect of client/server development. Since Microsoft Access 95 has opened up its reporting facilities to Visual Basic through the use of OLE, this chapter provides special solutions crafted around the use of Visual Basic 5, Microsoft Office, Access 95, and Crystal Reports.

Chapter 9: Sample Client/Server Applications

This book encompasses many topics that go into building client/server applications, and focuses heavily on building three-tier applications using the tools provided in Visual Basic 5. This chapter serves to pull together many of these concepts to demonstrate how all of these techniques can be combined.

Chapter 10: Basic SQL Server Management

This chapter focuses on the basics of building a database using Microsoft SQL Server 6.5, as well as optimizing its tips and tricks. This chapter's How-To's guide you through the graphical user interface portion of the SQL Enterprise Manager. In the "How It Works" sections, the Data Definition Language (DDL) equivalents are discussed.

Chapter 11: Activating Client/Server on the Web

Web technology today clearly provides a three-tier data access model with the browser as the client and provider of User services, the Web server as the provider of Business services, and any back-end data source as the provider of Data services. This chapter provides How-To's to help you become more productive today with this new technology.

ABOUT THE CD-ROM

The CD-ROM bundled with *Visual Basic 5 Client/Server How-To* contains all the source code from the How-To's developed in the book, as well as additional third-party utilities. Please refer to the file **README.1ST** on the root level of the CD-ROM to learn more.

What follows are directions for copying files to your hard drive for Windows NT 3.51, Windows 95, and Windows NT 4.0. Each operating system will be discussed in turn.

> **NOTE**
>
> The installation instructions assume your CD-ROM drive is the D: drive and C: is your hard drive. If your system is set up differently, please substitute the appropriate drive letters.

Windows NT 3.51

1. Open the File Manager.

2. In File Manager, locate the drive you want to copy to and click on it.

3. If you have a directory to which you want to copy the files, skip to Step 4. Otherwise, create a new directory by selecting File|Create Directory. Type

VB5CSHT

or type a directory name of your choice and press ENTER or click on the OK button.

4. Click on **VB5CSHT** or the directory you created.

5. Double-click on the D: drive icon. You will see a **SOURCE** directory. Click on the **SOURCE** directory to display its contents. Drag the contents to the destination drive. If you want to copy only a few directories, Ctrl-click on the directories and drag the selection to the destination drive.

> **NOTE**
>
> When Windows copies a CD-ROM, it does not change the Read-only attribute for the files it copies. You can view the files, but you cannot edit them until you remove this attribute. To do this, select the files. In File Manager, select File|Properties, click on the Read-only check box to deselect it, and then click OK.

Windows 95 and Windows NT 4.0

The easiest way to copy files using Windows 95 and Windows NT 4.0 is by using the desktop.

1. Double-click on the My Computer icon. Your drives will appear in a window on the desktop.

2. Double-click on your hard drive and create a new folder, such as *VB 5 Client Server How-To*, by selecting File|New|Folder from the window menu. A folder called *New Folder* will be created on your hard drive with the name highlighted. Type in the name you want and press the ⟨ENTER⟩ key.

3. Go back to your drive window and double-click on the icon that represents your CD-ROM drive. You will see a window that has a SOURCE folder in it. Double-click on the SOURCE folder to open it.

4. Select the directories you want to copy (⟨Ctrl⟩-click on the folders if you're not copying all of them) and drag your selection to the directory you created on your hard drive. You might need to reposition your windows to make your hard drive window visible.

NOTE
When Windows copies a CD-ROM, it does not change the Read-only attribute for the files it copies. You can view the files, but you cannot edit them until you remove this attribute. To do this, select the files. In File Manager, select File|Properties, click on the Read-only check box to deselect it, and then click OK.

VISUAL BASIC 5.0 NOTE
The projects in this book and on the CD-ROM were compiled using a late beta version of Visual Basic 5.0. If you experience difficulty running the provided programs, recompile the projects using the source code provided on the CD-ROM.

Third-Party Utilities Installation

In addition to source code, the CD-ROM contains Microsoft's® ActiveX™ Control Pad, selected ActiveX controls from Microsoft's® ActiveX™ Control Gallery, Computer Software Manufaktur's Alibaba Web server for Windows 95 and Windows NT 4.0, and the **Message Hook** control, required to run certain examples in the book. Installation instructions for Windows NT 3.51, Windows 95, and Windows NT 4.0 follow.

Windows NT 3.51
Install the ActiveX Control Pad by selecting File|Run from the Program Manager.

Type

```
d:\3rdparty\ctrlpad\setuppad.exe
```

into the dialog box and click OK. Follow the onscreen prompts to finish the installation.

Each ActiveX control from the Microsoft ActiveX Control Gallery is in its own directory along with an informational page (**INFO.HTM**) and a sample control page (**SAMPLE.HTM**). Install each control by using Internet Explorer 3.0 to open the **INFO.HTM** file in the control's directory. Then click the link to download and install the control. The control will be installed from the CD-ROM to the appropriate location on your hard drive.

To install the **Message Hook** control:

1. Launch File Manager.

2. Click on your C: drive icon.

3. Double-click on the directories necessary to bring you to **WINDOWS\SYSTEM32**.

4. Double-click on your CD-ROM icon then double-click on the **SOURCE** directory.

5. Drag the **MSGHOOK32.OCX** file to the C: icon.

6. Launch Visual Basic 5.

7. Select the Project menu and then select the Components listing from Visual Basic's menu.

8. Point to the Windows System32 folder. **MSGHoo32.OCX** will appear in your OCX list.

9. Select **MSGHoo32.OCX** from the listing.

Windows 95 and Windows NT 4.0

Install the ActiveX Control Pad by double-clicking on the CD-ROM icon, the 3RDPARTY folder, the CTRLPAD folder, and the **SETUPPAD.EXE** file. Follow the onscreen prompts to finish the installation.

Each ActiveX control from the Microsoft ActiveX Control Gallery is in its own directory along with an informational page (**INFO.HTM**) and a sample control page (**SAMPLE.HTM**). Install each control by using Internet Explorer 3.0 to open the **INFO.HTM** file in the control's directory. Then click the link to download and install the control. The control will be installed from the CD-ROM to the appropriate location on your hard drive.

Install the Alibaba Web server by double-clicking on the CD-ROM icon, the 3RDPARTY folder, the ALIBABA folder, and the **ALIBABAS.EXE** file. Follow the onscreen prompts to finish the installation.

To install the **Message Hook** control:

1. Double-click on the folders necessary to bring you to **WINDOWS\SYSTEM** in Windows 95 or **WINDOWS\SYSTEM32** in Windows NT 4.0.

2. Double-click on the CD-ROM icon.

3. Double-click on the SOURCE folder.

4. Right-click on the file **MSGHOOK.OCX** and select Copy.

5. Right-click within the SYSTEM (or system32 for Windows NT 4.0) folder and select Paste.

6. Launch Visual Basic 5.

7. Select the Project menu and then the Components listing from Visual Basic's menu.

8. Point to the Windows System (or system32 for Windows NT 4.0) folder. **MSGHoo32.OCX** will appear in your OCX list.

9. Select **MSGHoo32.OCX** from the listing.

CHAPTER 1
CLIENT/SERVER BASICS

by George Szabo

CLIENT/SERVER BASICS

How do I...

No one can ignore the incredible explosion of technological advances that has taken place over the last two decades. From the introduction of the personal computer, once derided as a toy, to today's gold rush happening on the global network known as the Internet, every facet of our lives is being touched by technology. The business reality is that to survive in today's market requires working smarter and adjusting quicker to market demands.

Here is the question: What does it take to modify your information systems to respond to business needs and opportunities? Even if your application is running on a handful of machines, redeploying your application each time you make a change to the business model can be costly. Now, consider an application deployed to 100 machines, 1000 machines, or more. Redeploying an application of this magnitude can be cost prohibitive if not impossible. So how can you craft applications that are robust, scalable, and maintainable?

Clearly, the future of corporate computing lies in standardized distributed components where the business logic can reside within its own tier and be located on centralized servers. Rather than recompiling and deploying 1000 client applications, you would modify and redeploy your business services on their own centralized servers. How will client applications be able to use business logic that exists on another machine? An object framework is essential to achieving this goal. This object framework is embodied in the Component Object Model (COM) and Microsoft's ActiveX standard. The Visual Basic 5 Professional and Enterprise Edition allows developers to exploit this object framework as they create a new generation of client/server solutions that take advantage of the latest technologies.

Microsoft has crafted Visual Basic to allow the creation of reusable components, invisible to the client, that can be deployed and accessed on remote machines of the components' services. This is done through Remote Automation. Services can be grouped into three logical categories: User services, Business services, and Data services. These logical areas can contain numerous physical components that can reside anywhere from the client's machine to a remote server across the world depending on what the business problem is that needs to be solved. Robust, scalable, maintainable systems are what it's all about.

This chapter will provide you with an introduction to client/server basics. If you are already well grounded in the issues and opportunities provided by this methodology, then you can jump right into the How-To's presented in this book. If, on the other hand, you are new to client/server development or just want to get a general overview of VB5's strategic role in the client/server model, read on. Here is a brief summary of the sections in this chapter.

1.1 Discover Client/Server and Other Computing Architectures

This section introduces three system architectures: centralized, file server, and client/server. You will explore a high-level view of these architectures and the weaknesses that encouraged the introduction of a client/server option.

1.2 Understand File Server vs. Client/Server Database Deployment

Some developers believe you can develop a client/server application using a Microsoft Access database file (MDB) placed on a network file server. This chapter will review the significant differences between deploying a database file on a file server and deploying an SQL database engine on a network server.

1.3 Learn About the Two-Tier vs. Three-Tier Client/Server Model

Many client/server systems have been developed and deployed. Most of these have been two-tier applications. The two-tier model has benefits as well as drawbacks. This section will explore the advantages and disadvantages of a two-tier versus a three-tier approach.

1.4 Investigate the Component Object Model

The key to a distributed client/server application is the ability to break apart the physical restrictions of a single compiled EXE and to partition the business model into shareable, reusable components. This section explores the critical importance that the Component Object Model (COM) plays in making this possible.

1.5 Discover the Service Model

Once an application no longer consists of a single physical entity but rather of a collection of partitioned logic, it is important to have a design strategy that allows a structured approach to the creation of client/server applications. The Service Model promotes the idea that all physical components fall into one of three categories based on the services they provide. The three service tiers are User services, Business services, and Data services. This section introduces you to this logic model that is integrated into the implementation strategy of Visual Basic.

1.6 Understand Client/Server Deployments Using Components

Understanding that application logic must be partitioned into physical components and that these components should be designed logically according to the Service Model, this section illustrates three typical client/server deployments: single server, business server, and a fully distributed deployment model.

1.7 Learn More About Client/Server Development Tools Included with Visual Basic 5

New ideas require new tools to help implement them. Visual Basic 5 Enterprise Edition comes with some special tools to allow the creation and remote deployment of components. This section will introduce you to these tools and their role in the development of a Visual Basic 5 client/server solution.

1.8 Create a SourceSafe Project

Developing component based client/server applications provides the opportunity for powerful team work. Each person will be building a piece of the puzzle. Visual Basic 5 comes with Visual SourceSafe which allows for the cataloging of code as well as the management of team projects in Visual Basic. This section provides a glimpse of this useful tool which extends Visual Basic into a new league of application development tools.

1.1 How do I...
Discover client/server and other computing architectures?

Contrary to many predictions over the past decade, the mainframe computer is here and is not going away anytime soon. During the sixties and seventies, companies that needed real computing power turned to the mainframe computer, which represents a "centralized" system architecture. Figure 1-1 shows a diagram of two critical components: the server and the client machines.

Of course, in this centralized architecture, the only thing that moves between the client and the host machine is the marshaling of keystrokes and the return of terminal characters. *Marshaling* is the process of packaging interface parameters and sending them across process boundaries. In the mainframe environment, keystrokes are marshaled from the terminal to the host. This is arguably not what people are referring to when they discuss client/server implementations. Pros for a centralized architecture include excellent security and centralized administration because both

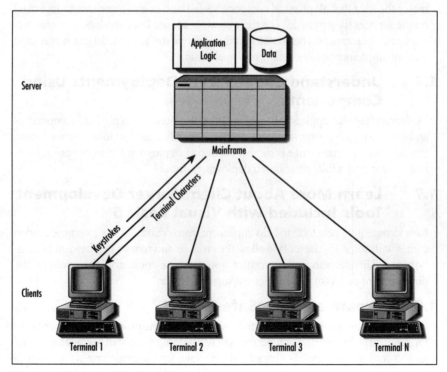

Figure 1-1 Centralized architecture

the application logic and the data reside on the same machine. Cons begin with the price tag. Mainframe computers are expensive to buy, lease, maintain, use, and the list goes on. Another disadvantage of this centralized architecture is the limitation that both the application and database live within the same mainframe process. There is no way to truly partition an application's logic beyond the mainframe's physical limitations.

During the 1980s, the personal computer charged into the business world. With it came a wealth of computing resources like printers, modems, and hard-disk storage. Businesses that could never have afforded a mainframe solution embraced the personal computer. Soon after the introduction of the personal computer to the business, came the introduction of the local area network (LAN) and the use of file server architectures. Figure 1-2 demonstrates a simple file server architecture.

The file server system created a 180-degree change in implementation from the mainframe. As depicted in Figure 1-2, application logic was now executed on the client workstation rather than on the server. In the file server architecture, a centralized server, or servers, provided access to computing resources like printers and large hard drives. Pros of this architecture are a low-cost entry point and flexible

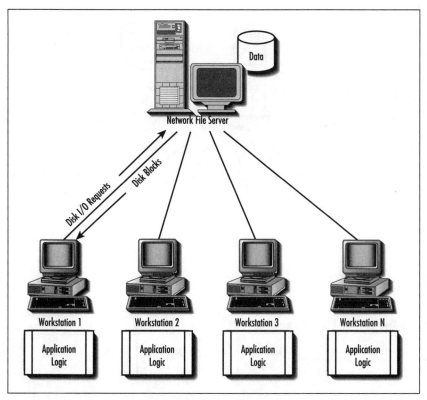

Figure 1-2 File server architecture

deployment. A business could buy a single computer, then two, and so on. A file server architecture allows you to add and reduce computer resources as needed, which makes it flexible. Cons for a file server architecture include the fact that all application logic is executed on the client machine. The file server serves files; that is the file server's job. Even though an application's files might be located on a network drive, the application is actually running in the client machine's memory space and using the client's processor. This means that the client machine must have sufficient power to run whatever application is needed or perform whatever task needs to be performed. Improving the performance and functionality of business applications is always a hot topic until the discussion includes the need to upgrade personal computers to take advantage of new application enhancements.

Although personal computers had become a powerful force in the business workplace they still lacked the powerful computing resources available within a mainframe. The client/server application architecture was introduced to address issues of cost and performance. Client/server applications allowed for applications to run on both the user workstation and the server (no longer referred to as a file server). See Figure 1-3.

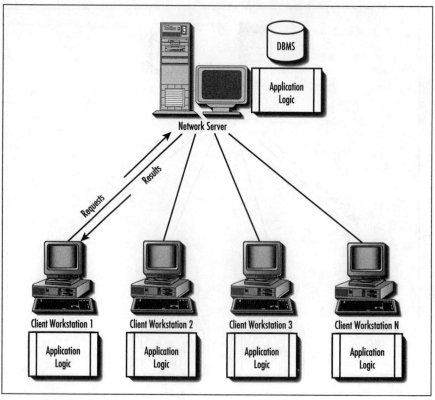

Figure 1-3 The client/server architecture

In this architecture, two separate applications operating independently could work together to complete a task. A well-known implementation of this concept is SQL-based Database Management Systems (DBMS). In Figure 1-3 you can see that, unlike the file server architecture, the request that goes out to the server is not simply a request for a file in the form of disk input/output requests which are returned as a series of input/output blocks. Instead, actual instructions can be communicated to an application running on the server, and the server can execute those instructions itself and send back a response.

Client/server refers to a process involving at least two independent entities; one is a client and the other a server. The client makes a request of the server, and the server services the request. A request may take the form of an SQL query submitted to an SQL database engine. The database engine in turn processes the request and returns a resultset. In this example, two independent processes work together to accomplish a single task. This exemplifies the client/server relationship.

Windows printing and the Print Manager is an example of a client/server relationship. A Windows application like Word or Excel prepares your document and submits it to the Print Manager. The Print Manager provides the service of queuing up requests and sending them to your printer as well as monitoring the job's progress. Once the job is complete, the Print Manager notifies the application that the job is complete. In this example, the Print Manager is the server; it provides the service of queuing and processing your print job. The application submitting the document for printing is the client. This example demonstrates how a client/server relationship can exist between applications that may not be database related.

The most popular client/server applications today revolve around the use of SQL Database Management Systems (DBMS) such as Oracle and Microsoft SQL Server. These applications, often referred to as *back-ends*, provide support for the storage, manipulation, and retrieval of the businesses' persistent data. These systems use Structured Query Language (SQL) as a standard method for submitting client requests. If you are not familiar with SQL, there are a number of good books that you can reference. Microsoft's SQL Server comes with an online help file that also can help you with proper SQL syntax.

Comments

Although both the mainframe and file server-based systems continue to provide service to business, they fail to provide a truly scalable framework for building competitive business solutions. The major factor is that logic must be executed on either the mainframe in a centralized architecture, or on the client in a file server-based architecture.

A client/server application is actually comprised of at least two pieces: a client that makes requests and a server that services the requests. These pieces can be separated and application logic distributed between the client and the server which provides for faster and more cost-effective application performance. In the next section you will review a critical difference between database deployment on a file server and implementing a database system such as SQL Server or Oracle on a network server that explains why the performance difference can be so dramatically better for client/server applications.

1.2 How do I...
Understand file server vs. client/server database deployment?

With the popularity of Microsoft Access and the proliferation of systems using the Microsoft database file (MDB) to store data, it must be mentioned that even though the MDB allows multiuser access, it is not a true client/server implementation. When you use an MDB as part of your application, you are using a file server implementation. It is important to understand the difference between a file server-based implementation and a client/server-based implementation in order to take full advantage of what a client/server architecture has to offer. Figures 1-4 and 1-5 demonstrate the fundamental difference between these two architectures.

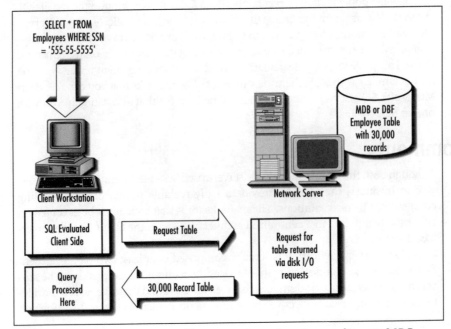

Figure 1-4 SQL process on a file server-based system using an MDB

In Figure 1-4, the query is never sent to the server. The query is actually evaluated and processed at the client. The query logic to access the MDB realizes it needs a table of data in order to process the request, so it requests the entire 30,000-row table across the network before it applies the **WHERE** clause of the **Select** statement, which specifies that you are looking for a record with a Social Security Number equal to "555-55-5555." So when an SQL statement is used against an MDB, it is processed by the client machine and only a file I/O request is sent across the network to retrieve the required data in the form of disk blocks. No logic is executed on the server except the transferring of file disk blocks. This is not what is referred to as client/server; this is simply a file server. It is true that placing an MDB out on a network drive does allow multiuse, but only because of client-side logic that references a shared record locking file for the MDB file in question. The lock file is comprised of the MDB name and an extension of LDB.

In the server-based architecture, the actual SQL statement is sent across the network and processed by an application running locally on the server machine, as shown in Figure 1-5. Because the SQL statement is processed on the server, only the results need to be sent back to the client. This is a vast improvement over the file-based architecture. If your query is looking to find an individual based on Social Security Number, a result set of one matching record would be passed back over the network rather than the whole 30,000-record table. So a major benefit of a client/server application is reduced network traffic and, in most cases, an incredibly quicker execution time.

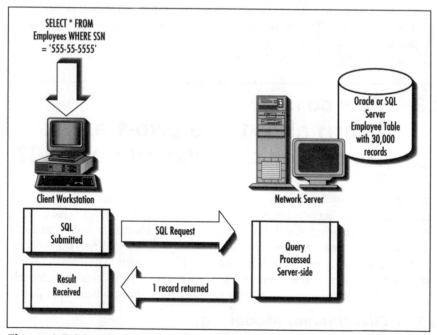

Figure 1-5 SQL process on a client/server-based system using an SQL database management system

The differences shown in Figures 1-4 and 1-5 clearly illustrate a significant advantage of a client/server implementation.

Consider the following: It would be impractical to give each employee a high-speed duplex laser printer but, by centralizing the printer and allowing people to share it as a resource, everyone benefits from it. The same is true with the database server. Since the query is processed by the server where the database engine is located and not on the clients' machine, a company can throw money into a powerful server and all the clients will benefit from the extra muscle.

Comments

Using an MDB on a file server does not mean that queries are actually processed by the server. Only when deploying full back-end database systems like Oracle and SQL Server does a query actually get processed by the server instead of the client. Deploying an MDB on a network file server is not always the wrong thing to do. Implementing true back-end database systems requires higher levels of expertise than a simple Microsoft Access MDB deployment. If the amount of data being stored and retrieved is small (you need to be the judge of this), then a file server solution may be a better solution. Clearly network traffic will become an issue as a system grows, but you can always graduate your MDB file to an SQL Server database when the time is right. Tools like the Upsizing Wizard available from Microsoft make the migration easier. Once you decide that implementing a client/server solution is the right choice, you will need to choose between a two-tier and three-tier model. In the next section you will review the differences between two-tier and three-tier client/server models.

1.3 How do I...
Learn about the two-tier vs. three-tier client/server model?

It is becoming clear that the issue is not one of simply processing transactions and generating reports, but rather of creating an information system that can change with business needs, needs that mandate tighter budgets and higher quality. To respond to the challenges being presented by the business environment, a new three-tier or N-tier client/server approach has been introduced. N-tier refers to the idea that there are no limits to the number of tiers that could be introduced to the client/server model. To begin this discussion, it is important to review the current two-tier approach.

Two-Tier Client/Server Model

The two-tier model is tied to the physical implementation, a desktop machine operating as a client and a network server housing the back-end database engine. In the two-tier model, logic is split between these two physical locations, the client and the server. In a two-tier model, the front-end piece is commonly being developed in PowerBuilder, Visual Basic, or some other 4GL. The key point to remember is that, in a two-tier model, business logic for your application must physically reside either on the client or be implemented on the back-end within the DBMS in the form of triggers and stored procedures. Both triggers and stored procedures are precompiled collections of SQL statements and control-of-flow statements. Consider a situation in which you set up a series of stored procedures to support a particular application's needs. Meanwhile, the developers of five other applications are making similar efforts to support their own needs, all in the same database. Sure, there are naming conventions and definitions of who owns what object, but the bottom line is that this scenario makes implementing and maintaining business rules downright ugly.

Paradigms, which implement a strict two-tier architecture, make developing client/server applications look easy, such as the data window in PowerBuilder where a graphical window of fields is magically bound to the back-end data source. In Visual Basic, using any of the data controls that provide a graphical link to the back-end data source creates a two-tier client/server application. This is because these implementations of application development directly tie the graphical user interface to back-end data access. The upside is that data access is simplified, allowing very rapid development of applications. The GUI is bound directly to the data source and all the details of data manipulation are handled automatically. This strength is also its weakness. While data access is simplified, it is also less flexible. Often you will not have complete control over your interactions with the data source because it is being managed for you. Of course, this extra management costs resources on the client and can result in poor performance of your applications.

There are three critical limitations of a two-tier client/server model.

1. **Not scalable.** The inability of a two-tier approach to grow beyond the physical boundaries of a client machine and a server machine prevents this model from being scalable.

2. **Unmanageable.** Since you cannot encapsulate business rules and deploy them centrally, sharing common processes and reusing your work is difficult at best.

3. **Poor performance.** The binding of the graphical interface to the data source consumes major resources on the client machine which results in poor performance and, unfortunately, unhappy clients.

Three-Tier Client/Server Model

The limited effectiveness of two-tier client/server solutions ushered in an improved model for client/server development. The three-tier client/server model is based on the ability to build partitioned applications. Partitioning an application breaks up your code into logical components. The Service Model, discussed later in this chapter, suggests that these components can be logically grouped into three tiers: User services, Business services, and Data services. Once an application has been developed using this model and technique, each component can then be deployed to whichever machine will provide the best performance depending on your situation and the current business need. Figure 1-6 shows a physical implementation of the three-tier client/server model. Sections 1.4 and 1.5 discuss partitioning, components, and the Service Model in depth.

So what is the value of distributed three-tier client/server development? There are essentially four benefits:

1. **Reuse.** The time you invest in designing and implementing components is not wasted because you can share them among applications.

2. **Performance.** Since you can deploy your components on machines other than the client workstation, you have the ability to shift processing load from a client machine that may be underpowered to a server with extra horsepower. This flexibility in deployment and design allows you, as a developer, to take advantage of the best possible methods for each aspect of your application's execution, resulting in better performance.

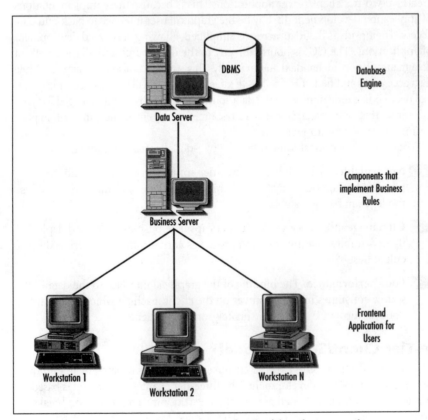

Figure 1-6 A three-tier client/server physical implementation

3. Manageability. Encapsulation of your application's services into components allows you to break down large, complex applications into more manageable pieces.

4. Maintenance. Centralizing components for reuse has an added benefit. They become easier to redeploy when modifications are made, which keeps pace with business needs.

Comments

Three-tier development is not the answer to every situation. Good partitioning and component design take time and expertise, both items that are in short supply. Additionally, three-tier client/server development, like any development, requires the support and commitment of the enterprise's powers that be. Two-tier client/server development is a much quicker way of taking advantage of SQL database engines and can fit the bill if both money and time are running out.

On the other hand, if you are looking to create systems to support a business as it grows and competes in today's marketplace, a component-based client/server model gives a great return on investment. As mentioned earlier, the benefits of a three-tier approach are the ability to reuse your work, manage large projects, simplify maintenance, and improve overall performance of your business solutions. The following section will introduce you to the Component Object Model and the concept of partitioning which play a key role in making three-tier client/server applications possible.

1.4 How do I...
Investigate the Component Object Model?

The Component Object Model (COM) is a general architecture for component software. This means that it is a standard, not an implementation. COM says this is how you should allow components to intercommunicate, but someone else (ActiveX) has to do it. ActiveX accomplishes the physical implementation of COM. Originally ActiveX was called OLE (Object Linking and Embedding). ActiveX includes the OLE implementation of COM but also improves on the OLE implementation by extending capabilities to take advantage of the Internet. This is done in the form of ActiveX controls as well as support for DCOM (Distributed Component Object Model) which is discussed later in this chapter.

Why is this important? So far the discussion of client/server has shown the need for a design model that allows encapsulation of critical business logic away from the mire of database design and front-end code. An example of logic used to support the business could be a rule that does not allow orders to be placed for amounts over $500 without a manager's approval. This business rule can now be implemented with code in a component that is centralized on its own server, making it easier to modify if necessary. If the rule changes to also allow supervisors to approve orders over $500, the change can be made much easier and quicker to a centralized component of code rather than redeploying a new executable to every desktop.

So the answer suggested is to partition the business logic out of the front-end and back-end applications and into its own set of components. The question is, how are these components supposed to talk to each other? How are you going to install these components on a network where your client applications can use them as if they were running locally on their machine? OLE and the Component Object Model are the answer.

In creating the COM, Microsoft sought to solve these four specific problems.

1. **Interoperability.** How can developers create unique components that work seamlessly with other components regardless of who creates them?

2. **Versioning.** Once a component is being used by other components or applications, how can you alter or upgrade the component without affecting all the components and applications that make use of it?

3. **Language independence.** How can components written in different languages still work together?

4. **Transparent cross-process interoperability.** How can developers write components to run in-process or out-of-process (and eventually cross-network), using one simple programming model? This is explained later in this section.

If you are using Visual Basic today, then you have no doubt experienced the benefits of the COM. All the third-party controls as well as Visual Basic itself take advantage of standards set by COM and implemented through what are referred to as ActiveX technologies. What this means to you is that objects based on the Component Object Model, objects you can write in Visual Basic, C++, or some other language, have the ability to work together regardless of the language used to create them. Since all these components know how to work together, you can purchase components from others or build them yourself and reuse them at any time during the business-system life cycle.

In-Process and Out-of-Process Servers

A component, also referred to as a server, is either *in-process,* which means its code executes in the same process space as the client application (this is a DLL), or *out-of-process,* which means it runs in another process on the same machine or in another process on a remote machine (this is an .EXE file). From these scenarios, you can see that there are actually three types of servers which can be created: in-process, local, and remote. Both local and remote servers must be out-of-process.

As you create components, you will need to choose the type of server based on the requirements of implementation and deployment. Components can be any size from encapsulating a few functions to larger, very robust implementations of a company's way of doing business. The powerful aspect of these component objects is that they look the same to client applications as well as to fellow components. The code used to access a component's services is the same regardless of whether the component is deployed as in-process, local, or remote.

Distributed Component Object Model (DCOM)

The Distributed Component Object Model (DCOM) was previously referred to as Network OLE. DCOM is a protocol that allows applications to make object-oriented remote procedure calls (RPC) in distributed computing environments (DCE). Using DCOM, an ActiveX component or any component that supports DCOM can communicate across multiple network transport protocols including the Internet Hypertext Transport Protocol (HTTP). DCOM provides a framework for:

- Data marshaling between components

- Client and server negotiated security levels based on the capabilities of distributed computing environments (DCEs) remote procedure calls (RPCs)

- Versioning of interfaces through the use of universally unique identifiers (UUIDs)

Comments

It is interesting to note that originally OLE was said to stand for Object Linking and Embedding. Microsoft backed off of that definition and said that objects that are written to support the Component Object Model are collectively called *component objects*. Since OLE supports the Component Object Model, OLE objects are referred to as component objects. Now Microsoft refers to these component objects as ActiveX. ActiveX components have been extended to support DCOM.

ActiveX is a physical implementation of the Component Object Model which provides the foundation for the creation of components which can encapsulate logic and be distributed to operate in-process, local, or remote. Visual Basic 5 has been extended to allow the creation of ActiveX servers. Visual Basic's ability to create components in the form of ActiveX DLLs (in-process servers) and ActiveX EXEs (local or remote servers) makes three-tier client/server applications easier to create than ever before.

Using Visual Basic, you can create applications that are partitioned into a number of separate physical components. Those components can then be placed transparently on any machine within your network as well as across the Internet. The following section will introduce you to the Service Model which suggests a logical rather than a physical way of viewing how applications should be partitioned into components.

1.5 How do I...
Discover the Service Model?

The Service Model is a logical way of grouping the components you create. Although his model is not language specific, for this book we will discuss the Service Model and how it is implemented using what is available in Visual Basic 5. The Service Model is based on the concept that every component is a collection of services that the component provides to others.

There are three types of services used in creating business solutions: User services, Business services, and Data services. Each of these types correlates to a tier in a three-tier client/server architecture. Figure 1-7 shows physical components (DLLs, EXEs, database triggers, and database stored procedures) grouped logically into the three service types. Note that DLL components and EXE components can be used to encapsulate logic in any tier. In fact, the only objects that are not in every tier are triggers and stored procedures because they are database specific.

Figure 1-7 also shows a very important benefit of using components, which is the ability to make a component's services available to more than a single application. Notice that the shaded areas overlap where components are used by both application 1 and 2. Reuse is a powerful aspect of the Service Model. Two basic rules for inter-component communication must be followed in the Service Model:

1. Components can request services from fellow components in their current tier and any tier below or above a component's tier.

2. Requests cannot skip tiers. User services components cannot communicate directly with components in the Data services tier and vice versa.

Often you may hear the Service Model referred to as a layered approach. The typical use of the term *layer* refers to a process in which one layer must speak to the next layer and move from top to bottom then back up. This does not correctly describe how components communicate within the Service Model because components can interact with other components in the same layer as well as those above and below it. The Service Model is meant to assist in deciding how to partition application logic into physical components but does not deal with the actual physical deployment of the software components. By understanding the three service tiers, you can begin to make decisions about which application logic you should deploy together within a single component as well as within the various tiers. The following section gives a brief overview of the three service types that comprise the Service Model: User services, Business services, and Data services.

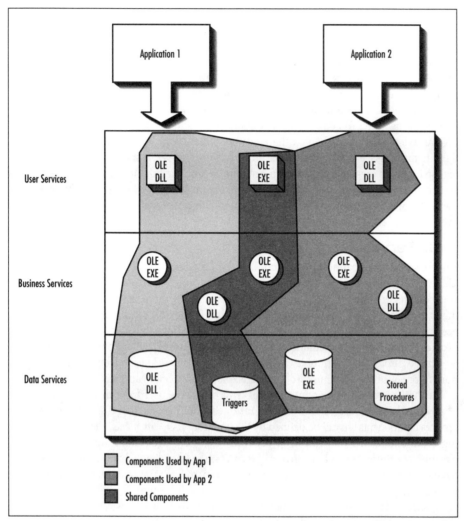

Figure 1-7 Physical components grouped logically within the Services tiers

User Services

Components that fall into the User services tier provide the visual interface that a client will use to view information and data. Components in this layer are responsible for contacting and requesting services from components in either the User services tier or the Business services tier. It is important to note that even though a component resides in the User services tier, one of the services provided to a user is the ability to perform business functions. User services play a role in doing business. Even though the business logic may be encapsulated in components of the Business services tier, it is the User services component that allows the user to have access to the whole process.

Although User services are normally contained within the user application, this is not always the case. A User service, like common company dialogs, could be compiled into a DLL and made available locally on a client's machine. Perhaps you wish to implement a standard set of error messages, but you don't want to deploy it to every machine. You could take that User service and compile it into an ActiveX EXE and deploy it remotely on a shared server so everyone could use it. Note that if the Error message component is placed on a central server, it should only contain text string error messages and should not display a dialog box. If a remote ActiveX server displays a dialog box, it would not appear on the user's workstation but on the server instead. Refer to Chapter 7, Business Objects, for more information on this.

Business Services

Since User services cannot directly contact the Data services tier, it is the responsibility of the Business services components to serve as bridges to alternate tiers. Business components provide business services that complete business tasks like validating that a customer is not over his or her credit limit. Rather than implementing business rules through a series of triggers and stored procedures, business components provide the service of implementing formal procedures and defined business rules. So why go through all the trouble to encapsulate the business logic in a business component or set of components? Robust, reusable, maintainable applications.

Business services components also serve to buffer the user from direct interaction with the database. The business tasks that will be executed by Business services components should be defined by the application's *requirements*, such as entering a patient record or printing a provider list. One overwhelming reason to partition out Business services into components is the knowledge that business rules have the highest probability for change and, in turn, have the highest probability for requiring the rewriting and redeployment of an application.

Business rules are defined as policies that control the flow of business tasks. An example of a business rule might be a procedure that applies a late charge to a person's bill if payment is not received by a certain date. It is very common for business rules to change more frequently than the tasks they support. This creates a good case for why business rules are excellent targets for encapsulation into components, thus separating the business logic from the application logic itself. The advantage here is that if the policy for applying late charges changes to include the stipulation that they cannot be sent to relatives of the boss, then you will only need to change the logic in your shared business component rather than in every client application.

Data Services

Data services involve all the typical data chores including the retrieval and modification of data as well as the full range of other database-related tasks. The key to Data services is that the rules of business are not implemented here. While a Data service component is responsible for managing and satisfying the requests submitted by a business component, or even a fellow Data services component, implementing the rules of business is not a responsibility.

Data services can be implemented as objects in a particular database management system (DBMS) in the form of triggers or stored procedures. Alternately, the Data services could provide access to heterogeneous data sources on multiple platforms on any number of servers or mainframes. A properly implemented Data services tier should allow changes in the Data services tier and related data sources to take place without affecting the services being provided to Business services components.

Comments

The Service Model is a logical view of working with components and application partitioning, not a physical one. Sometimes physical deployment of components may parallel the component's tier assignments but this is not necessary nor desired. In Figure 1-8, components within the Service Model have been mapped to one of three physical locations. Either they can reside on the client, on a network server (typically a business server), or a second network server (typically a database engine server).

Figure 1-8 helps to illustrate three key points with regard to the Service Model and physical deployment:

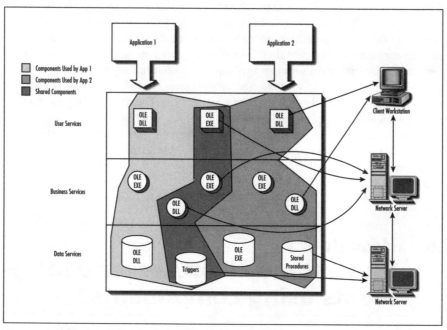

Figure 1-8 Simple physical deployment of components on a network

1. Triggers and stored procedures from the Data services tier must be deployed in the database back-end. This is because these objects are direct implementations of the database engine and are stored within the database itself. This is shown by the direct mapping of the stored procedures and triggers symbols within the Data services tier to the database server.

2. In order to share a single common source of services, a component must be an out-of-process remote Automation Server (ActiveX EXE) and be deployed on a central server so everyone can access it. In Figure 1-8 you will notice an ActiveX EXE within the User services tier. This ActiveX EXE is mapped to the business server so multiple users can access it.

3. Not all business logic is best deployed remotely. Due to performance considerations, an in-process DLL provides better performance than an ActiveX EXE and may be a wiser choice. In Figure 1-8 you will find a DLL within the Business services tier that represents this type of scenario. DLLs in general cannot be utilized remotely, so the Business services DLL must be deployed to the user's workstation rather than the business server.

One final comment should be made with regard to the idea of dual personality. Dual personality is a powerful aspect of components that affects their design. Any component can be both a client and a server. Consider a situation where you design a Business services component to calculate book royalties. The royalty calculation is a service that the Visual Basic component provides to any requester. In order to create the calculation, the business component requires information about the author's contract with the publisher. Your Business services component becomes a client of services rather than a server as it requests contract information from a Data services component. In this example, the royalty component is acting as a server of royalty information but also as a client of Data services. The royalty component is both a client and a server of services. This is a much more powerful implementation than the typical client/server understanding where the client/server relationship is more rigid and a client cannot be a server and vice versa. In the next section you will review three physical deployment scenarios available for client/server applications that utilize a three-tier client/server architecture.

1.6 How do I...
Understand client/server deployments using components?

The Service Model encourages the creation of components that encapsulate common reusable functionality in a physical package, the ActiveX DLL or ActiveX EXE. VB5 makes it possible to also create ActiveX controls in the form of OCXs as well as the creation of ActiveX documents. These ActiveX technologies are covered in Chapter

11, Activating Client/Server on the Web. Compiled into these physical formats, these pieces can be deployed on a practically infinite number of topologies. Before reviewing deployment options, it is important to understand the characteristics that accompany the ActiveX DLL and ActiveX EXE. Both are ActiveX component objects and share a common interface based on the standards defined by the Component Object Model.

When considering which is the proper container for a particular component, you should consider the following about these two physical component implementations. A DLL is an in-process server. *In-process* refers to the fact that the DLL operates in the same process space as the application using it. Because a DLL is operating in the same process, it loads much quicker than an EXE would. Additionally, a DLL cannot be deployed remotely, at least not without a trick or two. The trick being referred to is that a DLL can be deployed remotely if the DLL is parented by an EXE component. The EXE would instantiate the DLL on the remote machine and provide an interface to the DLL's methods and properties. This process is referred to as containment. The parent component marshals requests between a client and the DLL.

In the case of an EXE, it is important to know that there are basically two types of ActiveX EXEs. The first type of EXE is one that is deployed locally on a client machine (local ActiveX Automation Server); the second is a remotely deployed EXE (remote ActiveX Automation Server). ActiveX EXEs are always out-of-process servers which means that they run in their own process space. Out-of-process servers can be deployed remotely on a network server. This allows them to be shared among all applications that have access to that server. On the downside, ActiveX EXEs take significantly longer to load than a DLL. Accessing methods and properties of an ActiveX EXE component is much slower than working with a DLL. Once you place the EXE on a server, network traffic will become an additional concern with regard to execution speed.

One final consideration is crash protection. This is an important consideration when designing components. A DLL operates in-process and because of this, if it dies, it takes the application with it since they share the same process space. On the other hand, an ActiveX EXE runs out-of-process. This means that if a problem occurs, it may die, but the application or component calling it will not die. This allows the calling application or component to handle the problem by either restarting the EXE or performing some other type of recovery. Fault tolerance can be designed into your systems to provide greater support for mission critical execution. Table 1-1 highlights the considerations that have been presented thus far. You should keep these in mind when selecting the physical container for your component.

Table 1-1 ActiveX server types

COMPONENT	TYPE	PROS	CONS
DLL	In-process	Quick execution in-process	Local deployment only; no crash protection
EXE	Local out-of-process	Crash protection	Slower than DLL
EXE	Remote out-of-process	Remote execution, Crash protection	Up to 100 times slower; affected by network traffic

Physical Deployments

Three different client/server deployments use the three-tier strategy that is shown here.

Single server
Business server
Transaction server

All figures in this section include the Service Model diagram from Section 5 of this chapter. Each of the components has been given a letter from A to L to uniquely identify it. There is no specification as to whether the component is a DLL or EXE but you can refer to Figures 1-7 or 1-8 to reference this attribute.

Single Server Deployment

In the single server model shown in Figure 1-9 you will notice that all components are split between the client machine and the network server. *B, F, E,* and *J* are all shared items; therefore, they had to be deployed on the network server so that others could have access to them.

It is true that components installed on a workstation can be shared with other workstations in a peer-to-peer configuration, but this is a very poor implementation idea. A workstation usually has less processing power than a server. Another reason to avoid deploying shared components on workstations is the headache it causes when you are trying to keep track of it all.

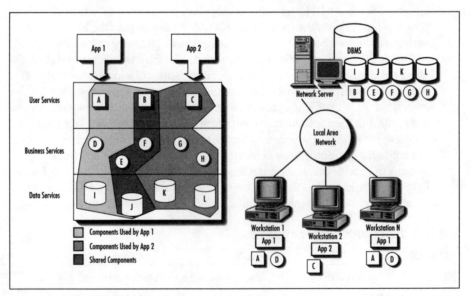

Figure 1-9 Single server deployment of components on a network

The single server deployment model also runs the DBMS back-end engine on the network server. All the Data services components are deployed on the network server as well. Application 1 is shown running on workstation 1. You will notice that not only is there a User services component on workstation 1, but also a Business services component, depicted by the letter D. This is to suggest that there might be a need for locally deployed Business services components perhaps due to the need for speed of execution. Although it is not a good idea to partition components based on speed, since this is not one of the factors considered on a logical Service Model level, you may find yourself in a situation where speed is the number one concern. In this case either local or in-process deployment of a component is possible. It doesn't take much to change a component from a DLL to an EXE with Visual Basic. Reference Chapter 7, Business Objects, for more information on this.

Business Server Deployment

A second step in the deployment scenario is the Business server deployment plan. In Figure 1-10 you will see the same Service Model diagram but this time the physical deployment includes an additional network server referred to as a business server. Its purpose is obvious: to provide a centralized location of all shared business components. Though the Business server is meant as a home for your business components, this server usually houses all components that must be centrally shared. This might include User services components as well as those shown by component B in Figure 1-10.

In Figure 1-10 you will notice that a User service component represented by letter B is on the Business server. This makes sense because the Business server is a good centralized location for deployment and maintenance in this scheme.

All of the Data services components have been deployed to the Data server. If you refer to Figure 1-7 or 1-8 of the previous section, you will note that two of the four Data services, trigger and store procedures, are labeled J and L in Figure 1-10. These components must be deployed on the same machine as the DBMS because they are integrated objects of the DBMS. In this deployment, all Data services have been kept together to allow centralized administration of these pieces.

The components kept on each workstation have not changed from the previous deployment scenario to this one. This is worth noting because it suggests that once you set up your workstations and their applications, you can continue to enhance deployment schemes in the server arena transparent to the workstations. This is a powerful feature and is made possible by the Remote Automation Connection Manager utility, which is discussed in the next section, Transaction Server Deployment.

One last point about this deployment diagram is that the connections of all workstations lead to the Business server. This may or may not be the actual physical implementation. Both the Business server and the Data server could be on the same network and be just as available, in which case, Figure 1-10 simply shows the allowed communication path: User services talk to Business services that talk to Data services and so on. This, however, does not have to be only a logical deployment. If

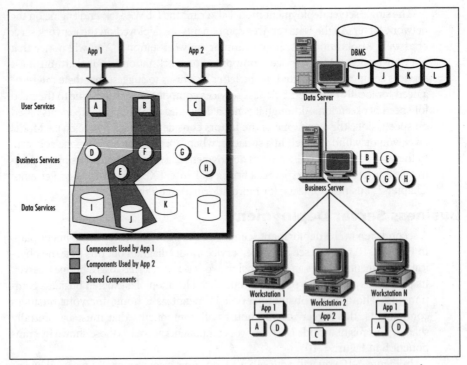

Figure 1-10 Business server deployment of components on a network

Open Database Connectivity (ODBC) drivers are not installed on any of the workstations, and all communication with the Data services components requires ODBC, then you have physically prevented this path. By eliminating a workstation's ability to directly access data you can create a much more secure environment, if that is a primary concern for your deployment. Remember that once ODBC is installed on a user's workstation he could effectively install any number of data accessing packages that utilize ODBC drivers, thus providing a potential security risk. There are a number of security measures that you could take to prevent a renegade user from directly accessing production or warehouse data. Avoiding the installation of ODBC on every workstation is one step you could take.

Transaction Server Deployment

The transaction server deployment scenario is the third and final scenario discussed in this section. Figure 1-11 shows a transaction server deployment scheme. What is a transaction server? A transaction server is an application whose purpose is to maintain and provide a pool of ActiveX server component objects in memory. Remember that EXE components must be started and loaded into their own process space each time they are used. This is a huge cost to incur when you need to use one.

In order to offset the load time cost of ActiveX EXEs, a transaction server creates a pool of these components. The transaction server then stands ready to pass clients an object reference to these preloaded components. Once the client receives a reference to a preloaded component, the client can use the component directly without funneling requests through the transaction server. This is an important point. If all requests had to be funneled through the transaction server, then the transaction server would soon become a bottleneck. The transaction server simply preloads components and hands their addresses out on request. When the client is done with the component, it is released and a new instance of the component is loaded into the pool to await the next client request for a component.

Figure 1-11 introduces the use of a transaction server. The transaction server becomes a type of switchboard operator passing component references to requesting clients. If workstation 1 in Figure 1-11 requested use of component *E*, then workstation 1 would be able to use component *E* directly until the reference was released. This is depicted by the dotted line from workstation 1 to component *E*.

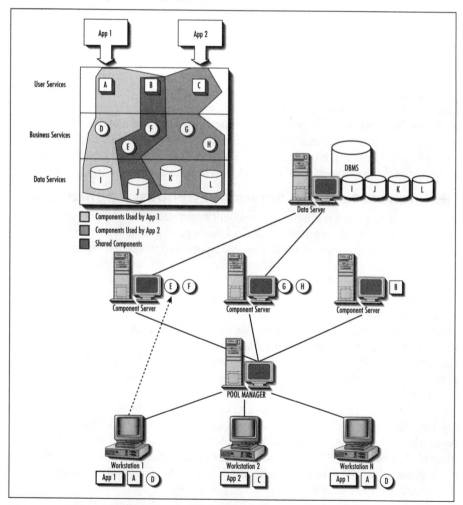

Figure 1-11 Physical deployment utilizing a transaction server

Another important aspect of the transaction server deployment scenario is that components can be moved from one component server to another based on load in order to improve performance. As the components are moved from one location to another, you will only need to register the new location with the transaction server. The transaction server has several responsibilities:

- Keep a pool of ActiveX servers instantiated

- Pass requesting applications a reference to these servers

- Terminate references to the ActiveX server when it is finished being used

- Validate usage of a component

The transaction server sits between the workstations and the business servers, which in this example are now called component servers.

Keep a Pool of ActiveX Servers Instantiated

In order for the transaction server to do its job, it must first be able to instantiate the components that it needs to maintain on the server. You will need to set up the transaction server machine so that it has access to all the other component servers. Additionally, you will need to use the Remote Connection Manager application to configure the network locations of these components. The benefit of this scenario is that you configure the location of the components at the transaction server machine. If a component is moved, you reconfigure the address at the transaction server, not at the workstation level. This is of huge importance in large deployments.

Pass References to These Servers to Request Applications

When a client requests a service of a component being maintained by the transaction server, the transaction server hands a reference to an available component in the pool. Depending on how many different components you have being managed by the transaction server, this may not be a minor activity. This introduces the question of granularity when designing and implementing components in your system.

Granularity refers to how finely you will partition your services. For example, will you put 100 services in a single EXE since they all have to do with financial calculations, or will you give each calculation its own EXE? The larger EXE is easier to locate since all the calculations are in a single physical package, but giving each calculation its own physical package makes it easier to test and debug. It also seems to be the case that smaller components or more granular components have a higher probability for reuse.

Note that each ActiveX out-of-process server takes about 500K to load in memory regardless of granularity. If the ActiveX component allows more than one connection to it, each connection is about another 10K. You can check memory consumption by using any number of memory monitoring programs. Consider the number of components that will need to be running at the same time when purchasing memory for your component servers.

Terminate References to the ActiveX Server When It Is Finished Being Used

Once a client is through using a component, it drops all references to the component. Once an ActiveX server has no references to it, this causes termination and it shuts down. When a component is terminated, the transaction server must adjust the pool and prepare for more requests. The transaction server can be created to maintain pool levels at different values throughout the day depending on expected demand.

Validate Usage of a Component

Another aspect of the transaction server is its ability to implement security. Part of the transaction server's design can and should be to know who is requesting a service. This information can be used to implement a security model. In this scenario, the transaction server could use the login and password to validate use of a component. This is not a great idea if the component is needed only for a second or two to perform a calculation. Checking security every time simply slows down the process of using the ActiveX server more.

Comments

In the single server, business server, and transaction server deployment scenarios, the components deployed to the workstations did not change. This emphasizes the goal, which is to centralize the application logic that will need to be maintained and updated. Rather than change the configuration on 100 workstations, it is much more cost effective to maintain components on a centralized server. However, this comes at a cost in execution time. So this is not a cure-all. Some components may need to be distributed to every workstation. The point being made is that the physical deployment opportunities are vast. Unfortunately, they are also fraught with uncertainty. Each situation in which you must deploy a component architecture and three-tier client/server application will require its own solution. Hopefully this section has provided you with some ideas.

1.7 How do I...

Learn more about client/server development tools included with Visual Basic 5?

There is a significant difference between what takes place in a two-tier client/ server application and the implementation and deployment of a three-tier application. In a two-tier approach, business logic is integrated into the application that sits on the user's workstation or the logic is integrated into the back-end database system in the form of triggers and stored procedures. With a three-tier approach, the business logic that represents what the company is all about is given its own tier. This tier is made possible by facilitating the ability to partition executable logic out of both the front-end application and the back-end database engine. So the difference resides in the partitioning of applications and the creation of components. The use of components, both on the local machine and deployed remotely, introduces a serious need for new tools. Visual Basic 5 comes with a variety of new tools:

Remote Automation Tools

Client Registration Utility
Remote Automation Connection Manager
Transaction Server
Component Manager
Automation Manager

Other Important Tools

Database Management Tools
Visual SourceSafe

The remainder of this section will provide a brief overview of the remote automation, data access, and team development tools that accompany Visual Basic 5.0 Enterprise Edition. These tools play a vital role in making three-tier client/server application development feasible and desirable.

Client Registration Utility

The registry of both NT and Windows 95 provides a library in which all objects used are registered. In order for a component to be available for use under Windows 95 or NT, it must be registered in the registry. This registration can take place several ways. If the component is an EXE, you only need to execute it and it will register itself on your system. If you have Visual Basic on your machine and compile a component into an EXE or DLL, it will be registered automatically. You can also use the Setup Wizard to create a setup program that will not only install the component but will register it in the registry and provide a method for un-installing the component as well.

The Client Registration Utility provided with Visual Basic allows you to register components from the command line. In order to use the Client Registration Utility, you will need to make sure that you compile your components with the Remote Server Support Files checked. This option is available when generating an EXE in Visual Basic by choosing the Options button. The Remote Server Support Files option will generate a file with the .VBR extension. This file provides a client machine's Windows registry with information it needs in order to run an ActiveX server that exists on a remote computer.

In today's world of choice, you get two versions of the Client Registration Utility: `CLIREG32.EXE` and `CLIREG16.EXE`. `CLIREG32.EXE` allows for registration that allows 32-bit applications to access the component you are registering.

`CLIREG16.EXE` is used to register your component for use by 16-bit applications. If you will be using both 16- and 32-bit applications to reference this component on the same machine, you will need to run both registration utilities. If you need to register a DLL on a client machine to run locally, you will want to use `Regsvr32.exe` for 32-bit Windows environments or `Regsvr16.exe` for 16-bit machines. This utility allows for local registration of ActiveX servers. Since a DLL cannot be executed like an EXE, nor can it be accessed directly via Remote Automation, you will need to install it using this utility. `Regsvr32` and `Regsvr16` can be found under your Visual Basic directory in the `Clisvr` subdirectory.

Remote Automation Connection Manager

The Remote Connection Manager is provided as an easy way of telling your system where to find a component. This is much like a phone directory. Figure 1-12 shows the Remote Automation Connection Manager's Server Connection tab and ActiveX classes list. You put in the connection information and this utility stores it in the registry. When an application or component tries to contact a component, it looks in the registry to find the information about the component. In this case, the important information is security related.

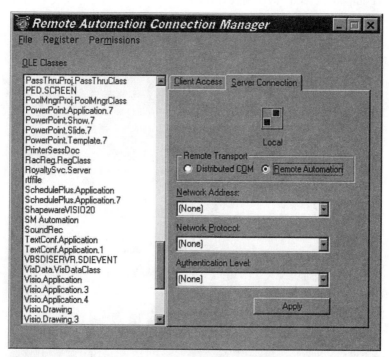

Figure 1-12 The Remote Automation Connection Manager

The list contains all the ActiveX classes that have been registered. To use the Remote Automation Connection Manager to set up access to a remote component class, you highlight the component's class name on the list and enter the network address, network protocol, and authentication level to be used (see Table 1-2). Additionally you can use either standard Remote Automation or the distributed component object protocol by simply selecting it from the Server Connection tab.

Table 1-2 Sample entries for the Remote Automation Connection Manager

OPTION	SAMPLE ENTRIES
Network Address	IP Address or Associated Name
Network Protocol	TCP/IP, Named Pipes, or other installed option
Authentication Level	No Authentication

The real power of the Remote Automation Connection Manager is in its ability to easily repoint the registry from a local reference to a remote reference of your component. Figure 1-13 shows the Remote Automation Connection Manager highlighting a component set up to be accessed remotely.

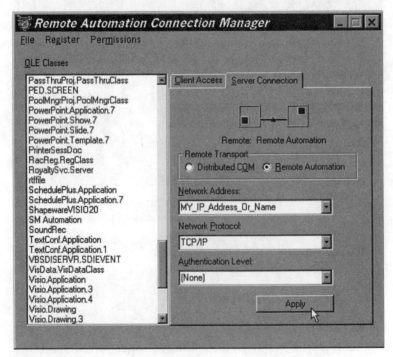

Figure 1-13 A remote configuration using the Remote Automation Connection Manager

Once the component's address within the registry has been changed to a remote machine, the Remote Automation Connection Manager displays two component symbols connected by a line and the label saying remote. To switch from local to remote access of a component is as easy as selecting Local or Remote from the Register menu list. What is taking place is that entries are being changed in the registry to point requests for service to a remote or local location. When you call someone on the phone, it really doesn't matter where they are as long as you have the phone number and they pick up the phone when you call. That is the idea with Remote Automation and components. Everyone uses a phone to talk to each other. Even if you are in the same house (on the same computer) you use the phone to talk. Doing this allows components to be deployed anywhere and all that needs to be done is to change the number in the phone book (registry) to the current phone number.

Security is worth mentioning here. The two types of security in Remote Automation are

1. **Access control.** This makes sure that only certain types of objects are remotely available. You can also make sure that only specified users can have access to certain objects.

2. **Authentication.** This ensures that data sent from one application is identical to the data received by the other. This allows protection from someone intercepting your data as it goes from one point to another.

There are many ways to implement security. On one end of the spectrum, you could implement no security and just trust that people won't access things they shouldn't. This method is easy to maintain because you simply ignore the risk.

On the other end of the spectrum, you could lock everything up and assign access to only the logged-on person at a single station. Figure 1-14 shows the contents of the Client Access tab of the Remote Automation Connection Manager.

If you are running Windows NT, you will want to set the System Security Policy to Allow Remote Creates by ACL. ACL stands for Access Control List and is a method used by NT to determine whether a user running an application has adequate permission to access the class. This is very powerful because it allows the NT operating system's security model to kick in allowing for a centralized method for handling security.

With Allow Remote Creates by ACL selected, a request for a remote ActiveX component object will be processed as usual by the Automation Manager (which will be discussed later in this section). The Automation Manager impersonates the client user and tries to open the remotely deployed object's class identification (CLSID) key with query permissions. If the open fails, the Automation Manager returns an error. On the other hand, if the open succeeds, the Automation Manager no longer impersonates the client user. It creates the requested object, and returns a reference as usual.

If you are using Windows 95, the client's ACL is not a valid choice so you will only be able to specify Allow Remote Creates by Key. If you select this option in the Remote Automation Connection Manager on the client and also check the Allow Remote

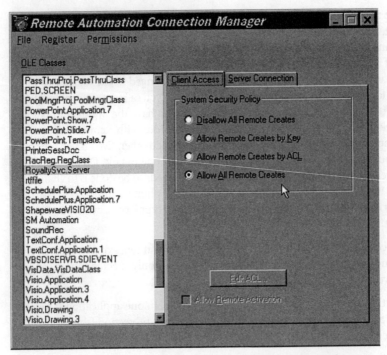

Figure 1-14 Client Access Tab of The Remote Automation
Connection Manager

Activation, then the system will grant access to an application that has the correct
value stored under the object's CLSID in the registry. If you use Windows 95 as a
server, you should also set the authentication level to No Authentication. Windows
95 does not support the full security model that NT does.

Automation Manager

The Automation Manager is an application responsible for connecting remote
clients to ActiveX Automation Servers. This application is multithreaded and must
be running on a machine that wishes to make components available for use from
other machines. Figure 1-15 shows the Automation Manager and the two visible values it presents.

As a client request is received by a machine running the Automation Manager,
the number of connections will be incremented. As ActiveX Automation Server component references are passed, the object's count will be incremented. As the
referenced objects are released, the counts are correspondingly reduced. The
Automation Manager can be found in your Windows `systems` directory with the
name `AUTMGR32.EXE`. This is a 32-bit application.

Component Manager

The promise of components is that they will make the long hours of work you put
into building them pay off by allowing reusability. The sad truth is that reuse is not

Figure 1-15 The
Automation Manager
waiting for a client request

a sure thing. For reuse to take place, you need to make sure it is easy for everyone to find components that are available for reuse and, once they are found, to be able to use them. The Component Manager is provided as a tool to accomplish this task. See Figure 1-16.

The Component Manager allows you to add and remove components from a catalog that everyone can share. You can also track important information about each component, allowing people to reuse the component. Finding the component is only half of the trick to using it. The other half is understanding the component's interface. The Component Manager allows you to store information about the component, including things like:

- **Sample Type**—Basic Concepts, Callback, Data Access, Object Ptr Passing, Pool Management, Work Distribution.

- **Technology**—Remote Data Objects, Jet/DAO, ODBC API, Office Integration

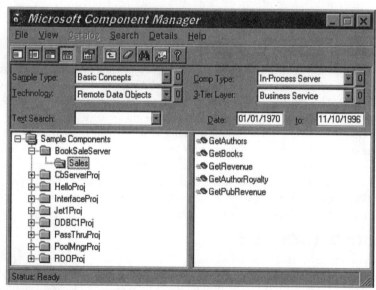

Figure 1-16 The Component Manager

- ■ **Component Type**—In-Process Server, Out-of-Process Server, MultiUse Instancing, SingleUse Instancing

- ■ **Three-Tier Layer**—User Service, Business Service, Data Service, All/App Service

Each component has a property sheet that allows you to enter information that describes the component and its interface. Additionally the Component Manager provides the ability to associate files with a component. This allows an open-ended method for a team of developers, or should we say component clients, to share sample code, functional specification, data maps, or any other types of information that may be useful to the component's reuse.

You and the people who will be creating and reusing components will have to decide on how to implement the Component Manager's features. It is easy to let the Component Manager Catalog get out of date, but this is your part in making sure that the effort invested in the development of components is one that is not wasted.

Database Management Tools

Communication between the Business services components and the Data services tier is a critical piece of the client/server puzzle. Visual Basic comes with three data access methods: Data Access Objects (DAOs), Remote Data Objects (RDOs), and Open Database Connectivity API (ODBC). Following is a brief description of each method. For a fuller discussion of these access methods, refer to Chapter 3, Remote Data Objects.

Data Access Objects (DAO)

Visual Basic 4 comes with support for the JET, Joint Engine Technology. JET provides an object-oriented implementation of data access called Data Access Objects (DAOs). This method of accessing data allows a developer to use data objects and collections to handle the tasks of data access. The implementation of data access objects is closely tied to the Microsoft database file structure called MDB. The MDB allows the storage of tables as well as query definitions, macros, forms, reports, and code. Data access objects only allow you to get at the tables and queries stored in the MDB. Data access objects automate much of the task of dealing with data, including managing connections, record locking, and fetching result sets. Data access objects provide for access to ODBC-compliant data sources as well.

Remote Data Objects

To optimize the methods for accessing ODBC-compliant data sources while at the same time simplifying the process is a huge task. *Remote Data Objects* (RDO) is provided to accomplish this task. Remote data objects is a thin layer that sits on top of the ODBC API. Because remote data objects is a thin layer, it does not impact the speed of execution for performing data access. This is critical to a production environment where one of the evaluating factors is the speed of execution. Remote data objects mirrors DAO object model and allows developers to use objects and collections to execute data-related tasks like submitting a query, processing results, and handling errors.

Open Database Connectivity (ODBC) API

Of all the methods for accessing data, the Open Database Connectivity (ODBC) API is the most efficient in terms of execution speed. In terms of programming, it requires the most time and the most caution. Since this is an application programming interface (API) you have full control over the very intimate details of data access. Both the DAO and the RDO use the ODBC API layer when accessing ODBC-compliant database engines like Oracle and Microsoft SQL Server. The ODBC API is cryptic and difficult to use but provides more control and better execution speed. It is generally recommended that remote data objects be used as it is the best balanced method. Its data access speed rivals using the ODBC API directly, and an ease of programming is provided by object-oriented syntax.

Visual SourceSafe

With the release of Visual Basic 4, Microsoft included a complete system for team development of enterprise-wide solutions. Of course this requires that the environment provide a mechanism of organizing team development. Visual SourceSafe provides the ability to manage large scale team development.

SourceSafe is actually comprised of two applications. The first is the Administrative module that allows you to maintain a roster of developers who work on various projects. Figure 1-17 shows this application. The second is the Visual SourceSafe Explorer.

The following rights can be assigned per user, per project:

- **Read.** User can use the file in read-only mode.

- **Check Out/Check In.** User can check out files for use and make modifications. The user can also check the files back in.

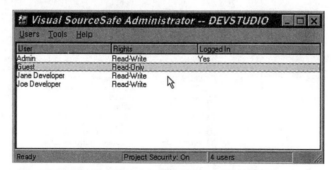

Figure 1-17 Visual SourceSafe Administrator

■ **Add/Rename/Delete.** User has the ability to add files to the project as well as rename and delete files within the project.

■ **Destroy.** User has the ability to permanently remove files in the project and physically destroy them.

The second application is the SourceSafe Explorer, which allows you to use a window that resembles the Windows Explorer. (See Figure 1-18.)

You can use this application to check in and check out files for a project. You can also view history of activity with a file, see the differences between files that have been changed, and create reports that allow you to manage a project.

Visual SourceSafe has also been provided as an add-in to the Visual Basic development environment. You can add it using the Add-In Manager from the Visual Basic menu bar. Visual SourceSafe will add four options to your Tools menu:

1. **Get.** This allows you to bring physical copies of files from the storage library maintained by SourceSafe on your network drive.

2. **Check Out.** Used for selecting files that you want to exclusively work with. Optionally you can either keep them checked out or release the files so others can check them out.

3. **Check In.** Once you have finished working on a file or project, you use the Check In command to update the SourceSafe code library with your changes.

4. **Undo Check Out.** This option allows you to effectively cancel a check out on the files you are working with. In a situation where you check out a file or project then make changes and decide that you wish to begin again, you can cancel the check out process with this option.

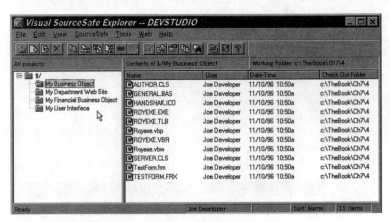

Figure 1-18 The Visual SourceSafe Explorer

Comments

The development of components is a very powerful idea whose time has come. Creating components is facilitated by the additional tools that make the management and implementation possible. It is important to note that all these tools are only available with the Enterprise Edition of Visual Basic. As a way to get started, the next section will walk you through the process of installing and adding a project to Visual SourceSafe.

1.8   How do I...
Create a SourceSafe project?

Problem

I would like to use source code control with my team but I don't know where to start.

Technique

Using source code control is an important part of team development but it also provides the individual developer with the benefit of having a secure place for code, the ability to share files between projects, an online history of changes, and more. Visual SourceSafe has been provided as part of the Visual Basic Enterprise Edition, but you can purchase it separately if you are using the Standard or Professional versions of Visual Basic. There are two methods for adding a project to Visual SourceSafe. The first method involves the use of the Visual SourceSafe Explorer and the second method is performed in the Visual Basic environment when you have the Visual SourceSafe Add-In installed. For this quick start on using Visual SourceSafe, you will use the Add-In method from Visual Basic.

Steps

In order to use Visual SourceSafe from the Visual Basic development environment, you will need to make sure that Visual SourceSafe has been installed on your machine and that a valid login for you exists in the SourceSafe Administrator. To add a login to SourceSafe, start the Visual SourceSafe Administrator program. Press [CTRL]+[A] to add a user. Enter your name and password and press OK. Now you have a valid login with SourceSafe. Once that is done, follow these steps.

1. Start Visual Basic. You do not need to specify a project at this time.

2. Select **Add-Ins** from the menu then select **Add-In Manager**. A dialog box will appear with the add-ins that are available on your system. If you do not see **Source Code Control Add-In**, then Visual SourceSafe has not been properly installed on your system. You will need to reinstall it before you can proceed.

3. **Check** the box next to the entry that reads `Source Code Control Add-In`, then press OK.

4. **Open** a project that you would like to add to Visual SourceSafe. As the project loads, you will be prompted automatically to add it to SourceSafe. For this How-To, reply No.

5. **Select** the `Add-Ins` menu again. You will notice a new entry on the menu for SourceSafe. Select this option. (See Figure 1-19.)

The SourceSafe Add-In Menu Has These Four Entries:

1. **Open New SourceSafe Project.** This menu option allows you to open a project already in SourceSafe but that has never been checked out to you.

2. **Run SourceSafe.** This runs the Visual SourceSafe Explorer.

3. **Add Project to SourceSafe.** This adds the current project to the SourceSafe code library.

4. **Options.** Use this to set options for SourceSafe.

5. Select `Add Project to SourceSafe`. You will be prompted by a SourceSafe dialog box.

6. Enter the name of this project in the Project field and press OK.

7. You will be prompted to select the files that make up the project. Select them and press OK.

8. SourceSafe will add your project to the source code control library.

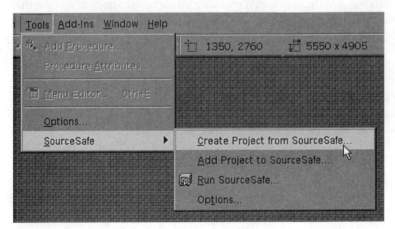

Figure 1-19 The SourceSafe Add-In menu

How It Works

When you install Visual SourceSafe on your machine, it also installs the Source Code Control Add-In. When you install this add-in into the Visual Basic development environment it allows you to add a project from the Visual Basic menus instead of starting the Visual SourceSafe Explorer and creating the project there. Selecting to add the currently open project to Source Code Control automatically starts Visual SourceSafe and prompts you to create a project entry in the source code library. Once the entry is made, you are prompted to add the files that comprise the project and then you are done.

Comments

The add-in for Visual SourceSafe does a great deal to simplify the process of using source code control. Much of the process is automated, including prompts that urge you to add projects to the source code library. Once a project is part of Visual SourceSafe, you will be able to check files in and out right from the Visual Basic development environment. Simply highlight the file in the Project window and use the right mouse button to see a menu of options for checking files in and out from SourceSafe. (See Figure 1-20.)

Figure 1-20 Menu choices available when you right-click on a file in the Project window

Before adding your projects, one suggestion is to add all developers to the SourceSafe Administrator first. This will allow you to set access rights for them on the projects. The SourceSafe Administrator does allow you to set individual rights by project. A shortcoming of Visual SourceSafe is the lack of group rights. Everything is on an individual basis, which can become a pain if you deal with a large number of people or projects and wish to control access to the code.

CHAPTER 2
GETTING CONNECTED

by Don Kiely

GETTING CONNECTED

How do I...

The introduction of VB 3.0 in 1993 introduced a whole new world to Windows programmers when Microsoft added native database features to the language, giving programmers the ability to work with database objects directly in the language itself. With VB 5, the explosion of the Internet, and rapidly changing and maturing client/server technologies, you have an almost baffling variety of choices for connecting to database servers. The How-To's in this chapter demonstrate how to use several of the most common database connections you'll use in VB. Most of the examples aren't sophisticated database applications (although a couple of the ODBC examples are), but are intended to showcase the connection techniques and related issues. Four of the How-To's produce essentially the same small application, highlighting the differences among the four connections used.

Microsoft has designed JET so that you can use it to directly access the .MDB or ISAM databases only, so that you can't use the JET engine and ODBC together to access database files. You can, however, use the ODBC API or Remote Data Objects alone, without JET, to access these databases.

The How-To's in this chapter demonstrate the various ways you can make a connection to a database. Since the Enterprise Edition's remote data objects are based on ODBC, the examples here discuss the different ways to make a connection with connect strings, the ODBC API, and other ODBC techniques. The final How-To discusses ways to determine the best connection for your particular application given the hardware, software, and network setup you have.

SQL Server ODBC Driver Requirements

Some of the How-To's in this chapter use an SQL Server ODBC driver, so you'll need to have both SQL Server and this driver installed so that you can use them either on the local machine or on the network. If not, you'll need to modify the code to use the ODBC data source and driver that you do have. You can see a list of ODBC drivers installed by running the ODBC Administrator, ODBCAD32.EXE, and clicking the ODBC Drivers tab.

The How-To's in this chapter assume that you are using the ODBC SDK 3.0 or later. If you are using version 2.x or earlier, you can download the latest version from Microsoft's Web site or get it from the Microsoft Developer Network CDs.

Remote Data Object Errors

Several of the How-To's in this chapter use the VB `RemoteData` control, remote data objects (RDOs), or both. When an error occurs with a remote connection, VB will update the `rdoErrors` collection of `rdoError` objects with information about the source of the error, a brief description, and so on to help you track down the source of the error. So before the first How-To, I'll describe in this section how to create a form you can use in any application to display all the details about an RDO error. Most of the How-To's in this chapter will use this form to report and handle connection errors.

1. Insert a new form into a VB project, saving it as **ERRORRDO.FRM** and naming it **frmRDOErrors**. Add the controls shown in Figure 2-1 to this form, with property settings as listed in Table 2-1. Using Project|Components... from the VB main menu, add the Microsoft Outline Control by checking the box to the left of the name, and clicking OK to close the window.

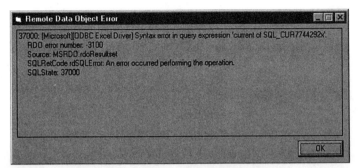

Figure 2-1 Reporting remote data object errors using an outline control

Table 2-1 Objects and properties for ERRORRDO.FRM

OBJECT	PROPERTY	SETTING
Form	Name	frmRDOErrors
	Caption	"Remote Data Object Error"
	MaxButton	0 'False
CommandButton	Name	cmdQuit
	Caption	"OK"
Outline	Name	outErrors
	Style	0

2. Add the following code to the Declarations section of the form. **Option Explicit** tells Visual Basic to make sure that you declare all variables and objects before using them, in order to avoid naming problems. You can have VB automatically add this statement to your code modules by checking the Require Variable Declaration check box in Tools|Options under the Editor tab. The form will use a **Property Let** procedure to receive the **rdoErrors** collection when an error occurs.

```
Option Explicit

'PRIVATE: *****************************************
'Private data members
Private mrdoErrs As rdoErrors
```

3. Add the following code to the form's **Load** event procedure, which simply centers the form.

```
Private Sub Form_Load()
    'Center the form
    Me.Top = (Screen.Height - Me.Height) / 2
    Me.Left = (Screen.Width - Me.Width) / 2
End Sub
```

4. The form uses a `Resize` event procedure so that the end-user can stretch or shrink the form to view the error data. Even though the outline control is loaded with one piece of information per line, some ODBC drivers insist upon returning long lines of data. Since the outline control has no word-wrapping, the end-user can at least stretch the form to see all the error data.

```
Private Sub Form_Resize()
   If Me.WindowState = vbNormal Then
      If Me.ScaleHeight < (4 * cmdQuit.Height) Then
         Me.Height = (6 * cmdQuit.Height)
      End If
      If Me.ScaleWidth < (4 * cmdQuit.Width) Then
         Me.Width = (4 * cmdQuit.Width)
      End If

      'Redraw the controls
      cmdQuit.Top = Me.ScaleHeight - (1.25 * cmdQuit.Height)
      cmdQuit.Left = Me.ScaleWidth _
         - (cmdQuit.Width + 0.25 * cmdQuit.Height)

      outErrors.Top = 0.25 * cmdQuit.Height

      outErrors.Left = 0.25 * cmdQuit.Height

      outErrors.Width = Me.ScaleWidth - 0.5 * cmdQuit.Height

      outErrors.Height = cmdQuit.Top - 0.5 * cmdQuit.Height

   End If

End Sub
```

5. Enter the following code to the **Public ErrorColl Property Let** procedure. When an RDO error occurs in another module, that module can set the **ErrorColl** property of this form to the **rdoErrors** collection containing information about the error. Since this collection can include several errors from different parts of the link to the database, this procedure adds a section to the outline control for each error, using the properties of the **rdoError** object. Once the Outline control is fully populated, the procedure expands all levels of the outline.

```
Public Property Let ErrorColl(rdoEr As rdoErrors)
Dim sText As String
Dim rdoE As rdoError
Dim i As Integer

   Set mrdoErrs = rdoEr

   'Load the Outline control with error members
   For Each rdoE In mrdoErrs
      Me.outErrors.AddItem rdoE.Description
      Me.outErrors.Indent(Me.outErrors.ListCount - 1) = 1

      sText = "RDO error number: " & rdoE.Number
      Me.outErrors.AddItem sText
      Me.outErrors.Indent(Me.outErrors.ListCount - 1) = 2
```

```
        If rdoE.Source = "" Then
            sText = "Source: Unknown"
        Else
            sText = "Source: " & rdoE.Source
        End If
        Me.outErrors.AddItem sText
        Me.outErrors.Indent(Me.outErrors.ListCount - 1) = 2

        Me.outErrors.AddItem ReturnCode(rdoE.SQLRetcode)
        Me.outErrors.Indent(Me.outErrors.ListCount - 1) = 2
        Me.outErrors.AddItem "SQLState: " & rdoE.SQLState
        Me.outErrors.Indent(Me.outErrors.ListCount - 1) = 2
    Next

    'Expand all of the outline levels
    For i = 0 To Me.outErrors.ListCount - 1
        Me.outErrors.Expand(i) = True
    Next

    Me.Show vbModal

End Property
```

6. The `rdoError` object used in the `ErrorColl Property Let` procedure contains a return code with information about the nature of the error. This procedure converts this return code to text that will be at least slightly more intelligible to the end-user.

```
Private Function ReturnCode(iRetCode As Integer) As String
Dim sText As String

    Select Case iRetCode
        Case rdSQLSuccess
            sText = "SQLRetCode rdSQLSuccess: The operation is successful."
        Case rdSQLSuccessWithInfo
            sText = "SQLRetCode rdSQLSuccessWithInfo: The operation is
successful, and additional information is available."
        Case rdSQLNoDataFound
            sText = "SQLRetCode rdSQLNoDataFound: No additional data is
available."
        Case rdSQLError
            sText = "SQLRetCode rdSQLError: An error occurred performing the
operation."
        Case rdSQLInvalidHandle
            sText = "SQLRetCode rdSQLInvalidHandle: The handle supplied is
invalid."
        Case Else
            sText = "SQLRetCode: Unknown Return Code"
    End Select

    ReturnCode = sText
End Function
```

7. Add this code to the `cmdQuit` command button's `Click` procedure to unload this form when the end-user is finished viewing the error information.

```
Private Sub cmdQuit_Click()
    Unload Me
End Sub
```

To use the **frmRDOErrors** form, check for errors in the normal VB way using an **On Error** statement around statements which use RDOs. In the error handler, call **frmRDOErrors** like this:

```
FormLoadError:
    frmRDOErrors.ErrorColl = rdoErrors
```

This statement assigns the **rdoErrors** collection to the **ErrorColl** property of the form, which executes the **ErrorColl Property Let** procedure listed above, displaying the error information. I demonstrate this technique in each of the How-To's which use this error form.

2.1 Write a Connect String

With a fully formed connect string, your application can connect directly to any ODBC data source name available on the local computer. But the trick is discovering what information ODBC needs to make the connection, and the driver's documentation as often as not doesn't provide enough information. This How-To will show how you can discover this string, and even paste it directly into your application.

2.2 Access Data with the JET Engine, ODBC, and the Data Control

One of the simplest ways of connecting to databases through ODBC is with the good old VB Data control. You'll see how to make the connection in this How-To and discover some of the limitations of doing things this way.

2.3 Make a Connection with the JET Engine, ODBC, and DAO

Where the VB Data control provides an easy but limited way to connect to data, VB's data access objects (DAOs) provide a flexible method that takes some coding work. This How-To will create the same small application as How-To 2.2 but with DAOs instead of the Data control so you can explore the differences between the two techniques.

2.4 Use the SQL Passthrough Option

Most modern client/server databases use some form of Structured Query Language (SQL) to retrieve and update information stored in the server. The SQL dialects are almost as varied as the number of database servers. This How-To will show you how to make sure your SQL statements are executed by the right tier in your enterprise application.

2.5   Open an ODBC Source Using the ODBC API

Sometimes you have to get down and dirty with low-level APIs to get the results you need in your application. You can learn the dozen or so server APIs that a medium enterprise probably uses or you can learn one, the ODBC API. This How-To builds an application you can use to explore what features an ODBC data source and driver use to give you access to data.

2.6   Make a Connection Using the RemoteData Control

When Microsoft first introduced the VB Enterprise Edition in 1995, it gave the world a new **RemoteData** control. This control has been described as "the regular VB Data control on steroids," giving you much more flexibility and power. This How-To rebuilds the application of How-To's 2.2 and 2.3 to use the **RemoteData** control and shows how its new features make your code simpler and more reliable.

2.7   Make a Connection Using Remote Data Objects

While the **RemoteData** control substantially improved upon the VB Data control, it still has its limitations. Remote data objects, however, provide both power and flexibility to data access. This How-To demonstrates how to use RDOs and shows some of the features they offer.

2.8   Benchmark My Connection Options

The number of ways to access data seems to be growing exponentially, making it harder to decide what method to use in a particular application. The answer is highly data-dependent, but you can benchmark database connections using your own live data to discover the best way to connect to your data.

COMPLEXITY

INTERMEDIATE

2.1   How do I...
Write a connect string?

Problem

I need to connect to a remote database using ODBC, but the driver documentation is just no help in giving me the information that it needs to make a connection. I need my application to make the connection (if at all possible), without users making any decisions about how to respond to the dialog boxes. How can I write a connect string without wasting time guessing?

Technique

The ODBC Manager, an integral part of ODBC, is designed so that it will prompt the end-user for any information it needs to make a connection to a database. Simply by structuring the **OpenDatabase** method, ODBC will respond by prompting for information about what data source you want (from those data sources installed on the system). Then you can make the connection and examine the Visual Basic Connect property. The **Connect** property at that point contains the fully formed connect string required to make a connection to that data source and can be copied and used directly in future attempts to connect to the database.

Steps

Open and run the **CONNSTR.VBP** Visual Basic project file. The Retrieve ODBC Connect String window will open. Click on the Connect to Data Source command button, and the ODBC Select Data Source window will appear, prompting you to select an installed data source name. Click on the Machine Data Source tab and select one of the listed data sources. Visual Basic and ODBC will obtain a list of tables available from this data source, and put them in the Tables Available listbox on the main form. After closing the Data Sources windows, either double-click on one of the tables or select one and click on the Get Connect String command button. The application will establish a connection to that database table and return the complete connect string, placing it in the Connect String text box, as shown in Figure 2-2. Click on the Copy Connect String command button to put the string in the Windows Clipboard, then paste it into your application.

1. Create a new project **CONNSTR.VBP**. Add the form **ERRORS.FRM** and the code module **ODBCAPI.BAS** (these modules are described in How-To 2.5), using Visual Basic's Project|Add File... menu command. The code module contains all the declarations needed for the ODBC API functions and the constants used in many of the functions.

2. Using Project|Components... from the VB main menu, select the custom controls shown in Table 2-2. Uncheck all others so that your project isn't cluttered with controls you aren't using, and so that the Setup Wizard doesn't include a lot of extra dead weight with your application.

Table 2-2 Custom controls used in CONNSTR.VBP

CONTROL
Microsoft Outline Control
Microsoft Windows Common Controls 5.0

3. Using Project|References... from the VB main menu, select the references shown in Table 2-3. Uncheck all others so your project isn't cluttered with DLLs you aren't using, and so the Setup Wizard doesn't include a lot of extra dead weight with your application.

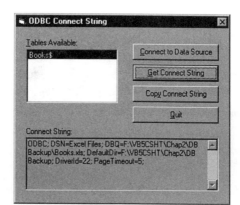

Figure 2-2 ODBC connect string for a data source using an Excel ODBC driver

Table 2-3 References used in CONNSTR.VBP

REFERENCE
Microsoft Visual Basic for Applications
Visual Basic Runtime Objects and Procedures
Microsoft Outline Control
Microsoft Windows Common Controls 5.0
Microsoft DAO 3.5 Object Library

4. Name the default form **frmConnect** and save the file as **CONNSTR.FRM**. Add the controls as shown in Figure 2-2, setting the properties as shown in Table 2-4.

Table 2-4 Objects and properties for CONNSTR.FRM

OBJECT	PROPERTY	SETTING
Form	Name	frmConnect
	BackColor	&H00C0C0C0&
	BorderStyle	3'Fixed Dialog
	Caption	"ODBC Connect String"
	MaxButton	0 'False
	MinButton	0 'False
	ShowInTaskbar	0 'False
CommandButton	Name	cmdCopyConnect
	Caption	"Cop&y Connect String"
	Enabled	0 'False

continued on next page

continued from previous page

OBJECT	PROPERTY	SETTING
CommandButton	Name	cmdGetConnect
	Caption	"&Get Connect String"
	Enabled	0 'False
CommandButton	Name	cmdQuit
	Caption	"&Quit"
TextBox	Name	txtConnect
	BackColor	&H00C0C0C0&
	MultiLine	-1 'True
	ScrollBars	2 'Vertical
	TabStop	0 'False
CommandButton	Name	cmdConnect
	Caption	"&Connect to DataSource"
ListBox	Name	lstTables
	Sorted	-1 'True
Label	Name	Label2
	BackColor	&H00C0C0C0&
	Caption	"Connect String:"
Label	Name	Label1
	BackColor	&H00C0C0C0&
	Caption	"&Tables Available:"

5. Add the following code to the Declarations section of **frmConnect**. **Option Explicit** tells Visual Basic to make sure that you declare all variables and objects before using them, in order to avoid naming problems. You can have VB automatically add this statement to your code modules by checking the Require Variable Declaration check box in Tools|Options under the Editor tab. The two module-level global variables will contain the connection information so that the records can be used throughout the module.

```
Option Explicit

'PRIVATE: ****************************************
'Private data members

'Module level globals to hold connection info
Private mDB As Database
Private mTbl As Recordset
```

6. Add this code to the form's **Load** event. After centering the form, the code allocates memory and a handle for the ODBC environment and connection. If either of these fail, there isn't much use in proceeding, so the program exits.

```
Private Sub Form_Load()
'Log on to an ODBC data source
'First, allocate ODBC memory and get handles
Dim iResult As Integer
Dim iTop As Integer, iLeft As Integer

    'Center the form
    iLeft = (Screen.Width - Me.Width) / 2
    iTop = (Screen.Height - Me.Height) / 2
    Me.Move iLeft, iTop

    'Allocate the ODBC environment handle
    iResult = ODBCAllocateEnv(ghEnv)
    If iResult <> SQL_SUCCESS Then
        End
    End If

    iResult = SQLAllocConnect(ghEnv, ghDbc)
    If iResult <> SQL_SUCCESS Then
        iResult = ODBCError("Dbc", ghEnv, ghDbc, 0, _
            iResult, "Error allocating connection handle.")
        End
    End If

    Me.Show
End Sub
```

7. Add the following code to the **cmdConnect** command button's **Click** event. Before getting the connection data, the end-user has to select a data source name for connection information. For this procedure, the built-in ODBC dialog boxes do all the work. The code that comes with the dialog includes this **OpenDatabase** statement:

```
Set mDB = OpenDatabase("", False, False, "ODBC;")
```

This line tells Visual Basic to open a database, but gives no information about which one, other than the fact that it is an ODBC database. ODBC responds by opening its Select Data Source dialog box for selection of a data source, as shown in Figure 2-3.

Once the end-user selects a data source name, the procedure loops through all the tables in the database—the **TableDefs** collection—using a Visual Basic **For Each... Next** loop, retrieves the table name of each table available in that data source, and adds each to the **lstTables** listbox. If a connection is made and there are any tables available, the **cmdGetConnect** command button is enabled for the next step of retrieving the connection information. The error handler routine is important in this procedure, and is discussed with the APIConnect procedure code in Step 13.

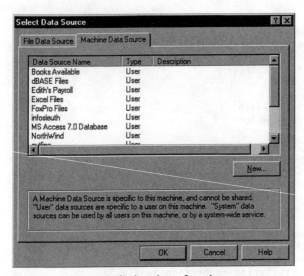

Figure 2-3 ODBC dialog box for data source selection

```
Private Sub cmdConnect_Click()
'Connect to a data source and populate lstTables
Dim i As Integer
'Dim sConnect As String
Dim iSaveCursor As Integer
Dim td As TableDef

    iSaveCursor = Screen.MousePointer
    Screen.MousePointer = vbHourglass

    lstTables.Clear

    On Error GoTo ErrHandler
    Set mDB = OpenDatabase("", False, False, "ODBC;")
    On Error GoTo 0

    For Each td In mDB.TableDefs
        lstTables.AddItem td.Name
    Next

    Screen.MousePointer = iSaveCursor

    If lstTables.ListCount Then
        cmdGetConnect.Enabled = True
    Else
        MsgBox "No tables available. Please connect " _
            & "to another data source."
    End If

    Exit Sub
```

```
ErrHandler:
    Screen.MousePointer = iSaveCursor
    Select Case Err.Number
        Case 3423
            'This data source can't be attached, (or the
            'user clicked Cancel, so use ODBC API to let
            'the user select a data source.
            APIConnect
            Resume
        Case 3059
            'The user clicked on Cancel
            Exit Sub
        Case Else
            'The error is something else, so send it back to
            'the VB exception handler
            Error Err.Number
            Resume
    End Select
End Sub
```

8. Add the following code to the `cmdGetConnect`'s `Click` event. This command button is only enabled once a connection is made and tables are available for selection. Assuming that a table name has been selected, a connection is made to that table by creating a recordset. This makes the connection information available, which can be retrieved by copying the value of the database's `Connect` property to the txtConnect text box, running it through the AddSpaces function shown in Step 9. Finally, the `cmdCopyConnect` command button is enabled.

```
Private Sub cmdGetConnect_Click()
Dim iSaveCursor As Integer

    iSaveCursor = Screen.MousePointer
    Screen.MousePointer = vbHourglass

    txtConnect.Text = ""

    If Len(lstTables.Text) Then
        Set mTbl = mDB.OpenRecordset(lstTables.Text)
        txtConnect.Text = AddSpaces(mDB.Connect)
    Else
        MsgBox "Please select a table first."
    End If

    cmdCopyConnect.Enabled = True
    Screen.MousePointer = iSaveCursor
End Sub
```

9. Add the following `Sub` procedure to the code section of `frmConnect`. When the program gets the raw connect string back from ODBC after making the connection to the database table, it is strung together with no spaces, unless a space happens to be in any of the strings enclosed in double quotes. Sometimes the connect string is quite long, so the text box has the `MultiLine` property set to `True`. But even with that, an unbroken

string with no spaces can exceed any text box width. So this function simply loops through the length of the string, replacing all the semicolon
separators with a semicolon-space pair of characters. ODBC uses semicolons to separate the different phrases in a connect string.

```
Function AddSpaces(sConnect As String)
Dim i As Integer
Dim sNew As String
Dim sNextChar As String

    For i = 1 To Len(sConnect)
        sNextChar = Mid$(sConnect, i, 1)
        If sNextChar = ";" Then
            sNew = sNew & sNextChar & " "
        Else
            sNew = sNew & sNextChar
        End If
    Next
    AddSpaces = sNew
End Function
```

10. Add the code for **cmdCopyConnect**'s **Click** event as shown here. This is
added as a convenience for the programmer. Once you have connected to
the data source and have received the connect string, just click on the Copy
Connect String command button, and the full string is copied to the
Windows Clipboard, ready to paste into your application wherever you
need to set up the connection.

```
Private Sub cmdCopyConnect_Click()

    'Select the text in txtConnect
    txtConnect.SetFocus
    txtConnect.SelStart = 0
    txtConnect.SelLength = Len(txtConnect.Text)

    'Copy selected text to Clipboard.
    Clipboard.SetText Screen.ActiveControl.SelText

End Sub
```

11. Add the following code to the form's **Unload** event and the **cmdQuit** command button's event. The **cmdQuit** command button ends the program by
unloading the form. As usual for Visual Basic applications that make direct
calls to the ODBC API, the code needs to clean up after itself, releasing the
memory and handles needed for connection to ODBC. The **iResult** variables are just a place to dump the return values; because the program is
ending anyway, you don't need to care about return values.

```
Private Sub cmdQuit_Click()
    Unload Me
End Sub


Private Sub Form_Unload(Cancel As Integer)
Dim iResult As Integer
```

```
    iResult = ODBCDisconnectDS(ghEnv, ghDbc, ghStmt)
    iResult = ODBCFreeEnv(ghEnv)
End Sub
```

12. Add the following code to the **DblClick** event procedure of the **lstTables** listbox. This simply adds the convenience of double-clicking a table in **lstTables** to retrieve the connect string, saving the work of also clicking the **cmdGetConnect** command button.

```
Private Sub lstTables_DblClick()
    cmdGetConnect_Click
End Sub
```

13. Add the following code to the code section of the form. ODBC error handling is covered in some detail in the introduction to this chapter, but sometimes it is necessary to handle errors generated by Visual Basic but caused by the ODBC system. This is one example of such a situation.

Two sorts of Visual Basic errors need to be handled in the **cmdConnect_Click** procedure. The first is for a problem making the connection to the data source for any of a number of causes: the database is not available, the connection couldn't be made because of network traffic, and so on. One common error of this type is attempting to open an ODBC database that is one of the databases that Visual Basic handles natively, such as an Access **.MDB** file or one of the ISAM databases.

This is where the **APIConnect** procedure comes in. Even though the error is generated by the Visual Basic error handler, there is some reason lurking in ODBC why the connection can't be made, and a call to the ODBC **SQLError** function will usually give more information about the problem (though ODBC can't always determine the reason for the error).

APIConnect calls the ODBC API function **SQLError** from within the error procedure, gets whatever additional information can be obtained, disconnects the ODBC connection (but not the handle—it may be needed again for another attempt to make a connection), and returns to **frmConnect**.

The other error that has to be handled is if the end-user clicks on Cancel when ODBC's SQL Data Sources dialog box is shown. ODBC lets you know this happened by returning an error. In this case the code exits the **Sub** procedure and returns to the main form.

```
Sub APIConnect()
'Can't connect through VB, so go direct
Dim iResult As Integer
Dim sConnectIn As String
Dim sConnectOut As String * SQL_MAX_OPTION_STRING_LENGTH
Dim lOutConnect As Long

    sConnectIn = ""

    iResult = SQLDriverConnect(ghDbc, Me.hWnd, _
```

continued on next page

continued from previous page

```
          sConnectIn, Len(sConnectIn), sConnectOut, _
          Len(sConnectOut), lOutConnect, SQL_DRIVER_PROMPT)
      If iResult <> SQL_SUCCESS Then
          iResult = ODBCError("Dbc", ghEnv, ghDbc, 0, _
              iResult, "Problem with call to SQLDriverConnect.")
          Exit Sub
      End If
      txtConnect.Text = AddSpaces(sConnectOut)

      'Free the connection, but not the handle
      iResult = SQLDisconnect(ghDbc)
      If iResult <> SQL_SUCCESS Then
          iResult = ODBCError("Dbc", ghEnv, ghDbc, 0, _
              iResult, "Problem with call to SQLDriverConnect.")
      End If

      cmdCopyConnect.Enabled = True
  End Sub
```

14. In the Project|[Project Name] Options menu item, set the startup form to `frmConnect`. You can also set an application description, but that is not required for the operation of this application.

How It Works

Three ODBC API functions make a connection to a data source: `SQLConnect`, `SQLBrowseConnect`, and `SQLDriverConnect`, shown in Table 2-5, and are used in the `ODBCAPI.BAS` procedures used in this How-To.

Table 2-5 ODBC functions for establishing data source connections

FUNCTION	VERSION	CONFORMANCE	PRIMARY ARGUMENTS
SQLConnect	1.0	Core	hDbc, data source name, user ID, authorization string
SQLDriverConnect	1.0	1	hDbc, window handle (hwnd), connect string in, connect string out, completion option
SQLBrowseConnect	1.0	2	hDbc, connect string in, connect string out

`SQLConnect` is the standard way of connecting to an ODBC data source. All of the arguments must be complete and correct, because if anything is wrong, ODBC generates an error. If everything is right, a connection is established. Valid return codes are `SQL_SUCCESS`, `SQL_SUCCESS_WITH_INFO`, `SQL_ERROR`, or `SQL_INVALID_HANDLE`. The only flexibility that `SQLConnect` provides is that if the specified data source name can't be found, the function looks for a default driver and loads that if one is defined in `ODBC.INI`. If not, `SQL_ERROR` is returned, and more information about the problem can be obtained with a call to `SQLError`. `SQLConnect` is the workhorse function of ODBC connections.

SQLDriverConnect offers a bit more flexibility for making ODBC connections. This function can handle data sources that require more information than the three arguments of **SQLConnect** (other than the connection handle **hDbc**, which all three functions require). It provides dialog boxes to prompt for any missing information needed for the connection and can handle connections not defined in the **ODBC.INI** file or registry. **SQLDriverConnect** provides three connection options:

1. A connection string provided in the function call that contains all the data needed, including data source name, multiple user IDs, multiple passwords, and any other custom information required by the database.

2. A connection string that only provides some of the data required to make the connection. The ODBC Driver Manager and the driver then can prompt for any additional information that each needs to make the connection.

3. A connection that is not defined in **ODBC.INI** or the registry. If any partial information is provided, the function will make whatever use of it that it can.

When a connection is successfully established, the function will then return **SQL_SUCCESS** and returns a completed connection string that may be used to make future connections to that database. It is a safe bet that **SQLDriverConnect** is the function that Visual Basic uses to discover the connect string when this How-To is employed because of the similarity in their operation.

SQLDriverConnect can return **SQL_SUCCESS**, **SQL_SUCCESS_WITH_INFO**, **SQL_NO_DATA_FOUND**, **SQL_ERROR**, or **SQL_INVALID_HANDLE**. Valid choices for the completion option argument are **SQL_DRIVER_PROMPT**, **SQL_DRIVER_COMPLETE**, **SQL_DRIVER_COMPLETE_REQUIRED**, or **SQL_DRIVER_NOPROMPT**.

The third function, **SQLBrowseConnect**, is perhaps the most interesting of the three functions. This function initiates an interactive method of discovering what it takes to connect to a particular database. Each time **SQLBrowseConnect** is called, the function returns additional attributes that are needed to make a connection. An application making the call can parse out the resulting string containing missing attributes (which are marked as required or optional), and return successively more fully complete connect strings. Attributes that involve selection from a fixed list of items are returned as that full list, so an application can present a listbox of choices to the end-user.

Comments

You can't make an ODBC connection through an attached table to a JET database that Visual Basic natively supports, like a Microsoft Access **.MDB** file or ISAM databases like **Btrieve** and **dBase** files. There normally isn't any reason to do so, although it can always be done using the ODBC API directly, bypassing JET.

2.2 How do I...
Access data with the JET engine, ODBC, and the Data control?

Problem

I have a database that I need to use in my application for simple browsing and updating data. How can I link to the data without spending a lot of time writing data access code and learning a whole new API?

Technique

The VB Data control provides a quick and easy way to link your application to a database, at the cost of speed and flexibility. The steps to bind the Visual Basic Data control and other bound controls to an ODBC data source are quite simple, not that much different from connecting to one of Visual Basic's native data formats using the JET database engine. This How-To shows exactly what is necessary to set up the controls to make the connection.

Steps

Open and run the **BOOKS.VBP** project file as shown in Figure 2-4. Use the Visual Basic Data control's navigation buttons at the bottom of the form to move through the SQL Server PUBS database, then click on Quit when you are finished.

1. This How-To uses an ODBC SQL Server driver and the sample PUBS database included with SQL Server. You can use any other ODBC data source or database, but you'll need to change the fields connected to the form's text boxes.

2. Create a data source name in ODBC for the PUBS database. Start the ODBC Adminstrator, **ODBCAD32.EXE**, most likely located in the Windows System directory in Windows 95 or the System32 directory in Windows NT. ODBC Administrator loads the ODBC Data Source Administrator window as shown in Figure 2-5. Here you define and maintain data source names available on this system.

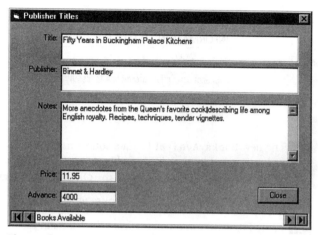

Figure 2-4 Using ODBC with the Visual Basic data control to review a book database

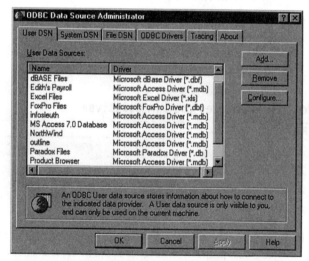

Figure 2-5 Main ODBC Administrator window

3. Click the Add... button so the Add Data Source window appears. The driver you need will be listed as something like **SQL Server** or **SQL Server (32-bit)**. Click this driver, then click OK so the ODBC SQL Server Setup window appears. Each ODBC driver has its own version of this setup window, prompting for the particular information that the driver needs to make a connection with its database. Click the Options>> button to show the full form, then enter the information as shown in Table 2-6. You may have to adjust other entries not listed in the table for your system setup. Then click OK to create the data source name.

Table 2-6 Books Available data source name setup information

PROMPT	INFORMATION TO ENTER
Data Source Name	Books Available
Description	[Optional description information to identify the data source]
Server	[The server where SQL Server is located]
Database Name	PUBS

4. The new `Books Available` data source name will appear in the `Data Sources` window as something like `Books Available` with a driver listed as `SQL Server`. Click OK to end the ODBC Administrator.

5. Start VB. Create a new project `BOOKS.VBP`.

6. Using Project|Components... from the VB main menu, unselect all the custom controls listed so your project isn't cluttered with controls you aren't using, and so the Setup Wizard doesn't include unneeded files with your application. This VB project uses only the native custom controls.

7. Using Project|References... from the VB main menu, select the references shown in Table 2-7. Uncheck all others so that your project isn't cluttered with DLLs you aren't using, and so the Setup Wizard doesn't include unneeded files with your application.

Table 2-7 References used in `BOOKS.VBP`

REFERENCE
Microsoft Visual Basic for Applications
Visual Basic Runtime Objects and Procedures
Visual Basic Objects and Procedures
Microsoft DAO 3.5 Object Library

8. Add the controls shown in Figure 2-4 to the default form in the new project, with property settings as listed in Table 2-8. Save the form as file `BOOKS.FRM`.

Table 2-8 Objects and properties for `BOOKS.FRM`

OBJECT	PROPERTY	SETTING
Form	Name	frmBooks
	BackColor	&H00C0C0C0&
	BorderStyle	3 'Fixed Dialog
	Caption	"Publisher Titles"
	MaxButton	0 'False

OBJECT	PROPERTY	SETTING
	MinButton	0 'False
TextBox	Name	txtPublisher
	DataSource	"Data1"
	MultiLine	-1 'True
CommandButton	Name	cmdClose
	Caption	"Close"
	Default	-1 'True
TextBox	Name	txtAdvance
	DataSource	"Data1"
TextBox	Name	txtPrice
	DataSource	"Data1"
TextBox	Name	txtNotes
	DataSource	"Data1"
	MultiLine	-1 'True
	ScrollBars	2 'Vertical
TextBox	Name	txtTitle
	DataSource	"Data1"
	MultiLine	-1 'True
Data	Name	Data1
	Align	2 'Align Bottom
	Caption	"Books Available"
	Connect	""
	DatabaseName	""
	Exclusive	0 'False
	Options	0
	ReadOnly	0 'False
	RecordsetType	1 'Dynaset
	RecordSource	""
Label	Name	Label9
	Alignment	1 'Right Justify
	BackColor	&H00C0C0C0&
	Caption	"Publisher:"
Label	Name	Label6
	Alignment	1 'Right Justify
	BackColor	&H00C0C0C0&
	Caption	"Advance:"
Label	Name	Label5

continued on next page

continued from previous page

OBJECT	PROPERTY	SETTING
	Alignment	1 'Right Justify
	BackColor	&H00C0C0C0&
	Caption	"Price:"
Label	Name	Label3
	Alignment	1 'Right Justify
	BackColor	&H00C0C0C0&
	Caption	"Notes:"
Label	Name	Label1
	Alignment	1 'Right Justify
	BackColor	&H00C0C0C0&
	Caption	"Title:"

9. Add the following code to the Declarations section of the form. `Option Explicit` tells Visual Basic to make sure that you declare all variables and objects before using them, in order to avoid naming problems. You can have VB automatically add this statement to your code modules by checking the Require Variable Declaration check box in Tools|Options under the `Editor` tab.

```
Option Explicit
```

10. Add the following code to the form's `Load` event procedure. After centering the form, the Data control's `Connect` property is set to the ODBC connection string and the `RecordSource` property is set to the SQL query to execute. Then the text boxes' `DataField` properties are set to the fields which each will hold. This is the step that links each field to the text boxes that hold each record's data. These properties could be set at design time, but when the `Data` control is not bound to a physical table, the code is less confusing.

```
Private Sub Form_Load()
'Set up the form and connect to data source
Dim db As Database
Dim rs As Recordset
Dim sSQL As String

    'Center the form
    Me.Top = (Screen.Height - Me.Height) / 2
    Me.Left = (Screen.Width - Me.Width) / 2

    'Connect to the database.
    Data1.Connect = "ODBC;DSN=Books Available;UID=sa;PWD="

    'Set the data control's RecordSource property
    sSQL = _
```

```
          "SELECT titles.*, publishers.* " _
        & "FROM titles, publishers " _
        & "WHERE publishers.pub_id = titles.pub_id " _
        & "ORDER BY titles.Title ASC;"
    Data1.RecordSource = sSQL

    'Connect each of the text boxes with the appropriate fieldname
    txtAdvance.DataField = "Advance"
    txtNotes.DataField = "Notes"
    txtPrice.DataField = "Price"
    txtPublisher.DataField = "Pub_Name"
    txtTitle.DataField = "Title"

End Sub
```

11. Add the following code to the **Click** event of the **cmdQuit** command button. This is the exit point that terminates the program.

```
Private Sub cmdClose_Click()
    Unload Me
End Sub
```

12. In the Project|[Project Name] Options menu item, set the startup form to **frmBooks**. You can also set an application description, but that is not required for the operation of this application.

How It Works

This is all the code required to use ODBC with Visual Basic's Data control. When the form is loaded, you can move about the database with the built-in navigation buttons.

There are several important details in setting up this procedure for use with ODBC. Note that I chose to do most of the setup and initialization in code in this How-To, but you can also set the properties of the Data control and bound text boxes when designing the form and then simply load the form. In this case, Visual Basic will make the connection for you and display the data directly, and you don't even need any code in the form's **Load** event.

■ The data control's **DatabaseName** property must be left blank to use an ODBC data source. If you enter a database name here, Visual Basic attempts to open the database using its native data format before you can set it to an empty string in code.

■ The **Connect** property of the Data control is set to the connect string that ODBC needs to connect to the database. This is the same connect string that other How-To's in this chapter use to set up other uses of ODBC directly. You can also simply set this property to **ODBC**. ODBC will prompt the end-user at runtime for information it needs to make the connection.

■ The Data control's `RecordSource` property is set to the SQL statement used to select the data from the database. This can be any SQL statement that creates a result set that Visual Basic can use to populate the bound text boxes.

■ Each text box's `DataSource` is set to the name of the Data control; in this How-To, `Data1`. This is the normal Visual Basic way of binding a control to a Data control. You can have as many Data controls on a form as you want, with different sets of controls bound to different bound controls and therefore to different databases.

■ Each text box's `DataField` property is set to the particular field name in the result set of data records. Note that this may be the name of the field in the database itself, but it is actually the name of the field returned in the result-set. The two can be the same, but the SQL statement can rename the fields or even return calculated fields that don't exist in the database.

Comments

You can actually perform some complex operations using the VB Data control, but you usually have to do a lot more coding to get around its limitations than if you used other techniques such as data access objects (DAOs). Some of the later How-To's in this chapter cover these other techniques.

COMPLEXITY
INTERMEDIATE

2.3   How do I...
Make a connection with the JET engine, ODBC, and DAO?

Problem

I have a database that I need to use in my application for data entry and editing. The VB Data control is easy to use, but I end up writing a ton of code to get around its limitations. Isn't there some way of coding more flexibility into my application?

Technique

When the VB Data control falls short of your needs—and it will for any sophisticated, modern application—VB provides data access objects (DAOs), which let you have almost complete flexibility accessing data. It is more work to code, but many of the routines can be used repeatedly in different forms in different applications.

The biggest change is that you have to code retrieving a record's data and putting it into controls on a form, then code saving changed data back to the record. It is harder to describe the process than to actually do it, though. Once you have a basic understanding of how DAOs work in this How-To, however, you should have no trouble using them in your own applications.

This How-To implements the same user interface used in How-To 2.2, which used the VB Data control, but modifies the code to use DAOs, and adds a few features to demonstrate how to use DAOs.

Steps

Open and run the **BOOKS.VBP** project file. Use the navigation buttons at the bottom of the form to move through the database, then add, delete, and update records. Then click on Quit when you are finished. The Publisher Titles windows is shown in Figure 2-6.

1. This How-To uses an ODBC SQL Server driver and the sample PUBS database included with SQL Server. You can use any other ODBC data source or database, but you'll need to change the fields connected to the form's text boxes.

2. Create a data source name in ODBC for the PUBS database. Start the ODBC Adminstrator, **ODBCAD32.EXE**, most likely located in the Windows System directory in Windows 95 or the System32 directory in Windows NT. ODBC Administrator loads the Data Sources window as shown in Figure 2-7. Here you define and maintain data source names available on this system.

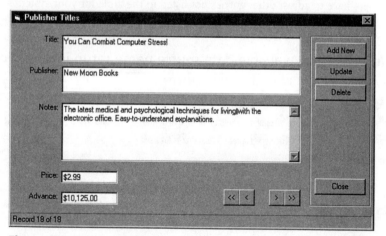

Figure 2-6 Using ODBC with Visual Basic data access objects to review a book database

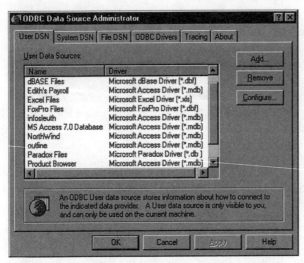

Figure 2-7 Main ODBC Administrator window

3. Click the Add... button so the Add Data Source window appears. The driver you need will be listed as something like `SQL Server` or `SQL Server (32-bit)`. Click this driver, then click `OK` so that the ODBC SQL Server Setup window appears. Each ODBC driver has its own version of this setup window, prompting for the particular information that the driver needs to make a connection with its database. Click the Options>>> button to show the full form, then enter the information as shown in Table 2-9. You may have to adjust other entries not listed in the table for your system setup. Then click OK to create the data source name.

Table 2-9 Books Available data source name setup information

PROMPT	INFORMATION TO ENTER
Data Source Name	Books Available
Description	[Optional description information to identify the data source]
Server	[The server where SQL Server is located]
Database Name	PUBS

4. The new Books Available data source name will appear in the Data Sources window as something like `Books Available` with a driver listed as `SQL Server`. Click OK to end the ODBC Administrator.

5. Start VB. Create a new project `BOOKS.VBP`.

6. Using Project|Components... from the VB main menu, select the custom controls shown in Table 2-10. Uncheck all others so your project isn't cluttered with controls you aren't using, and so the Setup Wizard doesn't include a lot of dead weight with your application.

Table 2-10 Custom control used in BOOKS.VBP

CONTROL
Microsoft Windows Common Controls 5.0

7. Using Project|References… from the VB main menu, select the references shown in Table 2-11. Uncheck all others so your project isn't cluttered with DLLs you aren't using, and so the Setup Wizard doesn't include unneeded files with your application.

Table 2-11 References used in BOOKS.VBP

REFERENCE
Microsoft Visual Basic for Applications
Visual Basic Runtime Objects and Procedures
Visual Basic Objects and Procedures
Microsoft DAO 3.5 Object Library

8. Add the controls shown in Figure 2-6 to the form in the new project, with property settings as listed in Table 2-12. Save the form as file BOOKS.FRM.

Table 2-12 Objects and properties for BOOKS.FRM

OBJECT	PROPERTY	SETTING
Form	Name	frmBooks
	BackColor	&H00C0C0C0&
	BorderStyle	3 'Fixed Dialog
	Caption	"Publisher Titles"
	MaxButton	0 'False
	MinButton	0 'False
TextBox	Name	txtTitle
	MultiLine	-1 'True
TextBox	Name	txtNotes
	MultiLine	-1 'True
	ScrollBars	2 'Vertical
TextBox	Name	txtPrice
TextBox	Name	txtAdvance
TextBox	Name	txtPublisher
	MultiLine	-1 'True

continued on next page

continued from previous page

OBJECT	PROPERTY	SETTING
Frame	Name	Frame1
CommandButton	Name	cmdClose
	Caption	"Close"
CommandButton	Name	cmdDelete
	Caption	"Delete"
CommandButton	Name	cmdUpdate
	Caption	"Update"
CommandButton	Name	cmdAddNew
	Caption	"Add New"
CommandButton	Name	cmdMove
	Caption	">>"
	Index	3
	TabStop	0 'False
CommandButton	Name	cmdMove
	Caption	">"
	Index	2
	TabStop	0 'False
CommandButton	Name	cmdMove
	Caption	"<"
	Index	1
	TabStop	0 'False
CommandButton	Name	cmdMove
	Caption	"<<"
	Index	0
	TabStop	0 'False
Label	Name	Label1
	Alignment	1 'Right Justify
	BackColor	&H00C0C0C0&
	Caption	"Title:"
Label	Name	Label3
	Alignment	1 'Right Justify
	BackColor	&H00C0C0C0&
	Caption	"Notes:"
Label	Name	Label5
	Alignment	1 'Right Justify
	BackColor	&H00C0C0C0&
	Caption	"Price:"

OBJECT	PROPERTY	SETTING
Label	Name	Label6
	Alignment	1 'Right Justify
	BackColor	&H00C0C0C0&
	Caption	"Advance:"
Label	Name	Label9
	Alignment	1 'Right Justify
	BackColor	&H00C0C0C0&
	Caption	"Publisher:"
StatusBar	Name	StatusBar1
	Align	2 'Align Bottom
	AlignSet	-1 'True
	Style	1
	SimpleText	""

9. Add the following code to the Declarations section of the form. **Option Explicit** tells Visual Basic to make sure that you declare all variables and objects before using them, in order to avoid naming problems. You can have VB automatically add this statement to your code modules by checking the Require Variable Declaration check box in Tools|Options under the Editor tab. The first two variables are references to database objects so code throughout the module can manipulate the data. The next two variables track the total number of records and the current location in the recordset. The last variable, **mDirty**, records whether the end-user has made any changes to the current data.

```
Option Explicit

'Database and Recordset objects that will contain
'the books table.
Dim db As Database
Dim rs As Recordset

'Variables to track the position in recordset.
Dim lTotRec As Long
Dim lCurrRec As Long

'Variable to indicated if data needs to be saved.
Dim mDirty As Boolean
```

10. Add the following code to the form's **Load** event procedure. After centering the form, **OpenDatabase** makes a connection to the ODBC data source, then the **rs Recordset** is opened using an SQL query. To prevent problems when there is no current record, a new record is added if the **Recordset** is empty.

The code uses the `lCurrRec` and `lTotRec` to keep track of the position in the recordset. You can implement this technique when using the Data control, but the logic gets to be a bit more convoluted since VB is handling part of the record navigation work for you. (VB and the JET engine are oriented to work on sets of records rather than individual records, so keeping track of the current record number is a concept foreign to VB.)

Finally, the `Load` event procedure calls the `DataLoad` procedure to load the form's controls with data from the current record.

```
Private Sub Form_Load()
'Set up the form and connect to data source
Dim sSQL As String

    'Center the form
    Me.Top = (Screen.Height - Me.Height) / 2
    Me.Left = (Screen.Width - Me.Width) / 2

    'Connect to the database.
    Set db = OpenDatabase("Books Available", _
        False, False, "ODBC;UID=sa;PWD=")

    'Create the recordset.
    sSQL = _
        "SELECT DISTINCTROW titles.*, publishers.* " _
        & "FROM publishers " _
        & "INNER JOIN titles " _
        & "ON publishers.pub_id = titles.pub_id " _
        & "ORDER BY titles.Title;"
        Set rs = db.OpenRecordset(sSQL)

    'If the recordset is empty, add a record.
    If rs.EOF And rs.BOF Then
        rs.AddNew
        rs.Update
        lTotRec = 1
    Else
        rs.MoveLast
        lTotRec = rs.RecordCount
    End If

    rs.MoveFirst
    lCurrRec = 1
    SetRecNum

    DataLoad

'    txtTitle.SetFocus

End Sub
```

11. Since the VB code is handling all the data management details, it needs to take care of properly saving data that is *dirty*, or has changed. You have several options: Let the end-user worry about it, manually updating the data when he or she changes it, or you can handle it entirely in code. Or you can use some combination of the two, which is the way I've implemented this program. The code responds to the form's controls' **Change** events and the end-user can manually save the data by clicking an Update button. Add the following code to the **Change** event procedure for all the text boxes on the form.

```
Private Sub txtAdvance_Change()

    mDirty = True

End Sub


Private Sub txtNotes_Change()

    mDirty = True

End Sub


Private Sub txtPrice_Change()

    mDirty = True

End Sub


Private Sub txtPublisher_Change()

    mDirty = True

End Sub


Private Sub txtTitle_Change()

    mDirty = True

End Sub
```

12. Add the following code to the **DataLoad Sub** procedure. This is the code that loads the current record's data into the form each time the end-user moves to a new record. The procedure finishes by setting the **mDirty** flag to **False**, since the data was just loaded, then updating the record counter at the bottom of the form.

```
Private Sub DataLoad()
'Copy the record's data to the text boxes.

    txtAdvance.Text = Format$(rs("Advance") & "", "Currency")
    txtNotes.Text = rs("Notes") & ""
    txtPrice.Text = Format$(rs("Price") & "", "Currency")
    txtPublisher.Text = rs("Pub_Name") & ""
    txtTitle.Text = rs("Title") & ""

    mDirty = False
    SetRecNum
End Sub
```

13. What goes in must come out, so add the following code to the **DataSave** procedure, which saves the data in the form to the current record, whenever the data is dirty or the end-user clicks the Update button. The **mDirty** flag is also set to **False** here, since the data in the form is again the same as that in the record.

```
Private Sub DataSave()
'Copy the current control contents to the record.
'ODBC driver and database has to support editing
'(most do).
    rs.Edit
    rs("Advance") = txtAdvance.Text
    rs("Notes") = txtNotes.Text
    rs("Price") = txtPrice.Text
    rs("Pub_Name") = txtPublisher.Text
    rs("Title") = txtTitle.Text
    rs.Update

    mDirty = False
End Sub
```

14. The form has an Update button the end-user can use to manually update data, which simply executes the **DataSave** procedure. The lines commented out here can be used to protect the end-user against himself or herself by only saving data when it is dirty. This is a user interface issue. If the user wants to save the data, you should go ahead and save it rather than essentially ignoring their wishes, whether or not the data is dirty. You may, however, have a good programmatic reason to not save clean data. In that case, and if you un-comment the two lines, at least let the end-user know that the data isn't being saved, and why.

```
Private Sub cmdUpdate_Click()
'    If mDirty Then
        DataSave
'    End If
End Sub
```

15. The next few procedures take care of navigating through the recordset. The navigation keys, a control array of command buttons, execute this **Click** event procedure which starts by checking whether the end-user wants to save any dirty data. Then it calls the **MoveRecord** procedure with the control index to actually reposition the record. Since there is a new current record, the **DataLoad** procedures loads the new data into the form.

```
Private Sub cmdMove_Click(Index As Integer)
Dim iResponse As Integer

    If mDirty Then
        iResponse = MsgBox("Dirty data. Save changes?", _
            vbYesNo + vbExclamation, "Update Data?")
        If iResponse = vbYes Then
            DataSave
```

```
        End If
    End If

    lCurrRec = MoveRecord(rs, Index, lCurrRec)

    DataLoad
End Sub
```

16. Enter the following code into the **MoveRecord Function** procedure. This code is a reusable function to move around a recordset, implementing code to move to the first or last record, and to the next and previous records. If the first record is current and the end-user clicks the Move Previous button, a beep sounds; a beep also sounds at the last record when the end-user clicks the Move Next button. You can get as creative as you want here, allowing the end-user to move forward or backward a fixed number of records or to go to a specific record number.

```
Public Function MoveRecord( _
    rs As Recordset, _
    Index As Integer, _
    Optional lCurrRec As Variant) As Long

    If IsMissing(lCurrRec) Then
        lCurrRec = 0
    End If

    Select Case Index
        Case 0 'MoveFirst
            rs.MoveFirst
            MoveRecord = 1

        Case 1 'MovePrevious
            rs.MovePrevious
            If rs.BOF Then
                Beep
                rs.MoveFirst
                MoveRecord = 1
            Else
                MoveRecord = lCurrRec - 1
            End If

        Case 2 'MoveNext
            rs.MoveNext
            If rs.EOF Then
                Beep
                rs.MoveLast
                MoveRecord = rs.RecordCount
            Else
                MoveRecord = lCurrRec + 1
            End If

        Case 3 'MoveLast
            rs.MoveLast
            MoveRecord = rs.RecordCount

    End Select
End Function
```

17. At the bottom of the form, a `StatusBar` control shows the end-user where he is in the recordset, indicating **Record 5 of 120** or whatever. Here the `lCurrRec` and `lTotRec` module variables finally become visibly useful.

```
Private Sub SetRecNum()
    StatusBar1.SimpleText = "Record " & _
        lCurrRec & " of " & lTotRec
End Sub
```

18. To add a new record, the **cmdAddNew** button's **Click** event checks to see whether dirty data should be saved, then adds a new record to the recordset. After updating the **lTotRec** count and the **lCurrRec** position in the recordset, the **DataLoad** procedure loads data from the new record. Since it is a new record and has no data, this clears the form's controls, making them ready to accept the end-user's input.

```
Private Sub cmdAddNew_Click()
Dim iResponse As Integer

    If mDirty Then
        iResponse = MsgBox("Dirty data. " _
            & "Save before adding a new record?", _
            vbYesNo + vbExclamation, "Dirty Data")
        If iResponse = vbYes Then
            DataSave
        End If
    End If

    rs.AddNew
    rs.Update
    rs.Move 0, rs.LastModified
    lTotRec = lTotRec + 1
    lCurrRec = rs.RecordCount

    DataLoad
End Sub
```

19. A Delete button allows the end-user to remove records from the recordset. This is very similar to the **AddNew** procedure. If after deleting the record the recordset is empty, a new record is added so there is always at least one record. Either way, the position is moved to the first record, and its data loaded into the form.

```
Private Sub cmdDelete_Click()
Dim iResponse As Integer

    iResponse = MsgBox("Are you sure that you " _
        & "want to delete this record?", _
        vbYesNo + vbExclamation, "Delete Record")
    If iResponse = vbYes Then
        rs.Delete
        lTotRec = lTotRec - 1
        If (rs.BOF And rs.EOF) Or lTotRec = 0 Then
            'If there aren't any records in the table, add an empty record
            'to avoid problems with "No current record" errors.
```

```
            rs.AddNew
            rs.Update
            rs.MoveLast <moved statement below>
            lCurrRec = rs.RecordCount
            lTotRec = lCurrRec
        Else
            lCurrRec = 1
        End If
    End If


    rs.MoveFirst
    DataLoad
End Sub
```

20. Add the following code to the `Click` event of the `cmdClose` command button. This is the exit point that terminates the program. After checking one
last time whether dirty data should be saved, the procedure unloads itself.

```
Private Sub cmdClose_Click()
Dim iResponse As Integer

    If mDirty Then
        iResponse = MsgBox("Dirty data. Save before closing?", _
            vbYesNo + vbExclamation, "Dirty Data")
        If iResponse = vbYes Then
            DataSave
        End If
    End If
    Unload Me
End Sub
```

21. In the Project|[Project Name] Options menu item, set the startup form to
`frmBooks`. You can also set an application description, but that is not
required for the operation of this application.

How It Works

If you compare this code with that in How-To 2.2, you'll find that many of the features you might take for granted with the Data control have to be handled by your
code. This is a bit more work but gives you far greater flexibility with how your application uses and navigates data.

The details of using ODBC are similar to those when using the Data control. All
the work of making the connection is handled in this code from the form's **Load** event
procedure as shown below:

```
'Connect to the database.
    Set db = OpenDatabase("Books Available", _
        False, False, "ODBC;UID=sa;PWD=")

    'Create the recordset.
    sSQL = _
        "SELECT DISTINCTROW titles.*, publishers.* " _
        & "FROM publishers " _
```

continued on next page

continued from previous page

```
        & "INNER JOIN titles " _
        & "ON publishers.pub_id = titles.pub_id " _
        & "ORDER BY titles.Title;"
Set rs = db.OpenRecordset(sSQL)
```

If ODBC needs more information in the `Connect` string (the last parameter of the `OpenDatabase` method), include it after the `ODBC;` entry, separating multiple entries with semicolons. If you need to figure out what connection information a database needs, see How-To 2.1 for code which makes a connection and then exposes the full connect string.

Incidentally, for larger applications, you should put this database initialization code in a separate procedure instead of in `Form_Load` to give you more flexibility connecting with the database, particularly to handle error conditions such as if the ODBC data source no longer points to the right database location. In a small sample application like this, it works well in the `Load` procedure.

Comments

VB's DAOs give your application enormous flexibility as compared to the limitations of the Data control, along with better speed if you code your applications carefully, at the cost of a bit more work coding. As a practical matter, the Data control is rarely used extensively in full-size applications, except perhaps for a simple form or two, because it just doesn't give you much help providing ease-of-use and data management features required of modern Windows applications.

COMPLEXITY
INTERMEDIATE

2.4 How do I...
Use the SQL passthrough option?

Problem

Every time I try to use the powerful features of my database server, I get error messages (from JET, I think) saying that my SQL statements are not valid. Even if the statements work, it takes forever to process the query. How can I be sure that my SQL statements are passing directly to the database server so that Visual Basic won't protect me from myself?

Technique

With the different tiers of a typical client/server database application, it isn't always easy to get the right statement to the right tier in the system because each layer may try to execute the statement itself. This is a problem if you are using any specialized features of the database server. For example, the Access JET database engine, left to its own way of doing things, will attempt to execute the SQL statements you pass its way. You need to "pass the statement through" JET, bypassing it but still letting JET manage the connection, thus creating a passthrough query.

The passthrough technique uses Visual Basic's native data access methods as shown in this How-To, using **CreateQueryDef** and **OpenRecordset**. Using this technique, you can execute any SQL syntax supported by the database, including stored procedures in SQL Server and extensions to SQL.

Steps

Open and run the **PASSTHRU.VBP** Visual Basic project file. The project automatically connects with the ODBC database and loads the bound data grid with two fields selected in the SQL string. Click Quit to end the program.

1. This How-To uses an ODBC SQL Server driver and the sample PUBS database included with SQL Server. You can use any other ODBC data source or database, but you'll need to change the fields connected to the form's text boxes.

2. Create a data source name in ODBC for the PUBS database. Start the ODBC Adminstrator, **ODBCAD32.EXE**, most likely located in the Windows System directory in Windows 95 or the System32 directory in Windows NT. ODBC Administrator loads the ODBC Data Source Administrator window as shown in Figure 2-8. Here you define and maintain data source names available on this system.

3. Click the Add... button so that the Add Data Source window appears. The driver you need will be listed as something like **SQL Server** or **SQL Server (32-bit)**. Click this driver, then click OK so the ODBC SQL Server Setup window appears. Each ODBC driver has its own version of this setup window, prompting for the particular information that the driver needs to make a connection with its database. Click the Options>>> button to show the full form, then enter the information as shown in Table 2-13. You may have to adjust other entries not listed in the table for your system setup. Then click OK to create the data source name.

Table 2-13 Books Available data source name setup information

PROMPT	INFORMATION TO ENTER
Data Source Name	Books Available
Description	[Optional description information to identify the data source]
Server	[The server where SQL Server is located]
Database Name	PUBS

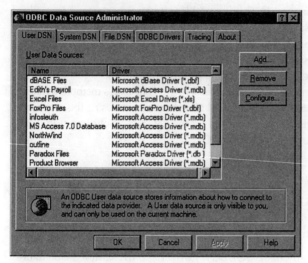

Figure 2-8 Main ODBC Administrator window

4. The new Books Available data source name will appear in the Data Sources window as something like **Books Available** with a driver listed as **SQL Server**. Click OK to end the ODBC Administrator.

5. Start VB and create a new project **PASSTHRU.VBP**.

6. Using Project|Components... from the VB main menu, select the custom controls shown in Table 2-14. Uncheck all others so your project isn't cluttered with controls you aren't using, and so the Setup Wizard doesn't include unused custom controls with your application.

Table 2-14 Custom control used in PassThru

CONTROL
Microsoft Data Bound Grid Control

7. Using Project|References... from the VB main menu, select the references shown in Table 2-15. Uncheck all others so your project isn't cluttered with DLLs you aren't using, and so the Setup Wizard doesn't include a lot of extra dead weight with your application.

Table 2-15 References used in PassThru

REFERENCE
Microsoft Visual Basic for Applications
Visual Basic Runtime Objects and Procedures
Visual Basic Objects and Procedures

REFERENCE

| Microsoft Data Bound Grid Library |
| Microsoft DAO 3.5 Object Library |

8. Name the default form `frmPassThru` and save the file as `PASSTHRU.FRM`. Add the controls shown in Figure 2-9, setting the properties as shown in Table 2-16.

Table 2-16 Objects and properties for `PASSTHRU.FRM`

OBJECT	PROPERTY	SETTING
Form	Name	frmPassthru
	Caption	"Passthrough Query"
CommandButton	Name	cmdQuit
	Caption	"Quit"
Data	Name	Data1
	Caption	"Data1"
	Connect	""
	DatabaseName	""
	Exclusive	0 'False
	Options	0
	ReadOnly	0 'False
	RecordsetType	1 'Dynaset
	RecordSource	""
DBGrid	Name	DBGrid1
	DataSource	Data1

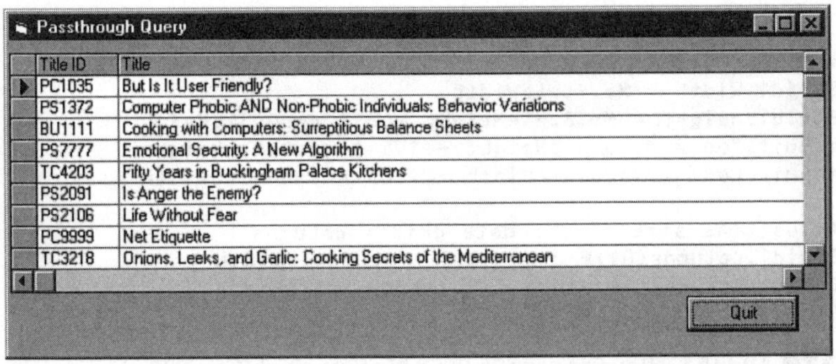

Figure 2-9 Dialog box to test SQL passthrough queries

9. Insert the following code in the Declarations section of the form. `Option Explicit` tells Visual Basic to make sure that you declare all variables and objects before using them, in order to avoid naming problems. You can have VB automatically add this statement to your code modules by checking the Require Variable Declaration check box in Tools|Options under the Editor tab.

```
Option Explicit
```

10. Add the following code in the `Load` event procedure of the form. This code centers the form, then sets the properties of the `Data` control to access the `Books Available` data source name.

```
Private Sub Form_Load()
'Dim dbPub As Database
'Dim qdPub As QueryDef
Dim sConnect As String
Dim iLeft As Integer
Dim iTop As Integer

    'Resize and center the form
    iLeft = (Screen.Width - Width) / 2
    iTop = (Screen.Height - Height) / 2

    Move iLeft, iTop

    sConnect = "ODBC;DSN=Books Available;UID=sa;PWD="
    data1.Options = dbSQLPassThrough
    data1.Connect = sConnect
    data1.RecordsetType = vbRSTypeSnapShot
    data1.RecordSource = "SELECT title_id AS 'Title ID', " _
        & "Title FROM Titles ORDER BY Title;"
    data1.Refresh
End Sub
```

11. Add the following code to the form's `Resize` event. This code expands and contracts the `DBGrid` control and relocates the `cmdQuit` command button as the end-user resizes the form.

```
Private Sub Form_Resize()
    DBGrid1.Width = Me.ScaleWidth
    DBGrid1.Height = Me.ScaleHeight - 2 * cmdQuit.Height
    cmdQuit.Top = Me.ScaleHeight - 1.5 * cmdQuit.Height
    cmdQuit.Left = Me.ScaleWidth - 1.25 * cmdQuit.Width

    'Adjust the size of the data grid's columns
    DBGrid1.Columns(0).Width = 0.1 * Me.ScaleWidth
    DBGrid1.Columns(1).Width = 0.9 * Me.ScaleWidth
End Sub
```

12. Add the following code to the `Click` event of the `cmdQuit` command button:

```
Private Sub cmdQuit_Click()
    Unload Me
End Sub
```

13. In the Project|[Project Name] Options menu item, set the startup form to `frmPassThru`. You can also set an application description, but that is not required for the operation of the application.

How It Works

There are essentially three ways to execute a query in Visual Basic using ODBC: execute the query using Visual Basic through the JET database engine, pass the query straight through ODBC to the database system and/or driver and let JET manage the connection, or use remote data objects. This How-To showed how to pass the query directly to ODBC and the database system.

Visual Basic normally uses the JET database engine to process queries before they are passed on to the database. When you use a passthrough query, however, the JET engine is bypassed entirely, except that Visual Basic still uses its recordset processor to create and manage the result sets of the query.

The major advantage of a passthrough query is to take advantage of any specific capabilities of the database. For example, you can only execute a SQL Server's stored procedures by using a passthrough query. In this case, the grammar of the query is not valid under the SQL grammar used by either Visual Basic or ODBC, so an error would result if Visual Basic processed the query before sending it on.

Passthrough queries also are advantageous for databases located in distant locations over the network. Rather than passing a huge amount of data through the network, the database itself does all the processing, returning only a resultset (if there is one) back to ODBC and Visual Basic.

Other uses for passthrough queries are

■ Creating a new database, table, or index on an external server.

■ Creating or managing triggers, defaults, rules, or stored procedures, all of which are different forms of small programs which are part of the back-end database.

■ Maintaining user accounts or performing other System Administrator tasks.

■ Running maintenance operations like Microsoft SQL Server's DBCC.

■ Executing multiple **INSERT** or **UPDATE** statements in a single batch command.

This How-To used the Data control to make the connection, but you can also use these techniques with data access objects (DAOs). When using DAOs, all that is needed to execute a passthrough SQL statement is to use only a name argument in **CreateQueryDef**. You then assign the SQL command as a string to the SQL property of the **QueryDef**. The following code illustrates the general procedure.

```
Dim db as Database
Dim qd As QueryDef
```

continued on next page

continued from previous page

```
Use the first argument, name, only in CreateQueryDef:
Set qd = MyDb.CreateQueryDef("MYODbCQuery")

qd.Connect = "ODBC;" "DSN=MyServer;UID=sa;PWD=hithere;DATABASE=pubs"
qd.SQL = "Exec SELECT * FROM pubs"
qd.ReturnsRows = True

Dim rs As Recordset
Set rs = qd.OpenRecordset()
```

Note the use of the `ReturnsRows` property in the above code. This property, when set to `True`, tells Visual Basic to use the JET engine to be ready to receive and manage the recordset (if any) that ODBC and the database returns from the query. `ReturnsRows` should be set to `False` for action queries or other commands that do not return records to Visual Basic.

The SQL string assigned to the SQL property of the `QueryDef` object `qd` is the syntax of the external database, which may or may not be different from the syntax normally required by Visual Basic. This statement will be passed directly to the external database, as will all other SQL statements you make using this instance of the `QueryDef` object. This also means that your application must be ready to handle any errors that the database returns.

Note also that previous versions of Visual Basic included a `DB_SQLPASSTHROUGH` or `dbSQLPassthrough` (in Visual Basic 4) constant for use with `CreateDynaset`, `CreateSnapshot`, or `ExecuteSQL` methods. With the latest version of the JET database engine, it is now recommended that you use the technique demonstrated above instead of using these constants.

COMPLEXITY
ADVANCED

2.5 How do I...
Open an ODBC source using the ODBC API?

Problem

What do I do if I want to get close to the metal with ODBC so I don't have to pay VB's performance penalties? How can I use the OBDC API to improve the performance of my applications?

Technique

The ODBC API is a complex set of functions that serves to provide a common interface you can use to access virtually any back-end database system. The problem in contemporary client/server applications is that each system has its own interface. The versions of SQL Server from Microsoft and Sybase are somewhat similar since they started life as the same product, but they have headed down different paths. But Oracle, DB2, and other heavy-duty database servers have radically different interfaces. A single programmer can't hope to master all these interfaces in a normal lifetime, certainly not when each system is significantly enhanced every year or two.

ODBC grew out of a need to bring order to the madness. By adding an additional layer (really two more, but it's all ODBC), you have one set of functions to learn and master, which will give you access to most of the features of any given database server. Don't think I'm saying it is simpler. ODBC's benefit is a single interface, not simplicity.

If you are going to get into ODBC in any serious way, crack open a copy of the latest version of the standard, which is part of the Microsoft Developer Network CDs or usually available on their Web site. I'll cover a few of the main points here about how ODBC works, but a single How-To isn't near enough. Other How-To's throughout this book touch on different aspects of using ODBC. And before you make a final decision to use the ODBC API directly, look at VB's remote data objects which provide a thin layer on top of ODBC. For some applications, that might be all you need.

ODBC Architecture

The ODBC architecture is shown in Error! Reference source not found. When your application calls one of the ODBC API functions, the ODBC Administrator or Driver Manager or both pass the commands to the appropriate driver, which then issues commands to the back-end database server in whatever language or code it understands, as shown in Figure 2-10. Any results or resultsets pass back through ODBC in the opposite direction.

Like all things in Windows, you manipulate objects with a handle which you must obtain from ODBC or Windows before you can do anything. ODBC has four handles: environment, connection, statement, and descriptor. An environment handle is an allocation of resources that manage ODBC overall. A connection handle allocates resources for the actual connection to the database. A statement handle is used to manage the actual requests that you make of the system. Statement handles must be associated with a connection, and connections must be associated with the environment. A descriptor handle provides information about either columns in a resultset or dynamic parameters in an SQL statement.

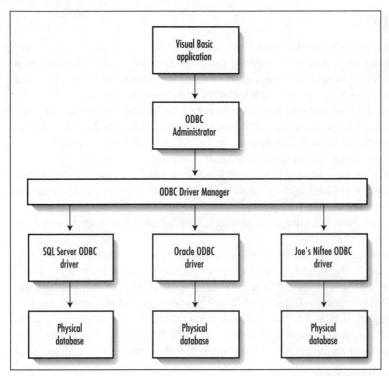

Figure 2-10 The ODBC API presents a layer between your application and the physical databases

Data Types

If you've used VB for any nontrivial projects, you've probably realized that VB data types don't correspond directly to almost any other system of data types; only a casual relationship exists between Windows's own data types and VB's. ODBC is no exception. While ODBC has a good variety of data types, you might have to do some conversions as you pass data back and forth between your application and the database. The most common types won't be a problem, but keep it in mind as you work with the API. All ODBC API functions used in this How-To are called directly. In this How-To, you'll get an idea of how to make direct use of the API while developing some useful *wrapper* functions to make the continued use of the ODBC API easier.

Steps

Load and run the Visual Basic project **ODBCAPI.VBP**. When the ODBC Database window appears, click on the Get ODBC Status button to retrieve a list of the installed data sources and ODBC drivers, as shown in Figure 2-11. Click on one of the registered ODBC databases. After a moment the Data Source window appears, shown in Figure 2-12, listing all the ODBC API functions that the data source and driver support, a count of the number of functions, and a selected list of settings and capabilities of the data source. Click on the Quit button to return to the ODBC Database window, then click Quit again to exit the program.

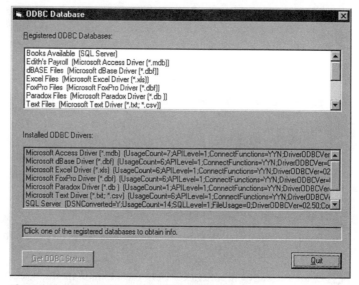

Figure 2-11 ODBC data information form

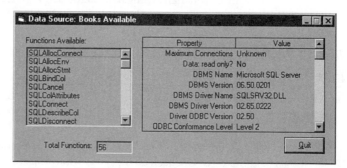

Figure 2-12 Attributes form showing information about a data source name

1. Create a new project **ODBCAPI.VBP**. Add the form **ERRORS.FRM** and the code module **ODBCAPI.BAS** from the accompanying CD using Visual Basic's Project|Add File... menu command. The code module contains all the declarations needed for the ODBC API functions and the constants used in many of the functions. Here is a brief description of the procedures in this code module.

■ The **ODBCALlocateEnv Function** procedure calls the **SQLALlocEnv** function. Before calling any ODBC API function, you have to start by getting an environment handle. ODBC will use this handle and a small bit of memory to communicate with our application.

■ The **ODBCConnectDriver Function** procedure sets up a connection to the database once an environment handle is established. This function does double duty: first to allocate memory and receive a database connection handle (**hDbc**), and then to make a connection with the data source driver passed to the function in the Server argument.

■ **ODBCConnectDS** provides an alternative to **ODBCConnectDriver**.

■ The **ODBCDisconnectDS** function both releases and frees connection handles. This function doesn't release the ODBC environment handle, so these wrapper functions can be used as needed within an application while keeping the environment handle available for use.

The **ODBCFreeEnv** function releases the environment handle and memory, making a call to the **SQLFreeEnv ODBC** function.

In addition to these wrapper functions, **ODBCAPI.BAS** has a number of support functions.

2. Using Project|Components... from the VB main menu, select the custom controls shown in Table 2-17. Uncheck all others so your project isn't cluttered with controls you aren't using, and so the Setup Wizard doesn't include unneeded custom controls with your application.

Table 2-17 Custom controls used in ODBCAPI.VBP

CONTROL
Microsoft Outline Control
Microsoft Grid Control

3. Using Project|References... from the VB main menu, select the references shown in Table 2-18. Uncheck all others so your project isn't cluttered with DLLs you aren't using, and so the Setup Wizard doesn't include a lot of extra dead weight with your application.

Table 2-18 References used in `ODBCAPI`

REFERENCE
Microsoft Visual Basic for Applications
Visual Basic Runtime Objects and Procedures
Visual Basic Objects and Procedures
Microsoft Outline Control
Microsoft Grid Control
Microsoft DAO 3.5 Object Library

4. Name the project's default form **frmODBCAPI** and save the file as **API.FRM**. Add the controls shown in Figure 2-11, setting the properties as shown in Table 2-19.

Table 2-19 Objects and properties for `API.FRM`

OBJECT	PROPERTY	SETTING
Form	Name	frmODBCAPI
	BackColor	&H00C0C0C0&
	BorderStyle	3 'Fixed Dialog
	Caption	"ODBC Database"
	MaxButton	0 'False
	MinButton	0 'False
ListBox	Name	lstODBCDrivers
	BackColor	&H00C0C0C0&
	Sorted	-1 'True
	TabStop	0 'False
TextBox	Name	txtODBCStatus
	BackColor	&H00C0C0C0&
	TabStop	0 'False
ListBox	Name	lstODBCDbs
CommandButton	Name	cmdGetStatus
	Caption	"&Get ODBC Status"
CommandButton	Name	cmdQuit
	Caption	"&Quit"
	Default	-1 'True
Label	Name	lblDrivers
	BackColor	&H00C0C0C0&
	Caption	"Installed ODBC Drivers:"

continued on next page

continued from previous page

OBJECT	PROPERTY	SETTING
Label	Name	lblDatabases
	BackColor	&H00C0C0C0&
	Caption	"&Registered ODBC
		Databases:"

5. Insert the following code in the **Declarations** section of **frmODBCAPI**. **Option Explicit** tells Visual Basic to make sure that you declare all variables and objects before using them, in order to avoid naming problems. You can have VB automatically add this statement to your code modules by checking the Require Variable Declaration check box in Tools|Options under the Editor tab. The dynamic arrays will be used to hold various pieces of information about the ODBC system and driver.

```
Option Explicit

'PRIVATE: ****************************************
'Private data members

'Dynamic arrays to hold data
Dim dbName() As String
Dim dbDesc() As String
Dim sDriverDesc() As String
Dim sDriverAttr() As String
```

6. Add the following code to the **Load** event procedure of the form. The **txtODBCStatus.Text** box gives the end-user instructions about the next steps to take to gather information about the data sources.

```
Private Sub Form_Load()
    txtODBCStatus.Text = _
        "Select Get ODBC Status to begin."

    'Center the form
    Me.Top = (Screen.Height - Me.Height) / 2
    Me.Left = (Screen.Width - Me.Width) / 2
End Sub
```

7. Put the following code in the **GetODBCdvrs** subroutine. This is the first of two procedures (the other is **GetODBCdbs**) which executes after the end-user clicks the **cmdGetStatus** button. **GetODBCdvrs** establishes a connection with the ODBC API and gets from it a list of all the data sources (drivers) that are registered in the **ODBC.INI** file or the Windows Registry. In the **Do** loop, each call to the API function **SQLDataSources** gets one data source name and description. This data is put into new elements of the global **dbName** and **dbDesc** arrays.

```
Private Sub GetODBCdvrs()
'Variables for ODBC API calls
Dim szDriverDesc As String * 512
Dim cbDriverDescMax As Integer
```

```
Dim pcbDriverDesc As Long
Dim szDriverAttributes As String * 2048
Dim cbDrvrAttrMax As Integer
Dim pcbDrvrAttr As Long

'Variables for procedure processing
Dim i As Integer
Dim iResult As Integer
Dim iErrResult As Integer

    cbDriverDescMax = 512
    cbDrvrAttrMax = 2048
    iResult = SQL_SUCCESS
    i = 0

    Do While iResult <> SQL_NO_DATA_FOUND
        iResult = SQLDrivers(ghEnv, _
            SQL_FETCH_NEXT, szDriverDesc, _
            cbDriverDescMax, pcbDriverDesc, _
            szDriverAttributes, cbDrvrAttrMax, pcbDrvrAttr)
        If iResult = SQL_ERROR Then
            iErrResult = ODBCError("Env", ghEnv, 0, 0, _
                iResult, "Error getting list of registered drivers.")
            Exit Sub
        End If

        ReDim Preserve sDriverDesc(i)
        sDriverDesc(i) = Left(szDriverDesc, pcbDriverDesc)
        ReDim Preserve sDriverAttr(i)
        sDriverAttr(i) = DeNull(Left(szDriverAttributes, _
            pcbDrvrAttr))

        lstODBCDrivers.AddItem sDriverDesc(i) _
            & "  (" & sDriverAttr(i) & ")"

        i = i + 1
    Loop

End Sub
```

8. Add the following code to the **Click** event of the **cmdGetStatus** button. This code calls the **GetODBCdbs** and **GetODBCdvrs** functions which populate the form's listboxes.

```
Private Sub cmdGetStatus_Click()
Dim iResult As Integer

    'Open the ODBC connection
    iResult = ODBCAllocateEnv(ghEnv)
    If iResult = SQL_SUCCESS Then
        GetODBCdbs
        GetODBCdvrs

        cmdGetStatus.Enabled = False
        txtODBCStatus.Text = "Click one of the " _
```

continued on next page

continued from previous page

```
            & "registered databases to obtain info."
    Else
        txtODBCStatus.Text = _
            "ODBC Information could not be retrieved."
        Exit Sub
    End If

End Sub
```

9. Put the following code in the **GetODBCdbs** subroutine. This code is similar to the above **GetODBCdvrs** code (which gets a list of ODBC drivers), getting the list of ODBC data source names that are registered in the **ODBC.INI** file.

```
Private Sub GetODBCdbs()
'Variables for ODBC API calls
Dim cbDSNMax As Integer
Dim szDSN As String * 33
Dim pcbDSN As Long
Dim pcbDescription As Long
Dim szDescription As String * 512
Dim cbDescriptionMax As Integer

'Variables for procedure processing
Dim iResult As Integer
Dim i As Integer
Dim iErrResult

    cbDSNMax = SQL_MAX_DSN_LENGTH + 1
    cbDescriptionMax = 512
    iResult = SQL_SUCCESS
    i = 0

    Screen.MousePointer = vbHourglass
    Do While iResult <> SQL_NO_DATA_FOUND
        'Get next data source (on the first call to
        'SQLDataSources, SQL_FETCH_NEXT gets the first
        'data source
        iResult = SQLDataSources(ghEnv, _
            SQL_FETCH_NEXT, szDSN, cbDSNMax, pcbDSN, _
            szDescription, cbDescriptionMax, pcbDescription)
        If iResult = SQL_ERROR Then
            iErrResult = ODBCError("Env", ghEnv, 0, 0, _
                iResult, "Error getting list of data sources.")
            Screen.MousePointer = vbDefault
            Exit Sub
        End If

        ReDim Preserve dbName(i)
        dbName(i) = Left(szDSN, pcbDSN)
        ReDim Preserve dbDesc(i)
        dbDesc(i) = Left(szDescription, pcbDescription)

        lstODBCdbs.AddItem dbName(i) & "  (" & dbDesc(i) & ")"
```

```
      i = i + 1
   Loop
   Screen.MousePointer = vbDefault

End Sub
```

10. Put the following code in the **lstODBCDbs Click** event subroutine. After the list of data sources and drivers is available, the end-user can click on any of the data source names to get a window listing the ODBC API SQL functions that can be called with that data source and various properties of the data source. This procedure loads the **frmAttributes** form and fills its listbox and grid with the data about the data source. Modally, **frmAttributes** is shown, meaning that the end-user must respond to the form by clicking Quit before being able to retrieve data about another data source.

```
Private Sub lstODBCDbs_Click()
Dim sDataSource As String
Dim sUserID As String
Dim sPassword As String
Dim iResult As Integer
Dim iErrResult As Integer
ReDim aiFuncList(100) As Integer
Dim i As Integer
Dim j As Integer

   Screen.MousePointer = vbHourglass
   sDataSource = dbName(lstODBCdbs.ListIndex)

   iResult = ODBCConnectDS(ghEnv, ghDbc, ghStmt, _
      sDataSource, sUserID, sPassword)
   If iResult <> SQL_SUCCESS Then
      Screen.MousePointer = vbDefault
      Exit Sub
   End If

   'Now get the list of functions
   iResult = SQLGetFunctions(ghDbc, _
      SQL_API_ALL_FUNCTIONS, aiFuncList(0))
   If iResult <> SQL_SUCCESS Then
      iErrResult = ODBCError("Dbc", ghEnv, _
         ghDbc, 0, iResult, _
         "Error getting list of ODBC functions")
      Screen.MousePointer = vbDefault
      Exit Sub
   End If

   Load frmAttributes

   j = 0
   For i = 0 To 99
      If aiFuncList(i) <> 0 Then
         frmAttributes.lstFunctions.AddItem ODBCFuncs(0, i)
```

continued on next page

continued from previous page

```
            j = j + 1
        End If
    Next

    frmAttributes.txtFuncCount.Text = j
    frmAttributes.Caption = "Data Source: " & sDataSource

    frmAttributes.Show vbModal

    Screen.MousePointer = vbDefault

End Sub
```

11. Add a `Function` procedure with the following code to remove nulls from the strings and name it `DeNull`. The SQLState information returned in the `GetODBCdvrs Sub` procedure contains embedded nulls to separate the parts of the state information. The `DeNull` function *denulls* the strings, replacing the nulls with a semicolon.

```
Private Function DeNull(sText As String) As String
'Replace embedded nulls with semi-colons.
Dim iInStr As Integer

    iInStr = InStr(sText, Chr$(0))
    Do While iInStr 'And iInStr =
        Mid(sText, iInStr, 1) = ";"
        iInStr = InStr(sText, Chr$(0))
    Loop

    'Lop off the trailing semi-colon.
    If Right$(sText, 1) = ";" Then
        sText = Left$(sText, Len(sText) - 1)
    End If

    DeNull = sText
End Function
```

12. Put the following code in the `cmdQuit_Click` subroutine. This command ends the program by unloading its main form.

```
Private Sub cmdQuit_Click()
    Unload Me
End Sub
```

13. Put the following code in the `Form_Unload` event subroutine. Since this form is the start-up form for the program, the time to do any final cleaning up after the program is when the form is unloaded. The code calls wrapper functions to release memory used by the ODBC API, and disconnects the program from any open data sources.

```
Private Sub Form_Unload(Cancel As Integer)
    'Clean up the ODBC connections and allocations
    Dim iResult As Integer
```

```
    iResult = ODBCDisconnectDS(ghEnv, ghDbc, ghStmt)
    iResult = ODBCFreeEnv(ghEnv)
End Sub
```

14. Add a new form to the project with the controls listed in Table 2-20 and save it as **ATTR.FRM**. This form will be used to display information about the data source. Figure 2-12 shows the form when running the program.

Table 2-20 Objects and properties for ATTR.FRM

OBJECT	PROPERTY	SETTING
Form	Name	frmAttributes
	BackColor	&H00C0C0C0&
	BorderStyle	1 'Fixed Single
	Caption	"Attributes"
	MaxButton	0 'False
CommandButton	Name	cmdQuit
	Caption	"&Quit"
	Default	-1 'True
TextBox	Name	txtFuncCount
	BackColor	&H00C0C0C0&
	TabStop	0 'False
ListBox	Name	lstFunctions
	BackColor	&H00C0C0C0&
MSGrid	Name	Grid grdGI
	FixedCols	0
	ScrollBars	2
Label	Name	Label1
	BackColor	&H00C0C0C0&
	Caption	"Functions Available:"
Label	Name	lblFuncCount
	Alignment	1 'Right Justify
	BackColor	&H00C0C0C0&
	Caption	"Total Functions:"

15. Insert the following code in the Declarations section of **frmAttributes**. **Option Explicit** tells Visual Basic to make sure that you declare all variables and objects before using them, in order to avoid naming problems. You can have VB automatically add this statement to your code modules by checking the Require Variable Declaration check box in Tools|Options under the Editor tab.

```
Option Explicit
```

16. Put the following code in the **Form_Load** event subroutine. The **frmAttributes** form is loaded into memory when the end-user clicks on an ODBC data source. This procedure sets up some of the properties of the grid control that must be set at runtime, and positions the form lower and to the right relative to the **frmODBCStatus** form.

```
Private Sub Form_Load()
    'Resize data here
    grdGI.ColWidth(0) = grdGI.Width / 2
    grdGI.ColWidth(1) = grdGI.Width / 2

    grdGI.ColAlignment(0) = 1
    grdGI.ColAlignment(1) = 0

    grdGI.Row = 0
    grdGI.Col = 0
    grdGI.Text = "Property"
    grdGI.Col = 1
    grdGI.Text = "Value"

    grdGI.FixedAlignment(0) = 2
    grdGI.FixedAlignment(1) = 2

    grdGI.HighLight = False

    'Other setup chores
    frmAttributes.Top = 1.5 * frmODBCAPI.Top
    frmAttributes.Left = 1.5 * frmODBCAPI.Left

    'Load other data source information
    ODBCInfo

End Sub
```

17. Add the following **ODBCInfo** procedure code to the project. This code uses the ODBC API function **SQLGetInfo** to retrieve individual pieces of information about the data source one at a time. The information gathered here is a representative sample of what can be retrieved. As each item is retrieved, a new row in the grid control is added for the data. Some of the data returned by the **SQLGetInfo** function is converted to a more user-friendly form.

```
Private Sub ODBCInfo()
Dim fInfoType As Integer

'return values
Dim ri As Integer
Dim rs As String * 255

Dim rgbInfoValue As Long
Dim cbInfoValueMax As Integer
Dim pcbInfoValue As Long
Dim result As Integer
Dim temp As String
```

```
        cbInfoValueMax = 255

    result = SQLGetInfo(ghDbc, SQL_ACTIVE_CONNECTIONS, ri, cbInfoValueMax,
pcbInfoValue)
    If result <> SQL_ERROR Then
        grdGI.AddItem "Maximum Connections " & Chr$(9) & IIf(ri = 0,
"Unknown", LTrim$(Str$(ri)))
    End If

    result = SQLGetInfo(ghDbc, SQL_DATA_SOURCE_READ_ONLY, ByVal rs,
cbInfoValueMax, pcbInfoValue)
    If result <> SQL_ERROR Then
        grdGI.AddItem "Data: read only? " & Chr$(9) & convCh(rs,
pcbInfoValue)
    End If

    result = SQLGetInfo(ghDbc, SQL_DBMS_NAME, ByVal rs, cbInfoValueMax,
pcbInfoValue)
    If result <> SQL_ERROR Then
        grdGI.AddItem "DBMS Name " & Chr$(9) & convCh(rs, pcbInfoValue)
    End If

    result = SQLGetInfo(ghDbc, SQL_DBMS_VER, ByVal rs, cbInfoValueMax,
pcbInfoValue)
    If result <> SQL_ERROR Then
        grdGI.AddItem "DBMS Version " & Chr$(9) & convCh(rs, pcbInfoValue)
    End If

    result = SQLGetInfo(ghDbc, SQL_DRIVER_NAME, ByVal rs, cbInfoValueMax,
pcbInfoValue)
    If result <> SQL_ERROR Then
        grdGI.AddItem "DBMS Driver Name " & Chr$(9) & convCh(rs,
pcbInfoValue)
    End If

    result = SQLGetInfo(ghDbc, SQL_DRIVER_VER, ByVal rs, cbInfoValueMax,
pcbInfoValue)
    If result <> SQL_ERROR Then
        grdGI.AddItem "DBMS Driver Version " & Chr$(9) & convCh(rs,
pcbInfoValue)
    End If

    result = SQLGetInfo(ghDbc, SQL_DRIVER_ODBC_VER, ByVal rs,
cbInfoValueMax, pcbInfoValue)
    If result <> SQL_ERROR Then
        grdGI.AddItem "Driver ODBC Version " & Chr$(9) & convCh(rs,
pcbInfoValue)
    End If

    result = SQLGetInfo(ghDbc, SQL_ODBC_API_CONFORMANCE, ri, cbInfoValueMax,
pcbInfoValue)
    If result <> SQL_ERROR Then
        Select Case ri
            Case SQL_OAC_NONE
                temp = "Core Only"
```

continued on next page

continued from previous page

```
                Case SQL_OAC_LEVEL1
                    temp = "Level 1"
                Case SQL_OAC_LEVEL2
                    temp = "Level 2"
            End Select
            grdGI.AddItem "ODBC Conformance Level " & Chr$(9) & temp
        End If

        result = SQLGetInfo(ghDbc, SQL_ODBC_SQL_CONFORMANCE, ri, cbInfoValueMax,
pcbInfoValue)
        If result <> SQL_ERROR Then
            Select Case ri
                Case SQL_OSC_MINIMUM
                    temp = "Minimum Grammar"
                Case SQL_OSC_CORE
                    temp = "Core Grammar"
                Case SQL_OSC_EXTENDED
                    temp = "Extended Grammar"
            End Select
            grdGI.AddItem "SQL Grammar Level " & Chr$(9) & temp
        End If

        If grdGI.Rows > 2 Then
            grdGI.RemoveItem 1
        End If
End Sub
```

18. Add the `ConvCh` function to the form. This procedure is called by `ODBCInfo` and simply converts a `Y` to `Yes`, `N` to `No`, and passes the character back unchanged if it is anything else.

```
Private Function ConvCh(inChar As String, num As Variant)
    inChar = LTrim$(Left$(inChar, num))

    Select Case inChar
        Case "Y"
            ConvCh = "Yes"
        Case "N"
            ConvCh = "No"
        Case Else
            ConvCh = inChar
    End Select

End Function
```

19. Put the following code in the `cmdQuit_Click` event subroutine. This simply unloads the form when the end-user clicks on the `Quit` command button.

```
Private Sub cmdQuit_Click()
    Unload Me
End Sub
```

20. Set the `frmODBCAPI` form as the start-up form for the project. Select Project|[Project Name] Options from the Visual Basic menu, and select `frmODBCAPI` from the list of startup form options, then click OK to close the window.

How It Works

This How-To gives an example of using several of the most common ODBC API functions, from initializing the connection to the data sources and drivers, through getting the specific information needed and putting it into a presentable form, and then releasing memory. Many of the techniques can easily be adapted for obtaining properties for doing the real work of connecting to a data source and extracting its data in meaningful forms. Using the ODBC API directly involves more work initially in writing the code, but that work is rewarded by the speed of processing and the easy portability as data is moved and changed into different formats on different machines.

COMPLEXITY
INTERMEDIATE

2.6   How do I...
Make a connection using the RemoteData control?

Problem

I need to access a database on another computer on the network. ODBC is too complex for a simple application, and the regular VB Data control can't handle the network well. How can I make a connection for simple database access?

Technique

The VB Enterprise Edition provides some nifty new tools for connecting with remote databases via ODBC. In this How-To, I'll modify the Books sample application used in How-To's 2.2 and 2.3, using instead the RemoteData control available only in the Enterprise Edition. As you'll see, it is only slightly more complex than using a VB Data control but reaps many benefits, not the least of which is performance.

Steps

Open and run the **BOOKS.VBP** project file. Use the Visual Basic `RemoteData` control's navigation buttons at the bottom of the form to move through the database, as shown in Figure 2-13. Click on Close when you are finished. (These figures show vertical bars in some of the text notes of the **BIBLIO.MDB** file. These are embedded carriage return and line feed characters, which the VB TextBox doesn't handle elegantly. If they bother you, you can programmatically strip them out of the text.)

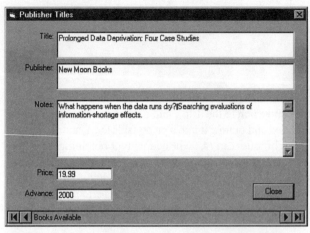

Figure 2-13 Using ODBC with the Visual Basic
`RemoteData` control to review a book database

1. This How-To uses an ODBC SQL Server driver and the sample PUBS database included with SQL Server. You can use any other ODBC data source or database, but you'll need to change the fields connected to the form's text boxes.

2. Create a data source name in ODBC for the PUBS database. Start the ODBC Adminstrator, **ODBCAD32.EXE**, most likely located in the Windows System directory in Windows 95 or the System32 directory in Windows NT. ODBC Administrator loads the Data Sources window as shown in Figure 2-14. Here you define and maintain data source names available on this system.

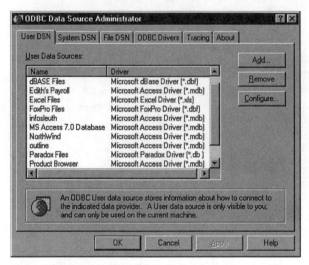

Figure 2-14 Main ODBC Administrator window

3. Click the Add… button so the Add Data Source window appears. The driver you need will be listed as something like **SQL Server** or **SQL Server (32-bit)**. Click this driver, then click OK so the ODBC SQL Server Setup window appears. Each ODBC driver has its own version of this setup window, prompting for the particular information the driver needs to make a connection with its database. Click the Options>>> button to show the full form, then enter the information as shown in Table 2-21. You may have to adjust other entries not listed in the table for your system setup. Then click OK to create the data source name.

Table 2-21 Books Available data source name setup information

PROMPT	INFORMATION TO ENTER
Data Source Name	Books Available
Description	[Optional description information to identify the data source]
Server	[The server where SQL Server is located]
Database Name	PUBS

4. The new **Books Available** data source name will appear in the Data Sources window as something like **Books Available** with a driver listed as **SQL Server**. Click OK to end the ODBC Administrator.

5. Start VB. Create a new project **BOOKS.VBP**. Add the form **ERRORRDO.FRM** (see the introduction to this chapter for a description of this form), using Visual Basic's Project|Add File... menu command. This form handles RDO errors.

6. Using Project|Components... from the VB main menu, select the custom controls shown in Table 2-22. Uncheck all others so your project isn't cluttered with controls you aren't using, and so the Setup Wizard doesn't include a lot of extra dead weight with your application.

Table 2-22 Custom controls used in BOOKS.VBP

CONTROL
Microsoft Outline Control
Microsoft RemoteData Control 2.0

7. Using Project|References... from the VB main menu, select the references shown in Table 2-23. Uncheck all others so your project isn't cluttered with DLLs you aren't using, and so the Setup Wizard doesn't include a lot of extra dead weight with your application.

Table 2-23 References used in BOOKS.VBP

REFERENCE
Microsoft Visual Basic for Applications
Visual Basic Runtime Objects and Procedures
Visual Basic Objects and Procedures
Microsoft RemoteData Control 2.0
Microsoft Outline Control
Microsoft Remote Data Object 1.0

8. Add the controls shown in Figure 2-13 to the form in the new project, with property settings as listed in Table 2-24. Save the form as file **BOOKS.FRM**.

Table 2-24 Objects and properties for BOOKS.FRM

OBJECT	PROPERTY	SETTING
Form	Name	frmBooks
	BackColor	&H00C0C0C0&
	BorderStyle	3 'Fixed Dialog
	Caption	"Publisher Titles"
	MaxButton	0 'False
	MinButton	0 'False
TextBox	Name	txtTitle
	DataSource	"rdcBooks"
	MultiLine	-1 'True
TextBox	Name	txtNotes
	DataSource	"rdcBooks"
	MultiLine	-1 'True
	ScrollBars	2 'Vertical
TextBox	Name	txtPrice
	DataSource	"rdcBooks"
TextBox	Name	txtAdvance
	DataSource	"rdcBooks"
CommandButton	Name	cmdClose
	Caption	"Close"
	Default	-1 'True
TextBox	Name	txtPublisher
	DataSource	"rdcBooks"
	MultiLine	-1 'True
Label	Name	Label1
	Alignment	1 'Right Justify

OBJECT	PROPERTY	SETTING
	BackColor	&H00C0C0C0&
	Caption	"Title:"
Label	Name	Label3
	Alignment	1 'Right Justify
	BackColor	&H00C0C0C0&
	Caption	"Notes:"
Label	Name	Label5
	Alignment	1 'Right Justify
	BackColor	&H00C0C0C0&
	Caption	"Price:"
Label	Name	Label6
	Alignment	1 'Right Justify
	BackColor	&H00C0C0C0&
	Caption	"Advance:"
Label	Name	Label9
	Alignment	1 'Right Justify
	BackColor	&H00C0C0C0&
	Caption	"Publisher:"
MSRDC	Name	rdcBooks
	Align	2 'Align Bottom
	DataSourceName	""
	RecordSource	""
	Connect	""
	ReadOnly	0 'False
	UserName	""
	Password	""
	Caption	"Books Available"

9. Add the following code to the Declarations section of the form. `Option Explicit` tells Visual Basic to make sure that you declare all variables and objects before using them, in order to avoid naming problems. You can have VB automatically add this statement to your code modules by checking the Require Variable Declaration check box in Tools|Options under the Editor tab.

```
Option Explicit
```

10. Add the following code to the form's **Load** event procedure. After centering the form, the **RemoteData** control's **DataSourceName** property is set to connect to the Books Available ODBC data source name and the SQL property is set with the query to execute against the database. Other `RemoteData` control properties specify a `Keyset` resultset, optimistic locking, whether to use the ODBC or server-side cursors, options relating to the `Keyset` and `Rowset` sizes, and a synchronous query, all features of how the ODBC database responds to a query. Then the text boxes' `DataField` properties are set to the fields which each will hold. This is the step that links each field to use with the text boxes that hold each record's data.

```
Private Sub Form_Load()
'Set up the form and connect to data source
Dim sSQL As String

    'Center the form
    Me.Top = (Screen.Height - Me.Height) / 2
    Me.Left = (Screen.Width - Me.Width) / 2

    sSQL = _
        "SELECT titles.*, publishers.* " _
        & "FROM titles, publishers " _
        & "WHERE publishers.pub_id = titles.pub_id " _
        & "ORDER BY titles.Title ASC;"

    rdcBooks.Connect = "DSN=Books Available;UID=sa;PWD="
    rdcBooks.SQL = sSQL
    rdcBooks.ResultsetType = rdOpenKeyset
    rdcBooks.LockType = rdConcurRowver
    rdcBooks.CursorDriver = rdUseIfNeeded
    rdcBooks.KeysetSize = 0
    rdcBooks.RowsetSize = 100
    rdcBooks.Options = 0

    'Connect each of the text boxes with the appropriate fieldname
    txtAdvance.DataField = "Advance"
    txtNotes.DataField = "Notes"
    txtPrice.DataField = "Price"
    txtPublisher.DataField = "Pub_Name"
    txtTitle.DataField = "Title"

    On Error GoTo FormLoadError
    rdcBooks.Refresh

    Exit Sub

FormLoadError:
    frmRDOErrors.ErrorColl = rdoErrors
End Sub
```

11. Add the following code to the `Click` event of the `cmdQuit` command button. This is the exit point that terminates the program.

```
Private Sub cmdClose_Click()
    Unload Me
End Sub
```

12. In the Project|[Project Name] Options menu item, set the startup form to **frmBooks**. You can also set an application description, but that is not required for the operation of this application.

How It Works

If you worked with How-To 2.2, this How-To should have looked remarkably familiar. The only real difference is that the **RemoteData** control provides more options you can use to control the connection to the ODBC data source. And if you read How-To 2.5 about using the ODBC API, you'll never go back to coding the API directly because of the sheer amount of coding required, even if you use wrapper functions or VB classes.

COMPLEXITY

INTERMEDIATE

2.7 How do I...

Make a connection using remote data objects?

Problem

How can I use the remote data features of the VB Enterprise Edition to connect to and manage databases over a network? People seem to rave about what they can do, but it all seems like a mystery to me.

Technique

The VB Enterprise Edition's remote data objects essentially provide a thin layer over the ODBC API by providing a set of objects that you can manipulate much like DAOs and other VB objects. As such, RDOs strike a balance between the two methods of accessing data, giving much of the best of both worlds. Figure 2-15 shows the hierarchy of remote data objects.

On the one hand, the hierarchy of remote data objects makes it relatively easy to create and manipulate objects, set their properties, and enumerate collections using VB's collection objects. On the other hand, RDOs expose the underlying structure of the ODBC API—such as by providing environment, connection, and statement handles—so you can use individual API functions if you want. RDOs provide the rarest of benefits: the best of both worlds.

RDOs are a bit more complex than JET's DAOs but in compensation they open many more options for remote data access than DAOs with ODBC.

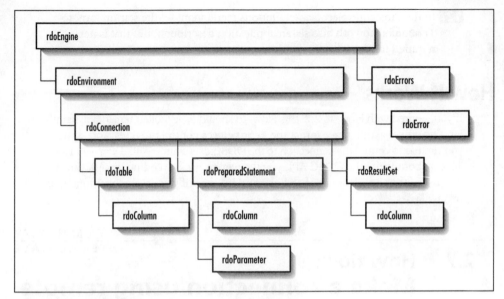

Figure 2-15 The remote data objects hierarchy

Steps

Open and run the **BOOKS.VBP** project file. Use the navigation buttons at the bottom of the form to move through the database, then add, delete, and update records. Then click on Close when you are finished. The Publisher Titles windows is shown in Figure 2-16.

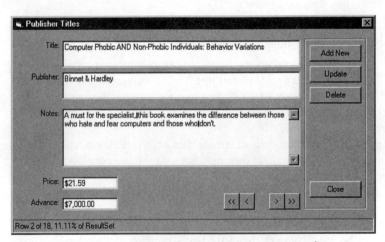

Figure 2-16 Using ODBC with Visual Basic remote data objects to review a book database

1. This How-To uses an ODBC SQL Server driver and the sample PUBS database included with SQL Server. You can use any other ODBC data source or database, but you'll need to change the fields connected to the form's text boxes.

2. Create a data source name in ODBC for the PUBS database. Start the ODBC Adminstrator, **ODBCAD32.EXE**, most likely located in the Windows System directory in Windows 95 or the System32 directory in Windows NT. ODBC Administrator loads the Data Sources window as shown in Figure 2-17. Here you define and maintain data source names available on this system.

3. Click the Add... button so the Add Data Source window appears. The driver you need will be listed as something like **SQL Server** or **SQL Server (32-bit)**. Click this driver, then click OK so the ODBC SQL Server Setup window appears. Each ODBC driver has its own version of this setup window, prompting for the particular information that the driver needs to make a connection with its database. Click the Options>>> button to show the full form, then enter the information as shown in Table 2-25. You may have to adjust other entries not listed in the table for your system setup. Then click OK to create the data source name.

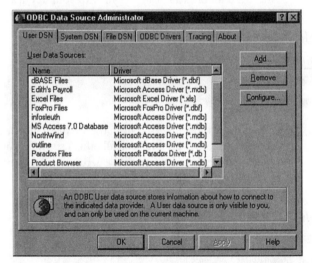

Figure 2-17 Main ODBC Administrator window

Table 2-25 Books Available data source name setup information

PROMPT	INFORMATION TO ENTER
Data Source Name	Books Available
Description	[Optional description information to identify the data source]
Server	[The server where SQL Server is located.]
Database Name	PUBS

4. The new **Books Available** data source name will appear in the Data Sources window as something like **Books Available** with a driver listed as **SQL Server**. Click OK to end the ODBC Administrator.

5. Start VB. Create a new project **BOOKS.VBP**. Add the form **ERRORRDO.FRM** (see the introduction to this chapter for a description of this form), using Visual Basic's Project|Add File... menu command. This form handles RDO errors.

6. Using Project|Components...from the VB main menu, select the custom controls shown in Table 2-26. Uncheck all others so your project isn't cluttered with controls you aren't using, and so the Setup Wizard doesn't include a lot of extra dead weight with your application.

Table 2-26 Custom controls used in BOOKS.VBP

CONTROL
Microsoft Outline Control
Microsoft Windows Common Controls 5.0

7. Using Project|References... from the VB main menu, select the references shown in Table 2-27. Uncheck all others so your project isn't cluttered with DLLs you aren't using, and so the Setup Wizard doesn't include a lot of extra dead weight with your application.

Table 2-27 References used in BOOKS.VBP

REFERENCE
Microsoft Visual Basic for Applications
Visual Basic Runtime Objects and Procedures
Visual Basic Objects and Procedures
Microsoft Windows Common Controls 5.0
Microsoft Remote Data Object 1.0
Microsoft Outline Control

8. Add the controls shown in Table 2-28 to the default form in the new project, with property settings as listed in Figure 2-16. Save the form as file BOOKS.FRM.

Table 2-28 Objects and properties for BOOKS.FRM

OBJECT	PROPERTY	SETTING
Form	Name	frmBooks
	BackColor	&H00C0C0C0&
	BorderStyle	3 'Fixed Dialog
	Caption	"Publisher Titles"
	MaxButton	0 'False
	MinButton	0 'False
Frame	Name	Frame1
CommandButton	Name	cmdAddNew
	BackColor	&H80000005&
	Caption	"Add New"
CommandButton	Name	cmdUpdate
	BackColor	&H80000005&
	Caption	"Update"
CommandButton	Name	cmdDelete
	BackColor	&H80000005&
	Caption	"Delete"
CommandButton	Name	cmdClose
	Caption	"Close"
CommandButton	Name	cmdMove
	Caption	"<<"
	Index	0
	TabStop	0 'False
CommandButton	Name	cmdMove
	Caption	"<"
	Index	1
	TabStop	0 'False
CommandButton	Name	cmdMove
	Caption	">"
	Index	2
	TabStop	0 'False
CommandButton	Name	cmdMove
	Caption	">>"

continued on next page

continued from previous page

OBJECT	PROPERTY	SETTING
	Index	3
	TabStop	0 'False
TextBox	Name	txtPublisher
	MultiLine	−1 'True
TextBox	Name	txtAdvance
TextBox	Name	txtPrice
TextBox	Name	txtNotes
	MultiLine	−1 'True
	ScrollBars	2 'Vertical
TextBox	Name	txtTitle
	MultiLine	−1 'True
Label	Name	Label9
	Alignment	1 'Right Justify
	BackColor	&H00C0C0C0&
	Caption	"Publisher:"
Label	Name	Label6
	Alignment	1 'Right Justify
	BackColor	&H00C0C0C0&
	Caption	"Advance:"
Label	Name	Label5
	Alignment	1 'Right Justify
	BackColor	&H00C0C0C0&
	Caption	"Price:"
Label	Name	Label3
	Alignment	1 'Right Justify
	BackColor	&H00C0C0C0&
	Caption	"Notes:"
Label	Name	Label1
	Alignment	1 'Right Justify
	BackColor	&H00C0C0C0&
	Caption	"Title:"
StatusBar	Name	StatusBar1
	Align	2 'Align Bottom
	AlignSet	−1 'True
	Style	1
	SimpleText	""

9. Add the following code to the Declarations section of the form. Option Explicit tells Visual Basic to make sure you declare all variables and objects before using them, in order to avoid naming problems. You can have VB automatically add this statement to your code modules by checking the Require Variable Declaration check box in Tools|Options under the Editor tab. The mrdo* variables will hold the remote data object handles.

```
Option Explicit

'Remote Data Object variables
Private mrdoEnv As rdoEnvironment
Private mrdoConn As rdoConnection
Private mrdoRS As rdoResultset

'Variable to indicated if data needs to be saved.
Dim mDirty As Boolean
```

10. Add the following code to the form's **Load** event procedure. After centering the form, the remote data objects that will link the application to the database are created using the default **rdoEnvironment(0)** and the **OpenConnection** method. The method uses the **rdDriverNoPrompt** option so that if enough information is given in the connect string ODBC won't present the end-user with dialogs to enter connect information. If the connect string is not complete, ODBC will prompt for whatever it needs.

Finally, the **Load** event procedure calls the **DataLoad** procedure to load the form's controls with data from the current record.

```
Private Sub Form_Load()
'Set up the form and connect to data source
Dim sSQL As String

    'Center the form
    Me.Top = (Screen.Height - Me.Height) / 2
    Me.Left = (Screen.Width - Me.Width) / 2

    'Allocate an ODBC environment handle
    Set mrdoEnv = rdoEnvironments(0)
    Set mrdoConn = mrdoEnv.OpenConnection("Books Available", _
        rdDriverNoPrompt, False, "ODBC;UID=sa;PWD=")

    sSQL = _
        "SELECT titles.*, publishers.* " _
        & "FROM titles, publishers " _
        & "WHERE publishers.pub_id = titles.pub_id " _
        & "ORDER BY titles.Title ASC;"
    Set mrdoRS = mrdoConn.OpenResultset(sSQL, _
        rdOpenKeyset, rdConcurRowver, 0)

    mrdoRS.MoveFirst
    SetRecNum

    DataLoad

End Sub
```

11. Since your VB code is handling all the data management details, it needs to take care of properly saving data that is *dirty*, or has changed. The code responds to the form's controls' **Change** events and the end-user can manually save the data by clicking an Update button. Add the following code to the **Change** event procedure for all the text boxes on the form.

```
Private Sub txtAdvance_Change()
    mDirty = True
End Sub

Private Sub txtNotes_Change()
    mDirty = True
End Sub

Private Sub txtPrice_Change()
    mDirty = True
End Sub

Private Sub txtPublisher_Change()
    mDirty = True
End Sub

Private Sub txtTitle_Change()
    mDirty = True
End Sub
```

12. Add the following code to the **DataLoad Sub** procedure. This is the code that loads the current record's data into the form each time the end-user moves to a new record. The procedure finishes by setting the **mDirty** flag to **False**, since the data was just loaded, then updating the record counter at the bottom of the form.

```
Private Sub DataLoad()
'Copy the record's data to its text box.
    txtAdvance.Text = Format$(mrdoRS("Advance") & "", "Currency")
    txtNotes.Text = mrdoRS("Notes") & ""
    txtPrice.Text = Format$(mrdoRS("Price") & "", "Currency")
    txtPublisher.Text = mrdoRS("Pub_Name") & ""
    txtTitle.Text = mrdoRS("Title") & ""

    mDirty = False
    SetRecNum
End Sub
```

13. Add the following code to the **DataSave** procedure, which saves the data in the form to the current record, whenever the data is dirty or the end-user clicks the Update button. The **mDirty** flag is also set to **False** here, since the data in the form is again the same as that in the record. The procedure uses the **frmRDOErrors** form in case of an error when saving the data.

```
Private Sub DataSave()
'Copy the current control contents to the record.
'ODBC driver and database has to support editing
'(most do).
```

```
mrdoRS.Edit
mrdoRS("Advance") = txtAdvance.Text
mrdoRS("Notes") = txtNotes.Text
mrdoRS("Price") = txtPrice.Text
mrdoRS("Pub_Name") = txtPublisher.Text
mrdoRS("Title") = txtTitle.Text
mrdoRS.Update

On Error GoTo DataSaveError
mrdoRS.Update

mDirty = False

Exit Sub

DataSaveError:
    frmRDOErrors.ErrorColl = rdoErrors

End Sub
```

14. The form has an Update button the end-user can use to manually update data, which simply executes the **DataSave** procedure. The lines commented out here can be used to protect the end-user against himself by only saving data when it is dirty.

```
Private Sub cmdUpdate_Click()
'    If mDirty Then
        DataSave
'    End If
End Sub
```

15. The next few procedures take care of navigating through the recordset. The navigation keys, a control array of command buttons, execute this **Click** event procedure which starts by checking whether the end-user wants to save any dirty data. Then it calls the **MoveRecord** procedure with the control index to actually reposition the record. Since there is a new current record, the **DataLoad** procedures loads the new data into the form.

```
Private Sub cmdMove_Click(Index As Integer)
Dim iResponse As Integer
Dim lRow As Long

    If mDirty Then
        iResponse = MsgBox("Dirty data. Save changes?", _
            vbYesNo + vbExclamation, "Update Data?")
        If iResponse = vbYes Then
            DataSave
        End If
    End If

    MoveRecord mrdoRS, Index

    DataLoad
End Sub
```

16. Enter the following code into the **MoveRecord Function** procedure. This
code is a reusable function to move around a recordset, implementing code
to move to the first or last record, and to the next and previous records. If
the first record is current and the end-user clicks the Move Previous button,
a beep sounds; a beep also sounds at the last record when the end-user
clicks the Move Next button. You can get as creative as you want here,
allowing the end-user to move forward or backward a fixed number of
records or to go to a specific record number.

```
Public Sub MoveRecord( _
    mrdoRS As rdoResultset, _
    Index As Integer)

    Select Case Index
        Case 0 'MoveFirst
            mrdoRS.MoveFirst

        Case 1 'MovePrevious
            mrdoRS.MovePrevious
            If mrdoRS.BOF Then
                Beep
                mrdoRS.MoveFirst
            End If

        Case 2 'MoveNext
            mrdoRS.MoveNext
            If mrdoRS.EOF Then
                Beep
                mrdoRS.MoveLast
            End If

        Case 3 'MoveLast
            mrdoRS.MoveLast

    End Select
End Sub
```

17. At the bottom of the form, a **StatusBar** control shows the end-user where
he is in the recordset, indicating **Record 5 of 120, 4% of ResultSet** or
whatever. This code demonstrates two of the nice features of RDOs, the
AbsolutePosition and **PercentPosition** properties. Rather than keeping track of the position in the **ResultSet** as the end-user navigates about,
RDOs keep track and expose the information in these two properties. This
is "un-SQL-like" behavior since it deals with individual rows rather than
whole resultsets, but it is convenient if you have to provide this information.

```
Private Sub SetRecNum()
    StatusBar1.SimpleText = "Row " _
        & mrdoRS.AbsolutePosition _
        & " of " & mrdoRS.RowCount _
        & ", " & Format$(mrdoRS.PercentPosition, "#0.00") _
        & "% of ResultSet"
End Sub
```

18. To add a new record, the **cmdAddNew** button's **Click** event checks to see
whether dirty data should be saved, then adds a new record to the recordset. The **DataLoad** procedure loads data from the new record. Since it is a
new record and has no data, this clears the form's controls, ready to accept
the end-user's input. The error handler uses the **frmRDOErrors** form for
RemoteData error handling.

```
Private Sub cmdAddNew_Click()
Dim iResponse As Integer

    If mDirty Then
        iResponse = MsgBox("Dirty data. " _
            & "Save before adding a new record?", _
            vbYesNo + vbExclamation, "Dirty Data")
        If iResponse = vbYes Then
            DataSave
        End If
    End If

    On Error GoTo AddNewError
    mrdoRS.AddNew
    mrdoRS.Update
    mrdoRS.Move 0, mrdoRS.LastModified

    DataLoad

    Exit Sub

AddNewError:
    frmRDOErrors.ErrorColl = rdoErrors

End Sub
```

19. A Delete button allows the end-user to remove records from the recordset.
This is very similar to the **AddNew** procedure. If after deleting the record the
Recordset is empty, a new record is added so there is always at least one
record. Either way, the position is moved to the first record, and its data
loaded into the form. **frmRDOErrors** is again used for error handling.

```
Private Sub cmdDelete_Click()
Dim iResponse As Integer

    iResponse = MsgBox("Are you sure that you " _
        & "want to delete this record?", _
        vbYesNo + vbExclamation, "Delete Record")
    If iResponse = vbYes Then
        On Error GoTo DeleteError
        mrdoRS.Delete
        If (mrdoRS.BOF And mrdoRS.EOF) Or mrdoRS.RowCount = 0 Then
            mrdoRS.AddNew
            mrdoRS.Update
            mrdoRS.MoveLast
        Else
```

continued on next page

continued from previous page

```
            mrdoRS.MoveFirst
        End If
    End If

    DataLoad

    Exit Sub

DeleteError:
    frmRDOErrors.ErrorColl = rdoErrors
End Sub
```

20. Add the following code to the **Click** event of the **cmdClose** command button. This is the exit point that terminates the program. After checking one last time whether dirty data should be saved, the procedure unloads itself.

```
Private Sub cmdClose_Click()
Dim iResponse As Integer

    If mDirty Then
        iResponse = MsgBox("Dirty data. Save before closing?", _
            vbYesNo + vbExclamation, "Dirty Data")
        If iResponse = vbYes Then
            DataSave
        End If
    End If
    Unload Me
End Sub
```

21. In the Project|[Project Name] Options menu item, set the startup form to **frmBooks**. You can also set an application description, but that is not required for the operation of this application.

Comments

Using the VB remote data objects is similar in many ways to JET DAOs but provide much finer control over databases, particularly over a network. If you compare the techniques used to navigate data in How-To's 2.2, 2.3, and 2.6 you'll find that the technique in this How-To is the most generally applicable to virtually any data source you need to access with VB. In many cases, it also gives the best performance.

COMPLEXITY
ADVANCED

2.8 How do I...
Benchmark my connection options?

Problem

I have so many different options for getting at my data on the server: attaching to JET databases, ODBC, remote data objects, and so on. How can I decide the best way (usually meaning fastest) to make database connections?

Technique

This How-To sets up a simple form for comparing two database connections; one using ODBC through JET and the other using remote data objects (RDOs). The **VB Timer** functions, saved to **Single-type** variables, provide the stopwatch. The program is designed to allow an unlimited number of repetitions, which can be set independently, so you get reliable results.

Steps

Open and run the **PERFORM.VBP** Visual Basic project file. The Connection Performance window will open. Select an ODBC data source name from the combo box, enter a query in the **Query** text box, and enter the number of repetitions for each connection. Then click the Run Benchmark Tests button. The number of iterations will show in the Results section, including intermediate minimum, maximum, and average time for each connection. Figure 2-18 shows the results for one test using 10 repetitions.

1. Create a new project **PERFORM.VBP**. Add the form **ERRORS.FRM** and the code module **ODBCAPI.BAS** (these modules are described in How-To 2.5), using Visual Basic's Project|Add File... menu command. The code module contains all the declarations needed for the ODBC API functions and the constants used in many of the functions.

2. Using Project|Components... from the VB main menu, select the custom controls shown in Table 2-29. Uncheck all others so your project isn't cluttered with controls you aren't using, and so the Setup Wizard doesn't include a lot of extra dead weight with your application.

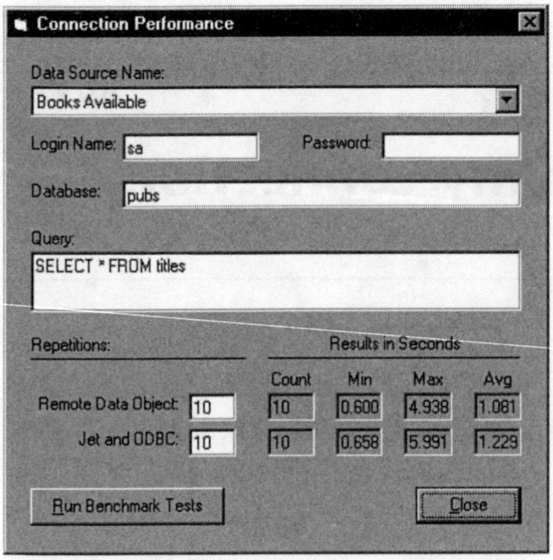

Figure 2-18 Results of benchmarking database connections using the PUBS SQL Server database over a Windows 95 and NT network

Table 2-29 Custom control used in Perform

CONTROL
Microsoft Outline Control

3. Using Project|References from the VB main menu, select the references shown in Table 2-30. Uncheck all others so your project isn't cluttered with DLLs you aren't using, and so the Setup Wizard doesn't include a lot of extra dead weight with your application.

Table 2-30 References used in Perform

REFERENCE
Microsoft Visual Basic for Applications
Visual Basic Runtime Objects and Procedures
Visual Basic Objects and Procedures
Microsoft Remote Data Object 1.0
Microsoft Outline Control
Microsoft DAO 3.5 Object Library

4. Name the default form **frmPerformance** and save the file as **PERFORM.FRM**. Add the controls as shown in Figure 2-18, setting the properties as shown in Table 2-31.

Table 2-31 Objects and properties for PERFORM.FRM

OBJECT	PROPERTY	SETTING
Form	Name	frmPerformance
	BorderStyle	3 'Fixed Dialog
	Caption	"Connection Performance"
	MaxButton	0 'False
	MinButton	0 'False
TextBox	Name	txtDatabase
TextBox	Name	txtPassword
TextBox	Name	txtLoginName
TextBox	Name	txtQuery
	MultiLine	-1 'True
TextBox	Name	txtJetResult
	BackColor	&H00C0C0C0&
	Locked	-1 'True
	TabStop	0 'False
TextBox	Name	txtRDOResult
	BackColor	&H00C0C0C0&
	Index	3
	Locked	-1 'True
	TabStop	0 'False
TextBox	Name	txtJetResult
	BackColor	&H00C0C0C0&
	Index	2
	Locked	-1 'True
	TabStop	0 'False
TextBox	Name	txtRDOResult
	BackColor	&H00C0C0C0&
	Index	2
	Locked	-1 'True
	TabStop	0 'False
TextBox	Name	txtJetResult
	BackColor	&H00C0C0C0&
	Index	1
	Locked	-1 'True
	TabStop	0 'False

continued on next page

continued from previous page

OBJECT	PROPERTY	SETTING
TextBox	Name	txtRDOResult
	BackColor	&H00C0C0C0&
	Index	1
	Locked	-1 'True
	TabStop	0 'False
TextBox	Name	txtJetResult
	BackColor	&H00C0C0C0&
	Index	0
	Locked	-1 'True
	TabStop	0 'False
TextBox	Name	txtRDOResult
	BackColor	&H00C0C0C0&
	Index	0
	Locked	-1 'True
	TabStop	0 'False
TextBox	Name	txtJetCount
TextBox	Name	txtRDOCount
CommandButton	Name	cmdRDC
	Caption	"&Run Benchmark Tests"
CommandButton	Name	cmdClose
	Caption	"&Close"
ComboBox	Name	cmbDSN
	Sorted	-1 'True
	Style	2 'Dropdown List
Label	Name	Label13
	Caption	"Database:"
Label	Name	Label12
	Alignment	1 'Right Justify
	Caption	"Password:"
Label	Name	Label11
	Caption	"Login Name:"
Label	Name	Label10
	Caption	"Query:"
Label	Name	Label9
	Alignment	2 'Center
	Caption	"Count"

OBJECT	PROPERTY	SETTING
Label	Name	Label8
	Alignment	2 'Center
	Caption	"Avg",
Label	Name	Label6
	Alignment	2 'Center
	Caption	"Max"
Label	Name	Label5
	Alignment	2 'Center
	Caption	"Min"
Line	Name	Line2
Label	Name	Label7
	Alignment	2 'Center
	Caption	"Results in Seconds"
Line	Name	Line1
Label	Name	Label4
	Caption	"Repetitions:"
Label	Name	Label2
	Alignment	1 'Right Justify
	Caption	"Jet and ODBC:"
Label	Name	Label3
	Alignment	1 'Right Justify
	Caption	"Remote Data Object:"
Label	Name	Label1
	Caption	"Data Source Name:"

5. Add the following code to the Declarations section of **frmPerformance**. **Option Explicit** tells Visual Basic to make sure you declare all variables and objects before using them, in order to avoid naming problems. You can have VB automatically add this statement to your code modules by checking the Require Variable Declaration check box in Tools|Options under the Editor tab.

```
Option Explicit
```

6. Add this code to the form's **Load** event. After centering the form, the code sets default values in the form's text boxes for the connection to be benchmarked. Then it calls the **GetODBCdbs** procedure, which is discussed next.

```
Private Sub Form_Load()

    Me.Left = (Screen.Width - Me.Width) / 2
    Me.Top = (Screen.Height - Me.Height) / 2

    'Set the starting defaults.
    txtRDOCount.Text = 10
    txtJetCount.Text = 10
    txtQuery.Text = "SELECT * FROM titles"
    txtLoginName.Text = "sa"
    txtPassword.Text = ""
    txtDatabase.Text = "pubs"

    'Load the cmbDSN with data source names.
    GetODBCdbs

End Sub
```

7. The `GetODBCdbs Sub` procedure uses some of the ODBC wrapper functions in `ODBCAPI.BAS` to obtain an environment handle, then queries ODBC for the list of available data source names. The `SQLDataSources` API function enumerates the data source names, providing information about each name. If the function call generates an error, the `ODBCErrors` function in `ODBCAPI.BAS` loads a form displaying the error to the end-user.

```
Private Sub GetODBCdbs()
'Variables for ODBC API calls
Dim cbDSNMax As Integer
Dim szDSN As String * 33
Dim pcbDSN As Long
Dim pcbDescription As Long
Dim szDescription As String * 512
Dim cbDescriptionMax As Integer

'Variables for procedure processing
Dim iResult As Integer
Dim iErrResult

    'Open a connection to an ODBC Environment handle
    iResult = ODBCAllocateEnv(ghEnv)
    If iResult <> SQL_SUCCESS Then
        MsgBox "Could not make connection to ODBC " _
            & "environment. Exiting application.", _
            vbOKOnly + vbCritical, "ODBC Problem"
        Unload Me
        End
    End If

    cbDSNMax = SQL_MAX_DSN_LENGTH + 1
    cbDescriptionMax = 512
    iResult = SQL_SUCCESS
    cmbDSN.Clear

    Screen.MousePointer = vbHourglass
    Do While iResult <> SQL_NO_DATA_FOUND
        'Get next data source (on the first call to
```

```
    'SQLDataSources, SQL_FETCH_NEXT gets the first
    'data source)
    iResult = SQLDataSources(ghEnv, _
        SQL_FETCH_NEXT, szDSN, cbDSNMax, pcbDSN, _
        szDescription, cbDescriptionMax, pcbDescription)

    If iResult = SQL_ERROR Then
        iErrResult = ODBCError("Env", ghEnv, 0, 0, _
            iResult, "Error getting list of data sources.")
        Screen.MousePointer = vbDefault
        Exit Sub
    End If

    cmbDSN.AddItem Left(szDSN, pcbDSN)
Loop

    iResult = ODBCFreeEnv(ghEnv)

    cmbDSN.ListIndex = 0
    Screen.MousePointer = vbDefault

End Sub
```

8. Add the following code to the `Click` event of the `cmdRDC` command button. Once the end-user has entered or changed any information for the
connection, he or she can click this button. The procedure starts by verifying that it has all the information it needs to start the test: a DSN is selected
and the number of repetitions for each test is one or more. Entries in the
other controls are up to the end-user, but all the information needed for a
valid connection is needed so that ODBC doesn't have to prompt for any
missing data. Then the procedure disables some of the controls for the
duration of the test, and calls the **Benchmark** procedure.

```
Private Sub cmdRDC_Click()
Dim iRDOCount As Integer
Dim iJetCount As Integer

    'Make sure that everything is set
    If cmbDSN.Text = "" Then
        MsgBox "Please select an ODBC data source name, " _
            & "then try again.", vbOKOnly + vbCritical, _
            "Data Source Name"
        cmbDSN.SetFocus
        Exit Sub
    End If

    iRDOCount = Val(txtRDOCount.Text)
    iJetCount = Val(txtJetCount.Text)
    If iRDOCount < 1 Or iJetCount < 1 Then
        MsgBox "You must enter at least one repetition " _
            & "for each connection method.", _
            vbOKOnly + vbCritical, "Data Source Name"
        If iRDOCount Then
            txtJetCount.SetFocus
```

continued on next page

continued from previous page

```
        Else
            txtRDOCount.SetFocus
        End If
        Exit Sub
    End If

    'Everything is hunky dory, so let's do it.
    txtRDOCount.Locked = True
    txtJetCount.Locked = True
    txtLoginName.Locked = True
    txtPassword.Locked = True
    cmdRDC.Enabled = False
    cmbDSN.Enabled = False
    cmdClose.Enabled = False

    Benchmark iRDOCount, iJetCount

    txtRDOCount.Locked = False
    txtJetCount.Locked = False
    txtLoginName.Locked = False
    txtPassword.Locked = False
    cmdRDC.Enabled = True
    cmbDSN.Enabled = True
    cmdClose.Enabled = False

End Sub
```

9. The **Benchmark Sub** procedure takes care of recording benchmark values and then running the **OpenRDO** and **OpenJet** procedures the specified number of repetitions. As each connection is made, this code records the elapsed time in Single data types, **fRDOTime** and **fJetTime**, so that fractions of seconds are recorded. It is critical that you benchmark connections that have minimum durations greater than the timing resolution on your system (usually 10 milliseconds for Windows NT and 55 milliseconds for Windows 95, according to the respective documentation). The statistics variables record information so that the minimum, maximum, and average times can be updated over the course of the test and displayed in the form.

Note that included are a couple of **DoEvents** statements outside the timing loops so that everything can catch up and stay in synch.

```
Private Sub Benchmark(iRDOReps As Integer, iJetReps As Integer)
Dim iRDOCount As Integer
Dim iJetCount As Integer
Dim iCount As Integer
Dim i As Integer
Dim sConnect As String

'Statistics variables
Dim fRDOTime As Single
Dim fJetTime As Single
Dim fRDOTotalTime As Double
Dim fJetTotalTime As Double
```

```vb
Dim fRDOMinTime As Single
Dim fJetMinTime As Single
Dim fRDOMaxTime As Single
Dim fJetMaxTime As Single
Dim fRDOAvgTime As Single
Dim fJetAvgTime As Single

    If iRDOReps > iJetReps Then
        iCount = iRDOReps
    Else
        iCount = iJetReps
    End If

    sConnect = "ODBC;DSN=" & cmbDSN.Text _
        & ";UID=" & txtLoginName.Text _
        & ";PWD=" & txtPassword.Text _
        & ";DATABASE=" & txtDatabase.Text

    For i = 1 To iCount
        If iRDOCount < iRDOReps Then
            fRDOTime = Timer

            If Not OpenRDO(sConnect) Then
                ClearResults
                Exit Sub
            End If

            fRDOTime = Timer - fRDOTime
            fRDOTotalTime = fRDOTotalTime + fRDOTime
            iRDOCount = iRDOCount + 1
        End If

        DoEvents

        If iJetCount < iJetReps Then
            fJetTime = Timer

            If Not OpenJet(sConnect) Then
                ClearResults
                Exit Sub
            End If

            fJetTime = Timer - fJetTime
            fJetTotalTime = fJetTotalTime + fJetTime
            iJetCount = iJetCount + 1
        End If

        'Update statistics so far
        txtRDOResult(0).Text = iRDOCount
        txtJetResult(0).Text = iJetCount

        'Minimum time
        If fRDOMinTime = 0 Then
            fRDOMinTime = fRDOTime
        ElseIf fRDOMinTime > fRDOTime Then
            fRDOMinTime = fRDOTime
```

continued on next page

continued from previous page

```
        End If
        txtRDOResult(1).Text = fRDOMinTime
        If fJetMinTime = 0 Then
            fJetMinTime = fJetTime
        ElseIf fJetMinTime > fJetTime Then
            fJetMinTime = fJetTime
        End If
        txtJetResult(1).Text = fJetMinTime

        'Maximum time
        If fRDOMaxTime < fRDOTime Then
            fRDOMaxTime = fRDOTime
        End If
        txtRDOResult(2).Text = fRDOMaxTime
        If fJetMaxTime < fJetTime Then
            fJetMaxTime = fJetTime
        End If
        txtJetResult(2).Text = fJetMaxTime

        txtRDOResult(3).Text = fRDOTotalTime / iRDOCount
        txtJetResult(3).Text = fJetTotalTime / iJetCount

        Me.Refresh
        DoEvents
    Next

End Sub
```

10. The `OpenJet Function` procedure actually opens the JET connection by opening the database and creating a recordset, then moving around a bit and recording some values. Since this is a timed test, if any error happens while making the connection, the test is ended by setting `OpenJet` to `False`. Note that the `db` and `rs` objects created are set to `Nothing` so their memory is released.

```
Private Function OpenJet(sConn As String) As Boolean
Dim db As Database
Dim rs As Recordset
Dim vValue As Variant

    On Error GoTo OpenJetError
    Set db = OpenDatabase("", False, False, sConn)

    'Create the recordset.
    Set rs = db.OpenRecordset(txtQuery.Text)

    rs.MoveLast
    vValue = rs(0)
    rs.MoveFirst
    vValue = rs(0)
    rs.MoveLast
    vValue = rs(0)

    Set db = Nothing
```

```
    Set rs = Nothing

    OpenJet = True
    Exit Function

OpenJetError:
    MsgBox "Error making Jet connection. Ending test.", _
        vbCritical, "Connect Error"
    OpenJet = False
End Function
```

11. The `OpenRDO` function serves essentially the same purpose as `OpenJet`, retrieving environment and connection handles from ODBC, then creating a `ResultSet`.

```
Private Function OpenRDO(sConn As String) As Boolean
Dim rdoEnv As rdoEnvironment
Dim rdoConn As rdoConnection
Dim rdoRS As rdoResultset
Dim vValue As Variant

    On Error GoTo OpenRDOError

    'Allocate an ODBC environment handle
    Set rdoEnv = rdoEnvironments(0)
    Set rdoConn = rdoEnv.OpenConnection("", _
        rdDriverNoPrompt, False, sConn)
    Set rdoRS = rdoConn.OpenResultset(txtQuery.Text, _
        rdOpenKeyset, rdConcurRowver, 0)

    rdoRS.MoveLast
    vValue = rdoRS(0)
    rdoRS.MoveFirst
    vValue = rdoRS(0)
    rdoRS.MoveLast
    vValue = rdoRS(0)

    rdoConn.Close

    Set rdoEnv = Nothing
    Set rdoConn = Nothing
    Set rdoRS = Nothing

    OpenRDO = True
    Exit Function

OpenRDOError:
    MsgBox "Error making RDO connection. Ending test.", _
        vbCritical, "Connect Error"
    OpenRDO = False
End Function
```

12. When an error occurs when making a database connection, the `Benchmark` procedure ends the test. `ClearResults` simply clears the results text boxes so that no confusing intermediate results are displayed to the end-user.

```
Private Sub ClearResults()
Dim i As Integer

    txtRDOResult(0).Text = ""
    txtJetResult(0).Text = ""

    For i = 0 To 3
        txtRDOResult(i).Text = ""
        txtJetResult(i).Text = ""
    Next
End Sub
```

13. Add the following code to the **Click** event procedure of the **cmdClose** command button. This code ends the program by unloading the form from memory.

```
Private Sub cmdClose_Click()
    Unload Me
End Sub
```

14. In the Project|[Project Name] Options menu item, set the startup form to **frmPerformance**. You can also set an application description, but that is not required for the operation of this application.

Comments

Benchmarking database connection is at best an art form, at worst misleading and confusing. You have two big strikes against you before you even start:

▪ Windows is a multitasking operating system, and both Windows 95 and NT are *preemptively* multitasking. This means that if Windows decides that it should devote some processor time to other applications or services, the benchmarking times are skewed. In older versions of Windows you could usually minimize this effect by closing all other applications, but modern versions have so many services and OLE functions happening that it is hard to eliminate all influences.

▪ Database connections, particularly over a network, are subject to traffic and errors that could be caused at any point on the network.

These conditions are complicated further because different types of database connections can be affected by the type of data returned and the form of the resultsets if any. A number of discussions can be seen online with one person claiming that one type of connection is clearly superior to another, while another person swears the opposite, and both have the data to prove their argument. The point is that you have to test how you access your databases using real data under real conditions to discover what works best for *your* data with *your* network under *your* system demands.

VB Enterprise Edition includes a data benchmarking application on the VB EE CD in the tools directory.

CHAPTER 3
REMOTE DATA OBJECTS

by George Szabo

REMOTE DATA OBJECTS

How do I...

If you were fortunate (or unfortunate) enough to have worked with Visual Basic 1.0 you will remember that it lacked any type of database access. Other than disk file access, Visual Basic was devoid of any true database capabilities. Visual Basic 2.0 introduced the Open Database Connectivity (ODBC) application programming interface (API). ODBC was promoted as a standard method for accessing any relational database engine that supported ODBC. All you needed was an ODBC driver for the database you wanted to access. But who supported ODBC 1.0? Using the ODBC API was cryptic and not for the faint of heart, and the ODBC 1.0 drivers that were available were limited in functionality and unstable.

It was not until the release of Microsoft Access 1.0 that ODBC started to get any real attention. Within the Access application was Joint Engine Technology (JET), which provided an object-oriented implementation for data access referred to as Data Access Objects (DAO). The JET engine was added to Visual Basic 3.0. DAO created a simple programming interface by which data could be retrieved and manipulated with minimal effort and a great deal of stability. Notice that speed was not mentioned. For all of its powerful features, when it comes to speed, JET is more like a jalopy. This was especially true when using JET as a conduit to ODBC database sources. Unfortunately ODBC, rather than JET itself, received the brunt of the bad rap and was labeled as a substandard method for accessing data from real database engines like Oracle, Informix, and so on. Even the rank and file SQL Server users found JET a poor second to the use of VBSQL.VBX, a Microsoft-provided control for Visual Basic that provided proprietary access to SQL Server using DBLIB.DLL, a dynamic link library of data access methods specific to SQL Server.

It is important to mention a few points about ODBC before proceeding. In an effort to promote ODBC, Microsoft has provided direct support for ODBC in SQL Server as its native connection. The ODBC API provides the same or better speed and functionality as VBSQL in SQL Server 6.0 and greater. Additionally the use of VBSQL is being discouraged by Microsoft. About 9 to 12 months before the release of Visual Basic 4.0, several articles were published in Visual Basic magazines outlining the use of the ODBC API from within Visual Basic. These articles demonstrated the speed and power that truly could be attained using the ODBC API without the JET layer. The ODBC API consistently outperformed JET anywhere from 10 times faster on up when accessing a back-end engine like SQL Server. This is still true with Visual Basic 5.0.

Microsoft Access and JET had opened the door to a large market desiring ODBC drivers for the array of heterogeneous data sources that corporate America faced each day. But it was Visual Basic and the ODBC API that provided the greatest possibility for serious enterprise development using these drivers. Unshackled from JET, many developers proceeded to use the ODBC API to create powerful front-ends to a variety of ODBC-compliant data sources that have come of age, including Oracle and MS SQL Server. But the ODBC API still suffered from complexity of implementation and the lack of a simple object model. Additionally, the ODBC API did not provide a link to using bound controls, which are controls that are automatically linked to a data source and are very useful for many simple applications.

What VB programmers clamored for was an object-oriented data access method that looked like JET and performed like ODBC. Additionally it needed to work with bound controls. Not a small task. What was delivered with Visual Basic Enterprise Edition were Remote Database Objects (RDOs) and the Remote Database Control (RDC).

RDO is arguably the single most important inclusion of Visual Basic 5.0 with regards to serious enterprise client/server development. RDO is a thin *wrapper* that uses the ODBC API directly, bypassing the JET database engine, while maintaining the simplicity and ease of use found in JET's data access objects. Figure 3-1 shows the RDO Object Model that simplifies use of the ODBC API. But what truly makes RDO so compelling is its ability to easily provide access and control over aspects of the server that previously could only be done using the ODBC API directly. These features include support for stored procedures with input and output variables, multiple resultsets, setting of engine isolation levels, creation and control of cursors, management of connections, and speed.

In this chapter you will explore basic RDO methods along with more advanced topics such as stored procedures, resultset management, and asynchronous queries. It is recommended that you create a data source name for this database. For information on connecting to a data source refer to Chapter 2, Getting Connected. Please note that all projects utilize the PUBS sample database that comes with Microsoft SQL Server. For your convenience, an MDB file containing the PUBS tables and data have been included on the CD that accompanies this book. Note, however, that several of the How-To's, primarily those that utilize stored procedures, will not work with an Access data source since this is not a true back-end engine and does not provide support for stored procedures or server-side cursors. For an explanation of server-side cursors please refer to How-To 3.5.

3.1   Create and Run an SQL Query

The whole process of client/server development is based on the ability of a client to submit a request to a server. In the world of database engines, this takes the form of Structured Query Language (SQL). In this How-To you will walk through the steps needed for an RDO to submit an SQL query to an ODBC-compliant data source.

3.2   Use an RDO to Insert, Update, and Delete Records

A fundamental aspect of SQL is the ability to insert, update, and delete records from a data source. This project will guide you through the creation of a simple data entry form complete with your own navigation buttons all linked to your ODBC source through the RDO's powerful **rdoResultset** object.

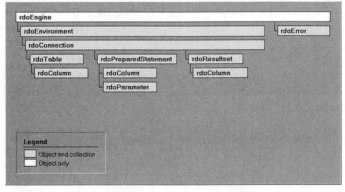

Figure 3-1 The remote database object model

3.3 Execute a Stored Procedure

A stored procedure can be any combination of SQL and flow-control statements saved under a single name within a Relational Database Management System (RDBMS). These statements are precompiled for speed of execution and can contain input and output parameters. In this How-To you will create an application that allows you to use a stored procedure called SP_HELPTEXT to retrieve information on other stored procedures found within your database.

3.4 Use an rdoPreparedStatement to Parameterize a Query

The benefit of parameterizing queries is similar to the benefit of creating parameterized functions. A single SQL statement or stored procedure can be used multiple times and modify its execution based on parameters you pass to it, allowing you to centralize logic in your application and make it more maintainable. This project will create a query form that allows you to enter search criteria and retrieve authors and their information from the PUBS database.

3.5 Control the Number of Rows Returned in a Resultset

The concept of load balancing is central to the client/server development question. If you have a client and a server, how do you balance the processing work so that the client and the server perform optimally? RDO provides control over data access load balancing through the rdoPreparedStatement object. This How-To creates a form where you can explore each option and combination with immediate feedback from your choices.

3.6 Create an RDO with Multiple Resultsets

Business activities can be grouped into a unit of work. These work units are better modeled by the submission of multiple requests and the receipt of multiple resultsets within a single call. This project will walk you through the mechanics of submitting multiple requests at once and handling the resultsets that are returned.

3.7 Perform an Asynchronous Query

Have you ever executed a query that took more than a few seconds to execute? If you submitted the query using a synchronous method, then you know that your application is unavailable until the request is filled. This How-To shows you how to submit asynchronous queries. Once the request is submitted, control is returned to your application. Additionally you will learn how to cancel a request that is processing.

3.1 How do I...
Create and run an SQL query?

Problem

I understand how to write SQL statements, but how do I use RDO to submit a statement to my database server?

Technique

The client/server process is comprised of requests and answers. SQL queries are an intricate part of this client/server process. There are two standard ways you can submit queries using RDO. Both methods require you to establish a connection to your data source. Once a connection is made, you can submit an SQL query by using the **OpenResultset** method against either an **rdoPreparedStatement** object or the **rdoConnection** object directly. In this How-To you will use the **OpenPreparedResultset** method directly on your **open connection** object. For information on using the **rdoPreparedStatement** object see How-To 3.4.

Steps

Open and run project **SUBMIT.VBP**. The running program appears as shown in Figure 3-2. As the application loads, you will be prompted for a data source name. Select a data source name (DSN) that connects to the PUBS database. Now the form will appear. Enter an SQL Select statement in the text box and press the Submit SQL button to send it to the backend database engine. If the Select statement returns records, they will be displayed in the **dbGrid** control. If no results are found, then the status bar will be updated to reflect the execution time of the query and will state that no records were returned.

1. Create a new project called **SUBMIT.VBP**. Select **Form1**, and add objects and set properties as shown in Table 3-1.

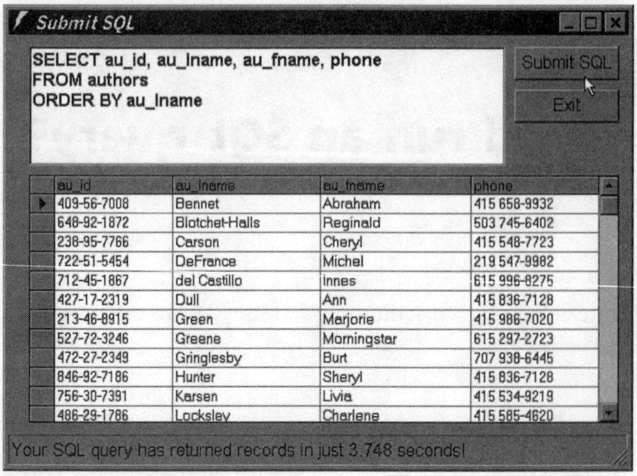

Figure 3-2 The form as it appears at runtime

Table 3-1 SUBMIT...FRM form and controls properties

OBJECT	PROPERTY	SETTING
Form	Name	frmSubmitSQL
	Caption	"Submit SQL"
TextBox	Name	txtSQL
	MultiLine	True
CommandButton	Name	cmdSubmitSQL
	Caption	"Submit SQL"
CommandButton	Name	cmdExit
	Caption	"Exit"
MSRDC	Name	rdcDisplay
DBGrid	Name	DBGrid1
	DataSource	rdcDisplay
StatusBar	Name	StatusBar1
	Align	Align Bottom
	Style	single panel
	SimpleText	""

2. The first thing you need to do is to dimension object variables for the environment and the connection. This is done by adding the following code to the General Declarations section of the form.

```
Option Explicit
Dim Env As rdoEnvironment
Dim Cn As rdoConnection
```

3. The form will use the environment and connection variables dimensioned in the General section of the form. This is done by adding the following code to the **Form_Load** event. In this example you will use the **OpenConnection** method to prompt the user to select a DSN at runtime.

```
Private Sub Form_Load()
    '
    'first you need to setup the RDO environment
    Set Env = rdoEnvironments(0)
    '
    'open a connection to a data source.
    Set Cn = Env.OpenConnection("", rdDriverPrompt, True, "")
End Sub
```

4. Enter the following code for the Submit SQL button **Click** event. This code performs the action of submitting the SQL query from the text box to the selected data source. This code also takes advantage of the new **rdoErrors** collection and **rdoError** objects to view errors generated during the RDO process. Notice that a **Timing** object is used to time the execution of the SQL statement. The **Timing** class is described later in this How-To.

```
Private Sub cmdSubmitSQL_Click()
    StatusBar1.SimpleText = "Processing Request ..."
    StatusBar1.Refresh
    On Error GoTo cmdSubmitSQL_error
    'you will use the timing object to time the whole process including
    'connect time.
    Dim oTiming As Timing
    Set oTiming = New Timing
    Call oTiming.Start
    '
    'the following routine is everything that must
    'be done to submit an SQL statement using
    'RDO.
    Dim Rst As rdoResultset
    '
    'submit the SQL statement and get the results
    Set Rst = Cn.OpenResultset(txtSQL.Text)
    '
    'finish timing of submission
    oTiming.Finish
    '
    'Check rowcount property to see if any records were returned.
    If Rst.RowCount > 0 Then
        StatusBar1.SimpleText = "Your SQL query has returned records" _
                & " in just " & oTiming.ElapsedTime & " seconds!"
        Set rdcDisplay.Resultset = Rst
    Else
        StatusBar1.SimpleText = "Query took " & oTiming.ElapsedTime _
                & "seconds - No records returned."
    End If
```

continued on next page

continued from previous page

```
cmdSubmitSQL_Exit:
    Set oTiming = Nothing
    Exit Sub

cmdSubmitSQL_error:
    'if error occurs check the RDO Collection for errors.
    Dim i As Integer
    For i = 0 To rdoErrors.Count - 1
    MsgBox rdoErrors(i).Description
    Next i
    'when done close all objects
    GoTo cmdSubmitSQL_Exit
End Sub
```

5. Enter the following code for the Exit button **Click** event. At the conclusion of your application it is an important practice to release the connection to your data source as well as the ODBC environment variable. This is done with the **Close** method shown below.

```
Private Sub cmdExit_Click()
    '
    'close out all objects in reverse order.
    Cn.Close
    Env.Close
    End
End Sub
```

6. Use Insert Class Module from Visual Basic's menu bar to add a class module to this project. The class will appear in the project window. Open the class module and press F4 to view the class's properties. Set these properties as shown in Table 3-2.

Table 3-2 TIMING.CLS **class module property setting**

OBJECT	PROPERTY	SETTING
Class Module	Name	"Timing"

7. Add the following code to the General Declarations section of the **Timing** class module. You will need to declare the **timeGetTime** API function in order to have access to a method that returns timing values with a millisecond resolution. The standard **Time()** function in Visual Basic only provides for seconds.

```
Option Explicit
'
'dimension readonly variables for timing events
Dim mStartTime As Long
Dim mFinishTime As Long
Dim mElapsedTime As Long
'
'declare API to get time in milliseconds.
Private Declare Function timeGetTime Lib "winmm.dll" () As Long
```

8. Add the following methods and properties to the `Timing` class. These methods and properties will allow you to time execution of SQL queries and have access to the elapsed time values in milliseconds.

```
'method to store start time
Public Sub Start()
    mStartTime = timeGetTime
End Sub

'method to store finish time and calculate elapsed time in milliseconds
Public Sub Finish()
    mFinishTime = timeGetTime
    mElapsedTime = mFinishTime - mStartTime
End Sub

'read-only property to access elapsed time.
Public Property Get ElapsedTime()
    ElapsedTime = mElapsedTime / 1000
End Property
```

How It Works

The RDO model is followed to allow execution of an SQL query. First an environment variable is set and a connection opened to a data source using the `OpenConnection` method. Once a connection is made, any SQL statements entered in the text box control are submitted to the data source using the `OpenResultset` method, which returns the results into an `rdoResultset` object variable labeled `Rst` for this project. The project uses a class module called `Timing` to actually time the execution of SQL queries in milliseconds. The resultset and elapsed time of the query are presented to the user via a remote data control and bound DBGrid control. This is accomplished by binding the DBGrid control to the RDC and setting the RDC's resultset property to the `Resultset` generated by the `OpenResultset` method that is coded behind the Execute SQL button. Figure 3-3 shows the path that your SQL statement must travel using the RDO model.

Comments

This project used the default values of many of the RDOs to demonstrate the fundamental steps required in executing SQL queries using RDO. A great number of options can be set for each object and method used in this How-To. Try submitting a variety of SQL statements including `Insert`, `Update`, and `Delete` statements and see how this implementation handles these statements. Try submitting procedures like `Use Master` to change the current database in use by the connection. Finally you may want to try modifying this project to connect without prompting you for a DSN. This can be done by specifying either a DSN or a connection string in the `OpenConnection` method and then changing `rdDriverPrompt` to `rdDriverNoPrompt`. Give it a try.

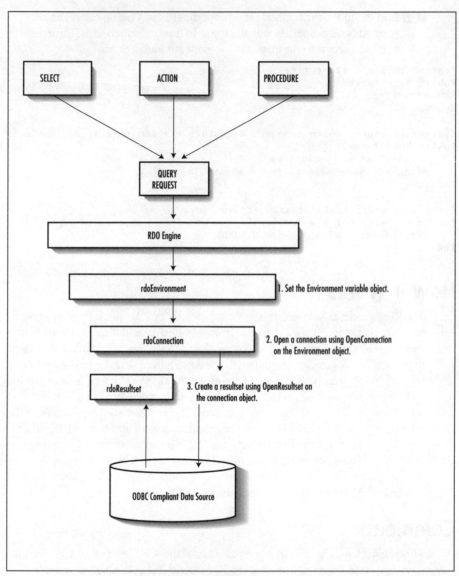

Figure 3-3 SQL query path to an ODBC data source

COMPLEXITY

INTERMEDIATE

3.2 How do I...
Use an RDO to insert, update, and delete records?

Problem

I am familiar with standard SQL statements like **Insert**, **Update**, and **Delete**. Is there an easier way to perform these functions using RDO?

Technique

RDO provides a special object called the **resultset** object. It provides some great functionality that can make simple data manipulation easier. Microsoft has gone to great lengths to mirror the object interface exposed by JET and Database Access Objects (DAO). The RDO contains methods like **AddNew**, **Update**, **Delete**, **MoveNext**, **MovePrevious**, **MoveFirst**, and **MoveLast**. All these methods should look very familiar to you if you have used DAO at all. This How-To uses an RDO **resultset** object to directly manipulate and view records in the Authors table of the PUBS database. Additionally, you create your own navigation buttons and display and collect information, all without using bound controls.

Steps

Open and run the project **AUTHINFO.VBP**. The running program appears as shown in Figure 3-4. Press the navigation buttons on the form to move from record to record. Try changing a record and moving to another record without selecting the Update button. Now move back to the record you changed. Your changes are gone. Now make changes and select Update before moving to another record. If you revisit the changed records you will see that your changes were stored. All of this is done without the use of bound controls.

1. Create a new project called **AUTHINFO.VBP**. Select **Form1**, and add objects and set properties as shown in Table 3-3.

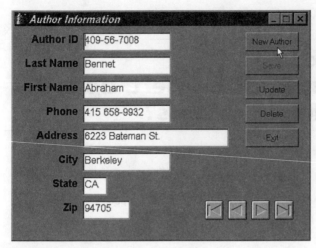

Figure 3-4 The form as it appears at runtime

Table 3-3 AUTHINFO.FRM form and controls properties

OBJECT	PROPERTY	SETTING
Form	Name	frmAuthorInf
	Caption	"Author Information"
	Icon	"books04.ico"
	Picture	"setup.bmp"
CommandButton	Name	cmdNewAuthor
	Caption	"New Author"
CommandButton	cmdExit	
	Caption	"E&xit"
CommandButton	cmdDelete	
	Caption	"Delete"
CommandButton	cmdUpdate	
	Caption	"Update"
CommandButton	cmdSave	
	Caption	"Save"
	Enabled	False
TextBox	txtAuthorID	
TextBox	txtLastName	
TextBox	txtFirstName	
TextBox	txtPhone	
TextBox	txtAddress	
TextBox	txtCity	

OBJECT	PROPERTY	SETTING
TextBox	txtState	
TextBox	txtZip	
AniPushButton	aniMoveLast	
	Picture Frame 1	"Arw02rt.ico"
	Picture Frame 2	"Arw02rtb.ico"
	PictDrawMode	1
AniPushButton	aniMoveNext	
	Picture Frame 1	"Arw01rt.ico"
	Picture Frame 2	
	PictDrawMode	1
AniPushButton	aniMovePrevious	
	Picture Frame 1	"Arw01lt.ico"
	Picture Frame 2	"Arw01ltb.ico"
	PictDrawMode	1
AniPushButton	aniMoveFirst	
	Picture Frame 1	"Arw02lt.ico"
	Picture Frame 2	"Arw02ltb.ico"
	PictDrawMode	1
Label	Label8	
	Alignment	Right Justify
	BackStyle	Transparent
	Caption	"Zip"
	ForeColor	&H00C0C0C0&
Label	Label7	
	Alignment	Right Justify
	BackStyle	Transparent
	Caption	"State"
	ForeColor	&H00C0C0C0&
Label	Label6	
	Alignment	Right Justify
	BackStyle	Transparent
	Caption	"City"
	ForeColor	&H00C0C0C0&
Label	Label5	
	Alignment	Right Justify
	BackStyle	Transparent

continued on next page

continued from previous page

OBJECT	PROPERTY	SETTING
	Caption	"Address"
	ForeColor	&H00C0C0C0&
Label	Label4	
	Alignment	Right Justify
	BackStyle	Transparent
	Caption	"Phone"
	ForeColor	&H00C0C0C0&
Label	Label3	
	Alignment	Right Justify
	BackStyle	Transparent
	Caption	"First Name"
	ForeColor	&H00C0C0C0&
Label	Label2	
	Alignment	Right Justify
	BackStyle	Transparent
	Caption	"Last Name"
	ForeColor	&H00C0C0C0&
Label	Label1	
	Alignment	Right Justify
	BackStyle	Transparent
	Caption	"Author ID"
	ForeColor	&H00C0C0C0&

2. The first thing you need to do is to dimension object variables for the environment, connection, and resultset. This is done by adding the following code to the General Declarations section of the form.

```
Option Explicit
'dimension your environment, connection and result
'object variables here. this will make them shareable
'within the form.
Dim Env As rdoEnvironment
Dim Cn As rdoConnection
Dim rstAuthor As rdoResultset
```

3. The form will use the environment and connection variables dimensioned in the General Declarations section of the form. This is done by adding the following code to the **Form_Load** event. In this example you will use the **OpenConnection** method to prompt the user to select a DSN at runtime.

```
Private Sub Form_Load()
    'set the environment variable to the default environment
    Set Env = rdoEnvironments(0)
    '
```

```
'since the application may potentially run against an MDB
'file which is not a true database server and does not
'support server-side cursors, here you will specify that
'the connection use ODBC cursors. This will work with
'SQL Server as well.
Env.CursorDriver = rdUseOdbc
'
'Open a connection. Since the DSN and Connection strings
'are empty, the ODBC Driver Selection Window will prompt you
'at runtime for a DSN etc.
Set Cn = Env.OpenConnection(dsname:="", _
                            Prompt:=rdDriverPrompt, _
                            ReadOnly:=False, _
                            Connect:="")
'
'with the connection complete you will now load the author
'information into the application
Call LoadAuthorInfo
End Sub
```

4. Create the following subroutine that retrieves all authors' information from the Authors tables located in the PUBS database. This subroutine is called during the **Form_Load** event.

```
Private Sub LoadAuthorInfo()
    Dim sSQL As String
    sSQL = "SELECT * FROM Authors ORDER BY au_lname"
    'using the connection opened earlier you will now create
    'an updateable resultset.Note that even though the online
    'VB help lists "Source" as the named parameter for the Open
    'Resultset method it is actually "Name".
    Set rstAuthor = Cn.OpenResultset(Name:=sSQL, _
                                     Type:=rdOpenDynamic, _
                                     LockType:=rdConcurRowver)
    'Check to see if any records were returned
    If rstAuthor.EOF <> True Then
        'display the records to the form
        Call DisplayRecord
    Else
        MsgBox "No records found"
    End If
End Sub
```

5. Enter the following routines to handle the **MoveNext** and **MovePrevious** navigation of records handled by the **rstAuthor** resultset. These routines will be used in the next step to prevent navigation beyond the first or last records of the resultset.

```
Private Sub aniMoveFirst_Click()
    rstAuthor.MoveFirst
    Call DisplayRecord
End Sub

Private Sub aniMoveLast_Click()
    rstAuthor.MoveLast
    Call DisplayRecord
End Sub
```

6. Handling the event of moving past the current resultset can be a bit tricky. Here you will use **MoveNext** and check if you have moved too far. If this is the case, then you will use **MoveLast**. Trying to use **MovePrevious** will not work because previous and next have no meaning when you are beyond the resultset at End Of File (EOF). **MoveLast** and **MoveFirst** both work because you are moving to a specific record.

```
Private Sub aniMoveNext_Click()
    If rstAuthor.EOF <> True Then
        rstAuthor.MoveNext
        If rstAuthor.EOF = True Then
            rstAuthor.MoveLast
            Beep
        Else
            Call DisplayRecord
        End If
    End If
End Sub

'same as the movenext routine.
Private Sub aniMovePrevious_Click()
    If rstAuthor.BOF <> True Then
        rstAuthor.MovePrevious
        If rstAuthor.BOF = True Then
            rstAuthor.MoveFirst
            Beep
        Else
            Call DisplayRecord
        End If
    End If
End Sub
```

7. Add the following code for each of the buttons that appear on the form.

```
'the New Author button and the Save button work in unison.
'First you clear the form and let the user enter new
'information. The Save button stores the information to
'the database.
Private Sub cmdNewAuthor_Click()
    Call ClearRecord
    Call DisableButtons
End Sub

'Once user selects save you will optimistically use
'the AddNew method of the resultset. Set the resultset
'to the new values and update (save).
Private Sub cmdSave_Click()
    rstAuthor.AddNew
    Call SetAuthorInfo
    rstAuthor.Update
    Call EnableButtons
End Sub

'this update routine is used to save changes to a
'currently present record. remember that you must call
'Edit before you set values and call Update.
```

```
Private Sub cmdUpdate_Click()
    rstAuthor.Edit
    Call SetAuthorInfo
    rstAuthor.Update
End Sub

'Deleting a record does not move you to the previous
'or next record. Your location simply becomes invalid
'Here you requery to adjust the set size. this also
'eliminates the need to move off the record you are
'deleting.
Private Sub cmdDelete_Click()
    rstAuthor.Delete
    rstAuthor.Requery
    Call DisplayRecord
End Sub

'As you exit you will need to close all of the object
'variables. Actually closing the form should take care
'of it for you just like closing the environment object
'automatically closes all object within it.
Private Sub cmdExit_Click()
    rstAuthor.Close
    Cn.Close
    Env.Close
    End
End Sub
```

8. Add the following routines to the form. These routines provide methods for displaying and retrieving information from the text boxes on the form.

```
'routine to display current row of resultset on form.
Private Sub DisplayRecord()
    txtAuthorID.Text = rstAuthor("au_id")
    txtLastName.Text = rstAuthor("au_lname")
    txtFirstName.Text = rstAuthor("au_fname")
    txtPhone.Text = rstAuthor("phone")
    txtAddress.Text = rstAuthor("address")
    txtCity.Text = rstAuthor("city")
    txtState.Text = rstAuthor("state")
    txtZip.Text = rstAuthor("zip")
End Sub


Private Sub ClearRecord()
    'this is a good place to set up default values
    txtAuthorID.Text = ""
    txtLastName.Text = ""
    txtFirstName.Text = ""
    txtPhone.Text = ""
    txtAddress.Text = ""
    txtCity.Text = ""
    txtState.Text = "WA"
    txtZip.Text = ""
End Sub
```

continued on next page

continued from previous page

```
'routine to set resultset to current values on form.
'This is a good place for validations.
Private Sub SetAuthorInfo()
    rstAuthor("au_id") = txtAuthorID.Text
    rstAuthor("au_lname") = txtLastName.Text
    rstAuthor("au_fname") = txtFirstName.Text
    rstAuthor("phone") = txtPhone.Text
    rstAuthor("address") = txtAddress.Text
    rstAuthor("city") = txtCity.Text
    rstAuthor("state") = txtState.Text
    rstAuthor("zip") = txtZip.Text
    rstAuthor("contract") = 0
End Sub
```

9. Add these routines to the form to enable and disable the navigation buttons. These routines are used to synchronize the navigation buttons with the corresponding navigation available for the underlying resultset.

```
'routine to disable the buttons on form.
Private Sub DisableButtons()
    cmdSave.Enabled = True

    cmdNewAuthor.Enabled = False
    cmdUpdate.Enabled = False
    aniMoveFirst.Enabled = False
    aniMovePrevious.Enabled = False
    aniMoveNext.Enabled = False
    aniMoveLast.Enabled = False
End Sub

'routine to enable the buttons on form.
Private Sub EnableButtons()
    cmdSave.Enabled = False

    cmdNewAuthor.Enabled = True
    cmdUpdate.Enabled = True
    aniMoveFirst.Enabled = True
    aniMovePrevious.Enabled = True
    aniMoveNext.Enabled = True
    aniMoveLast.Enabled = True
End Sub
```

How It Works

The `rdoResultset` object provides all the functionality to make this project work. First you step through the process of creating an `rdoResultset` by dimensioning and using both an environment and a connection. Once the connection to a data source is established, the `OpenResultset` method is used on the connection to create a dynamic resultset. To understand what a dynamic resultset refers to, you must first understand what a cursor is. A cursor in a resultset is similar in concept to a cursor in your word processing program. The cursor simply marks the current record you are on within a resultset. A dynamic cursor refers to cursors where the membership, order, and values in the resultset can constantly change. As rows are updated, deleted, or inserted these changes are detected by the cursor as data is accessed.

Cursors can be created and maintained by either the server database engine or the client ODBC driver manager. Be aware that, though dynamic cursors provide a great deal of functionality, they require a great deal of overhead from whoever is maintaining them. Finally, with an **rdoResultset** object populated, you are able to take advantage of the DAO-like methods of **MoveFirst**, **MovePrevious**, **MoveNext**, and **MoveLast** in order to easily navigate the records contained in the resultset. Additionally the application uses the **AddNew**, **Update**, and **Delete** methods to automate those activities as well.

Comments

Although the methods used in this How-To resemble those found in the DAO syntax, their implementation is significantly different. The DAO implementations automate the process with little flexibility whereas RDO provides the ability to control all aspects from the cursor type to the record-locking method. Take this application and try running it on two or more machines at the same time. Make changes to the Authors table using this project to see how changes made by one user can be seen by other users. This How-To works with an MDB file but, to truly see what implication cursor selection has on performance, you will need to use a true database server engine like Microsoft SQL Server.

COMPLEXITY
ADVANCED

3.3 How do I...
Execute a stored procedure?

Problem

In many situations I use stored procedures contained within the database to perform a variety of functions from granting rights to retrieving server information. How do I execute a stored procedure with an RDO?

Technique

Stored procedures are precompiled instructions that your database engine can execute. A stored procedure can contain anything from a single action query that returns no records to returning multiple resultsets with a single call. Additionally, stored procedures can contain logic. Before choosing the RDO method for running a stored procedure, it is important to answer the following questions: Does the stored procedure need input values? Does it need output values? Does it provide a return code? And, most importantly, does it return a resultset or multiple resultsets? Using these criteria you can then choose the method that is most appropriate to your need. In this How-To you will query the database you select for the names of all stored procedures it contains and load them into a listbox. Using a call to another stored procedure called **SP_HELPTEXT**, which comes with Microsoft SQL Server, you will be able to select any stored procedure from the listbox and view the SQL and flow control statements it contains as well as parameters it requires and default values it may provide. The result is a handy utility for developers.

Steps

Open and run project **EXECSP.VBP**. The running program appears as shown in Figure 3-5. As the program loads, you will be prompted to select a data source name (DSN). For this example you will need a connection that specifies the database where the stored procedure **SP_HELPTEXT** is found. For Microsoft SQL Server **SP_HELPTEXT** is found in the MASTER database. Do not specify an MDB file as a data source for this project since the Microsoft Database file does not support stored procedures and, therefore, will not work with this example. Once the application loads, click on the combo box and you will see a list of all the stored procedures that reside within the database. Select a stored procedure from the list and select the Execute button.

The application will return and present the code that comprises the stored procedure. You can see an example of this in Figure 3-6.

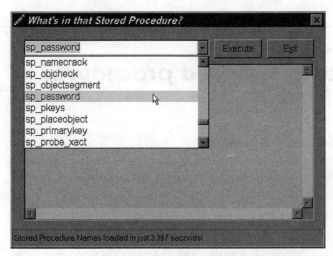

Figure 3-5 EXECSP as it appears listing all of the stored procedures within the selected database

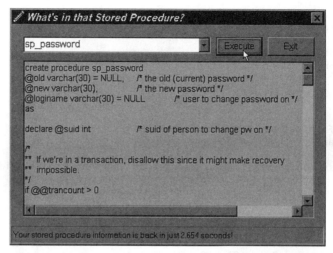

Figure 3-6 EXECSP after returning information on a selected stored procedure

This project is SQL Server specific. If you are running against Oracle or some other ODBC data source you can take the following stored procedure and re-create it for your DBMS with the appropriate syntax for that engine. **SP_HELPTEXT** resides in the MASTER database. This stored procedure accepts one parameter which is the name of an object in the database. For this example, stored procedure objects will be used. Once the **SP_HELPTEXT** stored procedure is executed and passed the name of a stored procedure object, it retrieves the actual select and flow control statements, variables, and text that comprise that stored procedure. Using this project, the following text was retrieved on **SP_HELPTEXT** itself.

```
create procedure sp_helptext
@objname varchar(92)
as
declare @dbname varchar(30)

set nocount on

/*
**   Make sure the @objname is local to the current database.
*/
if (@objname like '%.%.%' and
        substring(@objname, 1, charindex('.', @objname) - 1) <> db_name() )
        begin
                raiserror(15250,-1,-1)
                return (1)
        end

/*
**   See if @objname exists.
*/
```

continued on next page

continued from previous page

```
if (object_id(@objname) is null)
        begin
select @dbname = db_name()
raiserror(15009,-1,-1,@objname,@dbname)
                return (1)
        end

/*
**   Find out how many lines of text are coming back,
**   and return if there are none.
*/
if (select count(*) from syscomments where id = object_id(@objname)) = 0
        begin
                raiserror(15197,-1,-1,@objname)
                return (1)
        end

if (select count(*) from syscomments where id = object_id(@objname)
and texttype & 4 = 0) = 0
        begin
                print 'The object''s comments have been encrypted.'
                return (0)
        end

/*
**   Else get the text.
*/
select text from syscomments where id = object_id(@objname)

return (0)
```

1. Create a new project called **EXECSP.VBP**. Select **Form1**, and add objects and set properties as shown in Table 3-4.

Table 3-4 EXECSP.FRM form and control properties

OBJECT	PROPERTY	SETTING
Form	Name	frmExecSP
	BorderStyle	Fixed Single
	Caption	"What's in that Stored Procedure?"
	Icon	" Pencil01.ico"
TextBox	Name	txtDisplay
	BackColor	&H00C0C0C0&
	MultiLine	True
	ScrollBars	Both
CommandButton	Name	cmdExit
	Caption	"E&xit"
CommandButton	Name	cmdExecute

OBJECT	PROPERTY	SETTING
	Caption	"Execute"
ComboBox	Name	cmbStoredProcedureNames
StatusBar	Name	StatusBar1
	Align	Align Bottom
	Style	1
	SimpleText	""

2. You first need to dimension object variables for the environment, connection, prepared statement, and resultset. This is done by adding the following code to the General Declarations section of the form.

```
Option Explicit
'
'dimension environment and connection variables
Dim Env As rdoEnvironment
Dim Cn As rdoConnection
'
'Dimension object variables that will be needed to execute the
'stored procedure and store the results
Dim Rst As rdoResultset
Dim Ps As rdoPreparedStatement
'
'Dimension a variable for the timing object.
Dim oTiming As Timing
```

3. On loading the form you will set up the environment and require the user to specify a DSN to open a connection. This is accomplished by adding the following code to the **Form_load** event.

```
Sub Form_load()
    '
    'first you need to setup the RDO environment
    Set Env = rdoEnvironments(0)
    Env.CursorDriver = rdUseServer
    '
    'open a connection to a data source
    Set Cn = Env.OpenConnection(dsName:="", _
                                Prompt:=rdDriverPrompt, _
                                ReadOnly:=True, _
                                Connect:="")
    '
    'Initialize rdoPreparedStatement object
    Call InitializePS
    '
    'load combo box with stored procedure names
    Call LoadStoredProcedures

End Sub
```

4. Add the following code to the form. This code creates a prepared statement to execute the stored procedure **SP_HELPTEXT**. The prepared statement shown here as **Ps** will be used to retrieve the contents of the stored procedure by the **ExecuteStoredProcedure** subroutine found in Step 7.

```
Private Sub InitializePS()
    On Error GoTo InitializePS_error
    Dim sSQL As String
    '
    'The stored procedure has a single parameter which is the name
    'of the stored procedure selected in the combo box.
    sSQL = "{call master.dbo.sp_helptext (?)}"
    Set Ps = Cn.CreatePreparedStatement(Name:="", sqlstring:=sSQL)

    'you must set the rowsetsize to one. This is caused by the need to
    'prevent the use of server-side cursors when retrieving data from
    'a stored procedure.
    Ps.RowsetSize = 1

InitializePS_Exit:
    Exit Sub

InitializePS_error:
    'if error occurs check the RDO Collection for errors.
    Dim oRDOError As rdoError
    Dim sErr As String
    For Each oRDOError In rdoErrors
    sErr = sErr & oRDOError.Description
    Next
    MsgBox sErr

End Sub
```

5. Add the following code to your form. The **LoadStoredProcedures** routine uses an **rdoResultset** to retrieve stored procedure names that exist within the selected database. This routine is specific to SQL Server and uses the SYSOBJECTS table, which contains information about the current databases system objects. Procedures listed in the SYSOBJECTS table are marked with a **P** in the **TYPE** field, therefore, you will use a **SELECT** statement that retrieves objects with a **TYPE** field equal to P in order to return all stored procedures.

```
Public Sub LoadStoredProcedures()
    On Error GoTo LoadStoredProcedures_error
    'you will use the timing object to time the whole process including
    'connect time.
    Set oTiming = New Timing
    Call oTiming.Start
    '
    'the following routine is everything that must
    'be done to submit an SQL statement using
    'RDO.
    Dim Rst As rdoResultset
    Dim sSQL As String
    '
```

```
'The following Select statement works with MS SQL 6.0 and greater and
'returns the names of all stored procedures contained within
'the database connection.
Let sSQL = "SELECT name FROM sysobjects" _
        & " WHERE type = 'P' ORDER BY name"
'
'Use the connection object variable to create a resultset of
'stored procedures
Set Rst = Cn.OpenResultset(sSQL)
'
'finish timing of submission
oTiming.Finish
'
'Check rowcount property to see if any records were returned.
If Rst.RowCount <> 0 Then
    'load list
    cmbStoredProcedurenames.Clear
    While Not Rst.EOF = True
        cmbStoredProcedurenames.AddItem Rst("name")
        Rst.MoveNext
    Wend
    StatusBar1.SimpleText = "Stored Procedure Names loaded" _
            & " in just " & oTiming.ElapsedTime & " seconds!"
Else
    StatusBar1.SimpleText = "Query took " & oTiming.ElapsedTime _
            & "seconds - No Stored Procedures Found"
End If
'
'that's all there is to it
'
LoadStoredProcedures_Exit:
    Set oTiming = Nothing
    Exit Sub

LoadStoredProcedures_error:
    'if error occurs check the RDO Collection for errors.
    Dim oRDOError As rdoError
    Dim sErr As String
    For Each oRDOError In rdoErrors
    sErr = sErr & oRDOError.Description
    Next
    MsgBox sErr
End Sub
```

6. Enter the following text for the **Execute** button click event. The following
code executes the **ExecuteStoredProcedure** subroutine to retrieve the
detail information on the selected stored procedure using **SP_HELPTEXT**.

```
'calls a routine that executes the sp_helptext stored procedure.
Private Sub cmdExecute_Click()
    txtDisplay.Text = ""
    StatusBar1.SimpleText = "Processing Request ..."
    StatusBar1.Refresh
    txtDisplay.Refresh
    Call ExecuteStoredProcedure
End Sub
```

7. The `ExecuteStoredProcedure` subroutine passes in the selected stored procedure name from the combo box and uses `SP_HELPTEXT` to retrieve the actual text used to create the stored procedure. A prepared statement is used to execute the stored procedure. In this example, **Name** is assigned an empty string. The `rdoPreparedStatement` is appended to the `rdoPreparedStatements` collection. The `rdoPreparedStatement` can be used by referencing the prepared statement object variable or the `rdoPreparedStatement` object's ordinal value. Note: All `rdoPreparedStatement` objects are temporary and are lost when the `rdoConnection` object is closed.

```
Private Sub ExecuteStoredProcedure()
    On Error GoTo ExecuteStoredProcedure_Error
    '
    'you will use the timing object to time the whole process including
    'connect time.
    Dim oTiming As Timing
    Set oTiming = New Timing
    Call oTiming.Start
    '
    'set the single parameter for this prepared statement which is
    'a string variable which contains the name selected in the
    'combobox.
    Ps.rdoParameters(0) = cmbStoredProcedurenames.Text
    '
    'The prepared statement is executed by using the OpenResultset
    'method.
    Set Rst = Ps.OpenResultset(Type:=rdOpenForwardOnly, _
                               LockType:=rdConcurReadOnly)
    '
    'finish timing of submission
    oTiming.Finish
    '
    'Display the results
    Dim sResults As String
    Dim sFix As String
    Dim rc As Integer
    '
    'Check rowcount property to see if any records were returned.
    If Rst.RowCount <> 0 Then
        While Rst.EOF <> True
            sResults = sResults & Rst("text")
            Rst.MoveNext
        Wend
        'Pass resulting string to a routine that formats the output
        'correctly, then pass string to textbox for display.
        sFix = CvtCarrCtrl(sResults, rc%)
        txtDisplay.Text = sFix
        StatusBar1.SimpleText = "Your stored procedure information is back" _
                & " in just " & oTiming.ElapsedTime & " seconds!"
    Else
        StatusBar1.SimpleText = "Your stored procedure is back in " _
                & oTiming.ElapsedTime & " seconds - No records returned."
    End If
```

```
ExecuteStoredProcedure_Exit:
    Rst.Close
    Set oTiming = Nothing
    Exit Sub

ExecuteStoredProcedure_Error:

    'if error occurs check the RDO Collection for errors.
    Dim oRDOError As rdoError
    Dim sErr As String
    Dim sErrMsg As String

    For Each oRDOError In rdoErrors
    sErr = sErr & oRDOError.Description
    Next
    MsgBox sErr
    rdoErrors.Clear
End Sub
```

8. The `CvtCarrCtrl` function will accept a character string as input and convert any linefeed character to a carriage control character and a line feed. The number of line feeds converted will be passed back by reference. **SP_HELPTEXT** returns a series of rows that, when concatenated, display the text used to create the selected procedure. The strings that are returned, however, contain only linefeed characters without the carriage return character needed to properly display within the form's text box; therefore, conversion is required. Add this code to your form to take care of this process.

```
Function CvtCarrCtrl(InString As String, CharsConverted As Integer) As
String
'
'    Input:   Character String
'             Number of chars converted By Reference
'    Return: Converted Character String

    Dim tmp         As String
    Static inChar   As String * 1
    Dim i           As Integer
    Dim X           As Integer

    CharsConverted = 0

    ' Exit now if string does not contain a Carriage Return.
    If InStr(InString, Chr$(10)) = 0 Then
    CvtCarrCtrl = InString
    Exit Function
    End If

    ' Get the length of the string coming in.
    X = Len(InString)
    tmp = ""
```

continued on next page

continued from previous page

```
' Process string, add Carriage Return to linefeed
For i = 1 To X
inChar = Mid$(InString, i, 1)

If inChar = Chr$(10) Then
    tmp = tmp + Chr$(13) + Chr$(10)
    CharsConverted = CharsConverted + 1
Else
    tmp = tmp + inChar
End If
Next i

' Pass converted string back, right-trimmed.
CvtCarrCtrl = RTrim$(tmp)

End Function
```

9. As you exit it is a good practice to close all the object variables. Actually, closing the form should take care of it for you just like closing the environment object automatically closes all objects within it.

```
Private Sub cmdExit_Click()
    '
    'close out all objects in reverse order.
    Cn.Close
    Env.Close
    End
End Sub
```

10. Use Insert Class Module from Visual Basic's menu bar to add a class module to this project. The class will appear in the project window. Open the class module and press F4 to view the class's properties. Set these properties as shown in Table 3-5.

Table 3-5 TIMING.CLS **class module property settings**

OBJECT	PROPERTY	SETTING
Class Module	Name	"Timing"
	Creatable	False
	Public	False

11. Add the following code to the General Declarations section of the **Timing** class module. You will need to declare the **timeGetTime** API function in order to have access to a method that returns timing values with a millisecond resolution. The standard **Time()** function in Visual Basic only provides for seconds.

```
Option Explicit
'
'dimension readonly variables for timing events
Dim mStartTime As Long
```

```
Dim mFinishTime As Long
Dim mElapsedTime As Long
'
'declare API to get time in milliseconds.
Private Declare Function timeGetTime Lib "winmm.dll" () As Long
```

12. Add the following methods and properties to the **Timing** class. These methods and properties will allow you to time execution of SQL queries and have access to the elapsed time values in milliseconds.

```
'method to store start time
Public Sub Start()
    mStartTime = timeGetTime
End Sub

'method to store finish time and calculate elapsed time in milliseconds
Public Sub Finish()
    mFinishTime = timeGetTime
    mElapsedTime = mFinishTime - mStartTime
End Sub

'read-only property to access elapsed time.
Public Property Get ElapsedTime()
    ElapsedTime = mElapsedTime / 1000
End Property
```

How It Works

This project begins by creating and setting both an environment and connection variable. Once a connection is made to the database engine, an SQL Select statement is used to retrieve all the stored procedures that exist within the database specified at connect time. This is done by searching through the SYSOBJECTS tables for rows having a Type equal to **P**. The retrieved items are added to a listbox for easy perusal and selection.

Selecting a stored procedure with the combo box and clicking on the Execute button triggers the creation of an **rdoPreparedStatement** that specifically uses the **SP_HELPTEXT** stored procedure as follows.

```
sSQL = "{call master.dbo.sp_helptext (?)}"
Set Ps = Cn.CreatePreparedStatement(Name:="", sqlstring:=sSQL)
```

The curly braces and **call** are required parts of syntax when executing a stored procedure using the ODBC API; therefore, they are required when using an **rdoPreparedStatement** object. The following examples show valid syntax for various stored procedure types.

```
{call myStoredProcedure}              stored procedure with no parameters
{call myStoredProcedure (?)}          single parameter input or output
{? = call myStoredProcedure (?)}      single parameter with return value
{? = call myStoredProcedure (?, ?)}   multiple parameters with return value
```

Once the `rdoPreparedStatement` is created, the single parameter is set using the following syntax.

```
Ps.rdoParameters(0) = cmbStoredProcedurenames.Text
```

Now that the parameter is set, the resultset can be generated using the `rdoPreparedStatement` object. The text is retrieved for the selected stored procedure. The text returned must be converted to include carriage returns instead of only linefeed characters in order to display correctly in the text box. This is done with the `CvtCarrCtrl` function.

Comments

There are several gotcha's in working with stored procedures.

If your stored procedure returns records, you must use an `rdoPreparedStatement` in order to retrieve all the rows. Due to a limitation found somewhere in ODBC, a resultset executed against a connection object alone will execute properly but will not return more than a single row. If your stored procedure does not return any rows then this will work.

```
myResultset = myConnection.OpenResultset(sp_helptext parameter1)
```

A cursor is a collection of logical rows managed by either ODBC on the client machine or the database engine which resides on the server. No server-side cursors can be used when executing a stored procedure that contains anything other than a single SQL statement. This is due to a limitation in Microsoft SQL Server's cursor management that does not handle multiple resultsets. For more infomation on this refer to How-To's 3.5 and 3.6. Given this limitation, you have two options with regard to cursors in this situation. First, you could specifiy the use of ODBC cursors, since they are maintained on the client's machine, by setting the environment property `"CursorDriver = rdUseOdbc"` or, second, you could deactivate the use of server-side cursors by setting the `RowSetSize` of the `rdoPreparedStatement` object to 1, effectively disabling the cursor's use. Note that the cursor driver must be changed before opening a connection in order for it to take effect. In this project you specified the use of server-side cursors.

The final gotcha is the fact that to use a stored procedure with parameter binding in an `rdoPreparedStatement`, it must reside within the database specified by the connection object or it must use a fully qualified name like `master.dbo.sp_helptext`. This has a serious implication with regard to stored procedures that reside within the master database. The system-stored procedures reside in the MASTER database and can be executed from any database like PUBS. In the case of `sp_helptext`, the stored procedure relies on a function called `db_name()` to identify the current database. When the stored procedure is called using a fully qualified name, this function returns the name of the MASTER database rather than the name of the database currently in use when the call is made.

What this means is that in the case of `sp_helptext` you can only execute it against objects in the MASTER database. Try connecting to the PUBS database. Select a stored procedure from the combo box and press Execute. An error message is returned stating that the object specified, which was the stored procedure name, could not be found within the current database. Note that your connection database property will not reflect the change of execution nor will it affect it either. Additionally `sp_helptext` will not accept fully qualified object names as parameters.

So what choice do you have when it comes to using system-stored procedures that reside in the MASTER database? Well, you have three options. 1) You can copy affected stored procedures, like `sp_helptext`, to every database in which they will be used. Not a great solution. 2) You can rewrite these stored procedures to accept and handle fully qualified names or add an additional parameter that specifies the database to use. This might be a better solution. 3) You can sacrifice the benefit of a `PreparedStatement`, which is the ability to create it once and reuse it simply by setting the parameters using the `rdoParameter` object. Instead you could change the SQL to the following:

```
sSQL = Execute sp_helptext  & cmbPreparedStatementName.text
```

Then execute a `CreatePreparedStatement` each time you want to run the stored procedure with a different parameter rather than only once when you load the form. This works but, as was mentioned earlier, you are sacrificing the benefits of what the `rdoPreparedStatement` was supposed to provide, precompilation and parameter binding. Note that this problem has only been confirmed with SQL Server databases. You will need to evaluate your own needs to determine which is the best solution for you.

It is clear that stored procedures offer many opportunities for both encapsulation of functionality as well as frustration. Hopefully the information shared in this How-To will reduce the latter.

COMPLEXITY
BEGINNING

3.4 How do I...
Use an rdoPreparedStatement to parameterize a query?

Problem

I need to include a parameterized query (one that can accept variable information) in my application. I have been generating the SQL myself by concatenating strings based on options the user selects. The code is very ugly and, additionally, this does not allow me to create a prepared statement or bind parameters to get better performance. Is there a way to do this using RDO?

Technique

The `rdoPreparedStatement` object maps directly to the ODBC `SQLPrepare` function. Using this object, you can create parameterized queries and utilize a great deal of the power built into the RDO model. A powerful feature of any language is the ability to use parameters that can be set at the time of execution. SQL is no exception. Couple the ability to pass parameters with the ability to precompile a request, as with a prepared statement, and you can imagine the benefits with regard to execution time. In this How-To you will create a simple form that accepts three parameters that are used to retrieve book information by author from the PUBS database. You will not be able to use this project with an MDB database file because the Microsoft Access database engine does not support prepared statements.

Steps

Open and run project **PARAM.VBP**. When the application starts, you will be prompted to select a data source name. Specify a DSN that points to the PUBS database, which comes with Microsoft SQL Server. The tables found in the PUBS database can also be found on the accompanying CD in the /DATA directory. As you run this project you will see a message box showing the prepared statement that has been created. See Figure 3-7.

Once the application is running, you can select a Social Security Number from the combo box and specify a start date and end date that are used to retrieve the author's book sales information. The running program appears as shown in Figure 3-8.

1. Create a new project called **PARAM.VBP**. Select **Form1**, and add objects and set properties as shown in Table 3-6.

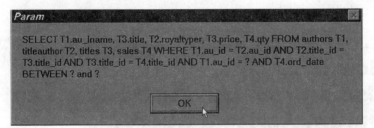

Param

SELECT T1.au_lname, T3.title, T2.royaltyper, T3.price, T4.qty FROM authors T1, titleauthor T2, titles T3, sales T4 WHERE T1.au_id = T2.au_id AND T2.title_id = T3.title_id AND T3.title_id = T4.title_id AND T1.au_id = ? AND T4.ord_date BETWEEN ? and ?

OK

Figure 3-7 The form that shows the prepared statement

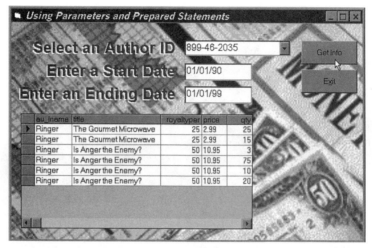

Figure 3-8 The form that allows runtime parameter input

Table 3-6 PARAMAPP.FRM form and controls properties

OBJECT	PROPERTY	SETTING
Form	Name	frmParamApp
	Caption	"Using Parameters and Prepared Statements"
	ForeColor	&H000000FF&
TextBox	Name	txtEndDate
TextBox	Name	txtStartDate
ComboBox	Name	cmbAuthorId
CommandButton	Name	cmdExit
	Caption	"E&xit"
CommandButton	Name	cmdGetInfo
	Caption	"Get Info"
DBGrid	Name	DBGrid1
	DataSource	rdcDisplay
Label	Name	Label6
	Alignment	Right Justify
	BackStyle	Transparent
	Caption	"Enter an Ending Date"
	ForeColor	&H00008000&

continued on next page

continued from previous page

OBJECT	PROPERTY	SETTING
Label	Name	Label5
	Alignment	Right Justify
	BackStyle	Transparent
	Caption	"Enter a Start Date"
	ForeColor	&H00008000&
Label	Name	Label4
	Alignment	Right Justify
	BackStyle	Transparent
	Caption	"Select an Author ID"
	ForeColor	&H00008000&
Label	Name	Label3
	Alignment	Right Justify
	BackStyle	Transparent
	Caption	"Enter an Ending Date"
	ForeColor	&H00FFFFFF&
Label	Name	Label2
	Alignment	Right Justify
	BackStyle	Transparent
	Caption	"Enter a Start Date"
	ForeColor	&H00FFFFFF&
Label	Name	Label1
	Alignment	Right Justify
	BackStyle	Transparent
	Caption	"Select an Author ID"
	ForeColor	&H00FFFFFF&
RemoteDataControl	Name	rdcDisplay
	DataSourceName	""
	RecordSource	""
	Connect	""

2. The first thing you need to do is to dimension object variables for the environment, connection, prepared statement, and resultset. This is done by adding the following code to the General Declarations section of the form.

```
Option Explicit
'dimension your environment and connection variables
Dim Env As rdoEnvironment
Dim cn As rdoConnection
```

```
Dim Ps As rdoPreparedStatement
Dim Rst As rdoResultset
```

3. On loading the form, you will set up the environment and require the user to specify a data source name to open a connection. This is accomplished by adding the following code to the **Form_load** event. This code also calls two procedures to load the authors' Social Security Numbers from the Authors table into a combo box and initialize the **rdoPreparedStatement** that will be used to return a resultset.

```
Private Sub Form_load()
    '
    'set the environment and connection objects
    Set Env = rdoEnvironments(0)
    Set cn = Env.OpenConnection("", rdDriverPrompt, True, "")
    '
    'Load the authors' social security number into the combo box
    'initialize the rdo prepared statement
    LoadAuthorIds
    '
    'initialize the rdo prepared statement
    InitializeStatement
    '
    'set default values
    txtStartDate = "01/01/90"
    txtEndDate = "01/01/99"
End Sub
```

4. Enter the following code into your form. The **LoadAuthorIds** procedure creates a resultset of all available author Social Security Numbers which are stored in the **au_id** field of the Authors table found in the PUBS database. The values are then added to the combo box list.

```
Private Sub LoadAuthorIds()
    Dim rstAuthorIds As rdoResultset
    Dim sSQL As String
    Dim i As Integer

    sSQL = "SELECT au_id FROM authors ORDER BY au_id"
    Set rstAuthorIds = cn.OpenResultset(sSQL)

    'Check rowcount property to see if any records were returned.
    If rstAuthorIds.RowCount <> 0 Then
        'load list
        cmbAuthorId.Clear
        While Not rstAuthorIds.EOF = True
            cmbAuthorId.AddItem rstAuthorIds("au_id")
            rstAuthorIds.MoveNext
        Wend
    Else
        MsgBox "Unable to load Author Ids"
    End If

    rstAuthorIds.Close
    '
    'that's all there is to it
End Sub
```

5. Add the following subroutine to your form. This code will create the
rdoPreparedStatement so that it is ready for use. This makes the most
sense since the purpose of using a prepared statement is to have it precompiled by the database engine and ready for execution once parameters
are set.

```
Private Sub InitializeStatement()
    'dimension variables for
    Dim sSQL As String
    '
    'construct SQL statement. Question marks are used as placeholders
    'for parameters.
    sSQL = "SELECT T1.au_lname, T3.title, T2.royaltyper, T3.price, T4.qty" _
        & " FROM authors T1, titleauthor T2, titles T3, sales T4" _
        & " WHERE T1.au_id = T2.au_id AND T2.title_id = T3.title_id" _
        & " AND T3.title_id = T4.title_id" _
        & " AND T1.au_id = ? AND T4.ord_date BETWEEN ? and ?"
    '
    'display the select statement so you can see what you are creating.
    MsgBox sSQL
    Set Ps = cn.CreatePreparedStatement("AuthInfo", sSQL)
End Sub
```

6. Add the following code to your form. This procedure handles the setting of
parameters and creation of the resultset. This code includes the setting of
various **rdoParameter** properties that you can adjust. They are included
here to illustrate their use although they are actually set to default values.

```
Private Sub cmdGetInfo_Click()
    'After an rdoPreparedStatement object has been set you must
    'provide values for each of the ? placeholders that is assigned
    'as an input value. All placeholders are input by default. Here
    'you will set all values of each parameter although it is not
    'necessary if the default settings are appropriate.
    'Set the parameters direction
    Ps.rdoParameters(0).Direction = rdParamInput
    Ps.rdoParameters(1).Direction = rdParamInput
    Ps.rdoParameters(2).Direction = rdParamInput
    '
    'You could use these statements to check the data type of each para
    'meter.
    'Ps.rdoParameters(0).Type      'rdTypeCHAR
    'Ps.rdoParameters(1).Type      'rdTypeDATE
    'Ps.rdoParameters(2).Type      'rdTypeDATE
    '
    'You could use these statements to check the parameter name.
    '"Paramn" where "n" is the ordinal number.
    'Ps.rdoParameters(0).Name      'Param0
    'Ps.rdoParameters(1).Name      'Param1
    'Ps.rdoParameters(2).Name      'Param2
    '
    'Set the parameters value
    Ps.rdoParameters(0).Value = cmbAuthorId.Text
    Ps.rdoParameters(1).Value = txtStartDate.Text
    Ps.rdoParameters(2).Value = txtEndDate.Text
```

```
    Set Rst = Ps.OpenResultset(rdConcurReadOnly, rdConcurReadOnly)
    Set rdcDisplay.Resultset = Rst
End Sub
```

7. As you exit, it is a good practice to close all the object variables. Actually, closing the form should take care of it for you just like closing the environment object automatically closes all objects within it.

```
Private Sub cmdExit_Click()
    cn.Close
    Env.Close
    End
End Sub
```

How It Works

Once the application is connected to a data source, the real work is performed by the `rdoPreparedStatement`. In this How-To the `rdoPreparedStatement` is created as the form loads so it is ready to be used immediately. The SQL used to create the `rdoPreparedStatement` includes three parameters, a string which is the Social Security Number of the author in question, and two dates specifying a date range which will limit the book sales information returned by the SQL query.

```
SELECT   T1.au_lname, T3.title, T2.royaltyper, T3.price, T4.qty
FROM     authors T1, titleauthor T2, titles T3, sales T4
WHERE    T1.au_id = T2.au_id
    AND T2.title_id = T3.title_id
    AND T3.title_id = T4.title_id
    AND T1.au_id = ?
    AND T4.ord_date BETWEEN ? and ?
```

A question mark is used to hold the place of parameters that will be provided prior to executing the statement. The syntax used for parameter placeholders in the prepared statement is identical to the syntax used when performing an ODBC `SQLPrepare` function. Once the statement is prepared and compiled on the server, parameters can be set and executed over and over.

This How-To introduces the use of the `rdoParameters` collection and the `rdoParameter` properties of **Name**, **Type**, **Direction**, and **Value**. If you are using default settings for these properties, you will only need to set the **Value** property. Once the prepared statement is executed, the resultset is passed to a Remote Data control with a bound DBGrid control to display the results to the user.

Comments

Parameterizing your queries is a very powerful feature. Using the `rdoPreparedStatement` object simplifies the process by allowing you to set values for parameters using the `rdoParameters` collection. The syntax is easier to read and also to debug. Additionally the `rdoPreparedStatement` object has the added benefit that accompanies any precompiled statement, that being speed of execution.

3.5 How do I...
Control the number of rows returned in a resultset?

Problem

The client machines that will run my applications have limited resources. I would like to optimize the performance of the client machines by controlling the number of rows that are buffered on the client machine. Additionally, I need a way to control how much the clients can request from the server. Is there a way to limit a resultset other than the **where** clause of the actual SQL?

Technique

The **rdoPreparedStatement** object provides several properties to give you control over the load balance of a request. *Load balancing* used in this context refers to the division of labor between the client and the server to process and handle a request. The properties that provide this control are **RowsetSize**, **KeysetSize**, and **MaxRows**. All of these properties work directly with a cursor. A *cursor* is a collection of logical rows managed by the ODBC cursor library or the database engine.

The **RowsetSize** property determines how many rows of the keyset are buffered by the application. **KeysetSize** controls the number of rows in the keyset buffer. The keyset buffer contains a set of only the key values used to retrieve rows of data contained within a server or ODBC cursor library. **MaxRows** does exactly that. It limits the maximum number of rows returned by any query executed using its **rdoPreparedStatement** object.

In this How-To you will create an application that accepts an SQL statement in a text box and processes it with the previously mentioned property settings. You can interactively adjust the **RowsetSize**, **KeysetSize**, and **MaxRows** as well as set the cursor driver, cursor type, and lock type. This will allow you to experiment with various combinations to see how different combinations affect execution of a query.

Steps

Open and run project **RETSET.VBP**. The running program appears as shown in Figure 3-9. Enter a **SELECT** statement like **SELECT * FROM Authors** and press Execute. The query will display the execution time in the form's caption and the results will appear in the text box below the query. Notice that the query only returned 5 rows of a possible 24 rows that exist in the Authors table. This is controlled by the **MaxRows** property setting. Set **MaxRows** to 10 and again press Execute. Ten rows are returned. Experiment with different cursor combinations to see how different combinations affect execution of the query.

1. Create a new project called **RETSET.VBP**. Select **Form1**, and add objects and set properties as shown in Table 3-7.

Table 3-7 RETSET.FRM form and controls properties

OBJECT	PROPERTY	SETTING
Form	Name	frmReturnSet
	Caption	"Controlling The Return Set"
	Icon	"wrench.ico"
ComboBox	Name	cmbLockType
	Style	Dropdown List
ComboBox	Name	cmbType
	Style	Dropdown List
ComboBox	Name	cmbCursorDriver
	Style	Dropdown List
TextBox	Name	txtDisplay
	BackColor	&H00C0C0C0&
	Locked	True
	MultiLine	True

continued on next page

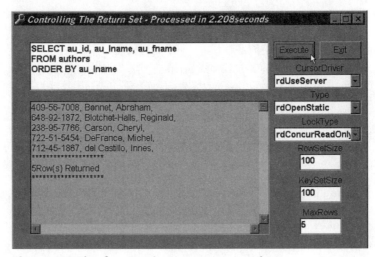

Figure 3-9 The form as it appears at runtime

continued from previous page

OBJECT	PROPERTY	SETTING
	ScrollBars	Both
TextBox	Name	txtKeySetSize
	Text	"100"
TextBox	Name	txtRowSetSize
	Text	"100"
TextBox	Name	txtMaxRows
	Text	"5"
TextBox	Name	txtSQL
	MultiLine	True
CommandButton	Name	cmdExit
	Caption	"E&xit"
CommandButton	Name	cmdExecute
	Caption	"Execute"
Label	Name	Label6
	Alignment	Center
	Caption	"LockType"
Label	Name	Label5
	Alignment	Center
	Caption	"Type"
Label	Name	Label4
	Alignment	Center
	Caption	"CursorDriver"
Label	Name	Label3
	Alignment	Center
	Caption	"KeySetSize"
Label	Name	Label2
	Alignment	Center
	Caption	"MaxRows"
Label	Name	Label1
	Alignment	Center
	Caption	"RowSetSize"

2. You first need to dimension object variables for the environment, connection, prepared statement, and resultset. This is done by adding the following code to the General Declarations section of the form.

```
Option Explicit
'
'dimension environment and connection variables
```

```
Dim Env As rdoEnvironment
Dim Cn As rdoConnection
'
'dimension object variables for a prepared statement and resultset
Dim Ps As rdoPreparedStatement
Dim Rst As rdoResultset
'
'holds the connect string created during initial startup.
Dim sConnect As String
```

3. On loading the form you will set up the environment and require the user to specify a data source name to open a connection. This is accomplished by adding the following code to the **Form_Load** event. This code also stores the connection string in **sConnect** so you can use it later when a new connection is needed.

```
Private Sub Form_Load()
    'set the environment variable and open a connection
    'by prompting user for DSN. This is done by leaving the
    'source parameter empty and the connect parameter empty
    'and specifying rdDriverPrompt.
    Set Env = rdoEnvironments(0)
    Env.CursorDriver = rdUseServer
    Set Cn = Env.OpenConnection(dsName:="", _
                                Prompt:=rdDriverPrompt, _
                                ReadOnly:=True, _
                                Connect:="")
    '
    'store the connection string for later use
    sConnect = Cn.Connect
    '
    'populate the combo boxes
    LoadComboBoxes
End Sub
```

4. Add the following subroutine to load default values into the combo boxes that correspond with the constants available for each of the properties you will be adjusting. You can review the listed constants in the Visual Basic Enterprise help file.

```
Private Sub LoadComboBoxes()
    '
    'load cmbCursorDriver with cursor driver options
    cmbcursordriver.List(0) = "rdUseIfNeeded"
    cmbcursordriver.ItemData(0) = 0
    cmbcursordriver.List(1) = "rdUseOdbc"
    cmbcursordriver.ItemData(1) = 1
    cmbcursordriver.List(2) = "rdUseServer"
    cmbcursordriver.ItemData(2) = 2
    '
    'set default
    cmbcursordriver.ListIndex = 2
    '
    'load cmbType with cursor type options
```

continued on next page

continued from previous page

```
        cmbtype.List(0) = "rdOpenForwardOnly"
        cmbtype.ItemData(0) = 0
        cmbtype.List(1) = "rdOpenStatic"
        cmbtype.ItemData(1) = 3
        cmbtype.List(2) = "rdOpenKeyset"
        cmbtype.ItemData(2) = 1
        cmbtype.List(3) = "rdOpenDynamic"
        cmbtype.ItemData(3) = 2
        '
        'set default
        cmbtype.ListIndex = 1
        '
        'load cmbLockType with cursor locktype options
        cmbLockType.List(0) = "rdConcurLock"
        cmbLockType.ItemData(0) = 2
        cmbLockType.List(1) = "rdConcurReadOnly"
        cmbLockType.ItemData(1) = 1
        cmbLockType.List(2) = "rdConcurRowver"
        cmbLockType.ItemData(2) = 3
        cmbLockType.List(3) = "rdConcurValues"
        cmbLockType.ItemData(3) = 4
        '
        'set default
        cmbLockType.ListIndex = 1
End Sub
```

5. Add the following code for the cursor driver combo box. If the choice in the cursor driver combo box changes, then the connection is closed, the cursor driver changed, and the connection reopened.

```
Private Sub cmbcursordriver_Click()
    '
    'check to see if anything has really changed.
    If cmbcursordriver.ItemData(cmbcursordriver.ListIndex) = _
        Env.CursorDriver Then
            Exit Sub
    End If
    '
    'close connection and reopen with new cursor driver
    Cn.Close
    '
    'reset the environment cursor to your selection
    Env.CursorDriver = cmbcursordriver.ItemData(cmbcursordriver.ListIndex)
    '
    'reuse connection string from initial prompt.
    Set Cn = Env.OpenConnection(dsName:="", _
                                Prompt:=rdDriverNoPrompt, _
                                ReadOnly:=True, _
                                Connect:=sConnect)
End Sub
```

6. Add the following code to your form for the Execute button's `Click` event. This code will apply all the property settings selected on the form and apply them to the `rdoPreparedStatement` object and the `rdoResultset` object before execution. Note that this subroutine creates an instance of the Timing class. You will need to include this class with this project.

```
Private Sub cmdExecute_Click()
    On Error GoTo cmdExecute_Error
    Dim oTiming As Timing
    Set oTiming = New Timing
    '
    'clear the text box that displays results
    txtDisplay.Text = ""
    txtDisplay.Refresh
    '
    'now you will create the prepared statement.
    Set Ps = Cn.CreatePreparedStatement("", txtSQL.Text)
    '
    'Here you will set the various options for number of rows
    'returned.rdOpenStatic, rdOpenKeyset, rdOpenForwardOnly
    'rdOpenDynamic
    Ps.RowsetSize = txtRowSetSize.Text
    Ps.KeysetSize = CLng(txtKeySetSize.Text)
    Ps.MaxRows = CLng(txtMaxRows.Text)
    '
    'start timing the request.
    oTiming.Start
    '
    'Resultset is opened using options from comboboxes.
    Set Rst = Ps.OpenResultset( _
            Type:=cmbtype.ItemData(cmbtype.ListIndex), _
            LockType:=cmbLockType.ItemData(cmbLockType.ListIndex))
    '
    'stop timing of request.
    oTiming.Finish
    '
    'Display the rows returned by the open resultset method
    Call DisplayResults

    Me.Caption = "Controlling The Return Set - Processed in " _
            & oTiming.ElapsedTime & "seconds"
    '
    'it is important to close the resultset since reusing it
    'without closing it simply appends results and DOES NOT
    'automatically reinitialize it.
    Rst.Close
    Ps.Close
    Exit Sub
cmdExecute_Error:
Dim oRDOError As rdoError
Dim sErr As String
    For Each oRDOError In rdoErrors
    sErr = sErr & vbCrLf & oRDOError.Description
    Next
    MsgBox sErr
    Exit Sub
End Sub
```

7. Once the resultset has been returned, the following code will take care of displaying it in the display text box.

```
Private Sub DisplayResults()
    Dim myCol As rdoColumn
    Dim sRst As String
    Dim iRstCount As Integer

    iRstCount = 0
    sRst = ""
    txtDisplay.Text = ""
    Do
        Do Until Rst.EOF = True
            'display results
            For Each myCol In Rst.rdoColumns
                sRst = sRst & myCol.Value & ", "
            Next
            sRst = sRst & vbCrLf
            iRstCount = iRstCount + 1
            Rst.MoveNext
        Loop
        sRst = sRst & "********************" & vbCrLf _
                    & iRstCount & "Row(s) Returned " & vbCrLf _
                    & "********************" & vbCrLf & vbCrLf

    Loop Until Rst.MoreResults = False
    txtDisplay.Text = txtDisplay.Text & sRst
    'Me.Caption = iRstCount & " Resultsets Returned!"
End Sub
```

8. As you exit, it is a good practice to close all the object variables. Actually closing the form should take care of it for you just like closing the environment object automatically closes all objects within it.

```
Private Sub cmdExit_Click()
    Cn.Close
    Env.Close
    End
End Sub
```

9. Use Insert Class Module from Visual Basic's menu bar to add a class module to this project. The class will appear in the project window. Open the class module and press F4 to view the class's properties. Set these properties as shown in Table 3-8.

Table 3-8 TIMING.CLS class module property setting

OBJECT	PROPERTY	SETTING
Class Module	Name	"Timing"

10. Add the following code to the General Declarations section of the **Timing** class module. You will need to declare the **timeGetTime** API function in order to have access to a method that returns timing values with a millisecond resolution. The standard **Time()** function in Visual Basic only provides for seconds.

```
Option Explicit
'
'dimension readonly variables for timing events
Dim mStartTime As Long
Dim mFinishTime As Long
Dim mElapsedTime As Long
'
'declare API to get time in milliseconds.
Private Declare Function timeGetTime Lib "winmm.dll" () As Long
```

11. Add the following methods and properties to the **Timing** class. These methods and properties will allow you to time execution of SQL queries and have access to the elapsed time values in milliseconds.

```
'method to store start time
Public Sub Start()
    mStartTime = timeGetTime
End Sub

'method to store finish time and calculate elapsed time in milliseconds
Public Sub Finish()
    mFinishTime = timeGetTime
    mElapsedTime = mFinishTime - mStartTime
End Sub

'read-only property to access elapsed time.
Public Property Get ElapsedTime()
    ElapsedTime = mElapsedTime / 1000
End Property
```

How It Works

This How-To allows you to explore the variety of options that affect performance when working with **rdoPreparedStatements**. Figure 3-10 shows how **KeysetSize**, **RowsetSize**, and **MaxRows** affect the client and the server's portion of the load in processing a request. It is worth noting that although the **KeysetSize** is depicted in the figure as affecting processing on the server, this is, in fact, determined by the choice in cursor drivers. If the cursor driver is ODBC, then the keyset is actually maintained by the client machine, versus the use of the server's cursor driver, which would then manage the keyset with the server's resources.

Although cursor driver and record locking options can apply to a resultset generated either with or without a prepared statement, limiting the number of rows returned by a query can only be done by using a **rdoPreparedStatement** and setting the **MaxRows** property.

On the server side of this project, the **KeysetSize** property controls the number of keysets buffered on the server if server-side cursors are set for the environment at the time the connection is established.

On the client side, the **RowsetSize** property determines how many rows of the keyset are buffered by the application. This property must be set before creating an **rdoResultset** object. Tuning the size of **RowsetSize** can affect performance and the amount of memory required to maintain the keyset buffer.

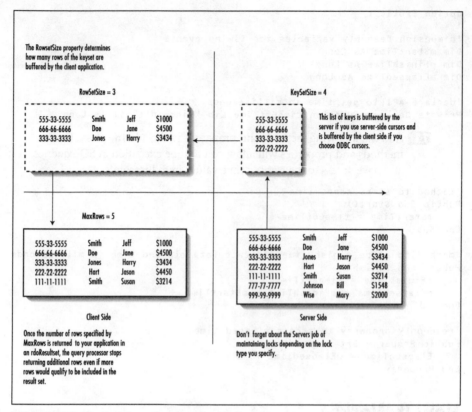

The RowsetSize property determines how many rows of the keyset are buffered by the client application.

RowSetSize = 3

555-33-5555	Smith	Jeff	$1000
666-66-6666	Doe	Jane	$4500
333-33-3333	Jones	Harry	$3434

KeySetSize = 4

| 555-33-5555 |
| 666-66-6666 |
| 333-33-3333 |
| 222-22-2222 |

This list of keys is buffered by the server if you use server-side cursors and is buffered by the client side if you choose ODBC cursors.

MaxRows = 5

555-33-5555	Smith	Jeff	$1000
666-66-6666	Doe	Jane	$4500
333-33-3333	Jones	Harry	$3434
222-22-2222	Hart	Jason	$4450
111-11-1111	Smith	Susan	$3214

555-33-5555	Smith	Jeff	$1000
666-66-6666	Doe	Jane	$4500
333-33-3333	Jones	Harry	$3434
222-22-2222	Hart	Jason	$4450
111-11-1111	Smith	Susan	$3214
777-77-7777	Johnson	Bill	$1548
999-99-9999	Wise	Mary	$2000

Client Side

Once the number of rows specified by MaxRows is returned to your application in an rdoResultset, the query processor stops returning additional rows even if more rows would qualify to be included in the result set.

Server Side

Don't forget about the Servers job of maintaining locks depending on the lock type you specify.

Figure 3-10 Illustrating the implications of RowSetSize, KeySetSize, and MaxRows

An additional aspect of RDO used in this How-To is that the rdoPreparedStatement object's MaxRows property is mapped to the ODBC statement option SQL_MAX_ROWS. When MaxRows is set to a value greater than 0, the maximum number of rows processed by Microsoft SQL Server is limited to the value of MaxRows. Once you change MaxRows for an rdoPreparedStatement, it stays set until you change it in code or close the object. Simply setting the rdoPreparedStatement using CreatePreparedStatement again does not reset the MaxRows property. If you insert, update, or delete by an action query using a rdoPreparedStatement with a MaxRows setting that is not set to the default, then the number of rows that will get processed will be limited to the number set in MaxRows.

Comments

Creating scalable applications requires the ability to control the balance of load. As an application's usage demands grow, adjustments must be made to optimize each configuration. You may consider setting these properties based on an external configuration file or registry entry either on a workstation or, better yet, at the business server where your RDO code will reside and provide communication between the business services and data services objects.

COMPLEXITY

INTERMEDIATE

3.6 How do I...

Create an RDO with multiple resultsets?

Problem

An SQL statement can contain any number of **SELECT** statements or stored procedures. Each **SELECT** statement returns a resultset. How can I handle multiple resultsets using RDO?

Technique

RDO provides a special method that can be used with the **rdoResultset** object. This method is called **MoreResults**. As you navigate forward through a resultset and finally hit the end of file (EOF), you can use the **MoreResults** method to find out if any additional results are pending. If **MoreResults** returns True, then you can proceed to retrieve additional results until no more exist.

Steps

Open and run project **MULTIRS.VBP**. The running program appears as shown in Figure 3-11. Enter multiple **SELECT** statements into the text box provided at the top. Make sure that you separate each SQL statement with a semicolon. Select the Retrieve Results button. The form's caption will change to display how many resultsets were returned. The resultsets will be displayed in the lower text box.

1. Create a new project called **MULTIRS.VBP**. Select **Form1**, and add objects and set properties as shown in Table 3-9.

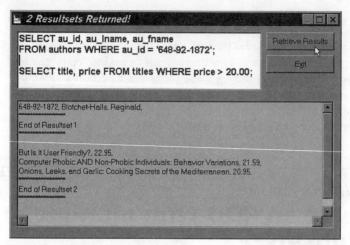

Figure 3-11 The form as it appears at runtime

Table 3-9 MULTIRS.FRM form and controls properties

OBJECT	PROPERTY	SETTING
Form	Name	frmMultiRS
	BorderStyle	Fixed Single
	Caption	"Multiple Result Sets"
	Icon	"note03.ico"
CommandButton	Name	cmdExit
	Caption	"E&xit"
TextBox	Name	txtDisplay
	BackColor	&H00C0C0C0&
	Locked	True
	MultiLine	True
	ScrollBars	Both
TextBox	Name	txtSQL
	MultiLine	True
CommandButton	Name	cmdRetrieveResults
	Caption	"Retrieve Results"

2. The first thing you need to do is to dimension object variables for the environment, connection, prepared statement, and resultset. This is done by adding the following code to the General Declarations section of the form.

```
Option Explicit
Dim Env As rdoEnvironment
Dim Cn As rdoConnection
Dim Ps As rdoPreparedStatement
Dim Rst As rdoResultset
```

3. On loading the form you will set up the environment and require the user to specify a data source name to open a connection. This is accomplished by adding the following code to the **Form_Load** event.

```
Private Sub Form_Load()
    Set Env = rdoEnvironments(0)
    'Env.CursorDriver = rdUseOdbc
    Set Cn = Env.OpenConnection("", rdDriverPrompt, True, "")
End Sub
```

4. Add the following code for the Retrieve Results command button **Click** event. This code deactivates the use of cursors thus allowing the receipt of multiple resultsets by creating a **rdoPreparedStatement** object and setting its **RowsetSize = 1**.

```
Private Sub cmdRetrieveResults_Click()
    Dim sSQL As String
    Dim iHowMany As Integer
    On Error GoTo cmdRetrieveResults_Error
    '
    'clear any results that are displayed within the lower text box.
    txtDisplay.Text = ""
    '
  'create a prepared statement
    sSQL = txtSQL.Text
    Set Ps = Cn.CreatePreparedStatement("", sSQL)
    '
    'set the rowsetsize to 1 in order to deactivate the use of cursors.
    Ps.RowsetSize = 1
    '
    'Process the SQL statements from the forms text box.
    Set Rst = Ps.OpenResultset(Type:=rdOpenForwardOnly, _
                        LockType:=rdConcurReadOnly)
    If Rst.EOF Then
        MsgBox "No results"
        GoTo cmdRetrieveResults_Exit
    Else
        DisplayResults
    End If

cmdRetrieveResults_Exit:
    Rst.Close
    Ps.Close
    Exit Sub
cmdRetrieveResults_Error:
    MsgBox rdoErrors(0).Description
End Sub
```

5. Once the SQL statement is processed and the results are available, you can gain access to each resultset with the following code which you should add to your project.

```
Private Sub DisplayResults()
    Dim myCol As rdoColumn
    Dim sRst As String
    Dim iRstCount As Integer

    iRstCount = 0
    sRst = ""

    Do
        Do Until Rst.EOF = True
            'display results
            For Each myCol In Rst.rdoColumns
                sRst = sRst & myCol.Value & ", "
            Next
            sRst = sRst & vbCrLf
            Rst.MoveNext
        Loop
        iRstCount = iRstCount + 1
        sRst = sRst & "*****************" & vbCrLf _
                    & "End of Resultset " & iRstCount & vbCrLf _
                    & "*****************" & vbCrLf & vbCrLf

    Loop Until Rst.MoreResults = False
    txtDisplay.Text = txtDisplay.Text & sRst
    Me.Caption = iRstCount & " Resultsets Returned!"
End Sub
```

6. As you exit, it is a good practice to close all the object variables. Actually closing the form should take care of it for you just like closing the environment object automatically closes all objects within it.

```
Private Sub cmdExit_Click()
Cn.Close
Env.Close
End
End Sub
```

How It Works

A simple form is created that allows you to enter an SQL statement. This statement is used to create an **rdoResultset**. If the SQL statement contains multiple **SELECT** statements, then it returns more than one resultset. A forward-only resultset is created with **RowsetSize** set to 1 so as to prevent the use of cursors on the back-end. As the application moves through the resultset using the **MoveNext** method, the program tests to see if the resultset is at End Of File (EOF). Once EOF is true, then the project uses the **MoreResults** method to begin processing the following set of results, if they exist. It is important to note that calling **MoreResults** at any point during the retrieval of results automatically discards the remaining rows in that resultset.

When no additional resultsets remain to be processed, the `MoreResults` method returns false and both the BOF and EOF properties of the `rdoResultset` object are set to true.

Comments

Business applications are centered on the concept of a unit of work. Whether that unit consists of loading a screen full of listboxes or processing a complex financial transaction, each would benefit from the ability to bundle multiple statements into a single call. There are some restrictions on the RDO implementation of handling multiple resultsets. One restriction is that you cannot use a server-side cursor to handle the resultset. A second restriction is that you must process the resultsets sequentially. Limitations aside, the ability of RDO to handle multiple resultsets is a powerful feature.

COMPLEXITY
ADVANCED

3.7   How do I...
Perform an asynchronous query?

Problem

Many times queries are submitted that require more than a second or two to be processed. When these queries are submitted, the client application enters a frozen state and no more work can be done within the client application until the query is complete and a resultset is generated. How can I submit SQL statements asynchronously?

Technique

RDO provides the ability to submit an SQL statement asynchronously to an ODBC source if the ODBC driver supports this functionality. This is accomplished by creating a resultset with `rdAsyncEnable` passed as a parameter. RDO uses a method of polling to see if a submitted request is complete. RDO polls the data source repeatedly to determine if the query has completed. The `AsyncCheckInterval` property allows you to change the duration of time between checks. Each time you check on the status of an asynchronous query, the server must respond. This response costs in processing time. Adjusting check times allows you to fine-tune performance by checking on a query's status only when necessary. This How-To will walk you through a fun exploration of asynchronous query submission.

Steps

Open and run project **FETCHIT.VBP**. The running program appears as shown in Figure 3-12. You will be prompted to select a data source name from a list. Once the form is up, select the File menu and select New Fetch Form. This will present you with an SQL submission form. Enter an SQL statement in the text box.

Once you have entered an SQL statement, select the Fetch button. The form will change in size and a spinning bone will appear. The spinning bone is meant to demonstrate at what point the client application regains control and how long it takes to actually get results. See Figure 3-13.

Once the query is complete, the bone stops spinning and the Fetch form is returned to its original size. Additionally, the execution time of the query is posted in the title bar of the child form. See Figure 3-14.

1. Create a new project called **FETCHIT.VBP**.

2. Select **Form1**, and add objects and set properties as shown in Table 3-10.

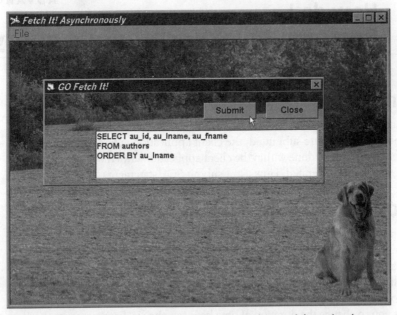

Figure 3-12 The form as it appears at runtime with a single Fetch form open

Figure 3-13 The form as it appears with several requests pending

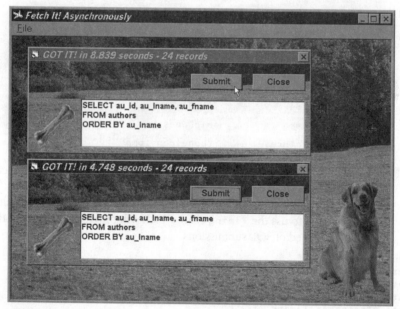

Figure 3-14 The form as it appears once results are available

Table 3-10 CFETCHIT.FRM form and control properties

OBJECT	PROPERTY	SETTING
Form	Name	cfrmFetchI
	BorderStyle	Fixed Single
	Caption	"GO Fetch It!"
	MaxButton	False
	MDIChild	True
	Picture	"meadow2.bmp"
CommandButton	Name	cmdClose
	Caption	"Close"
Timer	Name	Timer1
	Enabled	False
	Interval	250
CommandButton	Name	cmdSubmit
	Caption	"Submit"
TextBox	Name	txtSQL
	BackColor	&H00FFFFFF&
	MultiLine	True
Label	Name	lblMessage
	Alignment	Center
	BackStyle	Transparent
	Caption	"Click Bone to Cancel"
	ForeColor	&H000000FF&
Image	Name	imgBone
PictureClip	Name	picBones
	Picture	"boneicons.bmp"

3. You first need to dimension object variables for the environment, connection, and resultset. This is done by adding the following code to the General Declarations section of the form. Additionally, an object variable is dimensioned to use the **Timing** class, which will provide the ability to time execution speed of SQL submissions.

```
Option Explicit
Private Env As rdoEnvironment
Private Cn As rdoConnection
Private Rst As rdoResultset
Private oTiming As Timing
Private mFrmOrigWidth As Long
```

4. On loading the form, you will set up the environment and require the user to specify a data source name to open a connection. This is accomplished by adding the following code to the **Form_Load** event.

```
Private Sub Form_Load()
    'setup the environment
    Set Env = rdoCreateEnvironment(Str$(gEnvCount), rdoDefaultUser,
rdoDefaultPassword)
    gEnvCount = gEnvCount + 1
    'use odbc cursors
    Env.CursorDriver = rdUseOdbc

    'Since you want asynchronous handling of a query you will need
    'a seperate connection per request. This line simply prompts for
    'a Data Source Name (DSN).
    Set Cn = Env.OpenConnection("", rdDriverPrompt, True, "")
    Cn.AsyncCheckInterval = 5000
    '
End Sub
```

5. Add the following code to your form for the Submit button's **Click** event to handle the details of displaying the bone graphic and resizing the form during the time that the form waits for the submission to be completed.

```
Private Sub cmdSubmit_Click()
    Dim rc As Integer

    If txtSQL.Text = "" Then
        MsgBox "You must enter a SQL Statement to process"
        Exit Sub
    End If
    Set oTiming = New Timing
    oTiming.Start
    '
    'submit sql request
    rc = SubmitRequest
    If rc 0> True Then
        Me.Caption = "Unable to process request..."
        Exit Sub
    End If
    '
    'set GUI stuff to demonstrate the ability to
    'do other processes while SQL request is being
    'processed asynchronously.
    Timer1.Enabled = True
    mFrmOrigWidth = Me.Width
    Me.Width = txtSQL.Left
    lblMessage.Visible = True
End Sub
```

6. Add this code to the image control's `Click` event. This code allows the user to handle the asynchronous query process at will. This is done by using the `Cancel` method against the connection variable object.

```
Private Sub imgBone_Click()
    'cancel submitted query.
    Cn.Cancel
    Timer1.Enabled = False
    Me.Width = mFrmOrigWidth
    lblMessage.Visible = False
    Me.Caption = "Last Request Cancelled..."
    Set oTiming = Nothing
    Rst.Close
End Sub
```

7. Add the following code to the `Timer1` control's `Timer` event. This code is responsible for cycling through the pictures of the bone causing it to appear to rotate. Additionally, this routine checks the `StillExecuting` property of the resultset to see if the query has completed yet.

```
Private Sub Timer1_Timer()
    Static i As Integer
    If i = 8 Then
        If Rst.StillExecuting = False Then
            Timer1.Enabled = False
            oTiming.Finish
            DisplayResults
            Exit Sub
        End If
        i = 0
    End If
    imgBone.Picture = Me.picBones.GraphicCell(i)
    i = i + 1
End Sub
```

8. Add the following code to your form. This code actually submits the query taken from the form's text box and submits it to the back-end engine.

```
Private Function SubmitRequest() As Integer
    Dim i As Integer
    On Error GoTo SubmitRequest_Error
    '
    'Open resultset static so you can get a rowcount, note that
    'rdAsyncEnable is passed as the fourth argument when opening a
    'resultset directly against the connection.
    Set Rst = Cn.OpenResultset(txtSQL.Text, _
                            rdOpenStatic, _
                            rdConcurReadOnly, _
                            rdAsyncEnable)

    SubmitRequest = True

SubmitRequest_exit:
    Exit Function

SubmitRequest_Error:
    Dim Er As rdoError
```

```
    Dim sErrText As String
    For Each Er In rdoErrors
        sErrText = sErrText & Er.Description & vbCrLf
    Next
    MsgBox sErrText
    SubmitRequest = False
End Function
```

9. Add this code to your form to display the timing results and row count of the asynchronous query results.

```
Private Sub DisplayResults()
    Me.Caption = "GOT IT! in " & oTiming.ElapsedTime & " seconds"
    Me.Width = mFrmOrigWidth
    lblMessage.Visible = False
    Set oTiming = Nothing
    If Rst.StillExecuting = False Then
        Me.Caption = Me.Caption & " - " & Rst.RowCount & " records"
        Rst.Close
    End If
End Sub
```

10. As you exit, it is a good practice to close all the object variables. Actually closing the form should take care of it for you just like closing the environment object automatically closes all objects within it.

```
Private Sub cmdClose_Click()
    Cn.Close
    Env.Close
    Unload Me
End Sub
```

11. Insert an MDI form, and add objects and set properties as shown in Table 3-11.

Table 3-11 FETCHIT.FRM form and control properties

OBJECT	PROPERTY	SETTING
MDIForm	Name	mfrmFetchIt
	BackColor	&H8000000C&
	Caption	"Fetch It! Asynchronously"
	Picture	"meadow.bmp"
mFile	Caption	"&File"
mFNewFetchForm	Caption	"&New Fetch Form"
mFExit	Caption	"E&xit"

12. Dimension an object variable for the MDI child form.

```
Option Explicit
Dim ocfrmFetchForm As cfrmFetchIt
```

13. Enter the following code for the **New Fetch Form** menu **Click** event. This
code will create a new instance of the MDI child form.

```
Private Sub mFNewFetchForm_Click()
    Set ocfrmFetchForm = New cfrmFetchIt
    ocfrmFetchForm.Show
End Sub

Private Sub mFExit_Click()
    End
End Sub
```

14. Insert a new standard module and set the name to **General** as shown in
Table 3-12.

Table 3-12 GENERAL.BAS module properties

OBJECT	PROPERTY	SETTING
Module	Name	"General"

15. Each child form will have its own environment, connection, and resultset.
Enter the following code into the standard module called **GENERAL.BAS**.
The **genvCount** variable is used to generate a unique name for each child
form created.

```
Option Explicit
Global gEnvCount As Integer

Public Sub Main()
    'show main form
    mfrmFetchIt.Show
End Sub
```

16. Use Insert Class Module from Visual Basic's menu bar to add a class module
to this project. The class will appear in the project window. Open the class
module and press [F4] to view the class's properties. Set these properties as
shown in Table 3-13.

Table 3-13 TIMING.CLS class module property settings

OBJECT	PROPERTY	SETTING
Class Module	Name	"Timing"
	Creatable	False
	Public	False

17. Add the following code to the General Declarations section of the **Timing**
class module. You will need to declare the **timeGetTime** API function in
order to have access to a method that returns timing values with a millisecond resolution. The standard **Time()** function in Visual Basic only provides
for seconds.

```
Option Explicit
'
'dimension readonly variables for timing events
Dim mStartTime As Long
Dim mFinishTime As Long
Dim mElapsedTime As Long
'
'declare API to get time in milliseconds.
Private Declare Function timeGetTime Lib "winmm.dll" () As Long
```

18. Add the following methods and properties to the **Timing** class. These methods and properties will allow you to time execution of SQL queries and have access to the elapsed time values in milliseconds.

```
'method to store start time
Public Sub Start()
    mStartTime = timeGetTime
End Sub

'method to store finish time and calculate elapsed time in milliseconds
Public Sub Finish()
    mFinishTime = timeGetTime
    mElapsedTime = mFinishTime - mStartTime
End Sub

'read-only property to access elapsed time.
Public Property Get ElapsedTime()
    ElapsedTime = mElapsedTime / 1000
End Property
```

How It Works

The project consists of two forms, a parent MDI form and a child MDI form. The parent form serves as a container for any number of child forms that can be instantiated by way of the menu bar option New Fetch Form. Once a Fetch form has been created, a data source selected, and an SQL statement entered into the text box, the asynchronous query submission can be made by selecting the Submit button. There are two main pieces to the asynchronous puzzle. First you need to submit the SQL statement using the **CreateResultset** method and set the **rdAsyncEnable** option. This only works if your ODBC driver supports this functionality (Microsoft Access ODBC drivers do not support this functionality).

The second step takes place once a query has been submitted. This step involves methods for notifying the user when the request is done. The two styles available for this type of notification are server-side callbacks and polling. Server-side callbacks involve the server receiving a handle to a client application object, which is used to notify the client when the request is complete. You can see an example of this type of callback in How-To 7.7. Polling is a method in which the client checks back with the server periodically to see what the status is on the request. This How-To utilized the Polling method by checking the status on the request using the **StillExecuting** property of the resultset object. Additionally, polling intervals can be fine-tuned using the **AsyncCheckInterval** property of the **rdoConnection** object.

Comments

It is important to note that polling too often can negatively affect your server as well as workstation performance. If, on the other hand, you choose to poll less frequently you will get better performance, but affect the speed of getting results. Asynchronous queries make a lot of sense for any request that will take more than a few seconds to process. It is important to consider the question of asynchronous processing within the three-tier client/server architecture. In this model, RDO is providing connectivity between the Business services layer and the Data services layer. Within these layers, some processes make sense to be executed asynchronously, especially decision support queries or batch processing queries. You will need to examine the task at hand and decide which tool in your toolbox to use.

CHAPTER 4

USER INTERFACE DESIGN

by Noel Jerke

USER INTERFACE DESIGN

How do I...

4.1   Create a simple MDI application?

4.2   Build a toolbar to simplify access to menu functions?

4.3   Implement right mouse button context menus?

4.4.   Make an application drag-and-drop capable?

4.5   Organize form contents using the tab control?

The *client* tier of three-tier architectures can determine the difference between a program that is readily accepted and produces a productive end user and a program that is difficult to use and produces a frustrated end user. The Windows 95 interface, and most popular Windows 95 applications, such as Office 97, provide for a common set of user interface elements that help make an application useful and familiar.

The five How-To's in this chapter will demonstrate standard user interface design for your client-tier applications. Each How-To will build on the last to produce a fully integrated and feature-rich application interface. The sample application used throughout this chapter is a simple image-tracking database. This program will allow you to categorize and track all bitmap (BMP) and icon (ICO) format files on your system. In this chapter, we will not be strictly adhering to the three-tier client/server structure. For simplicity's sake, the Microsoft Remote Data Control (MSRDC) will be used to connect to a Microsoft Access 7.0 or SQL Server (6.5) database through an ODBC connection. Note that the final application provided in this chapter will be extended to be a true three-tier client/server application in Chapter 9, Sample Client/Server Applications.

The first How-To will demonstrate building Multiple Document Interface (MDI) applications. It will demonstrate techniques such as tiling and cascading MDI child windows and menu negotiation. But, what client application would be complete without the familiar toolbar for accessing the features of the application? The second How-To will add a toolbar to the program to provide this familiar application interface. Another important context-rich feature provided in Windows 95 is the use of the right mouse click. How-To 4.3 will demonstrate how adding right mouse-click support to your applications can provide for quick and simple access to common features.

How-To 4.4 demonstrates how drag-and-drop support for an application from the Windows Explorer provides easy and common-sense integration of your application with the Windows 95 environment. Support for dragging image files from the Windows Explorer to the application will be demonstrated through some simple API calls and an add-on OCX control (MSGHOOK.OCX). Also, drag-and-drop inside an application can be implemented for moving controls and data between objects. The final How-To will use the tab control to provide a simple and easy method for organizing and presenting information to the user.

An interesting comparison can be made between the first and last How-To's of this chapter. Each implements the same basic image-tracking application, but the interface of the first pales in comparison to that of the last. A rich user interface can truly make the difference between a mediocre application and an intuitive one.

> **NOTE**
>
> Each How-To in this chapter uses the `Idata.mdb` Access 7.0 database with an ODBC 32-bit driver. You will need to have an Image Database ODBC data source connected to either the Access database or a similar database on your SQL server. The first How-To details the simple database which can be easily replicated on any database platform.

4.1   Create a Simple MDI Application

Windows 95 Multiple Document Interface (MDI) applications are common and include just about any standard word processor or spreadsheet program. Providing many different child windows within a parent window is the key to providing support for working on different documents within an application. In this example, an image viewer and a data entry screen will be provided for the image database.

4.2 Build a Toolbar to Simplify Access to Menu Functions

The simple image inventory program built in the last How-To provides for many different menu options for navigating through the program. To make these menu features easier to navigate, a toolbar with appropriate icons will be added to the interface to simplify use of the program.

4.3 Implement Right Mouse Button Context Menus

Context-sensitive, right mouse clicks can be a very useful feature for providing access to application features within the context of where the click took place. In this example, menu features will pop up within the context of the right mouse click and, in one example, with the left mouse click also.

4.4 Make an Application Drag-and-Drop Capable

The image view application developed in the previous How-To's will benefit greatly from a little drag-and-drop magic. Being able to drag several bitmap image files from a directory listed in (for example) the Windows Explorer to the program, and automatically having them added to the database, will immeasurably speed up the categorization of images on a system. And, being able to preview an image before it is placed into the database will also be a powerful tool. A preview window will be added which will preview a dropped image and then allow that image to be dragged to the database.

4.5 Organize Form Contents Using the Tab Control

Our image inventory program is missing a couple of key features that will be provided together with a nice interface via the tab control. The user needs to have a simple way to select sort options and to view several images at once. With the tab control, these features can be added to different tabs on the control.

COMPLEXITY
BEGINNING

4.1 How do I...
Create a simple MDI application?

Problem

Multiple Document Interfaces (MDIs) are a standard for the Windows 95 user interface. How do I build a Windows MDI application that provides support for multiple menus based on the current child form and that provides features such as window tiles and cascades?

Technique

Multiple Document Interfaces consist of a parent window which typically shows the menus of the program and *contains* child windows. The child windows cannot be moved outside the frame of the parent window. Visual Basic provides for a simple way to create MDI parent and child forms. One of the standard objects that can be added to a project is an MDI form. The standard Visual Basic form can become the child of an MDI form simply by setting its MDIChild property to True. Visual Basic then automatically handles showing the menus for the child window in the MDI form. The `Arrange` method of the MDI form will be used to arrange the child windows.

Steps

Open and run 4-1.VBP. The running program appears as shown in Figure 4-1. This figure shows the MDI form without the child windows being shown. Note that there are only two primary menu groups to choose from. Select the Open Database menu option under the File menu to open the image database.

Once the image database is opened, there are two child windows shown. The first window shows the standard image file information for the current image, including an editable field for adding comments to the image. The second shows a view of the image currently being edited. To browse the database, select the record menu for the various options as shown in Figure 4-2.

Figure 4-1 The MDI form at runtime

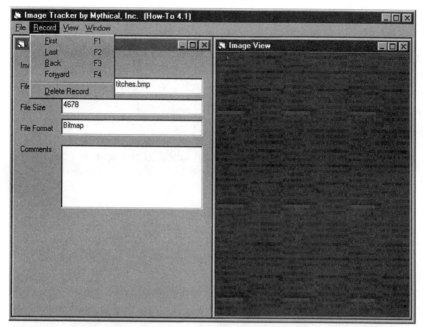

Figure 4-2 The child windows with the Record menu shown

Try out the options on the View menu to see the image in different sizes. You can use the Windows menu to tile the windows and see how the form's appearance changes. You can also cascade the child windows.

1. Create a new project called **4-1.VBP**. Add the objects and properties listed in Table 4-1 to the MDI form, **ImageTracker**.

Table 4-1 The form's objects and properties

OBJECT	PROPERTY	SETTING
MDIForm	Name	ImageTracker
	AutoShowChildren	0 'False
	Caption	"Image Tracker by Mythical, Inc."
		(How-To 4.1)"

2. Add the menus shown in Table 4-2 to the **ImageTracker** MDI form.

Table 4-2 The **ImageTracker** form's menus

CONTROL NAME	CAPTION
mFile	"&File"
mOpenImage	"&Open Image Database"

continued on next page

continued from previous page

CONTROL NAME	CAPTION
mBar	"-"
mExit	"E&xit"
mWindow	"&Window"
mImageData	"Image &Data"
mImageView	"Image &View"

3. Insert a new form into the project and save it as **IView.frm**. Add the objects and properties listed in Table 4-3 to the **ImageData** form.

Table 4-3 The `ImageView` form's objects and properties

OBJECT	PROPERTY	SETTING
Form	Name	ImageView
	Caption	"Image View"
	MDIChild	-1 'True
PictureBox	Name	DispPict
	Appearance	0 'Flat
	AutoSize	-1 'True
	BackColor	&H00FF0000&
	ForeColor	&H80000008&
	Picture	"pastel.bmp"
	ScaleMode	3 'Pixel
PictureBox	Name	BackPict
	AutoRedraw	-1 'True
	AutoSize	-1 'True
	BackColor	&H000000FF&
	BorderStyle	0 'None
	ScaleMode	3 'Pixel
	Visible	0 'False

4. Add the following menus from Table 4-4 to the **ImageView** form.

Table 4-4 The `ImageView` form's menus

CONTROL NAME	CAPTION
mFile	"&File"
mNewImage	"&New Image"
mBar	"-"
mExit	"E&xit"

CONTROL NAME	CAPTION	INDEX	CHECKED	SHORTCUT KEY
mRecord	"&Record"			
mBrowse	"&First"	0		F1
mBrowse	"&Last"	1		F2
mBrowse	"&Back"	2		F3
mBrowse	"For&ward"	3		F4
mBar2	"-"			
mDelete	"&Delete Record"			
mView	"&View"			
mSize	"&Fit in Window"	0		
mSize	"&Actual Size"	1	−1 'True	
mSize	"&50 Percent"	2		
mSize	"&200 Percent"	3		
mWindow	"&Window"			
mTile	"&Tile"			
mCascade	"&Cascade"			
mBar1	"-"			
mShowWindow	"Image &Data"	0		
mShowWindow	"Image &View"	1		

5. Insert a new form into the project and save it as `IData.frm`. Add the objects and properties listed in Table 4-5 to the `ImageData` form.

Table 4-5 The `ImageData` form's objects and properties

OBJECT	PROPERTY	SETTING
Form	Name	ImageData
	Caption	"Image Data"
	MDIChild	−1 'True
	Visible	0 'False
TextBox	Name	ImageInfo
	DataField	"Comments"
	DataSource	"MSRDC1"
	Index	4
	MultiLine	−1 'True
TextBox	Name	ImageInfo
	DataField	"FileFormat"
	DataSource	"MSRDC1"
	Index	3

continued on next page

continued from previous page

OBJECT	PROPERTY	SETTING
TextBox	Name	ImageInfo
	DataField	"FileSize"
	DataSource	"MSRDC1"
	Index	2
	Locked	-1 'True
TextBox	Name	ImageInfo
	DataField	"FileName"
	DataSource	"MSRDC1"
	Index	1
TextBox	Name	ImageInf
	DataField	"ImageID"
	DataSource	"MSRDC1"
	Index	0
	Locked	-1 'True
CommonDialog	Name	CommonDialog1
	DefaultExt	".bmp"
	DialogTitle	"Find Image File"
	Filter	"*.bmp; *.wmf"
	FilterIndex	1
	InitDir	"c:\windows"
MSRDC	Name	MSRDC1
	Visible	0 'False
	DataSourceName	"Image Database"
	RecordSource	"select * from ImageData
		order by ImageID"
	RecordsetType	1
	KeysetSize	0
	ReadOnly	0 'False
	UserName	""
	Password	""
	CursorDriver	2
	EOFAction	1
	BOFAction	1
	Caption	"MSRDC1"
	Prompt	3

OBJECT	PROPERTY	SETTING
	LockType	3
	Appearance	1
Label	Name	Comment
	AutoSize	-1 'True
	Caption	"Comments"
Label	Name	FileFormat
	AutoSize	-1 'True
	Caption	"File Format"
Label	Name	FileSize
	AutoSize	-1 'True
	Caption	"File Size"
Label	Name	FileName
	AutoSize	-1 'True
	Caption	"File Name"
Label	Name	ImageID
	AutoSize	-1 'True
	Caption	"Image ID"

6. Add the menus from Table 4-6 to the **ImageData** form.

Table 4-6 The ImageData form's menus

CONTROL NAME	CAPTION	INDEX	CHECKED	SHORTCUT KEY
mFile	"&File"			
mNewImage	"&New Image"			
mBar	"-"			
mExit	"E&xit"			
mRecord	"&Record"			
mBrowse	"&First"	0		F1
mBrowse	"&Last"	1		F2
mBrowse	"&Back"	2		F3
mBrowse	"For&ward"	3		F4
mBar2	"-"			
mDelete	"&Delete Record"			
mView	"&View"			
mSize	"&Fit in Window"	0		
mSize	"&Actual Size"	1	-1 'True	

continued on next page

continued from previous page

CONTROL NAME	CAPTION	INDEX	CHECKED	SHORTCUT KEY
mSize	"&50 Percent"	2		
mSize	"&200 Percent"	3		
mWindow	"&Window"			
mTile	"&Tile"			
mCascade	"&Cascade"			
mBar1	"-"			
mShowWindow	"Image &Data"	0		
mShowWindow	"Image &View"	1		

7. Add the following code to the MDI form. When the MDI form is loaded, the **ImageData** form is hidden to ensure that only the MDI form is visible. This provides the user with the option of whether or not to open the database.

```
Private Sub MDIForm_Load()

'  Hide the ImageData form when
'  the MDI form is first loaded
ImageData.Hide

End Sub
```

8. When the MDI form is unloaded or the Exit menu is selected, the program needs to be ended by calling the **MenuExit** method.

```
Private Sub MDIForm_QueryUnload(Cancel As Integer, UnloadMode As Integer)

'  Call the MenuExit program to
'  end the program
MenuExit

End Sub

Private Sub MDIForm_Unload(Cancel As Integer)

'  Call the MenuExit Yes, procedure> to
'  end the program
MenuExit

End Sub

Private Sub mExit_Click()

'  Call the MenuExit program to
'  end the program
MenuExit

End Sub
```

9. When the Image Data menu option is selected, the `MenuOpenData` method is called to open the image database. Note the next two procures are additional ways of opening the database from the program.

```
Private Sub mImageData_Click()

'   Call the MenuOpenData method to open the
'   Image database
MenuOpenData

End Sub
```

10. When the Image View menu option is selected, the `MenuOpenData` method is called to open the image database.

```
Private Sub mImageView_Click()

'   Call the MenuOpenData method to open the
'   Image database
MenuOpenData

End Sub
```

11. When the Open Image Database menu option is selected, the `MenuOpenData` method is called to open the image database.

```
Private Sub mOpenImage_Click()

'   Call the MenuOpenData method to open the
'   Image database
MenuOpenData

End Sub
```

12. Add the following code to the `ImageView` form. Insert the following `SizeViewPict` routine into the general declarations section of the form. This routine handles moving and sizing the display picture to fit on the viewable area of the form. It also calls the `SetView` routine to show the appropriate image from the database with the selected viewer options.

```
Public Sub SizeViewPict()

'   Allow for a small border
'   around the display picture
DispPict.Top = 5
DispPict.Left = 5
DispPict.Width = Me.Width - 5
DispPict.Height = Me.Height - 5

'   Set the view to the current
'   view option
SetView IView

End Sub
```

13. When the form is loaded, the view is set to Actual Size (1). Also, the **MenuBrowse** function is called to set the database to the first record.

```
Private Sub Form_Load()

'  Intially set IView to 1.
IView = 1

'  Call the MenuBrowse function
'  to show the first record
MenuBrowse 1

End Sub
```

14. When the display picture is painted, the size of the picture is set and the image redrawn using the **SizeViewPict** method. Note that this also handles updating the image when the form is resized, because the resized event triggers the **Paint** event.

```
Private Sub DispPict_Paint()

'  Size the view picture
SizeViewPict

End Sub
```

15. When the form would otherwise be unloaded by this procedure, the unload is canceled and the window is minimized. This ensures that the form cannot be unloaded while the application is still running. There is no need to unload the form except when the program is ended.

```
Private Sub Form_Unload(Cancel As Integer)

'  Cancel the unload.  We don't want the
'  form to be unloaded while the program is
'  running so that it does not have to be
'  re-initialized.  Instead, the form will be
'  minimized.
Cancel = -1
Me.WindowState = 1

End Sub
```

16. When one of the browse options for the database is selected from the menu (or through hot keys such as F1), the **MenuBrowse** routine is called to manipulate the database appropriately. Note that the index of the menu option selected is passed into the **MenuBrowse** routine to indicate the action to take.

```
Private Sub mBrowse_Click(Index As Integer)

'  Browse the record set depending on the
'  menu option chosen.
MenuBrowse Index

End Sub
```

17. When the user selects the Cascade menu option, the **MenuCascade** routine is called. Also, the **SizeViewPict** function is called to ensure that the displayed image is updated.

```
Private Sub mCascade_Click()

'  Cascade the windows
MenuCascade

'  Size the view picture after the cascade
SizeViewPict

End Sub
```

18. The user can delete a record in the database by selecting the Delete menu option. When this happens, the **MenuDelete** routine is called to delete the current record.

```
Private Sub mDelete_Click()

'  Call the MenuDelete function to
'  delete the selected record.
MenuDelete

End Sub
```

19. When the Exit menu option is selected, the **MenuExit** routine is called.

```
Private Sub mExit_Click()

'  Call the MenuExit function to
'  exit the program.
MenuExit

End Sub
```

20. The New Image menu option intiates the addition of a new image to the database by calling the **MenuNewImage** routine.

```
Private Sub mNewImage_Click()

'  Call the MenuNewImage function to get
'  a new image
MenuNewImage

End Sub
```

21. The **mShowWindow** control array of menu options allows for either the **ImageData** or **ImageView** child windows to be shown by calling the **MenuShowWindow** routine.

```
Private Sub mShowWindow_Click(Index As Integer)

'  Call the MenuShowWindow function to show
'  the selected window.
MenuShowWindow Index

End Sub
```

22. The Tile menu option calls the **MenuTile** function to tile the MDI child windows.

```
Private Sub mTile_Click()

'  Call the menu tile function to
'  tile the windows
MenuTile

End Sub
```

23. The **mSize** menu options allow for the view to be sized as either fit in window – **0** index, actual size – **1** index, 50% – **2** index, or 200% – **3** index. Note the index indicates which value will be passed into to set the view appropriately.

```
Private Sub mSize_Click(Index As Integer)

'  Set the view depending on the menu option
'  selected
SetView Index

End Sub
```

24. Add the following set of code to **IData.frm**. The form's resize event ensures that the data-entry fields are resized to fit on the form.

```
Private Sub Form_Resize()

Dim N As Integer

'  Resize the Image Info controls to
'  fit on the form when it is resized
For N = 1 To 4
    ImageData.ImageInfo(N).Width = ImageData.Width – ⇐
ImageData.ImageInfo(N).Left – 300
Next N

End Sub
```

25. When the form is unloaded by the user, the **UNLOAD** event is cancelled and the form is minimized. We do not want the form to be unloaded while the primary MDI application is still running; we simply want the form to be minimized. In some MDI applications, you may indeed want to have the form (i.e., a document) closed.

```
Private Sub Form_Unload(Cancel As Integer)

'  We don't want the form to be unloaded so that
'  it will not have to be re-initialized
Cancel = –1

'  Instead minimize the form
Me.WindowState = 1
End Sub
```

26. When one of the browse options for the database is selected from the menu (or through hot keys such as F1), the **MenuBrowse** routine is called to manipulate the database appropriately. Note the index of the menu option selected is passed into the **MenuBrowse** routine to indicate the action to take.

```
Private Sub mBrowse_Click(Index As Integer)

'   Browse the result set depending
'   on the menu selected
MenuBrowse Index

End Sub
```

27. The Cascade menu calls the **MenuCascade** routine to cascade the child windows.

```
Private Sub mCascade_Click()

'   Cascade the windows
MenuCascade

End Sub
```

28. The Delete menu option calls the **MenuDelete** routine to delete the current record of the resultset.

```
Private Sub mDelete_Click()

'   Delete the current record
'   of the result set
MenuDelete

End Sub
```

29. The Exit menu option calls the **MenuExit** routine to exit the application.

```
Private Sub mExit_Click()

'   Call the MenuExit method to
'   exit the program
MenuExit

End Sub
```

30. The New Image menu option calls the **MenuNewImage** routine to open the common file dialogue to find a new image to add to the database.

```
Private Sub mNewImage_Click()

'   Call the MenuNewImage function to allow
'   the user to select a new image to add to the
'   database
MenuNewImage

End Sub
```

31. The Image Data and Image View menu options invoke the
`MenuShowWindow` routine to show the specified window indicated by the
index.

```
Private Sub mShowWindow_Click(Index As Integer)

'   Call the MenuShowWindow function to show
'   the window selected
MenuShowWindow Index

End Sub
```

32. The View menu provides several size options for the image view. The index
indicates the view option.

```
Private Sub mSize_Click(Index As Integer)

'   Set the view based on the menu
'   selection
SetView Index

End Sub
```

33. The Tile menu option calls the `MenuTile` routine to tile the child windows.

```
Private Sub mTile_Click()

'   Tile the windows
MenuTile

End Sub
```

34. Insert a new module into the project and save it as **MenLogic.bas**. This
module will hold the primary routines for performing the various menu
tasks. The module consolidates the logic needed to perform the menu
options for both the **ImageData** and **ImageView** forms. Add the
StretchBlt API function to the global declarations section of the module.
This function will be used for stretching the viewed image.

```
'   StretchBlit will be used for the Image Viewer
Private Declare Function StretchBlt Lib "gdi32" (ByVal hdc As Long, ⇐
ByVal x As Long, ByVal y As Long, ByVal nWidth As Long, ByVal nHeight ⇐
As Long, ByVal hSrcDC As Long, ByVal xSrc As Long, ByVal ySrc As Long, ⇐
ByVal nSrcWidth As Long, ByVal nSrcHeight As Long, ByVal dwRop As Long) ⇐
As Long

Const SRCCOPY = &HCC0020

'   IView globally stores the current view for
'   the image I.E.  Fit in Window, 50%


Public IView As Integer
```

35. The `MenuExit` routine ends the program.

```
'   Handles ending the program when
'   users select exit from the menu
Public Sub MenuExit()
     End
End Sub
```

36. The `MenuTile` routine handles calling the `Arrange` method of the MDI form. The `VBTileVertical` constant is used to tile the child forms.

```
'   Handles tiling the windows
'   on the MDI form
Public Sub MenuTile()

'   Do a vertical tile
ImageTracker.Arrange vbTileVertical

End Sub
```

37. The `MenuCascade` routine handles calling the `Arrange` method of the MDI form. The `VBTileVertical` constant is used to cascade the child forms.

```
Public Sub MenuCascade()

'   Cascade the child forms
ImageTracker.Arrange vbCascade

End Sub
```

38. The `SetView` routine handles setting the view indicated by the index. First, the menu option for the last view is unchecked and the current index is checked. The current picture is cleared and, depending on the index, the image is copied from the `BackPict` picture box to the `DispPict` picture box. `StretchBlt` is used to perform the image stretching. Finally, the palette from the `BackPict` is copied to the display picture to ensure that the displayed image colors are correct.

```
Public Sub SetView(Index)

'   When a new image view is selected,
'   the original menu selection is
'   unchecked
ImageView.mSize(IView).Checked = False
ImageData.mSize(IView).Checked = False

'   Set the new view to the index
'   parameter
IView = Index

'   Check the new menu option for the
'   selected view.
ImageData.mSize(IView).Checked = True
ImageView.mSize(IView).Checked = True
```

continued on next page

continued from previous page

```
'  Clear the displayed picture
ImageView.DispPict.Cls


'  Depending on the view selected, the
'  original image will be copied to the
'  display picture appropriately
Select Case IView

    Case 0  'Fit in the Window
        Call StretchBlt(ImageView.DispPict.hdc, 0, 0, ⇐
    ImageView.DispPict.ScaleWidth, ImageView.DispPict.ScaleHeight, ⇐
    ImageView.BackPict.hdc, 0, 0, ImageView.BackPict.ScaleWidth, ⇐
    ImageView.BackPict.ScaleHeight, SRCCOPY)


    Case 1  'Actual Size
        Call StretchBlt(ImageView.DispPict.hdc, 0, 0, ⇐
    ImageView.BackPict.ScaleWidth, ImageView.BackPict.ScaleHeight, ⇐
    ImageView.BackPict.hdc, 0, 0, ImageView.BackPict.ScaleWidth, ⇐
    ImageView.BackPict.ScaleHeight, SRCCOPY)


    Case 2 '50%
        Call StretchBlt(ImageView.DispPict.hdc, 0, 0, ⇐
    ImageView.BackPict.ScaleWidth * 0.5, ImageView.BackPict.ScaleHeight ⇐
    * 0.5, ImageView.BackPict.hdc, 0, 0, ImageView.BackPict.ScaleWidth, ⇐
    ImageView.BackPict.ScaleHeight, SRCCOPY)


    Case 3 '200%
        Call StretchBlt(ImageView.DispPict.hdc, 0, 0, ⇐
    ImageView.BackPict.ScaleWidth * 2, ImageView.BackPict.ScaleHeight ⇐
    2, ImageView.BackPict.hdc, 0, 0, ImageView.BackPict.ScaleWidth, ⇐
    ImageView.BackPict.ScaleHeight, SRCCOPY)


End Select

'  Copy the palette from the holding picture
'  to the displayed picture.  This ensures that
'  the image's colors are displayed correctly.
ImageView.DispPict.Picture.hPal = ImageView.BackPict.Picture.hPal


End Sub
```

39. The `MenuShowWindow` function handles showing the appropriate form.

```
Public Sub MenuShowWindow(Index)

'  Check to see which Windows (Form)
'  is to be displayed.
Select Case Index

    Case 0  'Show ImageData
        ImageData.Show
        ImageData.WindowState = 0

    Case 1  'Show ImageView
        ImageView.Show
        ImageView.WindowState = 0
```

```
End Select

End Sub
```

40. The `MenuOpenData` routine queries the users whether they want to open the database. If so, the `ImageData` and `ImageView` forms are shown.

```
Public Sub MenuOpenData()

Dim Msg As String
Dim Style As Integer
Dim Title As String
Dim Response As Integer

'   Set the Message, Style, and Title
'   of the message box
Msg = "Do you want to open the Image Database ?"
Style = vbYesNo + vbCritical + vbDefaultButton1
Title = "Open Image Database"

'   Retrieve the user's response
Response = MsgBox(Msg, Style, Title)

'   If it was a yes, then show the ImageData
'   and ImageView forms.  Also start the view
'   in Tiled mode.
If Response = vbYes Then
    ImageView.Show
    ImageData.Show
    MenuTile
End If

End Sub
```

41. The `MenuBrowse` routine handles browsing through the database by manipulating the remote data control. First a check is done to ensure that there are available records to browse. If not, the New Image dialogue is shown. Otherwise the appropriate **move** method of the resultset is called. Once the move has been made, a check is done to see whether the database is at the end of file (eof) or beginning of file (bof) and, if so, the `MoveLast` and `MoveFirst` methods are called to ensure there is a current record. Then, the image is loaded into the `BackPict` picture, and the new view is set with the `SetView` method.

```
Public Sub MenuBrowse(MoveType)

Dim ImageName As String

'   Check the RowCount.  If it is 0
'   then there are no images in the
'   database.  We then need to show the New Image
'   dialog to add the first image.
If ImageData.MSRDC1.Resultset.RowCount = 0 Then MenuNewImage: Exit Sub
```

continued on next page

continued from previous page

```
' Depending on the type of move
' selected by the user, the result set
' is manipulated appropriately.
Select Case MoveType

    Case 0  'Move to First Record
        ImageData.MSRDC1.Resultset.MoveFirst

    Case 1  'Move to Last Record
        ImageData.MSRDC1.Resultset.MoveLast

    Case 2  'Move to Previous Record
        ImageData.MSRDC1.Resultset.MovePrevious

    Case 3  'Move to Next Record
        ImageData.MSRDC1.Resultset.MoveNext

End Select

' Check to see if the End of File or
' Beginning of File has been reached in
' the result set.  If so, then move first or
' last to ensure that a current record is
' always visible
If ImageData.MSRDC1.Resultset.EOF = True Then ⇐
ImageData.MSRDC1.Resultset.MoveLast
If ImageData.MSRDC1.Resultset.BOF = True Then ⇐
vImageData.MSRDC1.Resultset.MoveFirst

' Get the Image name from the database
ImageName = ImageData.MSRDC1.Resultset("FileName")

' Depending on whether or not the image file
' name is set or not, the picture display is
' set appropriately.
If ImageName <> "" Then
    ImageView.BackPict.Picture = LoadPicture(ImageName): SetView IView
Else
    ImageView.BackPict.Picture = LoadPicture(""): SetView IView
End If

End Sub
```

42. The `MenuNewImage` function handles setting up the Common File Dialog box to help the user find BMP or ICO files to track. Once a BMP or ICO file is selected, a new record is added to the database and the appropriate data for the image file is stored.

```
Public Sub MenuNewImage()

Dim ImageID As Integer
Dim ImageType As String

' Ensure an Update is done
ImageData.MSRDC1.Resultset.MoveNext
```

```
'  Set the filter type of the dialog
'  box
ImageData.commondialog1.Filter = "Bitmaps (*.bmp)|*.bmp|Icons ⇐
(*.ico)|*.ico|⇐
All Files (*.*)|*.*"

'  Set the title of the dialog
ImageData.commondialog1.DialogTitle = "New Image File"

'  Set the filter index to that of the
'  bitmap
ImageData.commondialog1.FilterIndex = 1

'  Set the flags to ensure that the
'  file must exist
ImageData.commondialog1.Flags = cdlOFNFileMustExist

'  Show the dialog box
ImageData.commondialog1.ShowOpen

'  Check to see if the filename was set
If ImageData.commondialog1.filename <> "" Then

    '  Add a new record
    ImageData.MSRDC1.Resultset.AddNew

    '  Set the file name
    ImageData.MSRDC1.Resultset("FileName") = ⇐
    ImageData.commondialog1.filename

    '  Set the file size
    ImageData.MSRDC1.Resultset("FileSize") = ⇐
    FileLen(ImageData.commondialog1.filename)

    '  Get the extension of the image
    ImageType = Right$(ImageData.commondialog1.filename, 3)

    '  Set the file format depending on
    '  the the extension
    Select Case UCase$(ImageType)

        Case "BMP"   'Standard bitmap
            ImageData.MSRDC1.Resultset("FileFormat") = "Bitmap"

        Case "ICO"   'Standard Icon
            ImageData.MSRDC1.Resultset("FileType") = "Icon"

    End Select

    '  Update the result set
    ImageData.MSRDC1.Resultset.Update

    '  Select SQL statement to get the
    '  new result set
    ImageData.MSRDC1.SQL = "select * from ImageData order by ImageID"
```

continued on next page

continued from previous page

```
'  Refresh the result set
ImageData.MSRDC1.Refresh

'  Move to the last record which was
'  just added.
MenuBrowse 1

End If

End Sub
```

43. The `MenuDelete` routine deletes the current record and moves to the next record.

```
Public Sub MenuDelete()

'  Delete the current record
ImageData.MSRDC1.Resultset.Delete

'  Move to the next record.
MenuBrowse 3

End Sub
```

How It Works

The Multiple Document Interface provides a framework for working with multiple windows of information. The fundamentals of making the application succesful fall into these three areas.

Menu Setup—The menu setup is the key to interfacing with the application. Note that the MDI menu is different from the menus for the `ImageData` and `ImageView` forms. When the `ImageData` or `ImageView` forms are loaded, their menus take over the menus for the MDI form. In order to make sure the code for the similar menu options works the same and is easily maintable, a BAS module is added with routines for each menu option.

Control and Image Resizing—Part of the key to ensuring that child windows appear correctly when they are resized, tiled, or cascaded is ensuring that the controls on those forms are also resized. In the `ImageData form resize` event, the controls on the form are sized to fit on the form. For the Image View `DispPict` picture which shows the image, its resize event handles calling the `SizeViewPict` routine to ensure the image is updated and fits in the window.

Database Interface—The database interface in this example is provided more for basic functionality than for demonstrating sophisticated database manipulation. The Microsoft Remote Data Control is used with a 32-bit ODBC connection, Image Database. In this case the database, `IData.MDB`, is provided in Microsoft Access 7.0 format and the ODBC driver is for Access 7.0. The database has the fields shown in Table 4-7.

Table 4-7 The `IData` database format

FIELD	FORMAT	DESCRIPTION
ImageID	AutoNumber	Auto count field
FileName	Text	The name of the file including the path
FileSize	Number	The size of the image file
FileFormat	Text	The image format of the file
Comments	Text	Image comments

Note that the database does not have to be in Access and can reside on any ODBC-compatible database such as Microsoft SQL Server.

The image is stretched and sized using the standard Windows API **StretchBlt** function with the SRCCOPY raster operation to copy the image source. In order to ensure that the image apprears correctly, the palette from the back picture where the actual image is stored is copied to the display picture. The palette can be retrieved from the picture object (**picture.hpal**) of the picture box.

Comments

This example adds a few extra touches that would not be necessary in a real application. For example, there is no need to ask users whether they wish to open the database, and, in fact, the database could open automatically when the application starts up. But the method used serves to show the different menu options for the MDI form versus the child windows. In this case, the child windows' menus are the same, but later How-To's in the chapter will show how the menus can diverge.

COMPLEXITY
INTERMEDIATE

4.2 How do I...
Build a toolbar to simplify access to menu functions?

Problem

Most popular Windows 95 user interfaces implement the use of a toolbar. How can I add an integrated toolbar to the MDI **ImageTracking** database application? The toolbar should facilitate easy use of all the program features.

Technique

The toolbar control, combined with the **ImageList** control, provides for an effective method for adding toolbars to an MDI application. The **ImageList** will hold a list of the icons for the buttons on the toolbar. The toolbar will also provide for the use of tool tips for the various button options.

Steps

Open and run **4-2.VBP**. The running program appears as shown in Figure 4-3.

Figure 4-4 shows the MDI child forms cascaded after selecting the Cascade toolbar button. Also note that the menu for the MDI form is hidden. This is done by selecting the Hide Menu option, which is the last tool button.

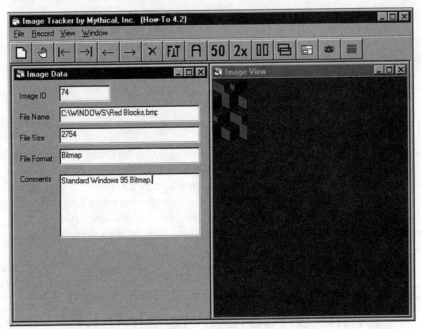

Figure 4-3 The form as it appears at runtime

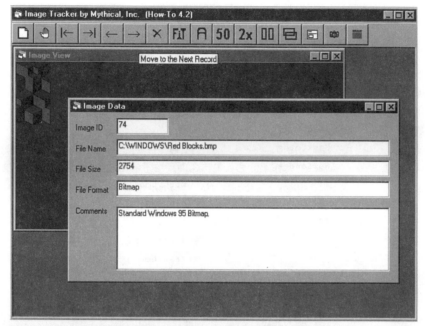

Figure 4-4 The MDI form without the toolbar visible

1. Create a new project called 4-2.VBP. Add the objects and properties listed in Table 4-8 to Form1 and save the form as **4-2.FRM**.

Table 4-8 The MDI form's objects and properties

OBJECT	PROPERTY	SETTING
MDIForm	Name	ImageTracker
	AutoShowChildren	0 'False
	BackColor	&H8000000C&
	Caption	"Image Tracker by Mythical, Inc.
		(How-To 4.2)"
Toolbar	Name	ImageTool
	Align	1 'Align Top
	Negotiate	-1 'True
	ImageList	"MDIButtons"
	ButtonWidth	926
	ButtonHeight	847
	AllowCustomize	0 'False

continued on next page

continued from previous page

OBJECT	PROPERTY	SETTING
	NumButtons	17 *(See ImageList for image icons)*
	AlignSet	-1 'True
	Wrappable	0 'False
ImageList	Name	MDIButtons
	ImageWidth	28
	ImageHeight	26
	MaskColor	12632256
	NumImages	17
	i1	open.bmp
	i2	new.bmp
	i3	hand.bmp
	i4	first.bmp
	i5	last.bmp
	i6	prev.bmp
	i7	next.bmp
	i8	delete.bmp
	i9	fit.bmp
	i10	actual.bmp
	i11	50.bmp
	i12	2x.bmp
	i13	tile.bmp
	i14	cascade.bmp
	i15	data.bmp
	i16	camera.bmp
	i17	menu.bmp

2. Add the menus shown in Table 4-9 to the **ImageTracker** MDI form.

Table 4-9 The form's menus

CONTROL NAME	CAPTION	INDEX	CHECKED	SHORTCUT KEY
mFile	"&File"			
mOpenImage	"&Open Image Database"			
mBar	"-"			
mExit	"E&xit"			
mWindow	"&Window"			
mImageData	"Image &Data"			
mImageView	"Image &View"			

CONTROL NAME	CAPTION	INDEX	CHECKED	SHORTCUT KEY
mBar3	"-"			
mShowTool	"Show Toolbar"	-1	'True	
mShowMenu	"Show Menu"	-1	'True	

3. Insert a new form into the project and save it as `IView.frm`. Add the objects and properties listed in Table 4-10 to the form.

Table 4-10 The form's objects and properties

OBJECT	PROPERTY	SETTING
Form	Name	ImageView
	Caption	"Image View"
	MDIChild	-1 'True
PictureBox	Name	DispPict
	Appearance	0 'Flat
	AutoSize	-1 'True
	BackColor	&H00FF0000&
	ForeColor	&H80000008&
	Picture	"pastel.bmp"
	ScaleMode	3 'Pixel
PictureBox	Name	BackPict
	AutoRedraw	-1 'True
	AutoSize	-1 'True
	BackColor	&H000000FF&
	BorderStyle	0 'None
	ScaleMode	3 'Pixel
	Visible	0 'False

4. Add the menus in Table 4-11 to the `ImageView` form.

Table 4-11 The form's objects and properties

CONTROL NAME	CAPTION	INDEX	CHECKED	SHORTCUT KEY
mFile	"&File"			
mNewImage	"&New Image"			
mBar	"-"			
mExit	"E&xit"			
mRecord	"&Record"			

continued on next page

continued from previous page

CONTROL NAME	CAPTION	INDEX	CHECKED	SHORTCUT KEY
mBrowse	"&First"	0		F1
mBrowse	"&Last"	1		F2
mBrowse	"&Back"	2		F3
mBrowse	"For&ward"	3		F4
mBar2	"-"			
mDelete	"&Delete Record"			
mView	"&View"			
mSize	"&Fit in Window"	0		
mSize	"&Actual Size"	1	-1 'True	
mSize	"&50 Percent"	2		
mSize	"&200 Percent"	3		
mWindow	"&Window"			
mTile	"&Tile"			
mCascade	"&Cascade"			
mBar1	"-"			
mShowWindow	"Image &Data"	0		
mShowWindow	"Image &View"	1		
mBar3	"-"			
mShowTool	"Show Toolbar"		-1 'True	
mShowMenu	"Show Menu"		-1 'True	

5. Insert a new form into the project and save it as `IData.frm`. Add the objects and properties listed in Table 4-12 to the form.

Table 4-12 The form's objects and properties

OBJECT	PROPERTY	SETTING
Form	Name	ImageData
	Caption	"Image Data"
	MDIChild	-1 'True
	Visible	0 'False
TextBox	Name	ImageInfo
	DataField	"Comments"
	DataSource	"MSRDC1"
	Index	4
	MultiLine	-1 'True
TextBox	Name	ImageInfo
	DataField	"FileFormat"

OBJECT	PROPERTY	SETTING
	DataSource	"MSRDC1"
	Index	3
TextBox	Name	ImageInfo
	DataField	"FileSize"
	DataSource	"MSRDC1"
	Index	2
	Locked	-1 'True
TextBox	Name	ImageInfo
	DataField	"FileName"
	DataSource	"MSRDC1"
	Index	1
TextBox	Name	ImageInfo
	DataField	"ImageID"
	DataSource	"MSRDC1"
	Index	0
	Locked	-1 'True
CommonDialog	Name	CommonDialog1
	DefaultExt	".bmp"
	DialogTitle	"Find Image File"
	Filter	"*.bmp; *.wmf"
	FilterIndex	1
	InitDir	"c:\windows"
MSRDC	Name	MSRDC1
	Visible	0 'False
	DataSourceName	"Image Database"
	RecordSource	"select * from ImageData order byImageID"
	RecordsetType	1
	KeysetSize	0
	ReadOnly	0 'False
	UserName	""
	Password	""
	CursorDriver	2
	EOFAction	1
	BOFAction	1
	Caption	"MSRDC1"
	Prompt	3

continued on next page

continued from previous page

OBJECT	PROPERTY	SETTING
	LockType	3
Label	Name	Comments
	AutoSize	-1 'True
	Caption	"Comments"
Label	Name	FileFormat
	AutoSize	-1 'True
	Caption	"File Format"
Label	Name	FileSize
	AutoSize	-1 'True
	Caption	"File Size"
Label	Name	FileName
	AutoSize	-1 'True
	Caption	"File Name"
Label	Name	ImageID
	AutoSize	-1 'True
	Caption	"Image ID"

6. Add the menus in Table 4-13 to the **ImageView** form.

Table 4-13 The form's objects and properties

CONTROL NAME	CAPTION	INDEX	CHECKED	SHORTCUT KEY
mFile	"&File"			
mNewImage	"&New Image"			
mBar	"-"			
mExit	"E&xit"			
mRecord	"&Record"			
mBrowse	"&First"	0		F1
mBrowse	"&Last"	1		F2
mBrowse	"&Back"	2		F3
mBrowse	"For&ward"	3		F4
mBar2	"-"			
mDelete	"&Delete Record"			
mView	"&View"			
mSize	"&Fit in Window"	0		
mSize	"&Actual Size"	1	-1 'True	
mSize	"&50 Percent"	2		
mSize	"&200 Percent"	3		

CONTROL NAME	CAPTION	INDEX	CHECKED		SHORTCUT KEY
mWindow	"&Window"				
mTile	"&Tile"				
mCascade	"&Cascade"				
mBar1	"-"				
mShowWindow	"Image &Data"	0			
mShowWindow	"Image &View"	1			
mBar3	"-"				
mShowTool	"Show Toolbar"		-1	'True	
mShowMenu	"Show Menu"		-1	'True	

> **NOTE**
>
> Only code that is different from or added to the last How-To will be described. If you need additional information regarding the other code, see the last How-To for a complete explanation.

7. Add the following set of code to the **ImageTracker** form. The toolbar has a button collection that defines the buttons for the toolbar. By referencing the index of the button, we can determine which button was selected and call the appropriate function. Note that the toolbar buttons each reference a corresponding menu option. Thus, the original code for each menu option can be called. For the Image Data and Image View buttons, when only the MDI form is loaded, the database is opened; otherwise, the corresponding form is shown.

```
Private Sub ImageTool_ButtonClick(ByVal Button As Button)

Select Case Button.Index

    Case 1
        '   Open the Image Database
        MenuOpenData

    Case 2

        '   Call the MenuNewImage function to get
        '   a new image
        MenuNewImage

    Case 3
        '   Exit the program
        MenuExit

    Case 4
        '   Move to the first record
        MenuBrowse 0
```

continued on next page

continued from previous page

```
Case 5
    '   Move to the last record
    MenuBrowse 1


Case 6
    '   Move back a record
    MenuBrowse 2


Case 7
    '   Move forward a record
    MenuBrowse 3


Case 8
    '   Delete the current record
    '   of the result set
    MenuDelete


Case 9
    '   Set the View to fit in the Window
    SetView 0


Case 10
    '   Set the View to actual size
    SetView 1


Case 11
    '   Set the View to 50 %
    SetView 2


Case 12
    '   Set the View to 200 %
    SetView 3


Case 13
    '   Tile the windows
    MenuTile


Case 14
    '   Cascade the Windows
    MenuCascade


Case 15
    '   If the ImageData form is not
    '   visible then call the
    '   MenuOpenData function to open
    '   the database.  Otherwise, show
    '   the ImageData Window (0)
    If ImageData.Visible = False Then
        MenuOpenData
    Else
        MenuShowWindow 0
    End If


Case 16
    '   If the ImageData form is not
```

```
        '   visible then call the
        '   MenuOpenData function to open
        '   the database.  Otherwise, show
        '   the ImageView Window (1)
        If ImageData.Visible = False Then
            MenuOpenData
        Else
            MenuShowWindow 1
        End If

    Case 17
        '   Show or hide the Menu depending
        '   on the current setting.
        MenuShowMenu

End Select

End Sub
```

8. When the `ImageTool` toolbar is double-clicked, the toolbar will become invisible. But, it is important to ensure that the MDI forms menu is visible. If it is not, then the toolbar should not be hidden.

```
Private Sub ImageTool_DblClick()

'   If the menu or ImageTracker is
'   visible then hide the toolbar.
'   Note we can not hide the toolbar
'   if the menu is also hidden.  the
'   user would be lost at that point.
If Me.mWindow.Visible = True Then
    MenuShowTool
End If

End Sub


Private Sub MDIForm_Load()

'   Hide the ImageData form when
'   the MDI form is first loaded
ImageData.Hide

End Sub

Private Sub MDIForm_QueryUnload(Cancel As Integer, UnloadMode As Integer)

'   Call the MenuExit program to
'   end the program
MenuExit

End Sub

Private Sub MDIForm_Unload(Cancel As Integer)
```

continued on next page

continued from previous page

```
'  Call the MenuExit program to
'  end the program
MenuExit

End Sub

Private Sub mExit_Click()

'  Call the MenuExit program to
'  end the program
MenuExit

End Sub


Private Sub mImageData_Click()

'  Call the MenuOpenData method to open the
'  Image database
MenuOpenData

End Sub

Private Sub mImageView_Click()

'  Call the MenuOpenData method to open the
'  Image database
MenuOpenData

End Sub

Private Sub mOpenImage_Click()

'  Call the MenuOpenData method to open the
'  Image database
MenuOpenData

End Sub
```

9. When the Show Menu option is selected, the **MenuShowMenu** routine is called to handle either showing or hiding the form's menus.

```
Private Sub mShowMenu_Click()

'  Show or hide the Menu
MenuShowMenu

End Sub
```

10. The Show ToolBar menu option calls the **MenuShowTool** routine to handle showing and hiding the toolbar.

```
Private Sub mShowTool_Click()

'  Show or hide the Toolbar
MenuShowTool

End Sub
```

11. Add the following set of code to the **ImageView** form.

```
Public Sub SizeViewPict()

'   Allow for a small border
'   around the display picture
DispPict.Top = 5
DispPict.Left = 5
DispPict.Width = Me.Width - 5
DispPict.Height = Me.Height - 5

'   Set the view to the current
'   view option
SetView IView

End Sub

Private Sub DispPict_Paint()

'   Size the view picture
SizeViewPict

End Sub

Private Sub Form_Load()

'   Intially set IView to 1.
IView = 1

'   Call the MenuBrowse function
'   to show the first record
MenuBrowse 1

End Sub

Private Sub Form_Unload(Cancel As Integer)

'   Cancel the unload.  We don't want the
'   form to be unloaded while the program is
'   running so that it does not have to be
'   re-initialized.  Instead, the form will be
'   minimized.
Cancel = -1
Me.WindowState = 1

End Sub


Private Sub mBrowse_Click(Index As Integer)

'   Browse the record set depending on the
'   menu option chosen.
MenuBrowse Index

End Sub
```

continued on next page

continued from previous page

```
Private Sub mCascade_Click()

' Cascade the windows
MenuCascade

' Size the view picture after the cascade
SizeViewPict

End Sub

Private Sub mDelete_Click()

' Call the MenuDelete function to
' delete the selected record.
MenuDelete

End Sub


Private Sub mExit_Click()

' Call the MenuExit function to
' exit the program.
MenuExit

End Sub


Private Sub mNewImage_Click()

' Call the MenuNewImage function to get
' a new image
MenuNewImage

End Sub
```

12. The Show Menu option calls the **MenuShowWindow** routine to show and hide the form's menu.

```
Private Sub mShowMenu_Click()

' Show or hide the Menu
MenuShowMenu

End Sub
```

13. The Show Tool option calls the **MenuShowTool** routine to show and hide the toolbar.

```
Private Sub mShowTool_Click()

' Show or hide the toolbar
MenuShowTool

End Sub
```

```
Private Sub mShowWindow_Click(Index As Integer)

'   Call the MenuShowWindow function to show
'   the selected window.
MenuShowWindow Index

End Sub


Private Sub mTile_Click()

'   Call the menu tile function to
'   tile the windows
MenuTile

End Sub


Private Sub mSize_Click(Index As Integer)

'   Set the view depending on the menu option
'   selected
SetView Index

End Sub
```

14. Add the following set of code to the **ImageData** form.

```
Private Sub Form_Resize()

Dim N As Integer

'   Resize the Image Info controls to
'   fit on the form when it is resized
For N = 1 To 4
    ImageData.ImageInfo(N).Width = ImageData.Width – ⇐
....ImageData.ImageInfo(N).Left - 300
Next N

End Sub


Private Sub Form_Unload(Cancel As Integer)

'   We don't want the form to be unloaded so that
'   it will not have to be re-initialized
Cancel = -1

'   Instead minimize the form
Me.WindowState = 1
End Sub


Private Sub mBrowse_Click(Index As Integer)

'   Browse the result set depending
'   on the menu selected
MenuBrowse Index

End Sub
```

continued on next page

continued from previous page

```vb
Private Sub mCascade_Click()

'   Cascade the windows
MenuCascade

End Sub

Private Sub mDelete_Click()

'   Delete the current record
'   of the result set
MenuDelete

End Sub

Private Sub mExit_Click()

'   Call the MenuExit method to
'   exit the program
MenuExit

End Sub

Private Sub mNewImage_Click()

'   Cal the MenuNewImage function to allow
'   the user to select a new image to add to the
'   database
MenuNewImage

End Sub
```

15. The Show Menu option handles calling the **MenuShowMenu** routine to show and hide the form's menus.

```vb
Private Sub mShowMenu_Click()

'   Show or hide the Menu
MenuShowMenu

End Sub
```

16. The Show ToolBar menu option handles calling the **MenuShowTool** routine to show and hide the toolbar.

```vb
Private Sub mShowTool_Click()

'   Show or hide the toolbar
MenuShowTool

End Sub

Private Sub mShowWindow_Click(Index As Integer)

'   Call the MenuShowWindow function to show
'   the window selected
```

```
MenuShowWindow Index

End Sub

Private Sub mSize_Click(Index As Integer)

'  Set the View based on the menu
'  selection
SetView Index

End Sub

Private Sub mTile_Click()

'  Tile the windows
MenuTile

End Sub
```

17. Insert a new module into the project and save it as `MenLogic.bas`. Add the following code to the General Declarations section of the module.

```
'  StretchBlit will be used for the Image Viewer
Private Declare Function StretchBlt Lib "gdi32" (ByVal hdc As Long, ⇐
ByVal x As Long, ByVal y As Long, ByVal nWidth As Long, ByVal nHeight ⇐
As Long, ByVal hSrcDC As Long, ByVal xSrc As Long, ByVal ySrc As Long, ⇐
ByVal nSrcWidth As Long, ByVal nSrcHeight As Long, ByVal dwRop As Long) ⇐
As Long

Const SRCCOPY = &HCC0020


'  IView globally stores the current view for
'  the image  I.E.  Fit in Window, 50%
Public IView As Integer


'  Handles ending the program when
'  users select exit from the menu
Public Sub MenuExit()
    End
End Sub


'  Handles tiling the windows
'  on the MDI form
Public Sub MenuTile()

'  Do a vertical tile
ImageTracker.Arrange vbTileVertical

End Sub


Public Sub MenuCascade()
```

continued on next page

continued from previous page

```
'  Cascade the child forms
ImageTracker.Arrange vbCascade

End Sub


Public Sub SetView(Index)

'  When a new image view is selected,
'  the original menu selection is
'  unchecked
ImageView.mSize(IView).Checked = False
ImageData.mSize(IView).Checked = False

'  Set the new view to the index
'  parameter
IView = Index

'  Check the new menu option for the
'  selected view.
ImageData.mSize(IView).Checked = True
ImageView.mSize(IView).Checked = True

'  Clear the displayed picture
ImageView.DispPict.Cls

'  Depending on the view selected, the
'  original image will be copied to the
'  display picture appropriately
Select Case IView

    Case 0  'Fit in the Window
        Call StretchBlt(ImageView.DispPict.hdc, 0, 0, ⇐
        ImageView.DispPict.ScaleWidth, ImageView.DispPict.ScaleHeight, ⇐
        ImageView.BackPict.hdc, 0, 0, ImageView.BackPict.ScaleWidth, ⇐
        ImageView.BackPict.ScaleHeight, SRCCOPY)

    Case 1  'Actual Size
        Call StretchBlt(ImageView.DispPict.hdc, 0, 0, ⇐
        ImageView.BackPict.ScaleWidth, ImageView.BackPict.ScaleHeight, ⇐
        ImageView.BackPict.hdc, 0, 0, ImageView.BackPict.ScaleWidth, ⇐
        ImageView.BackPict.ScaleHeight, SRCCOPY)

    Case 2 '50%
        Call StretchBlt(ImageView.DispPict.hdc, 0, 0, ⇐
        ImageView.BackPict.ScaleWidth * 0.5, ⇐
        ImageView.BackPict.ScaleHeight ⇐
        0.5, ImageView.BackPict.hdc, 0, 0, ⇐
        ImageView.BackPict.ScaleWidth, ⇐
        ImageView.BackPict.ScaleHeight, SRCCOPY)

    Case 3 '200%
        Call StretchBlt(ImageView.DispPict.hdc, 0, 0, ⇐
        ImageView.BackPict.ScaleWidth * 2, ImageView.BackPict.ScaleHeight ⇐
```

```
            2, ImageView.BackPict.hdc, 0, 0, ImageView.BackPict.ScaleWidth, ⇐
        ImageView.BackPict.ScaleHeight, SRCCOPY)

End Select

'   Copy the palette from the holding picture
'   to the displayed picture.  This ensures that
'   the image's colors are displayed correctly.
ImageView.DispPict.Picture.hPal = ImageView.BackPict.Picture.hPal

End Sub

Public Sub MenuShowWindow(Index)

'   Check to see which Windows (Form)
'   is to be displayed.
Select Case Index

    Case 0   'Show ImageData
        ImageData.Show
        ImageData.WindowState = 0

    Case 1   'Show ImageView
        ImageView.Show
        ImageView.WindowState = 0

End Select

End Sub

Public Sub MenuOpenData()

Dim Msg As String
Dim Style As Integer
Dim Title As String
Dim Response As Integer
Dim N As Integer

'   Set the Message, Style and Title
'   of the message box
Msg = "Do you want to open the Image Database ?"
Style = vbYesNo + vbCritical + vbDefaultButton1
Title = "Open Image Database"

'   Retrieve the user's response
Response = MsgBox(Msg, Style, Title)

'   If it was a yes, then show the ImageData
'   and ImageView forms.  Also start the view
'   in Tiled mode.
If Response = vbYes Then
    ImageView.Show
    ImageData.Show
    MenuTile
```

continued on next page

continued from previous page

```
      ImageTracker.ImageTool.Buttons(1).Visible = False

      For N = 2 To ImageTracker.ImageTool.Buttons.Count

          ImageTracker.ImageTool.Buttons(N).Visible = True

      Next N

      '  Ensure that the menu item's the same
      '  for the ImageData and ImageView forms
      ImageView.mShowMenu.Checked = ImageTracker.mShowMenu.Checked
      ImageData.mShowMenu.Checked = ImageTracker.mShowMenu.Checked
      ImageView.mShowTool.Checked = ImageTracker.mShowTool.Checked
      ImageData.mShowTool.Checked = ImageTracker.mShowTool.Checked

End If

End Sub


Public Sub MenuBrowse(MoveType)

Dim ImageName As String

'  Check the RowCount.  If it is 0
'  then there are no images in the
'  database.  We then need to show the New Image
'  dialog to add the first image.
If ImageData.MSRDC1.Resultset.RowCount = 0 Then MenuNewImage: Exit Sub

'  Depending on the type of move
'  selected by the user, the result set
'  is manipulated appropriately.
Select Case MoveType

    Case 0  'Move to First Record
        ImageData.MSRDC1.Resultset.MoveFirst

    Case 1  'Move to Last Record
        ImageData.MSRDC1.Resultset.MoveLast

    Case 2  'Move to Previous Record
        ImageData.MSRDC1.Resultset.MovePrevious

    Case 3  'Move to Next Record
        ImageData.MSRDC1.Resultset.MoveNext

End Select

'  Check to see if the End of File or
'  Beginning of File has been reached in
'  the result set.  If so, then move first or
'  last to ensure that a current record is
'  always visible
If ImageData.MSRDC1.Resultset.EOF = True Then ⇐
```

```
ImageData.MSRDC1.Resultset.MoveLast

If ImageData.MSRDC1.Resultset.BOF = True Then ⇐
ImageData.MSRDC1.Resultset.MoveFirst

'  Get the Image name from the database
ImageName = ImageData.MSRDC1.Resultset("FileName")

'  Depending on whether or not the image file
'  name is set or not, the picture display is
'  set appropriately.
If ImageName <> "" Then
    ImageView.BackPict.Picture = LoadPicture(ImageName): SetView IView
Else
    ImageView.BackPict.Picture = LoadPicture(""): SetView IView
End If

End Sub

Public Sub MenuNewImage()

Dim ImageID As Integer
Dim ImageType As String

'  Ensure an Update is done
ImageData.MSRDC1.Resultset.MoveNext

'  Set the filter type of the dialog
'  box
ImageData.commondialog1.Filter = "Bitmaps (*.bmp)|*.bmp|Icons ⇐
(*.ico)|*.ico| All Files (*.*)|*.*"

'  Set the title of the dialog
ImageData.commondialog1.DialogTitle = "New Image File"

'  Set the filter index to that of the
'  bitmap
ImageData.commondialog1.FilterIndex = 1

'  Set the flags to ensure that the
'  file must exist
ImageData.commondialog1.Flags = cdlOFNFileMustExist

'  Show the dialog box
ImageData.commondialog1.ShowOpen

'  Check to see if the filename was set
If ImageData.commondialog1.filename <> "" Then

    '  Add a new record
    ImageData.MSRDC1.Resultset.AddNew

    '  Set the file name
    ImageData.MSRDC1.Resultset("FileName") = ⇐
    ImageData.commondialog1.filename
```

continued on next page

continued from previous page

```
    '  Set the file size
    ImageData.MSRDC1.Resultset("FileSize") = ⇐
      FileLen(ImageData.commondialog1.filename)

    '  Get the extension of the image
    ImageType = Right$(ImageData.commondialog1.filename, 3)

    '  Set the file format depending on
    '  the the extension
    Select Case UCase$(ImageType)

        Case "BMP"  'Standard bitmap
            ImageData.MSRDC1.Resultset("FileFormat") = "Bitmap"

        Case "ICO"  'Standard Icon
            ImageData.MSRDC1.Resultset("FileType") = "Icon"

    End Select

    '  Update the result set
    ImageData.MSRDC1.Resultset.Update

    '  Select SQL statement to get the
    '  new result set
    ImageData.MSRDC1.SQL = "select * from ImageData order by ImageID"

    '  Refresh the result set
    ImageData.MSRDC1.Refresh

    '  Move to the last record which was
    '  just added.
    MenuBrowse 1

End If

End Sub

Public Sub MenuDelete()

'  Delete the current record
ImageData.MSRDC1.Resultset.Delete

'  Move to the next record.
MenuBrowse 3

End Sub
```

18. The **MenuShowTool** routine handles showing and hiding the toolbar. The current status is set by the check status of the **mShowTool** menu option. If the menu is checked then the toolbar is to be hidden and all of the Show ToolBar menu options are unchecked. If the menu is unchecked then the Show ToolBar menu items are checked and the toolbar shown.

```
Public Sub MenuShowTool()

'  If the toolbar is checked then
'  do the logic to hide the toolbar
If ImageTracker.mShowTool.Checked = True Then

     '  Hide the toolbar
     ImageTracker.ImageTool.Visible = False

     '  Change the menu check
     ImageTracker.mShowTool.Checked = False

     '  If the ImageData and ImageView forms
     '  are visible then handle setting their
     '  menu check marks.  If they are not
     '  visible, they are not loaded.
     If ImageData.Visible = True Then
         ImageData.mShowTool.Checked = False
         ImageView.mShowTool.Checked = False
     End If

Else

     '  Make the toolbar visible
     ImageTracker.ImageTool.Visible = True

     '  Change the menu check
     ImageTracker.mShowTool.Checked = True

     '  If the ImageData and ImageView forms
     '  are visible then handle setting their
     '  menu check marks.  If they are not
     '  visible, they are not loaded.
     If ImageData.Visible = True Then
         ImageData.mShowTool.Checked = True
         ImageView.mShowTool.Checked = True
     End If

End If

End Sub
```

19. The `MenuShowMenu` routine handles showing and hiding the menus for the forms. If the Show Menu menu item is checked, then the menus will be hidden; otherwise the menus will be shown. It is important to ensure that the toolbar is visible if the menu is to be hidden. If both the menu and toolbar were hidden, the user would be stuck.

```
Public Sub MenuShowMenu()

'  Check to see If the menu is already visible
If ImageTracker.mShowMenu.Checked = True Then

     '  If the tool bar is not visible,
     '  we do not want to also make the
     '  menu invisible
```

continued on next page

continued from previous page

```
        If ImageTracker.ImageTool.Visible = False Then Exit Sub

            ' Make the ImageTracker menus
            ' invisible and set the menu
            ' check mark appropriately
        ImageTracker.mFile.Visible = False
        ImageTracker.mShowMenu.Checked = False
        ImageTracker.mWindow.Visible = False

            ' If the ImageData and ImageView forms
            ' are visible then handle setting their
            ' menu check marks and visible properties.
            ' If they are not visible, they are not
            ' loaded.
        If ImageData.Visible = True Then
            ImageData.mShowMenu.Checked = False
            ImageView.mShowMenu.Checked = False
            ImageView.mFile.Visible = False
            ImageData.mFile.Visible = False
            ImageData.mWindow.Visible = False
            ImageView.mWindow.Visible = False
            ImageData.mRecord.Visible = False
            ImageView.mRecord.Visible = False
            ImageData.mView.Visible = False
            ImageView.mView.Visible = False
        End If

    Else

            ' Make the ImageTracker menus
            ' visible and set the menu
            ' check mark appropriately
        ImageTracker.mFile.Visible = True
        ImageTracker.mShowMenu.Checked = True
        ImageTracker.mWindow.Visible = True

            ' If the ImageData and ImageView forms
            ' are visible then handle setting their
            ' menu check marks and visible properties.
            ' If they are not visible, they are not
            ' loaded.
        If ImageData.Visible = True Then
            ImageData.mShowMenu.Checked = True
            ImageView.mShowMenu.Checked = True
            ImageData.mFile.Visible = True
            ImageView.mFile.Visible = True
            ImageData.mWindow.Visible = True
            ImageView.mWindow.Visible = True
            ImageData.mRecord.Visible = True
            ImageView.mRecord.Visible = True
            ImageView.mView.Visible = True
            ImageData.mView.Visible = True
        End If

    End If

    End Sub
```

How It Works

If you take a moment to compare the basic MDI application developed in the How-To before this one, you can easily see the benefits the toolbar interface provides to the user. Database browsing becomes obvious and easy to access through the toolbar buttons. Quickly switching between the different image views also becomes obvious as well as browsing the database.

Part of what makes the implementation of the toolbar possible is the use of the **ImageList** control. An **ImageList** simply holds a list of images. In this case the images are the bitmap button icons. The **ToolBar** control references the image list for defining the icon to be placed on the buttons. Note that the button icons are provided in the application directory.

The routines called to implement the different menu functions also implement the toolbar functionality. An added feature to help customize the interface to the user's liking is to allow either the menu or the toolbar to be hidden. It is important to ensure that at least one is visible.

Comments

The **ToolBar** control allows for a customize feature to organize the buttons on the toolbar. In this example, the property is set to **False**. To allow your user to customize the interface to your application, you might want to consider providing this functionality.

COMPLEXITY

INTERMEDIATE

4.3 How do I...
Implement right mouse button context menus?

Problem

The Windows 95 interface provides a rich set of features with the use of the right mouse click. How can I provide right mouse click context menus to help the user navigate the interfaces of my programs?

Technique

Visual Basic, starting with version 4, provides the `PopupMenu` method for providing instant pop-up menus based on the form's menus. With pop-up menus, based on the context of the mouse click, the appropriate menu can be shown with the *most likely* selection in bold. This How-To will add context-rich pop-up menus to the MDI application developed in the last How-To's.

Steps

Open and run 4-3.VBP. The running program appears as shown in Figure 4-6.

Figure 4-5 shows the toolbar pop-up menu for setting the toolbar, menu, and window options. Figure 4-6 shows the right-click option for the Image View window. You can also perform a left-click to show the menu options to flip the image horizontally and vertically.

Figure 4-7 shows the right-click option for the Image Data window. This provides for quick selection of the database browse functions of the program.

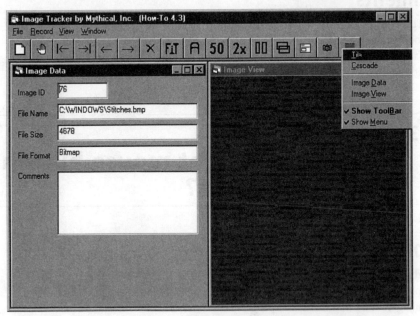

Figure 4-5 The form with the right-click pop-up menu for the toolbar

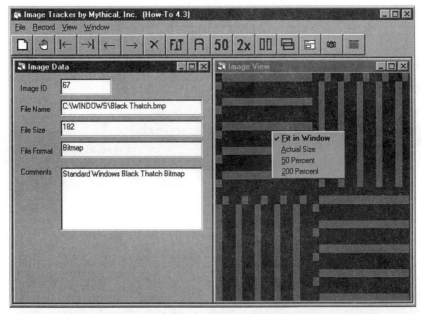

Figure 4-6 The form with the right-click pop-up menu for the Image View window

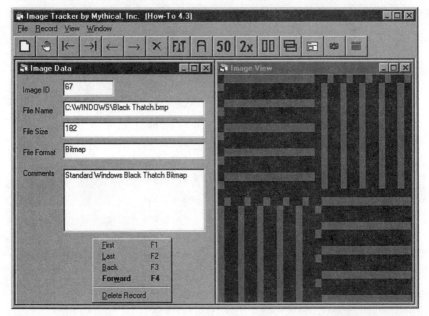

Figure 4-7 The form with the right-click pop-up menu for the Image Data window

1. Create a new project called 4-3.VBP. Add the objects and properties listed in Table 4-14 to the form and save the form as **4-3.FRM**.

Table 4-14 The MDI form's objects and properties

OBJECT	PROPERTY	SETTING
MDIForm	Name	ImageTracker
	AutoShowChildren	0 'False
	Caption	"Image Tracker by Mythical, Inc. (How-To 4.3)"
Toolbar	Name	ImageTool
	Align	1 'Align Top
	Negotiate	-1 'True
	ImageList	"MDIButtons"
	ButtonWidth	926
	ButtonHeight	847
	AllowCustomize	0 'False
	NumButtons	17 (See ImageList for button icons)
	AlignSet	-1 'True
	Wrappable	0 'False
ImageList	Name	MDIButtons
	ImageWidth	28
	ImageHeight	26
	MaskColor	12632256
	NumImages	17
	i1	open.bmp
	i2	new.bmp
	i3	hand.bmp
	i4	first.bmp
	i5	last.bmp
	i6	prev.bmp
	i7	next.bmp
	i8	delete.bmp
	i9	fit.bmp
	i10	actual.bmp
	i11	50.bmp
	i12	2x.bmp
	i13	tile.bmp
	i14	cascade.bmp

OBJECT	PROPERTY	SETTING
	i15	data.bmp
	i16	camera.bmp
	i17	menu.bmp

2. Add the menus shown in Table 4-15 to the `ImageTracker` form.

Table 4-15 The `ImageTracker` form's menus

CONTROL NAME	CAPTION	INDEX	CHECKED	SHORTCUT KEY
mFile	"&File"			
mOpenImage	"&Open Image Database"			
mBar	"-"			
mExit	"E&xit"			
mWindow	"&Window"			
mImageData	"Image &Data"			
mImageView	"Image &View"			
mBar3	"-"			
mShowTool	"Show Toolbar"		-1 'True	
mShowMenu	"Show Menu"		-1 'True	

3. Insert a new form into the project and save it as `IView.frm`. Add the objects and properties listed in Table 4-16 to the form.

Table 4-16 The `ImageView` form's objects and properties

OBJECT	PROPERTY	SETTING
Form	Name	ImageView
	Caption	"Image View"
	MDIChild	-1 'True
PictureBox	Name	DispPict
	BackColor	&H00C00000&
	BorderStyle	0 'None
	Picture	"pastel.bmp"
	ScaleMode	3 'Pixel
PictureBox	Name	BackPict
	AutoRedraw	-1 'True
	AutoSize	-1 'True
	BackColor	&H000000FF&

continued on next page

continued from previous page

OBJECT	PROPERTY	SETTING
	BorderStyle	0 'None
	Picture	"pastel.bmp"
	ScaleMode	3 'Pixel
	Visible	0 'False

4. Add the menus shown in Table 4-17 to the `ImageView` form.

Table 4-17 The `ImageView` form's menus

CONTROL NAME	CAPTION	INDEX	CHECKED	SHORTCUT KEY
mFile	"&File"			
mNewImage	"&New Image"			
mBar	"-"			
mExit	"E&xit"			
mRecord	"&Record"			
mBrowse	"&First"	0		F1
mBrowse	"&Last"	1		F2
mBrowse	"&Back"	2		F3
mBrowse	"For&ward"	3		F4
mBar2	"-"			
mDelete	"&Delete Record"			
mView	"&View"			
mSize	"&Fit in Window"	0		
mSize	"&Actual Size"	1	-1 'True	
mSize	"&50 Percent"	2		
mSize	"&200 Percent"	3		
mViewSet	"Viewer Settings"			
Flip	"Flip &Horizontal"	0		
Flip	"Flip &Vertical"	1		
mWindow	"&Window"			
mTile	"&Tile"			
mCascade	"&Cascade"			
mBar1	"-"			
mShowWindow	"Image &Data"	0		
mShowWindow	"Image &View"	1		
mBar3	"-"			
mShowTool	"Show Tool&Bar"			
mShowMenu	"Show &Menu"		-1 'True	

5. Insert a new form into the project and save it as `IData.frm`. Add the objects and properties listed in Table 4-18 to the form.

Table 4-18 The `ImageData` form's objects and properties

OBJECT	PROPERTY	SETTING
Form	Name	ImageData
	Caption	"Image Data"
	MDIChild	-1 'True
	Visible	0 'False
TextBox	Name	ImageInfo
	DataField	"Comments"
	DataSource	"MSRDC1"
	Index	4
	MultiLine	-1 'True
TextBox	Name	ImageInfo
	DataField	"FileFormat"
	DataSource	"MSRDC1"
	Index	3
TextBox	Name	ImageInfo
	DataField	"FileSize"
	DataSource	"MSRDC1"
	Index	2
	Locked	-1 'True
TextBox	Name	ImageInfo
	DataField	"FileName"
	DataSource	"MSRDC1"
	Index	1
TextBox	Name	ImageInfo
	DataField	"ImageID"
	DataSource	"MSRDC1"
	Index	0
	Locked	-1 'True
CommonDialog	Name	CommonDialog1
	DefaultExt	".bmp"
	DialogTitle	"Find Image File"
	Filter	"*.bmp; *.wmf"
	FilterIndex	1
	InitDir	"c:\windows"

continued on next page

continued from previous page

OBJECT	PROPERTY	SETTING
MSRDC	Name	MSRDC1
	Visible	0 'False
	DataSourceName	"Image Database"
	RecordSource	"select * from ImageData order by ImageID"
	RecordsetType	1
	KeysetSize	0
	ReadOnly	0 'False
	UserName	""
	Password	""
	CursorDriver	2
	EOFAction	1
	BOFAction	1
	Prompt	3
	LockType	3
Label	Name	Comments
	AutoSize	-1 'True
	Caption	"Comments"
Label	Name	FileFormat
	AutoSize	-1 'True
	Caption	"File Format"
Label	Name	FileSize
	AutoSize	-1 'True
	Caption	"File Size"
Label	Name	FileName
	AutoSize	-1 'True
	Caption	"File Name"
Label	Name	ImageID
	AutoSize	-1 'True
	Caption	"Image ID"

6. Add the menus shown in Table 4-19 to the **ImageData** form.

Table 4-19 The **ImageData** form's menus

CONTROL NAME	CAPTION	INDEX	CHECKED	SHORTCUT KEY
mFile	"&File"			
mNewImage	"&New Image"			
mBar	"-"			

CONTROL NAME	CAPTION	INDEX	CHECKED		SHORTCUT KEY
mExit	"E&xit"				
mRecord	"&Record"				
mBrowse	"&First"	0			F1
mBrowse	"&Last"	1			F2
mBrowse	"&Back"	2			F3
mBrowse	"For&ward"	3			F4
mBar2	"-"				
mDelete	"&Delete Record"				
mView	"&View"				
mSize	"&Fit in Window"	0			
mSize	"&Actual Size"	1	-1	'True	
mSize	"&50 Percent"	2			
mSize	"&200 Percent"	3			
mWindow	"&Window"				
mTile	"&Tile"				
mCascade	"&Cascade"				
mBar1	"-"				
mShowWindow	"Image &Data"	0			
mShowWindow	"Image &View"	1			
mBar3	"-"				
mShowTool	"Show Tool&Bar"		-1	'True	
mShowMenu	"Show &Menu"		-1	'True	

NOTE

Only the new code added to the project will be commented. If you need additional information regarding the other code, see the previous How-To's for a complete explanation.

7. Add the following set of code to the **ImageTracker** form.

```
Private Sub ImageTool_ButtonClick(ByVal Button As Button)

Select Case Button.Index

    Case 1
        '   Open the Image Database
        MenuOpenData

    Case 2
```

continued on next page

continued from previous page

```
          '  Call the MenuNewImage function to get
          '  a new image
          MenuNewImage

     Case 3
          '  Exit the program
          MenuExit

     Case 4
          '  Move to the first record
          MenuBrowse 0

     Case 5
          '  Move to the last record
          MenuBrowse 1

     Case 6
          '  Move back a record
          MenuBrowse 2

     Case 7
          '  Move forward a record
          MenuBrowse 3

     Case 8
          '  Delete the current record
          '  of the result set
          MenuDelete

     Case 9
          '  Set the View to fit in the Window
          SetView 0

     Case 10
          '  Set the View to actual size
          SetView 1

     Case 11
          '  Set the View to 50 %
          SetView 2

     Case 12
          '  Set the View to 200 %
          SetView 3

     Case 13
          '  Tile the windows
          MenuTile

     Case 14
          '  Cascade the Windows
          MenuCascade

     Case 15
          '  If the ImageData form is not
```

```
'    visible then call the
'    MenuOpenData function to open
'    the database.  Otherwise, show
'    the ImageData Window (0)
If ImageData.Visible = False Then
     MenuOpenData
Else
     MenuShowWindow 0
End If


Case 16
'    If the ImageData form is not
'    visible then call the
'    MenuOpenData function to open
'    the database.  Otherwise, show
'    the ImageView Window (1)
If ImageData.Visible = False Then
     MenuOpenData
Else
     MenuShowWindow 1
End If


Case 17
'    Show or hide the Menu depending
'    on the current setting.
MenuShowMenu


End Select

End Sub
```

8. The following code checks to see if the right mouse click was performed on the toolbar. If so, then the **mWindow** menu is shown over the toolbar. Note that this menu provides the option to hide the toolbar.

```
Private Sub ImageTool_MouseDown(Button As Integer, Shift As Integer, X As ⇐
Single, Y As Single)

'  Check for the right mouse
'  button click
If Button = vbPopupMenuRightButton Then

    '  If the ImageData form is not visible then
    '  show the popup menu for ImageTracker form.
    '  Otherwise show the pop up menu for the
    '  ImageData form.
    If ImageData.Visible = False Then
         Me.PopupMenu mWindow, vbPopupMenuCenterALign, , , mShowTool
    Else
         ImageData.PopupMenu ImageData.mWindow, vbPopupMenuCenterALign, , ⇐
         , ImageData.mShowTool
    End If

End If
```

continued on next page

continued from previous page

```
End Sub

Private Sub MDIForm_Load()

'  Hide the ImageData form when
'   the MDI form is first loaded
ImageData.Hide

End Sub
```

9. The following code checks to see if a right mouse click was performed on
the MDI form. The context of the click in this case is important. If the
image database has not yet been opened, then the **mFile** menu is shown to
give the user the option of opening the database or exiting the program.
Otherwise the **mWindow** menu is shown to provide the user with the standard window menu options.

```
Private Sub MDIForm_MouseDown(Button As Integer, Shift As Integer, X As ⇐
Single, Y As Single)

'  If the ImageData form is not visible,
'  then show the File menu from the
'  ImageTracker form
If (Button = vbPopupMenuRightButton) And (ImageData.Visible <> True) Then
    Me.PopupMenu mFile, vbPopupMenuCenterAlign, , , mOpenImage
    Exit Sub
End If

'  If the ImageData form is visible,
'  then show the Window menu from the
'  ImageData form
If (Button = vbPopupMenuRightButton) And (ImageData.Visible = True) Then
    ImageData.PopupMenu ImageData.mWindow, vbPopupMenuCenterAlign ', , ⇐
    , ImageData.mImageData
End If

End Sub


Private Sub MDIForm_QueryUnload(Cancel As Integer, UnloadMode As Integer)

'  Call the MenuExit program to
'  end the program
MenuExit

End Sub

Private Sub MDIForm_Unload(Cancel As Integer)

'  Call the MenuExit program to
'  end the program
MenuExit

End Sub
```

```
Private Sub mExit_Click()

'   Call the MenuExit program to
'   end the program
MenuExit

End Sub

Private Sub mImageData_Click()

'   Call the MenuOpenData method to open the
'   Image database
MenuOpenData

End Sub

Private Sub mImageView_Click()

'   Call the MenuOpenData method to open the
'   Image database
MenuOpenData

End Sub

Private Sub mOpenImage_Click()

'   Call the MenuOpenData method to open the
'   Image database
MenuOpenData

End Sub

Private Sub mShowMenu_Click()

'   Show or hide the Menu
MenuShowMenu

End Sub

Private Sub mShowTool_Click()

'   Show or hide the Toolbar
MenuShowTool

End Sub
```

10. Add the following set of code to the **ImageView** form.

```
Public Sub SizeViewPict()

'   Allow for a small border
'   around the display picture
disppict.Top = 5
disppict.Left = 5
disppict.Width = Me.Width - 5
disppict.Height = Me.Height - 5
```

continued on next page

continued from previous page

```
'  Set the view to the current
'  view option
SetView IView

End Sub

Private Sub DispPict_Paint()

'  Size the view picture
SizeViewPict

End Sub
```

11. The following code checks to see which mouse button was clicked on the display picture. If it was the right mouse button, then the **mView** menu is shown to provide the different viewing options for the image. If the left mouse button was clicked, then the **mViewSet** menu is shown to provide the user with the options of flipping the image horizontally or vertically.

```
Private Sub DispPict_MouseDown(Button As Integer, Shift As Integer, X As ⇐
Single, Y As Single)

'  If the right mouse button is selected, then
'  the different image size options are shown.  If
'  it is a left mouse click then the flip options
'  are shown
If Button = vbPopupMenuRightButton Then
    Me.PopupMenu mView, vbPopupMenuCenterAlign, , , mSize(0)
Else
    Me.PopupMenu mViewSet, vbPopupMenuCenterAlign
End If

End Sub
```

12. The flip menu options provide the user with the option of flipping the displayed image either horizontally or vertically. A check is done to ensure that only one of the flip options can be selected at any one point. The **SizeViewPict** routine is called to display the image in the new state.

```
Private Sub Flip_Click(Index As Integer)

'  When the flip menu is clicked, the
'  check on the menu is set appropriately
If flip(Index).Checked = False Then
    flip(Index).Checked = True
Else
    flip(Index).Checked = False
End If

'  It is important to ensure that only
'  a vertical or horizotal flip can be
'  performed.  Thus, the menu item that
'  was not clicked is unchecked.
```

```vb
If Index = 1 Then
    flip(0).Checked = False
Else
    flip(1).Checked = False
End If

'  Based on the selection,
'  the image is redisplayed.
SizeViewPict

End Sub

Private Sub Form_Load()

'  Intially set IView to 0.
IView = 1

'  Call the MenuBrowse function
'  to show the first record
MenuBrowse 1

End Sub

Private Sub Form_Unload(Cancel As Integer)

'  Cancel the unload.  We don't want the
'  form to be unloaded while the program is
'  running so that it does not have to be
'  re-initialized.  Instead, the form will be
'  minimized.
Cancel = -1
Me.WindowState = 1

End Sub

Private Sub mBrowse_Click(Index As Integer)

'  Browse the record set depending on the
'  menu option chosen.
MenuBrowse Index

End Sub

Private Sub mCascade_Click()

'  Cascade the windows
MenuCascade

'  Size the view picture after the cascade
SizeViewPict

End Sub

Private Sub mDelete_Click()

'  Call the MenuDelete function to
```

continued on next page

continued from previous page

```
'   delete the selected record.
MenuDelete

End Sub

Private Sub mExit_Click()

'   Call the MenuExit function to
'   exit the program.
MenuExit

End Sub

Private Sub mNewImage_Click()

'   Call the MenuNewImage function to get
'   a new image
MenuNewImage

End Sub

Private Sub mShowMenu_Click()

'   Show or hide the Menu
MenuShowMenu

End Sub

Private Sub mShowTool_Click()

'   Show or hide the toolbar
MenuShowTool

End Sub

Private Sub mShowWindow_Click(Index As Integer)

'   Call the MenuShowWindow function to show
'   the selected window.
MenuShowWindow Index

End Sub

Private Sub mTile_Click()

'   Call the menu tile function to
'   tile the windows
MenuTile

End Sub

Private Sub mSize_Click(Index As Integer)

'   Set the view depending on the menu option
'   selected
SetView Index

End Sub
```

13. Add the following set of code to the **ImageData** form. The **MouseDown** event of the form checks to see if a right mouse click was performed on the form. If so, then the **mRecord** menu is shown to provide the user with options for browsing the records of the database.

```
Private Sub Form_MouseDown(Button As Integer, Shift As Integer, X As ⇐
Single, Y As Single)

If Button = vbPopupMenuRightButton Then
    '   Show the Record menu for moving
    '   through the image records in the
    '   database
    Me.PopupMenu mRecord, vbPopupMenuCenterAlign, , , mBrowse(3)

End If

End Sub

Private Sub Form_Resize()

Dim N As Integer

'   Resize the Image Info controls to
'   fit on the form when it is resized
For N = 1 To 4
    ImageData.ImageInfo(N).Width = ImageData.Width - ⇐
    ImageData.ImageInfo(N).Left - 300
Next N

End Sub

Private Sub Form_Unload(Cancel As Integer)

'   We don't want the form to be unloaded so that
'   it will not have to be re-initialized
Cancel = -1

'   Instead minimize the form
Me.WindowState = 1
End Sub

Private Sub mBrowse_Click(Index As Integer)

'   Browse the result set depending
'   on the menu selected
MenuBrowse Index

End Sub

Private Sub mCascade_Click()

'   Cascade the windows
MenuCascade

End Sub
```

continued on next page

continued from previous page

```
Private Sub mDelete_Click()

' Delete the current record
' of the result set
MenuDelete

End Sub

Private Sub mExit_Click()

' Call the MenuExit method to
' exit the program
MenuExit

End Sub

Private Sub mNewImage_Click()

' Cal the MenuNewImage function to allow
' the user to select a new image to add to the
' database
MenuNewImage

End Sub

Private Sub mShowMenu_Click()

' Show or hide the Menu
MenuShowMenu

End Sub

Private Sub mShowTool_Click()

' Show or hide the toolbar
MenuShowTool

End Sub

Private Sub mShowWindow_Click(Index As Integer)

' Call the MenuShowWindow function to show
' the window selected
MenuShowWindow Index

End Sub

Private Sub mSize_Click(Index As Integer)

' Set the View based on the menu
' selection
SetView Index

End Sub
```

```
Private Sub mTile_Click()

'  Tile the windows
MenuTile

End Sub
```

14. Insert a new module into the program and save it as `MenLogic.bas`. Add the following code to the General Declarations section of the form.

```
'  StretchBlit will be used for the Image Viewer Private Declare Function ⇐
StretchBlt Lib "gdi32" (ByVal hdc As Long, ByVal X As Long, ByVal Y As ⇐
Long, ByVal nWidth As Long, ByVal nHeight As Long, ByVal hSrcDC As Long, ⇐
ByVal xSrc As Long, ByVal ySrc As Long, ByVal nSrcWidth As Long, ByVal ⇐
nSrcHeight As Long, ByVal dwRop As Long) As Long

Const SRCCOPY = &HCC0020

'  IView globally stores the current view for
'  the image  I.E.  Fit in Window, 50%
Public IView As Integer

'  Handles ending the program when
'  users select exit from the menu
Public Sub MenuExit()
     End
End Sub

'  Handles tiling the windows
'  on the MDI form
Public Sub MenuTile()

'  Do a vertical tile
ImageTracker.Arrange vbTileVertical

End Sub

Public Sub MenuCascade()

'  Cascade the child forms
ImageTracker.Arrange vbCascade

End Sub
```

15. The `SetView` routine handles setting the view indicated by the index. Note that the menu option for the last view is unchecked and the current index is checked. The current picture is cleared and, depending on the index, the image is copied from the `BackPict` picture box to the `DispPict` picture box. `StretchBlt` is used to perform the image stretching or the `PaintPicture` method of the `Picture` object is used to perform the horizontal and vertical flips of the image. Finally, the palette from `BackPict` is copied to the display picture to ensure that the image colors are correct.

```
Public Sub SetView(Index)

'  When a new image view is selected,
'  the original menu selection is
'  unchecked
ImageView.mSize(IView).Checked = False
ImageData.mSize(IView).Checked = False

'  Set the new view to the index
'  parameter
IView = Index

'  Check the new menu option for the
'  selected view.
ImageData.mSize(IView).Checked = True
ImageView.mSize(IView).Checked = True

'  Clear the displayed picture
ImageView.disppict.Cls

'  Depending on the view selected, the
'  original image will be copied to the
'  display picture appropriately
Select Case IView

'  Note that for the vertical and
'  horizontal flips, the height or
'  width is set to a negative value
'  and the starting point is set to
'  the height or width for the image
'  to be displayed.

    Case 0   'Fit in the Window
        If ImageView.flip(0).Checked = True Then
            '  Flip Horizontal
            ImageView.disppict.PaintPicture ImageView.backpict.Picture, ⇐
            ImageView.disppict.ScaleWidth, 0, -1 * ⇐
            ImageView.disppict.ScaleWidth, ⇐
            ImageView.disppict.ScaleHeight, ⇐
0, 0, ImageView.backpict.ScaleWidth,
 ImageView.backpict.ScaleHeight
        Else

            If ImageView.flip(1).Checked = True Then
                '  Flip Vertical
                ImageView.disppict.PaintPicture ⇐
                ImageView.backpict.Picture, ⇐
0, ImageView.disppict.ScaleHeight, ⇐
                ImageView.disppict.ScaleWidth, -1 * ⇐
                ImageView.disppict.ScaleHeight, 0, 0, ⇐
                ImageView.backpict.ScaleWidth,
                ImageView.backpict.ScaleHeight
            Else
                '  Normal Display
                Call StretchBlt(ImageView.disppict.hdc, 0, 0, ⇐
```

```
                    ImageView.disppict.ScaleWidth, ⇐
                    ImageView.disppict.ScaleHeight, ⇐
                    ImageView.backpict.hdc, 0,⇐
                    ImageView.backpict.ScaleHeight, SRCCOPY)
              End If
          End If

      Case 1    'Actual Size
          If ImageView.flip(0).Checked = True Then
                  '   Flip Horizontal
                  ImageView.disppict.PaintPicture ImageView.backpict.Picture, ⇐
                  ImageView.backpict.ScaleWidth, 0, -1 * ⇐
                  ImageView.backpict.ScaleWidth, ⇐
                  ImageView.backpict.ScaleHeight, ⇐
                  0, 0, ImageView.backpict.ScaleWidth,
ImageView.backpict.ScaleHeight
          Else
                  If ImageView.flip(1).Checked = True Then
                      '   Flip Vertical
                      ImageView.disppict.PaintPicture ⇐
                      ImageView.backpict.Picture, ⇐
                      ImageView.backpict.ScaleWidth, -1 * ⇐
                      ImageView.backpict.ScaleHeight, 0, 0, ⇐
                      ImageView.backpict.ScaleWidth,
ImageView.backpict.ScaleHeight
                  Else
                      '   Normal Display
                      Call StretchBlt(ImageView.disppict.hdc, 0, 0, ⇐
End If
          End If

      Case 2  '50%
          If ImageView.flip(0).Checked = True Then
                  '   Flip Horizontal
                  ImageView.disppict.PaintPicture ImageView.backpict.Picture, ⇐
              ImageView.backpict.ScaleWidth * 0.5, 0, -1 * ⇐
              ImageView.backpict.ScaleWidth * 0.5, ⇐
              ImageView.backpict.ScaleHeight * 0.5, 0, 0, ⇐
              ImageView.backpict.ScaleWidth, ImageView.backpict.ScaleHeight
          Else
                  If ImageView.flip(1).Checked = True Then
                      '   Flip Vertical
                      ImageView.disppict.PaintPicture ⇐
                      ImageView.backpict.Picture, ⇐
                  0, ImageView.backpict.ScaleHeight * 0.5, ⇐
                  ImageView.backpict.ScaleHeight * 0.5, 0, 0, ⇐
                  ImageView.backpict.ScaleWidth,
ImageView.backpict.ScaleHeight
                  Else
                      '   Normal Display
                      Call StretchBlt(ImageView.disppict.hdc, 0, 0, ⇐
                      ImageView.backpict.ScaleWidth * 0.5, ⇐
                      ImageView.backpict.ScaleHeight * 0.5,
```

continued on next page

continued from previous page

```
ImageView.backpict.hdc, ⇐
               0, 0, ImageView.backpict.ScaleWidth, ⇐
ImageView.backpict.ScaleHeight, SRCCOPY)
           End If
       End If

    Case 3 '200%
        If ImageView.flip(0).Checked = True Then
            ' Flip Horizontal
            ImageView.disppict.PaintPicture ImageView.backpict.Picture, ⇐
            ImageView.backpict.ScaleWidth * 2, 0, -1 * ⇐
            ImageView.backpict.ScaleWidth * 2, ⇐
        ImageView.backpict.ScaleHeight ⇐
      2, 0, 0, ImageView.backpict.ScaleWidth, ⇐
    ImageView.backpict.ScaleHeight
        Else
            If ImageView.flip(1).Checked = True Then
                ' Flip Vertical
                ImageView.disppict.PaintPicture ⇐
                ImageView.backpict.Picture, ⇐
                    0, ImageView.backpict.ScaleHeight * 2, ⇐
                    ImageView.backpict.ScaleWidth * 2, -1 * ⇐
                    ImageView.backpict.ScaleHeight * 2, 0, 0, ⇐
                    ImageView.backpict.ScaleWidth, ⇐
                    ImageView.backpict.ScaleHeight
            Else
                ' Normal Display
                Call StretchBlt(ImageView.disppict.hdc, 0, 0, ⇐
          ImageView.backpict.ScaleWidth * 2, ⇐
          ImageView.backpict.ScaleHeight * 2, ⇐
          ImageView.backpict.hdc, ⇐
          0, 0, ImageView.backpict.ScaleWidth, ⇐
          ImageView.backpict.ScaleHeight, SRCCOPY)
            End If
        End If

End Select

' Copy the palette from the holding picture
' to the displayed picture.  This ensures that
' the image's colors are displayed correctly.
ImageView.disppict.Picture.hPal = ImageView.backpict.Picture.hPal

End Sub

Public Sub MenuShowWindow(Index)

' Check to see which Windows (Form)
' is to be displayed.
Select Case Index

    Case 0   'Show ImageData
        ImageData.Show
        ImageData.WindowState = 0
```

```
    Case 1   'Show ImageView
        ImageView.Show
        ImageView.WindowState = 0

End Select

End Sub

Public Sub MenuOpenData()

Dim Msg As String
Dim Style As Integer
Dim Title As String
Dim Response As Integer
Dim N As Integer

'  Set the Message, Style and Title
'  of the message box
Msg = "Do you want to open the Image Database ?"
Style = vbYesNo + vbCritical + vbDefaultButton1
Title = "Open Image Database"

'  Retrieve the user's response
Response = MsgBox(Msg, Style, Title)

'  If it was a yes, then show the ImageData
'  and ImageView forms.  Also start the view
'  in Tiled mode.
If Response = vbYes Then
    ImageView.Show
    ImageData.Show
    MenuTile

    ImageTracker.ImageTool.Buttons(1).Visible = False

    For N = 2 To ImageTracker.ImageTool.Buttons.Count

        ImageTracker.ImageTool.Buttons(N).Visible = True

    Next N

    '  Ensure that the menu item's the same
    '  for the ImageData and ImageView forms
    ImageView.mShowMenu.Checked = ImageTracker.mShowMenu.Checked
    ImageData.mShowMenu.Checked = ImageTracker.mShowMenu.Checked
    ImageView.mShowTool.Checked = ImageTracker.mShowTool.Checked
    ImageData.mShowTool.Checked = ImageTracker.mShowTool.Checked

End If

End Sub

Public Sub MenuBrowse(MoveType)

Dim ImageName As String
```

continued on next page

continued from previous page

```
'   Check the RowCount.  If it is 0
'   then there are no images in the
'   database.  We then need to show the New Image
'   dialog to add the first image.
If ImageData.MSRDC1.Resultset.RowCount = 0 Then MenuNewImage: Exit Sub

'   Depending on the type of move
'   selected by the user, the result set
'   is manipulated appropriately.
Select Case MoveType

    Case 0   'Move to First Record
        ImageData.MSRDC1.Resultset.MoveFirst

    Case 1   'Move to Last Record
        ImageData.MSRDC1.Resultset.MoveLast

    Case 2   'Move to Previous Record
        ImageData.MSRDC1.Resultset.MovePrevious

    Case 3   'Move to Next Record
        ImageData.MSRDC1.Resultset.MoveNext

End Select

'   Check to see if the End of File or
'   Beginning of File has been reached in
'   the result set.  If so, then move first or
'   last to ensure that a current record is
'   always visible
If ImageData.MSRDC1.Resultset.EOF = True Then ⇐
ImageData.MSRDC1.Resultset.MoveLast
If ImageData.MSRDC1.Resultset.BOF = True Then ⇐
ImageData.MSRDC1.Resultset.MoveFirst

'   Get the Image name from the database
ImageName = ImageData.MSRDC1.Resultset("FileName")

'   Depending on whether or not the image file
'   name is set or not, the picture display is
'   set appropriately.
If ImageName <> "" Then
    ImageView.backpict.Picture = LoadPicture(ImageName): SetView IView
Else
    ImageView.backpict.Picture = LoadPicture(""): SetView IView
End If

End Sub

Public Sub MenuNewImage()

Dim ImageID As Integer
Dim ImageType As String

'   Ensure an Update is done
```

```
If ImageData.MSRDC1.Resultset.RowCount <> 0 Then
ImageData.MSRDC1.Resultset.MoveNext

'  Set the filter type of the dialog
'  box
ImageData.commondialog1.Filter = "Bitmaps (*.bmp)|*.bmp|Icons ⇐
(*.ico)|*.ico| All Files (*.*)|*.*"

'  Set the title of the dialog
ImageData.commondialog1.DialogTitle = "New Image File"

'  Set the filter index to that of the
'  bitmap
ImageData.commondialog1.FilterIndex = 1

'  Set the flags to ensure that the
'  file must exist
ImageData.commondialog1.Flags = cdlOFNFileMustExist

'  Show the dialog box
ImageData.commondialog1.ShowOpen

'  Check to see if the filename was set
If ImageData.commondialog1.filename <> "" Then

    '  Add a new record
    ImageData.MSRDC1.Resultset.AddNew

    '  Set the file name
    ImageData.MSRDC1.Resultset("FileName") = ⇐
    ImageData.commondialog1.filename

    '  Set the file size
    ImageData.MSRDC1.Resultset("FileSize") = ⇐
     FileLen(ImageData.commondialog1.filename)

    '  Get the extension of the image
    ImageType = Right$(ImageData.commondialog1.filename, 3)

    '  Set the file format depending on
    '  the extension
    Select Case UCase$(ImageType)

        Case "BMP"  'Standard bitmap
            ImageData.MSRDC1.Resultset("FileFormat") = "Bitmap"

        Case "ICO"  'Standard Icon
            ImageData.MSRDC1.Resultset("FileType") = "Icon"

    End Select

    '  Update the result set
    ImageData.MSRDC1.Resultset.Update

    '  Select SQL statement to get the
```

continued on next page

continued from previous page

```
        ' new result set
        ImageData.MSRDC1.SQL = "select * from ImageData order by ImageID"

        ' Refresh the result set
        ImageData.MSRDC1.Refresh

        ' Move to the last record which was
        ' just added.
        MenuBrowse 1

End If

End Sub

Public Sub MenuDelete()

' Delete the current record
ImageData.MSRDC1.Resultset.Delete

' Move to the next record.
MenuBrowse 3

End Sub

Public Sub MenuShowTool()

' If the toolbar is checked then
' do the logic to hide the toolbar
If ImageTracker.mShowTool.Checked = True Then

    If ImageTracker.mShowMenu.Checked = False Then Exit Sub

    ' Hide the toolbar
    ImageTracker.ImageTool.Visible = False

    ' Change the menu check
    ImageTracker.mShowTool.Checked = False

    ' If the ImageData and ImageView forms
    ' are visible then handle setting their
    ' menu check marks.  If they are not
    ' visible, they are not loaded.
    If ImageData.Visible = True Then
        ImageData.mShowTool.Checked = False
        ImageView.mShowTool.Checked = False
    End If

Else

    ' Make the toolbar visible
    ImageTracker.ImageTool.Visible = True

    ' Change the menu check
    ImageTracker.mShowTool.Checked = True

    ' If the ImageData and ImageView forms
```

```
      '   are visible then handle setting their
      '   menu check marks.  If they are not
      '   visible, they are not loaded.
      If ImageData.Visible = True Then
          ImageData.mShowTool.Checked = True
          ImageView.mShowTool.Checked = True
      End If

  End If

  End Sub

  Public Sub MenuShowMenu()

  '  Check to see If the menu is already visible
  If ImageTracker.mShowMenu.Checked = True Then

      '   If the tool bar is not visible,
      '   we do not want to also make the
      '   menu invisible
      If ImageTracker.ImageTool.Visible = False Then Exit Sub

      '   Make the ImageTracker menus
      '   invisible and set the menu
      '   check mark appropriately
      ImageTracker.mFile.Visible = False
      ImageTracker.mShowMenu.Checked = False
      ImageTracker.mWindow.Visible = False

      '   If the ImageData and ImageView forms
      '   are visible then handle setting their
      '   menu check marks and visible properties.
      '   If they are not visible, they are not
      '   loaded.
      If ImageData.Visible = True Then
          ImageData.mShowMenu.Checked = False
          ImageView.mShowMenu.Checked = False
          ImageView.mFile.Visible = False
          ImageData.mFile.Visible = False
          ImageData.mWindow.Visible = False
          ImageView.mWindow.Visible = False
          ImageData.mRecord.Visible = False
          ImageView.mRecord.Visible = False
          ImageData.mView.Visible = False
          ImageView.mView.Visible = False
          ImageView.mViewSet.Visible = False
      End If

  Else

      '   Make the ImageTracker menus
      '   visible and set the menu
      '   check mark appropriately
      ImageTracker.mFile.Visible = True
      ImageTracker.mShowMenu.Checked = True
```

continued on next page

continued from previous page

```
      ImageTracker.mWindow.Visible = True

      '   If the ImageData and ImageView forms
      '   are visible then handle setting their
      '   menu check marks and visible properties.
      '   If they are not visible, they are not
      '   loaded.
      If ImageData.Visible = True Then
          ImageData.mShowMenu.Checked = True
          ImageView.mShowMenu.Checked = True
          ImageData.mFile.Visible = True
          ImageView.mFile.Visible = True
          ImageData.mWindow.Visible = True
          ImageView.mWindow.Visible = True
          ImageData.mRecord.Visible = True
          ImageView.mRecord.Visible = True
          ImageView.mView.Visible = True
          ImageData.mView.Visible = True
          ImageView.mViewSet.Visible = True
      End If

  End If

  End Sub
```

How It Works

The key to making pop-up menus useful to the user is providing an intuitive use for already provided menus. It should become a natural habit for the user to attempt a right mouse click to bring up menu options applicable to the context of where the click was performed. In this example, each of the major user interface elements of the program are supported through right-click pop-up menus.

The `ImageView` form can be easily manipulated through both the left and right mouse buttons which provide quick access to the different methods available to manipulate the images. Because there is no specific use for the left mouse click on the `ImageView` form, it is logical to provide additional pop-up menu access to the provided manipulation methods.

The `ImageData` form pop-up menu is an intuitive one. The options for manipulating the records in the database are displayed. But, there is one additional right-click feature automatically provided by the text controls on the form. You can right-click on the text boxes and the control automatically provides the standard edit, copy, and paste menu options for manipulating the text in the control.

The example also provides the toolbar with a right-click pop-up menu which shows the Window menu options. This is useful for easily accessing all the user interface options of the program such as showing and hiding the toolbar and menus.

Comments

In this example, a user might become so comfortable with the use of the toolbar and the pop-up menu support that they no longer wish to see the menus of the forms at all, perhaps to maximize screen work space, etc. It would be a nice feature to allow the user to turn on and off the features of the interface that they do or do not wish to use.

COMPLEXITY

ADVANCED

4.4 How do I...
Make an application drag-and-drop capable?

Problem

So far my MDI application supports toolbars and pop-up menus. My users would also like to be able to manipulate images directly by dragging them to appropriate locations. How do I support drag-and-drop both in the program interface and for outside objects dropped onto the application?

Technique

Providing drag-and-drop support for an application can be implemented in two ways. The first is the simple concept of dragging and dropping the user interface elements of an application around within the application. For example, you can drag-and-drop the MDI child windows of an MDI application. Or, as this example shows, you can drag-and-drop the toolbar to either the top or the bottom of the MDI window. The other type of drag-and-drop is support for dragging objects from outside the application onto your program. In this example, it would be logical to drop image files onto the program and have them automatically added to the database. Visual Basic does not provide explicit support for this kind of drag-and-drop support. But, with a few API calls and a special custom control, **Msghook**, this can be readily accomplished.

Steps

Open and run 4-4.VBP.

Select the drag button on the toolbar to intiate the dragging of the toolbar. The toolbar can be dragged from the top to the bottom of the form or vice versa. Figure 4-8 shows the Windows Explorer with a file that has been dragged from the Explorer to the Image View window and added to the database.

Note that in the above example, multiple images can be dragged to the Image View window and all will be added to the database. However, users may want to look at a group of images without committing themselves to adding them to the database. We are going to add an Image Preview window for this purpose. Figure 4-9 shows the preview window of the program which supports images being dragged to it and displayed, but not added to the database. Note that the image from the preview window can be dragged to the Image View window and added to the database.

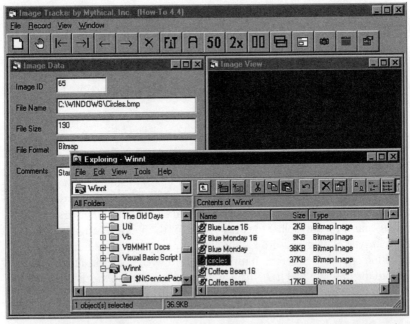

Figure 4-8 The Windows Explorer with a new image dragged and added to the database

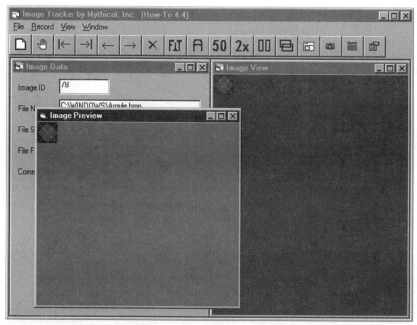

Figure 4-9 The Image Preview window

1. Create a new project called 4-4.VBP. Add the objects and properties listed in Table 4-20 to the form and save the form as **4-4.FRM**.

Table 4-20 The MDI form's objects and properties

OBJECT	PROPERTY	SETTING
MDIForm	Name	ImageTracker
	AutoShowChildren	0 'False
	BackColor	&H8000000C&
	Caption	"Image Tracker by Mythical, Inc.
		(How-To 4.4)"
Toolbar	Name	ImageTool
	Align	1 'Align Top
	Negotiate	-1 'True
	ImageList	"MDIButtons"
	ButtonWidth	926
	ButtonHeight	847
	AllowCustomize	0 'False
	NumButtons	18 (See ImageList for Button Icons)
	AlignSet	-1 'True
	Wrappable	0 'False
ImageList	Name	MDIButtons
	ImageWidth	28
	ImageHeight	26
	MaskColor	12632256
	NumImages	18
	i1	open.bmp
	i2	new.bmp
	i3	hand.bmp
	i4	first.bmp
	i5	last.bmp
	i6	prev.bmp
	i7	next.bmp
	i8	delete.bmp
	i9	fit.bmp
	i10	actual.bmp
	i11	50.bmp
	i12	2x.bmp
	i13	tile.bmp

OBJECT	PROPERTY	SETTING
	i14	cascade.bmp
	i15	data.bmp
	i16	camera.bmp
	i17	menu.bmp
	i18	prop.bmp

2. Add the menus shown in Table 4-21 to the **ImageTracker** form.

Table 4-21 The **ImageTracker** form's menus

CONTROL NAME	CAPTION	INDEX	CHECKED	SHORTCUT KEY
mFile	"&File"			
mOpenImage	"&Open Image Database"			
mBar	"-"			
mExit	"E&xit"			
mWindow	"&Window"			
mImageData	"Image &Data"			
mImageView	"Image &View"			
mBar3	"-"			
mShowTool	"Show Toolbar"		-1 'True	
mShowMenu	"Show Menu"		-1 'True	

3. Insert a new form into the project and save it as **IView.frm**. Add the objects and properties listed in Table 4-22 to the form.

Table 4-22 The Image View form's objects and properties

OBJECT	PROPERTY	SETTING
Form	Name	ImageView
	Caption	"Image View"
	MDIChild	-1 'True
PictureBox	Name	DispPict
	BackColor	&H00C00000&
	BorderStyle	0 'None
	Picture	"pastel.bmp"
	ScaleMode	3 'Pixel
PictureBox	Name	BackPict
	AutoRedraw	-1 'True

continued on next page

continued from previous page

OBJECT	PROPERTY	SETTING
	AutoSize	−1 'True
	BackColor	&H000000FF&
	BorderStyle	0 'None
	Picture	"pastel.bmp"
	ScaleMode	3 'Pixel
	Visible	0 'False
Msghook	Name	Msghook

4. Add the menus shown in Table 4-23 to the **ImageView** form.

Table 4-23 The **ImageView** form's menus

CONTROL NAME	CAPTION	INDEX	CHECKED	SHORTCUT KEY
mFile	"&File"			
mNewImage	"&New Image"			
mBar	"-"			
mExit	"E&xit"			
mRecord	"&Record"			
mBrowse	"&First"	0		F1
mBrowse	"&Last"	1		F2
mBrowse	"&Back"	2		F3
mBrowse	"For&ward"	3		F4
mBar2	"-"			
mDelete	"&Delete Record"			
mView	"&View"			
mSize	"&Fit in Window"	0		
mSize	"&Actual Size"	1	−1 'True	
mSize	"&50 Percent"	2		
mSize	"&200 Percent"	3		
mViewSet	"Viewer Settings"			
Flip	"Flip &Horizontal"	0		
Flip	"Flip &Vertical"	1		
mWindow	"&Window"			
mTile	"&Tile"			
mCascade	"&Cascade"			
mBar1	"-"			
mShowWindow	"Image &Data"	0		

CONTROL NAME	CAPTION	INDEX	CHECKED		SHORTCUT KEY
mShowWindow	"Image &View"	1			
mPreview	"Image &Preview"				
mBar3	"-"				
mShowTool	"Show Tool&Bar"		-1	'True	
mShowMenu	"Show &Menu"		-1	'True	

5. Insert a new form into the project and save it as **IData.frm**. Add the objects and properties listed in Table 4-24 to the form.

Table 4-24 The **ImageData** form's objects and properties

OBJECT	PROPERTY	SETTING
Form	Name	ImageData
	Caption	"Image Data"
	MDIChild	-1 'True
	Visible	0 'False
TextBox	Name	ImageInfo
	DataField	"Comments"
	DataSource	"MSRDC1"
	Index	4
	MultiLine	-1 'True
TextBox	Name	ImageInfo
	DataField	"FileFormat"
	DataSource	"MSRDC1"
	Index	3
TextBox	Name	ImageInfo
	DataField	"FileSize"
	DataSource	"MSRDC1"
	Index	2
	Locked	-1 'True
TextBox	Name	ImageInfo
	DataField	"FileName"
	DataSource	"MSRDC1"
	Index	1
TextBox	Name	ImageInfo
	DataField	"ImageID"
	DataSource	"MSRDC1"

continued on next page

continued from previous page

OBJECT	PROPERTY	SETTING
	Index	0
	Locked	-1 'True
CommonDialog	Name	CommonDialog1
	DefaultExt	".bmp"
	DialogTitle	"Find Image File"
	Filter	"*.bmp; *.wmf"
	FilterIndex	1
	InitDir	"c:\windows"
MSRDC	Name	MSRDC1
	Visible	0 'False
	DataSourceName	"Image Database"
	RecordSource	"select * from ImageData order by ImageID"
	RecordsetType	1
	KeysetSize	0
	ReadOnly	0 'False
	UserName	""
	Password	""
	CursorDriver	2
	EOFAction	1
	BOFAction	1
	Prompt	3
	LockType	3
Label	Name	ImageLabel
	AutoSize	-1 'True
	Caption	"Comments"
	DataSource	"MSRDC1"
	Index	4
Label	Name	ImageLabel
	AutoSize	-1 'True
	Caption	"File Format"
	DataSource	"MSRDC1"
	Index	3
Label	Name	ImageLabel
	AutoSize	-1 'True
	Caption	"File Size"
	DataSource	"MSRDC1"
	Index	2

OBJECT	PROPERTY	SETTING
Label	Name	ImageLabel
	AutoSize	-1 'True
	Caption	"File Name"
	DataSource	"MSRDC1"
	Index	1
Label	Name	ImageLabel
	AutoSize	-1 'True
	Caption	"Image ID"
	DataSource	"MSRDC1"
	Index	0

6. Add the menus shown in Table 4-25 to the `ImageData` form.

Table 4-25 The `ImageData` form's menus

CONTROL NAME	CAPTION	INDEX	CHECKED	SHORTCUT KEY
mFile	"&File"			
mNewImage	"&New Image"			
mBar	"-"			
mExit	"E&xit"			
mRecord	"&Record"			
mBrowse	"&First"	0		F1
mBrowse	"&Last"	1		F2
mBrowse	"&Back"	2		F3
mBrowse	"For&ward"	3		F4
mBar2	"-"			
mDelete	"&Delete Record"			
mView	"&View"			
mSize	"&Fit in Window"	0		
mSize	"&Actual Size"	1	-1 'True	
mSize	"&50 Percent"	2		
mSize	"&200 Percent"	3		
mWindow	"&Window"			
mTile	"&Tile"			
mCascade	"&Cascade"			
mBar1	"-"			

continued on next page

continued from previous page

CONTROL NAME	CAPTION	INDEX	CHECKED	SHORTCUT KEY
mShowWindow	"Image &Data"	0		
mShowWindow	"Image &View"	1		
mPreview	"Image &Preview"			
mBar3	"-"			
mShowTool	"Show Tool&Bar"		-1 'True	
mShowMenu	"Show &Menu"		-1 'True	

7. Insert a new form into the project and save it as `Preview.frm`. This form will become the Image Preview window. Add the objects and properties listed in Table 4-26 to the form.

Table 4-26 The `Preview` form's objects and properties

OBJECT	PROPERTY	SETTING
Form	Name	Preview
	Caption	"Image Preview"
PictureBox	Name	PrevPict
	Appearance	0 'Flat
	BackColor	&H00808080&
	BorderStyle	0 'None
	DragIcon	"pastel.bmp"
	DragMode	1 'Automatic
	ForeColor	&H80000008&
Msghook	Name	Msghook

> **NOTE**
>
> Only the new code added to the project will be commented. If you need additional information regarding the other code, see the previous How-To's for a complete explanation.

8. Add the following set of code to the `ImageTracker` form. The `ButtonClick` event of the toolbar handles calling the appropriate routines for each toolbar button. Note that the last button initiates the drag process for the toolbar control.

```
Private Sub ImageTool_ButtonClick(ByVal Button As Button)

Select Case Button.Index

    Case 1
```

```
     '  Open the Image Database
     MenuOpenData

Case 2

     '  Call the MenuNewImage function to get
     '  a new image
     MenuNewImage

Case 3
     '  Exit the program
     MenuExit

Case 4
     '  Move to the first record
     MenuBrowse 0

Case 5
     '  Move to the last record
     MenuBrowse 1

Case 6
     '  Move back a record
     MenuBrowse 2

Case 7
     '  Move forward a record
     MenuBrowse 3

Case 8
     '  Delete the current record
     '  of the result set
     MenuDelete

Case 9
     '  Set the View to fit in the Window
     SetView 0

Case 10
     '  Set the View to actual size
     SetView 1

Case 11
     '  Set the View to 50 %
     SetView 2

Case 12
     '  Set the View to 200 %
     SetView 3

Case 13
     '  Tile the windows
     MenuTile
```

continued on next page

continued from previous page

```
    Case 14
        ' Cascade the Windows
        MenuCascade

    Case 15
        ' If the ImageData form is not
        ' visible then call the
        ' MenuOpenData function to open
        ' the database.  Otherwise, show
        ' the ImageData Window (0)
        If ImageData.Visible = False Then
            MenuOpenData
        Else
            MenuShowWindow 0
        End If

    Case 16
        ' If the ImageData form is not
        ' visible then call the
        ' MenuOpenData function to open
        ' the database.  Otherwise, show
        ' the ImageView Window (1)
        If ImageData.Visible = False Then
            MenuOpenData
        Else
            MenuShowWindow 1
        End If

    Case 17
        ' Show or hide the Menu depending
        ' on the current setting.
        MenuShowMenu

    Case 18
        ' Start the drag process for the
        ' toolbar.
        ImageTool.Drag

End Select

End Sub

Private Sub ImageTool_MouseDown(Button As Integer, Shift As Integer, X ⇐
As Single, Y As Single)

' Check for the right mouse
' button click
If Button = vbPopupMenuRightButton Then

    ' If the ImageData form is not visible then
    ' show the popup menu for ImageTracker form.
    ' Otherwise show the pop up menu for the
    ' ImageData form.
    If ImageData.Visible = False Then
        Me.PopupMenu mWindow, vbPopupMenuCenterAlign, , , mShowTool
```

```
    Else
        ImageData.PopupMenu ImageData.mWindow, vbPopupMenuCenterAlign, , ⇐
        , ImageData.mShowTool
    End If

End If

End Sub
```

9. When the MDI form has a control dropped on it, which in this case is the toolbar, a check is done to see whether the toolbar is dropped on the top half or the bottom half of the MDI form. Depending on which half, the alignment of the toolbar is changed.

```
Private Sub MDIForm_DragDrop(Source As Control, X As Single, Y As Single)

'   Check to see if the drop was on
'   the top or bottom half of the
'   MDI form
If (Y - (ImageTool.Height / 2)) > (ImageTracker.Height / 2) Then
    ImageTool.Align = 2
Else
    ImageTool.Align = 1
End If

End Sub


Private Sub MDIForm_Load()

'   Hide the ImageData form when
'   the MDI form is first loaded
ImageData.Hide

End Sub


Private Sub MDIForm_MouseDown(Button As Integer, Shift As Integer, X As ⇐
Single, Y As Single)

'   If the ImageData form is not visible,
'   then show the File menu from the
'   ImageTracker form
If (Button = vbPopupMenuRightButton) And (ImageData.Visible <> True) Then
    Me.PopupMenu mFile, vbPopupMenuCenterAlign, , , mOpenImage
    Exit Sub
End If

'   If the ImageData form is visible,
'   then show the Window menu from the
'   ImageData form
If (Button = vbPopupMenuRightButton) And (ImageData.Visible = True) Then
    ImageData.PopupMenu ImageData.mWindow, vbPopupMenuCenterAlign ', , ⇐
    , ImageData.mImageData
End If

End Sub
```

continued on next page

continued from previous page

```
Private Sub MDIForm_QueryUnload(Cancel As Integer, UnloadMode As Integer)

'   Call the MenuExit program to
'   end the program
MenuExit

End Sub

Private Sub MDIForm_Unload(Cancel As Integer)

'   Call the MenuExit program to
'   end the program
MenuExit

End Sub

Private Sub mExit_Click()

'   Call the MenuExit program to
'   end the program
MenuExit

End Sub

Private Sub mImageData_Click()

'   Call the MenuOpenData method to open the
'   Image database
MenuOpenData

End Sub

Private Sub mImageView_Click()

'   Call the MenuOpenData method to open the
'   Image database
MenuOpenData

End Sub

Private Sub mOpenImage_Click()

'   Call the MenuOpenData method to open the
'   Image database
MenuOpenData

End Sub

Private Sub mShowMenu_Click()

'   Show or hide the Menu
MenuShowMenu

End Sub
```

```
Private Sub mShowTool_Click()

'   Show or hide the Toolbar
MenuShowTool

End Sub
```

10. Add the following set of code to the `ImageView` form. The `DragDrop` event of the `DispPict` control handles the drag-and-drop of the toolbar as well as the drop of a picture control from the preview picture. For the toolbar, a check is done to see which half of the display picture the toolbar has been dropped on, and the toolbar is aligned appropriately. If the toolbar was not the dropped object, then the only other object that can be dropped onto the picture is the preview image. In that case, the `PreviewFileName` public property of the `Preview` form is checked to see whether there is a current image loaded into the preview window. If so, then the `DropNewImage` function is called.

```
Private Sub DispPict_DragDrop(Source As Control, X As Single, Y As Single)

'   If the dropped control is the
'   toolbar then we need to do the
'   necessary checking to see if the
'   toolbar should be re-aligned
If Source.Name = "ImageTool" Then

    '   Check to see if the toolbar drop
    '   was on the top or bottom half of the
    '   picture box.  Note that the picture
    '   box is in pixel mode so we need to
    '   convert the coordinates to twips.
    If ((Y * Screen.TwipsPerPixelY) - (ImageTracker.ImageTool.Height / 2)) ⇐

        > (ImageTracker.Height / 2) Then
        ImageTracker.ImageTool.Align = 2
    Else
        ImageTracker.ImageTool.Align = 1
    End If

    Exit Sub

End If

'   Otherwise a new file should have
'   been dropped on the picture box
'   from the preview window.  We need
'   to check to ensure that there is
'   a picture file associated with the
'   preview.  If so then add the image to
'   the database.
If Preview.PreviewFileName <> "" Then
    DropNewImage Preview.PreviewFileName
End If

End Sub
```

11. The Show Preview menu option shows the preview window.

```
Private Sub mPreview_Click()

'   Show the preview window
Preview.Show

End Sub
```

12. The `Msghook` control handles processing messages to the control's parent window. In this case, we will be checking for the `WM_DROPFILES` message which indicates that a file has been dropped from the Windows Explorer. The `DragQueryFile` API function is first used to retrieve the number of files dragged from the Explorer `DragQueryFile` is also used to return the filename of the specified dropped file. It is then checked to see whether it is a bitmap or an icon. If it is an image file, then the `DropNewImage` routine is called to add the image to the database.

```
Private Sub Msghook_Message(ByVal msg As Long, ByVal wp As Long, ByVal lp ⇐
As Long, result As Long)

Dim NumFiles As Integer
Dim Buffer As String 'Byte
Dim N As Integer
Dim NameLen As Integer

'   Set the buffer up to recieve the
'   filename
Buffer = Space$(256)

'   See if the drop file message was
'   sent
If msg = WM_DROPFILES Then

    '   Retrieve the number of files
    '   dropped.
    NumFiles = DragQueryFile(wp, -1&, Buffer, Len(Buffer))

    '   Loop through the files and add them to
    '   the image database.
    For N = 0 To (NumFiles - 1)

        '   Get the filename of the file and
        '   retrieve the length of the
        '   filename
        NameLen = DragQueryFile(wp, N, Buffer, 128)

        '   Check to see if the file is a
        '   bitmap or icon.
        If (UCase(Right((Left(Buffer, NameLen)), 3)) = "BMP") ⇐
    Or (UCase(Right((Left(Buffer, NameLen)), 3)) = "ICO") Then

            '   Add the image to the database
            DropNewImage Left(Buffer, NameLen)
```

```
        End If

    Next N

    ' Tell the system the drag is done
    Call DragFinish(wp)

    '  Set the result
    result = 0

End If

End Sub

Public Sub SizeViewPict()

'  Allow for a small border
'  around the display picture
disppict.Top = 5
disppict.Left = 5
disppict.Width = Me.Width - 5
disppict.Height = Me.Height - 5

'  Set the view to the current
'  view option
SetView IView

End Sub

Private Sub DispPict_Paint()

'  Size the view picture
SizeViewPict

End Sub

Private Sub DispPict_MouseDown(Button As Integer, Shift As Integer, X As ⇐
Single, Y As Single)

'  If the right mouse button is selected, then
'  the different image size options are shown.  If
'  it is a left mouse click then the flip options
'  are shown
If Button = vbPopupMenuRightButton Then
    Me.PopupMenu mView, vbPopupMenuCenterAlign, , , mSize(0)
Else
    Me.PopupMenu mViewSet, vbPopupMenuCenterAlign
End If

End Sub

Private Sub Flip_Click(Index As Integer)

'  When the flip menu is clicked, the
'  check on the menu is set appropriately
If flip(Index).Checked = False Then
```

continued on next page

continued from previous page

```
        flip(Index).Checked = True
Else
        flip(Index).Checked = False
End If


'  It is important to ensure that only
'  a vertical or horizontal flip can be
'  performed.  Thus, the menu item that
'  was not clicked is unchecked.
If Index = 1 Then
        flip(0).Checked = False
Else
        flip(1).Checked = False
End If


'  Based on the selection,
'  the image is redisplayed.
SizeViewPict

End Sub
```

13. When the form is loaded, the **EnableFileDrop** routine is called to enable the form to accept the drop files message from the system. Also, the **Msghook** control is set up to handle the messages for the form and sets the control to receive the **WM_DROPFILES** message.

```
Private Sub Form_Load()

'  Enable the form to accept
'  file drops
EnableFileDrop Me.hwnd

'  Setup MsgHook control
Msghook.HwndHook = Me.hwnd
Msghook.Message(WM_DROPFILES) = True

'  Intially set IView to 0.
IView = 1

'  Call the MenuBrowse function
'  to show the first record
MenuBrowse 1

End Sub

Private Sub Form_Unload(Cancel As Integer)

'  Cancel the unload.  We don't want the
'  form to be unloaded while the program is
'  running so that it does not have to be
'  re-initialized.  Instead, the form will be
'  minimized.
Cancel = -1
Me.WindowState = 1
```

```
End Sub

Private Sub mBrowse_Click(Index As Integer)

'   Browse the record set depending on the
'   menu option chosen.
MenuBrowse Index

End Sub

Private Sub mCascade_Click()

'   Cascade the windows
MenuCascade

'   Size the view picture after the cascade
SizeViewPict

End Sub

Private Sub mDelete_Click()

'   Call the MenuDelete function to
'   delete the selected record.
MenuDelete

End Sub

Private Sub mExit_Click()

'   Call the MenuExit function to
'   exit the program.
MenuExit

End Sub

Private Sub mNewImage_Click()

'   Call the MenuNewImage function to get
'   a new image
MenuNewImage

End Sub

Private Sub mShowMenu_Click()

'   Show or hide the Menu
MenuShowMenu

End Sub

Private Sub mShowTool_Click()

'   Show or hide the toolbar
MenuShowTool
```

continued on next page

continued from previous page

```vb
End Sub

Private Sub mShowWindow_Click(Index As Integer)

' Call the MenuShowWindow function to show
' the selected window.
MenuShowWindow Index

End Sub

Private Sub mTile_Click()

' Call the menu tile function to
' tile the windows
MenuTile

End Sub

Private Sub mSize_Click(Index As Integer)

' Set the view depending on the menu option
' selected
SetView Index

End Sub
```

14. Add the following set of code to the **ImageData** form.

```vb
Private Sub Form_MouseDown(Button As Integer, Shift As Integer, X As ⇐
Single, Y As Single)

If Button = vbPopupMenuRightButton Then
    ' Show the Record menu for moving
    ' through the image records in the
    ' database
    Me.PopupMenu mRecord, vbPopupMenuCenterAlign, , , mBrowse(3)

End If

End Sub

Private Sub Form_Resize()

Dim n As Integer

' Resize the Image Info controls to
' fit on the form when it is resized
For n = 1 To 4
    ImageData.ImageInfo(n).Width = ImageData.Width - ⇐
    ImageData.ImageInfo(n).Left - 300
Next n

End Sub
```

```vb
Private Sub Form_Unload(Cancel As Integer)

'  We don't want the form to be unloaded so that
'  it will not have to be re-initialized

Cancel = -1

'  Instead minimize the form
Me.WindowState = 1

End Sub

Private Sub mBrowse_Click(Index As Integer)

'  Browse the result set depending
'  on the menu selected
MenuBrowse Index

End Sub

Private Sub mCascade_Click()

'  Cascade the windows
MenuCascade

End Sub

Private Sub mDelete_Click()

'  Delete the current record
'  of the result set
MenuDelete

End Sub

Private Sub mExit_Click()

'  Call the MenuExit method to
'  exit the program
MenuExit

End Sub

Private Sub mNewImage_Click()

'  Cal the MenuNewImage function to allow
'  the user to select a new image to add to the
'  database
MenuNewImage

End Sub
```

15. The Show Preview menu option handles showing the Preview window.

```
Private Sub mPreview_Click()

'   Show the Preview form
Preview.Show

End Sub

Private Sub mShowMenu_Click()

'   Show or hide the Menu
MenuShowMenu

End Sub

Private Sub mShowTool_Click()

'   Show or hide the toolbar
MenuShowTool

End Sub

Private Sub mShowWindow_Click(Index As Integer)

'   Call the MenuShowWindow function to show
'   the window selected
MenuShowWindow Index

End Sub

Private Sub mSize_Click(Index As Integer)

'   Set the View based on the menu
'   selection
SetView Index

End Sub

Private Sub mTile_Click()

'   Tile the windows
MenuTile

End Sub
```

16. Add the following set of code to the **Preview** form. The **PreviewFileName**
public variable will hold the name of the dropped image onto the Preview
window. This will be used when the preview picture is dropped onto the
database viewer. The filename in the variable will be used as a reference to
the image to be tracked.

```
'   Public property that will indicate
'   what filename is associated with
'   the preview

Public PreviewFileName As String
```

17. When the form is loaded, the `EnableFileDrop` routine is called to enable the form to accept the drop files message from the system. Also, the `Msghook` control is set up to handle the messages for the `Preview` form and set the control to receive the `WM_DROPFILES` message.

```vb
Private Sub Form_Load()

'   Enable the preview to accept
'   file drag and drop
EnableFileDrop Me.hwnd

'   Setup the MsgHook control
Msghook.HwndHook = Me.hwnd
Msghook.Message(WM_DROPFILES) = True

'   Move the preview picture to the
'   top left
PrevPict.Top = 0
PrevPict.Left = 0

'   Set the preview picture width
'   and height
PrevPict.Width = Preview.Width
PrevPict.Height = Preview.Height

End Sub

Private Sub Form_Resize()

'   When the form is resized,
'   resize the picture
PrevPict.Width = Preview.Width
PrevPict.Height = Preview.Height

End Sub

Private Sub Form_Unload(Cancel As Integer)

'   When the preview is unloaded,
'   make sure the ImageTracker form
'   is visible
ImageTracker.Show

End Sub
```

18. The `Msghook` control handles processing messages to the control's parent window. In this case, we will be checking for the `WM_DROPFILES` message which indicates that a file has been dropped from the Windows Explorer. The `DragQueryFile` API function is first used to retrieve the number of files dragged from the Explorer. `DragQueryFile` is also used to return the filename of the specified dropped file. It is then checked to see whether it is a bitmap or an icon. If it is an image file, then the `DropNewImage` routine is called to add the image to the database.

```vb
Private Sub Msghook_Message(ByVal msg As Long, ByVal wp As Long, ByVal lp ⇐
As Long, result As Long)

Dim NumFiles As Integer
Dim Buffer As String 'Byte
Dim N As Integer
Dim NameLen As Integer

' Set the buffer up to recieve the
' filename
Buffer = Space$(256)

' See if the drop file message was
' sent
If msg = WM_DROPFILES Then

    ' Retrieve the number of files
    ' dropped.
    NumFiles = DragQueryFile(wp, -1&, Buffer, Len(Buffer))

    ' Get the filename of the file and
    ' retrieve the length of the
    ' filename
    NameLen = DragQueryFile(wp, N, Buffer, 128)

    ' Check to see if the file is a
    ' bitmap or icon.
    If (UCase(Right((Left(Buffer, NameLen)), 3)) = "BMP") Or ⇐
    (UCase(Right((Left(Buffer, NameLen)), 3)) = "ICO") Then

        ' Load the picture into the preview
        PrevPict.Picture = LoadPicture(Left(Buffer, NameLen))

        ' Set the filename of the form
        PreviewFileName = Left(Buffer, NameLen)

    End If

    ' Tell the system the drag is done.
    Call DragFinish(wp)

    ' Set the result
    result = 0

End If

End Sub
```

19. Insert a new module into the project and save it as `MenLogic.bas`. This code handles most of the menu logic for the **ImageData** and **ImageView** forms.

```vb
' StretchBlit will be used for the Image Viewer
Private Declare Function StretchBlt Lib "gdi32" (ByVal hdc As Long, ⇐
ByVal X As Long, ByVal Y As Long, ByVal nWidth As Long, ByVal nHeight ⇐
```

```
As Long, ByVal hSrcDC As Long, ByVal xSrc As Long, ByVal ySrc As Long, ⇐
ByVal nSrcWidth As Long, ByVal nSrcHeight As Long, ByVal dwRop As Long) ⇐
As Long

Const SRCCOPY = &HCC0020

'   IView globally stores the current view for
'   the image I.E.  Fit in Window, 50%
Public IView As Integer

'   Handles ending the program when
'   users select exit from the menu
Public Sub MenuExit()
    End
End Sub

'   Handles tiling the windows
'   on the MDI form
Public Sub MenuTile()

'   Do a vertical tile
ImageTracker.Arrange vbTileVertical

End Sub

Public Sub MenuCascade()

'   Cascade the child forms
ImageTracker.Arrange vbCascade

End Sub

Public Sub SetView(Index)

'   When a new image view is selected,
'   the original menu selection is
'   unchecked
ImageView.mSize(IView).Checked = False
ImageData.mSize(IView).Checked = False

'   Set the new view to the index
'   parameter
IView = Index

'   Check the new menu option for the
'   selected view.
ImageData.mSize(IView).Checked = True
ImageView.mSize(IView).Checked = True

'   Clear the displayed picture
ImageView.disppict.Cls

ImageView.disppict.Picture.hPal = ImageView.backpict.Picture.hPal
```

continued on next page

continued from previous page

```
'   Depending on the view selected, the
'   original image will be copied to the
'   display picture appropriately
Select Case IView

'   Note that for the vertical and
'   horizontal flips, the height or
'   width is set to a negative value
'   and the starting point is set to
'   the height or width for the image
'   to be displayed.

    Case 0   'Fit in the Window
        If ImageView.flip(0).Checked = True Then
            '   Flip Horizontal
            ImageView.disppict.PaintPicture ImageView.backpict.Picture, ⇐
        ImageView.disppict.ScaleWidth, 0, -1 * ⇐
        ImageView.disppict.ScaleWidth, ImageView.disppict.ScaleHeight, ⇐
        0, 0, ImageView.backpict.ScaleWidth, _
          ImageView.backpict.ScaleHeight
        Else

            If ImageView.flip(1).Checked = True Then
                '   Flip Vertical
                ImageView.disppict.PaintPicture ⇐
        ImageView.backpict.Picture, ⇐
        0, ImageView.disppict.ScaleHeight, ⇐
        ImageView.disppict.ScaleWidth, -1 * ⇐
        ImageView.disppict.ScaleHeight, 0, 0, ⇐
        ImageView.backpict.ScaleWidth, ⇐
        ImageView.backpict.ScaleHeight
            Else
                '   Normal Display
                Call StretchBlt(ImageView.disppict.hdc, 0, 0, ⇐
        ImageView.disppict.ScaleWidth, ⇐
        ImageView.disppict.ScaleHeight, ImageView.backpict.hdc, 0, ⇐
        0, ImageView.backpict.ScaleWidth, ⇐
        ImageView.backpict.ScaleHeight, SRCCOPY)
            End If
        End If

    Case 1   'Actual Size
        If ImageView.flip(0).Checked = True Then
            '   Flip Horizontal
            ImageView.disppict.PaintPicture ImageView.backpict.Picture, ⇐
        ImageView.backpict.ScaleWidth, 0, -1 * ⇐
        ImageView.backpict.ScaleWidth, ImageView.backpict.ScaleHeight, ⇐
        0, 0, ImageView.backpict.ScaleWidth, ImageView.backpict.ScaleHeight
        Else
            If ImageView.flip(1).Checked = True Then
                '   Flip Vertical
                ImageView.disppict.PaintPicture ⇐
                ImageView.backpict.Picture, ⇐
        0, ImageView.backpict.ScaleHeight, ⇐
```

```
        ImageView.backpict.ScaleWidth, -1 * ⇐
        ImageView.backpict.ScaleHeight, 0, 0, ⇐
        ImageView.backpict.ScaleWidth, ImageView.backpict.ScaleHeight
         Else
              '  Normal Display
              Call StretchBlt(ImageView.disppict.hdc, 0, 0, ⇐
        ImageView.backpict.ScaleWidth, ⇐
        ImageView.backpict.ScaleHeight,  ImageView.backpict.hdc, 0, ⇐
        0, ImageView.backpict.ScaleWidth, ⇐
        ImageView.backpict.ScaleHeight, SRCCOPY)
         End If
      End If

Case 2 '50%
    If ImageView.flip(0).Checked = True Then
          '  Flip Horizontal
          ImageView.disppict.PaintPicture ImageView.backpict.Picture, ⇐
        ImageView.backpict.ScaleWidth * 0.5, 0, -1 * ⇐
        ImageView.backpict.ScaleWidth *0.5, ⇐
        ImageView.backpict.ScaleHeight * 0.5, 0, 0, ⇐
        ImageView.backpict.ScaleWidth, ImageView.backpict.ScaleHeight
      Else
          If ImageView.flip(1).Checked = True Then
              '  Flip Vertical
            ImageView.disppict.PaintPicture ImageView.backpict.Picture, ⇐
            0, ImageView.backpict.ScaleHeight * 0.5, ⇐
            ImageView.backpict.ScaleWidth * 0.5, -1 * ⇐
            ImageView.backpict.ScaleHeight * 0.5, 0, 0, ⇐
            ImageView.backpict.ScaleWidth, ImageView.backpict.ScaleHeight
          Else
              '   Normal Display
              Call StretchBlt(ImageView.disppict.hdc, 0, 0, ⇐
            ImageView.backpict.ScaleWidth * 0.5, ⇐
            ImageView.backpict.ScaleHeight * 0.5, ⇐
            ImageView.backpict.hdc, 0, 0, ⇐
            ImageView.backpict.ScaleWidth, ⇐
           ImageView.backpict.ScaleHeight, SRCCOPY)
          End If
      End If

Case 3 '200%
    If ImageView.flip(0).Checked = True Then
          '  Flip Horizontal
        ImageView.disppict.PaintPicture ImageView.backpict.Picture, ⇐
        ImageView.backpict.ScaleWidth * 2, 0, -1 * ⇐
        ImageView.backpict.ScaleWidth * 2, ⇐
        ImageView.backpict.ScaleHeight ⇐
        2, 0, 0, ImageView.backpict.ScaleWidth, ⇐
        ImageView.backpict.ScaleHeight
      Else
          If ImageView.flip(1).Checked = True Then
              '  Flip Vertical
              ImageView.disppict.PaintPicture ⇐
              ImageView.backpict.Picture, ⇐
```

continued on next page

continued from previous page

```
                        0, ImageView.backpict.ScaleHeight * 2, ⇐
                        ImageView.backpict.ScaleWidth * 2, -1 * ⇐
                        ImageView.backpict.ScaleHeight * 2, 0, 0, ⇐
                        ImageView.backpict.ScaleWidth, ⇐
                        ImageView.backpict.ScaleHeight
                Else
                    '  Normal Display
                     Call StretchBlt(ImageView.disppict.hdc, 0, 0, ⇐
                        ImageView.backpict.ScaleWidth * 2, ⇐
                        ImageView.backpict.ScaleHeight * 2, ⇐
                        ImageView.backpict.hdc, ⇐
                        0, 0, ImageView.backpict.ScaleWidth, ⇐
                        ImageView.backpict.ScaleHeight, SRCCOPY)
                End If
            End If

End Select

'  Copy the palette from the holding picture
'  to the displayed picture.  This ensures that
'  the images colors are displayed correctly.
ImageView.disppict.Picture.hPal = ImageView.backpict.Picture.hPal

End Sub

Public Sub MenuShowWindow(Index)

'  Check to see which Windows (Form)
'  is to be displayed.
Select Case Index

    Case 0  'Show ImageData
        ImageData.Show
        ImageData.WindowState = 0

    Case 1  'Show ImageView
        ImageView.Show
        ImageView.WindowState = 0

End Select

End Sub

Public Sub MenuOpenData()

Dim msg As String
Dim Style As Integer
Dim Title As String
Dim Response As Integer
Dim N As Integer

'  Set the Message, Style and Title
'  of the message box
```

```
msg = "Do you want to open the Image Database ?"
Style = vbYesNo + vbCritical + vbDefaultButton1
Title = "Open Image Database"

'  Retrieve the users response
Response = MsgBox(msg, Style, Title)

'  If it was a yes, then show the ImageData
'  and ImageView forms.  Also start the view
'  in Tiled mode.
If Response = vbYes Then
    ImageView.Show
    ImageData.Show
    MenuTile

    ImageTracker.ImageTool.Buttons(1).Visible = False

    For N = 2 To ImageTracker.ImageTool.Buttons.Count

        ImageTracker.ImageTool.Buttons(N).Visible = True

    Next N

    '  Ensure that the menu item's the same
    '  for the ImageData and ImageView forms
    ImageView.mShowMenu.Checked = ImageTracker.mShowMenu.Checked
    ImageData.mShowMenu.Checked = ImageTracker.mShowMenu.Checked
    ImageView.mShowTool.Checked = ImageTracker.mShowTool.Checked
    ImageData.mShowTool.Checked = ImageTracker.mShowTool.Checked

End If

End Sub

Public Sub MenuBrowse(MoveType)

Dim ImageName As String

'  Check the RowCount.  If it is 0
'  then there are no images in the
'  database.  We then need to show the New Image
'  dialog to add the first image.
If ImageData.MSRDC1.Resultset.RowCount = 0 Then MenuNewImage: Exit Sub

'  Depending on the type of move
'  selected by the user, the result set
'  is manipulated appropriately.
Select Case MoveType

    Case 0  'Move to First Record
        ImageData.MSRDC1.Resultset.MoveFirst

    Case 1  'Move to Last Record
        ImageData.MSRDC1.Resultset.MoveLast
```

continued on next page

continued from previous page

```
      Case 2  'Move to Previous Record
            ImageData.MSRDC1.Resultset.MovePrevious

      Case 3  'Move to Next Record
            ImageData.MSRDC1.Resultset.MoveNext

End Select

' Check to see if the End of File or
' Beginning of File has been reached in
' the result set.  If so, then move first or
' last to ensure that a current record is
' always visible
If ImageData.MSRDC1.Resultset.EOF = True Then ⇐
ImageData.MSRDC1.Resultset.MoveLast

If ImageData.MSRDC1.Resultset.BOF = True Then ⇐
ImageData.MSRDC1.Resultset.MoveFirst

' Get the Image name from the database
ImageName = ImageData.MSRDC1.Resultset("FileName")

' Depending on whether or not the image file
' name is set or not, the picture display is
' set appropriately.
If ImageName <> "" Then
    ImageView.backpict.Picture = LoadPicture(ImageName): SetView IView
Else
    ImageView.backpict.Picture = LoadPicture(""): SetView IView
End If

End Sub

Public Sub MenuNewImage()

Dim ImageID As Integer
Dim ImageType As String

' Ensure an Update is done
If ImageData.MSRDC1.Resultset.RowCount <> 0 Then
ImageData.MSRDC1.Resultset.MoveNext

' Set the filter type of the dialog
' box
ImageData.commondialog1.Filter = "Bitmaps (*.bmp)|*.bmp|Icons ⇐
(*.ico)|*.ico|All Files (*.*)|*.*"

' Set the title of the dialog
ImageData.commondialog1.DialogTitle = "New Image File"

' Set the filter index to that of the
' bitmap
ImageData.commondialog1.FilterIndex = 1
```

```
'   Set the flags to ensure that the
'   file must exist
ImageData.commondialog1.Flags = cdlOFNFileMustExist

'   Show the dialog box
ImageData.commondialog1.ShowOpen

'   Check to see if the filename was set
If ImageData.commondialog1.FileName <> "" Then

    '   Add a new record
    ImageData.MSRDC1.Resultset.AddNew

    '   Set the file name
    ImageData.MSRDC1.Resultset("FileName") = ⇐
    ImageData.commondialog1.FileName

    '   Set the file size
    ImageData.MSRDC1.Resultset("FileSize") = ⇐
      FileLen(ImageData.commondialog1.FileName)

    '   Get the extension of the image
    ImageType = Right$(ImageData.commondialog1.FileName, 3)

    '   Set the file format depending on
    '   the the extension
    Select Case UCase$(ImageType)

        Case "BMP"  'Standard bitmap
            ImageData.MSRDC1.Resultset("FileFormat") = "Bitmap"

        Case "ICO"  'Standard Icon
            ImageData.MSRDC1.Resultset("FileType") = "Icon"

    End Select

    '   Update the result set
    ImageData.MSRDC1.Resultset.Update

    '   Select SQL statement to get the
    '   new result set
    ImageData.MSRDC1.SQL = "select * from ImageData order by ImageID"

    '   Refresh the result set
    ImageData.MSRDC1.Refresh

    '   Move to the last record which was
    '   just added.
    MenuBrowse 1

End If

End Sub

Public Sub MenuDelete()
```

continued on next page

continued from previous page

```
'   Delete the current record
ImageData.MSRDC1.Resultset.Delete

'   Move to the next record.
MenuBrowse 3

End Sub

Public Sub MenuShowTool()

'   If the toolbar is checked then
'   do the logic to hide the toolbar
If ImageTracker.mShowTool.Checked = True Then

    If ImageTracker.mShowMenu.Checked = False Then Exit Sub

    '   Hide the toolbar
    ImageTracker.ImageTool.Visible = False

    '   Change the menu check
    ImageTracker.mShowTool.Checked = False

    '   If the ImageData and ImageView forms
    '   are visible then handle setting their
    '   menu check marks.  If they are not
    '   visible, they are not loaded.
    If ImageData.Visible = True Then
        ImageData.mShowTool.Checked = False
        ImageView.mShowTool.Checked = False
    End If

Else

    '   Make the toolbar visible
    ImageTracker.ImageTool.Visible = True

    '   Change the menu check
    ImageTracker.mShowTool.Checked = True

    '   If the ImageData and ImageView forms
    '   are visible then handle setting their
    '   menu check marks.  If they are not
    '   visible, they are not loaded.
    If ImageData.Visible = True Then
        ImageData.mShowTool.Checked = True
        ImageView.mShowTool.Checked = True
    End If

End If

End Sub

Public Sub MenuShowMenu()

'   Check to see If the menu is already visible
```

```
If ImageTracker.mShowMenu.Checked = True Then

    '  If the tool bar is not visible,
    '  we do not want to also make the
    '  menu invisible
    If ImageTracker.ImageTool.Visible = False Then Exit Sub

    '  Make the ImageTracker menus
    '  invisible and set the menu
    '  check mark appropriately
    ImageTracker.mFile.Visible = False
    ImageTracker.mShowMenu.Checked = False
    ImageTracker.mWindow.Visible = False

    '  If the ImageData and ImageView forms
    '  are visible then handle setting their
    '  menu check marks and visible properties.
    '  If they are not visible, they are not
    '  loaded.
    If ImageData.Visible = True Then
        ImageData.mShowMenu.Checked = False
        ImageView.mShowMenu.Checked = False
        ImageView.mFile.Visible = False
        ImageData.mFile.Visible = False
        ImageData.mWindow.Visible = False
        ImageView.mWindow.Visible = False
        ImageData.mRecord.Visible = False
        ImageView.mRecord.Visible = False
        ImageData.mView.Visible = False
        ImageView.mView.Visible = False
        ImageView.mViewSet.Visible = False
    End If

Else

    '  Make the ImageTracker menus
    '  visible and set the menu
    '  check mark appropriately
    ImageTracker.mFile.Visible = True
    ImageTracker.mShowMenu.Checked = True
    ImageTracker.mWindow.Visible = True

    '  If the ImageData and ImageView forms
    '  are visible then handle setting their
    '  menu check marks and visible properties.
    '  If they are not visible, they are not
    '  loaded.
    If ImageData.Visible = True Then
        ImageData.mShowMenu.Checked = True
        ImageView.mShowMenu.Checked = True
        ImageData.mFile.Visible = True
        ImageView.mFile.Visible = True
        ImageData.mWindow.Visible = True
        ImageView.mWindow.Visible = True
        ImageData.mRecord.Visible = True
```

continued on next page

continued from previous page

```
            ImageView.mRecord.Visible = True
            ImageView.mView.Visible = True
            ImageData.mView.Visible = True
            ImageView.mViewSet.Visible = True
        End If

    End If

    End Sub
```

20. The `DropNewImage` routine handles adding the newly dropped image to the database. First, the next record in the database is moved to the next record, which ensures that the update is done for the current record. Then a new record is added to the database and the different fields set to the Image file information.

```
Public Sub DropNewImage(FileName)

Dim ImageID As Integer
Dim ImageType As String

'   Ensure an Update is done
ImageData.MSRDC1.Resultset.MoveNext

'   Add a new record
ImageData.MSRDC1.Resultset.AddNew

'   Set the file name
ImageData.MSRDC1.Resultset("FileName") = FileName

'   Set the file size
ImageData.MSRDC1.Resultset("FileSize") = FileLen(FileName)

'   Get the extension of the image
ImageType = Right$(FileName, 3)

'   Set the file format depending on
'   the extension
Select Case UCase$(ImageType)

    Case "BMP"   'Standard bitmap
        ImageData.MSRDC1.Resultset("FileFormat") = "Bitmap"

    Case "ICO"   'Standard Icon
        ImageData.MSRDC1.Resultset("FileType") = "Icon"

End Select

'   Update the result set
ImageData.MSRDC1.Resultset.Update

'   Select SQL statement to get the
'   new result set
ImageData.MSRDC1.SQL = "select * from ImageData order by ImageID"
```

```
'  Refresh the result set
ImageData.MSRDC1.Refresh

'  Move to the last record which was
'  just added.
MenuBrowse 1

End Sub
```

21. Insert a new module into the project and save it as **Dropfile.bas**. The appropriate API functions are declared for enabling the Visual Basic forms to accept the file drag messages from the system. See the How It Works section for further details.

```
'  Declare the API file functions
'  and constants for the file drag
'  and drop
Declare Function GetWindowLong Lib "user32" Alias "GetWindowLongA" (ByVal ⇐
hwnd As Long, ByVal nIndex As Long) As Long

Declare Function SetWindowLong Lib "user32" Alias "SetWindowLongA" (ByVal ⇐
hwnd As Long, ByVal nIndex As Long, ByVal dwNewLong As Long) As Long

Declare Sub DragAcceptFiles Lib "shell32.dll" (ByVal hwnd As Long, ByVal ⇐
fAccept As Long)

Declare Sub DragFinish Lib "shell32.dll" (ByVal HDROP As Long)

Declare Function DragQueryFile Lib "shell32.dll" Alias "DragQueryFileA" ⇐
(ByVal HDROP As Long, ByVal UINT As Long, ByVal lpStr As String, ByVal ch⇐
As Long) As Long

Public Const GWL_EXSTYLE = (-20)
Public Const WS_EX_ACCEPTFILES = &H10&
Public Const WM_DROPFILES = &H233
```

22. The **EnableFileDrop** routine handles enabling the Visual Basic forms to accept the drag file messages from the system. First, the window style for the form is retrieved. Then, the style is changed to accept dropped files by using the **SetWindowLong** API. The **DragAcceptFiles** API function is used to indicate to the system that the form will handle dropped files.

```
Sub EnableFileDrop(hwnd As Long)

Dim Style As Long

'  Get the Window style
Style = GetWindowLong(hwnd, GWL_EXSTYLE)

'  Set to the form to accept
'  dropped files
Style = SetWindowLong(hwnd, GWL_EXSTYLE, Style Or WS_EX_ACCEPTFILES)
```

continued on next page

continued from previous page

```
'  Indicate to the system that
'  dragged files will be accepted
'  by the form
DragAcceptFiles hwnd, True

End Sub
```

How It Works

The drag-and-drop user interface feature provides an intuitive method for the user to both preview and add images to the database. The Windows Explorer is a natural and familiar interface for the user to browse the file system. If the user has a lot of images to add to the database, to simply use the New Image menu option for adding files would be cumbersome. With the Windows Explorer, multiple files can be dragged to the **ImageView** form and added to the database. In fact, with the implementation in this example, all the files from a directory can be dragged to the viewer and only the BMP and ICO files will be added to the database.

The Preview window also provides a simple way of viewing image files without first adding them to the database. If the user wants to add the image to the database, then the user can drag the picture control on the Preview window to the Image View window which will then add the image to the database. The Image View **DispPict** picture control's **DragDrop** event handles checking to see whether a file should be added to the database.

Visual Basic does not directly support file drag-and-drop features from the Windows Explorer. To make the file drag-and-drop features work, we will have to use a special control, **Msghook**, and dip into the Windows API. Table 4-27 outlines the different API functions used to implement the drag-and-drop.

Table 4-27 The drag-and-drop APIs

FUNCTION	DESCRIPTION
GetWindowLong	Retrieves information about the specified window
ByVal hwnd As Long	Handle of the window
ByVal nIndex As Long	Offset of the value to retrieve
SetWindowLong	Changes an attribute of the specified window
ByVal hwnd As Long	Handle of the window
ByVal nIndex As Long	Offset of the value to set
ByVal dwNewLong As Long	The new value
DragAcceptFiles	Registers whether or not a window accepts dropped files
ByVal hwnd As Long	Handle of the window
ByVal fAccept As Long	True or False
DragFinish	Finishes drag by releasing allocated transfer memory
ByVal HDROP As Long	Handle to the dropped memory

FUNCTION	DESCRIPTION
DragQueryFile	Retrieves the names of the dropped files (returns the number dropped)
ByVal HDROP As Long	Handle of the structure for the dropped files
ByVal UINT As Long	Index of the file to query
ByVal lpStr As String	Buffer to receive the filename
ByVal ch As Long	Size of the buffer

The **EnableFileDrop** routine in the **DropFile** module handles setting the form style to accept drop files. But, the system also needs to be notified to send the drop file message to the form. This is done with the **DragAcceptFiles** API. Once the form is prepared to accept files, the **WM_DROPFILES** message is sent from the system. When this happens, the **Msghook** control, which has been set to monitor for the **WM_DROPFILES** message, fires its message event. When the event fires, we check the message to ensure the **WM_DROPFILES** message was sent to the form. If so, then the **DragQueryFile** API is used to determine the number of files dropped and then each filename can be retrieved. If it is an image, then it will be added to the database.

Visual Basic does support drag-and-drop methods for various custom controls. This is demonstrated in the example by dragging the preview picture to the Image View picture as well as dragging the toolbar to change its alignment. The toolbar and picture controls have a drag method that can be initiated to drag an outline of the control using the mouse. When the control is dropped, the **DragDrop** method of the object the control was dropped on is initiated. The **DragDrop** method provides the name of the object dropped as well as **X** and **Y** drop locations. The coordinates allow us to determine how to change the alignment of the toolbar. For the **DispPict** control, we can determine whether the preview picture or the toolbar was dropped onto it by checking the name of the dropped object.

Comments

The drag-and-drop methods Visual Basic provides can be used to customize the interface of a program. For example, if the user would like to have the Comments field as the first field on the data entry form, then the drag-and-drop method could be used to change the order of the data-entry controls.

COMPLEXITY
INTERMEDIATE

4.5 How do I...
Organize form contents using the tab control?

Problem

The ability to provide the user with quick and simple views of different information in limited screen space can be invaluable to a program's interface. Windows 95 makes ample use of tabs for presenting information to the user. How can I utilize the tab control in my programs?

Technique

Visual Basic provides the **SSTab** control for implementing tabbed information in your Visual Basic programs. The image database program implemented in the chapter is missing a few critical features to make the interface complete. These include database sort options and the ability to view several images selected from a list without searching through the database. The tab control provides an effective method for accomplishing this.

Steps

Open and run 4-5.VBP. Figure 4-10 shows the **ImageData** form and the tab control.

The **ImageData** form now has a tab control which provides the standard data entry fields for the displayed image, but also provides a tab for sort options and three views of different images in the database. Figure 4-11 shows the different sort options for the images in the database. Select one of the options to sort the data.

The three View tabs provide a listbox that contains all the images in the database and a picture control for viewing images selected in the listbox. Select an image from the list to view it. Figure 4-12 shows an image selected on the View 1 tab.

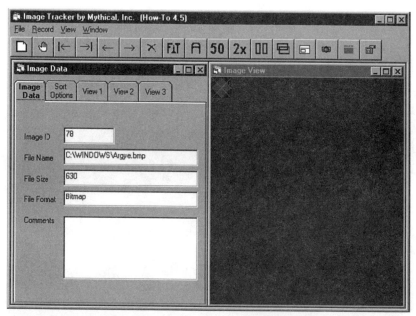

Figure 4-10 The form at runtime with the tab control

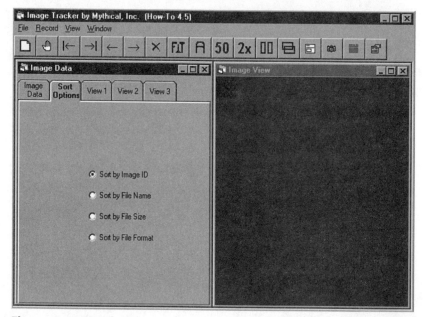

Figure 4-11 The form at runtime with the Sort Options tab control

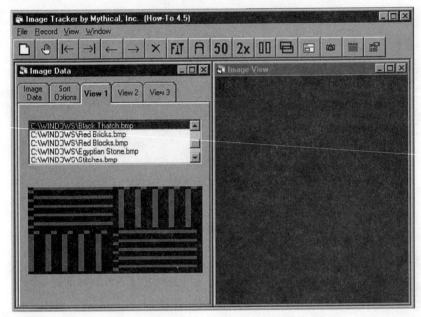

Figure 4-12 The form at runtime with the View 1 tab

1. Create a new project called 4-5.VBP. Add the objects and properties listed in Table 4-28 to the form and save the form as **4-5.FRM**.

Table 4-28 The MDI form's objects and properties

OBJECT	PROPERTY	SETTING
MDIForm	Name	ImageTracker
	AutoShowChildren	0 'False
	Caption	"Image Tracker by Mythical, Inc.
		(How-To 4.5)"
Toolbar	Name	ImageTool
	Align	1 'Align Top
	Negotiate	-1 'True
	ImageList	"MDIButtons"
	ButtonWidth	926
	ButtonHeight	847
	AllowCustomize	0 'False
	NumButtons	18
	AlignSet	-1 'True
	Wrappable	0 'False

OBJECT	PROPERTY	SETTING
ImageList	Name	MDIButtons
	ImageWidth	28
	ImageHeight	26
	MaskColor	12632256
	NumImages	18
	i1	open.bmp
	i2	new.bmp
	i3	hand.bmp
	i4	first.bmp
	i5	last.bmp
	i6	prev.bmp
	i7	next.bmp
	i8	delete.bmp
	i9	fit.bmp
	i10	actual.bmp
	i11	50.bmp
	i12	2x.bmp
	i13	tile.bmp
	i14	cascade.bmp
	i15	data.bmp
	i16	camera.bmp
	i17	menu.bmp
	i18	prop.bmp

2. Add the menus shown in Table 4-29 to the `ImageTracker` form.

Table 4-29 The `ImageTracker` form's menus

CONTROL NAME	CAPTION	INDEX	CHECKED	SHORTCUT KEY
mFile	"&File"			
mOpenImage	"&Open Image Database"			
mBar	"-"			
mExit	"E&xit"			
mWindow	"&Window"			
mImageData	"Image &Data"			
mImageView	"Image &View"			
mBar3	"-"			
mShowTool	"Show Toolbar"		-1	'True
mShowMenu	"Show Menu"		-1	'True

3. Insert a new form into the project and save it as **IView.frm**. Add the objects and properties shown in Table 4-30 to the form.

Table 4-30 The ImageView form's objects and properties

OBJECT	PROPERTY	SETTING
Form	Name	ImageView
	Caption	Image View"
	MDIChild	1 'True
PictureBox	Name	DispPict
	BackColor	H00C00000&
	BorderStyle	'None
	Picture	"pastel.bm"
	ScaleMode	'Pixel
PictureBox	Name	BackPict
	AutoRedraw	1 'True
	AutoSize	1 'True
	BackColor	H000000FF&
	BorderStyle	0 'None
	Picture	"pastel.bmp"
	ScaleMode	'Pixel
	Visible	'False
Msghook	Name	Msghook

4. Add the menus shown in Table 4-31 to the ImageView form.

Table 4-31 The ImageView form's menus

CONTROL NAME	CAPTION	INDEX	CHECKED	SHORTCUT KEY
mFile	"&File"			
mNewImage	&New Image"			
mBar	"-"			
mExit	"E&xit"			
mRecord	"&Record"			
mBrowse	"&First"	0		F1
mBrowse	"&Last"	1		F2

CONTROL NAME	CAPTION	INDEX	CHECKED	SHORTCUT KEY
mBrowse	"&Back"	2		F3
mBrowse	"For&ward"	3		F4
mBar2	"-"			
mDelete	"&Delete Record"			
mView	"&View"			
mSize	"&Fit in Window"	0		
mSize	"&Actual Size"	1	-1 'True	
mSize	"&50 Percent"	2		
mSize	"&200 Percent"	3		
mViewSet	"Viewer Settings"			
Flip	"Flip &Horizontal"	0		
Flip	"Flip &Vertical"	1		
mWindow	"&Window"			
mTile	"&Tile"			
mCascade	"&Cascade"			
mBar1	"-"			
mShowWindow	"Image &Data"	0		
mShowWindow	"Image &View"	1		
mPreview	"Image &Preview"			
mBar3	"-"			
mShowTool	"Show Tool&Bar"		-1 'True	
mShowMenu	"Show &Menu"		-1 'True	

5. Insert a new form into the project and save it as **IData.frm**. This implements the image data form as a tab control. Add the objects and properties shown in Table 4-32 to the form.

Table 4-32 The **ImageData** form's objects and properties

OBJECT	PROPERTY	SETTING
Form	Name	ImageData
	Caption	"Image Data"
	MDIChild	-1 'True
	Visible	0 'False
SSTab	Name	SSTab1
	Caption	"View 3"
	TabsPerRow	5

continued on next page

continued from previous page

OBJECT	PROPERTY	SETTING
	Tab	4
	TabOrientation	0
	Tabs	5
	Style	0
	TabMaxWidth	1323
	TabHeight	794
	TabCaption(0)	"Image Data"
	Tab(0).ControlCount	10
	Tab(0).ControlEnabled	0 'False
	Tab(0).Control(0)	"ImageInfo(0)"
	Tab(0).Control(1)	"ImageInfo(1)"
	Tab(0).Control(2)	"ImageInfo(2)"
	Tab(0).Control(3)	"ImageInfo(3)"
	Tab(0).Control(4)	"ImageInfo(4)"
	Tab(0).Control(5)	"ImageLabel(0)"
	Tab(0).Control(6)	"ImageLabel(1)"
	Tab(0).Control(7)	"ImageLabel(2)"
	Tab(0).Control(8)	"ImageLabel(3)"
	Tab(0).Control(9)	"ImageLabel(4)"
	TabCaption(1)	"Sort Options"
	Tab(1).ControlCount	4
	Tab(1).ControlEnabled	0 'False
	Tab(1).Control(0)	"Option1(0)"
	Tab(1).Control(1)	"Option1(1)"
	Tab(1).Control(2)	"Option1(2)"
	Tab(1).Control(3)	"Option1(3)"
	TabCaption(2)	"View 1"
	Tab(2).ControlCount	2
	Tab(2).ControlEnabled	0 'False
	Tab(2).Control(0)	"View(0)"
	Tab(2).Control(1)	"Thumb(0)"
	TabCaption(3)	"View 2"
	Tab(3).ControlCount	2
	Tab(3).ControlEnabled	0 'False
	Tab(3).Control(0)	"View(1)"
	Tab(3).Control(1)	"Thumb(1)"

OBJECT	PROPERTY	SETTING
	TabCaption(4)	"View 3"
	Tab(4).ControlCount	2
	Tab(4).ControlEnabled	-1 'True
	Tab(4).Control(0)	"View(2)"
	Tab(4).Control(1)	"Thumb(2)"
ListBox	Name	Thumb
	Index	2
ListBox	Name	Thumb
	Index	1
ListBox	Name	Thumb
	Index	0
OptionButton	Name	SortOpts
	Caption	"Sort by Image ID"
	Index	0
OptionButton	Name	SortOpts
	Caption	"Sort by File Name"
	Index	1
OptionButton	Name	SortOpts
	Caption	"Sort by File Size"
	Index	2
OptionButton	Name	SortOpts
	Caption	"Sort by File Format"
	Index	3
TextBox	Name	ImageInfo
	DataField	"ImageID"
	DataSource	"MSRDC1"
	Index	0
	Locked	-1 'True
TextBox	Name	ImageInfo
	DataField	"FileName"
	DataSource	"MSRDC1"
	Index	1
TextBox	Name	ImageInfo
	DataField	"FileSize"
	DataSource	"MSRDC1"
	Index	2

continued on next page

continued from previous page

OBJECT	PROPERTY	SETTING
	Locked	-1 'True
TextBox	Name	ImageInfo
	DataField	"FileFormat"
	DataSource	"MSRDC1"
	Index	3
TextBox	Name	ImageInfo
	DataField	"Comments"
	DataSource	"MSRDC1"
	Index	4
	MultiLine	-1 'True
Image	Name	View
	Index	
	Stretch	1 'True
Image	Name	View
	Index	1
	Stretch	-1 'True
Image	Name	View
	Index	0
	Stretch	-1 'True
Label	Name	ImageLabel
	AutoSize	-1 'True
	Caption	"Image ID"
	Index	0
Label	Name	ImageLabel
	AutoSize	-1 'True
	Caption	"File Name"
	Index	1
Label	Name	ImageLabel
	AutoSize	-1 'True
	Caption	"File Size"
	Index	2
Label	Name	ImageLabel
	AutoSize	-1 'True
	Caption	"File Format"
	Index	3
Label	Name	ImageLabel

OBJECT	PROPERTY	SETTING
	AutoSize	-1 'True
	Caption	"Comments"
	Index	4
CommonDialog	Name	CommonDialog1
	DefaultExt	".bmp"
	DialogTitle	"Find Image File"
	Filter	"*.bmp; *.wmf"
	FilterIndex	1
	InitDir	"c:\windows"
MSRDC	Name	MSRDC1
	Visible	0 'False
	DataSourceName	"Image Database"
	RecordSource	"select * from ImageData order by ImageID"
	RecordsetType	1
	KeysetSize	0
	ReadOnly	0 'False
	UserName	""
	Password	""
	CursorDriver	2
	EOFAction	1
	BOFAction	1
	Prompt	3
	LockType	3

6. Add the menus shown in Table 4-33 to the `ImageData` form.

Table 4-33 The `ImageData` form's menus

CONTROL NAME	CAPTION	INDEX	CHECKED	SHORTCUT KEY
mFile	"&File"			
mNewImage	"&New Image"			
mBar	"-"			
mExit	"E&xit"			
mRecord	"&Record"			
mBrowse	"&First"	0		F1
mBrowse	"&Last"	1		F2

continued on next page

continued from previous page

CONTROL NAME	CAPTION	INDEX	CHECKED	SHORTCUT KEY
mBrowse	"&Back"	2		F3
mBrowse	"For&ward"	3		F4
mBar2	"-"			
mDelete	"&Delete Record"			
mView	"&View"			
mSize	"&Fit in Window"	0		
mSize	"&Actual Size"	1	-1 'True	
mSize	"&50 Percent"	2		
mSize	"&200 Percent"	3		
mWindow	"&Window"			
mTile	"&Tile"			
mCascade	"&Cascade"			
mBar1	"-"			
mShowWindow	"Image &Data"	0		
mShowWindow	"Image &View"	1		
mPreview	"Image &Preview"			
mBar3	"-"			
mShowTool	"Show Tool&Bar"		-1 'True	
mShowMenu	"Show &Menu"		-1 'True	

7. Insert a new form into the project and save it as **Preview.frm**. Add the objects and properties shown in Table 4-34 to the form.

Table 4-34 The `Preview` form's objects and properties

OBJECT	PROPERTY	SETTING
Form	Name	Preview
	Caption	"Image Preview"
PictureBox	Name	PrevPict
	Appearance	0 'Flat
	BackColor	&H00808080&
	BorderStyle	0 'None
	DragIcon	"pastel.bmp"
	DragMode	1 'Automatic
	ForeColor	H80000008&
Msghook	Name	Msghook

> **NOTE**
>
> Only the new code added to the project will be commented. If you need additional information regarding the other code, see the previous How-To's for a complete explanation.

8. Add the following set of code to the **ImageTracker** form.

```
Private Sub ImageTool_ButtonClick(ByVal Button As Button)

Select Case Button.Index

    Case 1
        '   Open the Image Database
        MenuOpenData

    Case 2

        '   Call the MenuNewImage function to get
        '   a new image
        MenuNewImage

    Case 3
        '   Exit the program
        MenuExit

    Case 4
        '   Move to the first record
        MenuBrowse 0

    Case 5
        '   Move to the last record
        MenuBrowse 1

    Case 6
        '   Move back a record
        MenuBrowse 2

    Case 7
        '   Move forward a record
        MenuBrowse 3

    Case 8
        '   Delete the current record
        '   of the result set
        MenuDelete

    Case 9
        '   Set the View to fit in the Window
        SetView 0

    Case 10
        '   Set the View to actual size
        SetView 1
```

continued on next page

continued from previous page

```
      Case 11
          '  Set the View to 50 %
          SetView 2

      Case 12
          '  Set the View to 200 %
          SetView 3

      Case 13
          '  Tile the windows
          MenuTile

      Case 14
          '  Cascade the Windows
          MenuCascade

      Case 15
          '  If the ImageData form is not
          '  visible then call the
          '  MenuOpenData function to open
          '  the database.  Otherwise, show
          '  the ImageData Window (0)
          If ImageData.Visible = False Then
              MenuOpenData
          Else
              MenuShowWindow 0
          End If

      Case 16
          '  If the ImageData form is not
          '  visible then call the
          '  MenuOpenData function to open
          '  the database.  Otherwise, show
          '  the ImageView Window (1)
          If ImageData.Visible = False Then
              MenuOpenData
          Else
              MenuShowWindow 1
          End If

      Case 17
          '  Show or hide the Menu depending
          '  on the current setting.
          MenuShowMenu

      Case 18
          '  Start the drag process for the
          '  toolbar.
          ImageTool.Drag

  End Select

  End Sub

  Private Sub ImageTool_MouseDown(Button As Integer, Shift As Integer, X ⇐
  As Single, Y As Single)
```

```
'  Check for the right mouse
'  button click
If Button = vbPopupMenuRightButton Then

     '  If the ImageData form is not visible then
     '  show the popup menu for ImageTracker form.
     '  Otherwise show the pop up menu for the
     '  ImageData form.
     If ImageData.Visible = False Then
         Me.PopupMenu mWindow, vbPopupMenuCenterAlign, , , mShowTool
     Else
         ImageData.PopupMenu ImageData.mWindow, vbPopupMenuCenterAlign, , ⇐
         , ImageData.mShowTool
     End If

End If

End Sub

Private Sub MDIForm_DragDrop(Source As Control, X As Single, Y As Single)

'  Check to see if the drop was on
'  the top or bottom half of the
'  MDI form
If (Y - (ImageTool.Height / 2)) > (ImageTracker.Height / 2) Then
    ImageTool.Align = 2
Else
    ImageTool.Align = 1
End If

End Sub

Private Sub MDIForm_Load()

'  Hide the ImageData form when
'  the MDI form is first loaded
ImageData.Hide

End Sub

Private Sub MDIForm_MouseDown(Button As Integer, Shift As Integer, X As ⇐
Single, Y As Single)

'  If the ImageData form is not visible,
'  then show the File menu from the
'  ImageTracker form
If (Button = vbPopupMenuRightButton) And (ImageData.Visible <> True) Then
    Me.PopupMenu mFile, vbPopupMenuCenterAlign, , , mOpenImage
    Exit Sub
End If

'  If the ImageData form is visible,
'  then show the Window menu from the
'  ImageData form
```

continued on next page

continued from previous page

```
If (Button = vbPopupMenuRightButton) And (ImageData.Visible = True) Then
    ImageData.PopupMenu ImageData.mWindow, vbPopupMenuCenterAlign ', , , ⇐
        ImageData.mImageData
End If

End Sub

Private Sub MDIForm_QueryUnload(Cancel As Integer, UnloadMode As Integer)

' Call the MenuExit program to
' end the program
MenuExit

End Sub

Private Sub MDIForm_Unload(Cancel As Integer)

' Call the MenuExit program to
' end the program
MenuExit

End Sub

Private Sub mExit_Click()

' Call the MenuExit program to
' end the program
MenuExit

End Sub

Private Sub mImageData_Click()

' Call the MenuOpenData method to open the
' Image database
MenuOpenData

End Sub

Private Sub mImageView_Click()

' Call the MenuOpenData method to open the
' Image database
MenuOpenData

End Sub

Private Sub mOpenImage_Click()

' Call the MenuOpenData method to open the
' Image database
MenuOpenData

End Sub
```

```
Private Sub mShowMenu_Click()

'   Show or hide the Menu
MenuShowMenu

End Sub

Private Sub mShowTool_Click()

'   Show or hide the Toolbar
MenuShowTool

End Sub
```

9. Add the following set of code to the Image Data form. Add the
PopulateLists routine to the General Declarations section of the form.
The **PopulateLists** routine is a public method of the form that will populate the three view listboxes with a set of files in the database. Note that the
images are sorted by the current sort options selection.

```
Public Sub PopulateLists()

Dim N As Integer
Dim RS As rdoResultset

'   Get a copy of the record set
Set RS = MSRDC1.Resultset

'   Move to the first record.
RS.MoveFirst

'   Clear the list boxes.
For N = 0 To 2
    Thumb(N).Clear
Next

'   Move through the recordset and fill the
'   image list boxes for the thumb nails
Do Until RS.EOF

    '   Loop through and add the image names
    For N = 0 To 2
        Thumb(N).AddItem RS("Filename")
    Next

    '   Move to the next record
    RS.MoveNext

Loop

End Sub
```

10. When the form is loaded, the view listboxes are filled by calling the
PopulateLists routine.

```
Private Sub Form_Load()

'   Populate the list boxes
PopulateLists

End Sub

Private Sub Form_MouseDown(Button As Integer, Shift As Integer, X As ⇐
Single, Y As Single)

If Button = vbPopupMenuRightButton Then
    '   Show the Record menu for moving
    '   through the image records in the
    '   database
    Me.PopupMenu mRecord, vbPopupMenuCenterALign, , , mBrowse(3)

End If

End Sub

Private Sub Form_Resize()

Dim N As Integer

'   Size the tab control to fit in
'   the form.
SSTab1.Width = ImageData.Width - 110
SSTab1.Height = ImageData.Height - 500

'   Resize the other controls on the tab
For N = 1 To 4
    '   Resize the image info text
    '   boxes
    ImageData.ImageInfo(N).Width = SSTab1.Width - 1400

    '   Resize the thumb nail lists
    '   and the view image controls
    If N < 4 Then
        Thumb(N - 1).Width = SSTab1.Width - 450
        View(N - 1).Width = SSTab1.Width - 450
        View(N - 1).Height = SSTab1.Height - View(N - 1).Top - 750
    End If
Next N

End Sub

Private Sub Form_Unload(Cancel As Integer)

'   We don't want the form to be unloaded so that
'   it will not have to be re-initialized
Cancel = -1

'   Instead minimize the form
Me.WindowState = 1
```

```
End Sub

Private Sub mBrowse_Click(Index As Integer)

'   Browse the result set depending
'   on the menu selected
MenuBrowse Index

End Sub

Private Sub mCascade_Click()

'   Cascade the windows
MenuCascade

End Sub

Private Sub mDelete_Click()

'   Delete the current record
'   of the result set
MenuDelete

End Sub

Private Sub mExit_Click()

'   Call the MenuExit method to
'   exit the program
MenuExit

End Sub

Private Sub mNewImage_Click()

'   Cal the MenuNewImage function to allow
'   the user to select a new image to add to the
'   database
MenuNewImage

End Sub

Private Sub mPreview_Click()

'   Show the Preview form
Preview.Show

End Sub

Private Sub mShowMenu_Click()

'   Show or hide the Menu
MenuShowMenu

End Sub
```

continued on next page

continued from previous page

```
Private Sub mShowTool_Click()

'  Show or hide the toolbar
MenuShowTool

End Sub

Private Sub mShowWindow_Click(Index As Integer)

'  Call the MenuShowWindow function to show
'  the window selected
MenuShowWindow Index

End Sub

Private Sub mSize_Click(Index As Integer)

'  Set the View based on the menu
'  selection
SetView Index

End Sub

Private Sub mTile_Click()

'  Tile the windows
MenuTile

End Sub
```

11. The **Sort** options show up on the second tab of the tab control. There are several different methods provided for sorting the database. The SQL property of the remote data control is set to the appropriate SQL select statement for the sort. Then, the remote data control is refreshed and the view lists are repopulated.

```
Private Sub SortOpts_Click(Index As Integer)

Select Case Index

    Case 0
        MSRDC1.SQL = "select * from ImageData order by ImageID"

    Case 1
        MSRDC1.SQL = "select * from ImageData order by FileName"

    Case 2
        MSRDC1.SQL = "select * from ImageData order by FileSize"

    Case 3
        MSRDC1.SQL = "select * from ImageData order by FileFormat"

End Select

MSRDC1.Refresh
```

```
PopulateLists

'  Move to the last record which was
'  just added.
MenuBrowse 1

End Sub
```

12. When the thumbnail list of images on the image data form is clicked on, the name of the image to be viewed is retrieved from the list and the image is displayed in the image box. Note that the image box **stretch** property is set to **True** to stretch the image to fit in the box.

```
Private Sub Thumb_Click(Index As Integer)

    '  When the lists are clicked on
    '  load the files into the image
    '  controls
    View(Index).Picture = ⇐
LoadPicture(Thumb(Index).List(Thumb(Index).ListIndex))

End Sub
```

13. Add the following set of code to the **ImageView** form.

```
Private Sub DispPict_DragDrop(Source As Control, X As Single, Y As Single)

'  If the dropped control is the
'  toolbar then we need to do the
'  necessary checking to see if the
'  tool bar should be re-aligned
If Source.Name = "ImageTool" Then

    '  Check to see if the toolbar drop
    '  was on the top or bottom half of the
    '  picture box.  Note that the picture
    '  box is in pixel mode so we need to
    '  convert the coordinates to twips.
    If ((Y * Screen.TwipsPerPixelY) - (ImageTracker.ImageTool.Height / 2))⇐
        > (ImageTracker.Height / 2) Then
        ImageTracker.ImageTool.Align = 2
    Else
        ImageTracker.ImageTool.Align = 1
    End If

    Exit Sub

End If

'  Otherwise a new file should have
'  been dropped on the picture box
'  from the preview window.  We need
'  to check to ensure that there is
'  a picture file associated with the
```

continued on next page

continued from previous page

```
' preview.  If so, then add the image to
' the database.
If Preview.PreviewFileName <> "" Then
    DropNewImage Preview.PreviewFileName
End If

End Sub

Private Sub mPreview_Click()

' Show the preview window
Preview.Show

End Sub

Private Sub Msghook_Message(ByVal msg As Long, ByVal wp As Long, ByVal lp ⇐
As Long, result As Long)

Dim NumFiles As Integer
Dim Buffer As String 'Byte
Dim N As Integer
Dim NameLen As Integer

' Set up the buffer to receive the
' filename
Buffer = Space$(256)

' See if the drop file message was
' sent
If msg = WM_DROPFILES Then

    ' Retrieve the number of files
    ' dropped.
    NumFiles = DragQueryFile(wp, -1&, Buffer, Len(Buffer))

    ' Loop through the files and add them to
    ' the image database.
    For N = 0 To (NumFiles - 1)

        ' Get the filename of the file and
        ' retrieve the length of the
        ' filename
        NameLen = DragQueryFile(wp, N, Buffer, 128)

        ' Check to see if the file is a
        ' bitmap or icon.
        If (UCase(Right((Left(Buffer, NameLen)), 3)) = "BMP") Or ⇐
            (UCase(Right((Left(Buffer, NameLen)), 3)) = "ICO") Then

            ' Add the image to the database
            DropNewImage Left(Buffer, NameLen)

        End If

    Next N
```

```
        ' Tell the system the drag is done
        Call DragFinish(wp)

        '  Set the result
        result = 0

    End If

End Sub

Public Sub SizeViewPict()

'  Allow for a small border
'  around the display picture
disppict.Top = 5
disppict.Left = 5
disppict.Width = Me.Width - 5
disppict.Height = Me.Height - 5

'  Set the view to the current
'  view option
SetView IView

End Sub

Private Sub DispPict_Paint()

'  Size the view picture
SizeViewPict

End Sub

Private Sub DispPict_MouseDown(Button As Integer, Shift As Integer, X As ⇐
Single, Y As Single)

'  If the right mouse button is selected, then
'  the different image size options are shown.  If
'  it is a left mouse click then the flip options
'  are shown
If Button = vbPopupMenuRightButton Then
    Me.PopupMenu mView, vbPopupMenuCenterAlign, , , mSize(0)
Else
    Me.PopupMenu mViewSet, vbPopupMenuCenterAlign
End If

End Sub

Private Sub Flip_Click(Index As Integer)

'  When the flip menu is clicked, the
'  check on the menu is set appropriately
If flip(Index).Checked = False Then
    flip(Index).Checked = True
Else
    flip(Index).Checked = False
End If
```

continued on next page

continued from previous page

```
'   It is important to ensure that only
'   a vertical or horizotal flip can be
'   performed.  Thus, the menu item that
'   was not clicked is unchecked.
If Index = 1 Then
     flip(0).Checked = False
Else
     flip(1).Checked = False
End If


'   Based on the selection,
'   the image is redisplayed.
SizeViewPict

End Sub


Private Sub Form_Load()

'   Enable the form to accept
'   file drops
EnableFileDrop Me.hwnd

'   Setup MsgHook control
Msghook.HwndHook = Me.hwnd
Msghook.Message(WM_DROPFILES) = True

'   Intially set IView to 0.
IView = 1

'   Call the MenuBrowse function
'   to show the first record
MenuBrowse 1

End Sub



Private Sub Form_Unload(Cancel As Integer)

'   Cancel the unload.  We don't want the
'   form to be unloaded while the program is
'   running so that it does not have to be
'   re-initialized.  Instead, the form will be
'   minimized.
Cancel = -1
Me.WindowState = 1

End Sub

Private Sub mBrowse_Click(Index As Integer)

'   Browse the record set depending on the
'   menu option chosen.
MenuBrowse Index

End Sub
```

```vb
Private Sub mCascade_Click()

' Cascade the windows
MenuCascade

' Size the view picture after the cascade
SizeViewPict

End Sub

Private Sub mDelete_Click()

' Call the MenuDelete function to
' delete the selected record.
MenuDelete

End Sub

Private Sub mExit_Click()

' Call the MenuExit function to
' exit the program.
MenuExit

End Sub

Private Sub mNewImage_Click()

' Call the MenuNewImage function to get
' a new image
MenuNewImage

End Sub

Private Sub mShowMenu_Click()

' Show or hide the Menu
MenuShowMenu

End Sub

Private Sub mShowTool_Click()

' Show or hide the toolbar
MenuShowTool

End Sub

Private Sub mShowWindow_Click(Index As Integer)

' Call the MenuShowWindow function to show
' the selected window.
MenuShowWindow Index

End Sub
```

continued on next page

continued from previous page

```vb
Private Sub mTile_Click()

' Call the menu tile function to
' tile the windows
MenuTile

End Sub

Private Sub mSize_Click(Index As Integer)

' Set the view depending on the menu option
' selected
SetView Index

End Sub
```

14. Add the following set of code to the **Preview** form.

```vb
' Public property that will indicate
' what filename is associated with
' the preview
Public PreviewFileName As String

Private Sub Form_Load()

' Enable the preview to accept
' file drag and drop
EnableFileDrop Me.hwnd

' Setup the MsgHook control
Msghook.HwndHook = Me.hwnd
Msghook.Message(WM_DROPFILES) = True

' Move the preview picture to the
' top left
PrevPict.Top = 0
PrevPict.Left = 0

' Set the preview picture width
' and height
PrevPict.Width = Preview.Width
PrevPict.Height = Preview.Height

End Sub

Private Sub Form_Resize()

' When the form is resized,
' resize the picture
PrevPict.Width = Preview.Width
PrevPict.Height = Preview.Height

End Sub

Private Sub Form_Unload(Cancel As Integer)
```

```vb
'   When the preview is unloaded,
'   make sure the ImageTracker form
'   is visible
ImageTracker.Show

End Sub

Private Sub Msghook_Message(ByVal msg As Long, ByVal wp As Long, ByVal lp ⇐
As Long, result As Long)

Dim NumFiles As Integer
Dim Buffer As String 'Byte
Dim N As Integer
Dim NameLen As Integer

'   Set up the buffer to receive the
'   filename
Buffer = Space$(256)

'   See if the drop file message was
'   sent
If msg = WM_DROPFILES Then

    '   Retrieve the number of files
    '   dropped.
    NumFiles = DragQueryFile(wp, -1&, Buffer, Len(Buffer))

    '   Get the filename of the file and
    '   retrieve the length of the
    '   filename
    NameLen = DragQueryFile(wp, N, Buffer, 128)

    '   Check to see if the file is a
    '   bitmap or icon.
    If (UCase(Right((Left(Buffer, NameLen)), 3)) = "BMP") Or ⇐
    (UCase(Right((Left(Buffer, NameLen)), 3)) = "ICO") Then

        '   Load the picture into the preview
        PrevPict.Picture = LoadPicture(Left(Buffer, NameLen))

        '   Set the filename of the form
        PreviewFileName = Left(Buffer, NameLen)

    End If

    ' Tell the system the drag done.
    Call DragFinish(wp)

    '   Set the result
    result = 0

End If

End Sub
```

15. Insert a new module into the project and save it as **MenLogic.bas**.

```
'   StretchBlit will be used for the Image Viewer
Public Declare Function StretchBlt Lib "gdi32" (ByVal hdc As Long, ⇐
ByVal X As Long, ByVal Y As Long, ByVal nWidth As Long, ByVal nHeight ⇐
As Long, ByVal hSrcDC As Long, ByVal xSrc As Long, ByVal ySrc As Long, ⇐
ByVal nSrcWidth As Long, ByVal nSrcHeight As Long, ByVal dwRop As Long) ⇐
As Long

Global Const SRCCOPY = &HCC0020

'   IView globally stores the current view for
'   the image  I.E.  Fit in Window, 50%
Public IView As Integer

'   Handles ending the program when
'   users select exit from the menu
Public Sub MenuExit()
     End
End Sub

'   Handles tiling the windows
'   on the MDI form
Public Sub MenuTile()

'   Do a vertical tile
ImageTracker.Arrange vbTileVertical

End Sub

Public Sub MenuCascade()

'   Cascade the child forms
ImageTracker.Arrange vbCascade

End Sub

Public Sub SetView(Index)

'   When a new image view is selected,
'   the original menu selection is
'   unchecked
ImageView.mSize(IView).Checked = False
ImageData.mSize(IView).Checked = False

'   Set the new view to the index
'   parameter
IView = Index

'   Check the new menu option for the
'   selected view.
ImageData.mSize(IView).Checked = True
ImageView.mSize(IView).Checked = True

'   Clear the displayed picture
ImageView.disppict.Cls
```

```
ImageView.disppict.Picture.hPal = ImageView.backpict.Picture.hPal

'  Depending on the view selected, the
'  original image will be copied to the
'  display picture appropriately
Select Case IView

'  Note that for the vertical and
'  horizontal flips, the height or
'  width is set to a negative value
'  and the starting point is set to
'  the height or width for the image
'  to be displayed.

    Case 0   'Fit in the Window
        If ImageView.flip(0).Checked = True Then
            '  Flip Horizontal
            ImageView.disppict.PaintPicture ImageView.backpict.Picture, ⇐
            ImageView.disppict.ScaleWidth, 0, -1 * ⇐
            ImageView.disppict.ScaleWidth, ⇐
            ImageView.disppict.ScaleHeight, ⇐
            0, 0, ImageView.backpict.ScaleWidth, ⇐
            ImageView.backpict.ScaleHeight
        Else

            If ImageView.flip(1).Checked = True Then
                '  Flip Vertical
                ImageView.disppict.PaintPicture ⇐
                ImageView.backpict.Picture, ⇐
                0, ImageView.disppict.ScaleHeight, ⇐
                ImageView.disppict.ScaleWidth, -1 * ⇐
                ImageView.disppict.ScaleHeight, 0, 0, ⇐
                ImageView.backpict.ScaleWidth, ⇐
                ImageView.backpict.ScaleHeight
            Else
                '  Normal Display
                Call StretchBlt(ImageView.disppict.hdc, 0, 0, ⇐
            ImageView.disppict.ScaleWidth, ⇐
            ImageView.disppict.ScaleHeight, ⇐
            ImageView.backpict.hdc, 0, 0, ⇐
            ImageView.backpict.ScaleWidth, ⇐
            ImageView.backpict.ScaleHeight, SRCCOPY)
            End If
        End If

    Case 1   'Actual Size
        If ImageView.flip(0).Checked = True Then
            '  Flip Horizontal
            ImageView.disppict.PaintPicture ImageView.backpict.Picture, ⇐
            ImageView.backpict.ScaleWidth, 0, -1 * ⇐
            ImageView.backpict.ScaleWidth, ⇐
            ImageView.backpict.ScaleHeight, ⇐
            0, 0, ImageView.backpict.ScaleWidth, ⇐
            ImageView.backpict.ScaleHeight
```

continued on next page

continued from previous page

```
        Else
            If ImageView.flip(1).Checked = True Then
                ' Flip Vertical
                ImageView.disppict.PaintPicture ⇐
                ImageView.backpict.Picture, ⇐
                0, ImageView.backpict.ScaleHeight, ⇐
                ImageView.backpict.ScaleWidth, -1 * ⇐
                ImageView.backpict.ScaleHeight, 0, 0, ⇐
                ImageView.backpict.ScaleWidth, ⇐
                ImageView.backpict.ScaleHeight
            Else
                ' Normal Display
                Call StretchBlt(ImageView.disppict.hdc, 0, 0, ⇐
            ImageView.backpict.ScaleWidth, ⇐
            ImageView.backpict.ScaleHeight, ImageView.backpict.hdc, 0, ⇐
            0, ImageView.backpict.ScaleWidth, ⇐
            ImageView.backpict.ScaleHeight, SRCCOPY)
            End If
        End If

    Case 2 '50%
        If ImageView.flip(0).Checked = True Then
            ' Flip Horizontal
            ImageView.disppict.PaintPicture ImageView.backpict.Picture, ⇐
            ImageView.backpict.ScaleWidth * 0.5, 0, -1 * ⇐
            ImageView.backpict.ScaleWidth * 0.5, ⇐
            ImageView.backpict.ScaleHeight * 0.5, 0, 0, ⇐
            ImageView.backpict.ScaleWidth, ImageView.backpict.ScaleHeight
        Else
            If ImageView.flip(1).Checked = True Then
                ' Flip Vertical
                ImageView.disppict.PaintPicture ⇐
                ImageView.backpict.Picture, ⇐
                0, ImageView.backpict.ScaleHeight * 0.5, ⇐
                ImageView.backpict.ScaleWidth * 0.5, -1 * ⇐
                ImageView.backpict.ScaleHeight * 0.5, 0, 0, ⇐
                ImageView.backpict.ScaleWidth, ⇐
                ImageView.backpict.ScaleHeight
            Else
                ' Normal Display
                Call StretchBlt(ImageView.disppict.hdc, 0, 0, ⇐
            ImageView.backpict.ScaleWidth * 0.5, ⇐
            ImageView.backpict.ScaleHeight * 0.5, ⇐
            ImageView.backpict.hdc, ⇐
            0, 0, ImageView.backpict.ScaleWidth, ⇐
            ImageView.backpict.ScaleHeight, SRCCOPY)
            End If
        End If

    Case 3 '200%
        If ImageView.flip(0).Checked = True Then
            ' Flip Horizontal
            ImageView.disppict.PaintPicture ImageView.backpict.Picture, ⇐
            ImageView.backpict.ScaleWidth * 2, 0, -1 * ⇐
            ImageView.backpict.ScaleWidth * 2, ⇐
```

```
                ImageView.backpict.ScaleHeight ⇐
                2, 0, 0, ImageView.backpict.ScaleWidth, ⇐
                ImageView.backpict.ScaleHeight
        Else
            If ImageView.flip(1).Checked = True Then
                '  Flip Vertical
                ImageView.disppict.PaintPicture ⇐
                ImageView.backpict.Picture, ⇐
                0, ImageView.backpict.ScaleHeight * 2, ⇐
                ImageView.backpict.ScaleWidth * 2, -1 * ⇐
                ImageView.backpict.ScaleHeight * 2, 0, 0, ⇐
                ImageView.backpict.ScaleWidth, ⇐
                ImageView.backpict.ScaleHeight
            Else
                '  Normal Display
                Call StretchBlt(ImageView.disppict.hdc, 0, 0, ⇐
            ImageView.backpict.ScaleWidth * 2, ⇐
            ImageView.backpict.ScaleHeight * 2, ⇐
            ImageView.backpict.hdc, ⇐
            0, 0, ImageView.backpict.ScaleWidth, ⇐
            ImageView.backpict.ScaleHeight, SRCCOPY)
            End If
        End If

End Select

'  Copy the palette from the holding picture
'  to the displayed picture.  This ensures that
'  the images colors are displayed correctly.
ImageView.disppict.Picture.hPal = ImageView.backpict.Picture.hPal

End Sub

Public Sub MenuShowWindow(Index)

'  Check to see which Windows (Form)
'  is to be displayed.
Select Case Index

    Case 0  'Show ImageData
        ImageData.Show
        ImageData.WindowState = 0

    Case 1  'Show ImageView
        ImageView.Show
        ImageView.WindowState = 0

End Select

End Sub

Public Sub MenuOpenData()

Dim msg As String
Dim Style As Integer
```

continued on next page

continued from previous page

```
Dim Title As String
Dim Response As Integer
Dim N As Integer

'  Set the Message, Style, and Title
'  of the message box
msg = "Do you want to open the Image Database ?"
Style = vbYesNo + vbCritical + vbDefaultButton1
Title = "Open Image Database"

'  Retrieve the user's response
Response = MsgBox(msg, Style, Title)

'  If it was a yes, then show the ImageData
'  and ImageView forms.  Also start the view
'  in Tiled mode.
If Response = vbYes Then
    ImageView.Show
    ImageData.Show
    MenuTile

    ImageTracker.ImageTool.Buttons(1).Visible = False

    For N = 2 To ImageTracker.ImageTool.Buttons.Count

        ImageTracker.ImageTool.Buttons(N).Visible = True

    Next N

        '  Ensure that the menu item is the same
        '  for the ImageData and ImageView forms
    ImageView.mShowMenu.Checked = ImageTracker.mShowMenu.Checked
    ImageData.mShowMenu.Checked = ImageTracker.mShowMenu.Checked
    ImageView.mShowTool.Checked = ImageTracker.mShowTool.Checked
    ImageData.mShowTool.Checked = ImageTracker.mShowTool.Checked

End If

End Sub

Public Sub MenuBrowse(MoveType)

Dim ImageName As String

'  Check the RowCount.  If it is 0,
'  then there are no images in the
'  database.  We then need to show the New Image
'  dialog to add the first image.
If ImageData.MSRDC1.Resultset.RowCount = 0 Then MenuNewImage: Exit Sub

'  Depending on the type of move
'  selected by the user, the result set
'  is manipulated appropriately.
Select Case MoveType
```

```
        Case 0   'Move to First Record
            ImageData.MSRDC1.Resultset.MoveFirst

        Case 1   'Move to Last Record
            ImageData.MSRDC1.Resultset.MoveLast

        Case 2   'Move to Previous Record
            ImageData.MSRDC1.Resultset.MovePrevious

        Case 3   'Move to Next Record
            ImageData.MSRDC1.Resultset.MoveNext

End Select

'   Check to see if the End of File or
'   Beginning of File has been reached in
'   the result set.  If so, then move first or
'   last to ensure that a current record is
'   always visible
If ImageData.MSRDC1.Resultset.EOF = True Then ⇐
ImageData.MSRDC1.Resultset.MoveLast

If ImageData.MSRDC1.Resultset.BOF = True Then ⇐
ImageData.MSRDC1.Resultset.MoveFirst

'   Get the Image name from the database
ImageName = ImageData.MSRDC1.Resultset("FileName")

'   Depending on whether or not the image file
'   name is set, the picture display is
'   set appropriately.
If ImageName <> "" Then
    ImageView.backpict.Picture = LoadPicture(ImageName): SetView IView
Else
    ImageView.backpict.Picture = LoadPicture(""): SetView IView
End If

End Sub

Public Sub MenuNewImage()

Dim ImageID As Integer
Dim ImageType As String

'   Ensure an Update is done
If ImageData.MSRDC1.Resultset.RowCount <> 0 Then
ImageData.MSRDC1.Resultset.MoveNext

'   Set the filter type of the dialog
'   box
ImageData.commondialog1.Filter = "Bitmaps (*.bmp)|*.bmp|Icons ⇐
(*.ico)|*.ico|All Files (*.*)|*.*"

'   Set the title of the dialog
ImageData.commondialog1.DialogTitle = "New Image File"
```

continued on next page

continued from previous page

```
'  Set the filter index to that of the
'  bitmap
ImageData.commondialog1.FilterIndex = 1

'  Set the flags to ensure that the
'  file must exist
ImageData.commondialog1.Flags = cdlOFNFileMustExist

'  Show the dialog box
ImageData.commondialog1.ShowOpen

'  Check to see if the filename was set
If ImageData.commondialog1.FileName <> "" Then

    '  Add a new record
    ImageData.MSRDC1.Resultset.AddNew

    '  Set the file name
    ImageData.MSRDC1.Resultset("FileName") =
ImageData.commondialog1.FileName

    '  Set the file size
    ImageData.MSRDC1.Resultset("FileSize") = ⇐
      FileLen(ImageData.commondialog1.FileName)

    '  Get the extension of the image
    ImageType = Right$(ImageData.commondialog1.FileName, 3)

    '  Set the file format depending on
the extension
    Select Case UCase$(ImageType)

        Case "BMP"  'Standard bitmap
            ImageData.MSRDC1.Resultset("FileFormat") = "Bitmap"

        Case "ICO"  'Standard Icon
            ImageData.MSRDC1.Resultset("FileType") = "Icon"

    End Select

    '  Update the result set
    ImageData.MSRDC1.Resultset.Update

    '  Select SQL statement to get the
    '  new result set
    ImageData.MSRDC1.SQL = "select * from ImageData order by ImageID"

    '  Refresh the result set
    ImageData.MSRDC1.Refresh

    '  Since we have changed the record set
    '  the image lists need to be updated
    ImageData.PopulateLists

    '  Move to the last record which was
```

```
        '  just added.
        MenuBrowse 1

End If

End Sub

Public Sub MenuDelete()

'  Delete the current record
ImageData.MSRDC1.Resultset.Delete

'  Since we have changed the record set
'  the image lists need to be updated
ImageData.PopulateLists

'  Move to the next record.
MenuBrowse 1

End Sub

Public Sub MenuShowTool()

'  If the toolbar is checked then
'  do the logic to hide the toolbar
If ImageTracker.mShowTool.Checked = True Then

        '  If the menu is not shown, then don't
        '  hide the tool bar.
        If ImageTracker.mShowMenu.Checked = False Then Exit Sub

        '  Hide the toolbar
        ImageTracker.ImageTool.Visible = False

        '  Change the menu check
        ImageTracker.mShowTool.Checked = False

        '  If the ImageData and ImageView forms
        '  are visible then handle setting their
        '  menu check marks.  If they are not
        '  visible, they are not loaded.
        If ImageData.Visible = True Then
            ImageData.mShowTool.Checked = False
            ImageView.mShowTool.Checked = False
        End If

Else

        '  Make the toolbar visible
        ImageTracker.ImageTool.Visible = True

        '  Change the menu check
        ImageTracker.mShowTool.Checked = True

        '  If the ImageData and ImageView forms
```

continued on next page

continued from previous page

```
        ' are visible then handle setting their
        ' menu check marks.  If they are not
        ' visible, they are not loaded.
        If ImageData.Visible = True Then
            ImageData.mShowTool.Checked = True
            ImageView.mShowTool.Checked = True
        End If

    End If

End Sub

Public Sub MenuShowMenu()

' Check to see If the menu is already visible
If ImageTracker.mShowMenu.Checked = True Then

        ' If the tool bar is not visible,
        ' we do not want to also make the
        ' menu invisible
If ImageTracker.ImageTool.Visible = False Then Exit Sub

        ' Make the ImageTracker menus
        ' invisible and set the menu
        ' check mark appropriately
        ImageTracker.mFile.Visible = False
        ImageTracker.mShowMenu.Checked = False
        ImageTracker.mWindow.Visible = False

        ' If the ImageData and ImageView forms
        ' are visible then handle setting their
        ' menu check marks and visible properties.
        ' If they are not visible, they are not
        ' loaded.
        If ImageData.Visible = True Then
            ImageData.mShowMenu.Checked = False
            ImageView.mShowMenu.Checked = False
            ImageView.mFile.Visible = False
            ImageData.mFile.Visible = False
            ImageData.mWindow.Visible = False
            ImageView.mWindow.Visible = False
            ImageData.mRecord.Visible = False
            ImageView.mRecord.Visible = False
            ImageData.mView.Visible = False
            ImageView.mView.Visible = False
            ImageView.mViewSet.Visible = False
        End If

Else

        ' Make the ImageTracker menus
        ' visible and set the menu
        ' check mark appropriately
        ImageTracker.mFile.Visible = True
        ImageTracker.mShowMenu.Checked = True
```

```
        ImageTracker.mWindow.Visible = True

    '   If the ImageData and ImageView forms
    '   are visible then handle setting their
    '   menu check marks and visible properties.
    '   If they are not visible, they are not
    '   loaded.
    If ImageData.Visible = True Then
        ImageData.mShowMenu.Checked = True
        ImageView.mShowMenu.Checked = True
        ImageData.mFile.Visible = True
        ImageView.mFile.Visible = True
        ImageData.mWindow.Visible = True
        ImageView.mWindow.Visible = True
        ImageData.mRecord.Visible = True
        ImageView.mRecord.Visible = True
        ImageView.mView.Visible = True
        ImageData.mView.Visible = True
        ImageView.mViewSet.Visible = True
    End If

End If

End Sub

Public Sub DropNewImage(FileName)

Dim ImageID As Integer
Dim ImageType As String

'   Ensure an Update is done
ImageData.MSRDC1.Resultset.MoveNext

'   Add a new record
ImageData.MSRDC1.Resultset.AddNew

'   Set the file name
ImageData.MSRDC1.Resultset("FileName") = FileName

'   Set the file size
ImageData.MSRDC1.Resultset("FileSize") = FileLen(FileName)

'   Get the extension of the image
ImageType = Right$(FileName, 3)

'   Set the file format depending on
'   the the extension
Select Case UCase$(ImageType)

    Case "BMP"   'Standard bitmap
        ImageData.MSRDC1.Resultset("FileFormat") = "Bitmap"

    Case "ICO"   'Standard Icon
        ImageData.MSRDC1.Resultset("FileType") = "Icon"
```

continued on next page

continued from previous page

```
End Select

'  Update the result set
ImageData.MSRDC1.Resultset.Update

'  Select SQL statement to get the
'  new result set
ImageData.MSRDC1.SQL = "select * from ImageData order by ImageID"

'  Refresh the result set
ImageData.MSRDC1.Refresh

'  Move to the last record which was
'  just added.
MenuBrowse 1

End Sub
```

16. Insert a new module into the project and save it as **DropFile.bas**.

```
'  Declare the API file functions
'  and constants for the file drag
'  and drop
Declare Function GetWindowLong Lib "user32" Alias "GetWindowLongA" (ByVal ⇐
hwnd As Long, ByVal nIndex As Long) As Long

Declare Function SetWindowLong Lib "user32" Alias "SetWindowLongA" (ByVal ⇐
hwnd As Long, ByVal nIndex As Long, ByVal dwNewLong As Long) As Long

Declare Sub DragAcceptFiles Lib "shell32.dll" (ByVal hwnd As Long, ByVal ⇐
fAccept As Long)

Declare Sub DragFinish Lib "shell32.dll" (ByVal HDROP As Long)

Declare Function DragQueryFile Lib "shell32.dll" Alias "DragQueryFileA" ⇐
(ByVal HDROP As Long, ByVal UINT As Long, ByVal lpStr As String, ByVal ⇐
ch As Long) As Long

Public Const GWL_EXSTYLE = (-20)
Public Const WS_EX_ACCEPTFILES = &H10&
Public Const WM_DROPFILES = &H233

Sub EnableFileDrop(hwnd As Long)

Dim Style As Long

'  Get the Window style
Style = GetWindowLong(hwnd, GWL_EXSTYLE)

'  Set to the form to accept
'  dropped files
Style = SetWindowLong(hwnd, GWL_EXSTYLE, Style Or WS_EX_ACCEPTFILES)

'  Indicate to the system that
'  dragged files will be accepted
'  by the form
```

```
DragAcceptFiles hwnd, True

End Sub
```

How It Works

The tab control is a relatively easy tool to use in your applications. In this example, it provides a straightforward way to add different sort options for the application. Also the user may feel the need to be able to quickly view several images at once. The three View tabs provide thumbnail views of different images in the database. The listboxes provide a list of all the images in the database. The user can quickly flip between the images by clicking on the tabs. The tab control can be very useful for adding those features to your program that don't work well in a limited menu format, but don't need to be seen at all times.

Comments

Another tab could be provided to give the user options for searching the image database for particular recordsets. Or, another View tab could be provided to show all three of the thumbnails on a single tab. This type of multiview flexibility makes the tab control an invaluable tool.

CHAPTER 5
PRESENTING DATA TO THE USER

by David Jung

PRESENTING DATA TO THE USER

How do I...

When developing client/server applications in a distributed environment, there will be a major paradigm shift as to how business rules and functions are to be implemented. In the traditional two-tier model, you will find that business components are integrated into either the user interface or into the database components. Business logic integrated into the user interface becomes part of the application's program file. Business logic integrated into the database services takes the form of stored procedures and triggers. By having business logic in two separate layers, it can become difficult to manage when business rules change or get updated. In a distributed model, the business components can still be embedded in either component layer, but the proper deployment of business components should be completely separate from the other two layers. When designing business components, they will either physically

347

reside on the database layer or user interface layer, or they can reside on a separate application server altogether. Having the components separate from either layer, any change to business rules will only need to be applied to the business component and the change only needs to be applied once and in one location. If the business logic is embedded within each application, each application would need to be updated and redeployed throughout the enterprise.

As a practical example of the value of modularizing business components, consider the question of managing data display. The rate at which data is displayed to the user, especially large amounts of data, is an important factor in developing most client/server applications. A traditional way to retrieve information is to get all the information you've requested, no matter how many rows are returned, store it in arrays or controls, and synchronize the information through the use of primary and foreign keys. With large amounts of data, this can slow down your application considerably. Through the use of business components, optimizing your applications can become a lot easier. Working the business components separate from your application gives you the freedom to experiment with different methods of retrieving and manipulating data without affecting your production applications. Your front-end application does not need to be concerned with how the data is retrieved, just as long as it is retrieved.

This chapter's How-To's will demonstrate different methods for displaying the data for a fictitious hotel chain. The tables for the hotel database are stored in **Hotels7.MDB** located on the CD under Chapter 5 or if you run the SQL script under this chapter on SQL Server, the hotel database is **db_HotelSystem**. Because you are using ODBC, you will not need to be concerned whether you are using an MDB or an SQL Server database. Refer to Chapter 2, Getting Connected, to create an ODBC Data Source Name (DSN). The How-To's use the DSN **dsnWaiteSQL**. The business rules in the class modules are used as part of the actual program. In a real distributed component environment, they would not be part of the application but would be implemented as out-of-process OLE servers. Refer to Chapter 7, Business Objects, for more information on business objects and out-of-process OLE servers.

5.1 Load a List or Combo Box with the Results of a Query

Visual Basic 5.0 provides new list controls that bind to a database table. In a distributed component architecture, you want to avoid using these controls. Bound controls do not allow you to manage data on a transaction basis. They are linked to a database field and once you update the field, the database is updated. By developing business objects, the business components rather than the data layer will handle the way the data is retrieved and how it is placed in a control. This How-To will show you how to create a class module that will use the remote data object (RDO) to retrieve information from a database table and populate a combo box control.

5.2   Populate an Unbound Grid

Visual Basic 5.0 provides you with a new grid control that binds to a database table. In a distributed component architecture, you want to avoid using this control for the reasons given above. This How-To will show you how to create a class module that will use the remote data object to retrieve information from a database table and populate an unbound grid control.

5.3   Display Calculated Fields in an Unbound Grid

As part of some decision support systems, you want to be able to show the result of calculations in a spreadsheet-style format. In a distributed component architecture, retrieving data from a database table and making calculations are considered part of the business objects; they should be defined into two different class modules. This How-To will show you how to create a class that will use the remote data object to retrieve information from a database table and populate an unbound grid control. Also, it will show you how to create a class module that will be used to handle mathematical calculations.

5.4   Control the Number of Rows Displayed

When retrieving large amounts of data, displaying a small subset of information and controlling the amount the user will see at a given time can increase your application's performance and reduce network traffic. This How-To will show you how to use the remote data object's `GetRows` method to limit the amount of rows that are retrieved from the table and placed in the resultset.

5.5   Create a Master/Detail Form

Many times you have information in one table that drives information from another table. By retrieving only the information requested, you will speed up the user's perception of how fast the application operates. In this How-To, you will create a class module that will use the remote data object to retrieve information from database tables and display the information in the respective unbound grids. The information that is retrieved will be based on what the user selects in a combo box.

5.6   Create a Query by Example

Many times your users want to look up information in the system. Rather than taking the time to educate them on how the database is designed, how the tables relate to one another, and how to create queries to retrieve the information they want, you can develop a query form to help them perform their own lookups. In this How-To, you will create an interface so that by using a series of check boxes, radio buttons, and some user input, users can visually select the type of information they want with minimal knowledge of the database tables.

5.1 How do I...
Load a list or combo box with the results of a query?

Problem

I have a small amount of data I want to retrieve and use to populate a listbox or combo box. I would like to have a generic routine so I can use it throughout my application.

Technique

In versions 3.0 and earlier of Visual Basic, you would have placed the code for this routine in a standard module. With version 5, the routine should be placed in a class module. Class modules should be used to define procedures for all objects in your applications. Standard modules should contain procedures that do not pertain to any object. They should be used to contain any references to API functions.

The routine you are about to design is a simple one, designed to display information in a list-based control, such as a listbox or combo box. Essentially what this becomes is a data access object (DAO) you can reuse in other applications or that can become part of a business object that is an OLE automation server, which can be used by applications throughout your enterprise.

Steps

Open and run **CNTLFILL.VBP**. The form shown in Figure 5-1 will appear. When the combo box receives focus, it will be filled with the names of the hotels from the Hotels table in the Hotel database. Every time the combo box receives focus, either by clicking on it with the mouse or tabbing to it, the Hotels table will be required and the combo box will be populated with the list of hotel names. To exit the program, simply press OK.

This example uses a class that represents the physical database access and custom control manipulation used by this application.

1. Start Visual Basic and create a new project. Save the project as **CNTLFILL.VBP**. Select the default form, **Form1**, name it **frmHotelListing**, and save it as **CNTLFILL.FRM**. Assign the objects and properties for this form as listed in Table 5-1.

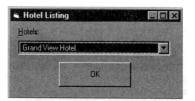

Figure 5-1 Combo box control filled via a class module

Table 5-1 Objects and properties of `CNTLFILL.FRM`

OBJECT	PROPERTY	SETTING
Form	Name	frmHotelListing
	Appearance	1 - 3D
	Caption	"Hotel Listing"
Label	Name	lblHotelListing
	Caption	"&Hotels:"
Combo Box	Name	cboHotels
	Style	2 - Dropdown List
Command Button	Name	cmdOK
	Caption	"OK"

2. Insert the following code into the General Declarations section of the `frmHotelListing`. This will create a new object of `CDataObjects` when the object variable is declared.

```
Option Explicit

' Assign the Hotel Name Member to Data Object
Private m_Hotels As CDataObjects
```

3. Insert the following code into the `Form_Load` event. As the form loads, this event creates the instance of the object, `CDataObject`. The object will be developed later in this How-To. If an error occurs, the error will be trapped and displayed through the `Error` subroutine.

```
Private Sub Form_Load()

On Error GoTo Err_Form_Load

    ' Create the instance
    Set m_Hotels = New CDataObjects
```

continued on next page

continued from previous page

```
Exit_Form_Load:
    Exit Sub


Err_Form_Load:
    Call afx_GenericError("Form_Load: ", Err)
    Resume Exit_Form_Load


End Sub
```

4. Insert the following code in the **Form_Unload** event. As the form gets unloaded, the reference to the object that was created in the **Form_Load**, **CDataObjects**, is terminated and the application is ended. If an error occurs, the error will be displayed through the **Error** procedure.

```
Private Sub Form_Unload(cancel As Integer)


    On Error GoTo Err_Form_Unload


    ' Clear the references
    Set m_Hotels = Nothing


Exit_Form_Unload:
    Exit Sub


Err_Form_Unload:
    Call afx_GenericError("Form_Unload:", Err)
    Resume Exit_Form_Unload
End Sub
```

5. Insert the following code in the **cboHotels_GotFocus** event. When the focus of the application is on the combo box, the **FillControl** method defined in **CDataObject** is performed using the **Select SQL** statement, and the combo box is populated with the names of the hotels.

```
Private Sub cboHotels_GotFocus()


Dim sSQL As String


    sSQL = "Select Hotel, Name from tbl_Hotels"


    ' Fill the combo box with the information from the database
    m_Hotels.FillControl cboHotels, sSQL, "hotel", "name"
End Sub
```

6. Insert the following code in the `cmdOK_Click` event. This will cause the `Form_Unload` event to be performed.

```
Private Sub cmdOK_Click()
    Unload Me
End Sub
```

7. Use the Insert Class Module menu item from the Visual Basic menu to add a new class module. Name it `CDataObjects` and save it as `CDATAOBJ.CLS`.

8. Add the following code to the General Declarations section of the `CDataObjects` class module. The first constant defines your database member. The next defines your connection member.

```
Option Explicit

' Database
Private m_env As rdoEnvironment

' Connection
Private m_con As rdoConnection
```

9. Insert the following code in the `Class_Initialize` event of `CDataObject`. When this class is initialized, a logical connection to ODBC is made. If an error occurs during any process of opening the database or establishing the resultset, the generic error handling routine will be called.

```
Private Sub Class_Initialize()

    Dim sSql As String

    On Error GoTo Err_Class_Initialize

    ' use the default environment
    Set m_env = rdoEnvironments(0)
    ' Open the connection
    Set m_con = m_env.OpenConnection(dsName:="dsnWaiteSQL", _
        Connect:="uid=sa;pwd=")

Exit_Class_Initialize:
    Exit Sub

Err_Class_Initialize:
    Call afx_GenericError("Class_Initialize:", Err)
    Resume Exit_Class_Initialize
End Sub
```

10. Add the following code to the `Class_Terminate` event of the
`CDataObject` class module. This event closes the RDO environment to the
object variables that were opened in the `Class_Initialize` procedure. By
closing the RDO environment, all connections and resultsets related to it
are also closed.

```
Private Sub Class_Terminate()

    On Error GoTo Err_Class_Terminate

    ' Close the RDO Environment
    If Not (m_env Is Nothing) Then
        m_env.Close
    End If

    ' Clear the references
    Set m_env = Nothing

Exit_Class_Terminate:
    Exit Sub

Err_Class_Terminate:
    Call afx_GenericError("Class_Terminate:", Err)
    Resume Exit_Class_Terminate
End Sub
```

11. Add the following public method to the `CDataObjects` class module. This
method is used to fill the desired list-based control with the requested
information. The control is first cleared before any information is added to
it. The `rdoResultset` is created based on the SQL query passed to this
procedure. As the resultset is processed, the selected control is populated.
When it is completed, the control's `ListIndex` property is set to the first
record. Note that this method passes through the use of the `ParamArray`
argument. The use of this allows you to provide an arbitrary number of
arguments. The information passed in the `ParamArray` consists of the
names of the columns that you will want to display in the control.

```
' Fill any list type control with the data
'
' Parameters:
'    cntl        list type control to fill
'    sSQL        SQL Statement
'    sIDColumn   name of the column containing the record ID
'    sColumns    name of the columns of data to display
Public Sub FillControl(cntl As Control, rs As rdoResultset, _
    sIDColumn As String, ParamArray sColumns() As Variant)
```

```
Dim sData As String
Dim i As Integer
Dim rs as rdoResultset


On Error GoTo Err_FillControl

' Clear the list
cntl.Clear


' open the resultset
Set rs = m_con.OpenResultset(sSQL)


' Add each record to control
' until the end of the file
If (Not rs.BOF) Then
    Do Until rs.EOF
        ' Concatenate each desired column
        sData = ""
        For i = 0 To UBound(sColumns)
            sData = sData & " " & rs(cstr(sColumns(i)))
        Next
        ' Add the item to the list
        cntl.AddItem sData
        cntl.ItemData(cntl.NewIndex) = rs(sIDColumn)

        ' Move to the next row
        rs.MoveNext
    Loop
End If
' Set control to highlight the first record
' in the list
cntl.ListIndex = 0

Exit_FillControl:
    Exit Sub


Err_FillControl:
    Call afx_GenericError("FillControl:", Err)
    Resume Exit_FillControl
End Sub
```

12. Use the Insert Module menu item from the Visual Basic menu to add a standard module to the project. This module will be used for error handling. Go to the module's property list by pressing [F4], name it **bError**, and save the file as **ERROR.BAS**. Add the following code to a public subprocedure.

Two values are going to be passed to this procedure. One is a string value, the name of the procedure in which the remote data object error occurred. The other is a long value, which is the error number that occurred. When an error occurs in any of the modules, this procedure is executed. The system will beep to notify the user that an error has occurred. The procedure the error occurred in, a description of the error, and the error number will be displayed in a message box.

```
' Generic Error routine
Public Sub afx_GenericError(sProcedure As String, lErr As Long)
    On Error GoTo Err_afx_GenericError

    Beep
    MsgBox sProcedure & " " & Error$(lErr) & ". " & vbCrLf _
        & "Error Nbr: " & CStr(lErr)
Exit_afx_GenericError:
    Exit Sub
Err_afx_GenericError:
    Call afx_GenericError("afx_GenericError:", Err)
    End
End Sub
```

How It Works

As the form loads, the **m_Hotels** member instantiates itself to the class module, **CDataObjects**. In that process, the connection to ODBC and the SQL Server database is made. Two controls can have focus—the combo box and command button. *Focus* refers to a control or window that can receive a mouse click or keyboard input at any one time. When the combo box receives focus, the **SQL** statement will be executed through the procedure, **FillControl**.

In the **FillControl** procedure, the control you wish to be filled is cleared and the **SQL** statement is executed. The **If** statement checks to make sure that data was returned by the **OpenResultset** statement. If data is returned, the **Do...Loop** will fill the control until there is no more data in the resultset. When you press the OK button, the **m_Hotels** member is set to nothing, which will cause the **Class_Terminate** event to be processed. This closes all your connections to the database.

Comments

The class that you just built, **CDataObjects**, can also populate a listbox. Simply change the name of the combo box to the name of the listbox.

COMPLEXITY

BEGINNING

5.2   How do I...
Populate an unbound grid?

Problem

In my reservation system, I want to display the reservation information of our guests in a grid format. I don't want it to be bound to a data control because I don't want the overhead that comes with using it. Also, I don't want to use a bound data control for there is no easy way to control the database transaction. How do I accomplish this?

Technique

The **DBGrid** control is a good control for displaying information in a spreadsheet format, but it would mean that you would have to bind it to a database through the use of the data control or remote data control. Since you don't want to bind the grid to a database like that, you are going to use the Microsoft **MSFlexGrid** control.

The Microsoft **MSFlexGrid** control is a more sophisticated grid control than the previous Microsoft grid control. It allows you to display your information in rows and columns just like any other original grid control, or you can have it bound to a database. When the grid is bound to a database, the data is displayed as read-only. The first thing you have to do is create an **rdoResultset** containing the rows and columns of interest. An **rdoResultset** is an object that contains the rows and columns of data that result from the query that was executed.

After the **rdoResultset** is created, you will use the **rdoResultset** method, **MoveNext**, to access the data. At any given time, a pointer will be looking at only one row of data within the **rdoResultset**. The **MoveNext** method is used to iterate over the records in the **rdoResultset**. Loop through the **rdoResultset** until you reach the **rdoResultset** property, **EOF**, which stands for End Of File.

As you pass through each row, you process each column of the **rdoResultset** through the **rdoColumns** collection. The **rdoColumns** collection contains **rdoResultset**'s column data based on which row you are pointing to. The two **rdoColumns** properties you use to get the column information are **Name** and **Value**. When you move to an active row as described earlier, you access the column **Value** by referencing the **Name** property of **rdoColumns'** column. For a more in-depth explanation of RDO, refer to Chapter 3, Remote Data Objects.

The information you will use is from the Reservations table from the Hotels database. You are interested only in a few of the columns in the table; therefore, our **SQL** statement will select only the columns you wish to display.

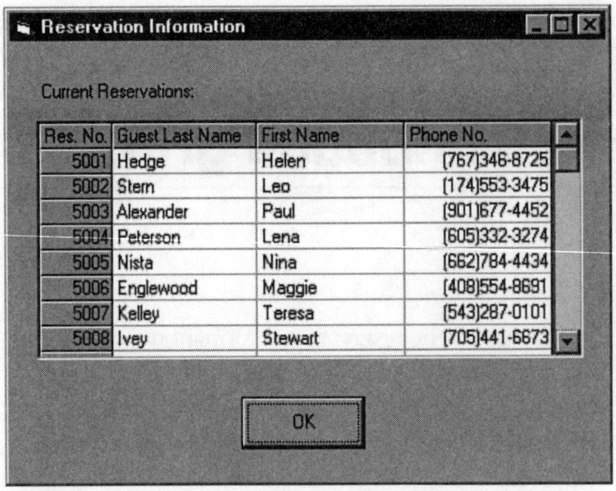

Figure 5-2 The unbound grid control filled
with data from an `rdoResultset`

Steps

Open and run **CUSTRESV.VBP**. The form shown in Figure 5-2 will appear. When the
form loads, the grid will be filled with the reservation number, the guest's first and
last name (last name first), and his phone number. To exit the program, simply
press OK.

This example uses a class module similar to the one developed in How-To 5.1.
A class module is used to perform the physical database access and custom control.

1. Create a new project and save it as **CUSTRESV.VBP**. Select the default form,
`Form1`, name it `frmResvInfo`, and save it as **RESVINFO.FRM**. Assign the
object and properties for this form as listed in Table 5-2.

Table 5-2 Objects and properties for RESVINFO.FRM

OBJECT	PROPERTY	SETTING
Form	Name	frmResvInfo
	Appearance	1 – 3D
	Caption	"Reservation Information"
Label	Name	lblCurResv
	Caption	"Current Reservations"
MSFlexGrid	Name	grdResvInfo
Command Button	Name	cmdOK
	Caption	"OK"

2. Insert the following code into the General Declarations section of **frmResvInfo**. This will create a new object of **CDataObjects** when the object variable, **m_Resv**, is declared.

```
Option Explicit

' Assign the Reservation Name Member to Data Object Class
Private m_Resv As CDataObjects
```

3. Insert the following code into the **Form_Load** event. As the form loads, the **Set** statement creates the instance of the object. The **With** statement executes a series of statements to set up the grid object's column widths and headers. The last statement performs the **FillGrid** method defined in **CDataObjects**, which populates the grid.

```
Private Sub Form_Load()

    Dim sSql as String

    On Error GoTo Err_Form_Load

    ' Create the instance
    Set m_Resvs = New CDataObjects

    ' Initialize Grid settings
    With grdResvInfo
        .ColWidth(0) = 720
        .ColWidth(1) = 1440
        .ColWidth(2) = 1440
        .ColWidth(3) = 1440
        .Row = 0
        .Col = 0
        .Text = "Res. No."
        .Col = 1
        .Text = "Guest Last Name"
        .Col = 2
        .Text = "First Name"
        .Col = 3
        .Text = "Phone No."
    End With

    sSql = "Select ResNo, LastName, FirstName, "
    sSql = sSql & "Phone from tbl_Reservations"
```

continued on next page

continued from previous page

```
      m_Resv.FillGrid grdResvInfo, sSql, "ResNo", "LastName", "FirstName", ⇐
"Phone"
Exit_Form_Load:
      Exit Sub


Err_Form_Load:
      Call afx_GenericError("Form_Load:", Err)
      Resume Exit_Form_Load


End Sub
```

4. Insert the following code in the **Form_Unload** event. As the form gets
unloaded, the reference to the object that was created in the **Form_Load**,
m_Resv, is terminated and the application ends. If an error occurs, the error
will be displayed through the **Error** procedure.

```
Private Sub Form_Unload(Cancel As Integer)

      On Error GoTo Err_Form_Unload

      Set m_Resv = Nothing

Exit_Form_Unload:
      Exit Sub


Err_Form_Unload:
      Call afx_GenericError("Form_Unload:", Err)
      Resume Exit_Form_Unload
End Sub
```

5. Insert the following code in the **cmdOK_Click** event. This will cause the
Form_Unload event to be performed.

```
Private Sub cmdOK_Click()

      On Error GoTo Err_cmdOK_Click

      Unload Me

Exit_cmdOK_Click:
      Exit Sub


Err_cmdOK_Click:
      Call afx_GenericError("cmdOK_Click:", Err)
      Resume Exit_cmdOK_Click
End Sub
```

6. Use the Insert Class Module menu item from the Visual Basic menu to add a new class module. Name it `CDataObjects` and save it as `CDATAOBJ.CLS`.

7. Add the following code to the General Declarations section of `CDataObjects`. The first constant defines your environment member. The last constant defines the database connection member.

```
Option Explicit

' Environment
Private m_env As rdoEnvironment

' Connection
Private m_con As rdoConnection
```

8. Insert the following code in the `Class_Initialize` event of the `CDataObject` class module. When this class is initialized, the environment and connection to the ODBC data source name is opened. If an error occurs during any process of opening the database or establishing the resultset, the error handling routine will be called. The `SQL` statement is going to return every record in the table to the resultset member.

```
Private Sub Class_Initialize()

    Dim sSql As String

    On Error GoTo Err_Class_Initialize

    ' use the default environment
    Set m_env = rdoEnvironments(0)
    ' Open the connection
    Set m_con = m_env.OpenConnection(dsn:="dsnWaiteSQL", _
        connect:="UID=sa;pwd=")

Exit_Class_Initialize:
    Exit Sub

Err_Class_Initialize:
    Call afx_GenericError("Class_Initialize:", Err)
    Resume Exit_Class_Initialize
End Sub
```

9. Add the following code to the `Class_Terminate` event of the `CDataObject` class module. This event closes the RDO environment to the object variables that were opened in the `Class_Initialize` procedure. By

closing the RDO environment, all connections and resultsets related to it
are also closed.

```
Private Sub Class_Terminate()
    On Error GoTo Err_Class_Terminate

' Close the resultset and database
    If Not (m_env Is Nothing) Then
        m_env.Close
    End If

    ' Clear the references
    Set m_env = Nothing

Exit_Class_Terminate:
    Exit Sub

Err_Class_Terminate:
    Call afx_GenericError("Class_Terminate:", Err)
    Resume Exit_Class_Terminate
End Sub
```

10. Add the following **Public** method to the **CDataObjects** class module to
fill the desired grid control with the requested information. The
OpenResultset executes the **SQL** statement that will get all the information contained in the **tbl_Reservations** table. The **If** statement checks
to make sure that data was returned to the resultset. If there is data, the
Do...Loop will process each row of information and the **For...Next** loop
will insert information into each column in the grid.

```
' Fill an unbound grid control with the data
'
' Parameters:
'    cntl        list type control to fill
'    sSQL        SQL statement to process
'    sColumns    name of the columns of data to display
Public Sub FillGrid(cntl As Control, sSql As String, ParamArray sColumns() ⇐
As Variant)

    Dim sData As String
    Dim i As Integer
    Dim j As Long
    Dim lMaxRows As Long
    Dim rs As rdoResultset
```

```
On Error GoTo Err_FillGrid

' Open the resultset
Set rs = m_con.OpenResultset(sSql)

' Add each record until the end of the file
j = 1
If (Not rs.BOF) Then
    Do Until rs.EOF
        cntl.Row = j
        For i = 0 To UBound(sColumns)
            With cntl
                .Col = i
                .Text = rs(sColumns(i))
            End With
        Next
        ' Get next row and add another row
        ' to the grid
        rs.MoveNext
        j = j + 1
        cntl.Rows = j + 1
    Loop
End If

Exit_FillGrid:
    Exit Sub

Err_FillGrid:
    Call afx_GenericError("FillGrid:", Err)
    Resume Exit_FillGrid

End Sub
```

11. Use the Insert Module menu item from the Visual Basic menu to add a standard module to the project. This module will be used for error handling. Go to the module's property list by pressing ⌨F4, name it **bError** and save the file as **ERROR.BAS**. Add the following code to a **Public Sub** procedure. Two values are going to be passed to this procedure. One is a string value and is the name of the procedure in which the remote data object error occurred. The other is a long value and is the error number that occurred. When an error occurs in any of the modules, this procedure is executed. The system will beep to notify the user that an error has occurred. The procedure the error occurred in, a description of the error, and the error number will be displayed in a message box.

```
' Generic Error routine
Public Sub afx_GenericError(sProcedure As String, lErr As Long)
    On Error GoTo Err_afx_GenericError

    Beep
    MsgBox sProcedure & " " & Error$(lErr) & ". " & CStr(lErr)
Exit_afx_GenericError:
    Exit Sub
Err_afx_GenericError:

    Call afx_GenericError("afx_GenericError:", Err)
    Stop
End Sub
```

How It Works

As the form loads, the **m_Resv** member instantiates itself to the class module, **CDataObjects**. In this process, the connection to ODBC and the SQL Server database is made. Then the grid settings are established with the number of columns, their width, and column headers. The form then calls **FillGrid** and passes the name of the grid, the **SQL** statement to be processed, and which columns are to be used in the grid to the procedure. The **FillGrid** procedure is based on the **FillControl** procedure used in How-To 5.1. Based on the arguments passed to it, a nested loop is used to fill in the grid with the appropriate information.

In the **FillGrid** procedure, the **rdoResultset** is opened based on the **SQL** statement passed to it. The **If** statement checks to make sure data was returned by the **OpenResultset** statement. If data is returned, the **For...Next** loop is used to insert information into the grid's columns, while the **Do...Loop** points the insertion to the correct row on the grid. The **MoveNext** method moves the data pointer to the next row in the resultset. Since it is not known how many rows are going to be returned by the resultset, a counter is used to add a row to the grid each time a data pointer moves to the next row.

When you click the OK button, the **m_Resv** member is set to nothing, which will cause the **Class_Terminate** event to be processed. This closes all your connections to the database.

Comments

This problem could have been solved using the **DBGrid** that also ships with VB 5.0; however, the **MsFlexGrid** control was designed with either bound or unbound data in mind. This means that **MsFlexGrid** is a lot easier to use in an unbound manner.

COMPLEXITY
BEGINNING

5.3 How do I...
Display calculated fields in an unbound grid?

Problem

I want to show marketing the percentage of how much people are paying to stay at any one of our hotels versus what the rooms actually cost. How can I show calculated information in a spreadsheet-like manner without using a bound control? I do not want to use a bound control because I do not want the overhead of binding my database connection to a data control and then linking that to a control.

Technique

As with any business function, certain sets of formulas and rules will apply to applications across the enterprise. By encapsulating these business rules in a class module outside the application, this function could be used in many other applications as well.

This example will be built upon what you learned in How-To 5.2. The same **FillGrid** procedure in **CDataObjects** will be used to fill the grid with the calculated information. Since calculations are different from data access, the process of calculating numbers is going to be placed in a separate class module. The **MsFlexGrid** control is going to be used as in How-To 5.2, because it works well with unbound data.

Steps

Open and run **CALCGRID.VBP**. The form shown in Figure 5-3 will appear. The grid will be filled with the hotel number, reservation number, last and first name of the guest, the amount the guest paid for the reservation, the actual cost of the room, and the percentage of markup (or down) the guest paid. To exit the program, click the OK button.

1. Create a new project and save it as **CALCGRID.VBP**. Select the default form, **Form1**, name it **frmMain**, and save it as **FMAIN.FRM**. Assign the objects and properties for this form as listed in Table 5-3.

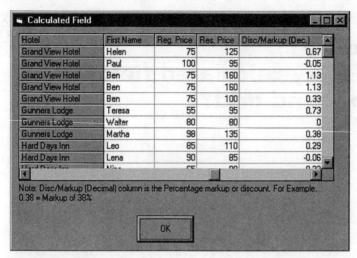

Figure 5-3 Payment markup or discount displayed in the grid

Table 5-3 Objects and properties of FMAIN.FRM

OBJECT	PROPERTY	SETTING
Form	Name	frmMain
	Appearance	1 - 3D
	Caption	"Calculated Field"
MsFlexGrid	Name	grdRoomRes
Command Button	Name	cmdOK
	Caption	"OK"
Label	Name	lblLegend
	Caption	"Note: Disc/Markup (Decimal) column is the Percentage markup or discount. For Example, 0.38 = Markup of 38%"

2. Insert the following code into the General Declarations section of the **frmMain**. This will create a new object of **CDataObjects** when the object variable, **m_RoomResv**, is declared.

```
Option Explicit


' Assign the member to the Data Object
Private m_RoomResv As CDataObjects
```

3. Insert the following code into the **Form_Load** event. As the form loads, the **Set** statement creates the instance of **CDataObject** to the member variable, **m_RoomResv**. The **With** statement prepares the grid with the appropriate number of columns and sets up their width. Then the **FillGrid** procedure is called and will fill the grid, **grdRoomRes**.

```
Private Sub Form_Load()

    On Error GoTo Err_Form_Load

    ' Create the instance
    Set m_RoomResv = New CDataObjects

    ' Initialize Grid Settings
    With grdRoomRes
        .Cols = 6
        .ColWidth(0) = 1800
        .ColWidth(1) = 720
        .ColWidth(2) = 1440
        .ColWidth(3) = 1080
        .ColWidth(4) = 900
        .ColWidth(5) = 900
        .Row = 0
        .Col = 0
        .Text = "Hotel"
        .Col = 1
        .Text = "Res. No"
        .Col = 2
        .Text = "Guest's Last Name"
        .Col = 3
        .Text = "First Name"
        .Col = 4
        .Text = "Reg. Price"
        .Col = 5
        .Text = "Res. Price"
    End With

    sSQL = "SELECT c.Name, b.ResNo, b.LastName, "
    sSQL = sSQL & "b.FirstName, b.Amount, a.Price "
    sSQL = sSQL & "From tbl_Rooms a, tbl_Reservations b "
    sSQL = sSQL & ", tbl_Hotels c "
    sSQL = sSQL & "Where a.Room = b.Room "
    sSQL = sSQL & "And a.Hotel = b.Hotel "
    sSQL = sSQL & "And b.Hotel = c.Hotel "
    sSQL = sSQL & "Order by c.Name"
```

continued on next page

continued from previous page

```
        m_RoomResv.FillGrid grdRoomRes, sSQL, "Hotel", _
            "ResNo", "LastName", "FirstName", "Amount", "Price"
        m_RoomResv.CalcPercent grdRoomRes      ' Fill the control

Exit_Form_Load:
    Exit Sub

Err_Form_Load:
    Call afx_GenericError("Form_Load:", Err)
    Resume Exit_Form_Load
End Sub
```

4. Insert the following code in the **Form_Unload** event. As the form gets
unloaded, the reference to the member that was created in the **Form_Load**,
m_RoomResv, is terminated and the application ends.

```
Private Sub Form_Unload(Cancel As Integer)

    Set m_RoomResv = Nothing

End Sub
```

5. Enter the following code in the **cmdOK** command button's **Click** event. This
procedure will invoke the **Form_Unload** event to end the sample program.

```
Private Sub cmdOK_Click()

    On Error GoTo Err_cmdOK_Click

    Unload Me

Exit_cmdOK_Click:
    Exit Sub

Err_cmdOK_Click:
    Call afx_GenericError("cmdOK_Click:", Err)
    Resume Exit_cmdOK_Click
End Sub
```

6. Use the Insert Class Module menu item from the Visual Basic menu to add
a new class module. Name it **CDataObjects** and save it as **CDATAOBJ.CLS**.

7. Add the following code to the General Declarations section of the
CDataObjects class module. The first constant defines your environment
member. The next constant defines your database connection.

```
Option Explicit

' Environment
Private m_env As rdoEnvironment

' Connect
Private m_con As rdoConnection
```

8. Insert the following code in the `Class_Initialize` event of the
`CDataObject` class module. When this class is initialized, the `Set` statement assigns the `m_Calcs` member to the `CCalculations` object. Then the
RDO environment and connection to your ODBC data source name is
opened. If an error occurs during any process of opening, the error handling routine will be called.

```
Private Sub Class_Initialize()

    Dim sSql As String

    On Error GoTo Err_Class_Initialize

    Set m_Calcs = New CCalculations

    ' use the default workspace and database
    Set m_env = rdoEnvironments(0)
    Set m_con = m_env.OpenConnection("dsnWaiteSQL", , , "UID=sa;PWD= ")

Exit_Class_Initialize:
    Exit Sub

Err_Class_Initialize:
    Call afx_GenericError("Class_Initialize:", Err)
    Resume Exit_Class_Initialize
End Sub
```

9. Add the following code to the `Class_Terminate` event of the
`CDataObject` class module. This event closes all the connections to the
object variables opened in the `Class_Initialize` procedure. By closing
the RDO environment, all connections and resultsets related to it are also
closed.

```
Private Sub Class_Terminate()

    On Error GoTo Err_Class_Terminate

' Close the RDO environment
    If Not (m_env Is Nothing) Then
        m_env.Close
    End If

    ' Clear the references
    Set m_env = Nothing
Exit_Class_Terminate:
    Exit Sub


Err_Class_Terminate:
    Call afx_GenericError("Class_Terminate:", Err)
    Resume Exit_Class_Terminate


End Sub
```

10. Add the following **Public** method to the **CDataObject** class module to fill the desired grid control with the requested information. The **OpenResultset** performs the **SQL** statement passed to it. The **If** statement checks to make sure that data was returned to the resultset. If there is data, the **Do...Loop** will process each row of information and the **For...Next** loop will insert information into each column of the grid.

```
' Fill an unbound grid control with the data
'
' Parameters:
'   cntl        list type control to fill
'   sSQL        SQL statement
'   sColumns    name of the columns of data to display
Public Sub FillGrid(cntl As Control, sSQL As String, _
    ParamArray sColumns() As Variant)

    On Error GoTo Err_FillGrid

    Dim sData As String
    Dim x As Long
    Dim y As Long
    Dim nMaxRows As Long
    Dim rs As rdoResultset

    ' Open the resultset
```

```
Set rs = m_con.OpenResultset(sSQL)

' Add each record until the end of the file
y = 1
If (Not rs.BOF) Then
    Do Until rs.EOF
        cntl.Row = y
        For x = 0 To UBound(sColumns)
            With cntl
                .Col = x
                .Text = rs(x)
            End With
        Next
        ' Get next row and add another row
        ' to the grid
        rs.MoveNext
        y = y + 1
        cntl.Rows = y + 1
    Loop
End If

Exit_FillGrid:
    Exit Sub
Err_FillGrid:
    Call afx_GenericError("FillGrid:", Err)
    Resume Exit_FillGrid

End Sub
```

11. Add the following **Private** method to the **CDataObjects** class module. This method performs the calculation of the price variance of how much the guest paid for the reservation versus what the room actually cost. The grid to be used is passed to this method through the **argument** variable. The first process adds one more row to the gird control to contain the percentage value of the discount and percentage is placed in the column's title. Next, to process the calculations, the fourth and fifth columns are looped through to get the dividend and divisor to calculate the percentage. The dividend and divisor are passed to the member, **m_Calcs** properties, **Dividend** and **Divisor**. The **m_Calcs** member has a method to calculate the percentage. The result of the calculation is placed in the percentage column by getting the **m_Calcs** property **Percentage**. If an error occurs during this method, the error handling routine will handle displaying the error to the user. The following steps explain how the **m_Calcs** handles the calculation of the percentage.

```vb
Private Sub CalcPercent(cntl As Control)

    Dim x As Long
    Dim y As Long

    On Error GoTo Err_CalcPercent

    ' Set up Discount/Markup column
    With cntl
        .Cols = .Cols + 1
        .Col = .Cols - 1
        .ColWidth(.Cols - 1) = 1740
        .Row = 0
        .Text = "Disc/Markup (Dec.)"
    End With
    ' Process the Discount/Markup
    For y = 1 To cntl.Rows - 1
        cntl.Row = y
        For x = 4 To 5
            cntl.Col = x
            If x = 5 Then
                m_Calcs.Divisor = CDbl(cntl.Text)
            Else
                m_Calcs.Dividend = CDbl(cntl.Text)
            End If
        Next x
        ' Add info to column
        With cntl
            .Col = 6
            .Text = m_Calcs.Percentage
        End With
    Next y

Exit_CalcPercent:
    Exit Sub

Err_CalcPercent:
    Call afx_GenericError("CalcPercent:", Err)
    Resume Exit_CalcPercent
End Sub
```

12. Use the Insert Class Module menu item from the Visual Basic menu to add a new class module. Name it `CCalculations` and save it as `CCALC.CLS`.

13. Add the following code to the General Declarations of the `CCalculations` class module. The members defined here are variables that will be used for calculating the percentage of price variance.

```
Option Explicit

Private m_Divisor As Double
Private m_Dividend As Double
Private m_Percentage As Double
```

14. Add the following **Public Property** procedures to the `CCalculations` class module. The **Property Let** and **Get** are used to define the **Divisor** member. These procedures expose the properties to the other parts of the application.

```
Public Property Let Divisor(dDivisor As Double)
    m_Divisor = dDivisor
End Property

Public Property Get Divisor() As Double
    Divisor = m_Divisor
End Property
```

15. Add the following **Public Property** procedures to the `CCalculations` class module. The **Property Let** and **Get** are used to define the **Dividend** member. These procedures expose the properties to the other parts of the application.

```
Public Property Let Dividend(dDividend As Double)
    m_Dividend = dDividend
End Property

Public Property Get Dividend() As Double
    Dividend = m_Dividend
End Property
```

16. Add the following **Public Property** procedures to the `CCalculations` class module. The **Property Let** and **Get** are used to define the **Percentage** member. These procedures expose the properties to the other parts of the application. In the **Property Get** procedure, the calculation for the percentage is performed and formatted to display up to two decimal places.

```
Public Property Let Percentage(dPercentage As Double)
    m_Percentage = dPercentage
End Property


Public Property Get Percentage() As Double

    Percentage = Format(((m_Divisor / m_Dividend) / m_Dividend), "#.00")

End Property
```

17. Use the Insert Module menu item from the Visual Basic menu to add a standard module to the project. This module will be used for error handling. Go to the module's property list by pressing F4, name it **bError**, and save the file as **ERROR.BAS**. Add the following code to a **Public Sub** procedure. Two values are going to be passed to this procedure. One is a string value and is the name of the procedure in which the remote data object error occurred. The other is a long value and is the error number that occurred. When an error occurs in any of the modules, this procedure is executed. The system will beep to notify the user that an error has occurred. The procedure the error occurred in, a description of the error, and the error number will be displayed in a message box.

```
' Generic Error routine
Public Sub afx_GenericError(sProcedure As String, lErr As Long)
    On Error GoTo Err_afx_GenericError


    Beep
    MsgBox sProcedure & " " & Error$(lErr) & ". " & CStr(lErr)


Exit_afx_GenericError:
    Exit Sub
Err_afx_GenericError:
    Call afx_GenericError("afx_GenericError:", Err)
    Stop
End Sub
```

How It Works

As the form loads, the **m_RoomResv** member variable is assigned the class module, **CDataObjects**. As **CDataObjects** gets initialized, the connection to ODBC and the SQL Server database is made. Then the grid control gets set up. The column headings and their widths are applied to the control. The **Form_Load** procedure then calls the **FillGrid** procedure. Based on the arguments passed to the procedure, a **For...Next** loop is used to fill the grid with the appropriate information.

In the **FillGrid** procedure, the **rdoResultset** is opened based on the **SQL** statement passed to it. The **If** statement checks to make sure data was returned by the **OpenResultset** statement. If data is returned, the **For...Next** loop is used to insert information into the grid's columns, while the **Do...Loop** points the insertion to the correct row on the grid. The **MoveNext** method moves the data pointer to the next row in the resultset. Since it is not known how many rows are going to be returned by the resultset, a counter is used to add a row to the grid each time the data pointer moves to the next row.

After the **FillGrid** procedure is performed, the **CalcPercent** procedure is called. First, a new column is added to the grid and its header information is set up. Then, the nested **For...Next** loops are used to process each row in the grid. The column header row and the last row will not be processed. The header row is not processed because it already has the value of the column title. The last row is not processed because there is no information to place in it. The first **For...Next** loop is used to process the rows and the second **For...Next** loop is used to process the columns. When the discount or markup value is calculated, the **Percentage** procedure is performed and the calculated value is added to the cell.

When you press the OK button, the **m_RoomResv** member is set to nothing, which will cause the **Class_Terminate** event to be processed. This closes all your connections to the database.

COMPLEXITY
BEGINNING

5.4   How do I...
Control the number of rows displayed?

Problem

I have a large amount of data I want to retrieve and use to populate a listbox or combo box. The problem I'm having is that the more information being retrieved into the resultset, the longer it takes to fill the control. I'm getting a lot of complaints from my users about how long this process is taking. Rather than retrieving all the records from the database tables based on my query, how do I limit the number of records retrieved into my resultset? Also, how do I get the rest of the records when the users want to see them?

Technique

One of the factors a lot of developers overlook when it comes to retrieving data is how much is actually needed at any one time. Using lookup controls like a listbox or combo box, there is a finite amount of space the user can see at one given time. For example, in a forecasting system, you might have over 10,000 different organizations to look at. One method of displaying this information is to break the organizations down by cost groups and have the information split into two or more different listboxes.

Another way of retrieving a controlled amount of data is by using cursors, or row pointers, to allow for moving up and down in a resultset with both relative and absolute positioning. *Relative positioning* refers to moving through a list of data through the use of a plus or minus value. *Absolute positioning* refers to moving the record pointer to an exact record number. For example, you have 5,000 rows of information and your record pointer is pointing at record 2,500. On your form, command buttons allow the user to move to the next or previous 100 rows. This is an example of relative positioning. Also on your form, command buttons allow the user to go to a specific record number. When you click the button, you enter the value 3,500 and press Enter. The record pointer now goes directly to record 3,500 and you display the record information for that record's row. This is an example of absolute positioning.

When retrieving a large amount of data, for example more than 1,000 rows, rather than displaying all the rows at once, fetch only the first 100 rows and display them in the listbox. As the user scrolls through the data, when he reaches the 100th row, then he can fetch the next 100, and so on.

This example will use the `rdoResultset` method `GetRows`. The `GetRows` method uses relative positioning. It retrieves the number of rows from an `rdoResultset` based on the argument you pass to it.

Steps

Open and run **CURSORS.VBP**. The form shown in Figure 5-4 will appear. When the form loads, a `rdoResultset` is created. The listbox is filled with the list of the guests of the hotel. Rather than displaying all the guests at once, only the first five guests are going to be displayed. To display more, press the command button and the next five will be displayed, and so on. When the listbox has all the rows from the `rdoResultset` in it, a message box will appear notifying you that you have retrieved all the records and you will not be able to press the button again.

1. Create a new project called **CURSORS.VBP**. Open the **Form1** and name it **fMain**. Save it as **FMAIN.FRM**. Add the objects and assign the properties to the form as listed in Table 5-4.

Figure 5-4 The first five records of registered guests

Table 5-4 Objects and properties of `FMAIN.FRM`

OBJECT	PROPERTY	SETTING
Form	Name	frmMain
	Caption	"Registered Guests"
List Box	Name	lstGuests
Command Button	Name	cmdGetMoreNames
	Caption	"Display More Guests"
Command Button	Name	cmdClose
	Caption	Close

2. Add the following code to the General Declarations section of **fMain**. The first variable is used to make the number of columns from the **SQL** statement available throughout the form. The next variable will be used to build a two-dimensional array which will contain the names of the guests. The last variable is for the **rdoResultset**.

```
Option Explicit

Dim nColumns As Integer
Dim vGuests As Variant
Dim rs As rdoResultset
```

3. Insert the following code in the **Form_Load** event. As the form loads, the **rdoResultset** is created. The **SQL** statement is not being built in the normal fashion, but through a function. This will be explained in a later step. After the **rdoResultset** is created, the first set of rows is retrieved and will be displayed by calling the **FetchRows** subroutine.

```
Private Sub Form_Load()

    Dim env As rdoEnvironment
    Dim con As rdoConnection
    Dim sSQL As String

    On Error GoTo Err_Form_Load

    ' Use the default environment
    Set env = rdoEnvironments(0)
    ' Open the connection
    Set con = env.OpenConnection(dsName:="dsnWaiteSQL",
Connect:="UID=sa;pwd=")

    ' Create the result set
    sSQL = "Select " & BuildSQL("FirstName", "LastName")
    sSQL = sSQL & " from tbl_Reservations Order by FirstName"
    Set rs = con.OpenResultset(sSQL)

    ' Get the first set of rows
    Call FetchRows

Exit_Form_Load:
    Exit Sub

Err_Form_Load:
    Call afx_GenericError("Form_Load:", Err)
    Resume Exit_Form_Load
End Sub
```

4. Insert the following code in the **Form_Unload** event. As the form gets unloaded, the reference to the RDO resultset created in the **Form_Load** is closed and set to **Nothing**.

```
Private Sub Form_Unload(Cancel as Integer)

    On Error GoTo Err_Form_Unload

    rs.Close
    Set rs = Nothing

Exit_Form_Unload
    Exit Sub

Err_Form_Unload
```

```
Call afx_GenericError(("Form_Unload:", Err)
Resume Exit_Form_Unload
```

5. Insert the following function, **BuildSQL**, to the form module. The function will return a string value, and since you do not know how many **select** items the query is going to have, the function accepts arguments via the **ParamArray**. This function has three purposes. First, it establishes how many **select** items are going to be used in the SQL statement. It will store that number in the module variable **nColumns**. Second, it puts the passed arguments into a contiguous string that will be used in the **SQL** statement. And since the SQL statement is dynamically built, it removes the last comma from the SQL statement. If the last comma were left in the statement, an error would result.

```
Function BuildSQL(ParamArray sSql() As Variant) As String

    Dim x As Integer
    Dim sSelect As String

    On Error GoTo Err_BuildSQL

    ' Get the Number of columns
    nColumns = UBound(sSql())
    ' Build the Select criteria
    For x = 0 To nColumns
        sSelect = sSelect & sSql(x) & ","
    Next
    ' Remove the last comma
    sSelect = Left(sSelect, Len(sSelect) - 1)

    BuildSQL = sSelect

Exit_BuildSQL:
    Exit Function

Err_BuildSQL:
    Call afx_GenericError("BuildSQL:", Err)
    Resume Exit_BuildSQL
End Function
```

6. Insert the following procedure code, **FetchRows**, to the form module. When an **rdoResultset** is first created, its **BOF** and **EOF** properties are set to **False**. If the **rdoResultset** is **True**, then there are no more rows to receive and you exit the procedure. Otherwise, the **rdoResultset** method, **GetRows**, is called and retrieves the specified number of rows. Then, using the number for columns from the **nColumns** variable and the **UBound** function, to get how many rows were actually retrieved using the **GetRows** method. The argument you assign the method is the number of rows returned; in this How-To you set it to **5**. The nested **For...Next** loop is used to populate the listbox.

```
Private Sub FetchRows()

    Dim y As Integer
    Dim x As Integer
    Dim sGuest As String

    On Error GoTo Err_FetchRows

    ' Check resultset for guests
    If rs.BOF Then
        MsgBox prompt:="No Guests found", Title:="Guest List"
        cmdGetMoreRows.Enabled = False
        Exit Sub
    ElseIf rs.EOF Then
        MsgBox prompt:="No more guests found", Title:="Guest List"
        cmdGetMoreRows.Enabled = False
        Exit Sub
    End If
    ' Get the next set of rows
    vGuests = rs.GetRows(5)

    ' Add the guest names to the list box
    For y = 0 To UBound(vGuests, 2)
        sGuest = ""
        For x = 0 To nColumns
            sGuest = sGuest & " " & vGuests(x, y)
        Next x
        lstGuests.AddItem sGuest
    Next y

Exit_FetchRows:
    Exit Sub
Err_FetchRows:
    Call afx_GenericError("FetchRows:", Err)
    Resume Exit_FetchRows
End Sub
```

7. Insert the following code in the `Click` event of the command button, `cmdClose`. This will unload the form which will trigger the `Form_Unload` event.

```
Private Sub cmdClose_Click()

    Unload Me

End Sub
```

8. Insert the following code in the `Click` event of the command button `cmdGetMoreRows`. This calls the `FetchRows` subprocedure.

```
Private Sub cmdGetMoreRows_Click()

    On Error GoTo Err_cmdGetMoreRows_Click

    Call FetchRows

Exit_cmdGetMoreRows_Click:
    Exit Sub

Err_cmdGetMoreRows_Click:
    Call afx_GenericError("cmdGetMoreRows_Click:", Err)
    Resume Exit_cmdGetMoreRows_Click
End Sub
```

9. Use the Insert Module menu item from the Visual Basic menu to add a standard module to the project. This module will be used for error handling. Go to the module's property list by pressing F4, name it **bError**, and save the file as **ERROR.BAS**. Add the following code to a **Public Sub** procedure. Two values are going to be passed to this procedure. One is a string value and is the name of the procedure in which the remote data object error occurred. The other is a long value and is the error number that occurred. When an error occurs in any of the modules, this procedure is executed. The system will beep to notify the user that an error has occurred. The procedure the error occurred in, a description of the error, and the error number will be displayed in a message box.

```
' Generic Error routine
Public Sub afx_GenericError(sProcedure As String, lErr As Long)
    On Error GoTo Err_afx_GenericError

    Beep
```

continued on next page

continued from previous page

```
        MsgBox sProcedure & " " & Error$(lErr) & ". " & CStr(lErr)


Exit_afx_GenericError:
    Exit Sub


Err_afx_GenericError:
    Call afx_GenericError("afx_GenericError:", Err)
    Resume Exit_afx_GenericError
End Sub
```

How It Works

When the form loads, connections to ODBC and the database are made. Then the **Load** event creates the **rdoResultset** based on the SQL query and retrieves the first five rows in the resultset. If the query was successful in retrieving information, the **FetchRows** procedure will continue. If no data was retrieved, the **rs.BOF** flag will be true and a message box will notify the user. If there is no more information in the resultset, the **rs.EOF** flag will be true and a message box will notify the user. In order to retrieve a group of rows at one time, the **GetRows** method is used. It retrieves the number of rows specified and places them into the array, **vGuests**. It then places a record pointer on the next row of information in the resultset. When the command button to get more guest names is pressed, the **FetchRows** procedure retrieves the next five rows based on where the record pointer lies. If there are only three rows left when the **GetRows** method is called, then only three rows will be retrieved and the **rdoResultset**'s **EOF** property will be set to **True**.

When you click the Close button, the RDO resultset is closed and is set to **Nothing**. Then the application ends.

Comments

There is a caveat you should to be aware of when using the **GetRows** method. If the **rdoResultset** contains a binary large object (BLOB) or the **rdoColumn** object has a data type of **rdTypeLONGVARBINARY** or **rdTypeLONGVARCHAR**, you will need to use the **GetChunk** method. If you use the **GetRows** method against such a resultset, you will receive the error message **Error 40036 Unbound Column – use GetChunk**.

5.5 How do I...
Create a Master/Detail form?

Problem

In Microsoft Access, I can design a form with an embedded child form. The main form would contain primary information, such as customer information, and the embedded child form would contain detail information, such as customer order information. This method uses bound controls so that when I change the primary information, the child information is updated because they are linked by a common key, typically the customer's account number. How would I implement something like this in Visual Basic?

Technique

Visual Basic, unlike Microsoft Access, does not allow you to embed a form within another form. You must design all the form's components onto one form. Rather than using bound controls to link different database tables together, you use the remote data object to createresultsets with the necessary information based on criteria that the user will select from a combo box.

Steps

Open and run **HOTEL.VBP**, and you will see the form shown in Figure 5-5. The combo box labeled Hotel will be filled with the names of the hotels from the database table, **tbl_Hotels**. The grid to the right of the combo box will display all the rooms that are available at the hotel that is selected in the Hotel combo box. The bottom grid displays all the reservations made at the hotel that is selected in the Hotel combo box.

1. Select **Form1** that was created when you first created this project. Name it **frmReservations** and save it as **HOTELRES.FRM**. Assign the objects and properties for this form as listed in Table 5-5. The form should look and be laid out similar to Figure 5-5.

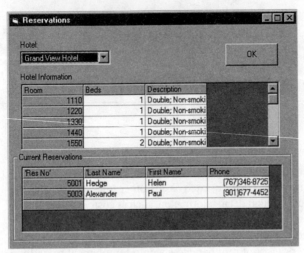

Figure 5-5 Hotel room and reservation information
displayed in two grids

Table 5-5 Objects and properties of `HOTELRES.FRM`

OBJECT	PROPERTY	SETTING
Form	Name	frmReservations
	Appearance	1 - 3D
	Caption	"Reservations"
Label	Name	lblHotel
	Caption	"&Hotel"
Label	Name	lblHotelInfo
	Caption	"Hotel &Info"
Combo Box	Name	cboHotels
	Style	2 - Dropdown List
Frame	Name	fraCurrentReservations
	Caption	"Current Reservations"
MsFlexGrid	Name	grdRoomInfo
MsFlexGrid	Name	grdResv
Command Button	Name	cmdOK
	Caption	"OK"

2. Insert the following code in the General Declarations section of
`frmReservations`. This will create a new object member for
`CDataObjects` when the object variable, `m_Resv`, is declared.

```
Option Explicit

' Assign the Resv member to the Data Object
Private m_Resv As CDataObjects
```

3. Insert the following code in the **Form_Load** event. As the form loads, this event creates the instance of the data access object for the **m_Resv** member variable. The **FillControl** method will perform the **SQL** statement and the **cboHotel** combo box will be populated with the name of the hotels.

```
Private Sub Form_Load()

    On Error GoTo Err_Form_Load

    ' Set the SQL Statment for Hotels
    sSQL = "Select Hotel, Name from tbl_Hotels"

    m_Resv.FillControl cboHotel, sSQL, "hotel", "name"

Exit_Form_Load:
    Exit Sub

Err_Form_Load:
    Call afx_GenericError("Form_Load:", Err)
    Resume Exit_Form_Load
End Sub
```

4. Insert the following code in the **Form_Unload** event. As the form gets unloaded, the reference to the members created in the **Form_Load**, **m_Resv**, is terminated and the application ends.

```
Private Sub Form_Unload(Cancel As Integer)

    On Error GoTo Err_Form_Unload

    ' Clear the reference
    Set m_Resv = Nothing

Exit_Form_Unload:
    Exit Sub

Err_Form_Unload:
    Call afx_GenericError("Form_Unload:", Err)
    Resume Exit_Form_Unload
End Sub
```

5. Enter the following code in the **cboHotel** combo box's **Click** event. This subroutine changes the pointer to an hourglass to provide feedback to the user that something is happening. Based on the hotel selected in the **cboHotel** combo box, the room and reservation information about the desired hotel will be displayed in their respective grids. Then the mouse pointer changes back to its default setting.

```
Private Sub cboHotel_Click()

    Dim sSQL As String

    On Error GoTo Err_cboHotel_Click

    Screen.MousePointer = vbHourglass

    sSQL = "Select Room, Beds, Description "
    sSQL = sSQL & "From tbl_Rooms a, tbl_Roomtypes b "
    sSQL = sSQL & "Where a.roomtype = b.roomtype "
    sSQL = sSQL & "And Hotel = " & cboHotel.ListIndex + 1
    m_Resv.FillGrid grdRoomInfo, sSQL, "Room", "Beds", "Description"

    ' Set the SQL Statment for Reservations
    sSQL = "Select ResNo as 'Res No', LastName as 'Last Name', "
    sSQL = sSQL & "FirstName as 'First Name', Phone "
    sSQL = sSQL & "From tbl_Reservations "
    sSQL = sSQL & "Where hotel = " & cboHotel.ListIndex + 1
    m_Resv.FillGrid grdResv, sSQL, "Res. No", "Last Name", "First Name", ⇐
"Phone"

    Screen.MousePointer = vbDefault

Exit_cboHotel_Click:
    Exit Sub
Err_cboHotel_Click:
    Call afx_GenericError("cboHotel_Click:", Err)
    Resume Exit_cboHotel_Click
End Sub
```

6. Add the following code to the form for the OK command button's **Click** event. This subroutine will cause the **Form_Unload** event to be triggered to end the program.

```
Private Sub cmdOK_Click()

    On Error GoTo Err_cmdOK_Click

    Unload Me

Exit_cmdOK_Click:
    Exit Sub

Err_cmdOK_Click:
    Call afx_GenericError("cmdOK_Click:", Err)
    Resume Exit_cmdOK_Click
End Sub
```

7. Use the Insert Class Module menu item to add a new class module. Name it `CDataObjects` and save it as `CDATAOBJ.CLS`.

8. Add the following code to the General Declarations section of `CDataObjects`. The first variable defines your RDO environment member. The next defines your RDO connection member.

```
Option Explicit

' Database
Private m_env As rdoEnvironment

' Connection
Private m_con As rdoConnection
```

9. Insert the following code in the `Class_Initialize` event of `CDataObject`. When this class is initialized, the RDO environment and connection are opened. If an error occurs during any process of opening, the error handling routine will be called.

```
Private Sub Class_Initialize()

    Dim sSql As String

    On Error GoTo Err_Class_Initialize

    ' use the default environment
    Set m_env = rdoEnvironments(0)
```

continued on next page

continued from previous page

```
    ' Open the connection
    Set m_con = m_env.OpenConnection(dsName:="dsnWaiteSQL",
Connect:="UID=sa;pwd=")

Exit_Class_Initialize:
    Exit Sub


Err_Class_Initialize:
    Call afx_GenericError("Class_Initialize:", Err)
    Resume Exit_Class_Initialize
End Sub
```

10. Add the following code to the **Class_Terminate** event of the **CDataObject**. This event closes the RDO environment to the object variables opened in the **Class_Initialize** procedure. By closing the RDO environment, all connections and resultsets related to it are also closed. If an error occurs during any process, the error handling routine will be called.

```
Private Sub Class_Terminate()

    On Error GoTo Err_Class_Terminate

    ' Close the resultset and database
    If Not (m_env Is Nothing) Then
        m_env.Close
    End If

    ' Clear the references
    Set m_env = Nothing
Exit_Class_Terminate:
    Exit Sub


Err_Class_Terminate:
    Call afx_GenericError("Class_Terminate:", Err)
    Resume Exit_Class_Terminate
End Sub
```

11. Add the following **Public** method to the **CDataObjects** class to fill the desired control, either a listbox or combo box, with the requested information. The **ParamArray** argument allows for an optional number of arbitrary arguments to be passed to this method. The control is cleared before any information is added to it. The **rdoResultset** is created based on the **SQL** statement that is passed to this procedure. As the resultset is processed, the selected control is populated. When the pointer has processed every record in the resultset, the control's **ListIndex** property is set to the first record.

```
' Fill any list type control with the data
'
' Parameters:
'    cntl         list type control to fill
'    sSQL         SQL Statement
'    sIDColumn    name of the column containing the record ID
'    sColumns     name of the columns of data to display
Private Sub FillControl(cntl As Control, sSQL as string, _
    sIDColumn As String, ParamArray sColumns() As Variant)

    Dim sData As String
    Dim i As Integer
    Dim rs as rdoResultset

    On Error GoTo Err_FillControl

    ' Clear the list
    cntl.Clear

    ' open the resultset
    Set rs = m_con.OpenResultset(sSQL)


    ' Add each record until the end of the file
    If (Not rs.BOF) Then
        Do Until rs.EOF
            ' Concatenate each desired column
            sData = ""
            For i = 0 To UBound(sColumns)
                sData = sData & " " & rs(cstr(sColumns(i)))
            Next
            ' Add the item to the list
            cntl.AddItem sData
            cntl.ItemData(cntl.NewIndex) = rs(sIDColumn)

            ' Move to the next row
            rs.MoveNext
        Loop
    End If

    ' Set control to highlight the first record
    ' in the list
    cntl.ListIndex = 0
```

continued on next page

continued from previous page

```
Exit_FillControl:
    Exit Sub


Err_FillControl:
    Call afx_GenericError("FillControl:", Err)
    Resume Exit_FillControl
End Sub
```

12. Add the following **Public** method to fill the desired grid control with the requested information. First, the procedure determines how many rows need to be added to the grid and adds one to the count to include the column headers. Using the **UBound** function against the **sColumns'** **ParamArray**, the number of columns for the grid is determined and the grid's row and column counts are adjusted accordingly. The width of the columns is set to one inch. The **rdoResultset** object has a collection called **rdoColumns** which represents the column information of the **rdoResultset**. By using the **Name** property of the **rdoColumns**, the database column name is returned and placed in the column heading of the grid. The record pointer is then reset to the beginning of the **rdoResultset** and is processed into the grid.

```
' Fill an unbound grid control with the data
'
' Parameters:
'   cntl        list type control to fill
'   sSQL        SQL statement
'   sColumns    name of the columns of data to display
Pbulic Sub FillGrid(cntl As Control, rs As rdoResultset, _
    ParamArray sColumns() As Variant)


    Dim sData As String
    Dim i As Integer
    Dim j As Long
    Dim lMaxRows As Long
    Dim rs As rdoResultset
    Dim sFieldName As String


    On Error GoTo Err_FillGrid


    ' Open the resultset
    Set rs = m_con.OpenResultset(sSQL)

' Set up the grid
    With cntl
        .Cols = UBound(sColumns) + 1
```

```
            .Rows = cntl.Rows
    End With
    For i = 0 To cntl.Cols - 1
        cntl.ColWidth(i) = 1440
    Next i


    ' Fill in the Column headers from the
    ' Database column names
    If (Not rs.BOF) Then
        cntl.Row = 0
        For i = 0 To cntl.Cols - 1
            cntl.Col = i
            sFieldName = rs.rdoColumns(i).Name
            cntl.Text = sFieldName
        Next


        ' Add each record until the end of the file
        j = 1
        Do Until rs.EOF
            cntl.Row = j
            For i = 0 To UBound(sColumns)
                With cntl
                    .Col = i
                    .Text = rs(i)
                End With
            Next
            ' Get next row
            rs.MoveNext
            j = j + 1
        Loop
    End If

Exit_FillGrid:
    Exit Sub
Err_FillGrid:
    Call afx_GenericError("FillGrid:", Err)
    Resume Exit_FillGrid
End Sub
```

13. Use the Insert Module menu item from the Visual Basic menu to add a standard module to the project. This module will be used for error handling. Go to the module's property list by pressing F4, name it **bError**, and save the file as **ERROR.BAS**. Add the following code to a **Public Sub** procedure. Two values are going to be passed to this procedure. One is a string value and is the name of the procedure in which the remote data object error occurred. The other is a long value and is the error number that occurred. When an error occurs in any of the modules, this procedure is executed. The system will beep to notify the user that an error has occurred. The procedure the error occurred in, a description of the error, and the error number will be displayed in a message box.

```
' Generic Error routine
Public Sub afx_GenericError(sProcedure As String, lErr As Long)
    On Error GoTo Err_afx_GenericError

    Beep
    MsgBox sProcedure & " " & Error$(lErr) & ". " & CStr(lErr)

Exit_afx_GenericError:
    Exit Sub

Err_afx_GenericError:
    Call afx_GenericError("afx_GenericError:", Err)
    Resume Exit_afx_GenericError
End Sub
```

How It Works

In this example, the detail form is the grid controls. When the form first loads, the **m_Resv** member is assigned to **CDataObjects**. **CDataObjects** gets initialized and the OBDC and SQL Server database connections are made. Then the **FillControl** procedure is called and it will process the **SQL** statement. The procedure will fill the **cboHotel** combo box with a list of the hotel names. When the **FillControl** procedure sets the first item in the list as the selected item, the **cboHotel_Click** event will be performed.

The **cboHotel_Click** event uses the combo box's selected items as part of the **Where** criteria of the **SQL** statement. This event calls the **FillGrid** procedure twice. Once is to fill the **grdRoomInfo** grid and the other is to fill the **grdResv** grid.

When the OK button is clicked, the **m_Resv** member is set to **Nothing**, which will cause the **Class_Terminate** event to be processed. This closes all your connections to the database.

Comments

Visual Basic is different from Microsoft Access when it comes to form design. One of the biggest paradigms Access programmers have to overcome is the fact that Visual Basic does not support the Form/Subform concept.

COMPLEXITY
INTERMEDIATE

5.6 How do I...
Create a query by example?

Problem

Occasionally, my users need to look up information using different search criteria. Often the resulting data from the query actually contains the same information, only the order in which the data is to be laid out or the date range on which to base the query is different. How can I accomplish this without rewriting the query each time they request this information?

Technique

This technique is often called Query by Example. It is not new; search engines within database programs have been using it for years. The technique is quite simple. Many times your users want to be able to create their own reports based on layouts they have received in other reports, but they are unfamiliar with how the data items are related to one another. The users would, therefore, have trouble specifying the exact criteria they need to get the results they want. By knowing what information users wish to retrieve and the possible variations of their request, your application can use combo boxes, check boxes, radio buttons, and text boxes to have the user select and deselect items for their search. The user basically builds a query from the components you provide.

Steps

Open and run **QBE.VBP**, and you will see the form shown in Figure 5-6. The information in the Hotel combo box comes from the **tbl_Hotels** table from the Hotels database. The information in the Payment Type combo box comes from the **tbl_PaymentTypes** table from the Hotels database. First, select a hotel where you want to see whether there are any reservations. Then select a payment type to help narrow the search. If you want to look up all payment types, select the item All. The other items, **Arrival Date**, **Departure Date**, and **Sort By**, are optional parameters. Press the **Find** command button to perform the search. If any information is found, it will be put in the grid with the frame (see Figure 5-7), **Results**. If no information is found, then a message box will appear notifying you that no records were found. The **Clear** command button will clear the results grid. The **End** command button will exit the program.

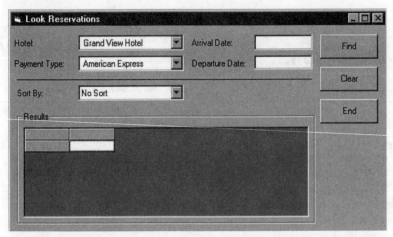

Figure 5-6 Reservation lookup form before a query

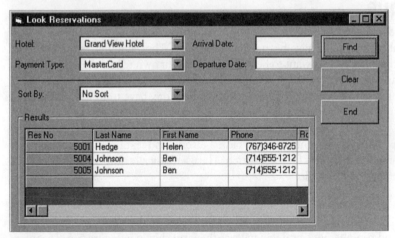

Figure 5-7 Results of a reservation lookup

1. Create a new project and save it as **QBE.VBP**. Select the default form,
   Form1, name it **frmMain** and save it as **FMAIN.FRM**. Assign the objects
   and properties for this form as listed in Table 5-6. The form should look
   similar to Figure 5-6 illustrated above. The **Line** object is not defined in the
   table because it was added just to show the separation of the **Where** criteria
   versus **Order By** criteria.

Table 5-6 Objects and properties of `FMAIN.FRM`

OBJECT	PROPERTY	SETTING
Form	Name	frmMain
	Appearance	1 - 3D
	Caption	"Lookup Reservations"
Command Button	Name	cmdFind
	Caption	"Find"
Command Button	Name	cmdClear
	Caption	"Clear"
Command Button	Name	cmdEnd
	Caption	"End"
Label	Name	lblHotel
	Caption	"&Hotel:"
Label	Name	lblPaymentType
	Caption	"&Payment Type:"
Label	Name	lblArrivalDate
	Caption	"&Arrival Date:"
Label	Name	lblDepartureDate
	Caption	"&Departure Date:"
Label	Name	lblSortBy
	Caption	"&Sort By:"
Combo Box	Name	cboHotels
	Style	2 - Dropdown List
Combo Box	Name	cboPaymentType
	Style	2 - Dropdown List
Combo Box	Name	cboSortBy
	Style	2 - Dropdown List
Line	Name	Line1
Text Box	Name	txtArrivalDate
	Text	""
Text Box	Name	txtDepartureDate
	Text	""
Frame	Name	fraResults
	Caption	"Results"
MsFlexGrid	Name	grdRes

2. Insert the following code into the General Declarations section of **frmMain**. This will create a new object of **CDataObjects** when the object variable, **m_Res**, is declared.

```
Option Explicit

' Assign the Res Name Member to the Data Object
Private m_Res As CDataObjects
```

3. Insert the following code in the **Form_Load** event. As the form loads, this event creates the instance of the data access object for the **m_Res** member variable. The Hotel combo box and Payment Type combo box are filled with data from their respective tables. The Sort By combo box is populated through the **AddItem** method and the control is set to display the first record in its list.

```
Private Sub Form_Load()

    Dim sSQL As String

    On Error GoTo Err_Form_Load

    ' Create the instance
    Set m_Res = New CDataObjects

    ' Fill the combo box with the information from the database
    sSQL = "Select Hotel, Name from tbl_Hotels"
    m_Res.FillControl cboHotels, sSQL, "Hotel", "Name"

    sSQL = "Select payment, descrip from tbl_PaymentTypes "
    sSQL = sSQL & "Order By descrip"
    m_Res.FillControl cboPaymentType, sSQL, "payment", "descrip"

    ' Fill the Sort By combo box
    cboSortBy.AddItem "No Sort"
    cboSortBy.AddItem "Last Name"
    cboSortBy.AddItem "First Name"
    cboSortBy.AddItem "Arrival Date"
    cboSortBy.AddItem "Departure Date"
    cboSortBy.ListIndex = 0


Exit_Form_Load:
    Exit Sub
```

```
Err_Form_Load:
    Call afx_GenericError("Form_Load: ", Err)
    Resume Exit_Form_Load

End Sub
```

4. Insert the following code in the **Form_Unload** event. As the form gets unloaded, the reference to the object that was created in the **Form_Load**, **CDataObjects**, is terminated and the application ends. If an error occurs, the error will be displayed through the **Error** procedure.

```
Private Sub Form_Unload(cancel As Integer)

    On Error GoTo Err_Form_Unload

    ' Clear the references
    Set m_Res = Nothing

Exit_Form_Unload:
    Exit Sub

Err_Form_Unload:
    Call afx_GenericError("Form_Unload:", Err)
    Resume Exit_Form_Unload
End Sub
```

5. Enter the following code in the form for the **Find** command button's **Click** event. This procedure first investigates the Sort By combo box to determine what type of sorting the query will require. Then the **SQL** statement is built by concatenating the **sSQL** variables so that part of the **Where** clause can be built dynamically. After it is built, the **FillGrid** procedure is executed to fill the **grdRes** grid. Note: In the Arrival and Departure dates section of the query, if you are using an Access database, replace the ticks (') with pound signs (#). Access uses these symbols when comparing date fields. All other database management systems use the tick marks.

```
Private Sub cmdFind_Click()

    Dim sSortBy As String

    On Error GoTo Err_cmdFind_Click

    ' Establish sort criteria
    Select Case cboSortBy.ListIndex
```

continued on next page

continued from previous page

```
        Case 0
            sSortBy = "No Sort"
        Case 1
            sSortBy = "LastName"
        Case 2
            sSortBy = "FirstName"
        Case 3
            sSortBy = "DateIn"
        Case 4
            sSortBy = "DateOut"
    End Select

    ' Fill the grid
    sSQL = "select resno as 'Res No', lastname as 'Last Name', "
    sSQL = sSQL & "firstname as 'First Name', Phone, "
    sSQL = sSQL & "room as 'Room Nbr', datein as 'Arrival', "
    sSQL = sSQL & "dateout as 'Depart' "
    sSQL = sSQL & "From tbl_reservations "
    sSQL = sSQL & "Where hotel = " & cboHotels.ListIndex + 1 & " "
    If cboPaymentType.ListIndex <> 5 Then ' All Payment Types
        sSQL = sSQL & "And Payment = "
        sSQL = sSQL & cboPaymentType.ItemData(cboPaymentType.ListIndex) ⇐
& " "
    End If
    If txtArrivalDate <> "" Then
        sSQL = sSQL & "and DateIn >= '" & txtArrivalDate & "' "
    End If
    If txtDepartureDate <> "" Then
        sSQL = sSQL & "and DateOut <= '" & txtDepartureDate & "' "
    End If
    If sSortBy <> "No Sort" Then
        sSQL = sSQL & "Order by " & sSortBy
    End If

    m_Res.FillGrid grdRes, sSQL, "Res No", "Last Name", "First Name", _
        "Phone", "Room Nbr", "Arrival", "Depart"

Exit_cmdFind_Click:
    Exit Sub
```

```
Err_cmdFind_Click:
    Call afx_GenericError("cmdFind_Click:", Err)
    Resume Exit_cmdFind_Click
End Sub
```

6. Add the following code to the form for the **End** command button's **Click** event. This subroutine will cause the **Form_Unload** event to be triggered to end the program.

```
Private Sub cmdEnd_Click()

    On Error GoTo Err_cmdEnd_Click

    Unload Me


Exit_cmdEnd_Click:
    Exit Sub


Err_cmdEnd_Click:
    Call afx_GenericError("cmdEnd_Click:", Err)
    Resume Exit_cmdEnd_Click
End Sub
```

7. Add the following code to the form's **Clear** command button's **Click** event. This procedure will clear all the data and leave the column headers intact.

```
Private Sub cmdClear_Click()

    Dim x As Integer
    Dim y As Integer

    On Error GoTo Err_cmdClear_Click

    With grdRes

        .Rows = 2

        For y = 0 To .Cols - 1
            .Col = y
            For x = 1 To .Rows - 1

                .Row = x
                .Text = ""
```

continued on next page

continued from previous page

```
                Next x
            Next y
        End With

Exit_cmdClear_Click:
        Exit Sub

Err_cmdClear_Click:
        Call afx_GenericError("cmdClear_Click:", Err)
        Resume Exit_cmdClear_Click
End Sub
```

8. Use the Insert Class Module menu item to add a new class module. Name it **CDataObjects** and save it as **CDATAOBJ.CLS**.

9. Add the following code to the General Declarations section of the **CDataObjects** class module. The first variable defines your **Environment** member. The next variable defines your database connection member.

```
Option Explicit


' Database
Private m_env As rdoEnvironment


' Connection
Private m_con As rdoConnection
```

10. Insert the following code in the **Class_Initialize** event of the **CDataObject** class module. When this class is initialized, the environment and connection to the ODBC data source name is opened. If an error occurs during any process of opening, the error handling routine will be called.

```
Private Sub Class_Initialize()

    On Error GoTo Err_Class_Initialize

    ' use the default environment
    Set m_env = rdoEnvironments(0)
    ' Open the connection
    Set m_con = m_env.OpenConnection(dsName:="dsnWaiteSQL",
Connect:="UID=sa;pwd=")
```

```
Exit_Class_Initialize:
    Exit Sub

Err_Class_Initialize:
    Call afx_GenericError("Class_Initialize:", Err)
    Resume Exit_Class_Initialize
End Sub
```

11. Add the following code to the **Class_Terminate** event of the **CDataObject**. This event closes the RDO environment object variables that were opened in the **Class_Initialize** procedure. By closing the RDO environment, all connections and resultsets related to it are also closed.

```
Private Sub Class_Terminate()

    On Error GoTo Err_Class_Terminate

    ' Close the resultset and database
    If Not (m_env Is Nothing) Then
        m_env.Close
    End If

    ' Clear the references
    Set m_env = Nothing


Exit_Class_Terminate:
    Exit Sub

Err_Class_Terminate:
    Call afx_GenericError("Class_Terminate:", Err)
    Resume Exit_Class_Terminate
End Sub
```

12. Add the following **Public** method to the **CDataObjects** class module to fill the desired control, either a listbox or combo box, with the requested information. The **ParamArray** argument allows for an optional amount of arbitrary arguments to be passed to this method. The control is cleared before any information is added to it. The **rdoResultset** is created based on the **SQL** statement passed to this procedure. After the resultset is created, its information is populated into the selected control. After the resultset is finished filling the control, the control's **ListIndex** property is set to the first item so that it is displayed to the user.

```
' Fill any list type control with the data
'
' Parameters:
'   cntl        list-type control to fill
'   sSQL        SQL statement
'   sIDColumn   name of the column containing the record ID
'   sColumns    name of the columns of data to display
Public Sub FillControl(cntl As Control, sSQL as string, _
    sIDColumn As String, ParamArray sColumns() As Variant)

    Dim sData As String
    Dim i As Integer
    Dim rs as rdoResultset

    On Error GoTo Err_FillControl

    ' Clear the list
    cntl.Clear

    ' open the resultset
    Set rs = m_con.OpenResultset(sSQL)


    ' Add each record until the end of the file
    If (Not rs.BOF) Then
        Do Until rs.EOF
            ' Concatenate each desired column
            sData = ""
            For i = 0 To UBound(sColumns)
                sData = sData & " " & rs(CStr(sColumns(i)))
            Next
            ' Add the item to the list
            cntl.AddItem sData
            cntl.ItemData(cntl.NewIndex) = rs(sIDColumn)

            ' Move to the next row
            rs.MoveNext
        Loop
    End If

    ' Set control to highlight the first record
    ' in the list
    cntl.ListIndex = 0

Exit_FillControl:
```

```
    Exit Sub

Err_FillControl:
    Call afx_GenericError("FillControl:", Err)
    Resume Exit_FillControl
End Sub
```

13. Add the following **Public** method to the **CDataObjects** class module to
fill the desired grid control with the requested information. The
OpenResultset performs the **SQL** statement passed to it. The **If** statement
checks to make sure that data was returned into the resultset. If there is
data, the **Do...Loop** will process each row of information and the
For...Next loop will insert information into each column of the grid. If
there is no information, a message box will notify the user.

```
' Fill an unbound grid control with the data
'
' Parameters:
'   cntl            list type control to fill
'   sSQL            SQL statement
'   sColumns        name of the columns of data to display
Private Sub FillGrid(cntl As Control, sSQL as String, _
    ParamArray sColumns() As Variant)

    Dim sData As String
    Dim i As Integer
    Dim j As Long
    Dim lMaxRows As Long
    Dim rs as rdoResultset
    Dim sFieldName As String


    On Error GoTo Err_FillGrid

    ' Open the resultset
    Set rs = m_con.OpenResultset(sSQL)
    ' Add each record until the end of file
    ' Set up the grid
    With cntl
        .Cols = UBound(sColumns) + 1
        .Rows =.Rows

        For i = 0 To cntl.Cols - 1
            cntl.ColWidth(i) = 1440
        Next i
        ' Clear the grid
```

continued on next page

continued from previous page

```
            .Rows = 2
            .Row = 1
            For i = 0 To .Cols - 1
                .Col = i
                .Text = ""
            Next


            ' Fill in the Column headers from the
            ' Database column names

            If (Not rs.BOF) Then
                .Row = 0
                For i = 0 To .Cols - 1
                    .Col = i
                    sFieldName = rs.rdoColumns(i).Name
                    .Text = sFieldName
                Next
                j = 1
                Do Until rs.EOF
                    cntl.Row = j
                    For i = 0 To UBound(sColumns)

                        .Col = i
                        .Text = rs(sColumns(i))

                    Next
                    ' Get next row
                    rs.MoveNext
                    j = j + 1
                Loop
            Else
                MsgBox prompt:="No information available", _
                    Title:=App.Title
            End If
        End With

Exit_FillGrid:
    Exit Sub
Err_FillGrid:
    Call afx_GenericError("FillGrid:", Err)
    Resume Exit_FillGrid
End Sub
```

14. Use the Insert Module menu item from the Visual Basic menu to add a standard module to the project to be used for error handling. Go to the module's property list by pressing F4, name it **bError**, and save the file as **ERROR.BAS**. Add the following code to a **Public Sub** procedure. Two values are going to be passed to this procedure. One is a string value and is the name of the procedure in which the remote data object error occurred. The other is a long value and is the error number that occurred. When an error occurs in any of the modules, this procedure is executed. The system will beep to notify the user that an error has occurred. The procedure the error occurred in, a description of the error, and the error number will be displayed in a message box.

```
' Generic Error routine
Public Sub afx_GenericError(sProcedure As String, lErr As Long)
    On Error GoTo Err_afx_GenericError

    Beep
    MsgBox sProcedure & " " & Error$(lErr) & ". " & CStr(lErr)

Exit_afx_GenericError:
    Exit Sub

Err_afx_GenericError:
    Call afx_GenericError("afx_GenericError:", Err)
    Resume Exit_afx_GenericError
End Sub
```

How It Works

When **frmMain** form loads, the Hotel and Payment Type combo boxes are populated with the information retrieved from the tables. Because there is no table for the **Sort By** options, they are added to the combo box hard-coded into the form.

The user needs to select a hotel, payment type, and method with which to sort by. The How-To defaults **Hotel** to **Grand View Hotel**, **Payment Type** to **American Express**, and the **Sort By** to **No Sort**, which stands for no sort order. The date ranges are optional parameters. When the Find button is clicked, the SQL query is built based on the provided information and the results are displayed in the grid. If no data is available, the grid will be cleared and a message box will notify the user that no information is available, as illustrated in Figure 5-8.

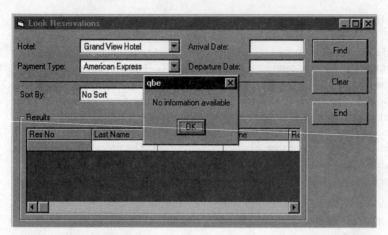

Figure 5-8 Reservation lookup notifies the user that no information is available

When the Clear button is pressed, the grid will be set back to two rows. All the rows will be cleared except for the column headers. When you press the End button, the m_Res member will be set to Nothing, which will cause the Class_Terminate event to be processed. This closes all your connections to the database.

Comments

In this example, you hard-coded the Sort By combo box with values. This is not a good programming practice. If the Sort By criteria changes later, you would have to change the source code and redistribute the application. A better practice is to have the list come from a reference table, similar to the Hotel and Payment Type combo boxes. When information changes, all you need to do is update the database table and the application will reflect the changes.

CHAPTER 6

OBJECT-ORIENTED APPLICATION DEVELOPMENT

6

by Noel Jerke

OBJECT-ORIENTED APPLICATION DEVELOPMENT

How do I...

6.1 Utilize the basics of object-oriented programming?

6.2 Implement a basic class module?

6.3 Utilize a collection of classes?

6.4 Implement an object model?

6.5 Build ActiveX components?

You cannot begin client/server development with Visual Basic 5.0 without thinking about objects. Microsoft is beginning to embrace the idea of object-oriented analysis and design throughout all its development products. Visual C++ and Visual J++ are based on the object-oriented methodology. Microsoft's important component integration strategy, ActiveX, is based on the concepts of a *world* of objects working together.

This chapter will serve to provide an introduction to the basic fundamentals of object-oriented analysis and design and, most importantly, how to apply these techniques to your client/server programs. The first How-To is a discussion of the basic fundamentals. How-To 6.2 is a simple example of using Visual Basic's fundamental object-oriented building tool, the class. How-To 6.3 will discuss the uses of a very flexible data type called the collection and how it relates to working with classes.

The last two How-To's provide two examples of implementing an object model and how to build a simple three-tier application that utilizes ActiveX components. Chapter 11, Activating Client/Server on the Web, provides a detailed explanation on how to design, build, and implement business objects using ActiveX components.

6.1   Utilize the Basics of Object-Oriented Programming

There are a few fundamental concepts to understand prior to doing object-oriented analysis and design. Certainly, this How-To cannot begin to discuss all the facets of good object-oriented programming. But it can serve to introduce the core concepts needed to move forward with Visual Basic 5.

6.2   Implement a Basic Class Module

The class module is the key tool used for implementing object techniques in your applications. This How-To will build a simple class that will encapsulate a set of properties and methods for working with disk files.

6.3   Utilize a Collection of Classes

The collection object provides a method for referring to a related group of items as a single unit or object. A collection of classes is a convenient method for dealing with a large set of instances of your class in a simple fashion. This section will demonstrate utilizing a collection of bitmap classes.

6.4   Implement an Object Model

A simple object model for browsing a set of bitmaps and performing such features as image fades will be implemented. Two new classes will be added to the `DiskFile` and `Bitmap` classes created earlier. This How-To will demonstrate how the classes work together to provide the functionality of the program.

6.5   Build ActiveX Components

The object model developed in the last How-To can be extended to provide even greater encapsulation based on out-of-process ActiveX executables and in-process ActiveX DLLs. A new class will be added to this example that will also store the bitmap data in an image database.

COMPLEXITY
BEGINNING

6.1 How do I...
Utilize the basics of object-oriented programming?

Object-oriented analysis and design is beginning to come of age for corporate systems development. With the development of tools such as Rational Rose, SmallTalk, C++, ActiveX, and so on, the idea of developing around *objects* is becoming easier and part of a fundamental part of our daily work as programmers. Now that something close to true objects has become an integral part of Visual Basic, starting with version 4.0, object techniques have become readily available to the thousands of Visual Basic programmers out there.

If you pick up a theoretical treatise on what object-oriented analysis and design is, you may quickly be confused by the detailed depth that makes up the object-oriented methodology. For large object-oriented systems development, a solid understanding of the theory and full implementation is needed and strongly recommended. But to get started with the tools that Microsoft has provided in Visual Basic, you only need to understand a few simple concepts.

The object-oriented methodology was conceived to help break down the complexity of complicated application systems. The fundamental concept is that complex *things* within an application system can be broken down into easily managed chunks. These things can be thought of as objects. For example, when you get on an airplane, do you think about the fuel subsystem, or how the wings are mechanically operating? No. You tend to think of the plane overall as a whole object. The *subsystems* that you do think about are things like extremely small seats or fold-out trays that your laptop will not fit on. These are the subsystems the airplane designers have *exposed* to you on the airplane object. As a passenger, there is no need for you to understand the underlying mechanics that make up a plane. In fact, if you think about all the objects you deal with on a day-to-day basis, if you had to understand and deal with all of them, you would be hopelessly overwhelmed.

Object-oriented programming seeks to break down the complexity of software systems so you will not be overwhelmed by all the different subsystems that go into building a small or large scale software project. If you think for a moment about Visual Basic, Microsoft has abstracted away most of the tedium of Windows programming and has only exposed certain aspects of Windows programming to you, as the programmer, so you don't have to worry about all the complexities of the Windows system. Abstracting away complexity makes a large system easier to deal with. After all, even the airplane pilot does not have to completely understand every detail of how an airplane works. He or she primarily needs to know how to operate the plane. Engineers and mechanics are available to deal with the contents of the various components of the instrumentation, flight control systems, engines, and so on. Abstraction is closely related to encapsulation. The best example of encapsulation is an ActiveX (OCX) custom control. A control completely hides or *encapsulates* the underlying logic behind the functionality exposed by the control. Likewise, the class module provides to the Visual Basic programmer the ability to encapsulate program code and only exposes the methods for utilizing the class.

The Class Module

Microsoft has provided a tool in Visual Basic that allows you, as the programmer, to provide this type of abstraction and encapsulation in your programs. This tool is called the class module. A *class* is any group of objects that fit a certain profile. An example could include the airplane wing in our earlier example or an employee in a company. The class module in Visual Basic provides a way for defining these classes and encapsulating their underlying functionality. The class also only exposes the functionality needed by the user to use the object effectively. With the airplane wing, the pilot has controls and settings that manipulate the wing.

A class module can have properties and methods. Methods define the functionality of the class. For example, the picture box control is an object that you use in your applications to display images. A method of the picture box control is `Circle`. This will draw a circle on the picture box. Your class objects can have their own methods that define the function of the object. With the picture box control, you can set the back and fore color properties of the picture box to change its appearance. Similarly, your class can have properties that define the attributes of the object. Note that these methods and properties do not have to be exposed to other objects. They can be either public or private. Private methods and properties are only accessible from within the class module. Public methods and properties are exposed to the rest of the program.

Relating Objects

Objects would be pretty boring and not very useful if you could not define relationships between them. For example, it would be pretty hard to model an airplane object if it could not be made up of many other objects that worked together to define the functionality of the plane. A control panel works with the mechanical parts of the plane to give feedback to the pilot. The engines work with the wings to provide flight for the plane.

There are several types of relationships to define how objects relate to each other. The first is the *is a* relationship. For example, we could define a class *wing* that has all the basic properties and methods for any type of airplane wing. But the wing of the new Boeing 777 could have additional properties and methods beyond those of a standard wing. So, the Boeing 777 wing is a type of standard wing. It would have all of the basic functionality of a wing, but would add to that definition. Another good example is that of the airplane seat. Each seat has arms, cushions, and so on. But the First Class seats would have additional properties that the Coach class seats do not.

The second is the *has a* relationship. In our airplane example, there are many *has a* relationships. For example, the airplane has a set of wings, engines, and landing gear. Classes with a *has a* relationship are composed of other classes to define their functionality.

The third is the *uses* relationship. This is where two objects work together or collaborate to provide functionality. For example, the airline uses the plane to transport passengers. The passengers use the airline to get to their destination. Each of these objects, the airline, plane, and passenger, collaborate.

Two object-oriented constructs allow us to define these relationships between classes. The first is inheritance. Inheritance was designed to remove redundancy in code between similar objects. In our airline example, we may have up to three types of passengers on the plane. These might include the First Class, Business Class, and Coach passenger. Each passenger has a set of common information and methods in our system. But each also has specific attributes and methods that uniquely define them. We could design three objects that all completely define each type of passenger. But we would certainly have redundancy with properties, such as name and address, and methods, such as bag check and check-in. Using inheritance, we would want to define a general passenger class and then define three classes for First, Business, and Coach passengers. These three classes would *inherit* the general passenger class and would add additional functionality specific to the specialized class. For example, the First Class passenger might automatically receive extra frequent flyer miles or a special check-in procedure.

The second idea is *polymorphism*. Let's say that the airline has now decided that the check-in method for First Class passengers is going to differ from that of any of the other passenger types. In our airline example of a general passenger object, we would need a way to override its *general* check-in method. A programming language that supports polymorphism would allow us to do this. So, for the First, Business, and Coach passenger classes, you would call the check-in method, but for the First Class passenger the functionality of the method would be different from that of the underlying passenger class.

Unfortunately the class module in Visual Basic does not readily support inheritance or polymorphism. One class module can contain another class module and certainly different class modules can work together. But, you cannot simply inherit all the attributes and methods from one class to another. Likewise, this makes polymorphism difficult to implement from direct class-to-class relationships. Visual Basic 5 does support creating polymorphism through the addition of the `implements` key word. By using class templates, which contain only an outline of all methods and properties, you can create polymorphism of methods and properties between classes.

The rest of this chapter will serve to introduce the class module, collections of classes, a simple object model, and how to build ActiveX components. While Visual Basic is not completely object oriented, the primary ideas of abstraction and encapsulation make a great leap forward in the way we will build our programs and we will be able to derive the primary benefits of object-oriented methodologies.

6.2 How do I...
Implement a basic class module?

Problem

The class module appears to be Microsoft's primary building tool for implementing three-tiered client/server systems. How do I utilize the class module in my projects?

Technique

To demonstrate, we will take the idea of an everyday disk file and encapsulate it in a class module. A disk file has many different properties such as directory location and file size. Also we can *perform* many methods on a file such as copying and deleting the file.

Steps

Open and run **6-2.VBP**. The running program appears as shown in Figure 6-1.

The text boxes on the form show the different properties of the **DiskFile** class created to encapsulate the **Clouds.bmp** file. There are two methods we can perform on the disk file. The first is to copy the file to a new location. Click on the Copy File to Root button to copy the clouds bitmap to the root directory. To delete the copy of the file, click on the Delete Copied File which uses the **Delete** method of the class.

How-To 6.2	
Full File Name	c:\windows\clouds.bmp
File Name	clouds.bmp
File Extension	bmp
File Directory	c:\windows\
File Size	307514
File Date	7/11/95 9:50:00 AM
File Description	Clouds Bitmap

Copy File to Root   Delete Copied File

Figure 6-1 The form as it appears at runtime

1. Create a new project called **6-2.VBP**. Add the objects and properties listed in Table 6-1 to **Form1** and save the form as **6-2.FRM**.

Table 6-1 The form's objects and properties

OBJECT	PROPERTY	SETTING
Form	Name	Form1
	Caption	"How-To 6.2"
CommandButton	Name	DelFile
	Caption	"Delete Copied File"
CommandButton	Name	Copy
	Caption	"Copy File to Root"
TextBox	Name	FileInfo
	Index	0 - 6
	Locked	-1 'True
Label	Name	FileLabels
	AutoSize	-1 'True
	Caption	"File Description"
	Index	6
Label	Name	FileLabels
	AutoSize	-1 'True
	Caption	"File Date"
	Index	5
Label	Name	FileLabels
	AutoSize	-1 'True
	Caption	"File Size"
	Index	4
Label	Name	FileLabels
	AutoSize	-1 'True
	Caption	"File Directory"
	Index	3
Label	Name	FileLabels
	AutoSize	-1 'True
	Caption	"File Extension"
	Index	2
Label	Name	FileLabels
	AutoSize	-1 'True
	Caption	"File Name"

continued on next page

continued from previous page

OBJECT	PROPERTY	SETTING
	Index	1
Label	Name	FileLabels
	AutoSize	-1 'True
	Caption	"Full File Name"
	Index	0

2. Add the following set of code to the General Declarations section of the form. We create two instances of the `DiskFile` class. One will be for the current clouds bitmap on the system. The second will be used for the copied file.

```
Option Explicit

'  Declare our two classes globally
Dim DF1 As DiskFile
Dim DF2 As DiskFile
```

3. When the copy button is selected, the `CopyFile` method of the first `DiskFile` class is called. The directory to copy the file to is passed in as an argument. In this case, the file is copied to the root of C.

```
Private Sub Copy_Click()

'  Copy the file to the root
DF1.CopyFile "c:\"

End Sub
```

4. When the `DelFile` button is selected, the second `DiskFile` class is set up to be created with the copied clouds bitmap. Then, the `DeleteFile` method of the class is called to delete the file.

```
Private Sub DelFile_Click()

'  Set the second class to the
'  copied file and then delete
'  it
DF2.FileName = "c:\clouds.bmp"
DF2.DeleteFile

End Sub
```

5. When the form is loaded, the two `DiskFile` classes are created. The first is set up to point to the clouds bitmap in the Windows directory. Also, the file description property of the class is set. Then, each of the properties of the `DiskFile` class is displayed in the text boxes on the form.

```
Private Sub Form_Load()

'  Create our two new classes
```

```
Set DF1 = New DiskFile
Set DF2 = New DiskFile

'  Set the class file name
DF1.FileName = "c:\windows\clouds.bmp"

'  Set the file name description
DF1.FileDesc = "Clouds Bitmap"

'  Show the full filename including
'  directory
FileInfo(0).Text = DF1.FileName

'  Show just the filename
FileInfo(1).Text = DF1.File

'  Show the file extension
FileInfo(2).Text = DF1.FileExt

'  Show the file directory
FileInfo(3).Text = DF1.Directory

'  Show the file size
FileInfo(4).Text = DF1.FileSize

'  Show the file date
FileInfo(5).Text = DF1.FileDate

'  Show the file description
FileInfo(6).Text = DF1.FileDesc

End Sub
```

6. Insert a new class module into the project by selecting the Insert menu and selecting Class Module. Set the name property of the class to `DiskFile` and save the class as `DiskFile.cls`. Add the following code to the General Declarations section of the class. These properties will help to define the attributes of the disk file for the class.

```
Option Explicit

'  Member property of the class that
'  stores the filename
Private m_FileName As String

'  Member property of the class that
'  stores the file description
Private m_FileDesc As String
```

7. The following public properties allow other programs to set and retrieve the file description for the class. Note that the description is stored in a private variable, `m_FileDesc`.

```
'  The get and set properties of the class
'  for the file description
Public Property Let FileDesc(s As String)
    m_FileDesc = s
End Property

Public Property Get FileDesc() As String
    FileDesc = m_FileDesc
End Property
```

8. The `File` property handles just returning the filename without the directory location of the file. Note we call the `ParseFile` routine to get the filename.

```
'  Get the file name by itself.
'  I.E. c:\windows\cloulds.bmp is clouds.bmp
Public Property Get File() As String
    File = ParseFile()
End Property
```

9. The `FileName` property can be retrieved and set.

```
'  Set and get the filename property for the
'  the class
Public Property Let FileName(s As String)
    m_FileName = s
End Property

Public Property Get FileName() As String
    FileName = m_FileName
End Property
```

10. The `FileSize` property returns the file size of the current file by calling the Visual Basic `FileLen` function.

```
'  Get the file size
Public Property Get FileSize() As Long
    FileSize = FileLen(m_FileName)
End Property
```

11. The `FileExt` property calls the `ParseExt` function which returns the extension for the current file.

```
'  Get the file extension
Public Property Get FileExt() As String
    FileExt = ParseExt()
End Property
```

12. The `Directory` property returns just the directory location of the file by calling the `ParseDir` function.

```
'  Get the directory of the file
Public Property Get Directory() As String
    Directory = ParseDir()
End Property
```

13. The `FileDate` property returns the file date by calling Visual Basic's
`FileDateTime` function.

```
'  Get the date of the file
Public Property Get FileDate() As Date
     FileDate = FileDateTime(m_FileName)
End Property
```

14. The `ParseFile` function is a private method of the class. The `m_FileName`
private property is searched to find just the filename and to exclude the
directory location.

```
'  Parse out the file name. Note that this is
'  a private method. It is only utilized in the
'  File property
Private Function ParseFile() As String

Dim N As Integer

ParseFile = ""

'  Start from the end of the file name
'  and look for the '\' character. Thus the
'  file part of the file name will be known
For N = Len(m_FileName) To 1 Step -1

    If Mid(m_FileName, N, 1) = "\" Then
        ParseFile = Right(m_FileName, Len(m_FileName) - N)
        N = -1
    End If

Next N

End Function
```

15. The `ParseDir` function is a private method of the class. The `m_FileName`
private property is searched to find just the directory location of the file and
excludes the filename.

```
'  Parse out the file directory. Note that
'  this is a private class method and is only
'  utilized by the Directory property
Private Function ParseDir() As String

Dim N As Integer

ParseDir = ""

'  Start from the end of the file name
'  and look for the first '\' character. Thus
'  the location of the file name will be known
'  and the rest is the directory location
For N = Len(m_FileName) To 1 Step -1
```

continued on next page

continued from previous page

```
        If Mid(m_FileName, N, 1) = "\" Then
            ParseDir = Left(m_FileName, N)
            N = -1
        End If

Next N

End Function
```

16. The `ParseExt` function is a private method of the class. The `m_FileName` private property is searched to find just the file extension and to exclude the directory location and filename.

```
'   GetExt retrieves the file extension if
'   there is one. This is only used by the
'   FileExt property
Private Function ParseExt() As String

Dim N As Integer

ParseExt = "(N/A)"

'   Start from the end of the file name
'   and look for the '.' character. Thus
'   the location of the extension will be known
'   in the file name string
For N = Len(m_FileName) To 1 Step -1

    If Mid(m_FileName, N, 1) = "." Then
        ParseExt = Right(m_FileName, Len(m_FileName) - N)
        N = -1
    End If

Next N

End Function
```

17. The `CopyFile` method of the class copies the current disk file to the specified location. Note that the `ParseFile` private method of the class is called to get just the filename for use in Visual Basic's `FileCopy` procedure.

```
'   Public method of the class to
'   copy the file to a new location
Public Sub CopyFile(NewLocation)
    FileCopy m_FileName, NewLocation + ParseFile
End Sub
```

18. The `DeleteFile` method deletes the current file.

```
'   Public method of the class to
'   delete the file
Public Sub DeleteFile()
    Kill m_FileName
End Sub
```

19. When the class is initialized, the filename and description are set to the appropriate defaults.

```
'  When the class is initialized
'  the filename, description and
'  extension will be set to
'  N/A.
Private Sub Class_Initialize()
m_FileName = "Uninitialized"
m_FileDesc = "N/A"
End Sub
```

How It Works

A simple class, `DiskFile`, is set up here to help encapsulate the use of disk files. By simply setting the `FileName` property of the class from the form, all the various properties of the file are just a simple class reference away. And the class provides two methods, `CopyFile` and `DeleteFile`, which make working with the file simple.

Let's examine the class in more detail. The properties are set up using the `Property` construct of Visual Basic. Using the `Property` construct, you can check the value sent in by the user, or you can execute other logic. Note that the property can be read, written, or both read and written depending on whether or not you use both the `Let` and `Get` properties. The `Let` property sets the value. The `Get` property retrieves the value. Note that if you are setting a property to an object, then use the `Set` keyword instead of `Let`. Also, the property can be set to public or private. The following example shows setting and retrieving the `FileName` property of the class.

```
'  Set and get the filename property for the
'  the class
Public Property Let FileName(s As String)
    m_FileName = s
End Property

Public Property Get FileName() As String
    FileName = m_FileName
End Property
```

The following code examples demonstrate returning just the directory location of the file. When the class property is called, the return value is actually the return value of the private `ParseDir` method. If we wanted, checking could be done to manipulate the `Directory`, such as setting it all to uppercase, or checking to ensure it is not null, and so on.

```
'  Get the directory of the file
Public Property Get Directory() As String
    Directory = ParseDir()
End Property
```

Methods of the class are identical in meaning to the familiar subroutines and functions of Visual Basic. The key is setting the method to be either public or private to indicate whether the method is visible to the rest of the program. You only want to expose those methods that you want other parts of your application to access.

Finally, note that the class module has two standard routines built in: `Initialize` and `Terminate`. The `Initialize` routine is called when the class is created and the `Terminate` routine is called when the class is destroyed. You can add appropriate code to these routines to handle class initialization and termination events.

In the form module, the class is easy to utilize. Note that the class is globally declared in the General Declarations section of the form. But the class is actually created by setting the global variable to a new instance of the class object when the form is loaded, or in subsequent processing. The following code demonstrates this.

```
Set DF1 = New DiskFile
Set DF2 = New DiskFile
```

Note that multiple instances of the class can be created. Once we have the class created, the various properties and methods can be utilized. The class module provides an invaluable tool for taking complex objects and encapsulating their functionality into an easy to implement and reuse object.

You may have noticed the `m` naming convention for the private variables of the class module. The `m` stands for member. These private properties of the class are `member` properties for the class that represents the properties or attributes.

Comments

The class module is the fundamental building block for constructing the functionality of your applications. The ability to abstract away and encapsulate complex segments of your code will become a powerful tool in your programming arsenal. Plus, you will be able to develop powerful business objects to implement the second tier of three-tier client server architecture.

COMPLEXITY
INTERMEDIATE

6.3 How do I...
Utilize a collection of classes?

Problem

Microsoft has provided another powerful tool beside the class module: the collection object. How can I utilize this collection object to extend the use of classes?

Technique

We are going to reuse the `DiskFile` class from the last How-To and add a new class module, `Bitmap` to the project. The `Bitmap` class will be a special type of disk file. While we cannot directly have the `Bitmap` class inherit the `DiskFile` class, the `Bitmap` class will be composed of a `DiskFile` class that will have the basic information about the bitmap file. We will add additional properties and methods to the bitmap class that are specific to image files.

Steps

Open and run **6-3.VBP**. The running program appears as shown in Figure 6-2.

The form shows a picture box that will display the various images when they are selected in the list box. Select the Oranges bitmap in the listbox and select the **Vertical** option. Then select the Rotate Bitmap button. The image is now flipped vertically as shown in Figure 6-3.

To remove images from the bitmap list, select the Remove Bitmap button. This removes images from the bitmap's collection as shown in Figure 6-4.

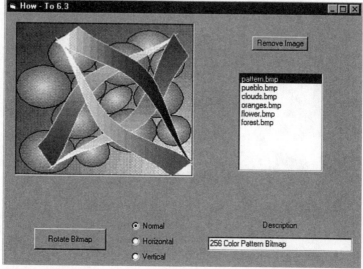

Figure 6-2 The form at runtime

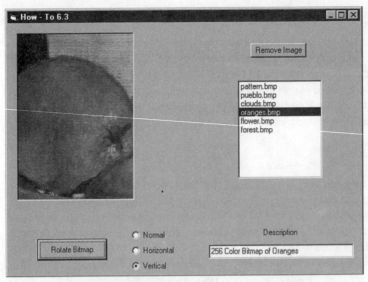

Figure 6-3 The Oranges bitmap flipped vertically

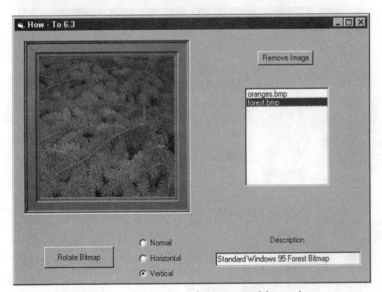

Figure 6-4 The list of images after several have been removed

1. Create a new project called **6-3.VBP**. Add the objects and properties listed in Table 6-2 to the form and save the form as **6-3.FRM**.

Table 6-2 The form's objects and properties

OBJECT	PROPERTY	SETTING
Form	Name	Form1
	Caption	"How – To 6.3"
CommandButton	Name	Remove
	Caption	"Remove Image"
CommandButton	Name	Display
	Caption	"Rotate Bitmap"
TextBox	Name	FileDesc
ListBox	Name	ImageList
OptionButton	Name	DisplayOpt
	Caption	"Vertical"
	Index	2
OptionButton	Name	DisplayOpt
	Caption	"Horizontal"
	Index	1
OptionButton	Name	DisplayOpt
	Caption	"Normal"
	Index	0
	Value	-1 'True
PictureBox	Name	DispPict
	AutoSize	-1 'True
	Picture	"pueblo.bmp"
PictureBox	Name	BackPict
	AutoSize	-1 'True
	Visible	0 'False
Label	Name	Label1
	AutoSize	-1 'True
	Caption	"Description"

NOTE

Only the new code added to the project will be commented. If you need additional information regarding the other code, see the previous How-To's for a complete explanation.

---

2. Add the following code to the General Declarations section of the form. A collection is created that will hold our series of bitmaps for the program.

```
Option Explicit

'   Bitmaps will be our collection of
'   bitmaps for viewing
Dim Bitmaps As Collection
```

3. Depending on the **Display** option, call the appropriate method of the
bitmap class to either flip the image or show it in the normal orientation.

```
Private Sub Display_Click()

'   Depending on the display option
'   show the bitmap appropriately
If DisplayOpt(0).Value = True Then Bitmaps.Item(ImageList.ListIndex +
1).Load
If DisplayOpt(1).Value = True Then Bitmaps.Item(ImageList.ListIndex +
1).Flip 1
If DisplayOpt(2).Value = True Then Bitmaps.Item(ImageList.ListIndex +
1).Flip 2

End Sub
```

4. When the form is loaded, a **bitmap** class is created and the Bitmaps collection is created. Then, all the bitmap images are set up and added to the
collection. The key for each collection member will be a simple counter.

```
Private Sub Form_Load()

Dim N As Integer
Dim BMP As Bitmap

'   Create the new collection of bitmaps
Set Bitmaps = New Collection

'   Create the bitmap object and add
'   it to the collection
For N = 1 To 6

    '   Create an instance of the bitmap
    Set BMP = New Bitmap

    '   Set the display picture
    '   properties
    Set BMP.BackPict = BackPict
    Set BMP.DispPict = DispPict

    '   Depending on the count, add the
    '   appropriate image and set the
    '   description
    Select Case N

        Case 1
            BMP.FileInfo.FileName = App.Path + "\pattern.bmp"
            BMP.FileInfo.FileDesc = "256 Color Pattern Bitmap"

        Case 2
            BMP.FileInfo.FileName = App.Path + "\pueblo.bmp"
```

```
                BMP.FileInfo.FileDesc = "Bitmap of an Pueblo Adobe Dwelling"

          Case 3
                BMP.FileInfo.FileName = App.Path + "\clouds.bmp"
                BMP.FileInfo.FileDesc = "Microsoft Clouds Bitmap"

          Case 4
                BMP.FileInfo.FileName = App.Path + "\oranges.bmp"
                BMP.FileInfo.FileDesc = "256 Color Bitmap of Oranges"

          Case 5
                BMP.FileInfo.FileName = App.Path + "\flower.bmp"
                BMP.FileInfo.FileDesc = "256 Color Bitmap of a Blossoming
Flower"

          Case 6
                BMP.FileInfo.FileName = App.Path + "\forest.bmp"
                BMP.FileInfo.FileDesc = "Standard Windows 95 Forest Bitmap"

    End Select

    '   Add the Bitmap class to the
    '   collection of bitmaps and set
    '   the key as the count
    Bitmaps.Add Item:=BMP, Key:=CStr(N)

    '   Add just the name of the image file
    '   to the list box
    ImageList.AddItem (BMP.FileInfo.File)

    '   Destroy the instance of the bitmap class
    Set BMP = Nothing

Next N

'   Set the image list to the first
'   selection
ImageList.ListIndex = 0

End Sub
```

5. When the form is unloaded, the members of the collection are removed. Note that the **For...Each...Next** construct is used to move through each object in the Bitmaps collection.

```
Private Sub Form_Unload(Cancel As Integer)

Dim N As Integer
Dim Obj as object

'   Destroy all of the bitmap instances
'   when the form is unloaded
For Each Obj In Bitmaps
    Bitmaps.Remove 1
Next

End Sub
```

6. When the `ImageList` box is clicked on, the new image is loaded by calling the `Load` function of the appropriate `bitmap` class. Then, the file description is shown by retrieving the file description property of the `FileInfo` class that is part of the `bitmap` class.

```
Private Sub ImageList_Click()

'  When an image in the list is
'  clicked on, load the image
Bitmaps.Item(ImageList.ListIndex + 1).Load

'  Set the file description in the
'  text box
FileDesc.Text = Bitmaps.Item(ImageList.ListIndex + 1).FileInfo.FileDesc
End Sub
```

7. When the Remove button is selected, the currently selected image from the `bitmap` class is removed.

```
Private Sub Remove_Click()

'  Always ensure there is at least
'  one entry in the list box
If ImageList.ListCount > 1 Then

    '  Remove the specified image from
    '  the collection and the list box
    Bitmaps.Remove ImageList.ListIndex + 1
    ImageList.RemoveItem ImageList.ListIndex
End If

'  Set the selection to the
'  first image
ImageList.ListIndex = 0

End Sub
```

8. Insert a new class module into the project and save it as `Bitmap.cls`. Add the following code to the General Declarations section of the class. Note that the `DiskFile` class is declared as a public property of the class. Thus, its methods and properties are exposed to the any of your code that uses the `bitmap` class.

```
Option Explicit

'  A Bitmap is a type of DiskFile
'  So, the Bitmap class will use
'  the properties and methods of
'  the DiskFile class for its
'  functionality
Public FileInfo As DiskFile

'  Declare the global properties of the
'  class. m_DispPict is the standard
'  display picture. m_BackPict is the
'  background picture that will be used
```

```
'  for the image flipping.
Private m_DispPict As Control
Private m_BackPict As Control
```

9. The `DispPict` property of the class handles taking in a picture box control for displaying the bitmap. Note that the `set` keyword is used since an object, in this case a control, is being passed into the property.

```
'  Get the Display picture control
Public Property Set DispPict(AControl As Control)
    Set m_DispPict = AControl
End Property
```

10. In order to do the image flips, we will need a working picture box that will not be visible to the user. So, when the property is set, the `AutoRedraw` property of the picture is set to True and the picture box is set to be invisible. This will create a working memory device context that will store the image in memory.

```
'  Get the Back ground picture control.
'  It is important to ensure that this
'  picture is invisible and that the
'  AutoRedraw property is true so that it
'  will act as a memory device context and
'  hold its image for later work
Public Property Set BackPict(AControl As Control)
    Set m_BackPict = AControl
    m_BackPict.AutoRedraw = True
    m_BackPict.Visible = False
End Property
```

11. The `Load` method of the class handles loading the bitmap into both the `BackPict` and `DispPict` picture boxes.

```
'  The load method of the class loads
'  the image into the two display pictures
Public Sub Load()
    m_BackPict.Picture = LoadPicture(FileInfo.FileName)
    m_DispPict.Picture = LoadPicture(FileInfo.FileName)
End Sub
```

12. The `Flip` method of the class will flip the image based upon the passed parameter. To rotate the image, use the `PaintPicture` method of the picture box.

```
'  The Flip method of the class will rotate
'  the picture accordingly
Public Sub Flip(Rotate)

'  Depending on the rotation selected, the
'  original image will be copied to the
'  display picture appropriately
Select Case Rotate

'  Note that for the vertical and
```

continued on next page

continued from previous page

```
'   horizontal flips, the height or
'   width is set to a negative value
'   and the starting point is set to
'   the height or width for the image
'   to be displayed. The PaintPicture
'   method of the picture box is used
'   to do the rotation
    Case 1   'Actual Size
            '   Flip Horizontal
            m_DispPict.PaintPicture m_BackPict.Picture, ⇐
        m_BackPict.ScaleWidth,   0, -1 * m_BackPict.ScaleWidth, ⇐
        m_BackPict.ScaleHeight, 0, 0, m_BackPict.ScaleWidth, ⇐
        m_BackPict.ScaleHeight

    Case 2
            '   Flip Vertical
            m_DispPict.PaintPicture m_BackPict.Picture, 0, ⇐
            m_BackPict.ScaleHeight, m_BackPict.ScaleWidth, -1 * ⇐
        m_BackPict.ScaleHeight, 0, 0, m_BackPict.ScaleWidth, ⇐
            m_BackPict.ScaleHeight

End Select

End Sub
```

13. When the class is initialized, the `DiskFile` class is created.

```
Private Sub Class_Initialize()
    '   When the class is intialized,
    '   the DiskFile class is created
    Set FileInfo = New DiskFile
End Sub
```

14. When the class is terminated, the `DiskFile` class is destroyed.

```
Private Sub Class_Terminate()
    '   When the class is terminated
    '   the DiskFile class is destroyed
    Set FileInfo = Nothing
End Sub
```

15. Insert a new class module into the project and save it as `DiskFile.cls`.

```
Option Explicit

'   Member property of the class that
'   stores the filename
Private m_FileName As String

'   Member property of the class that
'   stores the file description
Private m_FileDesc As String

'   The get and set properties of the class
'   for the file description
Public Property Let FileDesc(s As String)
    m_FileDesc = s
End Property
```

```
Public Property Get FileDesc() As String
    FileDesc = m_FileDesc
End Property


'  Get the file name by itself.
'  I.E. c:\windows\cloulds.bmp is clouds.bmp
Public Property Get File() As String
    File = ParseFile()
End Property


'  Set and get the filename property for the
'  the class
Public Property Let FileName(s As String)
    m_FileName = s
End Property


Public Property Get FileName() As String
    FileName = m_FileName
End Property


'  Get the file size
Public Property Get FileSize() As Long
    FileSize = FileLen(m_FileName)
End Property


'  Get the file extension
Public Property Get FileExt() As String
    FileExt = ParseExt()
End Property


'  Get the directory of the file
Public Property Get Directory() As String
    Directory = ParseDir()
End Property


'  Get the date of the file
Public Property Get FileDate() As Date
    FileDate = FileDateTime(m_FileName)
End Property


'  Parse out the file name. Note that this is
'  a private method. It is only utilized in the
'  File property
Private Function ParseFile() As String

Dim N As Integer

ParseFile = ""

'  Start from the end of the file name
'  and look for the '\' character. Thus the
'  file part of the file name will be known
For N = Len(m_FileName) To 1 Step -1

    If Mid(m_FileName, N, 1) = "\" Then
```

continued on next page

continued from previous page

```
            ParseFile = Right(m_FileName, Len(m_FileName) - N)
            N = -1
        End If

Next N

End Function

'   Parse out the file directory. Note that
'   this is a private class method and is only
'   utilized by the Directory property
Private Function ParseDir() As String

Dim N As Integer

ParseDir = ""

'   Start from the end of the file name
'   and look for the first '\' character. Thus
'   the location of the file name will be known
'   and the rest is the directory location
For N = Len(m_FileName) To 1 Step -1

    If Mid(m_FileName, N, 1) = "\" Then
        ParseDir = Left(m_FileName, N)
        N = -1
    End If

Next N

End Function

'   GetExt retrieves the file extension if
'   there is one. This is only used by the
'   FileExt property
Private Function ParseExt() As String

Dim N As Integer

ParseExt = "(N/A)"

'   Start from the end of the file name
'   and look for the '.' character. Thus
'   the location of the extension will be known
'   in the file name string
For N = Len(m_FileName) To 1 Step -1

    If Mid(m_FileName, N, 1) = "." Then
        ParseExt = Right(m_FileName, Len(m_FileName) - N)
        N = -1
    End If

Next N

End Function

'   Public method of the class to
```

```
'  copy the file to a new location
Public Sub CopyFile(NewLocation)
    FileCopy m_FileName, NewLocation + ParseFile
End Sub

'  Public method of the class to
'  delete the file
Public Sub DeleteFile()
    Kill m_FileName
End Sub

'  When the class is initialized
'  the filename, description and
'  extension will be set to
'  N/A.
Private Sub Class_Initialize()

m_FileName = "Uninitialized"
m_FileDesc = "N/A"

End Sub
```

How It Works

To demonstrate the collection object, we have added a new class, **bitmap**, to the project for working with bitmaps. This class will handle displaying bitmaps at different orientations. This class uses the **DiskFile** class created in the last How-To to provide a basic set of properties and methods for the bitmap file itself.

The collection object provides a method for referring to a related group of items as a single unit or object. A collection of classes is a convenient method for dealing with a large set of instances of our bitmap class in a simple fashion. In this case, we have a collection of bitmap classes. We will add each bitmap class to the collection and then, in our image manipulation, we will simply reference the collection.

To add items to the bitmap, use the **Add** method of the **bitmap** class. The **Item** property will indicate the item to be added and the **Key** property will give a name to the added item. In this case the item to be added is a **bitmap** class.

```
Bitmaps.Add Item:=BMP, Key:=CStr(N)
```

One of the ways to traverse the collection is to use the **For Each** syntax. The following code loops through each object in the collection and removes the object from the collection.

```
For Each Obj In Bitmaps
    Bitmaps.Remove 1
Next
```

The collection does not have to be of uniform objects. You can add many different types of objects to the collection. Each object's properties can be accessed through the collection.

```
If DisplayOpt(0).Value = True Then Bitmaps.Item(ImageList.ListIndex + ⇐
1).Load
```

The above code references the **bitmap** class. First, the collection is referenced, **Bitmaps**. Then the **item** property of the class is used to reference the appropriate item in the collection. Then, the method or property of the class is directly referenced which, in this case, is the **Load** method of the **bitmap** class.

Comments

The collection object provides one of the easiest ways to organize a collection of classes that are similarly related. Instead of trying to create arrays of classes, the collection object offers a dynamic and versatile way to work with groups of classes.

COMPLEXITY
ADVANCED

6.4 How do I...
Implement an object model?

Problem

Now that we have seen how to a build a class and use a collection of classes, how do I put this all together to implement an object model?

Technique

An object model represents how different objects in a software system interact with each other. And, as we have seen, it is a relatively easy matter to define a couple of classes to add functionality to your application. But things can get a little more complicated when working with multiple classes. In this example, we will combine the previously built **DiskFile** and **bitmap** classes with two new classes, **VertFade** and **PatBrush**. **VertFade** and **PatBrush** will add the ability to perform a vertical fade on the bitmap images. The **VertFade** class will utilize a collection of pattern brushes which are defined by the **PatBrush** class. The **bitmap** class will have a new fade method that will collaborate with the **VertFade** class to perform a fade on the bitmap. The primary form does not generally need to know about the **DiskFile**, **VertFade**, and **PatBrush** classes. These will be abstracted away from the client implementation. All of these classes working together define the object model for our project.

Steps

Open and run **6-4.VBP**. Figure 6-5 shows the form at load time and Figure 6-6 shows the pattern in mid-fade.

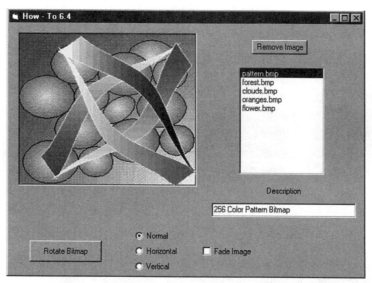

Figure 6-5 The running form

To show the vertical fade, select the Fade Image box. Then switch to another image. Each image will exit with a vertical fade before the next image is shown.

1. Create a new project called **6-4.VBP**. Add the objects and properties listed in Table 6-3 to the form and save the form as **6-4.FRM**.

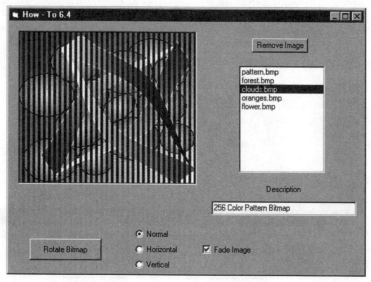

Figure 6-6 The pattern bitmap in mid-fade

Table 6-3 The form's objects and properties

OBJECT	PROPERTY	SETTING
Form	Name	Form1
	Caption	"How - To 6.4"
CheckBox	Name	FadeImage
	Caption	"Fade Image"
CommandButton	Name	Remove
	Caption	"Remove Image"
CommandButton	Name	Display
	Caption	"Rotate Bitmap"
TextBox	Name	FileDesc
ListBox	Name	ImageList
OptionButton	Name	DisplayOpt
	Caption	"Vertical"
	Index	2
OptionButton	Name	DisplayOpt
	Caption	"Horizontal"
	Index	1
OptionButton	Name	DisplayOpt
	Caption	"Normal"
	Index	0
	Value	-1 'True
PictureBox	Name	DispPict
	Picture	"pastel.bmp"
PictureBox	Name	BackPict
	AutoRedraw	-1 'True
	Picture	"pastel.bmp"
	Visible	0 'False
Label	Name	Label1
	AutoSize	-1 'True
	Caption	"Description"

NOTE

Only the new code added to the project will be commented. If you need additional information regarding the other code, see the previous How-To's for a complete explanation.

2. Add the following code to the General Declarations section of the form. The Bitmaps collection is declared for holding the list of images to be used in the application.

```
Option Explicit

'   Bitmaps will be our collection of
'   bitmaps for viewing
Dim Bitmaps As Collection
```

3. When the bitmap classes are set up, note the reference to the `FileInfo` `DiskFile` class which is contained in the `bitmap` class. This is done because Visual Basic does not offer true inheritance. If it did, we would not have to reference `FileInfo` directly.

```
Private Sub Display_Click()

'   Depending on the display option
'   show the bitmap appropriately
If DisplayOpt(0).Value = True Then Bitmaps.Item(ImageList.ListIndex +
1).Load
If DisplayOpt(1).Value = True Then Bitmaps.Item(ImageList.ListIndex +
1).Flip 1
If DisplayOpt(2).Value = True Then Bitmaps.Item(ImageList.ListIndex +
1).Flip 2

End Sub

Private Sub Form_Load()

Dim N As Integer
Dim BMP As Bitmap

'   Create the new collection of bitmaps
Set Bitmaps = New Collection

'   Create the bitmap object and add
'   it to the collection
For N = 1 To 5

    '   Create an instance of the bitmap
    Set BMP = New Bitmap

    '   Set the display picture
    '   properties
    Set BMP.BackPict = BackPict
    Set BMP.DispPict = DispPict

    '   Depending on the count, add the
    '   appropriate image and set the
    '   description
    Select Case N

        Case 1
            BMP.FileInfo.FileName = App.Path + "\pattern.bmp"
```

continued on next page

continued from previous page

```
                BMP.FileInfo.FileDesc = "256 Color Pattern Bitmap"

        Case 2
            BMP.FileInfo.FileName = App.Path + "\forest.bmp"
            BMP.FileInfo.FileDesc = "Standard Windows 95 Forest Bitmap"

        Case 3
            BMP.FileInfo.FileName = App.Path + "\clouds.bmp"
            BMP.FileInfo.FileDesc = "Microsoft Clouds Bitmap"

        Case 4
            BMP.FileInfo.FileName = App.Path + "\oranges.bmp"
            BMP.FileInfo.FileDesc = "256 Color Bitmap of Oranges"

        Case 5
            BMP.FileInfo.FileName = App.Path + "\flower.bmp"
            BMP.FileInfo.FileDesc = "256 Color Bitmap of a Blossoming
Flower"

    End Select

    '   Add the Bitmap class to the
    '   collection of bitmaps and set
    '   the key as the count
    Bitmaps.Add Item:=BMP, Key:=CStr(N)

    '   Add just the name of the image file
    '   to the list box
    ImageList.AddItem (BMP.FileInfo.File)

    '   Destroy the instance of the bitmap class
    Set BMP = Nothing

Next N

'   Set the image list to the first
'   selection
ImageList.ListIndex = 0

End Sub

Private Sub Form_Unload(Cancel As Integer)

Dim N As Integer

'   Destroy all of the bitmap instances
'   when the form is unloaded
For N = 1 To Bitmaps.Count
    Bitmaps.Remove 1
Next N

End Sub
```

4. When an image is selected, the **Fade** method of the **bitmap** class is called.

```
Private Sub imageList_Click()

'  Call the fade method of the class to
'  perform a vertical blind fade on the
'  image
If FadeImage.Value = 1 Then Bitmaps.Item(ImageList.ListIndex + 1).Fade

'  When an image in the list is
'  clicked on, load the image
Bitmaps.Item(ImageList.ListIndex + 1).Load

'  Set the file description in the
'  text box
FileDesc.Text = Bitmaps.Item(ImageList.ListIndex + 1).FileInfo.FileDesc

End Sub

Private Sub Remove_Click()

'  Always ensure there is at least
'  one entry in the list box
If ImageList.ListCount > 1 Then

    '  Remove the specified image from
    '  the collection and the list box
    Bitmaps.Remove ImageList.ListIndex + 1
    ImageList.RemoveItem ImageList.ListIndex
End If

'  Set the selection to the
'  first image
ImageList.ListIndex = 0

End Sub
```

5. Insert a new class into the project and save it as **Bitmap.cls**.

```
Option Explicit

'  A Bitmap is a type of DiskFile
'  So, the Bitmap class will use
'  the properties and methods of
'  the DiskFile class for its
'  functionality
Public FileInfo As DiskFile

'  Declare the global properties of the
'  class. m_DispPict is the standard
'  display picture. m_BackPict is the
'  background picture that will be used
'  for the image flipping.
Private m_DispPict As Control
Private m_BackPict As Control
```

continued on next page

continued from previous page

```
'  Get the Display picture control
Public Property Set DispPict(AControl As Control)
    Set m_DispPict = AControl
    m_DispPict.AutoSize = True
End Property


'  Get the Back ground picture control
'  It is important to ensure that this
'  picture is invisible and that the
'  AutoRedraw property is true so that it
'  will act as a memory device context and
'  hold its image for later work
Public Property Set BackPict(AControl As Control)
    Set m_BackPict = AControl
    m_BackPict.AutoRedraw = True
    m_BackPict.Visible = False
    m_BackPict.AutoSize = True
End Property
```

6. The `Fade` method of the `bitmap` class handles creating an instance of the `VertFade` class to perform the vertical fade. The class is set up to have the `BackPict` and `DispPict` picture boxes to perform the fade. The `Setup` method of the class is called and then the `Fade` method is run to perform the fade. Note that once the fade has finished, a slight pause is done to allow the viewer to see the full black image before the picture box is hidden. Then the picture box is hidden and a slight pause performed when the picture box is hidden. These two pauses help provide visual cues to the user as to when the fade is done and before the next image is loaded.

```
Public Sub Fade()

Dim T As Variant
Dim VF As VertFade

'  Create the vertical fade class
Set VF = New VertFade

'  Set the pictures used to perform
'  the fade
Set VF.BackPict = m_BackPict
Set VF.DispPict = m_DispPict

'  Setup the fade
VF.Setup

'  Perform the fade
VF.Fade

'  Get the current time
T = Time

'  Let the black fade show for
'  a few seconds
Do Until Time > (T + 0.0000001)
```

```
Loop

'  Delete the class
Set VF = Nothing

'  Make the displayed picture invisible
m_DispPict.Visible = False

'  For better effect, let the image
'  stay invisible for a few seconds
T = Time

Do Until Time > (T + 0.0000001)
Loop

End Sub

'  The load method of the class loads
'  the image into the two display pictures
Public Sub Load()
    m_DispPict.Picture = LoadPicture(FileInfo.FileName)
    m_BackPict.Picture = LoadPicture(FileInfo.FileName)
    m_DispPict.Visible = True
End Sub

'  The Flip method of the class will rotate
'  the picture accordingly
Public Sub Flip(Rotate)

'  Depending on the rotation selected, the
'  original image will be copied to the
'  display picture appropriately
Select Case Rotate

'  Note that for the vertical and
'  horizontal flips, the height or
'  width is set to a negative value
'  and the starting point is set to
'  the height or width for the image
'  to be displayed. The PaintPicture
'  method of the picture box is used
'  to do the rotation
    Case 1   'Actual Size
            '  Flip Horizontal
            m_DispPict.PaintPicture m_BackPict.Picture, ⇐
        m_BackPict.ScaleWidth, 0, -1 * m_BackPict.ScaleWidth, ⇐
        m_BackPict.ScaleHeight, 0, 0, m_BackPict.ScaleWidth, ⇐
        m_BackPict.ScaleHeight

    Case 2
            '  Flip Vertical
            m_DispPict.PaintPicture m_BackPict.Picture, 0, ⇐
        m_BackPict.ScaleHeight, m_BackPict.ScaleWidth, -1 * ⇐
        m_BackPict.ScaleHeight, 0, 0, m_BackPict.ScaleWidth, ⇐
        m_BackPict.ScaleHeight
```

continued on next page

continued from previous page

```
End Select

End Sub

Private Sub Class_Initialize()
    '  When the class is intialized,
    '  the DiskFile class is created
    Set FileInfo = New DiskFile
End Sub

Private Sub Class_Terminate()
    '  When the class is terminated
    '  the DiskFile class is destroyed
    Set FileInfo = Nothing
End Sub
```

7. Insert a new class into the project and save it as `DiskFile.cls`.

```
Option Explicit

'  Member property of the class that
'  stores the filename
Private m_FileName As String

'  Member property of the class that
'  stores the file description
Private m_FileDesc As String

'  The get and set properties of the class
'  for the file description
Public Property Let FileDesc(s As String)
    m_FileDesc = s
End Property

Public Property Get FileDesc() As String
    FileDesc = m_FileDesc
End Property

'  Get the file name by itself.
'  I.E. c:\windows\cloulds.bmp is clouds.bmp
Public Property Get File() As String
    File = ParseFile()
End Property

'  Set and get the filename property for the
'  the class
Public Property Let FileName(s As String)
    m_FileName = s
End Property

Public Property Get FileName() As String
    FileName = m_FileName
End Property

'  Get the file size
```

```
Public Property Get FileSize() As Long
    FileSize = FileLen(m_FileName)
End Property

'  Get the file extension
Public Property Get FileExt() As String
    FileExt = ParseExt()
End Property

'  Get the directory of the file
Public Property Get Directory() As String
    Directory = ParseDir()
End Property

'  Get the date of the file
Public Property Get FileDate() As Date
    FileDate = FileDateTime(m_FileName)
End Property

'  Parse out the file name. Note that this is
'  a private method. It is only utilized in the
'  File property
Private Function ParseFile() As String

Dim N As Integer

ParseFile = ""

'  Start from the end of the file name
'  and look for the '\' character. Thus the
'  file part of the file name will be known
For N = Len(m_FileName) To 1 Step -1

    If Mid(m_FileName, N, 1) = "\" Then
        ParseFile = Right(m_FileName, Len(m_FileName) - N)
        N = -1
    End If

Next N

End Function

'  Parse out the file directory. Note that
'  this is a private class method and is only
'  utilized by the Directory property
Private Function ParseDir() As String

Dim N As Integer

ParseDir = ""

'  Start from the end of the file name
'  and look for the first '\' character. Thus
'  the location of the file name will be known
'  and the rest is the directory location
For N = Len(m_FileName) To 1 Step -1
```

continued on next page

continued from previous page

```
        If Mid(m_FileName, N, 1) = "\" Then
            ParseDir = Left(m_FileName, N)
            N = -1
        End If

Next N

End Function

'   GetExt retrieves the file extension if
'   there is one. This is only used by the
'   FileExt property
Private Function ParseExt() As String

Dim N As Integer

ParseExt = "(N/A)"

'   Start from the end of the file name
'   and look for the '.' character. Thus
'   the location of the extension will be known
'   in the file name string
For N = Len(m_FileName) To 1 Step -1

    If Mid(m_FileName, N, 1) = "." Then
        ParseExt = Right(m_FileName, Len(m_FileName) - N)
        N = -1
    End If
End If

Next N

End Function

'   Public method of the class to
'   copy the file to a new location
Public Sub CopyFile(NewLocation)
    FileCopy m_FileName, NewLocation + ParseFile
End Sub

'   Public method of the class to
'   delete the file
Public Sub DeleteFile()
    Kill m_FileName
End Sub

'   When the class is initialized
'   the filename, description and
'   extension will be set to
'   N/A.
Private Sub Class_Initialize()

m_FileName = "Uninitialized"
m_FileDesc = "N/A"

End Sub
```

8. Insert a new class into the project and save it as **PatBrush.cls**. Add the following code to the General Declarations section of the class. The appropriate Win32 API functions, types, and constants are declared for creating bitmap pattern brushes.

```
Option Explicit

'   The BITMAPINFOHEADER contains basic informtion
'   about the bitmap we will create
Private Type BITMAPINFOHEADER '40 bytes
        biSize As Long
        biWidth As Long
        biHeight As Long
        biPlanes As Integer
        biBitCount As Integer
        biCompression As Long
        biSizeImage As Long
        biXPelsPerMeter As Long
        biYPelsPerMeter As Long
        biClrUsed As Long
        biClrImportant As Long
End Type

'   This data structure holds the header info as
'   well as the color data
Private Type BITMAPINFO
    bmiHeader As BITMAPINFOHEADER
    bmiColors As String * 8 ' Array length is arbitrary; may be changed
End Type

'   Selects an object into a device context
Private Declare Function SelectObject Lib "gdi32" (ByVal hdc As Long,⇐
ByVal hObject As Long) As Long

'   Creates a DIB Bitmap
Private Declare Function CreateDIBitmap Lib "gdi32" (ByVal hdc As Long, ⇐
lpInfoHeader As BITMAPINFOHEADER, ByVal dwUsage As Long, ByVal⇐
lpInitBits$, lpInitInfo As BITMAPINFO, ByVal wUsage As Long) As Long

'   Deletes a created object
Private Declare Function DeleteObject Lib "gdi32" (ByVal hObject As Long)⇐
As Long

'   Creates a pattern brush
Private Declare Function CreatePatternBrush Lib "gdi32" (ByVal HBITMAP As ⇐
Long) As Long

'   Paints a picture with the specified pattern
Private Declare Function PatBlt Lib "gdi32" (ByVal hdc As Long, ByVal x ⇐
As Long, ByVal y As Long, ByVal nWidth As Long, ByVal nHeight As Long,⇐
ByValdwRop As Long) As Long
```

continued on next page

continued from previous page

```
Const DIB_RGB_COLORS = 0        ' color table in RGBs
Const CBM_INIT = &H4&           ' initialize bitmap
Const PATCOPY = &HF00021        ' Used for Pattern Copy
Const BI_RGB = 0&               ' RGB Bitmap

' Declare m_BitInfoH as type BITMAPINFOHEADER
Dim m_BitInfoH As BITMAPINFOHEADER

' Declare m_BitInfo as type BITMAPINFO
Dim m_BitInfo As BITMAPINFO

' Holds the Screen data for building the bitmap
Dim m_Scrn As String * 32

' Holds the handle to the brush
Dim m_Hbr As Long
Dim m_OrgHbr As Long

' Declare our objects to be passed in
Private m_DispPict As Object
Private m_Array(8) As String * 8
```

9. The `SetupBitmap` method of the class will set up an 8x8 bitmap header with the two colors passed in as parameters. The bitmap header needs to be set up appropriately for creating a bitmap brush with two colors. More information about the type structures is provided in the How It Works section.

```
Public Sub SetupBitmap(r1, g1, b1, r2, g2, b2)

' Standard 40 Byte Header
m_BitInfoH.biSize = 40

' This will be an 8 by 8 bitmap
m_BitInfoH.biWidth = 8
m_BitInfoH.biHeight = 8

' One Plane
m_BitInfoH.biPlanes = 1

' Specifies the number of bits per pixel
m_BitInfoH.biBitCount = 1

' No Compression
m_BitInfoH.biCompression = BI_RGB

' These values are rarely used
m_BitInfoH.biSizeImage = 0
m_BitInfoH.biXPelsPerMeter = 0
m_BitInfoH.biYPelsPerMeter = 0

' Two colors used
m_BitInfoH.biClrUsed = 2

' This ensures that all colors are important
```

```
m_BitInfoH.biClrImportant = 0

'  Sets the colors for the bits
'  and background
m_BitInfo.bmiColors = Chr$(r1) + Chr$(g1) + Chr$(b1) + "0" + Chr$(r2) + ⇐
Chr$(g2) + Chr$(b2) + "0"

End Sub
```

10. The **BuildBitmap** function loops through the string array, **m_array**. This array is a series of 8 characters of either 1s or 0s. The 1s and 0s represent the bit pattern for the bitmap. The **m_Scrn** variable will have every fourth byte set to the calculated value, **V**. A string is created with the overall bit data to create the pattern with. From the bitmap created, the pattern brush is created.

```
Public Sub BuildBitmap()

Dim Counter as Integer
Dim V as integer
Dim C As Integer
Dim CompBitmap As Long

'  We will loop through each element in the array
For Counter = 1 To 8

    '  v will hold the value of the bit pattern, we
    '  need to reset it for each row
    V = 0

    '  We will loop through each row and set the bit values
    For C = 0 To 7

    '  We check for a 1 in the array and if it is one we
    '  then calculate the decimal value of the binary postion
    '  for example in 00000100, the 1 is = to 2^2 = 4
    If Mid$(m_Array(Counter), C + 1, 1) = "1" Then V = V + 2 ^ C

    Next C

    Mid$(m_Scrn, (Counter - 1) * 4 + 1, 1) = Chr$(V)

Next Counter

'  Set the BitmapInfoHeader field of m_BitInfo
m_BitInfo.bmiHeader = m_BitInfoH

'  Create the 8x8 bitmap specified by m_scrn
CompBitmap = CreateDIBitmap(m_DispPict.hdc, m_BitInfoH, CBM_INIT, m_Scrn,
m_BitInfo, DIB_RGB_COLORS)

'  Create the bitmap pattern from the screen
m_Hbr = CreatePatternBrush(CompBitmap)

End Sub
```

11. The `DeleteBrush` method deletes the current brush for the bitmap.

```
Public Sub DeleteBrush()

Dim Throw As Long

'  Select the original brush into the picture
Throw = SelectObject(m_DispPict.hdc, m_OrgHbr)

'  Delete the created brush
Throw = DeleteObject(m_Hbr)

End Sub
```

12. The `ShowPattern` method selects the brush into the display device context. The pattern is then copied into the device context using `PatBlt`.

```
Public Sub ShowPattern()

Dim m_OrgHbr, Throw As Long

'  Select the brush into the display
'  picture
m_OrgHbr = SelectObject(m_DispPict.hdc, m_Hbr)

'  Show the pattern screen
Throw = PatBlt(m_DispPict.hdc, 0, 0, m_DispPict.ScaleWidth,
m_DispPict.ScaleHeight, PATCOPY)

'  Select the original brush into the picture
Throw = SelectObject(m_DispPict.hdc, m_OrgHbr)

'  Delete the created brush
Throw = DeleteObject(m_Hbr)

End Sub
```

13. The `SetPattern` property sets and retrieves the string bit pattern for the pattern bitmap.

```
Public Sub SetPattern(s, index)
    '  Set the pattern sent in
    m_Array(index) = s
End Sub

'  Get the picture for display
Public Property Set DispPict(AControl As Object)
    Set m_DispPict = AControl
End Property
```

14. When the class is terminated, be sure and delete the brush.

```
Private Sub Class_Terminate()

'  Delete the brush if it exists
If m_Hbr <> 0 Then DeleteBrush

End Sub
```

15. Insert a new class into the project and save it as `VertFade.cls`. Add the following code to the General Declarations section of the class. A collection of pattern brushes is declared which will create the pattern bitmaps needed for the vertical fade. Also, the `BitBlt` API function is declared to copy the pattern bitmap to the display.

```
Option Explicit

'  PatBrushes is a collection of
'  bitmap brushes
Dim m_PatBrushes As Collection

'  BitBlt will be used for the image copies
Private Declare Function BitBlt Lib "gdi32" (ByVal hDestDC As Long, ByVal ⇐
x
As Long, ByVal y As Long, ByVal nWidth As Long, ByVal nHeight As Long, ⇐
ByVal hSrcDC As Long, ByVal xSrc As Long, ByVal ySrc As Long, ByVal ⇐
dwRop As Long)
As Long

'  Constants for the BitBlt copies
Const SRCCOPY = &HCC0020
Const SRCAND = &H8800C6

'  Globally declare the members of the class
Dim m_BackPict As Control
Dim m_DispPict As Control
```

16. The `BackPict` and `DispPict` picture box controls will be set for performing the fade on the images.

```
'  BackPict and DispPict are the picture
'  controls for performing the fade
Public Property Set BackPict(AControl As Control)
    Set m_BackPict = AControl
End Property

Public Property Set DispPict(AControl As Control)
    Set m_DispPict = AControl
End Property
```

17. The `CreateFade` method handles setting up the bitmap brushes in the `PatBrush` classes which will be used to perform the vertical fade. Each `PatBrush` class in the `PatBrushes` collection is looped through to create the patterns. Note that the `cnt` variable is only incremented with each brush. Thus the string in `Pat$` for each brush is used 8 times. Then the bitmap is set up for that brush and we move to the next brush.

```
Public Sub CreateFade()

Dim Cnt As Long
Dim N As Long
Dim Pat As String
Dim Brush
```

continued on next page

continued from previous page

```
Cnt = 0

' Create 10 transition brushes
For Each Brush In m_PatBrushes

Cnt = Cnt + 1

        ' Set up the 8x8 pattern
        For N = 1 To 8

            ' Depending on Cnt and N the appropriate row of
            ' the bitmap pattern is set.
            If Cnt = 1 Then Pat$ = "00000000"

            If Cnt = 2 Then Pat$ = "10000000"

            If Cnt = 3 Then Pat$ = "11000000"

            If Cnt = 4 Then Pat$ = "11100000"

            If Cnt = 5 Then Pat$ = "11110000"

            If Cnt = 6 Then Pat$ = "11111000"

            If Cnt = 7 Then Pat$ = "11111100"

            If Cnt = 8 Then Pat$ = "11111110"

            If Cnt = 9 Then Pat$ = "11111111"

            If Cnt = 10 Then Pat$ = "11111111"

            ' Set the row bits
            Brush.SetPattern Pat$, N

            Pat$ = ""

        Next N

    ' Call the setup bitmap function and
    ' pass in the colors
    Brush.SetupBitmap 255, 255, 255, 0, 0, 0

    ' Build the pattern bitmap
    Brush.BuildBitmap

Next Brush

End Sub
```

18. The `Fade` method of the class handles looping through the pattern brushes. First, the back picture is cleared. Then the next pattern bitmap is displayed in the back picture, by calling the `ShowPattern` method of the `PatBrush` class. Once the pattern is displayed in the hidden picture, the image is copied to the display picture. Note that the pattern is created out of the view of the user, so while the picture is cleared and the pattern is shown, no flickers will be seen in the process.

```
Public Sub Fade()

Dim Cnt As Integer
Dim Throw As Integer
Dim Brush As Object

'  Create the Vertical Patterns
CreateFade

'  Loop through the patterns and
'  display the pattern brush
For Cnt = 1 To 10

    '  Clear the back picture
    m_BackPict.Cls

    '  Display the pattern
    m_PatBrushes.Item(Cnt).ShowPattern

    '  Copy the Pattern to the screen
    Throw = BitBlt(m_DispPict.hdc, 0, 0, m_DispPict.ScaleWidth,⇐
        m_DispPict.ScaleHeight, m_BackPict.hdc, 0, 0, SRCAND)

Next Cnt

End Sub
```

19. The **Setup** method handles creating the **PatBrushes** collection. Each **PatBrush** class is set up and added to the collection of pattern brushes.

```
Public Sub Setup()

Dim N As Integer
Dim PB As PatBrush

'  Create the collection of vertical
'  pattern brushes
Set m_PatBrushes = New Collection

'  Set the picture widths
m_DispPict.Width = m_BackPict.Width
m_DispPict.Height = m_BackPict.Height

'  Set the picture autoredraw and visible
'  property
m_BackPict.AutoRedraw = True
m_BackPict.Visible = False

'  Set up the collection
For N = 1 To 10
```

continued on next page

continued from previous page

```
         ' Create the pattern brush
         Set PB = New PatBrush

         ' Set the display picture for
         ' the pattern. In this case it
         ' will be the working back picture
         Set PB.DispPict = m_BackPict

         ' Add the class to the collection
         m_PatBrushes.Add Item:=PB, Key:=CStr(N)

    Next N

    End Sub
```

20. When the class is terminated, the pattern brushes are deleted and the collection destroyed.

```
    Private Sub Class_Terminate()

    Dim Brush

    ' Delete the brushes
    For Each Brush In m_PatBrushes
        Brush.DeleteBrush
    Next Brush

    ' Delete the collection
    Set m_PatBrushes = Nothing

    End Sub
```

How It Works

There are two aspects of this How-To to explore. The first is the object-oriented model used to design the project. The second is the little bit of Windows API magic used to perform the vertical fade.

The object-oriented model used is based on exposing the **bitmap** class to the form. But, the **bitmap** class works with several other classes to build its functionality. The beauty of the project is that the primary program logic, that of browsing the bitmaps, is not filled with the underlying functionality of how the bitmaps are displayed, or for that matter, how the fade is performed.

The **bitmap** class utilizes the **DiskFile** class and is in fact a type of disk file. The bitmap class collaborates with the **VertFade** class to provide the fade functionality. The **Vertfade** class uses a collection of pattern brushes created by the **PatFade** class to provide the vertical fade patterns. Each class encapsulates a set of functionality that hides its complexity from the rest of the program. For example, the **VertFade** class does not have to know much about how to create pattern brushes; it only needs to know how to work with the **PatBrush** class. The form does not need to *understand* any of the underlying intricacies of a bitmap; it just calls the methods of the bitmap class. This simple object model serves to demonstrate the power of object-oriented programming and techniques. One of the primary side benefits of this methodology is that we now have a set of four classes that can be reused by any future applications and can be easily added to your applications. This is very similar to the concepts that made VBXs and OCXs so popular.

In case you are wondering how the underlying bitmap logic works, let's discuss the **VertFade** and **PatBrush** classes. The **PatBrush** class handles creating a Windows bitmap brush from a specified pattern.

Bitmaps can be built bit-by-bit using the Windows API. For a bitmap brush, an 8x8 bitmap can be built and used as a brush. There are four primary steps to be accomplished to do this:

1. Set up the bit pattern—**SetPattern** method of the class

2. Set up the bitmap structure—**SetupBitmap** method of the class

3. Build the bitmap object—**BuildBitmap** method of the class

4. Show the bitmap brush—**ShowPattern** method of the class

The first step is to define the pattern of the 8x8 bitmap. This is done by passing in a string which defines the vertical pattern of the pattern bitmap (i.e., "11000000"). This is a convenient way to define, bit by bit, the bitmap format. The **BuildBitmap** function handles converting the array into the data needed to build the bitmap. The following is one example of the vertical pattern array:

```
m_array(1) = "11110000"
m_array(2) = "11110000"
m_array(3) = "11110000"
m_array(4) = "11110000"
m_array(5) = "11110000"
m_array(6) = "11110000"
m_array(7) = "11110000"
m_array(8) = "11110000"
```

When the bitmap is set up, the Windows bitmap structures are initialized and the colors for the background and bits determined. Table 6-4 details the **BITMAP-INFO** API structures. Table 6-5 details the **BITMAPINFOHEADER** API structure.

Table 6-4 BITMAPINFO **API-type structure**

MEMBER	DESCRIPTION
biSize As Long	Specifies the number of bytes required by the structure.
biWidth As Long	Specifies the width of the bitmap, in pixels.
biHeight As Long	Specifies the height of the bitmap, in pixels.
biPlanes As Integer	Specifies the number of planes for the target device (always 1).
biBitCount As Integer	Specifies the number of bits per pixel: 1, 4, 8, 16, 24, or 32.

continued on next page

continued from previous page

MEMBER	DESCRIPTION
biCompression As Long	Specifies the type of compression for a compressed bottom-up bitmap.
biSizeImage As Long	Specifies the size, in bytes, of the image (usually 0).
biXPelsPerMeter As Long	Specifies the horizontal resolution, in pixels per meter (usually 0).
biYPelsPerMeter As Long	Specifies the vertical resolution, in pixels per meter (usually 0).
biClrUsed As Long	Specifies the number of color indices in the color table.
biClrImportant As Long	Specifies the number of important color indices (usually 0).

Table 6-5 BITMAPINFOHEADER **API-type structure**

MEMBER	DESCRIPTION
bmiHeader As BITMAPINFOHEADER	Points to a BITMAPINFOHEADER structure.
bmiColors() As Byte	Byte array that specifies colors.

Note that the bitmap colors are easily set as every four bytes for the **bmiColors** byte field. The first byte of the four is the red value, the second green, the third blue, and the last must be 0. The first set of four is color index 0 in the bitmap palette, the second set of four is color index 1 and so on.

The next step builds the bitmap and provides a handle for creating the brush. The key to building the bitmap is converting the **m_array** string into a format usable by the **CreateDIBitmap** function. The **CreateDIBitmap** function expects the bitmap data to be placed in 4-byte blocks such that every row in the bitmap image must end on a 4-byte boundary. Each element of **m_array** is converted into a binary number with the following loop.

```
For C = 0 To 7
If Mid$(m_Array(Counter), C + 1, 1) = "1" Then V = V + 2 ^ C
    Next C
```

The string array (**m_array**) essentially represents a binary number that must be converted into a single decimal value, which in this code is represented by **V**. That decimal value is then placed in every fourth byte of a string which will represent the bitmap data. The following code does this:

```
Mid$(m_Scrn, (Counter - 1) * 4 + 1, 1) = Chr$(V)
```

The **m_Scrn** variable will hold the bitmap values for each row of the pattern to be created (with each row being every four bytes). This can then be used in the **CreateDIBitmap** function as follows:

```
' Create the 8x8 bitmap specified by m_scrn
CompBitmap = CreateDIBitmap(m_DispPict.hdc, m_BitInfoH, CBM_INIT, m_Scrn, ⇐
m_BitInfo, DIB_RGB_COLORS)
```

The `CreateDIBitmap` function takes six parameters which will build the bitmap. Table 6-6 is a breakdown of each.

Table 6-6 `CreateDIBitmap` **parameters**

PARAMETER	DESCRIPTION
ByVal hDC As Long	The device context to build the bitmap in.
lpInfoHeader as BITMAPINFOHEADER	The bitmap format.
ByVal dwUsage As Long	Defines whether or not the bitmap is initialized.
ByVal lpInitBits$	Points to the bitmap bit data.
lpInitInfo as BITMAPINFO	Contains the BITMAPHEADER and color information.
ByVal wUsage As Long	Specifies whether the colors contain explicit red, green, blue (RGB) values or palette indices.

Once the handle of the bitmap is created, the bitmap pattern brush is easily created with the `CreatePatternBrush` function which only takes the handle to the bitmap as a parameter. Last, the pattern is easily displayed using the `PatBLT` function. First our new pattern brush must be selected into the device context by using the `SelectObject` API.

The `VertFade` class creates a series of pattern brushes. The `BitBrush` class builds the vertical patterns by building a set of pattern brushes based on a set of 10 strings sent into each consecutive pattern brush with each string representing a step in the vertical fade. Each of the `PatBrush` classes in the array will be set up to be a series of pattern bitmaps that get successively black, with a vertical pattern.

Once this series of bitmaps is created, the next step is to loop through them and build the next fade image. This is done in the `Fade` method. Then the pattern merely needs to be copied into our background picture box and then copied to the display image using `BitBlt`. This two-step process is done to reduce screen flickering during the fade process.

Comments

Additional functionality could be easily added to the program by adding new classes to give additional features, or the current classes could be easily extended. For example, a method could be added to the `VertFade` class to do a type of *reverse* fade to let the images fade in. In the next How-To, we will add an element of *persistence* to store the bitmap information in a database. Also, we will make this program into a simple three-tier application.

6.5 How do I...
Build ActiveX components?

Problem

The code from the last How-To implements a simple object model. How do I extend this application to store the image data in a database and how do I break out some of the classes to be in-process DLLs and out-of-process ActiveX components?

Technique

Amazingly enough, the database developed in Chapter 4, User Interface Design, **IData.mdb**, can be utilized with this application (funny how those things work out in well-planned books). An ActiveX component will be created that handles retrieving and storing data in the **IData.mdb** file. This ActiveX component will be registered in the system and called from the sample tier client application. We will also encapsulate the **DiskFile** class into an ActiveX DLL that can be called from our application.

Steps

Open and run **6-5.VBP**. Figure 6-7 shows the form at runtime.

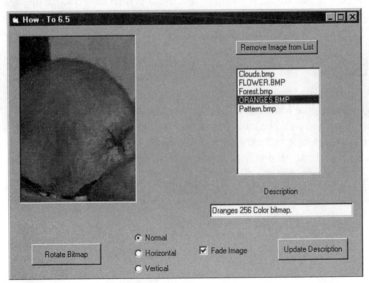

Figure 6-7 The form at runtime

The application has the same functionality as all the previous How-To's. But the underlying implementation has changed significantly. The persistent data about the bitmap images is being pulled from the database. As Figure 6-8 shows, if you want to change and store the description of the images in the database, simply click on the Update Description button.

1. Create a new project called 6-5.VBP. Add the objects and properties listed in Table 6-7 to the form and save the form as **6-5.FRM**.

Table 6-7 The form's objects and properties

OBJECT	PROPERTY	SETTING
Form	Name	Form1
	Caption	"How - To 6.5"
CommandButton	Name	UpdateDesc
	Caption	"Update Description"
CheckBox	Name	FadeImage
	Caption	"Fade Image"
	Value	1 'Checked
CommandButton	Name	Remove
	Caption	"Remove Image from List"
CommandButton	Name	Display
	Caption	"Rotate Bitmap"
TextBox	Name	FileDesc
ListBox	Name	ImageList
OptionButton	Name	DisplayOpt
	Caption	"Vertical"
	Index	2
OptionButton	Name	DisplayOpt
	Caption	"Horizontal"
	Index	1
OptionButton	Name	DisplayOpt
	Caption	"Normal"
	Index	0
	Value	-1 'True
PictureBox	Name	DispPict
	Picture	"pastel.bmp"
PictureBox	Name	BackPict
	AutoRedraw	-1 'True
	Picture	"pastel.bmp"

continued on next page

continued from previous page

OBJECT	PROPERTY	SETTING
	Visible	0 'False
Label	Name	Label1
	AutoSize	−1 'True
	Caption	"Description"

> **NOTE**
>
> Only the new code added to the project will be commented. If you need additional information regarding the other code, see the previous How-To's for a complete explanation.

2. Add the following code to the General Declarations section of the form. The **IData** object is created. Note that a reference to the **ImageData** server is needed in the project references.

```
Option Explicit

'  Bitmaps will be our collection of
'  bitmaps for viewing
Dim Bitmaps As Collection

'  Globally declare the ImageData
'  class
Dim IData As ImageData
```

3. The **UpdateDesc** button handles updating the image comments in both the bitmap class and the database.

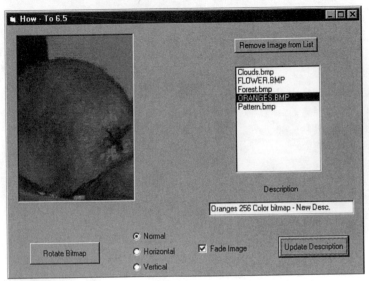

Figure 6-8 The image with the description updated

```
Private Sub UpdateDesc_Click()

'   Update the file description
Bitmaps.Item(ImageList.ListIndex + 1).FileInfo.FileDesc = FileDesc.Text

'   Store the new file description in
'   the database by calling the remote
'   servers UpdateComments method
IData.UpdateComments FileDesc.Text, Bitmaps.Item(ImageList.ListIndex + 1).ID

End Sub

Private Sub Display_Click()

'   Depending on the display option
'   show the bitmap appropriately
If DisplayOpt(0).Value = True Then Bitmaps.Item(ImageList.ListIndex +
1).Load
If DisplayOpt(1).Value = True Then Bitmaps.Item(ImageList.ListIndex +
1).Flip 1
If DisplayOpt(2).Value = True Then Bitmaps.Item(ImageList.ListIndex +
1).Flip 2

End Sub
```

4. When the form is loaded, the **ImageData** class is created. When the Bitmaps collection is set up, the collection is based on the current set of images in the database. The **bitmap** class is created with the specified Image ID, filename, and comments/description.

```
Private Sub Form_Load()

Dim N As Integer
Dim BMP As Bitmap
Dim ID As Integer

'   Create an instance of the
'   ImageData object
Set IData = New ImageData

'   Open the connecton in the
'   remote object
IData.InitConnect

'   Get the ID set
IData.GetIDSet

'   Intially set ID to true
ID = True

'   Create the new collection of bitmaps
Set Bitmaps = New Collection

'   Loop through the images in the
'   database until all are added to
```

continued on next page

continued from previous page

```
' our bitmaps collection
Do Until ID = False

    ' Create an instance of the bitmap
    Set BMP = New Bitmap

    ' Set the display picture
    ' properties
    Set BMP.BackPict = BackPict
    Set BMP.DispPict = DispPict

    ' Get the next image ID
    ID = IData.GetNextID

    ' Check to see if False was returned
    ' if so then end the Loop
    If ID = False Then Exit Do

    ' Set the bitmap filename
    BMP.FileInfo.filename = IData.GetFileName(ID)

    ' Set the bitmap description
    BMP.FileInfo.FileDesc = IData.GetComments(ID)

    ' Set the bitmaps ID
    BMP.ID = ID

    ' Add the Bitmap class to the
    ' collection of bitmaps and set
    ' the key as the count
    Bitmaps.Add Item:=BMP, Key:=CStr(ID)

    ' Add just the name of the image file
    ' to the list box
    ImageList.AddItem (BMP.FileInfo.File)

    ' Destroy the instance of the bitmap class
    Set BMP = Nothing

Loop

' Set the image list to the first
' selection
ImageList.ListIndex = 0

End Sub

Private Sub Form_Unload(Cancel As Integer)

Dim N As Integer

' Destroy all of the bitmap instances
' when the form is unloaded
For N = 1 To Bitmaps.Count
    Bitmaps.Remove 1
```

```
Next N

'  Kill the Idata instance
Set IData = Nothing

End Sub

Private Sub imageList_Click()

'  Call the fade method of the class to
'  perform a vertical blind fade on the
'  image
If FadeImage.Value = 1 Then Bitmaps.Item(ImageList.ListIndex + 1).Fade

'  When an image in the list is
'  clicked on, load the image
Bitmaps.Item(ImageList.ListIndex + 1).Load

'  Set the file description in the
'  text box
FileDesc.Text = Bitmaps.Item(ImageList.ListIndex + 1).FileInfo.FileDesc

End Sub

Private Sub Remove_Click()

'  Always ensure there is at least
'  one entry in the list box
If ImageList.ListCount > 1 Then

    '  Remove the specified image from
    '  the collection and the list box
    Bitmaps.Remove ImageList.ListIndex + 1
    ImageList.RemoveItem ImageList.ListIndex
End If

'  Set the selection to the
'  first image
ImageList.ListIndex = 0

End Sub
```

5. Insert a new class into the project and save it as **Bitmap.cls**. Note that the bitmap class utilizes the **DiskFile** object which is an ActiveX DLL file. A reference must be added to the project for the ActiveX DLL file.

```
Option Explicit

'  A Bitmap is a type of DiskFile
'  So, the Bitmap class will use
'  the properties and methods of
'  the DiskFile class for its
'  functionality
Public FileInfo As DiskFile

'  Declare the global properties of the
```

continued on next page

continued from previous page

```vb
'   class. m_DispPict is the standard
'   display picture. m_BackPict is the
'   background picture that will be used
'   for the image flipping.
Private m_DispPict As Control
Private m_BackPict As Control
Private m_ID As Integer


'   Provide a unique ID to reference the bitmap
Public Property Let ID(I As Integer)
    m_ID = I
End Property

Public Property Get ID() As Integer
    ID = m_ID
End Property


'   Get the Display picture control
Public Property Set DispPict(AControl As Control)
    Set m_DispPict = AControl
    m_DispPict.AutoSize = True
End Property


'   Get the Back ground picture control
'   It is important to ensure that this
'   picture is invisible and that the
'   AutoRedraw property is true so that it
'   will act as a memory device context and
'   hold its image for later work
Public Property Set BackPict(AControl As Control)
    Set m_BackPict = AControl
    m_BackPict.AutoRedraw = False
    m_BackPict.Visible = False
    m_BackPict.AutoSize = True
End Property


Public Sub Fade()

Dim T As Variant
Dim VF As VertFade

'   Create the vertical fade class
Set VF = New VertFade

'   Set the pictures used to perform
'   the fade
Set VF.BackPict = m_BackPict
Set VF.DispPict = m_DispPict

'   Setup the fade
VF.Setup

'   Perform the fade
VF.Fade
```

```
'  Get the current time
T = Time

'  Let the black fade show for
'  a few seconds
Do Until Time > (T + 0.0000001)
Loop

'  Delete the class
Set VF = Nothing

'  Make the displayed picture invisible
m_DispPict.Visible = False

'  For better effect, let the image
'  stay invisible for a few seconds
T = Time

Do Until Time > (T + 0.0000001)
Loop

End Sub

'  The load method of the class loads
'  the image into the two display pictures
Public Sub Load()
    m_DispPict.Picture = LoadPicture(FileInfo.FileName)
    m_BackPict.Picture = LoadPicture(FileInfo.FileName)
    m_DispPict.Visible = True
End Sub

'  The Flip method of the class will rotate
'  the picture accordingly
Public Sub Flip(Rotate)

'  Depending on the rotation selected, the
'  original image will be copied to the
'  display picture appropriately
Select Case Rotate

'  Note that for the vertical and
'  horizontal flips, the height or
'  width is set to a negative value
'  and the starting point is set to
'  the height or width for the image
'  to be displayed. The PaintPicture
'  method of the picture box is used
'  to do the rotation
    Case 1   'Actual Size
             '  Flip Horizontal
             m_DispPict.PaintPicture m_BackPict.Picture, ⇐
        m_BackPict.ScaleWidth, 0, -1 * m_BackPict.ScaleWidth, ⇐
        m_BackPict.ScaleHeight, 0, 0, m_BackPict.ScaleWidth, ⇐
        m_BackPict.ScaleHeight

    Case 2
             '  Flip Vertical
```

continued on next page

continued from previous page

```
                m_DispPict.PaintPicture m_BackPict.Picture, 0, ⇐
        m_BackPict.ScaleHeight, m_BackPict.ScaleWidth, -1 * ⇐
        m_BackPict.ScaleHeight, 0, 0, m_BackPict.ScaleWidth, ⇐
        m_BackPict.ScaleHeight

End Select

End Sub

Private Sub Class_Initialize()
    '  When the class is intialized,
    '  the DiskFile class is created
    Set FileInfo = New DiskFile
End Sub

Private Sub Class_Terminate()
    '  When the class is terminated
    '  the DiskFile class is destroyed
    Set FileInfo = Nothing
End Sub
```

6. Insert a new class into the project and save it as **PatBrush.cls**.

```
Option Explicit

'  The BITMAPINFOHEADER contains basic informtion
'  about the bitmap we will create
Private Type BITMAPINFOHEADER '40 bytes
        biSize As Long
        biWidth As Long
        biHeight As Long
        biPlanes As Integer
        biBitCount As Integer
        biCompression As Long
        biSizeImage As Long
        biXPelsPerMeter As Long
        biYPelsPerMeter As Long
        biClrUsed As Long
        biClrImportant As Long
End Type

'  This data structure holds the header info as
'  well as the color data
Private Type BITMAPINFO
    bmiHeader As BITMAPINFOHEADER
    bmiColors As String * 8 ' Array length is arbitrary; may be changed
End Type

'  Selects an object into a device context
Private Declare Function SelectObject Lib "gdi32" (ByVal hdc As Long, ⇐
ByVal hObject As Long) As Long

'  Creates a DIB Bitmap
Private Declare Function CreateDIBitmap Lib "gdi32" (ByVal hdc As Long, ⇐
lpInfoHeader As BITMAPINFOHEADER, ByVal dwUsage As Long, ByVal ⇐
lpInitBits$,
```

```
lpInitInfo As BITMAPINFO, ByVal wUsage As Long) As Long

'  Deletes a created object
Private Declare Function DeleteObject Lib "gdi32" (ByVal hObject As Long) ⇐
As Long

'  Creates a pattern brush
Private Declare Function CreatePatternBrush Lib "gdi32" (ByVal HBITMAP As ⇐
Long) As Long

'  Paints a picture with the specified pattern
Private Declare Function PatBlt Lib "gdi32" (ByVal hdc As Long, ByVal x ⇐
As Long, ByVal y As Long, ByVal nWidth As Long, ByVal nHeight As Long, ⇐
ByVal dwRop As Long) As Long

Const DIB_RGB_COLORS = 0        '  color table in RGBs
Const CBM_INIT = &H4&           '  initialize bitmap
Const PATCOPY = &HF00021        '  Used for Pattern Copy
Const BI_RGB = 0&               '  RGB Bitmap

'  Declare m_BitInfoH as type BITMAPINFOHEADER
Dim m_BitInfoH As BITMAPINFOHEADER

'  Declare m_BitInfo as type BITMAPINFO
Dim m_BitInfo As BITMAPINFO

'  Holds the Screen data for building the bitmap
Dim m_Scrn As String * 32

'  Holds the handle to the brush
Dim m_Hbr As Long
Dim m_OrgHbr As Long

'  Declare our objects to be passed in
Private m_DispPict As Object
Private m_Array(8) As String * 8

Public Sub SetupBitmap(r1, g1, b1, r2, g2, b2)

'  Standard 40 Byte Header
m_BitInfoH.biSize = 40

'  This will be an 8 by 8 bitmap
m_BitInfoH.biWidth = 8
m_BitInfoH.biHeight = 8

'  One Plane
m_BitInfoH.biPlanes = 1

'  Specifies the number of bits per pixel
m_BitInfoH.biBitCount = 1

'   No Compression
m_BitInfoH.biCompression = BI_RGB
```

continued on next page

continued from previous page

```
'  These values are rarely used
m_BitInfoH.biSizeImage = 0
m_BitInfoH.biXPelsPerMeter = 0
m_BitInfoH.biYPelsPerMeter = 0

'  Two colors used
m_BitInfoH.biClrUsed = 2

'  This ensures that all colors are important
m_BitInfoH.biClrImportant = 0

'  Sets the colors for the bits
'  and background
m_BitInfo.bmiColors = Chr$(r1) + Chr$(g1) + Chr$(b1) + "0" + Chr$(r2) + ⇐
Chr$(g2) + Chr$(b2) + "0"

End Sub

Public Sub BuildBitmap()

Dim Counter as integer
dim V as integer
dim C As Integer
Dim CompBitmap As Long

'  We will loop through each element in the array
For Counter = 1 To 8

    '  v will hold the value of the bit pattern, we
    '  need to reset it for each row
    V = 0

    '  We will loop through each row and set the bit values
    For C = 0 To 7

        '  We check for a 1 in the array and if it is one we
        '  then calculate the decimal value of the binary postion
        '  for example in 00000100, the 1 is = to 2^2 = 4
        If Mid$(m_Array(Counter), C + 1, 1) = "1" Then V = V + 2 ^ C
    Next C
    Mid$(m_Scrn, (Counter - 1) * 4 + 1, 1) = Chr$(V)

Next Counter

'  Set the BitmapInfoHeader field of m_BitInfo
m_BitInfo.bmiHeader = m_BitInfoH

'  Create the 8x8 bitmap specified by m_scrn
CompBitmap = CreateDIBitmap(m_DispPict.hdc, m_BitInfoH, CBM_INIT, m_Scrn, ⇐
m_BitInfo, DIB_RGB_COLORS)

'  Create the bitmap pattern from the screen
m_Hbr = CreatePatternBrush(CompBitmap)

End Sub
```

```
Public Sub DeleteBrush()
Dim Throw As Long

'   Select the original brush into the picture
Throw = SelectObject(m_DispPict.hdc, m_OrgHbr)

'   Delete the created brush
Throw = DeleteObject(m_Hbr)

End Sub

Public Sub ShowPattern()

Dim m_OrgHbr, Throw As Long

'   Select the brush into the display
'   picture
m_OrgHbr = SelectObject(m_DispPict.hdc, m_Hbr)

'   Show the pattern screen
Throw = PatBlt(m_DispPict.hdc, 0, 0, m_DispPict.ScaleWidth, ⇐
m_DispPict.ScaleHeight, PATCOPY)

'   Select the original brush into the picture
Throw = SelectObject(m_DispPict.hdc, m_OrgHbr)

'   Delete the created brush
Throw = DeleteObject(m_Hbr)

End Sub

Public Sub SetPattern(s, index)
    '   Set the pattern sent in
    m_Array(index) = s
End Sub

'   Get the picture for display
Public Property Set DispPict(AControl As Object)
    Set m_DispPict = AControl
End Property

Private Sub Class_Terminate()

'   Delete the brush if it exists
If m_Hbr <> 0 Then DeleteBrush

End Sub
```

7. Insert a new class module into the project and save it as **VertFade.cls**.

```
Option Explicit

'   PatBrushes is a collection of
'   bitmap brushes
Dim m_PatBrushes As Collection
```

continued on next page

continued from previous page

```
'   BitBlt will be used for the image copies
Private Declare Function BitBlt Lib "gdi32" (ByVal hDestDC As Long, ByVal ⇐
x As Long, ByVal y As Long, ByVal nWidth As Long, ByVal nHeight As Long, ⇐
ByVal hSrcDC As Long, ByVal xSrc As Long, ByVal ySrc As Long, ByVal ⇐
dwRop As Long)
As Long


'   Constants for the BitBlt copies
Const SRCCOPY = &HCC0020
Const SRCAND = &H8800C6


'   Globally declare the members of the class
Dim m_BackPict As Control
Dim m_DispPict As Control


'   BackPict and DispPict are the picture
'   controls for performing the fade
Public Property Set BackPict(AControl As Control)
    Set m_BackPict = AControl
End Property

Public Property Set DispPict(AControl As Control)
    Set m_DispPict = AControl
End Property


Public Sub CreateFade()

Dim Cnt As Long
Dim N As Long
Dim Pat As String
Dim Brush


Cnt = 0

'   Create 10 transition brushes
For Each Brush In m_PatBrushes

Cnt = Cnt + 1

    '   Set up the 8x8 pattern
    For N = 1 To 8

        '   Depending on Cnt and N the appropriate row of
        '   the bitmap pattern is set.
        If Cnt = 1 Then Pat$ = "00000000"

        If Cnt = 2 Then Pat$ = "10000000"

        If Cnt = 3 Then Pat$ = "11000000"

        If Cnt = 4 Then Pat$ = "11100000"

        If Cnt = 5 Then Pat$ = "11110000"
```

```vb
        If Cnt = 6 Then Pat$ = "11111000"

        If Cnt = 7 Then Pat$ = "11111100"

        If Cnt = 8 Then Pat$ = "11111110"

        If Cnt = 9 Then Pat$ = "11111111"

        If Cnt = 10 Then Pat$ = "11111111"

        '  Set the row bits
        Brush.SetPattern Pat$, N

        Pat$ = ""

    Next N

'  Call the setup bitmap function and
'  pass in the colors
Brush.SetupBitmap 255, 255, 255, 0, 0, 0

'  Build the pattern bitmap
Brush.BuildBitmap

Next Brush

End Sub

Public Sub Fade()

Dim Cnt As Integer
Dim Throw As Integer
Dim Brush As Object

'  Create the Vertical Patterns
CreateFade

'  Loop through the patterns and
'  display the pattern brush
For Cnt = 1 To 10

    '  Clear the back picture
    m_BackPict.Cls

    '  Display the pattern
    m_PatBrushes.Item(Cnt).ShowPattern

    '  Copy the Pattern to the screen
    Throw = BitBlt(m_DispPict.hdc, 0, 0, m_DispPict.ScaleWidth, ⇐
        m_DispPict.ScaleHeight, m_BackPict.hdc, 0, 0, SRCAND)

Next Cnt

End Sub

Public Sub Setup()
```

continued on next page

continued from previous page

```
Dim N As Integer
Dim PB As PatBrush

'  Create the collection of vertical
'  pattern brushes
Set m_PatBrushes = New Collection

'  Set the picture widths
m_DispPict.Width = m_BackPict.Width
m_DispPict.Height = m_BackPict.Height

'  Set the picture autoredraw and visible
'  property
m_BackPict.AutoRedraw = True
m_BackPict.Visible = False

'  Set up the collection
For N = 1 To 10

    '  Create the pattern brush
    Set PB = New PatBrush

    '  Set the display picture for
    '  the pattern. In this case it
    '  will be the working back picture
    Set PB.DispPict = m_BackPict

    ' Add the class to the collection
    m_PatBrushes.Add Item:=PB, Key:=CStr(N)

Next N

End Sub

Private Sub Class_Terminate()

Dim Brush

'  Delete the brushes
For Each Brush In m_PatBrushes
    Brush.DeleteBrush
Next Brush

'  Delete the collection
Set m_PatBrushes = Nothing

End Sub
```

8. Create a second project and save it as **6-5-DLL.vbp**. This project will be used to encapsulate the **DiskFile** class in an ActiveX DLL file. Insert a new BAS module into the project and save it as **module1.bas**. Add an empty **Sub Main** to the module.

```
Public Sub Main()

End Sub
```

9. Insert a new class into the project and save it as `DiskFile.cls`.

```
Option Explicit

'   Member property of the class that
'   stores the filename
Private m_FileName As String

'   Member property of the class that
'   stores the file description
Private m_FileDesc As String

'   The get and set properties of the class
'   for the file description
Public Property Let FileDesc(s As String)
    m_FileDesc = s
End Property

Public Property Get FileDesc() As String
    FileDesc = m_FileDesc
End Property

'   Get the file name by itself.
'   I.E. c:\windows\cloulds.bmp is clouds.bmp
Public Property Get File() As String
    File = ParseFile()
End Property

'   Set and get the filename property for the
'   the class
Public Property Let FileName(s As String)
    m_FileName = s
End Property

Public Property Get FileName() As String
    FileName = m_FileName
End Property

'   Get the file size
Public Property Get FileSize() As Long
    FileSize = FileLen(m_FileName)
End Property

'   Get the file extension
Public Property Get FileExt() As String
    FileExt = ParseExt()
End Property

'   Get the directory of the file
Public Property Get Directory() As String
    Directory = ParseDir()
End Property

'   Get the date of the file
Public Property Get FileDate() As Date
    FileDate = FileDateTime(m_FileName)
```

continued on next page

continued from previous page

```vb
End Property

'  Parse out the file name. Note that this is
'  a private method. It is only utilized in the
'  File property
Private Function ParseFile() As String

Dim N As Integer

ParseFile = ""

'  Start from the end of the file name
'  and look for the '\' character. Thus the
'  file part of the file name will be known
For N = Len(m_FileName) To 1 Step -1

    If Mid(m_FileName, N, 1) = "\" Then
        ParseFile = Right(m_FileName, Len(m_FileName) - N)
        N = -1
    End If

Next N

End Function

'  Parse out the file directory. Note that
'  this is a private class method and is only
'  utilized by the Directory property
Private Function ParseDir() As String

Dim N As Integer

ParseDir = ""

'  Start from the end of the file name
'  and look for the first '\' character. Thus
'  the location of the file name will be known
'  and the rest is the directory location
For N = Len(m_FileName) To 1 Step -1

    If Mid(m_FileName, N, 1) = "\" Then
        ParseDir = Left(m_FileName, N)
        N = -1
    End If

Next N

End Function

'  GetExt retrieves the file extension if
'  there is one. This is only used by the
'  FileExt property
Private Function ParseExt() As String

Dim N As Integer
```

```
ParseExt = "(N/A)"

'   Start from the end of the file name
'   and look for the '.' character. Thus
'   the location of the extension will be known
'   in the file name string
For N = Len(m_FileName) To 1 Step -1

    If Mid(m_FileName, N, 1) = "." Then
        ParseExt = Right(m_FileName, Len(m_FileName) - N)
        N = -1
    End If

Next N

End Function

'   Public method of the class to
'   copy the file to a new location
Public Sub CopyFile(NewLocation)
    FileCopy m_FileName, NewLocation + ParseFile
End Sub

'   Public method of the class to
'   delete the file
Public Sub DeleteFile()
    Kill m_FileName
End Sub

'   When the class is initialized
'   the filename, description and
'   extension will be set to
'   N/A.
Private Sub Class_Initialize()

m_FileName = "Uninitialized"
m_FileDesc = "N/A"

End Sub
```

10. Create a new project and save it as **6-5-srv.vbp**. This will be an ActiveX executable which will provide the database connectivity to the third tier of data. Insert a new BAS module into the project and save it as **Module1.bas**.

```
Public Sub Main()

End Sub
```

11. Add the following code to the General Declarations section of the project. Note that a global RDO environment, connection, and resultset are declared.

```
Option Explicit

'   Declare a global result set which
'   can be used to retrieve all of
'   the image IDs in the database
Dim m_IDResultSet As rdoResultset

'   Dim a remote data environment
Dim Env As rdoEnvironment

'   Dim a remote data connection
Dim Con As rdoConnection

'   Declare a remote data record set
Dim RS As rdoResultset
```

12. The **InitConnect** method of the class handles opening the connection to the database. The global RDO environment variable, **Env**, is set to the first member of the **rdoEnvironments** collection. Then the RDO connection, **con**, is set to the ODBC **ImageDatabase** connection. We now have our connection to the database established. This method should be first used when the class is called.

```
Public Sub InitConnect()

'   Set the remote data environment
Set Env = rdoEnvironments(0).

'   Open the ODBC connection
Set Con = Env.OpenConnection(dsName:="Image Database",
Prompt:=rdDriverNoPrompt)

End Sub
```

13. The private **DBExec** method handles executing the specified SQL command on the database.

```
Private Sub DBExec(cmd$)

'   Execute the specified SQL Command
Con.Execute cmd$

End Sub
```

14. The **DBOpenRec** private method handles opening a resultset based on the specified SQL command.

```
Private Sub DBOpenRec(cmd$)

'   Open a resulset based on the
'   SQL query. rdOpenKeySet indicates
'   that the rows can be updated.
Set RS = Con.OpenResultset(cmd$, rdOpenKeyset, rdConcurRowver)

End Sub
```

15. The `GetComments` method retrieves the comments for a specified image in the database. It uses the `DBOpenRec` method to retrieve the resultset. It then returns the value of the `Comments` field of the database.

```
Public Function GetComments(ImageID As Integer) As String

'   Get the comments field for the specified
'   image
DBOpenRec "Select * from ImageData Where ImageID = " + Trim(Str$(ImageID))

'   Return the value
GetComments = RS("Comments")

End Function
```

16. The `GetFileName` method retrieves the filename for a specified image in the database. It uses the `DBOpenRec` method to retrieve the resultset. It then returns the value of the `FileName` field of the database.

```
Public Function GetFileName(ImageID As Integer) As String

'   Get the file name for the specified
'   image
DBOpenRec "Select * from ImageData Where ImageID = " + Trim(Str$(ImageID))

'   Return the file name
GetFileName = RS("FileName")

End Function
```

17. The `GetFileFormat` method retrieves the comments for a specified image in the database. It uses the `DBOpenRec` method to retrieve the resultset. It then returns the value of the `FileFormat` field of the database.

```
Public Function GetFileFormat(ImageID As Integer) As String

'   Get the file format for the specified
'   image
DBOpenRec "Select * from ImageData Where ImageID = " + Trim(Str$(ImageID))

'   Return the file format
GetFileFormat = RS("FileFormat")

End Function
```

18. The `GetIDSet` method retrieves a resultset of all the images in the database. This is set to the private resultset, `m_IDResultSet` property.

```
Public Sub GetIDSet()

'   Select all of the images
'   in the database
DBOpenRec "Select * from ImageData"

'   Set the global IDResultSet class
```

continued on next page

continued from previous page

```
'  member to have the list of images
Set m_IDResultSet = RS

End Sub
```

19. The `GetNextID` method retrieves the next ID in the resultset. This method allows a calling application to be able to move through the database and retrieve all the entries. When the last record is reached, False is returned from the function.

```
Public Function GetNextID() As Integer

'  Check to see if the end of the
'  result set has been reached
If m_IDResultSet.EOF <> True Then
    '  Get the next Image ID and
    '  return the value
    GetNextID = m_IDResultSet("ImageID")

    '  Move to the next record
    m_IDResultSet.MoveNext
Else
    '  Close the result set if the
    '  end of the result set was reached.
    m_IDResultSet.Close

    '  Return False as the value
    GetNextID = False
End If

End Function
```

20. The `UpdateComments` method handles updating the comments of the image. The new comments and the image ID are passed in as parameters.

```
Public Sub UpdateComments(NewComments As String, ID As Integer)

'  Update the comments for the
'  specified Image
DBExec "Update ImageData set Comments = '" + NewComments + "' where ⇐
ImageID = " + LTrim(Str$(ID))

End Sub
```

How It Works

This How-To demonstrates how to break an application up into a three-tier architecture using the various tools provided in Visual Basic. The first tier is the client application which provides the basic functionality of the program. This tier uses the `Bitmap`, `VertFade`, and `PatBrush` classes, within the project. We have created two ActiveX components that are easy to reuse and incorporate into the client application. The `DiskFile` ActiveX DLL and the `ImageData` ActiveX executable comprise the second tier. Finally, the third tier is the data tier comprised of the database. With ODBC, the database in this example can reside in an Access MDB or on the SQL server.

To create the ActiveX DLL and ActiveX executable, be sure to add the classes to separate projects from your client application. For the ActiveX DLL file, simply compile the project as an ActiveX DLL instead of an EXE. Set the project options to include an appropriate project and application name. This name will show up in the references dialog in the client application.

For the ActiveX executable, under the Project menu select Disk Properties. Then select the Project tab. For the start mode, select the ActiveX executable option. Be sure and give the project a name and fill out the description. You will need to compile the program as an EXE file and then run the EXE to register the ActiveX executable. Once registered, the client project will show the ActiveX executable in the references dialog.

Note in the client application, the References menu is under the Tool menu. Be sure the `Disk` and `IData` objects are selected. Once you have done this, press the F2 key to bring up the object browser. Select either the `Disk` or `IData` objects and you can review the various properties and methods of each object. This will correspond directly to the public methods and properties in your ActiveX DLL and ActiveX executable projects.

Comments

The rest of the chapters in the book will expand on using ActiveX components to build business objects, collections, and so on. After the How-To's in this chapter you should have a strong feel for the object-oriented capabilities of Visual Basic and for the opportunities to rethink how your applications can be designed and built.

CHAPTER 7

BUSINESS OBJECTS

by George Szabo

BUSINESS OBJECTS

How do I...

7.1   **Set up an ActiveX business object project?**

7.2   **Encapsulate business rules into a class?**

7.3   **Encapsulate business rules into an in-process server (ActiveX DLL)?**

7.4   **Encapsulate business rules into an out-of-process server (ActiveX EXE)?**

7.5   **Move my business object to a remote server?**

7.6   **Pass variant arrays to and from a business object?**

What is a business object? A *business object* is a self-contained component of logic that encapsulates the business rules and processes of an organization's business model. In terms of Visual Basic 5.0, a business object is a class or classes used to encapsulate the business logic of your applications. This encapsulation of business logic can reside within the same executable as the user interface logic or it can be partitioned away from the user interface code by separating it into ActiveX DLLs (in-process servers) or ActiveX EXEs (out-of-process servers) that can be transparently called from your user interfaces with no code changes.

Using Remote Automation these business objects can then be deployed to different physical locations and still provide their encapsulated business logic to the client applications referencing them. All of this can be done transparently to the client application and its code.

Design Principles

There are a variety of techniques being used to create, design, and implement business objects today. This chapter provides the mechanical building blocks that will enable you to assemble the business objects that you need. It is important to note that the quality of an object, and its value, is really based on the time and thought given to its design. There are several activities that you must do before you are ready to use these building blocks. You will need to do the following:

- Define the objects that comprise the business you are dealing with.

- Clarify each object's characteristics and the relationship they have to each other.

- Group your objects into services (accounting, customers, sales).

- Define the interface that each of these objects will reveal.

Persistent Objects

Additionally you will need to decide whether a business object should be designed as a persistent object—an object that remembers activities between requests—or as a nonpersistent object that does not retain any information from request to request. Each type of business object has its benefits. Persistent objects have the benefit of remembering the state of properties between requests so you can execute multiple methods based on persistent properties. This means that you don't have to set these properties every time, thus reducing the number of calls you must make.

Nonpersistent objects have the benefit of simplicity—much like using a black box function that contains no static variables. If your object provides financial calculations that do not require tracking internal state information, then a nonpersistent model is the way to go.

Where Should the Object Reside?

Once you have defined your business objects, grouped them into services, and decided whether they are best implemented as persistent or nonpersistent objects, you are ready to enter into the discussion of physical partitioning of these objects. Prior to this point, all your work has been to define the logical design and implementation of your business object. Before you can move into architecting the final object, you need to consider how it will be physically deployed. What? You mean that you need to code differently based on where the object will eventually reside? Yes. You can code your business logic and move it from being in the same executable as the client interface to being accessed on a remote server via the Internet (or more likely an Intranet). But, as you partition your application's logic physically, execution time increases, requiring the use of special methods to bring execution speed back into acceptable parameters.

Making a thousand calls to an in-process server (ActiveX DLL) on your local machine may not be a big deal, but once you move to an out-of-process server (ActiveX EXE) and Remote Automation, you will need to consider special methods to make your business objects usable. This can be done by reducing the number of calls by packaging data into a single call. Calling a remote out-of-process server can take up to 100 times as long as the same call to an in-process ActiveX DLL. This chapter contains How-To information that will help you compare the differences in execution speed as well as optimize communication between the client application and your business objects.

It is fair to say that centralized business services (business rules) are a goal for most developers. Over the past several years, stored procedures—precompiled instructions that your database engine can execute—have been marketed as the vehicle for encapsulating and centralizing business logic. Many a database administrator and SQL specialist have spent, and continue to spend, long days and nights trying to re-create business logic using the limited syntax available to stored procedures. The result of this experiment has been an inadequate ability to duplicate the business process. In the three-tier client/server model, by contrast, stored procedures are used for the execution of base level activities (SELECT, INSERTs, UPDATEs, DELETEs) in the data tier while the true business logic resides in your business objects in the business tier.

Why not place all this logic in the client where you have the greatest control and flexibility with logic, rather than in a remote server? This might be fine if you are writing business systems for 5 workstations. Obviously, though, when you have 50 or even 500 workstations, deploying new versions of an application every time the business rules change is expensive if not impossible. The alternative, described in this chapter, is to implement centralized business rules located in business objects (components) that can be accessed by all your client applications. If a rule changes, you can go to one place, change it, and redeploy without redeploying to a thousand workstations. There is a server hit, with regard to execution speed, that comes from dealing with a remotely deployed business object but the benefits of maintainability and reuse provide enormous opportunities that competitive businesses must exploit.

Depending on your level of expertise, you may be able to use any of the How-To's in this chapter independently of the others. However, if you are new to the design of business objects, their use, and deployment, it is recommended that you work through these How-To's in order.

7.1 Set Up an ActiveX Business Object Project

The toughest part of building business objects is knowing where to start. You will walk through the creation of a template project that you can use as the starting point for all your business objects.

7.2   Encapsulate Business Rules into a Class

This project makes use of the template created in How-To 7.1. You will encapsulate logic to calculate an author's royalties for any given time period. You will do this with classes and implement both standard and optimized methods for communication between the client interface and the business object interface.

7.3   Encapsulate Business Rules into an In-Process Server (ActiveX DLL)

A key to the Component Object Model is the ability to partition logic into discrete components. One place to put these components is in a server application that runs in a library (DLL) on the same machine as the primary application. Building on How-To 7.2, you will see exactly what it takes to partition business logic out of a single executable into its own in-process server (ActiveX DLL).

7.4   Encapsulate Business Rules into an Out-of-Process Server (ActiveX EXE)

The other partitioning alternative is to use a server that runs as a remote executable on the network as an EXE file. Although in-process servers are faster than out-of-process servers, in order to deploy your business logic remotely it must be contained in an ActiveX executable or out-of-process server. This project will show you what you need to do to create such a server.

7.5   Move My Business Object to a Remote Server

Centralized business services cannot be realized until business objects can be deployed remotely. In How-To's 7.3 and 7.4, both in-process DLL and out-of-process EXE servers are built. These servers are running on the local machine. This How-To walks you through both the automatic and manual process of deploying your business objects on a remote machine.

7.6   Pass Variant Arrays to and from a Business Object

It is often vital to optimize the execution speed of the implementation of a business object, particularly when it is deployed remotely. The use of variant arrays can give you a real speed advantage over conventional Visual Basic syntax. You will make use of variant arrays to get and set information in a business object, resulting in execution times that are 2 to 3 times faster than standard dot operations. A *dot operation* is the syntax used to reference properties of an object using a dot between the two, for example, `MyList.Sortorder`.

You will implement the use of a collection object within an ActiveX server. Collections are a powerful feature in Visual Basic but implementing a collection within a business object is not a trivial matter. In order to maintain control over the object, you will implement a wrapper for the collection object. A *wrapper* is a function whose purpose is to provide an interface to another function. This is done to safeguard how a client can use the collection within your business object. This will provide the scenario in which methods using variant arrays make sense.

COMPLEXITY

INTERMEDIATE

7.1 How do I...
Set up an ActiveX business object project?

Problem

I am about to begin developing business components. How do I set up my projects in Visual Basic? Where do I start?

Technique

There are a series of steps that you should take when starting a project that will result in either an in-process server or an out-of-process server. Even if you are going to keep the business logic in the same executable as the interface, using this template and understanding the issues will make partitioning your application later on much smoother.

Steps

Open **BUSOBJ.VBP**. The form for testing your business object's functionality appears in Figure 7-1.

Run the project. The form contains two text boxes and several buttons that exercise the methods and properties of the component object. As you press a button, a resulting message is displayed in the text box to the left of the buttons. The text box above the buttons is used to adjust the number of repetitions that a test executes. Although you can run this project, it does not contain any business logic or usefulness until you apply it to your own projects. This will be done in How-To 7.2. The template project contains the following pieces:

- **SERVER.CLS**—This is the server class module which provides a secure entry point for your business component. This module also provides a reference to a second class module that will eventually hold the methods and properties that do the real work.

- **DEPOBJ.CLS**—This is a dependent class module that will eventually hold the methods and properties that will fill this business component. This class is not creatable by the public but must be created by the server class and passed to the requesting party.

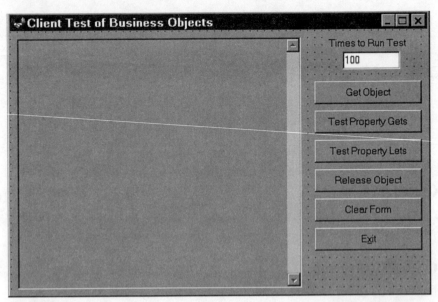

Figure 7-1 Internal test form for business object template

■ **GENERAL.BAS**—This is a standard code module that simply provides a subroutine called **MAIN**. Visual Basic projects must specify a startup form or procedure. Since a form cannot be specified for an ActiveX DLL or ActiveX EXE, you must use a subroutine called **MAIN**. This code module is included to hold the **MAIN** subroutine.

These three modules are all you need to create a business object, also referred to as a component. The template also includes a form to allow testing of the business object's methods and properties. The **TIMING.CLS** class module is included to provide support to the test form in timing execution speeds. The test form and timing class are included as key pieces to testing the functionality of your business object but are not required pieces. Here is how to set up the business object template:

1. Create a new standard EXE project called **BUSOBJ.VPB**.

2. Open the project property dialog box by selecting Project from the Visual Basic menu bar and selecting the Project's Properties. You can see the Project Properties dialog box containing the primary options you need to set for an ActiveX server project in Figure 7-2.

3. Set the properties listed in Table 7-1 for this project.

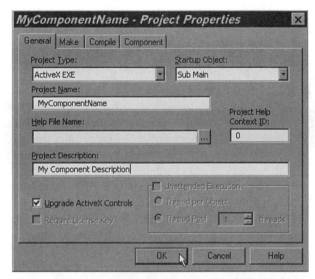

Figure 7-2 Visual Basic Project Properties General tab

Table 7-1 The project's general settings

OBJECT	PROPERTY	SETTING
General Tab	Project Type	ActiveX DLL
	Startup Object	Sub Main
	Project Name	MyComponentName
	Project Description	"My Component Description"
Component Tab	Project Compatibility	checked

4. Create a new code module and save it as `GENERAL.BAS`.

5. Add the following code to the General Declarations section of the `GENERAL.BAS` code module. You declare a global remote data object (RDO) environment and connection object at this level so that once you open a connection it will remain open until you specifically close it. If you declared the RDO connection and environment inside a function, it would be closed each time the function completed and moved out of scope. This avoids having to reconnect over and over again, costing you a lot of time.

```
Option Explicit

Global Env As rdoEnvironment
Global Cn As rdoConnection
```

continued on next page

continued from previous page

```
'Use this Global constant to easily repoint this business
'object towards a different data source.

Global Const DB_TARGET = "ConfiguredDataSourceName"
```

6. Add the following procedure called **MAIN** to the **GENERAL.BAS** code module. Visual Basic doesn't realize that a DLL's entry point is its creatable public class module; therefore, you are required to use a **SUB MAIN** procedure as its main entry point. The entry point was configured earlier by setting the startup form to **SUB MAIN** on the General tab. No code is required in the **MAIN** subprocedure. The code included here checks the start mode of the component. If the component has been compiled as an ActiveX EXE and is started by double-clicking on it or executing it from the command line, then the test form will be loaded. Here the evaluation code is commented out since you are going to be using the test form every time. Once you compile your object as a ActiveX DLL or ActiveX EXE, you will need to remove the comment marks in front of the **If** statement shown below.

```
Sub MAIN()

    'If App.StartMode = vbSModeStandalone Then
        frmTestClient.Show vbModal
    'End If

End Sub
```

7. Create a new class module and save it as **SERVER.CLS.** Set the properties listed in Table 7-2 for this class. These settings are important. A project must have at least one class module that is public and creatable.

Table 7-2 Class option settings

OPTION	SETTING
Name	Server
Instancing	5 - MultiUse

8. Add the following code to the General Declarations section of the **Server** class. The standard entry point into all business services objects is a creatable class module. All projects will use **Server** as this class's name. The following variables, properties, and methods are the starting point for all projects.

```
Option Explicit

'UserId is read-only by the client application. This will allow
'you to know who is using this object. This variable is set using the
'connect method.

Private m_UserId As String

'Password is neither read nor written by a client application. It is
'stored so that you can pass it on to other services or servers that
'may need a password supplied like a backend database server when
'you prepare a connection string.

Private m_Password As String

'Parent object is a reference to the object that instantiated this
'instance of this business object. It is neither read nor written by
'the client application. You will use this Object reference during
'termination to assure that this business object is properly
'released and replaced.

Private m_Parent As Object

'This declaration uses Early Binding to dimension an object
'variable that you will use to pass a reference to the client
'applications request. The reference to this member object
'variable is passed in the Load method of this class but could
'just as easily be passed as part of the Connect method.

Private m_DependentObject As DependentObject
```

9. The template you are now building is designed to provide a standard for the business objects you design and deploy. You have already taken the first step by creating a class module named **Server**. Now add the **Connect** method to your **Server** class module. Once your business object is instantiated, the client application or component must call the **Connect** method in order to gain access to the rest of the business object's properties and methods.

```
Sub Connect (UserId As String, _
                  Password As String, _
                  Optional Parent As Variant)

     Static Connected As Boolean
```

continued on next page

continued from previous page

```
'only allow this business object to be initialized once.

If Connected Then Exit Sub

'set the Connected flag to true.

Connected = True

'set all of the necessary variables declared earlier.

m_UserId = UserId
m_Password = Password

'check for optional Parent parameter. This will be present when
'the component is started by a pool manager.

If IsMissing(Parent) Then
    Set m_Parent = Nothing
Else
    Set m_Parent = Parent
End If

'You will use the User Id and Password to set up the
'environment for Remote Data Objects

rdoEngine.rdoDefaultUser = UserId
rdoEngine.rdoDefaultPassword = Password

'You will open a connection to the database. This
'connection will then be used to issue SQL to the
'Data Tier or to trigger Stored Procedures residing
'within the database engine. Note that DB_TARGET is set in the
'General.bas file. The DB_TARGET is the name of a valid ODBC
'data source name (DSN).

Set Env = rdoEngine.rdoEnvironments(0)
Set Cn = Env.OpenConnection(dsname:=DB_TARGET, _
                            Prompt:=rdDriverNoPrompt, _
                            ReadOnly:=False, _
                            Connect:="")

    End Sub
```

10. The User Id is a parameter provided to the Connect method which was added to the Server class module earlier. In order to allow the client or pool manager to check the User Id, you will need to create a property that can be read. This is done by adding the following code to the Server class module. Because there is no Let property for User Id in the Server class module, a client application cannot change the User Id. UserId is read-only.

```
Property Get UserId() As String

    'The UserId is read-only so you will only need to have this
    'routine to make it available to the client application.

    UserId = m_UserId

End Property
```

11. You need a method that allows the client to get a reference to dependent objects. Dependent classes are class modules that are set to public but not externally creatable. This is done by adding the following code to the Server class module. Note that this function could be part of the Connect method to reduce needed code.

```
Public Function Load() As DependentObject
'The Load Method of the Server Class creates a new instance
'of a dependent class and passes a reference to that class."

    Set m_DependentObject = New DependentObject
    Set Load = m_DependentObject

End Function
```

> **NOTE**
>
> Using mixed case when creating project names and other property names is done purposefully. Since VB checks your syntax as each line is completed, you can type these names all in lowercase when referencing them in later lines of code, and, as you leave the line, if the name is typed correctly it will be properly formatted with uppercase and lowercase. If you have not typed the name correctly, it will remain all lowercase. This will eliminate a great deal of pain that comes from debugging problems caused by mistyping object names and properties.

12. Create a new class module and save it as `DEPOBJ.CLS.` Set the properties listed in Table 7-3 for this class. This class is empty and contains no code. This will be the home of your business object's methods and properties. A client must call the `Connect` method of the `Server` class followed by the `Load` method to gain access to this class. If you follow this process for all of your business component objects, you will have a consistent process for controlling use of your components.

Table 7-3 Class option settings

OPTION	SETTING
Name	DependentObject
Instancing	2 - PublicNotCreatable

13. As mentioned earlier, all you need to create your business object is the `GENERAL.BAS` code module, the `SERVER.CLS` class module, and the `DEPOBJ.CLS` class module. These three files comprise the core of your business object. The following form and its code are used to test the functionality of the business object internally. Tools to test ActiveX components are in their infancy. This makes finding problems and fixing them very difficult. By testing your business object at every step of its development and deployment, you can catch problems early in the process, which will make life much easier later on.

14. Select Form1, and add objects and set properties as shown in Table 7-4. Save the form as `TESTFORM.FRM`.

Table 7-4 The project's objects and properties

OBJECT	PROPERTY	SETTING
Form	Name	frmTestClient
	Caption	"Client Test of Business Objects"
	Icon	Handshak.ico
Label	Name	label1
	Caption	"Times to Run Test"
TextBox	Name	txtTestReps
	Text	"100"
TextBox	Name	txtDisplay
	Text	""
	MultiLine	True
	ScrollBars	2 - Vertical

OBJECT	PROPERTY	SETTING
CommandButton	Name	cmdGetObject
	Caption	"Get Object"
CommandButton	Name	cmdTestPropertyGets
	Caption	"Test Property Gets"
CommandButton	Name	cmdTestPropertyLets
	Caption	"Test Property Lets"
CommandButton	Name	cmdReleaseObject
	Caption	"Release Object"
CommandButton	Name	cmdClear
	Caption	"Clear Form"
CommandButton	Name	cmdExit
	Caption	"E&xit"

14. The first thing you will need to do with the test form in order to use the classes that you created is to dimension object variables for the **Server** class as well as the **Dependent Object** class. This is done by adding the following code to the General Declarations section of the form.

```
Option Explicit
'dimension an object variable for the component
Dim oBusinessObject As MyComponentName.Server

'dimension an object variable for the main dependent object.
Dim oDependentObject As DependentObject

'Dimension a variable for the timing object
Dim oTiming As Timing
```

15. Add the following code to the test form **Load** event to make the timing class and its timing methods and properties available.

```
Private Sub Form_Load()

    'create an instance of the timing class so you can time tests.
    Set oTiming = New Timing

End Sub
```

16. The first thing you will need to do in order to test the methods and properties of the business component object is to create an instance of the classes that you can test. You need to create an instance of the **Server** class module and any dependent classes you will be testing. This is done by adding the **GetObjectReference** and **GetDependentObjectReference** methods to the test form.

```
Private Sub GetObjectReference()

    'starting timing event
    oTiming.Start

    'Instantiate the Business Object
    Set oBusinessObject = New MyComponentName.Server

    'finish timing event.
    oTiming.Finish

    'Make sure that you successfully got the object
    If oBusinessObject Is Nothing Then
        txtDisplay.Text = txtDisplay.Text _
                            & "Bummer, couldn't get it." _
                            & vbCrLf
    Else
        txtDisplay.Text = txtDisplay.Text _
                            & "Yahoo! Got the Business Object in " _
                            & oTiming.ElapsedTime _
                            & " seconds" & vbCrLf

    End If

End Sub

Private Sub GetDependentObjectReference()

    'Dimension any variables that you need to pass when
    'getting a reference to the main dependent business
    'object. Place those here...
    Dim MyParameters As Variant

    'start timing event.
    oTiming.Start
```

```
'Here you would set any parameters needed.
MyParameters = "Hello World"

'now you allow the Business Object to pass a reference
'to a newly created dependent object that represents the
'main body of your business services for this object.
Set oDependentObject = oBusinessObject.Load(MyParameters)

'finish timing event.
oTiming.Finish

'make sure you got a reference to the new dependent object.
If oDependentObject Is Nothing Then
    txtDisplay.Text = txtDisplay.Text _
                     & "Bummer, couldn't get Dependent Object." _
                     & vbCrLf
Else
    txtDisplay.Text = txtDisplay.Text _
                     & "Yahoo! Got the Dependent Object in " _
                     & oTiming.ElapsedTime _
                     & " seconds" & vbCrLf
End If

End Sub
```

17. Once you have an instance of the classes you will be testing, you then need routines that exercise the properties and methods of those classes. The following **PropertyGet** and **PropertySet** procedures are provided as examples but will need to be modified to work with your specific business component object. This will be done in How-To 7.2.

```
Private Sub PropertyGet()

    'insert a routine that retrieves properties from
    'your business object using individual dot commands.
    '    txtDisplay.text = oDependentObject.PropertyName

End Sub

Private Sub PropertySet()

    'insert a routine that sets properties from the
    'business object using individual dot commands.
    '    oDependentObject.PropertyName = MyNewValue

End Sub
```

18. The test form allows the user to specify the number of times to run a test. A centralized routine is needed to run the property and methods tests based on the number of repetitions specified on the form. Additionally, the tests must be timed and results displayed to the window. This is done by adding the following **RunTest** procedure to the test form.

```
Private Sub RunTest(sTestFunction As String, sDisplayText As String)
    'this routine will run the tests on properties and methods as
    'many times as are specified in the txtTestReps textbox. The
    'default is 100

    Dim i As Integer
    Dim iReps As Integer

    'Make sure you have an object reference before you start
    If oDependentObject Is Nothing Then
        txtDisplay.Text = txtDisplay.Text _
                            & "No reference to Dependent Object found." _
                            & vbCrLf

        Exit Sub
    Else

    End If

    'make sure that you have a valid value for number of repetitions
    'for the tests.
    If txtTestReps.Text <> "" Then
        iReps = CInt(txtTestReps.Text)
    Else
        iReps = 1
    End If

    '++++++++++++++++++++++++++++++++++++++++++++++++++'
    'test interface of server                          '
    '++++++++++++++++++++++++++++++++++++++++++++++++++'

    'start timing this event
    oTiming.Start

    'run test
```

```
    For i = 1 To iReps
        'Place the name of the functions you wish to test here
        Select Case sTestFunction
        Case "PropertyGet"
            PropertyGet
        Case "PropertySet"
            PropertySet
        End Select
    Next

    'stop timing event
    oTiming.Finish

    'display the time taken to retrieve the properties using
    'standard dot operation gets.
    txtDisplay.Text = txtDisplay.Text _
                        & Str(iReps) _
                        & " Rep(s) of " & sDisplayText & " in " _
                        & oTiming.ElapsedTime _
                        & " seconds" & vbCrLf

    'repeat this code for each function you wish to test.

End Sub
```

19. The test form currently has two buttons designated to start the testing process. You will need to add the following code to the **Click** events of those two buttons.

```
Private Sub cmdTestPropertyGets_Click()
    'call the RunTest procedure and provide it the name of the test
    'you wish to run as well as the text you want displayed with timing
    'results.

    Call RunTest("PropertyGet", "Standard Property Gets")

End Sub


Private Sub cmdTestPropertyLets_Click()

    Call RunTest("PropertySet", "Standard Property Lets")

End Sub
```

20. You will need a way to release your instances of the classes you are testing. This is done by setting your object variables equal to the keyword **Nothing**. This is done by adding the following method **ReleaseObjects**.

```
Private Sub ReleaseObjects()

    'start timing event
    oTiming.Start

    'de-reference ActiveX server objects that exist
    Set oDependentObject = Nothing
    Set oBusinessObject = Nothing

    'finish timing event.
    oTiming.Finish

    txtDisplay.Text = txtDisplay.Text _
                        & "Objects released in only " _
                        & oTiming.ElapsedTime _
                        & " seconds!" & vbCrLf

End Sub
```

21. Add the following code to the **Click** events of the **GetObject**, **ReleaseObject**, Exit, and Clear buttons on the test form. This code will connect the buttons to the corresponding procedures you have already added to the test form.

```
Private Sub cmdGetObject_Click()

    'Get a reference to the royaltysvc component
    GetObjectReference

    'Get a reference to the Main Dependent Object
    'in this component.
    GetDependentObjectReference

End Sub

Private Sub cmdReleaseObject_Click()

    ReleaseObjects

End Sub
```

```
Private Sub cmdExit_Click()

    'you can not use the END command in a DLL. During development
    'unload form and references to objects then manually stop the
    'project with the VB toolbar stop button.
    Unload frmTestClient

End Sub


Private Sub cmdClear_Click()

    'use to clear the textbox.
    txtDisplay.Text = ""

End Sub
```

22. Use Insert Class Module from Visual Basic's menu bar to add a class module to this project. The class will appear in the project window. Open the class module and press [F4] to view the class's properties. Set these properties as shown in Table 7-5.

Table 7-5 TIMING.CLS class module property settings

OBJECT	PROPERTY	SETTING
Class Module	Name	"Timing"
	Instancing	1 - Private

23. Add the following code to the General Declarations section of the **Timing** class module. You will need to declare the **timeGetTime** API function in order to have access to a method that returns timing values with a millisecond resolution. The standard **Time()** function in Visual Basic only provides for seconds.

```
Option Explicit
'
'dimension readonly variables for timing events
Dim mStartTime As Long
Dim mFinishTime As Long
Dim mElapsedTime As Long
'
'declare API to get time in milliseconds.
Private Declare Function timeGetTime Lib "winmm.dll" () As Long
```

24. Add the following methods and properties to the **Timing** class. These methods and properties will allow you to time execution of SQL queries and have access to the elapsed time values in milliseconds.

```
'method to store start time
Public Sub Start()
    mStartTime = timeGetTime
    mFinishTime = 0
    mElapsedTime = 0
End Sub

'method to store finish time and calculate elapsed time in milliseconds
Public Sub Finish()
    mFinishTime = timeGetTime
    mElapsedTime = mFinishTime - mStartTime
End Sub

'read-only property to access elapsed time.
Public Property Get ElapsedTime()
    ElapsedTime = mElapsedTime / 1000
End Property
```

How It Works

There are two things you must do in order to create an ActiveX server. First, you must set the startup form to **Sub Main**. Second, you must have a class module with its instancing property set to something other than private. If the ActiveX server project is going to be compiled as an ActiveX DLL you will additionally need to be sure that the **instancing** property is set to **5-MultiUse**.

It is important to note that ActiveX servers, especially those deployed remotely, often do not have forms that are used or visible. Additionally, all error messages should be handed back to the client and not displayed on the server. If the business object is running on a remote machine and pops up a message box, it will not return control to the client application until the message box is closed. There is no guarantee that anyone will be available to see or respond to it.

The form contained in the template is designed for use as a testing mechanism for the business logic contained in the project. As you develop your business objects, you will find that it is critical to use a phased approach to development and implementation. You need to test internal to the project, then you need to test on your local machine with a client calling your business object, and finally you need to test remotely. If you skip one of these steps, it will come back to haunt you. Finding the cause of errors once you deploy remotely is not a fun thing and can shorten anyone's life expectancy.

The `Server` class provides a standard entry point into all business objects. The entry point refers to the syntax used to reference your business object. Since your template project is called `MyComponent` and the single public class module is called `Server`, you would create the object by calling the `Server` class using the following syntax:

```
DIM ClientObject AS MyComponent.Server
SET ClientObject = NEW MyComponent.Server
ClientObject.Connect
```

In order to use any of the methods or access any of the properties, a client of the business object must instantiate the business object by dimensioning an object variable, setting the object variable to a new instance of the business object's `Server` class, and finally executing the `Connect` method. Standardizing on the use of a class module called `Server` allows you to control how people gain access to the methods and properties of your objects. The template uses a method called `Load` to allow public access to the dependent class found in the template. The dependent class is actually the future home of the properties and methods that will comprise the purpose of this component.

Comments

A template or boilerplate approach to starting a business object project is a good way to get over the hump. Of course, having written specifications and a plan helps, too. Take the template created in this How-To and copy it into a new directory. Using this template to create your business objects will get you up and running right away.

COMPLEXITY
ADVANCED

7.2 How do I...
Encapsulate business rules into a class?

Problem

I want to keep all the business logic in my application for now but still be able to partition it out of the application easily if I need to in the future.

Technique

There are significant architectural decisions that can facilitate easy (or easier) partitioning of an application's services. Unless you understand what these are and develop with these restrictions in mind, you are headed for trouble. This How-To will demonstrate how to encapsulate business rules into a class within your project. By applying the rules that will apply to an object destined for remote deployment, we will build a solid foundation for a maintainable and scalable application.

Steps

Open and run **MYROYSVC.VBP**. The running program appears as shown in Figure 7-3.

The form that appears is the test form for the business rules encapsulated in this project. Press the Get Object button. The action and execution time are displayed on the form in a large text area. Press the Test Property Gets button. This tests the ability to get information from the business object. Press the Test Property Lets button to test writing information to the business object. Finally press the Release Object button to release the business object and let it terminate.

The first step is to determine what the business question is that we need to answer. This component will provide the royalty amounts for a given author during a time period specified by the client application. For information focusing on how to access data from a database server like SQL Server, refer to Chapter 3, Remote Data Objects. For this example, we will hard code test data and a simple testing interface to allow us to focus on the mechanics of implementation and intercommunication between the client application and the services of the business object (component).

Although the encapsulation of business rules is often referred to as a business object it is actually better referred to as a component, since several objects (classes) exist within a single Visual Basic project. The project can actually be a wrapper around several objects that work together or are related by the services they provide. Refer to Figure 7-4 for a diagram of the business object you will build here and the eventual role it plays in a three-tier client/server architecture.

To build the Royalty Service business object, do the following:

1. Copy the template created with How-To 7.1 into a new directory.

2. Rename the VBP file from **BUSOBJ.VPB** to **MYROYSVC.VPB**.

3. Start the project.

4. Set the following options for the project. You can see the Option tab containing the primary options you need to set for an ActiveX server project (see Figure 7-4). Set the properties listed in Table 7-6 for this project.

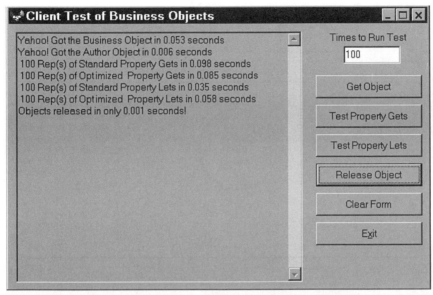

Figure 7-3 The Royalty Information Component's test form at runtime

Table 7-6 The project's option settings

OBJECT	PROPERTY	SETTING
General Tab	Project Type	ActiveX EXE
	Startup Object	Sub Main
	Project Name	Royaltysvc
	Project Description	"Royalty Information"
Component Tab	Project Compatibility	checked
	Start Mode	Standalone

5. When a project contains a class module with a public property set to **True**, compiling the project generates a registry entry. This is because setting a class module's public property to **True** implies that you want to access it from another application through ActiveX, which requires that the object be entered in the registry and assigned a class ID. Visual Basic automatically takes care of the registration for you—a great feature if that's what you really want to do. Since this project is not yet an ActiveX server, there is no need to generate a registry entry for this project. How-To 7.3 and 7.4 will introduce the steps for converting this project into an ActiveX server. For now you will tell Visual Basic to set the public property of all class modules in this project to **False** to avoid the generation of a registry entry. Steps 6 and 7 of this How-To take care of this for you.

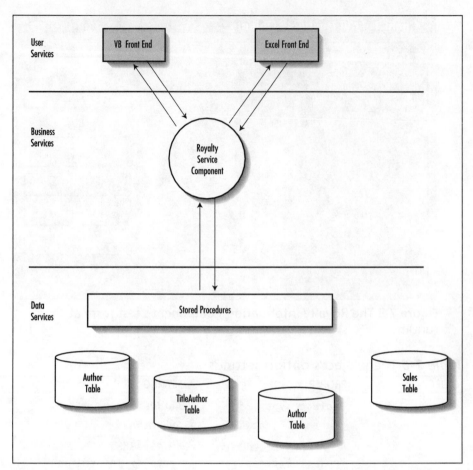

Figure 7-4 The Royalty Service business object within the Service Model diagram

> **6.** Open **SERVER.CLS** from the project window in Visual Basic. While your cursor is in the class module, press ⟨F4⟩ to display the property sheet. Set the following properties found in Table 7-7.

Table 7-7 Class option settings

OPTION	SETTING
Instancing	1 – Private
Name	Server

7. Add a new class module and save it as **AUTHOR.CLS**. Refer to Table 7-8 to configure settings for the **AUTHOR.CLS**.

Table 7-8 Class option settings

OPTION	SETTING
Instancing	1 - Private
Name	Author

8. The purpose of this project is to construct a business object that provides an author's royalty information based on a data range. You will need variables to store the author's information once it is retrieved. Add the following variables to the declarations section of the **AUTHOR.CLS**. These variables are declared as private. This forces people to use the properties of the **Author** class in order to alter the private memory variables found in the declarations section of the **Author** class.

```
Option Explicit

'These are private variables for the author class.
Private m_LastName As String
Private m_FirstName As String
Private m_AuthorId As String
Private m_StartDate As Date
Private m_EndDate As Date
Private m_TotalRoyalty As Currency
```

9. Add the following **Get** and **Let** properties to **AUTHOR.CLS** to provide controlled access to the private memory variables found in the declaration section of this class. A **Property Get** allows the client of your business object to read a property. A **Property Let** allows the client to write to a property. When the project is compiled, the client will be able to use the object browser that comes with Visual Basic to see your object's public interface.

```
Public Property Get StartDate() As Date
    'Read
    StartDate = m_StartDate
End Property

Public Property Let StartDate(dtNewStartDate As Date)
    'Write
    m_StartDate = dtNewStartDate
End Property
```

continued on next page

continued from previous page

```
Public Property Get EndDate() As Date
    'Read
    EndDate = m_EndDate
End Property


Public Property Let EndDate(dtNewEndDate As Date)
    'Write
    m_EndDate = dtNewEndDate
End Property


Public Property Get AuthorId() As String
    'Read
    AuthorId = m_AuthorId
End Property


Public Property Let AuthorId(sNewAuthorId As String)
    'Write
    m_AuthorId = sNewAuthorId
End Property


Public Property Get TotalRoyalty() As Currency
    'Read Only
    TotalRoyalty = m_TotalRoyalty
End Property


Public Property Get LastName() As String
    'Read
    LastName = m_LastName
End Property


Public Property Let LastName(sNewLastName As String)
    'Write
    m_LastName = sNewLastName
End Property


Public Property Get FirstName() As String
    'Read
    FirstName = m_FirstName
End Property


Public Property Let FirstName(sNewFirstName As String)
    'Write
    m_FirstName = sNewFirstName
End Property
```

10. The purpose of the **Author** class module is to provide an author's royalty information for a specified time period. Add the following public **GetInfo** method to the **Author** class module to accomplish the retrieval of the author's royalty information. For now you will provide hard coded values. The next step would be to include code to access a data source for the needed information. For examples on doing this, refer to Chapter 3, Remote Data Objects. Note that whenever your procedure includes optional parameters, you should check their existence in your code with the **IsMissing** function.

```
Public Sub GetInfo(ByVal sAuthorId As String, _
             Optional ByVal dtStartDate As Variant, _
             Optional ByVal dtEndDate As Variant)
    '
    'use author's id and date range to get royalty information
    'for this project you will hard code values for testing purposes.
    m_AuthorId = sAuthorId
    '
    'because these parameters are optional you will need to check if
    'they have been provided using the IsMissing function.
    If IsMissing(m_StartDate) Then
        m_StartDate = "01/01/1900"
    Else
        m_StartDate = dtStartDate
    End If
    If IsMissing(m_EndDate) Then
        m_EndDate = "01/01/1999"
    Else
        m_EndDate = dtEndDate
    End If
    '
    'At this point the above information would be used with a method
    'like Remote Data Objects to retrieve the author's name and
    'royalty information. For this example we will hard code the return
    'values.
    m_TotalRoyalty = 2500    'calculated value based on business logic
                             'qty * price
    m_LastName = "Shakespeare"
    m_FirstName = "William"

End Sub
```

11. Add the `PropertyGetAll` and `PropertySetAll` methods to the `Author` class module. These methods allow the client application to retrieve and write multiple properties with a single call. This is an optimized method that will become of greater importance as the user interface is separated from the business object.

```
Public Sub PropertyGetAll(Optional ByVal StartDate As Variant, _
                          Optional ByVal EndDate As Variant, _
                          Optional ByVal FirstName As Variant, _
                          Optional ByVal LastName As Variant, _
                          Optional ByVal TotalRoyalty As Variant, _
                          Optional ByVal AuthorId As Variant)


    If IsMissing(StartDate) Then
        'not requested
    Else
        StartDate = m_StartDate
    End If
    If IsMissing(EndDate) Then
        'not requested
    Else
        EndDate = m_EndDate
    End If
    If IsMissing(FirstName) Then
        'not requested
    Else
        FirstName = m_FirstName
    End If
    If IsMissing(LastName) Then
        'not requested
    Else
        LastName = m_LastName
    End If
    If IsMissing(TotalRoyalty) Then
        'not requested
    Else
        TotalRoyalty = m_TotalRoyalty
    End If
    If IsMissing(AuthorId) Then
        'not requested
```

```
    Else
        AuthorId = m_AuthorId
    End If

End Sub

Public Sub PropertySetAll(Optional ByVal StartDate As Variant, _
                      Optional ByVal EndDate As Variant, _
                      Optional ByVal FirstName As Variant, _
                      Optional ByVal LastName As Variant, _
                      Optional ByVal AuthorId As Variant)
    '
    'since parameters are optional, check to see if they exist using
    'the IsMissing function.
    If IsMissing(StartDate) Then
        'set a default here since it was not specified
    Else
        m_StartDate = StartDate
    End If
    If IsMissing(EndDate) Then
        'set a default here since it was not specified
    Else
        m_EndDate = EndDate
    End If
    If IsMissing(FirstName) Then
        'set a default here since it was not specified
    Else
        m_FirstName = FirstName
    End If
    If IsMissing(LastName) Then
        'set a default here since it was not specified
    Else
        m_LastName = LastName
    End If
    If IsMissing(AuthorId) Then
        'set a default here since it was not specified
    Else
        m_AuthorId = AuthorId
    End If

End Sub
```

12. The template that you are using for this project needs to be updated to contain references to the newly added **Author** class module. Open the **SERVER.CLS** class module and change the following code in the General Declarations section.

```
Private m_DependentObject As DependentObject
```

should be changed to

```
Private m_DependentObject As Author
```

13. The **Load** method of the **Server** class module creates an instance of the **Author** class module and passes the object reference to the client application. The **Load** method from your template needs to be modified to work with the newly added **Author** class module. Modify the **Load** function of the **SERVER.CLS** class module to the following.

```
Public Function Load(AuthorId As Variant, _
                     Optional StartDate As Variant, _
                     Optional EndDate As Variant _
                     ) As Author
    '
    'This method allows the client to get a reference
    'to the dependent author object. The author class is set to
    'public but is not externally creatable. Note that this function
    'could be part of the initialize method to reduce code needed
    'to get a reference to the author class.
    '
    Set m_DependentObject = New Author
    '
    'initialize the object with data
    '
    Call m_DependentObject.GetInfo(AuthorId, StartDate, EndDate)
    '
    'Pass the object reference back.
    '
    Set Load = m_DependentObject
    '
End Function
```

14. Highlight **frmTestClient** in the project window and select the View Code button.

15. You will need to change all references of `MyComponentName` to `RoyaltySvc`, since this is the project's new name. Do this by selecting Edit from the Visual Basic menu bar and clicking Replace. Set the Replace options to Current Module and Find Whole Word Only. Enter `MyComponentName` in the Find What box and enter `RoyaltySvc` in the Replace With box. Select Replace to complete the changes. Selecting Replace rather than Replace All will allow you to see what exactly is being changed. Repeat this process to replace `oDependentObject` with `oAuthor` and `DependentObject` with `Author`. This will update all generic object references to the actual names being used by this project.

16. Now that the business object's class modules have been modified to provide author royalty information based on a date range, it is time to modify the test form. The test form included with the template provides the framework for testing your business object. You will need to modify the form to specifically test the properties and methods that have been added. The `GetDependentObjectReference` procedure must be modified to support the three required parameters of the `Server` class module's `Load` method, which are `Author ID`, `Start Date`, and `End Date`. This is done by adding the following code to the test form.

```
Private Sub GetDependentObjectReference()

    'Dimension any variables that you need to pass when
    'getting a reference to the main dependent business
    'object. Place those here...
    Dim vAuthorId As Variant
    Dim vStartDate As Variant
    Dim vEndDate As Variant

    'start timing event.
    oTiming.Start

    'Here you would set any parameters needed.
    vAuthorId = "555-55-5555"
    vStartDate = #1/1/97#
    vEndDate = #6/30/97#

    'now you allow the Business Object to pass a reference
    'to a newly created dependent object that represents the
    'main body of your business services for this object.
    Set oAuthor = oBusinessObject.Load(vAuthorId, vStartDate, vEndDate)
```

continued on next page

continued from previous page

```
'finish timing event.
oTiming.Finish

'make sure you got a reference to the new dependent object.
If oAuthor Is Nothing Then
    txtDisplay.Text = txtDisplay.Text _
                    & "Bummer, couldn't get Dependent Object." _
                    & vbCrLf
Else
    txtDisplay.Text = txtDisplay.Text _
                    & "Yahoo! Got the Dependent Object in " _
                    & oTiming.ElapsedTime _
                    & " seconds" & vbCrLf
End If

End Sub
```

17. The following `PropertyGet` and `PropertySet` procedures read and write the author's properties. Add these procedures to the test form.

```
Private Sub PropertyGet()
'store property values in this variant
Dim vPropertyValues As Variant

'retrieve each property using a dot command
With oAuthor
    vPropertyValues = vPropertyValues & .AuthorId
    vPropertyValues = vPropertyValues & .LastName
    vPropertyValues = vPropertyValues & .FirstName
    vPropertyValues = vPropertyValues & .StartDate
    vPropertyValues = vPropertyValues & .EndDate
    vPropertyValues = vPropertyValues & .TotalRoyalty
End With

End Sub

Private Sub PropertySet()
'Hard code new values that will be set in the
'business object we are testing.

With oAuthor
    .AuthorId = "333-333-3333"
    .LastName = "King"
    .FirstName = "Stephen"
```

```
      .StartDate = #1/1/97#
      .EndDate = #6/30/97#
End With

End Sub
```

18. The following `PropertyGetAll` and `PropertySetAll` procedures provide an optimized method for retrieving and writing property values to the `Author` class. This is done by passing multiple parameters to allow the reading or writing of property values with a single call. Add the following procedures to the test form.

```
Private Sub PropertyGetAll()
Dim vPropertyValues As Variant
Dim vStartDate As Variant
Dim vEndDate As Variant
Dim vFirstName As Variant
Dim vLastName As Variant
Dim vTotalRoyalty As Variant
Dim vAuthorId As Variant

'this routine uses a method of the Author class to
'retrieve all properties with a single call.
Call oAuthor.PropertyGetAll(vStartDate, vEndDate, vFirstName, vLastName, _
                 vTotalRoyalty, vAuthorId)

    vPropertyValues = vPropertyValues & vAuthorId
    vPropertyValues = vPropertyValues & vLastName
    vPropertyValues = vPropertyValues & vFirstName
    vPropertyValues = vPropertyValues & vStartDate
    vPropertyValues = vPropertyValues & vEndDate
    vPropertyValues = vPropertyValues & vTotalRoyalty

End Sub

Private Sub PropertySetAll()
'Dimension variables to pass to Business Object
Dim vStartDate As Variant
Dim vEndDate As Variant
Dim vFirstName As Variant
Dim vLastName As Variant
Dim vAuthorId As Variant
```

continued on next page

continued from previous page

```
'Fill the variables with values for test
vStartDate = #1/1/97#
vEndDate = #6/30/97#
vFirstName = "Stephen"
vLastName = "King"
vAuthorId = "444-444-4444"

'this routine uses a method of the Author class to
'set all properties with a single call.
Call oAuthor.PropertySetAll(vStartDate, _
                            vEndDate, _
                            vFirstName, _
                            vLastName, _
                            vAuthorId)


End Sub
```

19. The `RunTest` procedure that you find in the template from How-To 7.1 must be modified to support the optimized methods, `PropertyGetAll` and `PropertySetAll`. Replace the template's `RunTest` procedure with this one.

```
Private Sub RunTest(sTestFunction As String, sDisplayText As String)
    'this routine will run the tests on GETS as many times as are
    'specified in the txtTestReps textbox. The default is 100

    Dim i As Integer
    Dim iReps As Integer

    'Make sure you have an object reference before you start
    If oAuthor Is Nothing Then
        txtDisplay.Text = txtDisplay.Text _
                        & "No reference to Dependent Object found." _
                        & vbCrLf

        Exit Sub
    Else

    End If

    'make sure that you have a valid value for number of repetitions
    'for the tests.
    If txtTestReps.Text <> "" Then
```

```
        iReps = CInt(txtTestReps.Text)
    Else
        iReps = 1
    End If


    ''''''''''''''''''''''''''''''''''''''''''''''''''''
    'test ability to get information from server  '
    ''''''''''''''''''''''''''''''''''''''''''''''''''''


    'start timing this event
    oTiming.Start

    'run test
    For i = 1 To iReps
        'Place the name of the functions you wish to test here
        Select Case sTestFunction
        Case "PropertyGet"
            PropertyGet
        Case "PropertySet"
            PropertySet
        Case "PropertyGetAll"
            PropertyGetAll
        Case "PropertySetAll"
            PropertySetAll

        End Select
    Next

    'stop timing event
    oTiming.Finish

    'display the time taken to retrieve the properties using
    'standard dot operation gets.
    txtDisplay.Text = txtDisplay.Text _
                    & Str(iReps) _
                    & " Rep(s) of " & sDisplayText & " in " _
                    & oTiming.ElapsedTime _
                    & " seconds" & vbCrLf

    'repeat this code for each function you wish to test.

End Sub
```

20. The `Click` event for the `cmdTestPropertyGets` and `cmdTestPropety-Lets` buttons must be updated to include the execution of tests for the optimized `PropertyGetAll` and `PropertySetAll` methods added earlier. Change each button's `Click` event to the following:

```
Private Sub cmdTestPropertyGets_Click()

    Call RunTest("PropertyGet", "Standard Property Gets")
    Call RunTest("PropertyGetAll", "Optimized Property Gets")

End Sub

Private Sub cmdTestPropertyLets_Click()

    Call RunTest("PropertySet", "Standard Property Lets")
    Call RunTest("PropertySetAll", "Optimized Property Lets")

End Sub
```

How It Works

This project comprises the `Server` class module, the `Author` class module, and the `GENERAL.BAS` code module on the business object side. The project also contains a single test form and a class module that assists in timing the execution of tests. The `Server` class module is the first class that must be created in order to work with this business object. The `Author` class contains all the author information that the client wishes to access. The business object interface used in this project requires the use of the `Load` method (which is part of the `Server` class) in order to create an instance of the `Author` class and access its properties and methods. This allows you to put code in the `Load` method that weeds out who can and can't get to the `Author` class module, its properties, and methods.

The first step to creating this project was to use the template created in How-To 7.1. Once the template was copied into a new directory, the public property of all class modules was set to `False` and the `creatable` property was set to `not creatable`. This prevents Visual Basic from automatically placing entries in the registry every time you compile the application. In later How-To's using this project, the public and `creatable` properties of the `Server` and `Author` class modules will be changed but this project attempted to show a self-contained implementation of a business object with an internal form to test the business object's interface.

The second step was to build the `Author` class, which encapsulates the functionality needed. For this project you were trying to create an object that would provide an author's royalties based on a data range. This functionality was encapsulated into the `Author` class module with access to its functionality controlled by the `Server` class module's `Load` method. The `Author` class provided properties for the author's ID number, last name, first name, and total royalties as well as the date range being used to calculate the amount of royalties due to the author.

Once the `Author` class is completed, the next step is to modify the test form to test the newly added functionality. A standardized name, `Server`, is used for the class module that will grant access to the rest of the business objects' functionality. Next the project was assigned a permanent project name, `RoyaltySvc`. Whenever the business object is created by the test form, the project name is used to explicitly identify the `Server` class. This prevents the need for rewriting code when the test form is removed and compiled into its own executable. Internally, you could code the following:

```
dim myObject as Server
```

This only works when called internally to the project. Or you could code this:

```
dim myObject as RoyaltySvc.Server
```

This will continue to work after the interface and business logic are separated into different components, as long as the business object retains the project name of `RoyaltySvc`.

Another important aspect of the way that this business object was implemented is the inclusion of two optimized methods for retrieving and setting information in the business object, `PropertyGetAll` and `PropertySetAll`. The key here is that the farther away you partition your business logic, the more costly dot operations become. A *dot operation* is the syntax used to reference properties of an object using a dot, as in the following:

```
myObject.LastName
myObject.FirstName
myObject.TotalRoyalty
```

The `PropertyGetAll` and `PropertyLetAll` methods of the `Author` class allow the passing of groups of variables utilizing one dot command rather than several. The `Timing` class that is part of the template used for this project displays the execution time for the reading and writing of properties. The execution times are displayed in the large text box that is part of the test form. The ability to view the execution times of various operations serves to familiarize you with the impact that partitioning and physical deployment have on the syntactical methods you can use when constructing your business object.

Comments

Business objects can implement a variety of interfaces. Figure 7-5 shows the object model for the `RoyaltySvc` business object as well as the public interface.

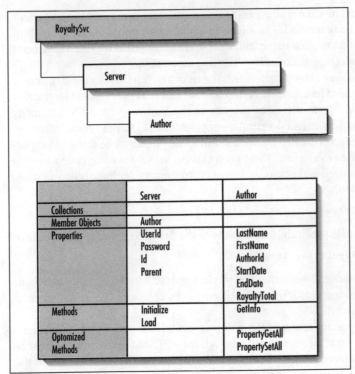

Figure 7-5 `RoyaltySvc` object model and public interface

In general, there are two types of interface models: broad base and deep design. A broad-based interface implements all the properties and methods through a single object that can be referenced. This allows the client to create a single connection to the object and access a variety of properties, not necessarily all related or grouped. The Microsoft Word ActiveX interface is based on a broad design. The deep design is one that will be explored in How-To 7.6. In a deep design, properties are grouped and tiered. In order to access features in a deeper layer you need to gain a reference to that object or collection of objects. Each reference is another connection. For information on the cost of each connection during remote deployment, refer to How-To 7.5. The Excel ActiveX interface implements a deep design.

Many decisions must be made in designing a business object but, until you understand the mechanical implementations of this new technology, those decisions remain at bay. This project allows you to set the number of iterations for the testing of **Get** and **Let** properties and methods. Try the test form using a variety of settings from 1 to 1000 repetitions. Review what impact volume has on the various techniques for accessing and setting business object values. Once you have worked through this How-To you will have a better understanding of just how all these variations can affect your project's performance. Understanding the strengths and limitations of this technology can only be to your advantage.

7.3   How do I...
Encapsulate business rules into an in-process server (ActiveX DLL)?

Problem

I have a Visual Basic project that contains code I would like to share with other applications on the same machine. I would like to use this project to create an ActiveX DLL that all the applications can use. How do I create an ActiveX DLL using this project?

Technique

Starting wth VB5, you can create ActiveX Dynamic Link Libraries (DLLs). This is a significant improvement over previous versions of VB. ActiveX objects provide an important component in the move to code reusability. As business rules are grouped into services and encapsulated into objects, these objects can be reused by various client applications, thus allowing you to write code that can truly be reused. Prior to VB4 and VB5 you would need to use a language like C++ to create DLLs. In this How-To you will take an existing project and compile it as an ActiveX DLL. Since DLLs operate as in-process servers (using the same processing space as the application), speed should not be impacted significantly. You will include a speed check on execution.

Steps

Open and run **TESTDLL.VBP**. The running program appears as shown in Figure 7-6.

What you are seeing is a client application referencing the business object in **ROYDLL.DLL**. Since an ActiveX DLL is an in-process server, it operates within the memory space of the client. The execution speed is affected minimally by the fact that it is now fully contained within a DLL. Note that a client cannot access a DLL directly if it is on a remote machine. This is because a DLL does not create its own process but relies on operating within the process space of the client. To create an ActiveX DLL perform the following steps:

1. Copy the template created with How-To 7.2 into a new directory.

2. Rename the VBP file from `MYROYSVC.VBP` to `ROYDLL.VBP`. Rename the VBW file from `MYROYSVC.VBW` to `ROYDLL.VBW`.

3. Start the project.

4. Make the following changes to the `GENERAL.BAS` file. Comment out the following code. Do not remove this code completely since you will need to uncomment those lines that show the test form if you ever work on this object and wish to test the functionality with the Visual Basic environment. You must remove this code to prevent the test form that is internal to the project from loading when the ActiveX DLL is used by a client.

```
'If App.StartMode = vbSModeStandalone Then
'    frmTestClient.Show vbModal
'End If.
```

5. Set the following options for the project. You can see the Option tab containing the primary options you need to set for an ActiveX server project. Set the properties listed in Table 7-9 for this project.

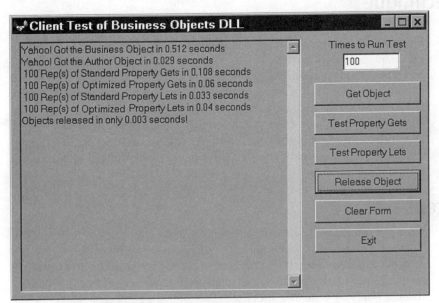

Figure 7-6 The TESTDLL project's test form at runtime

Table 7-9 The project's option settings

OBJECT	PROPERTY	SETTING
General Tab	Project Type	ActiveX DLL
	Startup Object	Sub Main
	Project Name	Royaltysvc
	Project Description	"Royalty Service Component DLL"
Component Tab	Project Compatibility	checked
	Start Mode	ActiveX Component

6. Set the following properties for the **Server** class and the **Author** class (see Tables 7-10 and 7-11).

Table 7-10 Class option settings for Server

OPTION	SETTING
Name	Server
Instancing	5 – MultiUse

Table 7-11 Class option settings for Author

OPTION	SETTING
Name	Author
Instancing	2 – PublicNotCreatable

7. From the File menu select Make RoyDLL.DLL (see Figure 7-7). Set the filename to **ROYDLL.DLL**.

8. Select the Option button from the ActiveX DLL dialog box. Modify the Title field to Royalty Service DLL (see Figure 7-8).

9. Generate the DLL. This will automatically create an entry in the registry. If you open a different project, then open your References list from the menu bar, you will see the newly created DLL listed. Search the list for the description of the Royalty Service Component DLL.

10. Select Project, RoyaltySvc Properties, Component tab. You will notice that the DLL you just compiled is already specified. This will allow you to recompile the project without generating a new class ID in the registry. Each time you compile this project, the DLL you specified will be used as a guide to verify that the changes you have made are backward compatible. Now that you have that out of the way, you can separate out the test form.

11. Create a new subdirectory called `TestForm` and start a new project. Select Standard EXE. Remove the default Form1 from the project.

12. Save the project as `TESTDLL.VBP`.

13. Copy the files `TESTFORM.FRM`, `TESTFORM.FRX`, and `TIMING.CLS` to the new directory for this project.

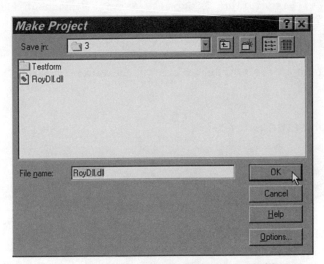

Figure 7-7 Visual Basic Make ActiveX DLL file dialog box

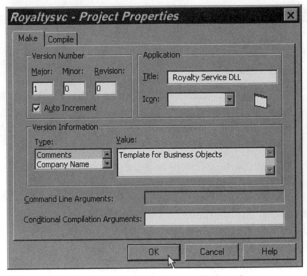

Figure 7-8 ActiveX DLL Options dialog box

14. Select Add File from the Project menu in Visual Basic. Add **TESTFORM.FRM** to the TESTDLL project.

15. Select Add File from the Project menu in Visual Basic. Add **TIMING.CLS** to the TESTDLL project.

16. Open **TESTFORM.FRM** and change the **Caption** property to read Client Test of Business Object DLL.

17. Select Project from the Visual Basic menu and select Project1 Properties. Choose the General tab and specify the startup form as **frmTestClient**. Select OK.

18. Now you will need to reference the business object. Select Project, References. A dialog box will appear that lists all the objects you can reference. Find Royalty Service Component DLL and select it. Select OK.

19. Select File from the Visual Basic menu bar and select Make TestDLL.EXE.

20. Enter the filename, **TESTDLL.EXE**.

21. Select the Options button and set the **Title** property to **TESTDLL**. Select OK.

22. Generate an executable.

23. Run **TESTDLL.EXE**. This is the same test form used to test your project in How-To 7.2. Select each button on the form in order from top to bottom. Start with the Get Object button which will tell you if your test form was able to create an instance of the **RoyaltySvc** business object. The Test Property Gets and Test Property Lets buttons will run tests to exercise the ability to retrieve and write properties to the **RoyaltySvc** business object. The Release Object button will release the **RoyaltySvc** business object so that it unloads from memory. Each of these actions provides visible feedback within the test form's display text box.

How It Works

You could have simply tried to compile the application as an ActiveX DLL and responded to the error messages until it worked. The main change is that the test form is prevented from appearing when the ActiveX DLL is called by a client application. This is done by commenting out the form load action in the **GENERAL.BAS** file. Both class modules were set to public and the server class module was set to Creatable **MultiUse**. At this point an ActiveX DLL is generated by selecting the Make ActiveX DLL from the File menu.

It is important to note that once you generate an ActiveX DLL or ActiveX EXE, entries are being made in the registry. In this How-To you are shown that Visual Basic sets the just generated DLL as the compatible ActiveX server. What this does is prevent Visual Basic from creating a different identification entry in the registry each time you compile.

Once an ActiveX DLL is generated, a second application is created to test the ability to utilize this business object from a client application. The test form and time class module are copied into a new directory. A new Visual Basic project is started and these files are added. The project, called **TESTDLL.VBP**, adds a reference to the new ActiveX DLL created earlier. This ActiveX DLL appears as Royalty Service Component DLL. Once the test form's project references the ActiveX DLL, the project is compiled as **TESTDLL.EXE**. The test form allows you to create an instance of the business object, run tests on the ability to retrieve and store information in the business object, and release the business object. The **Timing** class module provides timing methods to measure the execution speed of all tests.

Comments

Visual Basic has done a great job of simplifying the process for creating usable ActiveX objects. This project has allowed you to take the first step towards partitioning logic out of an application by taking you step-by-step through the process of generating an ActiveX DLL. The second part of the process was creating a client application that was able to utilize the RoyaltySvc ActiveX DLL. Now that you have completed this project, you can run a test to see how different execution times are for retrieving and storing information within the **RoyaltySvc** business object. Compare these times to the execution time from How-To 7.2. If your tests are similar to those shown in this book, then you will find only a slight decrease in execution time when using a DLL. Considering the benefits of using libraries of reusable code, it is very exciting to consider what aspects of your current projects you can first partition into DLLs.

COMPLEXITY
BEGINNING

7.4 How do I...
Encapsulate business rules into an out-of-process server (ActiveX EXE)?

Problem

There are a number of business functions that continuously change. Each time they change, I must rewrite a portion of code in every application. I decided to move these functions to an ActiveX DLL but I still must deploy the changes to every desktop. I would like to centralize these functions on a server where every application could use them. I know that I must create an out-of-process server (ActiveX EXE). How do I create an ActiveX EXE?

Technique

Code that changes on a regular basis is a good candidate for partitioning into an out-of-process server that can then be deployed on a remote machine. But before you can remotely deploy a business object, you must compile your business object as an ActiveX EXE. ActiveX DLLs are in-process servers, which means that they operate within the client application's process space. Since processes cannot span to a remote machine, a DLL could not be used on a remote machine; it must be on the local machine. This prevents it from being deployed centrally for all to use. Visual Basic allows you to take the same code that you used to generate an ActiveX DLL and recompile it as an ActiveX EXE without changing any code.

Steps

Open and run **TESTEXE.VBP**. The running program appears as shown in Figure 7-9.

Select the Get Object button first and then select the Test Property Gets and Test Property Lets buttons to retrieve and store information in the **RoyaltySvc** business object. Notice the difference in values between the normal dot operation methods and the parameterized methods that reduce calls between the client and server. The optimized methods provide significant savings in execution speed.

If you have worked through the earlier How-To's, you will see that the timings on this out-of-process server are significantly slower than the same operations against a DLL. The difference in execution time can range from 10 times slower to 100 times slower. This is important to understand when deciding what will run locally and what should run on a centralized server. Crafting your business objects to optimize performance for running remotely is critical if centralized business services is your goal. The first step to deploying a business object you create is to generate an out-of-process server that can run locally on the client machine. Only ActiveX EXEs can be directly accessed via Remote Automation. You could theoretically hang ActiveX DLLs off an ActiveX EXE on a remote machine to overcome this limitation. To generate an ActiveX EXE do the following:

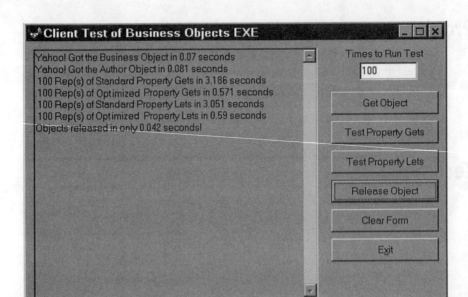

Figure 7-9 Client test of business object ActiveX EXE

1. Create a new directory, copy in project **ROYDLL.VBP** from How-To 7.3, and rename it **ROYEXE.VBP**. Rename the VBW file **ROYEXE.VBW**.

2. Once you compile this project as an ActiveX EXE, you will be able to activate it using two methods: standalone and ActiveX automation. *Standalone* means that the out-of-process server is being started directly and not being called by some other application. The following code checks the start mode of the ActiveX EXE and displays the test form when the ActiveX EXE is started directly by the user (standalone) and not by another application (ActiveX server). This is very powerful. Consider that Excel and Word operate similarly. To activate this feature, uncomment the following lines of code that exist in the **GENERAL.BAS** file.

```
If App.StartMode = vbSModeStandalone Then

    frmTestClient.Show vbModal

End If
```

3. Select Tools, Options, Project tab settings. Clear the compatible ActiveX Server field and change the **Description** property to Royalty Service Component EXE.

4. Select the Components tab and check the Remote Server Files check box. This will tell Visual Basic to generate three files when you compile: EXE, VBR, and TLB. These files are needed for deploying the ActiveX EXE on a remote server.

5. Open the **Server** class module and press F4 to show the property sheet. Change instancing to **3-SingleUse**. This can be set as either Single Use or Multi-Use. *Single Use* means that each time a client requests this business object, a new instance and new process will be started on the machine where the ActiveX EXE resides. *Multi-Use* means that only one instance of the ActiveX EXE will run on the machine where it resides. Each request for services from this ActiveX EXE will be handled by the same instance of this business object. For multiple users of the same business object for this project, we want Single Use, which will create a new instance of the ActiveX EXE server for each client requesting services.

6. Select File, Make ROYEXE File. When the Make EXE File dialog box appears, the filename should be set to **ROYEXE.EXE**. Change the application title to Royalty Service EXE. Check Auto Increment to activate version numbers. Press OK.

7. Generate the Executable. You will notice that three files were generated (EXE, VBR, and TLB). These files are necessary for remote deployment of this object.

8. Once the project has been compiled select Project, RoyaltySvc Properties, Component tab. You will notice that the just-compiled EXE, **ROYEXE.EXE**, is in the Version Compatibility box. This is important because it safeguards backward compatibility of the project and also prevents Visual Basic from generating a different ID for this project each time it is compiled.

9. Create a new directory for the client test form. Copy files into the new directory from the TESTDLL Visual Basic project created in How-To 7.3. You should have five files: **TESTDLL.VBP**, **TESTDLL.VBW**, **TESTFORM.FRM**, **TESTFORM.FRX**, and **TIMING.CLS**.

10. Rename **TESTDLL.VBP** to **TESTEXE.VBP** and **TESTDLL.VBW** to **TESTEXE.VBW**. Open **TESTEXE.VBP**.

11. Open the Project menu, open References, and uncheck Royalty Service Component DLL. Page down through the reference list and place a check next to Royalty Service Component EXE. Select OK to save these changes to your project references.

12. Open **frmTestClient** form and change the caption property to read Client Test of RoyaltySvc EXE.

13. Select File, Make EXE File. The name that appears will be Make TestDLL.EXE. This will be changed.

14. Enter the filename, **TESTEXE.EXE**.

15. Select the Options button and set the **Title** property to **TESTEXE**. Select OK.

16. Generate an executable.

17. Run **TESTEXE.EXE**. This is the same test form used to test your project in How-To 7.2 and How-To 7.3. Select each button on the form in order from top to bottom. Start with the Get Object button, which will tell you if your test form was able to create an instance of the **RoyaltySvc** business object. Remember that this is an out-of-process server, which means that the **RoyaltySvc** business object must load in its own process space. This takes time. The test form will display just how much time it does take. The Test Property Gets and Test Property Lets buttons will run tests to exercise the ability to retrieve and write properties to the **RoyaltySvc** business object. The Release Object button will release the **RoyaltySvc** business object so that it unloads from memory. Each of these actions provides visible feed-back within the test form's display text box.

How It Works

Creating an out-of-process server (ActiveX EXE) requires that you have at least one class module with its public property set to **True** and a **creatable** property set to either **Multi-Use** or **Single Use**. Setting a class's public property to **True** tells Visual Basic that you want other applications to be able to see and use the class's publicly declared properties and methods. Visual Basic takes the initiative and upon com-piling an ActiveX EXE Visual Basic makes the appropriate registry entries so ActiveX-aware applications can use your newly compiled business object. The **creatable** property of the class affects how the business object is loaded when a client needs to use the services provided by your business object. Multi-Use means that a single instance of the business object is loaded and multiple clients can use this single instance at one time. Setting a class to creatable **Single Use** means that each client needing the business object will have a separate copy loaded just for them. In this project the **SERVER.CLS** has a public property set to **True** and is configured as creatable **Single Use**.

Once you have created **ROYEXE.EXE**, you can use it from any ActiveX aware appli-cation. In this project, the client test form that was used in How-To 7.3 is modified to reference the new out-of-process server (ActiveX EXE). This is done by opening the reference list for the test form in Visual Basic and deselecting Royalty Service

Component DLL and selecting Royalty Service Component EXE instead. All of the code used by the test form to work with the **RoyaltySvc** business object remains untouched. Switching from a DLL to an EXE does not change how your client application refers to the business object. This is done transparently. This is an important point to understand. No changes to your client application's code need to be made to accommodate converting an ActiveX DLL to an ActiveX EXE. How-To 7.5 will explain how to move your out-of-process server to a remote machine.

One change was made to the **ROYEXE.VBP** project before it was compiled. The following code was added to the **GENERAL.BAS** file within the **Sub MAIN** procedure.

```
If App.StartMode = vbSModeStandalone Then

    frmTestClient.Show vbModal

End If
```

This code checks the start mode of the ActiveX EXE and displays the test form when the ActiveX EXE is started directly by the user (standalone). The ability to know how the program was started, either by direct execution or an ActiveX call, allows you to respond differently to each scenario. This is exactly what you experience with applications like Excel and Word. If you execute either of these applications, you are presented with the standard interface but, if you control them through ActiveX, this is not the case. This code change was not required in order to create an ActiveX EXE but provides a powerful enhancement to the project.

Beware of the missing reference error. As you add and remove ActiveX servers from your registry or recompile them with different class IDs, you may encounter a missing reference problem as shown in Figure 7-10.

To fix this missing reference you must deselect the reference that is missing and press OK. Now reopen the reference list. This refreshes the reference list. Scan the reference list for the properly registered Royalty Service Component EXE and select it. Now your reference to the business object is repaired.

Comments

There simply is no easier way for creating out-of-process servers. This is not to say that making business objects is easy. This is not the case. Since the goal is reuse, it is critical that enough time be allocated to properly design these service objects. Fortunately, once you have taken all the time to design and code your business object, Visual Basic makes it a pleasure to compile and use.

Generating an out-of-process server is the first major step in being able to deploy your business object remotely. How-To 7.5 takes you the rest of the way. Pay special attention to the performance of your object's every step made towards remote deployment. By running the client test applications, you can examine the

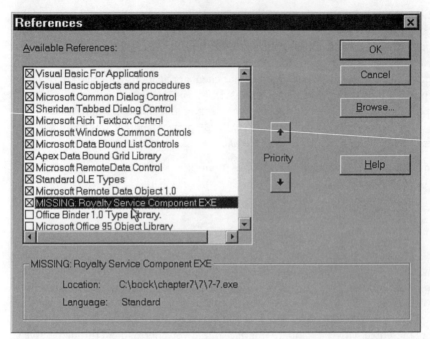

Figure 7-10 Missing reference in the TESTEXE.VBP project

execution times for both standard and optimized methods of retrieving and storing information in your business object. The more you understand what to expect, the more prepared you will be to handle the mechanics of coding for this new opportunity.

COMPLEXITY
BEGINNING

7.5 How do I...
Move my business object to a remote server?

Problem

I have a business object that needs to be used by many user workstations. How do I get it to run on its own server and allow everyone to be able to use it?

Technique

Visual Basic automatically adds your ActiveX server application to the registry of your machine each time you compile it. A new class ID is generated and references are placed in the registry. The real question is what does it take to get your business server object to run on a remote machine as well as a client machine that have never used Visual Basic before. Visual Basic comes with an automated set-up process to install your ActiveX business objects easily to any Windows NT or Windows 95 system.

Steps

Open and run **TESTEXE.VBP**. The running program appears as shown in Figure 7-11.

Select the Get Object button first and then select the Test Property Gets and Test Property Lets buttons to retrieve and store information in the **RoyaltySvc** business object. Notice the difference in values between the normal dot operation methods and the bulk methods that reduce calls between the client and server. The optimized methods provide dramatic savings in execution speed. Compare the times generated using the remotely deployed business object with the times generated against a DLL. You will notice that the optimized methods have a much greater impact when working with remotely deployed business objects.

The process of deploying a business object remotely can be a bit overwhelming if it doesn't work the first time. Therefore, this How-To outlines two methods for deploying your business objects. The first method uses the automated Setup Wizard that comes with Visual Basic. The second method is a manual method using

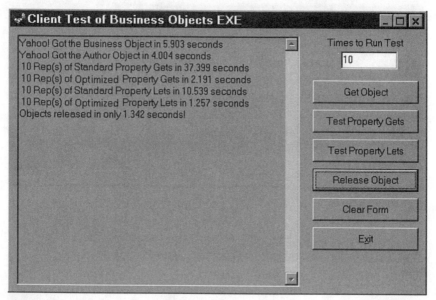

Figure 7-11 Client test of remotely deployed business object (ActiveX EXE)

step-by-step implementation techniques to catch and solve problems when they occur. First try the automatic process. If this doesn't work, then use the manual method.

Automatic Installation

1. Create a subdirectory. Name this directory **3-5Setup**.

2. Start the Visual Basic Setup Wizard, which you can find in your Visual Basic Program Group (see Figure 7-12).

3. Specify the project file used to create the business object you are going to deploy. In this case the business object is **ROYEXE.EXE** and was generated using **ROYEXE.VBP**. DO NOT select the Rebuild the project's EXE file option unless you are sure you have configured the project to reference the original ActiveX server for compatibility. To create an ActiveX server reference for your project you will need to open **ROYEXE.VBP** and select Tools, Options, Project tab and enter **ROYEXE.EXE**, in the Compatible ActiveX Server field. Otherwise a new class ID will be generated each time the project is compiled.

4. The Setup Wizard will process the VBP file and ask you where you wish to place the setup files. Specify the new subdirectory you created earlier. If you have not created it yet, you can specify a new directory now and it will create it for you. Select Directory and enter **C:\Chapter7\4\Setup**, for example, then select Next to continue.

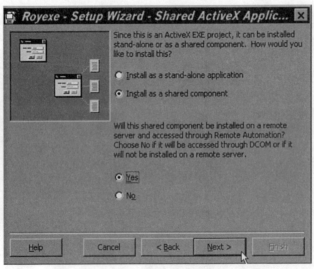

Figure 7-12 Visual Basic Setup Wizard

5. The Setup Wizard will attempt to find any ActiveX servers used by your application. Since this is the ActiveX Server itself, none will appear on the list. This server could very possibly reference other ActiveX servers or DLLs in which case they would appear here. Select Next to continue.

6. You will now have to select a deployment model. Select Install as ActiveX automation shared component. You will also need to check the box for Yes, install remote ActiveX automation server components if this is the first time you are installing this on the remote machine. This refers to the Remote Automation Connection Manager and the Automation Manager, which provide support for Remote Automation. Refer to Chapter 1, Client/Server Basics, for an overview of these tools.

7. At this point, you are presented with a list of the files that the Setup Wizard has determined are needed. You can save the template that was created by this process to reduce the time needed to create setup disks in the future. After you are done, press Finish to complete the process. It's just like magic. Unlike the Setup Wizard of Visual Basic 3.0, this one really does work (in most cases).

8. Now that you have the setup files ready, copy them to a network server, if available, so that the setup can be executed from all workstations where you must install support for the remotely deployed business object.

9. To complete the deployment, go to each machine and run the setup program from the network location containing the setup files. Installation will be automatic. You will, however, need to point the locally registered ActiveX server to the centralized remote location.

> **NOTE**
>
> The setup program generated by the wizard also provides a way to uninstall your component from the machine using ST5UNST.EXE. The uninstall command line refers to a log file that is created during setup.

Manual Installation

1. The following files are required on the server. Place them in a directory found in the path or place them in the **System32** directory on an NT machine or the **System** directory of a Windows 95 machine. This is only required if you have never installed a Visual Basic application on the machine or if you are preparing the machine as a home for remote business objects (see Table 7-12).

Table 7-12 Files to install on your server to run a remote business object

FILENAME	DESCRIPTION
CLIREG32.EXE	Registration program for Remote Automation on a client
AUTPRX32.DLL	Automation Proxy
AUTMGR32.EXE	Automation Manager
RACREG32.DLL	Support DLL for the Remote Automation Connection Manager
RACMGR32.EXE	Remote Automation Connection Manager

2. Unregister your server EXE from both the client and server machines so you have a clean start. Use the EXE name followed by **/UNREGSERVER** to unregister it from the registry. If you receive an error while trying to unregister the business object, you may have a corrupt registry. If this is the case, you will need to use **regedit32.exe** to find the problem. Try searching for all registry entries that contain the path to your business object. In this case it would be **ROYEXE.EXE**. Once you find them, delete the key that refers to your business object and start over. Do this on both the local and remote machines. Remember, all machines must be able to run VB applications.

3. Now register your business object again. From the command line execute **ROYEXE.EXE /REGSERVER**. Test the component locally. Start up the **TESTEXE.EXE** program and verify that it can reference the business object. If you have a problem at this point, there is a problem with the test app's ability to reference the object via the registry. Try opening the test application in Visual Basic and verifying that it contains a valid reference to the ActiveX server you are trying to deploy. If the reference is missing, then deselect it and find the current reference listing of the **ROYEXE** business object. Select it and recompile your test application.

4. Start the Remote Automation Connection Manager (**RACMGR32.EXE**) on the machine that will house the business object. **RACMGR32.EXE** can be found in the **VB/clisvr** directory and needs to be installed along with **AUTMGR32.EXE** and **CMPMGR32.EXE** in the directory, which is part of the path on the server machine, in order to support Remote Automation and the marshaling of requests to business objects. Once you can start the Remote Automation Connection Manager on the server, highlight the **RoyaltySvc.Server** entry. Click on Client Access tab and select Allow All Remote Creates. This will eliminate security issues as a possible connection problem. This setting should be changed once the components are installed successfully. Start the Automation Manager (**AUTMGR32.EXE**). The server is now ready to receive requests.

5. You have successfully installed and tested the ActiveX server locally on both the client and server workstations. All that is left is to point the client machine object reference to the server machine's copy of the business object. Start the Remote Automation Connection Manager on the client machine (see Figure 7-13).

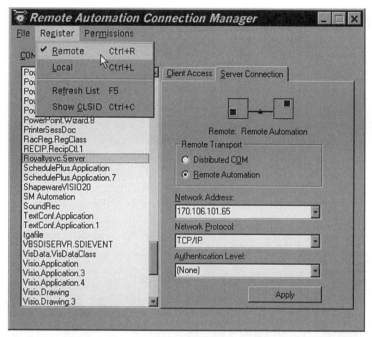

Figure 7-13 The Remote Automation Connection Manager configured to use a remote ActiveX server

6. Highlight the RoyaltySvc.Server ActiveX Class in the Remote Automation Connection Manager. Set the Network Address to the server machine's name. Set the Network Protocol to the appropriate protocol for your network. Set the Authentication Level to No Authentication for now. Once the business object has been set up successfully you can change this option to secure your system. For now, selecting No Authentication allows you to eliminate one possible reason why a remote automation server might not be accessible. Click on the Apply button. Choose Register from the menu and select Remote. Once this is done, the remote symbol will appear on the Server Connection tab associated with the `RoyaltySvc.Server` class.

7. Now that everything is configured properly, or so we hope, start the test application `TESTEXE.EXE`. Since you have verified that this test program worked successfully against the `ROYEXE.EXE` running on the local machine, it should now connect successfully to the `ROYEXE.EXE` located on the server workstation you specified in the Remote Automation Connection Manager. If you encounter an error, you are probably having a network connection problem. Verify that you have a good connection between the machines. Try to access a shared directory on the server machine from the client and then try to access the client from the server. If the problem persists, contact your network administrator for help.

How It Works

The key to deploying a business server object remotely is completely controlled by the registry and the Automation Manager. The registry provides the locally run client and server applications with a common address while the Remote Automation Connection Manager is used to set overall security settings and modify entries in the registry so calls to an ActiveX Server know where to go. The beauty of this is that a locally running application doesn't have any idea when it asks for an ActiveX object how it gets it. In Figure 7-14 you can see what the process path for a request looks like on both a single machine as well as with a remote machine involved.

The Automation Manager contains both a proxy and a stub that allow the Automation Manager to marshal requests and hand them to the regular ActiveX stub that unmarshals the information as it moves from the client to the server. A *proxy* is an object that packages parameters for a specific interface with the purpose of relaying a remote method call. The proxy is a DLL and runs in the process of the application sending a request. A stub operates in the process of the receiving

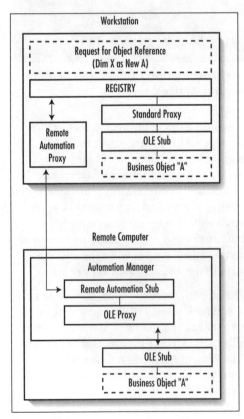

Figure 7-14 Remote automation
communication process

application. The *stub* application is a DLL that unpackages the parameters from the proxy and actually makes the method call to the component on the remote machine. *Marshaling* refers to the process that allows the packaged parameters to be transmitted across process boundaries.

On the trip back from the remote component, the ActiveX stub hands the marshaled values back to the Automation Manager, which then transmits them to the Remote Automation proxy which is responsible for unmarshaling the information to the ActiveX client. The bottom line here is that the Automation Manager, along with the registry, seamlessly allows a client application to use your business object without changing a line of code in your application. It doesn't matter if you are working with an ActiveX DLL on the local machine or an ActiveX EXE deployed on an NT Server across the network or Internet.

The Setup Wizard and the setup program it generates automate much of the task of installing the right pieces and making the right entries in the registry of each machine, but when this goes awry you can follow a manual process for stepping through the installation and deployment process. A manual installation may take a little longer initially but should a problem occur you are in a good position to identify what is going on.

Comments

There are many factors involved in the deployment of ActiveX servers to remote machines. Visual Basics implementation is by far the easiest to use. Problems may occur but are resolvable if the process is taken in controlled steps.

COMPLEXITY
ADVANCED

7.6 How do I...
Pass variant arrays to and from a business object?

Problem

Deploying my business object as a Remote ActiveX object has killed performance. Things that took one second now take 10 to 100 times longer to execute. How can I improve the performance?

Technique

The problem is that remotely deploying a business object requires that you deal with the limitation of Remote Procedure Call (RPC) access. Making an RPC requires a significant amount of overhead to establish and execute. The first step is to deal with the speed issues related to instantiating the object. The second step is to architect batch methods of setting and getting data to and from your object. The third step is to eliminate any values passed by reference.

Steps

Part of implementing this How-To is to create a situation that would take full advantage of the techniques that will be shown. You will add a collection to the business object developed in earlier How-To's. The collection object creates a situation where a greater amount of data must be passed between the client and the server. This will set up a situation where passing variant arrays can be evaluated clearly against other standard methods.

Open and run project COLLEXE.VBP. The running program appears as shown in Figure 7-15.

First you will need to select the Get Object button. Now select the Test Collection button. There are four result lines that are returned with timings. Two are for standard dot operation syntax methods; the other two are optimized methods that pass variant arrays to reduce the number of calls. Note that the text box now accepts a value to set how many objects to add to the collection. Try 50 and work your way up. See how size affects the difference in the various methods.

Now open and run the project TESTCOLL.VBP. The last project was operating against internal business objects. This project references the out-of-process server. Make sure that it is registered properly on your machine. Refer to How-To 7.5 if you

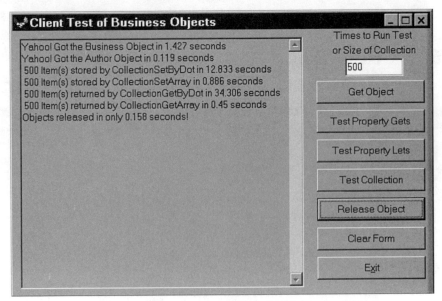

Figure 7-15 Client test of variant contained within a remotely deployed business object

need help. As you retry the Test Collection button, you will see a dramatic difference. Now the variant array methods drastically outperform the standard dot operation methods. If you move the ActiveX Server to a remote machine this will only serve to reinforce the value of the optimized methods.

1. Make the following changes to the **GENERAL.BAS** file. Comment out the following code. Do not remove this code completely since you will need to uncomment these lines that show the test form if you ever work on this object and wish to test the functionality with the Visual Basic environment. You must remove this code to prevent the test form that is internal to the project from loading when the ActiveX DLL is used by a client.

```
'If App.StartMode = vbSModeStandalone Then
'    frmTestClient.Show vbModal
'End If.
```

2. Set the following options for the project. You can see the Option tab containing the primary options you need to set for an ActiveX server project. Set the properties listed in Table 7-13 for this project.

Table 7-13 The project's option settings

OBJECT	PROPERTY	SETTING
General Tab	Project Type	ActiveX DLL
	Startup Object	Sub Main
	Project Name	Royaltysvc
	Project Description	"Royalty Service Component DLL"
Component Tab	Project Compatibility	checked
	Start Mode	ActiveX Component

3. Set the following properties for the **Server** class and the **Author** class (see Tables 7-14 and 7-15).

Table 7-14 Class option settings for **Server**

OPTION	SETTING
Name	Server
Instancing	5 - MultiUse

Table 7-15 Class option settings for **Author**

OPTION	SETTING
Name	Author
Instancing	2 - PublicNotCreatable

4. Start by copying all files from How-To 7.4 into a new directory.

5. Rename the VBP file from `ROYEXE.VBP` to `COLLEXE.VBP`. Rename the VBW file from `ROYEXE.VBW` to `COLLEXE.VBW`.

6. Start the project.

7. Select Project, RoyaltySvc Properties, General tab settings. Change the property description field to Royalty Service Component EXE w/COLL.

8. Add these constants to the Declarations area of the `GENERAL.BAS` file. These are positional constants used for the `CollectionGet` and `CollectionSet` arrays. Since these constants are global, they can be seen by the client application that uses this component. This will allow you to make changes to the array used to pass data and have the client piece automatically adjust.

```
Global Const royMaxColumns = 5
Global Const royTitlePosition = 1
Global Const royTitleIdPosition = 2
Global Const royRoyaltyPosition = 3
Global Const royBookPricePosition = 4
Global Const royQtySoldPosition = 5
```

9. Add the following method to the `AUTHOR.CLS` to provide a client with access to the `Royalties` class. The `Royalties` method creates a new instance of the `Royalties` class module and passes a reference back to the client.

```
Public Function Royalties() As Royalties

    Set Royalties = New Royalties

End Function
```

10. Add a new class module to the `ROYCOLL.VBP` project. Name the class `ROYALTIES.CLS`. Set the properties according to Table 7-16.

Table 7-16 Class option settings for `Royalties`

OPTION	SETTING
Name	Royalties
Instancing	2 - PublicNotCreatable

11. The `Royalties` class module provides a home for a collection object called `m_Royalties`. This collection will hold detailed information on the authors' books and royalties. You could simply make the collection public to allow external applications to access the collection directly but this would give you no control over how the collection is used. You would be unable to validate the type of information stored in the collection as well. By creating a class as a wrapper to the collection, you can create properties and methods to give controlled access to the collection. Add the following code to the General Declarations of the **Royalties** class module to dimension the private collection object that will hold the authors' detail information.

```
Option Explicit

'information about the author

'Declare the private collection that will hold royalty information.
Private m_Royalties As New Collection
```

12. Add the following four procedures to provide a public interface to the collection object that will contain author royalty information. Remember that a collection has four basic methods: **Count**, **Item**, **Remove**, and **Add**. The **Count** method provides you with the number of objects in the collection. The **Item** method allows you to access a particular object in the collection based on a key value. The **Remove** method allows you to remove an object from the collection and the **Add** method allows you to add new objects (information) to the collection. You can provide a controlled public interface to the collection's four basic methods by adding the following methods to **ROYALTIES.CLS**.

```
Public Function Count() As Variant
    Count = m_Royalties.Count
End Function

Public Function Item(Key As Variant) As Royalty
    Set Item = m_Royalties.Item(Key)
End Function

Public Sub Remove(Key As Variant)
    m_Royalties.Remove Key
End Sub

Public Function Add(Optional Title As Variant, _
                Optional TitleId As Variant, _
                Optional Royalty As Variant, _
                Optional BookPrice As Variant, _
                Optional QtySold As Variant) As Object
    Dim NewRoyalty As Royalty
    Set NewRoyalty = New Royalty
```

continued on next page

continued from previous page

```
With NewRoyalty
                If IsMissing(Title) = False Then .Title = Title
                If IsMissing(TitleId) = False Then .TitleId = TitleId
                If IsMissing(Royalty) = False Then .Royalty = Royalty
                If IsMissing(BookPrice) = False Then .BookPrice =
BookPrice
                If IsMissing(QtySold) = False Then .QtySold = QtySold
End With
m_Royalties.Add NewRoyalty
Set Add = NewRoyalty
End Function
```

13. Add the following `CollectionSet` method to `ROYALTIES.CLS` to set all values in a collection in a single pass. This method use a variant array to pass information back and forth between the client and the ActiveX Server. This method reduces the number of calls, thus accelerating the process of setting collection values.

```
Public Function CollectionSet(vRoyaltyArray As Variant)
    Dim ixRoyalty As Integer
    'erase old collection
    Do Until Me.Count = 0
        Me.Remove 1
    Loop
    'remember that me refers to the Royalties Class Object therefore
    'Me.Add executes the Add method contained in this class to add values
    'to the collection.
    Do
        ixRoyalty = ixRoyalty + 1
        'The add method below is using named parameters for greater
        'flexibility.
        Me.Add Title:=(vRoyaltyArray(royTitlePosition, ixRoyalty)), _
            TitleId:=(vRoyaltyArray(royTitleIdPosition, ixRoyalty)), _
            Royalty:=(vRoyaltyArray(royRoyaltyPosition, ixRoyalty)), _
            BookPrice:=(vRoyaltyArray(royBookPricePosition, ixRoyalty)), _
            QtySold:=(vRoyaltyArray(royQtySoldPosition, ixRoyalty))
    Loop Until ixRoyalty >= UBound(vRoyaltyArray, 2)
End Function
```

14. Add the following `CollectionGet` method to `ROYALTIES.CLS` to get all values in a collection in a single pass. This method use a variant array to pass information back and forth between the client and the ActiveX Server. This method reduces the number of calls, thus accelerating the process of retrieving collection values.

```
Public Function CollectionGet() As Variant
    Dim vRoyaltyArray As Variant
    Dim ixRoyalty As Integer
    'Dimension variant variables to hold data that will be
    'returned using the PropertyGet method of the Royalty Class.
    Dim Title As Variant
    Dim TitleId As Variant
    Dim Royalty As Variant
    Dim BookPrice As Variant
    Dim QtySold As Variant
    'ReDimension the Variant as an Array. RoyMaxColumns
    ReDim vRoyaltyArray(1 To royMaxColumns, 1 To Me.Count)
    Do
        ixRoyalty = ixRoyalty + 1
        Me.Item(ixRoyalty).PropertyGet Title:=Title, _
                                       TitleId:=TitleId, _
                                       Royalty:=Royalty, _
                                       BookPrice:=BookPrice, _
                                       QtySold:=QtySold
        vRoyaltyArray(royTitlePosition, ixRoyalty) = Title
        vRoyaltyArray(royTitleIdPosition, ixRoyalty) = TitleId
        vRoyaltyArray(royRoyaltyPosition, ixRoyalty) = Royalty
        vRoyaltyArray(royBookPricePosition, ixRoyalty) = BookPrice
        vRoyaltyArray(royQtySoldPosition, ixRoyalty) = QtySold
    Loop Until ixRoyalty >= Me.Count
    'Pass the variant array back to the client application.
    CollectionGet = vRoyaltyArray
End Function
```

15. Add a new class module to the **ROYCOLL.VBP** project. Name the class **ROYALTY.CLS**. Set the properties according to Table 7-17.

Table 7-17 Class option settings for Royalty

OPTION	SETTING
Name	Royalty
Instancing	2 - PublicNotCreatable

16. The **Royalty** class module provides the structure for the objects that will populate the private collection object that exists within the **Royalties** class module. The **Royalty** class resembles a database record. The **Royalty** class holds an author's Title (book name), Title ID (ISBN), royalty amount, book price, and quantity sold. Add the following code to the General Declarations of the **Royalty** class module to dimension the private variables needed to hold the author's detailed information.

```
Option Explicit
'dim the private variables that will hold royalty information.
Private m_Title As String
Private m_TitleId As Long
Private m_Royalty As Currency
Private m_BookPrice As Currency
Private m_QtySold As Long
```

17. In order to use this object to house an author's detailed information, you must be able to read and write the properties of the class. Add the following property **Gets** and **Lets** to **ROYALTY.CLS** to implement the ability to read and write values to this class.

```
Public Property Get Title() As String
    Title = m_Title
End Property


Public Property Let Title(NewTitle As String)
    m_Title = NewTitle
End Property


Public Property Get TitleId() As Long
    TitleId = m_TitleId
End Property


Public Property Let TitleId(NewTitleId As Long)
    m_TitleId = NewTitleId
End Property


Public Property Get BookPrice() As Currency
    BookPrice = m_BookPrice
End Property


Public Property Let BookPrice(NewBookPrice As Currency)
    m_BookPrice = NewBookPrice
End Property


Public Property Get QtySold() As Long
    QtySold = m_QtySold
End Property


Public Property Let QtySold(NewQtySold As Long)
    m_QtySold = NewQtySold
End Property
```

```
Public Property Get Royalty() As Currency
    Royalty = m_Royalty
End Property


Public Property Let Royalty(NewRoyalty As Currency)
    m_Royalty = NewRoyalty
End Property
```

18. This project includes the use of variant arrays and bulk read and write methods to improve the performance of remote ActiveX servers. The **PropertyGet** method is a bulk read method that is used by the **Royalties** class to populate a variant array sent back to the client application. This method helps to reduce the number of calls being made and increases execution speed for the remotely deployed business object.

```
Public Sub PropertyGet(Optional Title As Variant, _
                       Optional TitleId As Variant, _
                       Optional Royalty As Variant, _
                       Optional BookPrice As Variant, _
                       Optional QtySold As Variant)
    If IsMissing(Title) = False Then
        Title = m_Title
    End If
    If IsMissing(TitleId) = False Then
        TitleId = m_TitleId
    End If
    If IsMissing(Royalty) = False Then
        Royalty = m_Royalty
    End If
    If IsMissing(BookPrice) = False Then
        BookPrice = m_BookPrice
    End If
    If IsMissing(QtySold) = False Then
        QtySold = m_QtySold
    End If
End Sub
```

19. Compile **ROYCOLL.VBP** by selecting the File menu and choosing Make **ROYCOLL.EXE**. Generate an executable. This will automatically install the ActiveX server in your registry. For information on deploying this ActiveX automation server remotely refer to How-To 7.5.

20. Once the project has been compiled, select Project, RoyaltySvc Properties, Component tab and select Project Compatibility. Then enter the just-compiled EXE, `ROYCOLL.EXE`, in the field provided for the Compatible ActiveX Server. This is important because it safeguards backward compatibility of the project and also prevents Visual Basic from generating a different ID for this project each time it is compiled.

21. Create a new directory for the client test form. Copy files into the new directory from the TESTEXE Visual Basic project created in How-To 7.4. You should have five files: `TESTEXE.VBP`, `TESTEXE.VBW`, `TESTFORM.FRM`, `TESTFORM.FRX`, and `TIMING.CLS`.

22. Rename `TESTEXE.VBP` as `TESTCOLL.VBP` and `TESTEXE.VBW` as `TEST-COLL.VBW`. Open `TESTCOLL.VBP`.

23. Open the Project menu, open References, and uncheck Royalty Service Component EXE. Page down through the reference list and place a check next to Royalty Service Component EXE w/COLL. Select OK to save these changes to your project references (see Figure 7-16).

24. Open the `frmTestClient` form and change the `Caption` property to read Client Test of RoyaltySvc EXE w/COLL.

25. You will need to modify the Client test form in order to test the new collection and classes modules you have added to this project. Add the following controls and set the following properties found in Table 7-18. Refer to Figure 7-15 earlier in this How-To for the placement of the Test Collection button and the new labels.

Table 7-18 `frmTestClient` **form enhancements**

OBJECT	PROPERTY	SETTING
CommandButton	Name	cmdTestCollection
	Caption	"Test Collection"
Label	Name	Label1
	Caption	"Times to Run Test"
Label	Name	Label2
	Caption	"or Size of Collection"

26. Dimension a variable for the new `Royalties` class module that is now part of the business object. You can do this by adding the following code to the General Declarations section of the `frmTestClient` form.

```
Dim oRoyalties As Royalties
```

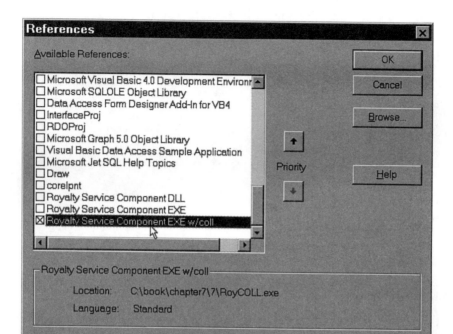

Figure 7-16 Setting references for the Client test form

27. Add the following code to the **cmdTestCollections Click** event to execute a test of the new **Royalties** class interface by reading and writing information to and from the **Royalties** class.

```
Private Sub cmdTestCollection_Click()
    Dim i As Integer
    Dim iReps As Integer

On Error GoTo cmdTestCollectionError
    'here you will get a reference to the royalties object ⇐
    Set oRoyalties = oAuthor.Royalties

    'Make sure you have an object reference before you start
    If oRoyalties Is Nothing Then
        txtDisplay.Text = txtDisplay.Text _
                    & "No reference to Royalties Collection Object
found." _
                    & vbCrLf

        Exit Sub
    End If
```

continued on next page

continued from previous page

```
''''''''''''''''''''''''''''''''''''''''''''''''''''''''''''''
'set collection data using dot operations            '
''''''''''''''''''''''''''''''''''''''''''''''''''''''''''''''

'run test
    CollectionSetByDot


''''''''''''''''''''''''''''''''''''''''''''''''''''''''''''''
'set collection data using variant array             '
''''''''''''''''''''''''''''''''''''''''''''''''''''''''''''''

'run test
    CollectionSetArray


''''''''''''''''''''''''''''''''''''''''''''''''''''''''''''''
'get collection data using dot operations            '
''''''''''''''''''''''''''''''''''''''''''''''''''''''''''''''

'run test
    CollectionGetByDot


''''''''''''''''''''''''''''''''''''''''''''''''''''''''''''''
'get collection data using variant array             '
''''''''''''''''''''''''''''''''''''''''''''''''''''''''''''''

'run test
    CollectionGetArray


'release the royalties object
Set oRoyalties = Nothing


Exit Sub


'simple error handler to display error and proceed on
cmdTestCollectionError:
    MsgBox Err.Number & " " & Err.Description
    Resume Next


End Sub
```

28. Add the `CollectionGetByDot` procedure to the `frmTestClient` form. This procedure will retrieve all of the author's royalty information from the `Royalties` collection, which exists inside the `Royalties` class module, by fetching each line individually using an object reference and a dot command.

```
Private Sub CollectionGetByDot()
    Dim vTitle As Variant
    Dim lTitleId As Long
```

```
Dim cRoyalty As Currency
Dim cBookPrice As Currency
Dim lQtySold As Long
Dim ixRoyaltyCount As Variant

'you are not using the repetitions field you are simply retrieving the
'rows that are in the royalties collection.

'start timing this event
oTiming.Start

'run test
For ixRoyaltyCount = 1 To oRoyalties.Count

    'grab a reference to the royalty item you are going to set.
    'retrieve the collection information on royalty line at a time.
    With oRoyalties.Item(ixRoyaltyCount)
        vTitle = .Title
        lTitleId = .TitleId
        cRoyalty = .Royalty
        cBookPrice = .BookPrice
        lQtySold = .QtySold
    End With

Next

'stop timing event
oTiming.Finish

'display the time taken to retrieve the properties using
'standard dot operation gets.
txtDisplay.Text = txtDisplay.Text _
                & Str(ixRoyaltyCount - 1) _
                & " Item(s) returned by CollectionGetByDot in " _
                & oTiming.ElapsedTime _
                & " seconds" & vbCrLf

End Sub
```

29. Add the `CollectionSetByDot` procedure to the `frmTestClient` form.
This will fill the `Royalties` collection with author royalty objects (records)
equal to the number specified on the test form. This is done by setting each
object in the `Royalties` collection individually using an object reference
and a dot command.

```
Private Sub CollectionSetByDot()
    Dim vTitle As Variant
    Dim vTitleId As Variant
    Dim vRoyalty As Variant
    Dim vBookPrice As Variant
    Dim vQtySold As Variant
    Dim iReps As Long
    Dim i As Long

    'make sure that you have a valid value for number of repetitions
    'for the tests.
    If txtTestReps.Text <> "" Then
        iReps = CInt(txtTestReps.Text)
    Else
        iReps = 1
    End If

    'start timing this event
    oTiming.Start

    ''''''''''''''''''''''''''''''''''''''
    ' RUN TEST                            '
    ''''''''''''''''''''''''''''''''''''''
    'erase old collection
    Do Until oRoyalties.Count = 0
        oRoyalties.Remove 1
    Loop

    'populate the collection one royalty line at a time.
    For i = 1 To iReps

        vTitle = "VB4 Client/Server How-To"
        vTitleId = 1234
        vRoyalty = 500
        vBookPrice = 50.5
        vQtySold = 5000

        oRoyalties.Add Title:=vTitle, _
                    TitleId:=vTitleId, _
                    Royalty:=vRoyalty, _
                  BookPrice:=vBookPrice, _
                    QtySold:=vQtySold
```

```
    Next

    'stop timing event
    oTiming.Finish

    'display the time taken to retrieve the properties using
    'standard dot operation gets.
    txtDisplay.Text = txtDisplay.Text _
                    & Str(iReps) _
                    & " Item(s) stored by CollectionSetByDot in " _
                    & oTiming.ElapsedTime _
                    & " seconds" & vbCrLf

End Sub
```

30. Get all royalty records from the `Royalty` collection—which exists inside
your business object—by fetching a variant array of data and parsing it on
the client side. To use this optimized retrieval method add the following
`CollectionGetArray` to the `frmTestClient` form.

```
Private Sub CollectionGetArray()

    Dim sTitle As String
    Dim lTitleId As Long
    Dim cRoyalty As Currency
    Dim cBookPrice As Currency
    Dim lQtySold As Long
    Dim ixRoyaltyRow As Long
    Dim iRowsInArray As Long
    Dim vRoyaltyArray As Variant

'start timing this event
    oTiming.Start

    'retrieve a variant array of data with all collection information
    vRoyaltyArray = oRoyalties.CollectionGet

    'get the array's dimensions. You could use the count property but that
    'would require another call which you don't want to make in order to
    'optimize speed. Remember that the ubound function need to know the ⇐
array
    'and the second set of dimensions that represent the number of actual
    'rows to which the variant array was redimensioned. That is why you ⇐
enter
```

continued on next page

continued from previous page

```
    'the number 2.
iRowsInArray = UBound(vRoyaltyArray, 2)

    'parse the variant array
    For ixRoyaltyRow = 1 To iRowsInArray

        'populate the collection one royalty line at a time.
        sTitle = vRoyaltyArray(royTitlePosition, ixRoyaltyRow)
        lTitleId = vRoyaltyArray(royTitleIdPosition, ixRoyaltyRow)
        cRoyalty = vRoyaltyArray(royRoyaltyPosition, ixRoyaltyRow)
        cBookPrice = vRoyaltyArray(royBookPricePosition, ixRoyaltyRow)
        lQtySold = vRoyaltyArray(royQtySoldPosition, ixRoyaltyRow)

    Next

    'stop timing event
    oTiming.Finish

    'display the time taken to retrieve the properties using
    'standard dot operation gets.
    txtDisplay.Text = txtDisplay.Text _
                    & Str(iRowsInArray) _
                    & " Item(s) returned by CollectionGetArray in " _
                    & oTiming.ElapsedTime _
                    & " seconds" & vbCrLf

End Sub
```

31. Set all royalty records from the `Royalty` collection—which exist inside of your business object—by sending a variant array of data to the business object. The business object then parses the variant array and applies the updates. This is done by adding the `CollectionSetArray` procedure to the `frmClientTest` form.

```
Private Sub CollectionSetArray()

    Dim vRoyaltyArray As Variant
    Dim ixRoyalties As Long
    Dim iReps As Long

    'make sure that you have a valid value for number of repetitions
    'for the tests.
```

```vb
If txtTestReps.Text <> "" Then
    iReps = CInt(txtTestReps.Text)
Else
    iReps = 1
End If

'start timing this event
oTiming.Start

'set up your variant array dimensions
ReDim vRoyaltyArray(royMaxColumns, iReps) 'add order

'run test
For ixRoyalties = 1 To iReps

    'stuff values into the array. The constants below that have
    'the word position in them are global constants found in
    'global bas file. This allows us to centralize information
    'about the position of each value within the array.
    vRoyaltyArray(royTitlePosition, ixRoyalties) = "VB How-To"
    vRoyaltyArray(royTitleIdPosition, ixRoyalties) = 55555
    vRoyaltyArray(royRoyaltyPosition, ixRoyalties) = 5000
    vRoyaltyArray(royBookPricePosition, ixRoyalties) = 55.5
    vRoyaltyArray(royQtySoldPosition, ixRoyalties) = 500

Next

'now that the array is full send it.
oRoyalties.CollectionSet vRoyaltyArray

'stop timing event
oTiming.Finish

'display the time taken to send a variant array and set properties
'in the business object.
txtDisplay.Text = txtDisplay.Text _
                    & Str(iReps) _
                    & " Item(s) stored by CollectionSetArray in " _
                    & oTiming.ElapsedTime _
                    & " seconds" & vbCrLf

End Sub
```

How It Works

There are two lessons implemented by this How-To. First is that a collection was added to the business object creating a much richer feature set and interface. Second, you implemented methods that passed variant arrays to optimize speed.

Adding a collection allows you to store and retrieve detail-level information about the authors' royalties. The business object can now store information about each title, its sales, and the book's price. Two class modules are added to the project, **Royalties** and **Royalty**, to handle the collection object that will store royalty information about the authors. Both of these classes are implemented as dependent classes. That means that external clients cannot simply create these objects at will. They can only be created by calling a method in the **Author** object. The **Royalty** class stores the actual royalty information and is added to a private collection that is part of the **Royalties** class. The **Royalties** class serves as a shell or wrapper for the collection and provides methods like **Count** that mirror the standard **Count** property of the collection. Because the client cannot directly manipulate the collection except through the methods and properties of the **Royalties** class, you have created a much more secure and hopefully stable business object. See Figure 7-17.

In How-To 7.2 you saw how setting and getting properties in batches improved the performance of ActiveX server objects that were deployed as out-of-process servers. This was especially evident on remotely deployed ActiveX servers. The technique of passing individual parameters as part of a method, as demonstrated in **PropertyGetAll** and **PropertySetAll**, works in limited situations. Once you start moving large amounts of data like those stored in a collection, you must use a new technique to pass information. The goal is still the same, to reduce the number of calls that need to be made. It should be noted that you cannot pass user-defined types to remotely deployed business objects. This is a big limitation that cannot be circumvented without a great deal of effort. In this How-To you implemented the strategy of using a variant array to pass data to and from the server.

Although using variant arrays can be faster for remotely deployed business objects, it may not be better when working with ActiveX DLLs deployed locally. This is because the variant array is passed by value to the server. This passes a full copy of the data once to the server. Passing by reference, on the other hand, would have copied all the data to the server and then back again, thus doubling the work. This is not the case when passing values by reference locally. In a local scenario, passing a value by reference simply passes a pointer to the object. This is much faster than making a copy. So what does this mean? If you are working with a collection in an ActiveX DLL, you will probably want to pass values by reference and you may not even want to implement an optimized method using variant arrays since the gains are minor until you deploy remotely. If you are deploying your business object remotely, these methods are critical to improving the usefulness of the business object.

In order to keep the focus clear, this How-To does not connect the data source to the business object. You can refer to Chapter 3, Remote Data Objects, for specifics on how to implement this aspect of the business object.

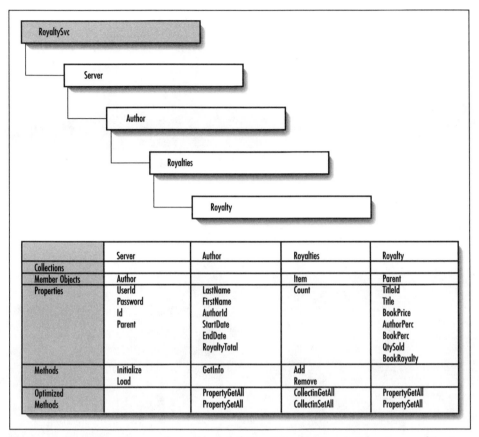

	Server	Author	Royalties	Royalty
Collections				
Member Objects	Author		Item	Parent
Properties	UserId Password Id Parent	LastName FirstName AuthorId StartDate EndDate RoyaltyTotal	Count	TitleId Title BookPrice AuthorPerc BookPerc QtySold BookRoyalty
Methods	Initialize Load	GetInfo	Add Remove	
Optimized Methods		PropertyGetAll PropertySetAll	CollectinGetAll CollectinSetAll	PropertyGetAll PropertySetAll

Figure 7-17 Properties and methods of the Royalty Service business object

Comments

There are tricks to every situation. If you are creating in-process servers that run on the client's machine, then you will want to tailor your methods to optimize that situation. If, on the other hand, you are deploying your business object remotely, then you will want to include methods that pass parameters by value and package large amounts of data into variant arrays to **Set** and **Get** properties. You will always need to include the standard **Get** and **Let** statements. After you have these done, you can proceed to add optimized methods as the situation dictates. Remember, ActiveX communication does not have to be slow. Methods like those demonstrated in this How-To dropped transfer times from numbers like 30 seconds to subsecond responses, depending on the situation. Try it out and see what you can eke out. This How-To has added a few more tricks to your remote bag.

CHAPTER 8

REPORTING AND DATA CONNECTION SUPPORT

by Don Kiely

REPORTING AND DATA CONNECTION SUPPORT

How do I...

8.1   **Create a report using Crystal Reports?**

8.2   **Create a detailed report with groups without Crystal Reports?**

8.3   **Create a multiple query report using Word 95 and OLE?**

8.4   **Create a pivot table and chart using Excel 95 and OLE?**

This chapter provides a series of How-To's for the decision support aspect of client/server development. Since Microsoft Access 95 has opened up its reporting facilities to Visual Basic through the use of OLE, this chapter provides special solutions crafted around the use of VB5, MS Office, Access 95, and Crystal Reports.

The How-To's in this chapter use different data sources to generate the reports, including both single Access .MDB files and remote data from a SQL Server. The source of the data doesn't really make much difference; however, all of the techniques are easily changed for any source. The biggest differences lie in how errors with the connection to the data are handled. When using the JET engine's data access objects (DAOs), errors need to be handled differently than with remote data objects (RDOs).

The four How-To's in this chapter provide you with a foundation for a variety of reporting techniques to use in your client/server applications. The methods you choose depend largely on the degree to which you desire to give the user control over the final report and the resources available on the end-user's computer, such as whether he or she have Microsoft Office available.

8.1   Create a Report Using Crystal Reports

The Crystal Reports report generator included with VB and most Microsoft database products gives you everything in a single package: a standalone report generator, a custom control you can use to run reports from a VB application, and an API for more control over a report. This How-To shows the creation of a database report using the Crystal Reports designer program.

8.2   Create a Detailed Report with Groups Without Crystal Reports

At times none of the packaged database reporting systems will work for your application, perhaps because they don't handle your situation very well, such as reports that don't easily fit a row and column format or that require special processing beyond the ability of the Crystal print engine. Or you don't want to deliver the required megabytes of support files with your applications. This How-To shows how you can use the Windows RichTextBox control to create complex reports grouped on the records in a different table than the one used for the main body of data.

8.3   Create a Multiple Query Report Using Word 95 and OLE

For client/server databases of anything more than trivial size, performance is always an issue. A busy network, while it is waiting for data to return from the server, can make your application seem sluggish to the end-user, even if you tell the end-user the reason for the delay. Using a multiple query can significantly improve the speed of queries to database servers. This How-To demonstrates a multiple query, using Microsoft Word to generate a report document with three different sections resulting from each of the multiple queries sent to the server.

8.4   Create a Pivot Table and Chart Using Excel 95 and OLE

A pivot table is a useful technique for analyzing and filtering data contained in many records. This How-To shows how to query a database and format the data to produce a pivot table and chart using OLE and Microsoft Excel.

COMPLEXITY
BEGINNING

8.1 How do I...
Create a report using Crystal Reports?

Problem

I need to create a quick report to report data in our client/server database system, and distribute it enterprise-wide with my application. How can I create a standard report quickly and easily?

Technique

The Crystal Reports program, included with VB since version 3 added database support, is a powerful and flexible report tool. The user interface is a bit quirky, however, so be prepared to spend some time fussing with your report to get it just how you want it. This How-To exercises many of Crystal's design features but there are many more hidden in its menus and dialog boxes. The best way to become comfortable with it is to experiment and try different ways of accomplishing things.

Steps

The steps in this How-To show in detail how to create a report listing the publishers and titles in the BIBLIO.MDB database included with VB. Upon completion, the report will look like Figure 8-1. To open and run a report in Crystal Reports, select File|Open from the main Crystal menu, and select the PUBS.RPT report. To print the report, click the print icon on the toolbar, or select File|Print from the main menu. To preview the report on screen, click the Print Preview icon on the toolbar, or select File|Print Preview from the Crystal Reports main menu.

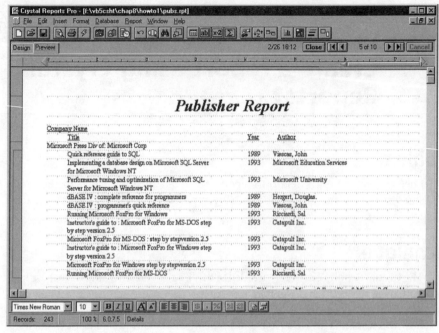

Figure 8-1 Print preview of finished publisher's report

1. This How-To uses the **BIBLIO.MDB** database included with VB. Start the Crystal Reports program. If you installed Visual Basic with the defaults, there is a Crystal Reports for Visual Basic icon in the Start menu or in Program Manager. Otherwise, start it by running the **CRW.EXE** file in the **C:\Program Files\DevStudio\VB\Report** directory (or wherever Visual Basic is installed).

2. The general design details are shown in the various tables throughout this How-To, stepping through the process needed to properly create the report. Figure 8-2 shows the main report elements in the Crystal Reports design window.

3. To make sure the steps you need to follow for this How-To correspond to your Crystal Reports setup, select File|Options from the Crystal Reports main menu and the New Report tab, and make sure that the Use Report Gallery for new reports option is checked. Set the Report Directory to the default location where you want to save reports. For your sanity, make sure that the Refresh data on every print option under the Reporting tab is unchecked, so the underlying query isn't run every time you preview the report as you put it together. You might want to experiment with the Show Field Names option under the Layout tab to see which you prefer as you design your report: a *cluttered* report with the field names showing or a

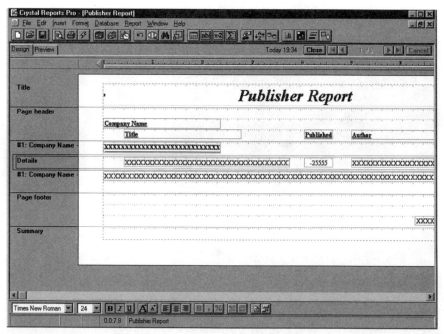

Figure 8-2 Crystal Reports design window for publisher's report

clean report with less information. Figures 8-3a through 8-3c show how the various options should appear.

4. As you work designing the report, be sure to periodically save your work by selecting File|Save (or File|Save As the first time) from the Crystal Reports main menu.

5. Click on the new report toolbar button or select File|New from the main menu. The Crystal Reports Create New Report dialog appears. This dialog lists a number of wizards, called experts, you can use to create different kinds of reports. Select the Standard expert. Figure 8-4 shows the Create New Report dialog.

6. When the Create Report Expert dialog appears, the Step 1: Tables tab will be selected so that you can select the database file used for the report. Click the Data File button, and select the **BIBLIO.MDB** database file, located in your VB program directory. Click the Done button after you select the file; Crystal lets you add additional files if you want, but this How-To will only use one. After a moment, the dialog will list the tables in the database, as shown in Figure 8-5, and will switch automatically to Step 2: Links.

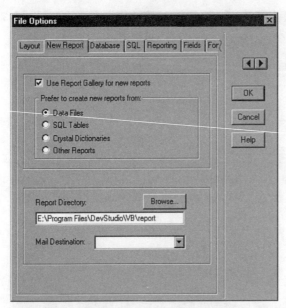

Figure 8-3a Crystal Reports File Options screen showing the New Report options

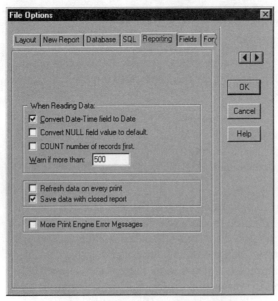

Figure 8-3b Crystal Reports File Options screen showing the Reporting options

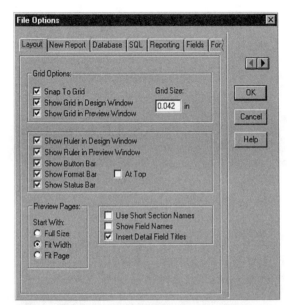

Figure 8-3c Crystal Reports File Options
screen showing the Layout options

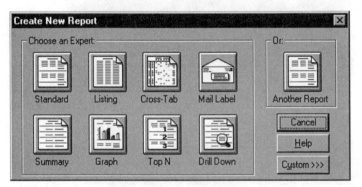

Figure 8-4 Create New Report window

7. Under the Step 2: Links tab, Crystal will list all the relationships defined between the tables of the database, shown in Figure 8-6. If the existing relationships in the database were not adequate for the report, you could add and edit them here. For this How-To, the default relationships are adequate.

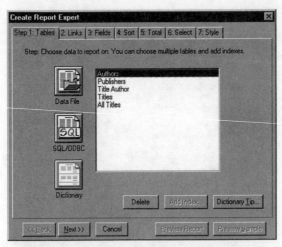

Figure 8-5 Use Step 1: Tables in the Create
Report Expert to select the database

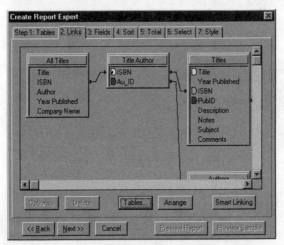

Figure 8-6 Use Step 2: Links in the Create
Report Expert dialog to maintain
relationships between tables

8. Click either the Step 3: Fields tab or the Next>> button, and select the
fields that you want to include in the table. This dialog uses standard
Windows selection methods, so you can add fields to the report by double-
clicking the field, clicking it and then clicking the Add -> button, or

selecting multiple fields by CTRL-clicking each one and then clicking the Add -> button. Use one of these methods to add the fields listed in Table 8-1 to the report.

Table 8-1 Fields from the Biblio database used in the report

TABLE NAME	FIELD NAME
Publishers	Company Name
Titles	Title
	Year Published
Authors	Author

9. Click either the Step 4: Sort tab or the Next>> button. Most database reports should be grouped and printed in some logical order, and this report will group all of a single publisher's titles together under the publisher's name. Add the Publishers.Company Name to the Group Fields: listbox, then add the Titles.Title field so that each publisher's books are listed alphabetically. The order in which you add these fields is important, because that will determine how the records are sorted in the final report. Figure 8-7 shows the Create Report Expert dialog at this point. Both of these fields should sort in ascending order, so accept that as the default in the Order: listbox.

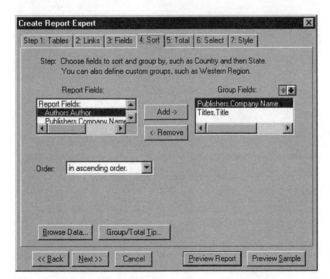

Figure 8-7 Use Step 4: Sort in the Create Report Expert dialog to control the order in which records are printed

10. Click either the Step 5: Total tab or the Next>> button. If this were a report with values such as money or counts of things, Crystal will automatically add group and grand totals to the report. In this case, however, totals aren't meaningful for any fields. But trying to be helpful, Crystal has automatically added the numeric Year Published field to the Total Fields: list. Since the sum of years is meaningless, click on the field and then click the <-Remove button. Also uncheck the Add Grand Totals check box. The Create Report Expert dialog should now look like Figure 8-8.

11. Click either the Step 6: Select tab or the Next>> button to show Figure 8-9. If you are interested in only a subset of the records in the tables you've selected, you can select them here. When you add a field to the Select Fields: list, options appear below for entering the criteria to use for the selection. For this report, we don't want any subsets. Since Crystal hasn't made any selections for us, nothing needs to be done.

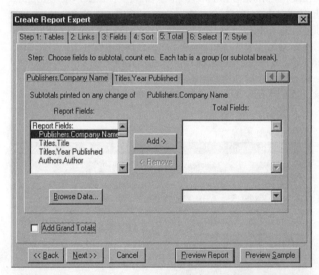

Figure 8-8 Use Step 5: Total in the Create Report Expert dialog to add group and grand totals to the report

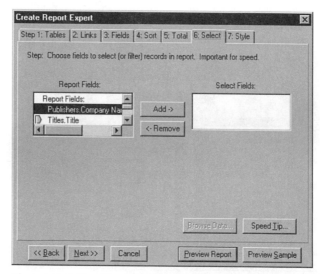

Figure 8-9 Use Step 6: Select to filter records for
the report

12. Click either the Step 7: Style tab or the Next>> button. Enter a report title,
Publisher Report, in the Title: text box. Crystal will create reports as simple
or as fancy as you want, using various combinations of highlighting, font
sizes, shading, and other effects. Leave the selection as Standard in the
Style: box, unless you want to experiment with other looks for the report.
Just be aware that if you pick another style, your final report probably
won't look like the report created in this How-To. As you select each of the
report styles, a vague approximation of the report appearance will display
to the right of the Style: list, as shown in Figure 8-10. You can also add an
image to the report by clicking the button showing the two mountains and
rising sun.

13. Click the Preview Sample button at the lower-right side of the Create
Report Expert dialog. The dialog disappears and another appears letting
you select to use all the records in the tables for the sample or just a limited
number. Leave the default as all the records and click the OK button to produce the sample report. The window shown in Figure 8-11 appears, letting
you examine your results so far. You might want to select Report|Zoom
from the main menu to get a clearer look at the contents of the report.
Although Crystal makes a valiant attempt to create a good report, it isn't yet
perfect so the next step is to make some adjustments to produce the desired
result.

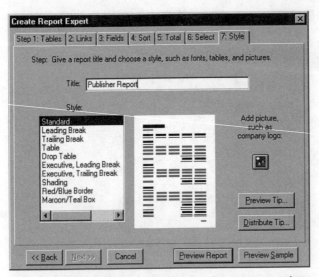

Figure 8-10 Use Step 7: Style to select among the predesigned report styles

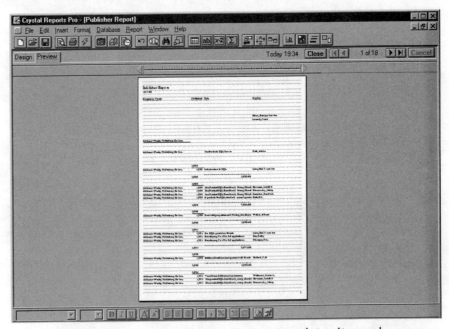

Figure 8-11 After the Create Report Expert completes its work, you can preview the report so far

14. First, however, this is a good time to save the report. Select File|Save from the main menu, or click the diskette icon, and save the report with the name **PUBS.RPT**.

15. Go to design mode by clicking on the Design tab. Take a moment to poke around the design view. Notice that the left side of the view has a wide gray area divided into sections. Each of these sections has a particular function within the report, as described in Table 8-2.

Table 8-2 Crystal Reports section descriptions

NAME	DESCRIPTION
Title	Information will appear only on the first page of the report
Page Header	Fields located here will appear at the top of every page
#1: Company Name	Prints at the beginning of each company's records
#2: Year Published	Prints at the beginning of each different year (this report won't use this section)
Details	This is where each title will print, grouped by publisher
#2: Year Published	Prints at the end of each different year (this report won't use this section)
#1: Company Name	Prints at the end of each company's records
Page Footer	Fields located here will appear at the bottom of every page
Summary	Information will appear only on the last page of the report

16. The default left and right margins for this report are 0.25". This report isn't terribly cluttered, so start by increasing the margins to 0.5" on each side. Select File|Page Margins... and set the left and right margins to 0.5" and click OK. One caution: Crystal has a nasty habit of making inaccessible fields that are outside the printable area of the page. So be sure to move any fields that might otherwise disappear before changing the margins. This isn't a problem with this report.

17. The next thing to do is get rid of a few extraneous fields that Crystal added to the report. (Some of these elements may not have been added to the report while others might have been added that we don't mention here. Crystal Services seems to be constantly refining the product, so your mileage may vary.) First, even though you told it not to add totals, it added a Total field for the years. So delete the field that looks like -5,555,555.55 (assuming you set the options described at the beginning of this How-To) and the label to the left of it by selecting the fields and pressing the Delete key.

18. Delete the extra Company Name field in the group footer section. Remember when you told Crystal to group by Company Names and Titles? Crystal adds this extra field so that the company name prints at the end of each company's records. A nice touch, but not necessary for this type of report.

19. After listing each publisher's titles, the report should state the number of titles for that publisher. This step adds two fields so that `Title count for <publisher name>: #` prints. Start by selecting one of the fields in the Details section of the report. Add the title count by selecting Insert|Summary... from the main menu. In the top combo box select Count. `Group #1: Publishers.Company Name -A` should already appear in the second combo box. Click OK. The field will appear automatically in the bottom `#1: Company Name` section. Move it so the field's right edge is at the right margin, and narrow it to hold three or four characters. Remember to save your work often.

20. Add the text for the title count by selecting Insert | Formula Field... from the main menu. Name the field `PublisherSubTotal` and click OK. In the Edit Formula: @PublisherSubTotal dialog, enter

```
"Title count for "  + TrimRight({Publishers.Company Name}) + ": "
```

and click Check then OK. This code creates a string which prints in the report, combining the text within the double quotes with the trimmed contents of the Publishers.Company Name field in the database. Position the new field so that its right edge just touches the Count of Titles.Title field in the Page Footer section of the report. Extend the left edge of the field to the report's left margin so there is room for any length of company name. Remember to save the report.

21. Crystal created two grouping fields, based on Company Name and Title, as indicated by the `#1: Company Name` and `#2: Year Published` headings in the gray area to the left of the report fields. The report doesn't need to include any data there, nor should there be spaces between titles. So right-click on both the header (first or top) `#2: Year Published` heading in the gray area, and select Hide Section. Do the same for the footer (second or bottom) `#2: Year Published` heading. At this point, the report should look like Figure 8-12.

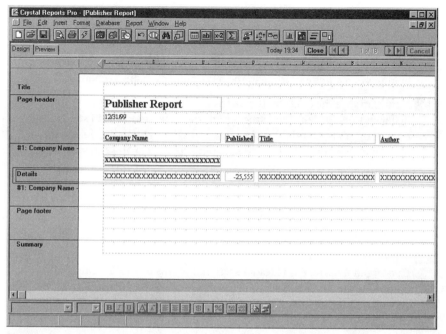

Figure 8-12 The design view of the report after some changes have been made

22. If necessary, scroll to the right of the report so the Page Number field, in the Page Footer section, is showing. The default page number simply says **1**, etc., but this report should show **Page 1**. Unfortunately, Crystal has no easy way to add text to the page number, so use a formula field with the **ToText** function, which is a Crystal function to convert a number to text. Select Insert | Formula Field... and name the field **PageNumber**. Enter this code in the Edit Formula dialog, which creates a string of the form **Page 1** by combining **"Page"** with the page number converted to text:

```
"Page " + ToText (PageNumber, 0)
```

Click Check and then OK, positioning the new field on the middle line of the Page Footer section of the report, with its right edge at the right margin. Click on the previously existing page number field, and press the DELETE key to delete it.

23. To look its best, the page number should appear right-justified in the field, but by default it is left-justified. Right-click on the **PageNumber** field and select Change Format... from the pop-up menu. Change the alignment to Right, and click OK.

24. Scroll back to the left side of the report if necessary. Crystal set up the report so the publisher's name prints on the same line as every book. Since it really only needs to print once at the beginning of each list of titles, delete that field from the Details section of the report. Be careful not to delete the bold `Company Name` heading in the #1: Company Name section.

25. Now rearrange the fields on the `Details` line so the `Title` prints about a half inch from the left side of the report, then the `Year Published` to the right of the `Title`, and the `Author` name to the right of that. Resize the fields and space them in a way that is pleasing to you. You can switch back and forth between the Design view and Preview to see how things look, then make adjustments. When you are done, move the header fields at the bottom of the Page Header section of the report so the proper heading is positioned over the correct field, as shown in Figure 8-2. Move the `Company Name` header one line up so that it is above the `Title` header.

26. The default for the report title is to print it at the top of every page, so Crystal put it in the Page Header section. For this report, the title should appear only on the first page, so move the field to the Title section of the report by dragging it with the left mouse button. While you're at it, either delete the data field or move it to a more convenient location on the report.

27. The Page Header section now has two blank lines between the report title and the column headers. Select all the column headers by clicking on one and holding down the (CTRL) key while clicking on the others, and move them as a group up one line. Then drag the bottom line of the Page Header section up as far as it will go, immediately below the column header fields. Save your work.

28. Now spruce up the report by changing fonts and field alignments. Start by right-clicking the report header (do this before widening the field so the right edge of the field won't disappear beyond the right margin when you enlarge the font) and select Change Font... from the pop-up menu. Set the font to 24-point bold italic. Click OK, then right-click the field again. Select Change Format... from the pop-up, and set the Alignment to Centered. Click OK. Finally, drag the right edge of the field to the right margin of the report.

29. Set the properties listed in Table 8-3 for the rest of the fields; leave the defaults for the other properties and fields not listed. Remember to right-click the field you want to edit, and select Change Format... to change the Alignment and related changes, and Change Font... to change the font. The Print on Multiple Lines option for the Titles.Title field will print the whole title on as many lines as it takes, so none of the titles are hidden. When you are finished, save your work.

Table 8-3 Publisher's report fields and formatting

REPORT ELEMENT	VALUES
Report Header	Centered alignment
Year Header	Centered alignment
Titles.Title	Print on multiple lines
Titles.Year Published	Centered alignment, no thousands separator
Count of Titles.Title	Left alignment, no negative
@PublisherSubtotal	Right alignment
@PageNumber	Right alignment

30. Test the layout of the report by clicking the Print Preview button on the toolbar or by selecting File|Print Preview from the Crystal main menu.

Comments

While the user interface of Crystal can be frustrating to work with, it is quite flexible. Even if there isn't an obvious way to do any given formatting feature using Crystal built-in functions (such as **ToText**, which was used in this How-To), you can usually achieve the end you want by either designing your database queries at the back-end of the server system or using Crystal's scripting language. The script is similar to VB code but different enough so you'll have some work getting used to it, but Crystal does provide list boxes for many selections. Since the product is available for almost every database server you're likely to encounter, you'll only have to learn its idiosyncrasies once.

COMPLEXITY
INTERMEDIATE

8.2 How do I...

Create a detailed report with groups without Crystal Reports?

Problem

I need to print a highly customized database report but can't use Crystal Reports because of its quirks and all the files that I'd need to distribute with my application. I can use the VB **Printer** object, but that means writing a lot of code to specify every detail of layout. How can I put together an attractive report with native VB and Windows tools, with enough flexibility to allow record groupings?

Technique

This How-To combines the Windows RichTextBox control with a couple of API calls to produce a What-You-See-Is-What-You-Get (WYSIWYG) display that shows what will be printed. It is far easier to code a report this way than using the VB **Printer** object and requires no large files be included with your application.

Grouping records is a powerful relational database technique which lets you create and display a hierarchy of data. In this How-To, the report groups books by authors. That is, it lists an author's name then groups that author's books under his or her name. In theory, you can use any number of grouping levels, depending on the type of data you want in the report.

Steps

Open and run the **RTFPRINT.VBP** project file. The Database Report window appears as shown in Figure 8-13. Set the margins for the report or accept the default one-inch margins. Click the Create Report button and watch as the report is generated in the RichTextBox window. When the report is complete, click the Set Form Width button to automatically size the form to the actual width of the report based on your settings. Then click Print to send the report to the default printer.

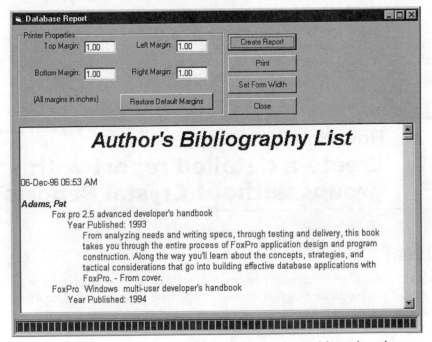

Figure 8-13 The Windows RichTextBox control provides a handy way to produce database reports with a print preview feature

1. Create a new project and name it `RTFPRINT.VBP`. Add the form `RTFPRINT.BAS` (located in the code directory for this How-To on the accompanying CD) using Visual Basic's Add File menu command. This code is adapted from Microsoft KnowledgeBase article Q146022. It provides two handy routines for printing formatted text from the RichTextBox control.

2. Using Project|Components... from the VB main menu, and select the custom controls shown in Table 8-4. Uncheck all others so your project isn't cluttered with controls you aren't using, and so the Setup Wizard doesn't include a lot of extra dead weight with your application.

Table 8-4 Custom controls used in `RTFPRINT.VBP`

CONTROL
Microsoft Common Dialog Control 5.0
Microsoft RichTextBox Control 5.0
Microsoft Windows Common Controls 5.0

3. Using Project|References... from the VB main menu, select the references shown in Table 8-5.

Uncheck all others so your project isn't cluttered with DLLs you aren't using, and so the Setup Wizard doesn't include a lot of extra dead weight with your application.

Table 8-5 References used in `RTFPRINT.VBP`

REFERENCE
Microsoft Visual Basic for Applications
Visual Basic Runtime Objects and Procedures
Microsoft Common Dialog Control 5.0
Microsoft RichTextBox Control 5.0
Microsoft Windows Common Controls 5.0
Microsoft DAO 3.5 Object Library

4. Name the default form `frmPrint` and save the file as `RTFPRINT.FRM`. Add the controls as shown in Figure 8-13, setting the properties as shown in Table 8-6.

Table 8-6 Objects and properties for RTFPRINT.FRM

OBJECT	PROPERTY	SETTING
Form	Name	frmPrint
	Caption	"Form1"
CommandButton	Name	cmdSetFormWidth
	Caption	"Set Form Width"
CommandButton	Name	cmdCreateReport
	Caption	"Create Report"
Frame	Name	fraSettings
	Caption	"Printer Properties"
CommandButton	Name	cmdDefaults
	Caption	"Restore Default Margins"
TextBox	Name	txtRightMargin
TextBox	Name	txtLeftMargin
TextBox	Name	txtTopMargin
TextBox	Name	txtBottomMargin
Label	Name	Label5
	Caption	"(All margins in inches)"
Label	Name	Label4
	Alignment	1 'Right Justify
	Caption	"Bottom Margin:"
Label	Name	Label3
	Alignment	1 'Right Justify
	Caption	"Top Margin:"
Label	Name	Label2
	Alignment	1 'Right Justify
	Caption	"Right Margin:"
Label	Name	Label1
	Alignment	1 'Right Justify
	Caption	"Left Margin:"

OBJECT	PROPERTY	SETTING
CommandButton	Name	cmdClose
	Caption	"Close"
CommandButton	Name	cmdPrint
	Caption	"Print"
ProgressBar	Name	progBar
	Align	2 'Align Bottom
CommonDialog	Name	cdDB
RichTextBox	Name	rtb1
	HideSelection	0 'False
	ReadOnly	-1 'True
	ScrollBars	2

5. Add the following code to the Declarations section of the form. Option Explicit tells Visual Basic to make sure that you declare all variables and objects before using them, in order to avoid naming problems. The two module level variables will contain a reference to the database file used for the report and RichTextBox's line width so that it can be kept consistent throughout the report.

```
Option Explicit

Dim mDB As Database
Dim mlLineWidth As Long
```

6. Add the following code to the form's Load event procedure. The code calls the cmdDefaults Click event procedure to format the initial defaults for the page margins.

```
Private Sub Form_Load()
    'Initialize Form and Command button
    Me.Caption = "Database Report"

    cmdDefaults_Click
End Sub
```

7. By including code in the form's Resize event procedure, any time the form is resized the RichTextBox will shrink or expand to fit the form. This will be handy for the cmdSetFormWidth button, which sizes the form to show the full width of the text in the control if the monitor and resolution allow it.

```
Private Sub Form_Resize()
Dim lTop As Long
Dim lHeight As Long
Dim lWidth As Long

    'Position the RTF on form
    lTop = frasettings.Top + frasettings.Height + 200
    lWidth = Me.ScaleWidth - 200
    lHeight = progBar.Top - lTop - 100
    rtb1.Move frasettings.Left, lTop, lWidth, lHeight
End Sub
```

8. Add this code to the `Click` event of the `cmdDefaults` command button, which gives the end-user an easy way to return to the document's starting state of one-inch margins, in case the end-user makes changes then later decides that the defaults were okay. The form's `Load` event uses this procedure to set the initial defaults.

```
Private Sub cmdDefaults_Click()
'Set the default margins to one inch
    txtTopMargin.Text = "1.00"
    txtBottomMargin.Text = "1.00"
    txtLeftMargin.Text = "1.00"
    txtRightMargin.Text = "1.00"

End Sub
```

9. The code in the `GotFocus` events of each of the text boxes makes it easier for the end-user to edit the margins for the report. As the end-user tabs among the text boxes, the code highlights the current entry so the end-user doesn't need to select the text before making a change. The `LostFocus` event code formats new entries in the margin text boxes in the format "`0.00`" so the information stays uniform in appearance. You can also add error-checking code to these events to prevent, for example, settings that allow no area on the page for text.

```
Private Sub txtTopMargin_GotFocus()
    txtTopMargin.SelStart = 0
    txtTopMargin.SelLength = Len(txtTopMargin.Text)
End Sub

Private Sub txtBottomMargin_GotFocus()
    txtBottomMargin.SelStart = 0
    txtBottomMargin.SelLength = Len(txtBottomMargin.Text)
End Sub

Private Sub txtLeftMargin_GotFocus()
    txtLeftMargin.SelStart = 0
    txtLeftMargin.SelLength = Len(txtLeftMargin.Text)
End Sub

Private Sub txtrightMargin_GotFocus()
    txtRightMargin.SelStart = 0
    txtRightMargin.SelLength = Len(txtRightMargin.Text)
End Sub
```

```
Private Sub txtTopMargin_LostFocus()
    txtTopMargin.Text = Format$(Str(Val(txtTopMargin.Text)), "#0.00")
End Sub

Private Sub txtbottomMargin_LostFocus()
    txtBottomMargin.Text = Format$(Str(Val(txtBottomMargin.Text)), "#0.00")
End Sub

Private Sub txtleftMargin_LostFocus()
    txtLeftMargin.Text = Format$(Str(Val(txtLeftMargin.Text)), "#0.00")
End Sub

Private Sub txtrightMargin_LostFocus()
    txtRightMargin.Text = Format$(Str(Val(txtRightMargin.Text)), "#0.00")
End Sub
```

10. Add the `SetupRTB` and `NormalRTF` Sub procedures, which set the RichTextBox to different formats. The `SetupRTB` Sub procedure sets up the RichTextBox control to a uniform beginning state. Putting this code into a single procedure avoids the need to change formatting commands in many places throughout the form's code. Anytime the code makes changes to the formatting, such as by entering bold text, `NormalRTF` sets it back to its *normal* state.

`SetupRTB` makes a call to the `WYSIWYG_RTF` procedure in the `RTFPRINT.BAS` code module. `WYSIWYG_RTF` establishes the line width for the text in the RichTextBox given the margins set in the form's code. It also sets the length of the line of text to appear the same in the RichTextBox and on the printer.

```
Private Sub SetupRTB()
Dim lLeftMargin As Long
Dim lRightMargin As Long

    rtb1.Text = ""

    'Set the RTF box to its normal formatting
    NormalRTF

    'Tell the RTF to base its display on  the printer dimensions
    '1440 Twips=1 Inch
    lLeftMargin = Val(txtLeftMargin.Text) * 1440
    lRightMargin = Val(txtRightMargin.Text) * 1440
    mlLineWidth = WYSIWYG_RTF(rtb1, lLeftMargin, lRightMargin)

End Sub

Private Sub NormalRTF()
'Reset the RTF box to our chosen default
    rtb1.SelAlignment = rtfLeft
    rtb1.SelBold = False
    rtb1.SelItalic = False
    rtb1.SelFontName = "Arial"
    rtb1.SelFontSize = 10
End Sub
```

11. Add a **LoadDB** function procedure to the **frmPrint** form and enter the
code below. This function locates the **BIBLIO.MDB** database included with
VB. It starts by checking to see if a file location has been stored in the registry when this program was run previously, under the **"VB5CSHT"** key
under the application's .EXE name. If there is no entry or if the file isn't at
the specified location, it uses the form's common dialog control to prompt
the end-user for the file's location. If the end-user cancels the dialog box,
the code pops up a warning message box and ends the procedure.
Otherwise, the procedure opens the database, stores the file location in the
registry, and sets the function's return value to the name of the file.

```
Public Function LoadDB(sDefaultFile As String) As String
'Returns the full file name if it can be found
Dim sAppFile As String

    sAppFile = GetSetting("VB5CSHT", App.EXEName, "DBPath", sDefaultFile)

    If Len(Dir(sAppFile)) = 0 Then
        cdDB.InitDir = sDefaultFile
        cdDB.filename = "biblio.mdb"
        cdDB.DialogTitle = "Open VB Biblio Database"
        cdDB.Filter = "Access (*.mdb)|*.mdb|All Files (*.*)|*.*"
        cdDB.Flags = cdlOFNPathMustExist + cdlOFNFileMustExist
        cdDB.ShowOpen
        sAppFile = cdDB.filename
        If Len(Dir(sAppFile)) = 0 Or Mid$(sAppFile, 3, 1) <> "\" Then
            'No file selected
            MsgBox "No file selected. Ending application.", _
                vbCritical, "No Database Selected"
            LoadDB = ""
            cmdClose_Click
            Exit Function
        End If
    End If

    'It is here, so open it
    Set mDB = OpenDatabase(sAppFile, False, False)

    'Save the file name and location for next execution
    SaveSetting "VB5CSHT", App.EXEName, "DBPath", sAppFile

    LoadDB = sAppFile
End Function
```

12. Add the following code to the **cmdCreateReport_Click** event procedure,
which generates the report in the RichTextBox control. It starts by opening
the **BIBLIO.MDB** database using the **LoadDB** procedure. Then it sets up the
RichTextBox with the starting format. It then calls the
PrintReportHeader to print the report name, in this case using bold ital-
ics, to print **"Author's Bibliography List"**.

This procedure uses two SQL statements to manage grouping titles for each
author. The first SQL statement simply retrieves the contents of the Authors

table, sorted by the author name. The names are in the form **"Last Name, First Name"** in this database, so this puts the authors in alphabetical order without any string concatenation. This recordset, **rsAuthors**, is then used for the main **Do While** loop.

Inside the author's loop, another SQL statement retrieves the author's titles from the Titles table. If this author has any titles, the **PrintAuthor** procedure is used to print the data. With each run through the author's loop the code updates the form's progress bar.

```
Private Sub cmdCreateReport_Click()
Dim sSQLAuthors As String
Dim sSQLTitles As String
Dim sSQL As String
Dim rsAuthors As Recordset
Dim rsTitles As Recordset
Dim i As Long

    rtb1.SetFocus

    'Open the database
    LoadDB "c:\vb5\biblio.mdb"

    'Set up the rich text box for the report
    SetupRTB
    PrintReportHeader

    'Create the authors query statement
    sSQLAuthors = "SELECT * FROM Authors ORDER BY Author"
    Set rsAuthors = mDB.OpenRecordset(sSQLAuthors, dbOpenSnapshot)

    progBar.Min = 0
    progBar.Max = rsAuthors.RecordCount
    progBar.Value = 0
    i = 0

    Do While Not rsAuthors.EOF
        sSQLTitles = "SELECT * FROM Titles " _
            & "INNER JOIN [Title Author] ON Titles.ISBN = [Title Author].ISBN
" _
            & "WHERE ([Title Author].Au_ID) = " & rsAuthors("Au_ID") & " " _
            & "ORDER BY Titles.Title;"
        Set rsTitles = mDB.OpenRecordset(sSQLTitles, dbOpenSnapshot)

' <fix spacing>        rsTitles.MoveLast
        If rsTitles.RecordCount Then
            PrintAuthor rsAuthors, rsTitles
        End If

        rsAuthors.MoveNext

        i = i + 1
        progBar.Value = i
    Loop

End Sub
```

13. The `PrintReportHeader` `Sub` procedure is the first of two procedures called by `cmdCreateReport` to print a report element. Isolating code like this makes it easier to write understandable code and localizes the formatting code you will likely need to tweak. This procedure sets the formatting options for the report title, prints the title, returns the formatting to normal by calling the `NormalRTF` procedure, and adds a date to the report. Note that all of the RichTextBox control's formatting options are set through its methods.

```
Private Sub PrintReportHeader()

    rtb1.SelAlignment = rtfCenter
    rtb1.SelBold = True
    rtb1.SelItalic = True
    rtb1.SelFontSize = 24

    rtb1.SelText = "Author's Bibliography List" _
        & vbCrLf & vbCrLf

    NormalRTF
    rtb1.SelText = Format$(Now, "Medium Date") & " " _
        & Format$(Now, "Medium Time") & vbCrLf & vbCrLf


End Sub
```

14. `cmdCreateReport` calls the `PrintAuthor` `Sub` procedure to print the author group header name and the list of titles. The code starts by printing the author name in bold italic then changes back to the normal text. The `Do While` loop prints each of the author's titles, year published, and comments. Note that by using the RichTextBox control, you don't have to write code to break lines at logical places as you would when using VB's `Printer` object. The RichTextBox handles all that for you, and you can fine-tune it by setting the margin widths and by using the `SelIndent` property of the RichTextBox.

```
Private Sub PrintAuthor(rsAuthors, rsTitles)
'Print each author's information. Assumes that the
'desired formatting is set before calling, and that
'line spacing before is set.
Dim sText As String

    rtb1.SelBold = True
    rtb1.SelItalic = True
    rtb1.SelText = rsAuthors("Author") & vbCrLf
    rtb1.SelBold = False
    rtb1.SelItalic = False

    rtb1.SelRightIndent = 720 'Half inch

    rsTitles.MoveFirst
    Do While Not rsTitles.EOF
        rtb1.SelIndent = 720 'Half inch
```

```
            rtb1.SelText = rsTitles("Title") & vbCrLf
            rtb1.SelIndent = 1080

            If Not IsNull(rsTitles("Year Published")) Then
                rtb1.SelText = "Year Published: " _
                    & rsTitles("Year Published") & vbCrLf
            End If

            rtb1.SelIndent = 1440
            If Not IsNull(rsTitles("Comments")) Then
                rtb1.SelText = rsTitles("Comments") & vbCrLf
            End If

            rsTitles.MoveNext
        Loop

        rtb1.SelText = vbCrLf
        rtb1.SelIndent = 0
        rtb1.SelRightIndent = 0

End Sub
```

15. As a convenience to the end-user, the `cmdSetFormWidth_Click` event resizes the form to show the report as it will appear when printed, including line breaks. If the monitor is not wide enough to show the full width of the form, it is sized to the width of the monitor. If for any reason `mlLineWidth` hasn't yet been set, then the form is not changed.

```
Private Sub cmdSetFormWidth_Click()
'Set the form width to match the line width, but only
'if mlLineWidth has been set.
Dim lWidth As Long

    If mlLineWidth Then
        lWidth = mlLineWidth + 200
        If lWidth > Screen.Width Then
            lWidth = Screen.Width
        End If

        Me.Width = lWidth
    End If
End Sub
```

16. Add the `cmdPrint_Click` event procedure to the form to send the report to the printer. Using the same margins used to create the report in the RichTextBox, the procedure calls the `PrintRTF` function in `RTFPRINT.BAS`. `PrintRTF` is roughly the equivalent of the `cmdCreateReport_Click` event procedure, but sends the output to the printer.

```
Private Sub cmdPrint_Click()
Dim lLeftMargin As Long
Dim lRightMargin As Long
Dim lTopMargin As Long
```

continued on next page

continued from previous page

```
Dim lBottomMargin As Long

    '1440 Twips=1 Inch
    lLeftMargin = Val(txtLeftMargin.Text) * 1440
    lRightMargin = Val(txtRightMargin.Text) * 1440
    lTopMargin = Val(txtTopMargin.Text) * 1440
    lBottomMargin = Val(txtBottomMargin.Text) * 1440

    ' Print the contents of the RichTextBox with a one inch margin
    PrintRTF rtb1, lLeftMargin, lTopMargin, _
        lRightMargin, lBottomMargin ' 1440 Twips = 1 Inch
End Sub
```

17. Add the following code to the `Click` event of the `cmdClose` command button. This code ends the application by unloading the form.

```
Private Sub cmdClose_Click()
    Unload Me
End Sub
```

18. In the Tools Project Options menu item, set the startup form to `frmPrint`. You can also set an application description, but that is not required for the operation of this application.

How It Works

The code in this How-To uses code from the Microsoft KnowledgeBase article Q146022 about setting up the RichTextBox control for WYSIWYG printing. If you look at the `RTFPRINT.BAS` file included on the code disk or at the KnowledgeBase article, you'll see how the displays are coordinated. The `WYSIWYG_RTF` procedure uses a Windows device context (DC) to send an `EM_SETTARGETDEVICE` message to the RichTextBox control to base its display on a printer DC, so the procedure returns the length of each line. The `PrintRTF` then uses an `EM_FORMATRANGE` message to send a page at a time to the printer.

The `PrintHeader` and `PrintAuthor Sub` procedures demonstrate one way to format and add text to the RichTextBox control for repeating information of a database table grouped in this case by author. Using the RichTextBox gives you complete control and flexibility as to how you present the information, nested as deeply as you want, without the constraints of report writing tools. You can achieve a similar degree of flexibility by using OLE and a word processor such as Word for Windows or WordPerfect, but then all users must have access to a copy of the word processor. Since the RichTextBox control is included with Windows 95 and NT, you don't need to include any other files or programs with your application.

Comments

Before VB 4, the only option you had to print any type of document was the VB `Printer` object if you didn't want to use a third-party product. Programming a database report with the `Printer` object was tortuous at best because you had to keep track of your current location and where you were on the page and coding for line breaks in the right places.

In theory you could use the regular Windows text box in the same way as the RichTextBox in this How-To, but the text box doesn't let you set different fonts and other formatting to different text in the document. It was also limited to 32K of text, although you could actually expand that to almost 64K. The text box option just isn't viable for a modern application.

The RichTextBox control provides many of the features needed for a database report. Besides handling line breaks, it lets you format the text almost any way you want. The first incarnation of the control has some fairly serious bugs, none of which affects this How-To, but limits your ability to add graphics to a report. The control also has hooks to save the text to an .RTF disk file automatically so you don't have to code to save files. Probably the best part of the control is that it can handle unlimited text sizes.

COMPLEXITY
INTERMEDIATE

8.3 How do I...
Create a multiple query report using Word 95 and OLE?

Problem

I have several queries that I need to send to an ODBC data source in order to produce a database report. But sending each query, producing its report, then sending the next query is *slow*. How can I consolidate the dissimilar queries to produce my report more quickly?

Technique

Microsoft Access's JET engine and most back-end database servers support multiple queries and multiple resultsets. Using multiple queries can have a dramatic effect on your application's performance, since sending multiple queries together in a single call to the back-end database system can obtain all of the information needed to populate result sets in your application. This How-To demonstrates how to combine multiple queries with VB's remote data objects (RDOs) sent all at once to SQL Server—although the technique works with any database server which supports multiple queries—and using Microsoft Word to produce a custom database report via OLE.

Steps

Open and run the **MULTIQ.VBP** Visual Basic project file. The Multiple Query Report window appears, shown in Figure 8-14, and the application makes a connection to the Books Available data source linked to the PUBS SQL Server sample database. The application then starts Microsoft Word and gets a **Word.Basic OLE** object used to create the report. Click on the Create Report button to create the three-part database report: a list of publishers, authors, and titles in the database. When the report is finished, as shown in Figure 8-15, the application automatically activates Word so that you can preview, edit, and print the document. Return to the MULTIQ application and click the Quit button to exit the application and leave Word running.

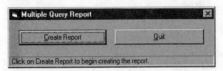

Figure 8-14 VB form used to create a database report based on a multiple rdoResultset query

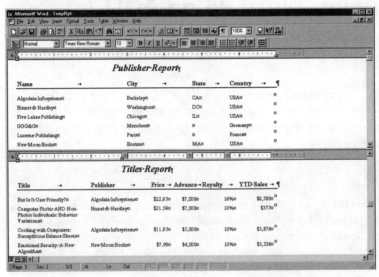

Figure 8-15 Using multiple queries and Microsoft Word to produce a database report

1. This How-To uses an ODBC SQL Server driver and the sample PUBS database included with SQL Server. You can use any other ODBC data source or database, but you'll need to change the fields connected to the form's text boxes.

2. Create a data source name in ODBC for the PUBS database. Start the ODBC Adminstrator, **ODBCAD32.EXE**, most likely located in the Windows System directory in Windows 95 or the System32 directory in Windows NT. ODBC Administrator loads the Data Source window as shown in Figure 8-16. Here you define and maintain data source names available on this system.

3. Click the Add… button so that the Add Data Source window appears. The driver you need will be listed as something like **SQL Server** or **SQL Server (32-bit)**. Click this driver, then click OK so the ODBC SQL Server Setup window appears. Each ODBC driver has its own version of this setup window, prompting for the particular information the driver needs to make a connection with its database. Click the Options>>> button to show the full form, then enter the information as shown in Table 8-7. You may have to adjust other entries not listed in the table for your system setup. Then click OK to create the data source name.

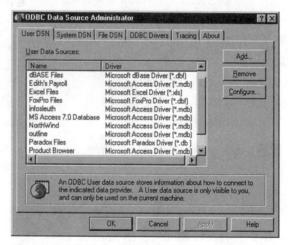

Figure 8-16 Main ODBC Administrator window

Table 8-7 Books Available data source name setup information

PROMPT	INFORMATION TO ENTER
Data Source Name	Books Available
Description	[Optional description information to identify the data source]
Server	[The server where SQL Server is located]
Database Name	PUBS

4. The new Books Available data source name will appear in the Data Sources window as something like Books Available with a driver listed as SQL Server. Click OK to end the ODBC Administrator.

5. Start VB. Create a new project MULTIQ.VBP. Add the form ERRORRDO.FRM (see the introduction to Chapter 2, Getting Connected, for a description of this form), using Visual Basic's Project|Add File... menu command. This form handles RDO errors.

6. Using Project|Components... from the VB main menu, select the custom controls shown in Table 8-8. Uncheck all others so your project isn't cluttered with controls you aren't using, and so the Setup Wizard doesn't include a lot of extra dead weight with your application.

Table 8-8 Custom controls used in MULTIQ.VBP

CONTROL
Microsoft Common Dialog Control 5.0
Microsoft Outline Control 5.0
Microsoft Windows Common Controls 5.0

7. Using Project|References... from the VB main menu, select the references shown in Table 8-9. Uncheck all others so your project isn't cluttered with DLLs you aren't using, and so the Setup Wizard doesn't include a lot of extra dead weight with your application.

Table 8-9 References used in MULTIQ.VBP

REFERENCE
Microsoft Visual Basic for Applications
Visual Basic Runtime Objects and Procedures
Microsoft Common Dialog Control 5.0
Microsoft Windows Common Controls 5.0
Microsoft Remote Data Object 1.0
Microsoft Outline Control

8. Add the controls shown in Figure 8-14 to the form in the new project, with property settings as listed in Table 8-10. Save the form as file MULTIQ.FRM.

Table 8-10 Objects and properties for MULTIQ.FRM

OBJECT	PROPERTY	SETTING
Form	Name	frmMultiQuery
	BackColor	&H00C0C0C0&
	Caption	"Multiple Query Report"
CommandButton	Name	cmdReport
	Caption	"&Create Report"
	Default	-1 'True
CommandButton	Name	cmdQuit
	Caption	"&Quit"
StatusBar	Name	StatusBar1
	Align	2 'Align Bottom
	AlignSet	-1 'True
	Style	1
	SimpleText	""

9. Add the following code to the Declarations section of the form. Option Explicit tells Visual Basic to make sure that you declare all variables and objects before using them, in order to avoid naming problems. The mobjWord object variable will hold the OLE object obtained from Microsoft Word. The mColumn array variables will be used in the three different parts of the report to format tabs and table columns. The third set of variables are the remote data objects used to make the connection with the Books Available SQL Server data source.

```
Option Explicit

Dim mobjWord As Object

Dim mColumnTabs() As String
Dim mColumnHeaders() As String
Dim mColumnWidths() As String

'Remote Data Object variables
Private mrdoEnv As rdoEnvironment
Private mrdoConn As rdoConnection
Private mrdoRS As rdoResultset
```

10. Add the following code to the form's **Load** event procedure. This procedure does two primary tasks in preparation for creating the report: making the connection to the **Books Available** data source and getting an OLE object from Microsoft Word. If the data source cannot be connected, the form unloads itself and ends the application.

```
Private Sub Form_Load()
Dim iSaveCursor As Integer

    cmdReport.Enabled = False
    cmdQuit.Enabled = False

    iSaveCursor = Me.MousePointer
    Me.MousePointer = vbHourglass

    Me.Show
    Me.Refresh

    'Open the Books Available data source
    Status "Connecting to Books Available data source."
    If Not OpenDataSource() Then
        MsgBox "Couldn't open Books Available data source. " _
            & "Ending application.", vbOKOnly, "Data Source Error"
        Unload Me
        Exit Sub
    End If
```

The next set of code makes the connection to Word, by first starting Word itself. This isn't strictly necessary for using a **Word.Basic** object, but in this case the application uses the Word user interface to display the report, let the end-user make changes, and print the report. These tasks can just as easily be controlled from your application by manipulating the **Word.Basic** object; the **GetObject** and **CreateObject** methods then start an invisible instance of Word.

```
    'Create a Microsoft Word object
    DoEvents
    Status "Starting Word."
    If Not StartWord() Then
        MsgBox "Couldn't start Word for Windows. " _
            & "Ending application.", vbOKOnly, "Error Starting Word"
        Unload Me
        Exit Sub
    End If
```

After Word starts, **GetObject** gets a **Word.Basic** object and sets it to the **mobjWord** object variable.

```
    Status "Creating a Word object"
    Set mobjWord = GetObject("", "Word.Basic")

    cmdReport.Enabled = True
    cmdQuit.Enabled = True

    Status "Click on Create Report to begin creating the report."
```

```
    Me.MousePointer = iSaveCursor
End Sub
```

11. Add the `OpenDataSource` function procedure. This is the procedure
which opens the connection to the **Books Available** data source using
VB's RDOs. After making the connection using the `OpenConnection`
method, the `rdoDefaultCursorDriver` is set to `rdUseServer`.
`rdUseServer` tells the RDO to use the back-end SQL Server database to
manage the resultset cursors, which will be retrieved one at a time.

The SQL statement in the code contains three queries. The first retrieves all
the publisher names from the Publisher table and sorts them on **pub_name**.
The second retrieves the list of authors from the Authors table and sorts the
list by last name then first name. The third query retrieves a list of titles
from the Titles table, pulling the associated publisher data from the
Publisher table. Note that in the final **sSQL** string, the three queries are separated by semicolons. You can use an essentially unlimited number of
queries, not all of which need to be the same type. I just as easily could
have included an **UPDATE** query to update a publisher's address at the same
time.

Once the SQL statement is ready, the code creates a prepared statement to
create a **psBooks** statement in SQL Server. You can also directly use the
`OpenResultset` statement without using a prepared statement.

In case of an error while making the remote data connection, the
frmRDOErrors displays the full error returned by SQL Server, the ODBC
driver, and the RDO using a VB outline control. Since any tier along the
connection path can raise an error, you need to be sure to obtain all errors
to pinpoint the problem.

```
Private Function OpenDataSource()
Dim sSQL As String
Dim rdoPS As rdoPreparedStatement

    'Allocate an ODBC environment handle
    Set mrdoEnv = rdoEnvironments(0)
    Set mrdoConn = mrdoEnv.OpenConnection("Books Available", _
        rdDriverNoPrompt, False, "ODBC;UID=sa;PWD=")
    rdoDefaultCursorDriver = rdUseServer
    sSQL = "SELECT * FROM publishers ORDER BY pub_name; "
    sSQL = sSQL & "SELECT * FROM authors ORDER BY au_lname, au_fname; "
    sSQL = sSQL & _
        "SELECT titles.*, publishers.* " _
        & "FROM titles, publishers " _
        & "WHERE publishers.pub_id = titles.pub_id " _
        & "ORDER BY titles.Title ASC;"
    On Error GoTo OpenDataSourceError
    Set rdoPS = mrdoConn.CreatePreparedStatement("psBooks", "")
    rdoPS.SQL = sSQL
    rdoPS.RowsetSize = 1
```

continued on next page

continued from previous page

```
    Set mrdoRS = rdoPS.OpenResultset(rdOpenForwardOnly)
    OpenDataSource = True
    Exit Function

OpenDataSourceError:
    frmRDOErrors.ErrorColl = rdoErrors
    OpenDataSource = False
End Function
```

12. Add the **StartWord** function procedure code shown below. This procedure starts Word so the end-user can use its features to modify and print the report rather than needing to code these features into the VB application. The procedure starts by using the Windows API function **FindExecutable** to find the program associated in the registry with ***.DOC** files. Since this function requires a full filename of a Word document, I've used the **TempRpt.doc** file generated by this How-To's program, located in the application directory. There are other ways to get this information, such as by searching the registry, but this technique will be reliable in most cases since most end-users will not change the association established by the Word installation program.

FindExecutable returns error codes between 0 and 32, so if the result code is greater than 32, **sFileName** contains the full path and filename for Word. The code strips the terminating null character from this string then uses VB's **Shell** function to start Word. The **AppActivate** statement sets focus to Word, then the form's **SetFocus** method returns to the **MultiQ** application so the end-user can start generating the report.

```
Private Function StartWord()
Dim sFileName As String
Dim iResult As Integer
Dim lResult As Long

    sFileName = Space$(128)
    iResult = FindExecutable("TempRpt.doc", App.Path, sFileName)
If iResult > 32 Then
    sFileName = Left$(sFileName, Len(sFileName) - 1)
    lResult = Shell(sFileName, vbNormalNoFocus)
    StartWord = True
    AppActivate App.Title
    Me.SetFocus
    Else
        StartWord = False
    End If
End Function
```

13. Once the connection to **Books Available** is made and Word has started, the end-user can click on the **cmdReport** command button to generate the report. Add the following code to the button's **Click** event procedure. The procedure starts by using the **mobjWord** object's **DocRestore** method to restore the active document's MDI child window in case it is minimized or maximized. If it is minimized, the end-user isn't able to see the report as it is generated, and if it is maximized you can't use the **AppActivate** statement to switch to Word because the document's name will be in the title bar.

The next bit of code sets the page formatting for all three of the reports. By setting these properties before adding any text to the document, the changes will apply to all three reports.

The code then generates the three reports in succession. The **mrdoRS** result-set variable contains the first of the three resultsets from the multiple query created in the **OpenDataSource** function. Once the code is finished with the first **rdoResultset**, it uses the **MoreResults** method to check if there are more results (no surprise there). But **MoreResults** also closes the first **rdoResultset**, making the second **rdoResultset** active and available for use. This is an example of how the RDO manages the SQL Server cursors for your application.

The rest of the code in this procedure saves the report, using a **TEMPRPT.DOC** filename, after first setting off Word's Summary prompt, then moves to the top of the document and makes Word the active application so the end-user can review the report.

```
Private Sub cmdReport_Click()
Dim sFileName As String
Dim iSaveCursor As Integer

    iSaveCursor = Me.MousePointer
    Me.MousePointer = vbHourglass

    cmdReport.Enabled = False

    Status "Creating a new Word document"
    mobjWord.FileNew
    'Restore the document so we can use AppActivate
    'with "Microsoft Word"
    On Error Resume Next
    mobjWord.DocRestore
    On Error GoTo 0

    With mobjWord
        .FilePageSetup TopMargin:="0.8" + Chr$(34), _
            BottomMargin:="0.8" + Chr$(34), _
            LeftMargin:="0.75" + Chr$(34), _
            RightMargin:="0.75" + Chr$(34), _
            ApplyPropsTo:=0, _
            DifferentFirstPage:=0
    End With
PrintPublishers

    If mrdoRS.MoreResults Then
        mobjWord.EndOfDocument
```

continued on next page

continued from previous page

```
        mobjWord.insertbreak Type:=2 'Break, new page
        PrintAuthors
    End If
    If mrdoRS.MoreResults Then
        mobjWord.EndOfDocument
        mobjWord.insertbreak Type:=2 'Break, new page
        PrintTitles
    End If

    'Save the Word document
    mobjWord.ToolsOptionsSave SummaryPrompt:=0

    sFileName = App.Path & "\TempRpt.doc"
    'Word won't let us save a file over an existing document
    If Len(Dir(sFileName)) Then
        Kill sFileName
    End If
    mobjWord.FileSaveAs Name:=sFileName

    Status "Report complete"
    mobjWord.StartOfDocument
    AppActivate "Microsoft Word"
    Me.MousePointer = iSaveCursor

End Sub
```

14. The next several procedures generate the three reports, using the **mobjWord** object variable and its methods and properties to format and insert text. I'll discuss the three procedures which generate the reports, then discuss the support procedures. The first report lists the **Publishers**, so enter this code for the **PrintPublishers Sub** procedure. The procedure uses the **mColumnTabs**, **mColumnHeaders**, and **mColumnWidths** arrays to set up the columns used for each field in the report. **mColumnTabs** sets the widths of the columns based on the tab spacing of the column header. The **SetColumnWidths** procedure will use this array to calculate the table's column widths.

The next set of code uses these arrays to print the report header and footer for the Publishers report, adding the **SortaMarvelous Software** company name to the bottom of the report. The **TableInsertTable** Word function inserts a table into the document. The code then formats the column widths of the new table, using the **mColumnWidths** array.

Once the table is formatted properly, a **Do While** loop moves through the current **mrdoRS rdoResultset**, adding field data to each cell in the table. Note that since the **mrdoRS** was created as a forward-only cursor to be more efficient, you can't move back and forth through the **rdoResultset**. For example, if you try to use the **MoveFirst** method on the **mrdoRS** object, the RDO will generate an error even if you are at the first record.

```
Private Sub PrintPublishers()
Dim sTitle As String
Dim iColumns As Integer
Dim i As Integer
Dim sInsertText As String
Dim iColCount As Integer

    sTitle = "Publisher Report"
    Status "Setting up report"

    'Set up standard layout information
    iColCount = 4
    ReDim mColumnTabs(iColCount - 1)
    mColumnTabs(0) = "3.0"
    mColumnTabs(1) = "4.75"
    mColumnTabs(2) = "5.75"
    mColumnTabs(3) = "7.0"

    ReDim mColumnHeaders(iColCount)
    mColumnHeaders(0) = "Name"
    mColumnHeaders(1) = "City"
    mColumnHeaders(2) = "State"
    mColumnHeaders(3) = "Country"

    ReDim mColumnWidths(iColCount)
    SetColumnWidths

    Status "Inserting header and footer information"

    'PrintHeader sTitle, mColumnTabs(), mColumnHeaders()
    PrintFooter "SortaMarvelous Software, Inc."
    PrintReportTitle sTitle
    PrintColHeaders mColumnTabs(), mColumnHeaders()

    'Start printing the report
    Status "Adding data to report"

    mobjWord.TableInsertTable NumColumns:=iColCount, _
    NumRows:=2, _
    InitialColWidth:="2 in"

    For i = 0 To iColCount
        With mobjWord
            .TableSelectColumn
            .TableColumnWidth ColumnWidth:=mColumnWidths(i)
            .NextCell
            .NextCell
        End With
    Next

    'Format the paragraph height
    mobjWord.TableSelectTable
    mobjWord.FormatParagraph Before:="6 pt"

    'Select the first cell in the table
```

continued on next page

continued from previous page

```
    'mobjWord.TableSelectColumn
    mobjWord.NextCell

    Do While Not mrdoRS.EOF
        With mobjWord
            sInsertText = mrdoRS("pub_name") & ""
            .Insert sInsertText
            .NextCell
            sInsertText = mrdoRS("City") & ""
            .Insert sInsertText
            .NextCell
            sInsertText = mrdoRS("State") & ""
            .Insert sInsertText
            .NextCell
            sInsertText = mrdoRS("Country") & ""
            .Insert sInsertText
            .NextCell
            .TableInsertRow
        End With
        mrdoRS.MoveNext
    Loop

End Sub
```

15. Add the following code for the **PrintAuthors Sub** procedure. This procedure works like the **PrintPublishers** procedure, changing only to use
the fields from the author's table.

```
Private Sub PrintAuthors()
Dim sTitle As String
Dim iColumns As Integer
Dim i As Integer
Dim sInsertText As String
Dim iColCount As Integer

    sTitle = "Author Report"
    Status "Setting up report"

    'Set up standard layout information
    iColCount = 3
    ReDim mColumnTabs(iColCount - 1)
    mColumnTabs(0) = "2.0"
    mColumnTabs(1) = "4.0"
    mColumnTabs(2) = "6.0"

    ReDim mColumnHeaders(iColCount)
    mColumnHeaders(0) = "Name"
    mColumnHeaders(1) = "Phone"
    mColumnHeaders(2) = "Address"

    ReDim mColumnWidths(iColCount)
    SetColumnWidths

    Status "Inserting header and footer information"
```

```
PrintReportTitle sTitle
PrintColHeaders mColumnTabs(), mColumnHeaders()

'Start printing the report
Status "Adding data to report"

mobjWord.TableInsertTable NumColumns:=iColCount, _
NumRows:=2, _
InitialColWidth:="2 in"

For i = 0 To iColCount
    With mobjWord
        .TableSelectColumn
        .TableColumnWidth ColumnWidth:=mColumnWidths(i)
        .NextCell
        .NextCell
    End With
Next

'Format the paragraph height
mobjWord.TableSelectTable
mobjWord.FormatParagraph Before:="6 pt"

'Select the first cell in the table
'mobjWord.TableSelectColumn
mobjWord.NextCell

Do While Not mrdoRS.EOF
    With mobjWord
        sInsertText = mrdoRS("au_fname") & " " _
            & mrdoRS("au_lname") & ""
        .Insert sInsertText
        .NextCell
        sInsertText = mrdoRS("phone") & ""
        .Insert sInsertText
        .NextCell
        sInsertText = mrdoRS("city") & ", " _
            & mrdoRS("state") & "  " _
            & mrdoRS("zip") & ""
        .Insert sInsertText
        .NextCell
        .TableInsertRow
    End With
    mrdoRS.MoveNext
Loop

End Sub
```

16. Add the following code for the **PrintTitles Sub** procedure. This procedure again works much like the **PrintPublishers** procedure, but has a few new twists to better format the numerical data included in this part of the report, using VB's **Format$** function to add dollar signs, percent signs, and to keep the numbers aligned vertically.

```
Private Sub PrintTitles()
Dim sTitle As String
Dim iColumns As Integer
Dim i As Integer
Dim sInsertText As String
Dim iColCount As Integer

    sTitle = "Titles Report"
    Status "Setting up report"

    'Set up standard layout information
    iColCount = 6
    ReDim mColumnTabs(iColCount - 1)
    mColumnTabs(0) = "2.0"
    mColumnTabs(1) = "3.65"
    mColumnTabs(2) = "4.25"
    mColumnTabs(3) = "5.0"
    mColumnTabs(4) = "6.0"
    mColumnTabs(5) = "7.0"

    ReDim mColumnHeaders(iColCount)
    mColumnHeaders(0) = "Title"
    mColumnHeaders(1) = "Publisher"
    mColumnHeaders(2) = "Price"
    mColumnHeaders(3) = "Advance"
    mColumnHeaders(4) = "Royalty"
    mColumnHeaders(5) = "YTD Sales"

    ReDim mColumnWidths(iColCount)
    SetColumnWidths

    Status "Inserting header and footer information for titles."

    PrintReportTitle sTitle
    PrintColHeaders mColumnTabs(), mColumnHeaders()

    'Start printing the report
    Status "Adding data to report"

    mobjWord.TableInsertTable NumColumns:=iColCount, _
    NumRows:=2, _
    InitialColWidth:="2 in"

    For i = 0 To iColCount
        With mobjWord
            .TableSelectColumn
            .TableColumnWidth ColumnWidth:=mColumnWidths(i)
            .NextCell
            .NextCell
        End With
    Next

    'Format the paragraph height
    mobjWord.TableSelectTable
    mobjWord.FormatParagraph Before:="6 pt"

    'Select the first cell in the table
```

```
'mobjWord.TableSelectColumn
mobjWord.NextCell

Do While Not mrdoRS.EOF
    With mobjWord
        sInsertText = mrdoRS("title") & ""
        .Insert sInsertText
        .NextCell
        sInsertText = mrdoRS("pub_name") & ""
        .Insert sInsertText
        .NextCell
        sInsertText = Format$(mrdoRS("price"), "Currency")
        .RightPara
        .Insert sInsertText
        .NextCell
        sInsertText = Format$(mrdoRS("advance"), "$#,##0")
        .RightPara
        .Insert sInsertText
        .NextCell
        sInsertText = Format$(mrdoRS("royalty") / 100, "#0%")
        .RightPara
        .Insert sInsertText
        .NextCell
        sInsertText = Format$(mrdoRS("ytd_sales"), "$#,##0")
        .RightPara
        .Insert sInsertText
        .NextCell
        .TableInsertRow
    End With
    mrdoRS.MoveNext
Loop

End Sub
```

17. The `SetColumnWidths` `Sub` procedure is the first of the *support* procedures used in all three of the report sections. This procedure takes the tabs set in the `mColumnTabs` array, which are text values, to easily use them with the `mobjWord` object, and calculates the distances between them to set the column widths.

```
Private Sub SetColumnWidths()
    Dim i As Integer
    For i = LBound(mColumnTabs) To UBound(mColumnTabs)
        If i Then
            mColumnWidths(i) = Str$(Val(mColumnTabs(i)) _
                - Val(mColumnTabs(i - 1)))
        Else
            mColumnWidths(i) = mColumnTabs(i)
        End If
    Next
End Sub
```

18. Add the following code for the `PrintHeader` `Sub` procedure. This code uses the `ViewHeader` and `ToggleHeaderFooterLink` to add headers and footers to this part of the report. It also calls the `PrintColHeaders` procedure to add column headings.

```
Private Sub PrintHeader(Title As String, Tabs() As String, _
    ColHeaders() As String)
Dim i As Integer

    'Insert the report header
    With mobjWord
        .ViewHeader
        .ToggleHeaderFooterLink
        .FormatTabs ClearAll:=1
        .FormatTabs Position:="7.0" + Chr$(34), _
            DefTabs:="0.5" + Chr$(34), _
            Align:=2
        .StartOfLine
        .SelectCurSentence
        .CharRight 1, 1
        .FormatFont Points:="12", _
            Font:="Times New Roman", _
            Bold:=1
        .StartOfLine
        .Insert Title + Chr$(9)
        .InsertDateTime DateTimePic:="d' 'MMMM', 'yyyy", _
            InsertAsField:=0
        .InsertPara
        .InsertPara
    End With

    PrintColHeaders Tabs(), ColHeaders()

    mobjWord.ViewHeader     'Closes if it is open

    'Now set DifferentFirstPage
'   mobjWord.FilePageSetup DifferentFirstPage:=1

    'Give it a chance to catch up
    DoEvents
End Sub
```

19. Add the following code to the **PrintFooter Sub** procedure. This procedure is similar to the **PrintHeader** procedure.

```
Private Sub PrintFooter(Company As String)

    'Insert the report footer
    mobjWord.ViewFooter
    mobjWord.FormatTabs ClearAll:=1
    mobjWord.FormatTabs Position:="7.0" + Chr$(34), _
        DefTabs:="0.5" + Chr$(34), _
        Align:=2, _
        Leader:=0
    mobjWord.StartOfLine
    mobjWord.Insert Company + Chr$(9) + "Page "
    mobjWord.InsertPageField
    mobjWord.SelectCurSentence
    mobjWord.FormatFont Points:="12", _
        Font:="Times New Roman", _
        Bold:=1
```

```
mobjWord.ViewFooter

'Give it a chance to catch up
DoEvents
End Sub
```

20. The `PrintReportTitle` `Sub` procedure prints the report title for this section of the report, printing the name in bold, unitalicized text.

```
Private Sub PrintReportTitle(Title As String)
    With mobjWord
        .InsertPara
        .LineUp
        .Insert Title
        .StartOfLine
        .SelectCurSentence
        .FormatFont Points:="18", _
            Font:="Times New Roman", _
            Bold:=1, _
            Italic:=1
        .CenterPara

        .FormatBordersAndShading ApplyTo:=0, _
            Shadow:=0

        'Leave the cursor on the following line
        .LineDown
    End With

    'Give it a chance to catch up
    DoEvents
End Sub
```

21. Add the following code for the `PrintColHeaders` `Sub` procedure. Using the column arrays, this procedure inserts the column headers for this part of the report.

```
Private Sub PrintColHeaders(Tabs() As String, ColHeaders() As String)
Dim i As Integer
Dim iAlign As Integer

    'Assumes cursor is at the beginning of the proper location
    mobjWord.InsertPara
    mobjWord.LineUp
    mobjWord.FormatParagraph Before:="12 pt", _
        After:="6 pt"

    For i = 0 To UBound(Tabs)
        Select Case Right$(Tabs(i), 1)
            Case "R"
                iAlign = 2 'Right align
                Tabs(i) = Left$(Tabs(i), Len(Tabs(i)) - 1)
            Case "C"
                iAlign = 1 'Center align
                Tabs(i) = Left$(Tabs(i), Len(Tabs(i)) - 1)
            Case "D"
```

continued on next page

continued from previous page

```
                iAlign = 3 'Decimal align
                Tabs(i) = Left$(Tabs(i), Len(Tabs(i)) - 1)
            Case "B"
                iAlign = 4 'Bar
                Tabs(i) = Left$(Tabs(i), Len(Tabs(i)) - 1)
            Case Else
                iAlign = 0 'Left align
        End Select

        mobjWord.FormatTabs Position:=Tabs(i) + Chr$(34), _
            Align:=iAlign
    Next
    For i = 0 To UBound(ColHeaders) - 1
        mobjWord.Insert ColHeaders(i) + Chr$(9)
    Next

    With mobjWord
        .StartOfLine
        .SelectCurSentence
        .CharRight 1, 1
        .FormatFont Points:="12", _
            Font:="Times New Roman", _
            Bold:=1
        .FormatBordersAndShading ApplyTo:=0, _
            BottomBorder:=2
        .LineDown
    End With

    'Give it a chance to catch up
    DoEvents
End Sub
```

22. Add the following code to the **Status Sub** procedure. At various points throughout the application, status messages are sent to the StatusBar control at the bottom of the form to keep the end-user apprised of what is happening.

```
Sub Status(sCaption)
    StatusBar1.SimpleText = sCaption
    StatusBar1.Refresh
End Sub
```

23. Add the following code for the **cmdQuit** command button **Click** event procedure and the form's **Unload** event procedure. This code ends the application by unloading the form and setting the module-level object variables to **Nothing**.

```
Private Sub cmdQuit_Click()
    Status "Ending application"
    Unload Me
End Sub

Private Sub Form_Unload(Cancel As Integer)
    'Shut down Word
    Set mobjWord = Nothing
```

```
      Set mrdoEnv = Nothing
      Set mrdoConn = Nothing
      Set mrdoRS = Nothing
End Sub
```

24. Add a new code module to the project by selecting Project|Add Module from the VB main menu. Save the file as **COMMON.BAS** and set its module name in the property's window as **basCommon**.

25. Add the following code to the Declarations section of the module. The sole purpose of the code module is to contain the **Declare** statement for the **FindExecutable** API function, which can't be placed in a form module.

```
Option Explicit

Declare Function FindExecutable Lib "shell32.dll" _
   Alias "FindExecutableA" (ByVal lpFile As String, _
   ByVal lpDirectory As String, _
   ByVal lpResult As String) As Long
```

26. In the Tools Project Options menu item, set the startup form to **frmMultiQuery**. You can also set an application description, but that is not required for the operation of this application.

How It Works

Many back-end database servers allow you to create multiple queries—strings which contain more than one query. One of the advantages of this technique is to reduce the amount of network traffic, since only one SQL statement string is sent to the database server, which can also manage the cursor for the resultsets. This How-To used an SQL string which looks like the following with all the VB operators used in the code stripped away:

```
SELECT * FROM publishers ORDER BY pub_name;
SELECT * FROM authors ORDER BY au_lname, au_fname;
SELECT titles.*, publishers.* FROM titles, publishers
   WHERE publishers.pub_id = titles.pub_id
   ORDER BY titles.Title ASC;"
```

Here is another example of a valid multiple query string which uses different types of queries in the same string:

```
SELECT * FROM publishers ORDER BY pub_name;
UPDATE Publishers SET City = 'Fairbanks' WHERE pub_id = '1389';
SELECT titles.*, publishers.* FROM titles, publishers
   WHERE publishers.pub_id = titles.pub_id
   ORDER BY titles.Title ASC;"
```

Some SQL Server stored procedures return multiple resultsets; you use the same technique with **MoreResults** with this type of query.

MoreResults clears the current **rdoResultset** and returns a Boolean value that indicates if one or more additional result sets are waiting. If there are no additional resultsets to process, the `MoreResults` method returns `False` and the RDO's `BOF` and `EOF` properties are set to `True`. Using the `MoreResults` method flushes the current `rdoResultset`, so be sure that you are finished with the current resultset before using the `MoreResults` method. You can also use the RDO's `Cancel` method to flush the contents of an `rdoResultset`, but `Cancel` also flushes any additional resultsets not yet processed.

The `FindExecutable` API function used in this How-To is only one way to find the WinWord application associated in Windows with a .DOC file. Using this method assumes that the end-user hasn't changed the association for .DOC files, and this is probably a pretty safe assumption. You can always fall back on other methods, such as prompting the end-user for the .EXE file location, searching the Windows registry directly, or even searching the hard drive directly. In any event, you should include code for the possibility that the computer doesn't have access to Word either locally or over the network via Remote Automation. You can include this check either in your application or in the installation program.

Most of the rest of the code in this How-To manages the `Word.Basic` object variable `mobjWord`. It's a lot of code, but still far less than trying to code the same features using the VB `Printer` object, taking advantage of the features built into Microsoft Word or any other word processor of choice. The use of the `Word.Basic` object is designed to use the monolithic object in Word 7.0 and earlier. Later versions of Word use a more complex object model that gives you finer control over the objects, but it should still work with this code.

COMPLEXITY
ADVANCED

8.4 How do I...
Create a pivot table and chart using Excel 95 and OLE?

Problem

I have a large database of information which includes a large number of pieces of data for each of the company's sales people, tracking their performance over the last 10 years. How can I analyze the data using VB to put it into a meaningful form and display it in such a way that even top management can use and understand it?

Technique

The code in this How-To demonstrates how to create a pivot table and chart using a VB remote data object (RDO) to query an SQL Server database, add the data to an Excel worksheet using a worksheet OLE object provided by Excel, and create a chart based on the pivot table, again through OLE. The code keeps the table and chart logic separate so you can easily just create a pivot table without a chart.

A pivot table is one way to display data that has a relatively small set of entities, each of which has a relatively high number of pieces of data in the database. A pivot table summarizes, or cross-tabulates, large amounts of data. For example, you might have a table with the percentage population change for the ten largest cities in the country for each of the last 15 years. By using a pivot table, you can display the data to show how the population changed by year or by city.

Steps

Start Microsoft Excel, then open and run the **PIVOT.VBP VB** project file. The project's Data Analysis form appears, shown in Figure 8-17, and the application obtains a worksheet object from the Excel object library. Click the Load Spreadsheet button; the application connects to the Books Available SQL Server database, producing the data and pivot table shown in Figure 8-18. The data on the left is the result of the query added to the worksheet, and the table on the right is the pivot table based on the data. Return to the Pivot application and click the Create Chart button to create a stacked column chart in Excel, as shown in Figure 8-19. Click the Quit button to quit the application.

Figure 8-17 VB form used to create a pivot table and chart using Microsoft Excel

	A	B	C	D	E	F	G	H	I	J	K
1	Last Name	First Name	Units	Year		Sum of Units		Year			
2	Bennet	Abraham	15	1994		Last Name	First Name	1992	1993	1994	Grand Total
3	Blotchet-H	Reginald	20	1992		Bennet	Abraham	0	0	15	15
4	Carson	Cheryl	30	1993		Blotchet-Halls	Reginald	20	0	0	20
5	DeFrance	Michel	40	1994		Carson	Cheryl	0	30	0	30
6	del Castillo	Innes	10	1993		DeFrance	Michel	0	0	40	40
7	Dull	Ann	50	1993		del Castillo	Innes	0	10	0	10
8	Green	Marjorie	35	1993		Dull	Ann	0	50	0	50
9	Green	Marjorie	15	1994		Green	Marjorie	0	35	15	50
10	Gringlesby	Burt	20	1992		Gringlesby	Burt	20	0	0	20
11	Hunter	Sheryl	50	1993		Hunter	Sheryl	0	50	0	50
12	Karsen	Livia	20	1993		Karsen	Livia	0	20	0	20
13	Locksley	Charlene	25	1993		Locksley	Charlene	0	25	0	25
14	MacFeath	Stearns	45	1993		MacFeather	Stearns	0	45	0	45
15	O'Leary	Michael	20	1992		O'Leary	Michael	20	25	0	45
16	O'Leary	Michael	25	1993		Panteley	Sylvia	40	0	0	40
17	Panteley	Sylvia	40	1992		Ringer	Albert	0	25	108	133
18	Ringer	Albert	25	1993		Singer	Anne	0	0	148	148
19	Ringer	Albert	108	1994		Straight	Dean	0	15	0	15
20	Singer	Anne	148	1994		White	Johnson	0	15	0	15
21	Straight	Dean	15	1993		Yokomoto	Akiko	20	0	0	20
22	White	Johnson	15	1993		Grand Total		120	345	326	791
23	Yokomoto	Akiko	20	1992							

Figure 8-18 Pivot table using a remote data object and Microsoft Excel

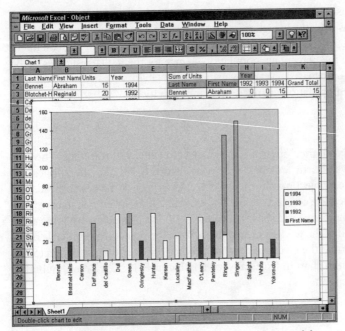

Figure 8-19 Editable chart based on the pivot table

1. This How-To uses an ODBC SQL Server driver and the sample PUBS database included with SQL Server. You can use any other ODBC data source or database, but you'll need to change the fields connected to the form's text boxes.

2. Create a data source name in ODBC for the PUBS database. Start the ODBC Adminstrator, **ODBCAD32.EXE**, most likely located in the Windows System directory in Windows 95 or the System32 directory in Windows NT. ODBC Administrator loads the Data Sources window as shown in Figure 8-20. Here you define and maintain data source names available on this system.

3. Click the Add... button so that the Add Data Source window appears. The driver you need will be listed as something like **SQL Server** or **SQL Server (32-bit)**. Click this driver, then click OK so the ODBC SQL Server Setup window appears. Each ODBC driver has its own version of this setup window, prompting for the particular information the driver needs to make a connection with its database. Click the Options>>> button to show the full form, then enter the information as shown in Table 8-11. You may have to adjust other entries not listed in the table for your system setup. Then click OK to create the data source name.

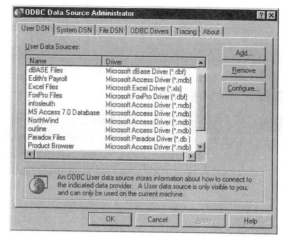

Figure 8-20 Main ODBC Administrator window

Table 8-11 Books Available data source name setup information

PROMPT	INFORMATION TO ENTER
Data Source Name	Books Available
Description	[Optional description information to identify the data source]
Server	[The server where SQL Server is located]
Database Name	PUBS

4. The new **Books Available** data source name will appear in the Data Sources window as something like **Books Available** with a driver listed as **SQL Server**. Click OK to end the ODBC Administrator.

5. Start VB. Create a new project **PIVOT.VBP**. Add the form **ERRORRDO.FRM** (see the introduction to Chapter 2, Getting Connected, for a description of this form), using Visual Basic's Add File menu command. This form handles RDO errors.

6. Using Project|Components... from the VB main menu, select the custom controls shown in Table 8-12. Uncheck all others so your project isn't cluttered with controls you aren't using, and so the Setup Wizard doesn't include a lot of extra dead weight with your application.

Table 8-12 Custom controls used in `PIVOT.VBP`

CONTROL
Microsoft Common Dialog Control 5.0
Microsoft Outline Control
Microsoft Windows Common Controls 5.0

7. Using Project|References… from the VB main menu, select the references shown in Table 8-13. Uncheck all others so your project isn't cluttered with DLLs you aren't using, and so the Setup Wizard doesn't include a lot of extra dead weight with your application.

Table 8-13 References used in `PIVOT.VBP`

REFERENCE
Microsoft Visual Basic for Applications
Visual Basic Runtime Objects and Procedures
Microsoft Common Dialog Control 5.0
Microsoft Excel 5.0 Object Library (or if you have a later version, that one)
Microsoft Windows Common Controls 5.0
Microsoft Remote Data Object 1.0
Microsoft Outline Control

8. Add the controls shown in Figure 8-17 to the form in the new project, with property settings as listed in Table 8-14. Save the form as file `PIVOT.FRM`.

Table 8-14 Objects and properties for `PIVOT.FRM`

OBJECT	PROPERTY	SETTING
Form	Name	frmPivot
	Caption	"Data Analysis"
CommandButton	Name	cmdChart
	Caption	"Create Chart"
CommandButton	Name	cmdLoadSS
	Caption	"&Load Spreadsheet"
	Enabled	0 'False
CommandButton	Name	cmdQuit
	Caption	"&Quit"
	Default	-1 'True
StatusBar	Name	StatusBar1
	Align	2 'Align Bottom
	AlignSet	-1 'True

OBJECT	PROPERTY	SETTING
	Style	1
	SimpleText	""

9. Add the following code to the **Declarations** section of the form. **Option Explicit** tells Visual Basic to make sure that you declare all variables and objects before using them, in order to avoid naming problems. The **mobjExcel** object variable will hold the worksheet OLE object obtained from Microsoft Excel. The set of **mrdo** variables are the remote data objects used to make the connection with the Books Available SQL Server data source.

```
Option Explicit

'Object variable for Excel worksheet
Dim mobjExcel As Object

'Remote Data Object variables
Private mrdoEnv As rdoEnvironment
Private mrdoConn As rdoConnection
Private mrdoRS As rdoResultset
```

10. Enter the following code in **frmPivot**'s **Load** event procedure. The main purpose of this procedure is to get a worksheet OLE object from Excel's object library.

```
Private Sub Form_Load()
    cmdLoadSS.Enabled = False
    cmdChart.Enabled = False
    cmdQuit.Enabled = True

    Me.Show
    Me.Refresh

    'Create a Microsoft Excel object
    Status "Creating an Excel object"
    Set mobjExcel = GetObject("", "Excel.Sheet.5")

    Status "Click on Load Spreadsheet to begin creating the report."
    cmdLoadSS.Enabled = True
End Sub
```

11. Add the following code to the **Click** event procedure of the **cmdLoadSS** command button. Once the form is loaded and **mobjExcel** contains a reference to a worksheet object, this procedure reads the database information and adds it to a database area of an Excel spreadsheet.

The **OpenDataSource** procedure, discussed below, makes the connection to the **Books Available** data source. If the connection isn't made for any reason, this function returns **False**, the end-user is notified, and the **Sub** procedure exits.

The next bit of code loops through the `rdoColumns` collection of the `mrdoRS rdoResultSet`, adding each field's name to the top of a column in the Excel worksheet. The `iRowNo` variable keeps track of the current row in the spreadsheet when the data from the resultset is added to the sheet.

The `Do While` loop then steps through the resultset containing the data for the pivot table, adding each record to a row in the worksheet. I've made this fairly generic so it will work with any number of fields in the resultset.

The next section of code selects the area of the worksheet containing the data just added. In the later call to Excel's `PivotTableWizard` method, you can specify an area containing the data as a range, or else the method uses the database named `range` by default. I've elected to define the database range name, then redefine `sRange` to the location where I want to place the pivot table. Be careful not to overwrite any of the data used for the pivot table; the generated table will use the changed data, resulting in garbage in the table.

The next section of code uses the `PivotTableWizard` method to create the actual pivot table, which I've named `AuthorsPivot`. The `SourceType` parameters tells Excel that I want to use an Excel database for the source data. You can also make an ODBC connection directly through Excel, specify a range in the worksheet, or use another pivot table. Since I'm the paranoid type, I've specified the database named `range` for the `SourceData` parameter, even though this is the default for a `SourceType` of `xlDatabase`.

Once the pivot table is created, you need to specify which fields the table uses for its different parts. `RowFields` are the data contained in the row headings and `ColumnFields` are for the columns.

Setting the table's `DataFields` is a less than intuitive process given the nice, simple `AddFields` method above. Even though the Units field hasn't explicitly been added to the pivot table's fields, use the `PivotFields` ("Units") method to return a reference to this object and set its orientation to `xlDataField`. This sets the data used in the main body of the table to the Units field, summing the units for the total number by author and year.

By default the `PivotTableWizard` includes a subtotal line for each unique `RowFields` line. Since this pivot table has only one author on each line, turn off the subtotals, which clutter the table needlessly. Setting the `Subtotals` array to all `False` values completely turns off subtotals. See the Access documentation for more information about the `Subtotals` property.

```
Private Sub cmdLoadSS_Click()
Dim iSaveCursor As Integer
Dim aConnect(1) As String
Dim sSQL As String
```

```
Dim irowNo As Integer
Dim j As Integer
Dim sRange As String

    iSaveCursor = Me.MousePointer
    Me.MousePointer = vbHourglass

    'Open the Books Available data source
    Status "Connecting to Books Available data source."
    If Not OpenDataSource() Then
        Status "Unable to connect to the Books Available data source."
        MsgBox "Couldn't open Books Available data source. " _
            & "Ending application.", vbOKOnly, "Data Source Error"
        Unload Me
        Exit Sub
    End If

    cmdLoadSS.Enabled = False

    'At the end of the loop, iRowNo will have the last row
    'of the range of cells and j will hold the number of
    'columns.
    irowNo = 1
    Status "Adding column names to pivot table data."
    For j = 0 To mrdoRS.rdoColumns.Count - 1
        mobjExcel.Cells(irowNo, j + 1).Value = mrdoRS.rdoColumns(j).Name
    Next

    Do While Not mrdoRS.EOF
        irowNo = irowNo + 1
        Status "Adding row to pivot table data: " _
            & mrdoRS.rdoColumns("Last Name").Value
        For j = 0 To mrdoRS.rdoColumns.Count - 1
            mobjExcel.Cells(irowNo, j + 1).Value = mrdoRS.rdoColumns(j).Value
        Next
        mrdoRS.MoveNext
    Loop

    With mobjExcel
        Status "Defining the Database range."
        sRange = "$A1:$" & Chr(Asc("A") + j - 1) & LTrim(Str(irowNo))
        .Range(sRange).Name = "Database"
        sRange = Chr(Asc("A") + j + 1) & "1"
        .Range(sRange).Select

        Status "Adding the pivot table to the worksheet."
        .PivotTableWizard SourceType:=xlDatabase, _
            SourceData:="Database", TableName:="AuthorsPivot", _
            RowGrand:=True, ColumnGrand:=True

        Status "Adding fields to pivot table."
        .PivotTables(1).AddFields _
            RowFields:=Array("Last Name", "First Name"), _
            ColumnFields:=Array("Year"), _
            AddToTable:=True
```

continued on next page

continued from previous page

```
        Status "Setting the data field for the pivot table."
        .PivotTables(1).PivotFields("Units").Orientation = xlDataField

        sRange = Chr(Asc("A") + j + 1) & "3"
        .Range(sRange).Select

        Status "Turning off the subtotal lines for each row."
        .PivotTables(1).PivotFields("Last Name").Subtotals = _
            Array(False, False, False, False, False, False, _
            False, False, False, False, False, False)

    End With

    Status "Pivot table completed."
    DoEvents
    AppActivate "Microsoft Excel"
    Me.MousePointer = iSaveCursor
    cmdChart.Enabled = True
    cmdLoadSS.Enabled = False

End Sub
```

12. Add the `OpenDataSource` function procedure. This is the procedure which opens the connection to the `Books Available` data source using VB's RDOs.

The code puts the `SQL SELECT` statement in the `sSQL` string variable. This query summarizes data in the authors, sales, and titles tables in the PUBS database, to create a resultset which contains a record for each author for every year in which he had sales. The data in the source tables ranges from 1992 through 1994, so each author could have zero to three records in the resultset. See the How It Works section later for more information about how this works.

```
Private Function OpenDataSource()
Dim sSQL As String
Dim rdoPS As rdoPreparedStatement

    'Allocate an ODBC environment handle
    Set mrdoEnv = rdoEnvironments(0)
    Set mrdoConn = mrdoEnv.OpenConnection("Books Available", _
        rdDriverNoPrompt, False, "ODBC;UID=sa;PWD=")

    sSQL = "SELECT authors.au_lname 'Last Name', " _
        & "authors.au_fname 'First Name', " _
        & "Sum(sales.qty) 'Units', " _
        & "datepart(year,(sales.ord_date)) 'Year' " _
        & "FROM authors, sales, titleauthor " _
        & "WHERE titleauthor.au_id = authors.au_id " _
        & "AND titleauthor.title_id = sales.title_id " _
        & "GROUP BY authors.au_lname, authors.au_fname, " _
        & "datepart(year,(sales.ord_date)) " _
        & "ORDER BY authors.au_lname, authors.au_fname"

    On Error GoTo OpenDataSourceError
```

```
    Set mrdoRS = mrdoConn.OpenResultset(sSQL, rdOpenForwardOnly)
    OpenDataSource = True

    Exit Function

OpenDataSourceError:
    frmRDOErrors.ErrorColl = rdoErrors
    OpenDataSource = False
End Function

Sub Status(sCaption)
    StatusBar1.SimpleText = sCaption
    StatusBar1.Refresh
End Sub
```

13. Once the pivot table is created in Excel, the `cmdLoadSS` enables the
`cmdChart` button on the form. Add the following code to the `cmdChart`
command button's `Click` event procedure. This procedure uses the new
pivot table to create the bar chart shown in Figure 8-19.

The code sets up the parameters needed by the Excel `ChartWizard`
method to create the bar chart. Since the Excel sheet is a new worksheet
and the code in this application just created a single pivot table, this code
references the first and only pivot table, `PivotTables(1)`. The
`TableRange1` method returns a reference to the full area of the table less
any page fields (this How-To doesn't use page fields). A companion
method, `TableRange2`, selects the entire table including the page fields.
But `TableRange1` includes the row and column totals which I don't want
to include in the chart, since those larger numbers skew the results and
make the chart harder to use. This means using the `Selection.Row` and
`.Column` properties, along with a count of the columns in the range (the
pivot table) to determine the size of the range and reduce it by one row and
one column. When I have this information, I rebuild the `sRange` string
variable to specify the range to be included in the chart.

The code can at last call the `ChartWizard` method to create the chart,
using the edited range of the table and a column chart of type 3 (stacked
bars).

```
Private Sub cmdChart_Click()
Dim iRow As Integer
Dim iCol As Integer
Dim iRowCount As Integer
Dim iColCount As Integer
Dim sRange As String
Dim iSaveCursor As Integer

    iSaveCursor = Me.MousePointer
    Me.MousePointer = vbHourglass

    With mobjExcel
        'Select the pivot table
```

continued on next page

continued from previous page

```
        .PivotTables(1).TableRange1.Select

        'TableRange1 includes cells we don't want,
        'so get the range of cells and cut it down
        'to exclude the row and column totals, and the
        'fields at the top of the table.
        iRow = .Application.Selection.Row
        iCol = .Application.Selection.Column
        iRowCount = .Application.Selection.Rows.Count
        iColCount = .Application.Selection.Columns.Count

        sRange = Chr(Asc("A") + iCol - 1) _
            & LTrim(Str(iRow + 1)) & ":" _
            & Chr(Asc("A") + iCol + iColCount - 3) _
            & LTrim(Str(iRow + iRowCount - 2))
        .Range(sRange).Select

        'Add the chart.
        .ChartObjects.Add(40, 40, 575, 325).Select
        .Application.CutCopyMode = False
        .Application.ActiveChart.ChartWizard Source:=.Range(sRange), _
            Gallery:=xlColumn, Format:=3, PlotBy:=xlColumns, _
            CategoryLabels:=1, SeriesLabels:=1, HasLegend:=1
    End With

    Status "Pivot chart completed."
    DoEvents
    AppActivate "Microsoft Excel"
    Me.MousePointer = iSaveCursor
    cmdChart.Enabled = False
End Sub
```

14. Add the following code to the `cmdQuit` command button's `Click` event to unload the form and thus end the application.

```
Private Sub cmdQuit_Click()
    Unload Me
End Sub
```

15. Add the following code to the form's `Unload` event procedure. This code sets the object and remote data object variables to `Nothing`, releasing their memory. In most cases it is best to release these variables in the form's `Unload` event so they are explicitly released even if the form isn't closing as a result of the end-user clicking the Quit button.

```
Private Sub Form_Unload(Cancel As Integer)
    'Release the module-level variable objects.
    Set mrdoEnv = Nothing
    Set mrdoConn = Nothing
    Set mrdoRS = Nothing
    Set mobjExcel = Nothing
End Sub
```

16. In the Tools Project Options menu item, set the startup form to `frmPivot`. You can also set an application description, but that is not required for the operation of this application.

How It Works

A pivot table is a useful way to analyze data that consists of multiple records for each entity of interest, in which you are interested in a couple of characteristics for each entity. For example, Table 8-15 lists the results of the query used in the code for this How-To:

```
SELECT authors.au_lname 'Last Name', authors.au_fname 'First Name',
    Sum(sales.qty) 'Units', datepart(year,(sales.ord_date)) 'Year'
FROM authors, sales, titleauthor
WHERE titleauthor.au_id = authors.au_id
    AND titleauthor.title_id = sales.title_id
GROUP BY authors.au_lname, authors.au_fname, datepart(year,(sales.ord_date))
ORDER BY authors.au_lname, authors.au_fname
```

This SQL statement takes a first step in summarizing the data into a form which can easily be used by Excel's Pivot Table Wizard. Notice that several of the authors have more than one record in the table, meaning that their book or books had at least one sale in each of multiple years. This format makes analyzing the data very difficult, all the more so when you are working with thousands of rows of data, such as when an individual author might have dozens of records in the data.

Table 8-15 Data from the PUBS SQL Server database used in this How-To

LAST NAME	FIRST NAME	UNITS	YEAR
Bennet	Abraham	15	1994
Blotchet-Halls	Reginald	20	1992
Carson	Cheryl	30	1993
DeFrance	Michel	40	1994
del Castillo	Innes	10	1993
Dull	Ann	50	1993
Green	Marjorie	35	1993
Green	Marjorie	15	1994
Gringlesby	Burt	20	1992
Hunter	Sheryl	50	1993
Karsen	Livia	20	1993
Locksley	Charlene	25	1993
MacFeather	Stearns	45	1993
O'Leary	Michael	20	1992
O'Leary	Michael	25	1993

continued on next page

continued from previous page

LAST NAME	FIRST NAME	UNITS	YEAR
Panteley	Sylvia	40	1992
Ringer	Albert	25	1993
Ringer	Albert	108	1994
Singer	Anne	148	1994
Straight	Dean	15	1993
White	Johnson	15	1993
Yokomoto	Akiko	20	1992

The resulting pivot table, shown in Table 8-16, provides a format much easier to analyze. In one glance, you can see each author's yearly sales.

Table 8-16 Pivot table generated from the data in Table 8-15

LAST NAME	FIRST NAME	1992	1993	1994	GRAND TOTAL
Bennet	Abraham	0	0	15	15
Blotchet-Halls	Reginald	20	0	0	20
Carson	Cheryl	0	30	0	30
DeFrance	Michel	0	0	40	40
del Castillo	Innes	0	10	0	10
Dull	Ann	0	50	0	50
Green	Marjorie	0	35	15	50
Gringlesby	Burt	20	0	0	20
Hunter	Sheryl	0	50	0	50
Karsen	Livia	0	20	0	20
Kiely	Don	50	75	95	220
Locksley	Charlene	0	25	0	25
MacFeather	Stearns	0	45	0	45
O'Leary	Michael	20	25	0	45
Panteley	Sylvia	40	0	0	40
Ringer	Albert	0	25	108	133
Singer	Anne	0	0	148	148
Straight	Dean	0	15	0	15
White	Johnson	0	15	0	15
Yokomoto	Akiko	20	0	0	20
Grand Total		170	420	421	1011

Most of the hard work in producing the pivot table takes place within Excel, so the Visual Basic code in this How-To serves mostly to read data and place it into the spreadsheet. Then the code calls the Excel Pivot Table Wizard to create the table. Then the Excel Chart Wizard charts the pivot table. This is an example of producing relatively simple code by using the sophisticated features of an OLE server, in this case Excel.

SAMPLE CLIENT/SERVER APPLICATIONS

by Noel Jerke

SAMPLE CLIENT/SERVER APPLICATIONS

How do I...

9.1 Build a three-tier client/server transaction processing application?

9.2 Build a three-tier client/server decision support system?

9.3 Build a three-tier client/server image tracking system?

This book encompasses many topics that go into building client/server applications and focuses heavily on building three-tier applications using the tools provided in Visual Basic 5. This chapter serves to pull together many of these concepts into three examples that help to demonstrate how all these techniques can be combined.

The first two examples used in this chapter will demonstrate building a simple inventory order entry and decision support system. Certainly a full inventory management system cannot be built and demonstrated within the scope of this chapter, but key components will be developed to demonstrate building three-tier applications.

The inventory system will be for a company, WeeSchool, Inc., a wholesaler of school supplies. The first How-To will implement two order transaction processes for selling and adding inventory. The first process will be an order system for filling orders taken from salespersons. The second process will be for taking restock orders from suppliers. The application will utilize basic user interface services for the first tier. Several second-tier business objects will be implemented for encapsulating the underlying business logic. Finally the third-tier Data services layer will consist of an SQL Server database and a series of stored procedures.

The second How-To will build on these same sets of business objects and the SQL database to implement a simple set of decision support utilities for the inventory system. The primary value of this example is to show how the same set of business objects developed in the first How-To can be reused to provide the new functionality. In this example, only the first tier needs to be completely redesigned; the second tier requires only minimal additional functionality; the third tier will require no modifications.

> **NOTE**
>
> To build the SQL database needed for these first two examples, run the WholeSale.SQL script located in the Chapter 9 folder on the CD. This script was built from a Microsoft SQL 6.5 database. Note that you must provide Stock Item, Suppliers, and Salespersons *seed* data to utilize the database. Example data is provided in both How-To's 9.1 and 9.2. Also, the applications will look for a 32-bit ODBC connection, WholeSale, for connecting to the database.

The third How-To will take the sample two-tier image tracking application built in Chapter 4, User Interface Design, and convert it into a three-tier application. This new example will abstract away the primary objects in the application into classes and will also utilize stored procedures and the SQL Server.

> **NOTE**
>
> To build the database for the third How-To, run the IData.SQL script located in the Chapter 9 folder on the CD. This script was built from an SQL 6.5 database. Also, the application will look for a 32-bit ODBC connection, Image Data, for connecting to the database.

9.1 Build a Three-Tier Client/Server Transaction Processing Application

Two-Tier Transaction processing applications are a familiar format for Visual Basic applications. But, with the addition of object-oriented features in Visual Basic and support for ActiveX components, these applications can be built, partitioned, and deployed in a new way that allows for a separate business logic tier. This How-To will utilize all three tiers to build a sample inventory transaction processing system.

9.2 Build a Three-Tier Client/Server Decision Support System

This How-To will build on the first and second tiers developed in the last How-To to implement several decision support tools for supporting the inventory system. A Sales Commission review tool will be developed for analyzing a salesperson's performance and adjusting the commission rate appropriately. Also, a review tool will be developed for analyzing the sales history of a stock item and adjusting the sale price appropriately. Finally, a tool is created for reviewing overall order history by date.

9.3 Build a Three-Tier Client/Server Image Tracking System

The example How-To's developed in Chapter 4, User Interface Design, were primarily created to demonstrate MDI user interface design techniques. These examples were not built to be three-tier client applications primarily because they utilized the remote data control and did not encapsulate important business objects into classes. This How-To will take the How-To 4.5 application and turn it into a true three-tier client/server application.

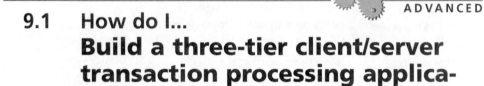

COMPLEXITY
ADVANCED

9.1 How do I...
Build a three-tier client/server transaction processing application?

Problem

With Visual Basic 5, Microsoft has provided many tools for doing enterprise client/server development. This book has demonstrated many new techniques for building my client/server applications. How can I combine all of this together to build a three-tier client/server transaction processing system?

Technique

The key to building a three-tier client/server application is dividing the programming logic between the user interface, the encapsulated business objects, and the Data services layer. In this example, the user interface will handle presenting the information to the user and receiving the user input. The business objects layer will encapsulate the different objects we will use in the inventory transaction system. Table 9-1 outlines the business objects that will be developed.

Table 9-1 Second-tier business objects

BUSINESS OBJECT	DESCRIPTION
clsData	Encapsulates the interface to the data services layer.
clsOrderItem	Encapsulates a single item in an order of school supplies.
clsSalesPerson	A salesperson.
clsStockItem	Encapsulates an inventory stock item.
clsStockOrder	An order for inventory stock.
clsSupplier	The supplier of stock items.
clsSupplyOrder	An order for supplies from inventory.

These business objects will collaborate with the user interface to provide the fundamental functionality of the application. These objects can be implemented in an ActiveX component at any point on the network and could be managed by a pool manager. The Data services layer will be implemented on an SQL Server and will utilize several stored procedures. Table 9-2 reviews each.

Table 9-2 Third-tier SQL Server stored procedures

STORED PROCEDURE	DESCRIPTION
Insert_Stock_Order	Inserts a new stock order and returns the order ID.
Insert_Supply_Order	Inserts a new supply order and returns the order ID.
InsertSaleItem	Inserts a new ordered item.
UpdateBackOrder	Updates the backorder quantity.
UpdateShelfQuantity	Updates the shelf inventory quantity.

By combining these tools we will have an object-oriented three-tier application that can be partitioned easily to fit the underlying network architecture and can be scaled for transaction load.

NOTE

Steps 107 through 112 will explain how to set up and seed the WholeSale database for this application. Also, you will need to have a 32-bit ODBC data source for the database. In this example, the database was set up in Microsoft SQL Server 6.5 as WholeSale and the ODBC DSN was also set to WholeSale. You may place the database tables and choose a name; just ensure the ODBC connection is set up properly (refer to Chapter 2, Getting Connected).

Steps

First open and run the 9-1-Srv.VBP project. This project will load the appropriate objects for the user interface project. Next, open the 9-1.VBP project. You will have to delete the current reference to WholeSale Objects and then add a reference to the currently running WholeSale Objects. Then run 9-1.VBP. The running program appears as shown in Figure 9-1.

This program has two functions: ordering from inventory by a salesperson to fulfill a customer order, and ordering from suppliers to restock inventory. To place an order for school supplies, click on the Supplies Order button. Figure 9-2 shows the data entry form for ordering items from inventory. Select the item you want to order and enter the quantity to order. The various fields show the purchase and sale price of the items as well as the quantity in stock and on back order. The bottom frame shows the TotalSale and Net profit.

When the supply order is placed, you will need to select the salesperson who is placing the order. The second tab will allow you to do this. This will also show the commission rate for the salesperson and the total commission for the sale as shown in Figure 9-3.

Figure 9-1 The form as it appears at runtime

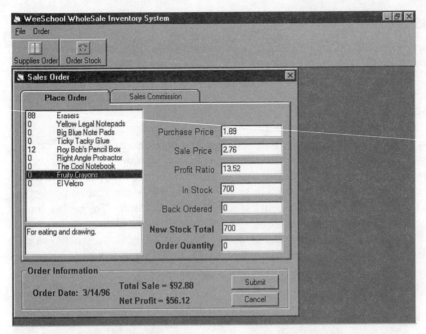

Figure 9-2 The Place Order tab for the Supply Order form

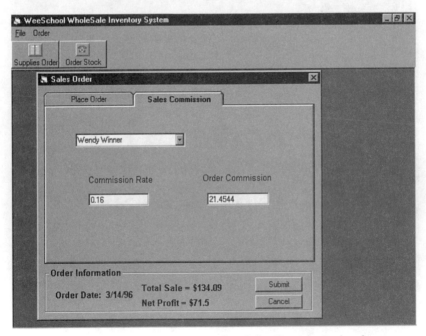

Figure 9-3 The Sales Commission tab of the Supply Order form

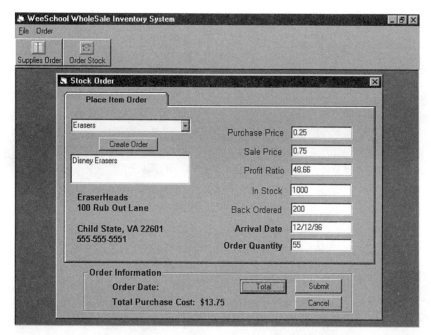

Figure 9-4 The Stock Order form

Once the order is finished, click on the Submit button to place the order. This process handles ordering items from inventory. To order stock for inventory, select the Order Stock button. Figure 9-4 shows the Stock Order form.

Select an item from the drop-down listbox. Click on the Create Order button to place an order for the item. Enter the Order Quantity and Arrival Date for the order. To get the Total Purchase price for the order, select the Total button. To submit the order, select Submit.

1. Create a new project called 9-1.VBP. Add the objects and properties listed in Table 9-3 to Form1 and save the form as 9-1.FRM.

Table 9-3 The form's objects and properties

OBJECT	PROPERTY	SETTING
MDIForm	Name	MDIForm1
	AutoShowChildren	0 'False
	Caption	"WeeSchool WholeSale Inventory System"
	WindowState	2 'Maximized
ImageList	Name	ImageList1

continued on next page

continued from previous page

OBJECT	PROPERTY	SETTING
	ImageWidth	24
	ImageHeight	22
	NumImages	2
	i1	"9-1.frx":0000
	i2	"9-1.frx":023F
Toolbar	Name	Toolbar1
	Align	1 'Align Top
	ImageList	"ImageList1"
	ButtonWidth	2011
	ButtonHeight	1111
	NumButtons	2

2. Add the menus in Table 9-4 to the MDI form.

Table 9-4 The ImageTracker form's menus

MENU NAME	CAPTION
mFile	"&File"
mOpenImage	"&Open Image Database"
mBar	"-"
mExit	"E&xit"
mWindow	"&Window"
mImageData	"Image &Data"
mImageView	"Image &View"
mFile	"&File"
mExit	"E&xit"
mOrder	"Order"
mSupplyOrd	"Supplies Order"
mStockOrd	"Order Stock"

3. Add a new form to the project and save it as StockOrd.frm. Add the objects and properties listed in Table 9-5 to the form.

Table 9-5 The StockOrd form's objects and properties

OBJECT	PROPERTY	SETTING
Form	Name	StockOrd
	BorderStyle	1 'Fixed Single

OBJECT	PROPERTY	SETTING
	Caption	"Stock Order"
	MaxButton	0 'False
	MDIChild	-1 'True
Frame	Name	Frame1
	Caption	"Order Information"
	Font	
	name	"Arial"
	weight	700
	size	9.75
CommandButton	Name	Total
	Caption	"Total"
CommandButton	Name	Submit
	Caption	"Submit"
CommandButton	Name	Cancel
	Caption	"Cancel"
Label	Name	OrderDate
	AutoSize	-1 'True
	Caption	"Order Date:"
	Font	
	name	"Arial"
	weight	700
	size	9.75
Label	Name	TotalPurch
	AutoSize	-1 'True
	Caption	"Total Purchase Cost: $"
	Font	
	name	"Arial"
	weight	700
	size	9.75
SSTab	Name	SSTab1
	Caption	"Place Item Order"
	TabsPerRow	3
	Tab	0
	TabOrientation	0
	Tabs	1
	Style	0

continued on next page

continued from previous page

OBJECT	PROPERTY	SETTING
	TabCaption(0)	"Place Item Order"
	Tab(0).ControlCount	18
	Tab(0).Control(0)	"Label3(2)"
	Tab(0).Control(1)	"Label2(1)"
	Tab(0).Control(2)	"Label3(1)"
	Tab(0).Control(3)	"Label3(0)"
	Tab(0).Control(4)	"Label2(0)"
	Tab(0).Control(5)	"Label1(0)"
	Tab(0).Control(6)	"Label1(1)"
	Tab(0).Control(7)	"Supplier"
	Tab(0).Control(8)	"ItemDesc"
	Tab(0).Control(9)	"ProfitRatio"
	Tab(0).Control(10)	"PPrice"
	Tab(0).Control(11)	"SPrice"
	Tab(0).Control(12)	"BackOrder"
	Tab(0).Control(13)	"InStock"
	Tab(0).Control(14)	"Quantity"
	Tab(0).Control(15)	"StockList"
	Tab(0).Control(16)	"ArrivalDate"
	Tab(0).Control(17)	"CreateOrder"
CommandButton	Name	CreateOrder
	Caption	"Create Order"
TextBox	Name	ArrivalDate
ComboBox	Name	StockList
TextBox	Name	Quantity
	Text	"0"
TextBox	Name	InStock
	Locked	-1 'True
	Text	"0"
TextBox	Name	BackOrder
	Locked	-1 'True
	Text	"0"
TextBox	Name	SPrice
	Locked	-1 'True
	Text	"0"

OBJECT	PROPERTY	SETTING
TextBox	Name	PPrice
	Locked	-1 'True
	Text	"0"
TextBox	Name	ProfitRatio
	Locked	-1 'True
	Text	"0"
TextBox	Name	ItemDesc
	Locked	-1 'True
	MultiLine	-1 'True
Label	Name	Supplier
	Font	
	name	"Arial"
	weight	700
	size	9.75
Label	Name	Label1
	AutoSize	-1 'True
	Caption	"Arrival Date"
	Font	
	name	"Arial"
	weight	700
	size	9.75
	Index	1
Label	Name	Label1
	AutoSize	-1 'True
	Caption	"Order Quantity"
	Font	
	name	"Arial"
	weight	700
	size	9.75
	Index	0
Label	Name	Label2
	AutoSize	-1 'True
	Caption	"In Stock"
	Font	
	name	"Arial"
	weight	400
	size	9.75

continued on next page

continued from previous page

OBJECT	PROPERTY	SETTING
	Index	0
Label	Name	Label3
	AutoSize	-1 'True
	Caption	"Back Ordered"
	Font	
	name	"Arial"
	weight	700
	size	9.75
	Index	0
Label	Name	Label3
	AutoSize	-1 'True
	Caption	"Sale Price"
	Font	
	name	"Arial"
	weight	400
	size	9.75
	Index	1
Label	Name	Label2
	AutoSize	-1 'True
	Caption	"Purchase Price"
	Font	
	name	"Arial"
	weight	400
	size	9.75
	Index	1
Label	Name	Label3
	AutoSize	-1 'True
	Caption	"Profit Ratio"
	Font	
	name	"Arial"
	weight	400
	size	9.75
	Index	2

4. Insert the following form into the project and save it as SupplyOrd.frm. Add the objects and properties listed in Table 9-6 to the form.

Table 9-6 The form's objects and properties

OBJECT	PROPERTY	SETTING
Form	Name	SupplyOrd
	BorderStyle	1 'Fixed Single
	Caption	"Sales Order"
	MDIChild	-1 'True
Frame	Name	Frame1
	Caption	"Order Information"
	Font	
	name	"Arial"
	weight	700
	size	9.75
CommandButton	Name	Cancel
	Caption	"Cancel"
CommandButton	Name	Submit
	Caption	"Submit"
Label	Name	NetProfit
	AutoSize	-1 'True
	Caption	"Net Profit:"
	Font	
	name	"Arial"
	weight	700
	size	9.75
Label	Name	TotalSale
	AutoSize	-1 'True
	Caption	"Total Sale:"
	Font	
	name	"Arial"
	weight	700
	size	9.75
Label	Name	OrderDate
	AutoSize	-1 'True
	Caption	"Order Date:"
	Font	
	name	"Arial"
	weight	700
	size	9.75

continued on next page

continued from previous page

OBJECT	PROPERTY	SETTING
SSTab	Name	SSTab1
	TabIndex	0
	Caption	"Sales Commission"
	TabsPerRow	3
	Tab	1
	TabOrientation	0
	Tabs	2
	Style	0
	TabCaption(0)	"Place Order"
	Tab(0).ControlCount	16
	Tab(0).Control(0)	"Label1(0)"
	Tab(0).Control(1)	"Label2(0)"
	Tab(0).Control(2)	"Label3(0)"
	Tab(0).Control(3)	"Label3(1)"
	Tab(0).Control(4)	"Label2(1)"
	Tab(0).Control(5)	"Label3(2)"
	Tab(0).Control(6)	"Label1(1)"
	Tab(0).Control(7)	"StockList"
	Tab(0).Control(8)	"Quantity"
	Tab(0).Control(9)	"InStock"
	Tab(0).Control(10)	"BackOrder"
	Tab(0).Control(11)	"SPrice"
	Tab(0).Control(12)	"PPrice"
	Tab(0).Control(13)	"ProfitRatio"
	Tab(0).Control(14)	"ItemDesc"
	Tab(0).Control(15)	"NewStock"
	TabCaption(1)	"Sales Commission"
	Tab(1).ControlCount	5
	Tab(1).Control(0)	"Label4"
	Tab(1).Control(1)	"Label5"
	Tab(1).Control(2)	"ComRate"
	Tab(1).Control(3)	"Sales"
	Tab(1).Control(4)	"OrderCom"
TextBox	Name	NewStock
	Text	"0"

OBJECT	PROPERTY	SETTING
TextBox	Name	ItemDesc
	Locked	-1 'True
	MultiLine	-1 'True
TextBox	Name	ProfitRatio
	Locked	-1 'True
	Text	"0"
TextBox	Name	PPrice
	Locked	-1 'True
	Text	"0"
TextBox	Name	SPrice
	Locked	-1 'True
	Text	"0"
TextBox	Name	OrderCom
	Locked	-1 'True
ComboBox	Name	Sales
TextBox	Name	ComRate
	Locked	-1 'True
TextBox	Name	BackOrder
	Locked	-1 'True
	Text	"0"
TextBox	Name	InStock
	Locked	-1 'True
	Text	"0"
TextBox	Name	Quantity
	Text	"0"
ListBox	Name	StockList
Label	Name	Label1
	AutoSize	-1 'True
	Caption	"New Stock Total"
	Font	
	name	"Arial"
	weight	700
	size	9.75
	Index	1
Label	Name	Label3
	AutoSize	-1 'True

continued on next page

continued from previous page

OBJECT	PROPERTY	SETTING
	Caption	"Profit Ratio"
	Font	
	name	"Arial"
	weight	400
	size	9.75
	Index	2
Label	Name	Label2
	AutoSize	-1 'True
	Caption	"Purchase Price"
	Font	
	name	"Arial"
	weight	400
	size	9.75
	Index	1
Label	Name	Label3
	AutoSize	-1 'True
	Caption	"Sale Price"
	Font	
	name	"Arial"
	weight	400
	size	9.75
	Index	1
Label	Name	Label5
	AutoSize	-1 'True
	Caption	"Order Commission"
	Font	
	name	"Arial"
	weight	400
	size	9.75
	Label	Label4
	AutoSize	-1 'True
	Caption	"Commission Rate"
	Font	
	name	"Arial"
	weight	400
	size	9.75

OBJECT	PROPERTY	SETTING
Label	Name	Label3
	AutoSize	-1 'True
	Caption	"Back Ordered"
	Font	
	name	"Arial"
	weight	400
	size	9.75
	Index	0
Label	Name	Label2
	AutoSize	-1 'True
	Caption	"In Stock"
	Font	
	name	"Arial"
	weight	400
	size	9.75
	Index	0
Label	Name	Label1
	AutoSize	-1 'True
	Caption	"Order Quantity"
	Font	
	name	"Arial"
	weight	700
	size	9.75
	Index	0

5. Add the following set of code to the MDI form. When the application is loaded, three functions are called to build collections of stock items, salespersons, and suppliers. These will be used throughout the application.

```
Private Sub MDIForm_Load()

'   Load up the collections for each
'   type of object
LoadStockItems
LoadSalesPersons
LoadSuppliers

End Sub
```

6. When the form is exited, the project is unloaded.

```
Private Sub mExit_Click()

'   Unload the project.
Unload Me

End Sub
```

7. When the Stock Order menu item is selected, a new stock order class is created and the stock order form is shown.

```
Private Sub mStockOrd_Click()

'   Create a new stock order by instantiating a new object of the
'   clsStockItemOrder class
Set StockOrder = New clsStockItemOrder

'   Show the form
StockOrd.Show

End Sub
```

8. When the Supply Order menu is selected, a new supply order class is created. Then the supply order form is shown.

```
Private Sub mSupplyOrd_Click()

'   Create a new supply order by instantiating a new
'   object of the clsSupplyOrder class
Set SupplyOrder = New clsSupplyOrder

'   Show the form
SupplyOrd.Show

End Sub
```

9. When the toolbar is selected, the appropriate order class is created and the
form is shown.

```
Private Sub Toolbar1_ButtonClick(ByVal Button As Button)

Select Case Button.Index

    Case 1
        '   Create a new supply order and
        '   show the form
        Set SupplyOrder = New clsSupplyOrder
        SupplyOrd.Show

    Case 2
        '   Create a new stock order and
        '   show the form
        Set StockOrder = New clsStockItemOrder
        StockOrd.Show

End Select

End Sub
```

10. Add the following set of code to the **StockOrd** form. The **SubmitFlag** will be used to record whether the order has been submitted. If it has, then the form will be unloaded without a query.

```
Option Explicit

'   Flag used for indicating that the order
'   has been submitted
Dim SubmitFlag As Integer
```

11. Add the following procedure to the General Declarations section of the stock order form. **TotalPurchase** handles setting the quantity ordered and displaying the total purchase price for the item.

```
Private Sub TotalPurchase()

'   Set the stock item that is to be
'   purchased
StockOrder.PurchaseItem = StockList.ItemData(StockList.ListIndex)

'   Set the quantity to be ordered
StockOrder.Quantity = Quantity.Text

'   Calculate the total purchase price
'   for the order and display it
totalpurch.Caption = "Total Purchase Cost:   $" & StockOrder.TotalPurchase

End Sub
```

12. When the Cancel button is selected, the form is unloaded.

```
Private Sub Cancel_Click()

'   Unload the form
Unload Me

End Sub
```

13. When the **CreateOrder** button is clicked, the list of stock items is disabled. Also, the order date is displayed.

```
Private Sub CreateOrder_Click()

'   When an item is to be ordered,
'   do not allow the user to select
'   another item to be ordered
StockList.Enabled = False

'   Show the order date
OrderDate.Caption = Date

End Sub
```

14. When the form is loaded, a listbox is filled with the stock items. The **ItemData** property will hold the item ID for later easy reference.

```
Private Sub Form_Load()

Dim SI As Object
Dim Cnt As Integer

'  When the form is loaded, the stock list
'  box is filled.  The item data property of
'  the listbox will have the Item ID of the
listed item

'  init array counter
Cnt=0

For Each SI In StockItems
    StockList.AddItem SI.ItemName
    StockList.ItemData(Cnt) = SI.ItemID
    Cnt = Cnt + 1
Next

End Sub
```

15. When the form is unloaded, if an order is in progress, a check is done to see whether the order has been submitted. If not, then the user is queried on whether they want to continue.

```
Private Sub Form_Unload(Cancel As Integer)

Dim MSG As String
Dim Style As Integer
Dim Title As Integer
Dim Response As Integer

'  Check to see if an order is in progress
If (StockList.Enabled = False) Then

    '  Check to see if the order has
    '  been submitted
    If SubmitFlag <> True Then

        '  Query the user to see if they really
        '  want to quit without submitting the
        '  order
        MSG = "Cancel Order and don't save?"   ' Define message.
        Style = vbYesNo + vbCritical + vbDefaultButton2 ' Define buttons.
        Title = "Cancel Order"   ' Define title.

        Response = MsgBox(MSG, Style, Title)

        If Response = vbNo Then     ' User chose Yes.
            Cancel = True
        Else
            '  Kill the order class when done
            Set StockOrder = Nothing
        End If

    End If
```

```
'  Kill the order class when done
Set StockOrder = Nothing

End If

End Sub
```

16. When each item in the stock list is selected, the sale price, shelf quantity, quantity on back order, product description, supplier, and profit ratio are shown. Notice that the **With** construct is used to make referencing the collection item easier.

```
Private Sub StockList_Click()

Dim SText As String

'  Set the index for the following
'  items
With StockItems.Item(CStr(StockList.ItemData(StockList.ListIndex)))

    '  Get the purchase price
    PPrice.Text = .PurchasePrice

    '  Get the sale price
    SPrice.Text = .SalePrice

    '  Get the number on back order
    BackOrder.Text = .BackOrder

    '  Get the quantity on the shelf
    InStock.Text = .ShelfQuantity

    '  Get the profit ratio and only show
    '  two decimal points.
    ProfitRatio.Text = Left(.ProfitPercentage, 5)

    '  Show the item description
    ItemDesc.Text = .ItemDesc

    '  The following lines build the address of the
    '  supplier
    SText = Suppliers.Item(.SupplierID).Name

    SText = SText + Chr$(13) + Suppliers.Item(.SupplierID).Address1

    SText = SText + Chr$(13) + Suppliers.Item(.SupplierID).Address2

    SText = SText + Chr$(13) + Suppliers.Item(.SupplierID).City

    SText = SText + ", " + Suppliers.Item(.SupplierID).State

    SText = SText + " " + Suppliers.Item(.SupplierID).Zip

    SText = SText + Chr$(13) + Suppliers.Item(.SupplierID).Phone
```

continued on next page

continued from previous page
```
End With

'   Show the address
Supplier.Caption = SText

End Sub
```

17. When the Submit button is clicked, a check is first done to make sure an order is in progress. If so, then a check is done to ensure an arrival date is entered as well as a quantity. Then the `TotalPurchase` function is called to get the total purchase price and the order and arrival date is set. Finally the order is stored and the `SubmitFlag` is set to `True`.

```
Private Sub Submit_Click()

'   Don't submit a job if we are not in
'   order mode for an item
If StockList.Enabled = True Then Exit Sub

'   Check to see if an arrival date
'   and quantity has been entered
If ArrivalDate.Text = "" Then MsgBox "You have not entered in an arrival ⇐
date.": Exit Sub

If Val(Quantity.Text) = 0 Then MsgBox "You have not entered in an ⇐
order quantity.": Exit Sub

'   Calculate the total purchase
TotalPurchase

'   Set the orderdate
StockOrder.OrderDate = Date

'   Set the arrival date
StockOrder.ArrivalDate = CDate(ArrivalDate.Text)

'   Save the order
StockOrder.StoreOrder

'   Set the submitflag so that
'   the form can be unloaded without
'   a query.
SubmitFlag = True

'   Unload the form
Unload Me

End Sub
```

18. When the total button is selected, the total purchase price is shown.

```
Private Sub Total_Click()

'   Calculate and display the
'   total purchase price
```

```
TotalPurchase

End Sub
```

19. Add the following set of code to the `SupplyOrd` form. The `SubmitFlag` will indicate whether the form should be unloaded without a cancel query. `CurrentItem` indicates the currently selected item in the stock listbox.

```
Option Explicit

'   The SubmitFlag is used to determine
'   if the order has been submitted.
Dim SubmitFlag As Integer

'   CurrentItem will keep track of the
'   current stock item being worked with
Dim CurrentItem As Integer
```

20. Add the following procedure to the General Declarations section of the form. The sales commission for the supply order is calculated by calling the `CalculateCommission` method of the salesperson class and sending in the total order price.

```
Private Sub UpdateCommission()

'   Set the sales commission for the order
If Sales.ListIndex <> -1 Then SupplyOrder.SalesCommission = ⇐
SalesPersons.Item(Sales.ListIndex + 1). ⇐
CalculateCommission(SupplyOrder.CalculateTotalOrderPrice)

'   Show the commission for the order
OrderCom.Text = SupplyOrder.SalesCommission

End Sub
```

21. Add the following code to the General Declarations section of the form. First, the quantity ordered is updated by calling `UpdateSaleItem` method of the `SupplyOrder` class. Then the listbox display is updated to show the current order quantity. Next, the sales commission is calculated and the total sale shown. The `NetProfit` is shown and calculated with the `CalculateNetProfit` method of the class. Also, the new shelf quantity for the item is calculated and displayed.

```
Private Sub UpdateOrderCount()

'   Update the sale item for this order to have
'   the new quantity for the order
SupplyOrder.UpdateSaleItem StockList.ItemData(CurrentItem),
Val(Quantity.Text)

'   Show the order count
StockList.List(CurrentItem) = Quantity.Text & " " & Chr$(9) &
```

continued on next page

continued from previous page

```
StockItems.Item(CStr(StockList.ItemData(CurrentItem))).ItemName

'   Update the commission figure
UpdateCommission

'   Calculate the total sale for the order
TotalSale.Caption = "Total Sale = $" & SupplyOrder.CalculateTotalOrderPrice

'   Calculate the net profit
NetProfit.Caption = "Net Profit = $" & SupplyOrder.CalculateNetProfit

'   Set the index for the following items
With StockItems.Item(CStr(StockList.ItemData(CurrentItem)))

    '   Show the new in stock count
    NewStock.Text = .ShelfQuantity -
SupplyOrder.GetSaleItemQuantity(StockList.ItemData(CurrentItem))

    '   Show the current quantity
    InStock.Text = .ShelfQuantity

End With

End Sub
```

22. When the Cancel button is selected, the form is unloaded.

```
Private Sub Cancel_Click()

'   Unload the form
Unload Me

End Sub
```

23. When the form is loaded, a listbox is filled with the stock items. The
ItemData property will hold the item ID for later easy reference. Also, a
listbox will be filled with the current set of salespersons.

```
Private Sub Form_Load()

Dim SI As Object
Dim SP As Object
Dim Cnt As Integer

'   Load the stock items into the
'   listbox.  The ItemData property
'   will contain the Item ID
For Each SI In StockItems
    StockList.AddItem "O " & Chr$(9) & SI.ItemName
    StockList.ItemData(Cnt) = SI.ItemID
    Cnt = Cnt + 1
Next

'   Load the sale persons in the
'   listbox
```

```
For Each SP In SalesPersons
    Sales.AddItem SP.FirstName + " " + SP.LastName
Next

'  Select the first item in the listbox
StockList.ListIndex = 0

'  Set the current stock item being
'  worked with
CurrentItem = 0

'  Set the order date
SupplyOrder.OrderDate = Date

' Show the order date
OrderDate.Caption = "Order Date:   " & Date

End Sub
```

24. When the form is unloaded, a check is done to see whether the order has been submitted. If not, the user is queried whether to continue.

```
Private Sub Form_Unload(Cancel As Integer)

Dim MSG As String
Dim Style As Integer
Dim Title As String
Dim Response As Integer

'  Check to see if the order has been submitted
If SubmitFlag <> True Then

    '  Query the user if they want to save the
    '  order or not.
    MSG = "Cancel Order and don't save?"    ' Define message.
    Style = vbYesNo + vbCritical + vbDefaultButton2 ' Define buttons.
    Title = "Cancel Order"   ' Define title.

    Response = MsgBox(MSG, Style, Title)

    If Response = vbNo Then      ' User chose Yes.
        Cancel = True
    Else
        '  Kill the order class if we are done
        Set SupplyOrder = Nothing
    End If

Else

    '  Kill the order class if we are done
    Set SupplyOrder = Nothing

End If

End Sub
```

25. On the salesperson tab, when the sales listbox is selected, the commission rate for the salesperson is shown and the `UpdateCommission` procedure is called to calculate the sales commission for the order.

```
Private Sub Sales_Click()

'   Show the commission rate
ComRate.Text = SalesPersons.Item(Sales.ListIndex + 1).CommissionRate

'   Update the order commission
UpdateCommission

End Sub
```

26. When the Tab button is selected, the order count and sales commission are updated.

```
Private Sub SSTab1_Click(PreviousTab As Integer)

'   Update the order count
UpdateOrderCount

'   Update the sales commission
UpdateCommission

End Sub
```

27. When a stock item is selected in the listbox, the order count is updated by calling `UpdateOrderCount`. Then the `CurrentItem` is updated to reflect the currently selected item. Next, the purchase price, sale price, description, profit ratio, back order quantity, shelf quantity, and new in-stock totals are shown.

```
Private Sub StockList_Click()

'   Update the order count
UpdateOrderCount

'   Get the current item
CurrentItem = StockList.ListIndex

'   Set the quantity for the new item
Quantity.Text =
SupplyOrder.GetSaleItemQuantity(StockList.ItemData(CurrentItem))

With StockItems.Item(CStr(StockList.ItemData(CurrentItem)))

'       Show the purchase price
PPrice.Text = .PurchasePrice

'       Show the sale price
SPrice.Text = .SalePrice

'       Show the quantity on back order
BackOrder.Text = .BackOrder
```

```
    '   Show the new stock count
    NewStock.Text = .ShelfQuantity - SupplyOrder.GetSaleItemQuantity( ⇐
      StockList.ItemData(CurrentItem))

    '   Show the current stock count
    InStock.Text = .ShelfQuantity

    '   Show the profit percentage
    ProfitRatio.Text = Left(.ProfitPercentage, 5)

    '   Show the description
    ItemDesc.Text = .ItemDesc

End With

End Sub
```

28. The Submit button `Click` event checks to see whether a salesperson is selected; if so, then the order count is updated and the order stored. Finally, the `SubmitFlag` is set to `True` so the form will be unloaded without a query.

```
Private Sub Submit_Click()

'   Check to ensure a salesperson is
'   selected
If Sales.ListIndex = -1 Then

MsgBox "You have not yet selected a salesperson for the order."

Exit Sub

End If

'   update the order count
UpdateOrderCount

'   Save the order
SupplyOrder.StoreOrder

'   Set the submit flag so no query
'   is given on the unload
SubmitFlag = True

'   unload the form
Unload Me

End Sub
```

29. Insert a new module into the project and save it as `Global.bas`. The `StockItems`, `SalesPersons`, and `Suppliers` collections are globally declared and will hold the current list for each. A class for both a supply order and stock order is globally declared for creating orders.

```
Option Explicit

Global StockItems As Collection
Global SalesPersons As Collection
Global SupplyOrder As clsSupplyOrder
Global StockOrder As clsStockItemOrder
Global Suppliers As Collection
```

30. When the project is loaded, the three classes are created and the MDI form shown.

```
Public Sub main()

'   Create the stock items collection
Set StockItems = New Collection

'   Create the salespersons collection
Set SalesPersons = New Collection

'   Create the suppliers collection
Set Suppliers = New Collection

'   Show the form
MDIForm1.Show

End Sub
```

31. The **LoadStockItems** procedure handles calling the **GetStockItems** method of the **clsStockItem** class. This method fills the referenced collection with a list of stock items. Note that we temporarily create a meta **clsStockItem** class to call the **GetStockItems** method. A meta class is usually utilized to work on an entire set of objects (in this case stock items), instead of a single item.

```
Public Sub LoadStockItems()

'   Create a meta stock class
Dim MetaSI As clsStockItem

Set MetaSI = New clsStockItem

'   Build the items in the class
MetaSI.GetStockItems StockItems

Set MetaSI = Nothing

End Sub
```

32. The **LoadSalesPersons** procedure handles calling the **GetSalesPersons** method of the **clsSalesPersons** class. This method fills the referenced collection with a list of salespersons. Note that we temporarily create a meta **clsSalesPersons** class to call the **GetSalesPersons** method.

```
Public Sub LoadSalesPersons()

'  Create a meta salespersons class
Dim MetaSP As clsSalesPerson

Set MetaSP = New clsSalesPerson

'  Get the salespersons
MetaSP.GetSalesPersons SalesPersons

Set MetaSP = Nothing

End Sub
```

33. The `LoadSuppliers` procedure handles calling the `GetSuppliers` method of the `clsSupplier` class. This method fills the referenced collection with a list of suppliers. Note that we temporarily create a meta `clsSupplier` class to call the `GetSuppliers` method.

```
Public Sub LoadSuppliers()

'  Create a meta supplier class
Dim MetaSI As clsSupplier

Set MetaSI = New clsSupplier

'  Get the suppliers
MetaSI.GetSuppliers Suppliers

Set MetaSI = Nothing

End Sub
```

34. Create a new project and save the project as 9-1-srv.vbp. Insert a new module into the project and save it as 9-1-srv.bas. Add the following code to the General Declarations section of the module. The `clsData` class is created for interfacing with the database.

```
Option Explicit

'  Globally declare the data class
Global DS As clsData

Public Sub Main()

'  Create the data class
Set DS = New clsData

End Sub
```

35. Insert a new class into the project and save it as `clsData.cls`. Add the following code to the General Declarations section of the class. A remote data environment, connection, and resultset are globally declared.

```
Option Explicit

' Dim a remote data environment
Dim Env As rdoEnvironment

' Dim a remote data connection
Dim Con As rdoConnection

' Declare a remote data record set
Dim RS As rdoResultset
```

36. The `InitConnect` method handles initializing a connection through ODBC to the SQL server. Note that you will need a 32-bit ODBC data source named WholeSale. Also, note that in order to use RDO–prepared statements that use multiple selects in the stored procedure, the cursors must be ODBC–based and not server-based. This is done by setting the RDO engines default cursor driver to use ODBC.

```
Public Sub InitConnect()

' Set the default engine cursor driver
' to ODBC.  This is needed to support calling
' stored procedures that use multiple select
' statments.
rdoEngine.rdoDefaultCursorDriver = rdUseOdbc

' Set the remote data environment
Set Env = rdoEnvironments(0)

' Open the ODBC connection
Set Con = Env.OpenConnection(dsName:="WholeSale", Prompt:=rdDriverNoPrompt)

End Sub
```

37. The `DBExec` method handles executing the specified command.

```
Private Sub DBExec(Cmd$)

' Execute the specified SQL Command
Con.Execute Cmd$

End Sub
```

38. The `DBOpenRec` method handles opening the specified resultset.

```
Private Sub DBOpenRec(Cmd$)

' Open a resulset based on the
' SQL query.  rdOpenKeySet indicates
' that the rows can be updated.
Set RS = Con.OpenResultset(Cmd$, rdOpenKeyset, rdConcurRowver)

End Sub
```

39. The `GetSuppliers` method returns a resultset of all the suppliers in the database.

```
Public Function GetSuppliers() As rdoResultset

' Get the list of suppliers
DBOpenRec "Select * from Suppliers"

Set GetSuppliers = RS

End Function
```

40. The `GetStockItems` method returns a resultset of all the stock items in a database.

```
Public Function GetStockItems() As rdoResultset

' Get the list of stock items
DBOpenRec "Select * from StockItem"

Set GetStockItems = RS

End Function
```

41. `GetBackOrder` returns the back ordered quantity for the specified stock item.

```
Public Function GetBackOrder(ItemID) As Long

' Get the back order quantity for the item
DBOpenRec "Select backorder from StockItem where itemid = " & ItemID

GetBackOrder = RS("backorder") & ""

End Function
```

42. `GetSalesPersons` returns a resultset of all the salespersons in the database.

```
Public Function GetSalesPersons() As rdoResultset

' Get the list of salespersons
DBOpenRec "Select * from SalesPerson"

Set GetSalesPersons = RS

End Function
```

43. `InsertSupplyOrder` inserts a new supply order into the database. It does this by using RDO–prepared statements. The first parameter in the `InsertSupplyOrder`–prepared statement is set up to be the return value. The next four parameters are set to be the total sale, salesperson ID, order date, and commission. Finally the prepared statement is executed and the order ID is returned.

```
Public Function InsertSupplyOrder(TotalSale, SalesID, OrderDate,
SalesCommission) As Integer
```

continued on next page

continued from previous page

```
Dim InsertSupplyOrderPS As rdoPreparedStatement

'   Create an RDO prepared statement for calling
'   the stored procedure
Set InsertSupplyOrderPS = Con.CreatePreparedStatement("INSERT_SUPPLY_ORDER"⇐
, "{ ? = call INSERT_SUPPLY_ORDER (?, ?, ?, ?) }")

'   The first parameter is the return value which
'   will be the order id
InsertSupplyOrderPS.rdoParameters(0).Direction = rdParamReturnValue

'   Set the four input parameters
InsertSupplyOrderPS.rdoParameters(1) = TotalSale
InsertSupplyOrderPS.rdoParameters(2) = SalesID
InsertSupplyOrderPS.rdoParameters(3) = OrderDate
InsertSupplyOrderPS.rdoParameters(4) = SalesCommission

'   Open the result set for the return
'   value from the stored procedure
Set RS = InsertSupplyOrderPS.OpenResultset(rdOpenStatic, rdConcurReadOnly)

'   Return the new order id
InsertSupplyOrder = RS(0)

    Close the prepared statement
InsertSupplyOrderPS.Close

End Function
```

44. `InsertStockOrder` inserts a new stock order into the database. It does this by using RDO–prepared statements. The "?" indicates the parameters to be passed in and returned. The first parameter is set up to be the return value. The next three parameters are set to be the total purchase price, order date, and arrival date. Finally, the prepared statement is executed and the order ID is returned.

```
Public Function InsertStockOrder(TotalPurchasePrice, OrderDate, ArrivalDate)
As Integer

Dim InsertStockOrderPS As rdoPreparedStatement

'   Create an RDO prepared statement for calling
'   the stored procedure
Set InsertStockOrderPS = Con.CreatePreparedStatement("INSERT_STOCK_ORDER"⇐
, "{ ? = call INSERT_STOCK_ORDER (?, ?, ?) }")

'   The first parameter is the return value which
'   will be the order id
InsertStockOrderPS.rdoParameters(0).Direction = rdParamReturnValue

'   Set the three input parameters
InsertStockOrderPS.rdoParameters(1) = TotalPurchasePrice
InsertStockOrderPS.rdoParameters(2) = OrderDate
```

```
InsertStockOrderPS.rdoParameters(3) = ArrivalDate

'  Open the result set for the return
'  value from the stored procedure
Set RS = InsertStockOrderPS.OpenResultset(rdOpenStatic, rdConcurReadOnly)

'  return the order id
InsertStockOrder = RS(0)

   Close the prepared statement
InsertStockOrderPS.Close

End Function
```

45. The `InsertSaleItem` method handles executing the `InsertSaleItem`
stored procedure on the database to insert a new supply sale item into the
database. Note that we do not need to use RDO–prepared statements since
this stored procedure does not return any data.

```
Public Sub InsertSaleItem(OrderID, ItemID, Quantity, SalePrice, OrderType)

'  Execute the stored procedure to
'  insert an ordered sale item
DBExec "exec insertsaleitem " & OrderID & ", " & ItemID & "⇐
, " & Quantity & ", " & SalePrice & ", " & OrderType

End Sub
```

46. The `GetShelfQuantity` method returns the shelf quantity for the specified stock item.

```
Public Function GetShelfQuantity(ItemID) As Long

'  Get the shelf quantity for the
'  for the product.
DBOpenRec "Select shelfquantity from StockItem where itemid = " & ItemID

GetShelfQuantity = RS("shelfquantity") & ""

End Function
```

47. The `UpdateShelfQuantity` method updates the shelf quantity for the
specified stock item.

```
Public Sub UpdateShelfQuantity(ItemID, UpdateQuantity)

Dim CurrentQuantity

'  Get the current quantity
CurrentQuantity = GetShelfQuantity(ItemID)

'  Update the shelf quantity
DBExec "exec updateshelfquantity " & ItemID & ", " & (CurrentQuantity ⇐
- UpdateQuantity)

End Sub
```

48. `UpdateBackOrder` updates the quantity on back order for a specified stock item.

```
Public Sub UpdateBackOrder(ItemID, UpdateQuantity)

Dim CurrentQuantity

'  Get the current back order
'  quantity
CurrentQuantity = GetBackOrder(ItemID)

'  Update the back order quantity
DBExec "exec updatebackorder " & ItemID & ", " & (CurrentQuantity ⇐
+ UpdateQuantity)

End Sub
```

49. `GetPurchPrice` returns the purchase price for a specified item.

```
Public Function GetPurchPrice(ItemID) As Double

'  Get the pruchase price for the item
DBOpenRec "Select PurchPrice from StockItem where ItemID = " & ItemID

GetPurchPrice = RS("PurchPrice") & ""

End Function

Private Sub Class_Initialize()

'  Initialize the connection
InitConnect

End Sub
```

50. Insert a new class into the project and save it as `clsOrderItem.cls`. Add the following code to the General Declarations section of the class. The global members of the class are declared.

```
Option Explicit

Dim m_OrderID As Integer
Dim m_ItemID As Integer
Dim m_Quantity As Long
Dim m_SalePrice As Double
Dim m_OrderType As Integer
```

51. The `OrderID` property of the class holds the ID for the current order.

```
'  The ID of the order for
'  the stock item
Public Property Let OrderID(I As Integer)
    m_OrderID = I
End Property

Public Property Get OrderID() As Integer
    OrderID = m_OrderID
End Property
```

52. The `ItemID` property holds the ID of the ordered item.

```
'  The ID of the ordered item
Public Property Let ItemID(I As Integer)
    m_ItemID = I
End Property

Public Property Get ItemID() As Integer
    ItemID = m_ItemID
End Property
```

53. The `Quantity` property identifies the quantity of the item ordered.

```
'  The quantity ordered
Public Property Let Quantity(L As Long)
    m_Quantity = L
End Property

Public Property Get Quantity() As Long
    Quantity = m_Quantity
End Property
```

54. The `OrderType` property indicates whether the item is a restock order or an order from inventory.

```
'  The type of order.  1 is a supply order
'   2 is a restock order
Public Property Let OrderType(I As Integer)
    m_OrderType = I
End Property

Public Property Get OrderType() As Integer
    OrderType = m_OrderType
End Property
```

55. The `SalePrice` property identifies the sale price for the item.

```
'  The sale price of the item
Public Property Let SalePrice(D as Double)
    m_SalePrice = D
End Property

Public Property Get SalePrice() As Double
    SalePrice = m_SalePrice
End Property
```

56. The `TotalSale` method calculates the total sale of the ordered quantity.

```
'  Calculates the total sale price for
'   the ordered quantity
Public Function TotalSale() As Double
    TotalSale = m_SalePrice * m_Quantity
End Function
```

57. The `StoreItem` method calls the `InsertSaleItem` method of the `clsData` class to store the ordered item.

```
Public Sub StoreItem(OrderID)

'  Save the ordered item
DS.InsertSaleItem OrderID, m_ItemID, m_Quantity, m_SalePrice, m_OrderType

End Sub
```

58. Insert a new class into the project and save it as `clsSalesPersons.cls`. Add the following code to the General Declarations section of the class. The global members of the class are declared.

```
Option Explicit

Dim m_SalesId As Integer
Dim m_FirstName As String
Dim m_LastName As String
Dim m_CommissionRate As Double
```

59. The `SalesID` property holds the ID for the salesperson.

```
'  salesperson ID
Public Property Get SalesID() As Integer
    SalesID = m_SalesId
End Property

Public Property Let SalesID(I As Integer)
    m_SalesId = I
End Property
```

60. The `FirstName` property sets and contains the first name for the salesperson.

```
'  First name of the salesperson
Public Property Get FirstName() As String
    FirstName = m_FirstName
End Property

Public Property Let FirstName(S As String)
    m_FirstName = S
End Property
```

61. The `LastName` property sets and contains the last name for the salesperson.

```
'  Last name of the salesperson
Public Property Get LastName() As String
    LastName = m_LastName
End Property

Public Property Let LastName(S As String)
    m_LastName = S
End Property
```

62. The `CommissionRate` property sets and retrieves the commission rate for the salesperson. Note that when the commission rate is to be retrieved, it is automatically read from the database in case it has been updated by another program.

```
'   The commission rate for the
'   salesperson
Public Property Get CommissionRate() As Double
    CommissionRate = m_CommissionRate
End Property

Public Property Let CommissionRate(D as Double)
    m_CommissionRate = D
End Property
```

63. GetSalesPersons is a meta function that handles retrieving the set of salespersons stored in the database. For each salesperson, a clsSalesPerson class is created and added to the passed in collection. An outside object that wishes to get all of the salespersons objects should call this function and pass in an initialized collection.

```
'   Meta function that gets all the
'   salespersons
Public Sub GetSalesPersons(SalesPersons As Object)

Dim RS As rdoResultset
Dim SP As clsSalesPerson

'   Get the record set of salespersons
Set RS = DS.GetSalesPersons

Do Until RS.EOF

    '   Create the new class
    Set SP = New clsSalesPerson

    '   set the sales id
    SP.SalesID = RS("salesid") & ""

    '   set the first name
    SP.FirstName = Trim(RS("firstname") & "")

    '   set the last name
    SP.LastName = Trim(RS("lastname") & "")

    '   set the commission rate
    SP.CommissionRate = Trim(RS("commissionrate") & "")

    '   add the class to the collection
    SalesPersons.ADD Item:=SP, Key:=CStr(RS("salesid") & "")

    '   move to the next record
    RS.MoveNext

Loop

Set SP = Nothing

End Sub
```

64. The `CalculateCommission` procedure calculates the commission based on the order sale.

```
' Calculates the commission for the sale
Public Function CalculateCommission(Sale) As Double
    CalculateCommission = CommissionRate * Sale
End Function
```

65. Insert a new class into the project and save is as **`clsStockItem.cls`**. This class will encapsulate an item in the inventory stock. Add the following code to the General Declarations section of the class. The global members of the class are declared.

```
Option Explicit

Dim m_ItemID As Integer
Dim m_ItemName As String
Dim m_ItemDesc As String
Dim m_ShelfQuantity As Long
Dim m_SalePrice As Double
Dim m_PurchasePrice As Double
Dim m_BackOrder As Long
Dim m_SupplierID As Integer
```

66. The `ItemID` sets and returns the stock item ID.

```
' The stock item id
Public Property Get ItemID() As Integer
    ItemID = m_ItemID
End Property

Public Property Let ItemID(I As Integer)
    m_ItemID = I
End Property
```

67. The `ItemName` property holds the name of the stock item.

```
' The item name
Public Property Get ItemName() As String
    ItemName = m_ItemName
End Property

Public Property Let ItemName(S As String)
    m_ItemName = S
End Property
```

68. The `ItemDesc` property contains the description of the item.

```
' The item description
Public Property Get ItemDesc() As String
    ItemDesc = m_ItemDesc
End Property

Public Property Let ItemDesc(S As String)
    m_ItemDesc = S
End Property
```

69. The ShelfQuantity property holds the current shelf quantity of the item. When the value is retrieved, the current value in the database is retrieved first to ensure the latest amount is retrieved.

```
'  The shelf quantity
Public Property Get ShelfQuantity() As Long
    m_ShelfQuantity = DS.GetShelfQuantity(m_ItemID)
    ShelfQuantity = m_ShelfQuantity
End Property

Public Property Let ShelfQuantity(L As Long)
    m_ShelfQuantity = L
End Property
```

70. The SupplierID property contains the ID of the supplier of the stock item.

```
'  The supplier id
Public Property Let SupplierID(I As Integer)
    m_SupplierID = I
End Property

Public Property Get SupplierID() As Integer
    SupplierID = m_SupplierID
End Property
```

71. The BackOrder property contains the quantity of the product on back order. Note that when the quantity is called for, the latest value from the database is retrieved.

```
'  The back order quantity
Public Property Get BackOrder() As Long
    '  Get the latest back order quantity
    m_BackOrder = DS.GetBackOrder(m_ItemID)
    BackOrder = m_BackOrder
End Property

Public Property Let BackOrder(L As Long)
    m_BackOrder = L
End Property
```

72. The PurchasePrice property handles setting and retrieving the purchase price for the stock item.

```
'  The purchase price
Public Property Get PurchasePrice() As Double
    PurchasePrice = m_PurchasePrice
End Property

Public Property Let PurchasePrice(D as Double)
    m_PurchasePrice = D
End Property
```

73. The SalePrice property handles setting and retrieving the sale price for the stock item.

```
'   The sale price
Public Property Get SalePrice() As Double
    SalePrice = m_SalePrice
End Property

Public Property Let SalePrice(D as Double)
    m_SalePrice = D
End Property
```

74. The `ProfitPercentage` property handles returning the calculated profit percentage for the stock item based on the current purchase price and sale price. Note, for this example, there are two values hard coded into this calculation. The first is the average commission rate of .1 The second is the overhead percentage of .08. These two figures would best be calculated through some type of decision support system such as the one represented in the next How-To.

```
Public Property Get ProfitPercentage() As Double

Dim CommissionAvg As Double
Dim Costs As Double
Dim OverHeadAdd As Double

'   Calculate the average commission
CommissionAvg = m_SalePrice * 0.1

'   Calculate the overhead addition
'   Note:   This should be supported
'   in an outside business object.  But,
'   is outside the scope of this How-To.
OverHeadAdd = m_SalePrice * 0.08

'   Total the costs
Costs = m_PurchasePrice + OverHeadAdd + CommissionAvg

'   Calculate the profit percentage
ProfitPercentage = ((m_SalePrice - Costs) / m_SalePrice) * 100

End Property
```

75. The `GetStockItems` is a meta method of the class that operates on each stock item. The procedure requires that a collection be passed in so that it can be filled with all the stock item classes. For each stock item in the database, a new class is created and added to the collection.

```
'   Meta function to retrieve the
'   the stock items
Public Sub GetStockItems(Stock As Object)

Dim RS As rdoResultset
Dim SI As clsStockItem

'   Get the items
Set RS = DS.GetStockItems
```

```
Do Until RS.EOF

    '  Create a new class
    Set SI = New clsStockItem

    '  Set the id
    SI.ItemID = RS("itemid") & ""

    '  Set the name
    SI.ItemName = Trim(RS("itemname") & "")

    '  Set the description
    SI.ItemDesc = Trim(RS("itemdesc") & "")

    '  Set the purchase price
    SI.PurchasePrice = RS("purchprice") & ""

    '  Set the sale price
    SI.SalePrice = RS("saleprice") & ""

    '  Set the supplier id
    SI.SupplierID = RS("supplierid") & ""

    '  add the class to the collection
    Stock.ADD Item:=SI, Key:=CStr(RS("itemid") & "")

    '  Move to the next record
    RS.MoveNext

Loop

Set SI = Nothing

End Sub
```

76. Insert a new class into the project and save it as `clsStockOrder.cls`. This class encapsulates an order for more inventory stock. Add the following code to the General Declarations section of the class. The global members of the class are declared. Note that this class contains one instance of the `clsOrderItem` class which will represent the item to be ordered.

```
Option Explicit

Dim m_OrderID As Integer
Dim m_TotalPurchase As Double
Dim m_OrderDate As Date
Dim m_ArrivalDate As Date
Dim SI As clsOrderItem
```

77. The `OrderID` property contains the ID of the stock order and the code below allows for getting and setting the property's value.

```
'  The order id
Public Property Let OrderID(I As Integer)
    m_OrderID = I
```

continued on next page

continued from previous page

```
End Property

Public Property Get OrderID() As Integer
    OrderID = m_OrderID
End Property
```

78. The `TotalPurchase` property handles setting the total purchase price based on the quantity of the stock item being ordered.

```
' The total purchase price
Public Property Get TotalPurchase() As Double

    ' Calculate the total purchase
    TotalPurchase = DS.GetPurchPrice(SI.ItemID) * SI.Quantity

End Property
```

79. The `OrderDate` property handles setting and retrieving the date of the order.

```
' The date of the order
Public Property Let OrderDate(D As Date)
    m_OrderDate = D
End Property

Public Property Get OrderDate() As Date
    OrderDate = m_OrderDate
End Property
```

80. The `ArrivalDate` property handles setting and retrieving the arrival date of the stock.

```
' The arrival date of the order
Public Property Let ArrivalDate(D As Date)
    m_ArrivalDate = D
End Property

Public Property Get ArrivalDate() As Date
    ArrivalDate = m_ArrivalDate
End Property
```

81. The `PurchaseItem` property returns and sets the ID of the stock item to be purchased.

```
' The item to be purchased
Public Property Get PurchaseItem() As Integer
    PurchaseItem = SI.ItemID
End Property

Public Property Let PurchaseItem(I As Integer)
    SI.ItemID = I
End Property
```

82. The `Quantity` property handles setting and retrieving the quantity of the item to be ordered.

```
'  The quantity to order
Public Property Let Quantity(L As Long)
    SI.Quantity = L
End Property

Public Property Get Quantity() As Long
    Quantity = SI.Quantity
End Property
```

83. The `StoreOrder` procedure handles storing the stock item order. The stock order is placed in the database and the order ID is returned. Then the ordered item is stored with the order ID indicating which order the item goes with. Finally, the quantity on back order is updated for the stock item.

```
Public Sub StoreOrder()

'  Insert the order
m_OrderID = DS.InsertStockOrder(Me.TotalPurchase, m_OrderDate,
m_ArrivalDate)

'  Store the ordered item
SI.StoreItem m_OrderID

'  Update the back order quantity
DS.UpdateBackOrder SI.ItemID, SI.Quantity

End Sub
```

84. When the class is initialized, the `clsOrderItem` class is initialized. Note the order type is set to **2** to indicate this is an order for inventory stock.

```
Private Sub Class_Initialize()

Set SI = New clsOrderItem

'  Set the order type to 2 for a stock order
SI.OrderType = 2

End Sub
```

85. Insert a new class into the project and save it as `clsSupplier.cls`. This class will encapsulate a supplier of stock items. Add the following code to the General Declarations section of the form. The global members of the class are declared.

```
Option Explicit

Dim m_SupplierID As Integer
Dim m_Name As String
Dim m_Address1 As String
Dim m_Address2 As String
Dim m_City As String
Dim m_State As String
Dim m_Zip As String
Dim m_Phone As String
```

86. The `SupplierID` property handles setting and retrieving the ID of the supplier.

```
'  The supplier id
Public Property Let SupplierID(I As Integer)
    m_SupplierID = I
End Property

Public Property Get SupplierID() As Integer
    SupplierID = m_SupplierID
End Property
```

87. The `Name` property handles setting and retrieving the name of the supplier.

```
'  The supplier name
Public Property Let Name(S As String)
    m_Name = S
End Property

Public Property Get Name() As String
    Name = m_Name
End Property
```

88. The `address1` and `address2` properties set and retrieve the address information for the supplier.

```
'  The supplier address1
Public Property Let Address1(S As String)
    m_Address1 = S
End Property

Public Property Get Address1() As String
    Address1 = m_Address1
End Property

'  The supplier address2
Public Property Let Address2(S As String)
    m_Address2 = S
End Property

Public Property Get Address2() As String
    Address2 = m_Address2
End Property
```

89. The `City` property sets and retrieves the supplier's city.

```
'  The supplier city
Public Property Let City(S As String)
    m_City = S
End Property

Public Property Get City() As String
    City = m_City
End Property
```

90. The `State` property sets and retrieves the supplier's state.

```
'  The supplier state
Public Property Let State(S As String)
    m_State = S
End Property

Public Property Get State() As String
    State = m_State
End Property
```

91. The `Zip` property sets and retrieves the supplier's zip code.

```
'  The supplier zip
Public Property Let Zip(S As String)
    m_Zip = S
End Property

Public Property Get Zip() As String
    Zip = m_Zip
End Property
```

92. The `Phone` property sets and retrieves the supplier's phone number.

```
'  The supplier phone
Public Property Let Phone(S As String)
    m_Phone = S
End Property

Public Property Get Phone() As String
    Phone = m_Phone
End Property
```

93. The `GetSuppliers` procedure is a meta method of the class that fills a collection with all the suppliers in the database. The method requires that a collection is passed into the procedure. The class then creates a class for each supplier and adds it to the collection.

```
'  Meta function to get the suppliers
Public Sub GetSuppliers(Suppliers As Object)

Dim RS As rdoResultset
Dim SI As clsSupplier

'  Get the record set of suppliers
Set RS = DS.GetSuppliers

Do Until RS.EOF

    '  Create the class
    Set SI = New clsSupplier

    '  Set the supplier id
    SI.SupplierID = RS("supplierid") & ""

    '  Set the supplier name
    SI.Name = Trim(RS("name") & "")
```

continued on next page

continued from previous page

```
'  Set the supplier address
SI.Address1 = Trim(RS("address1") & "")

'  Set the supplier address
SI.Address2 = Trim(RS("address2") & "")

'  Set the supplier city
SI.City = RS("city") & ""

'  Set the supplier state
SI.State = RS("State") & ""

'  Set the supplier zip
SI.Zip = RS("zip") & ""

'  Set the supplier phone
SI.Phone = RS("phone") & ""

'  Add the supplier to the collection
Suppliers.ADD Item:=SI, Key:=CStr(RS("supplierid") & "")

RS.MoveNext

Loop

Set SI = Nothing

End Sub
```

94. Insert a new class into the project and save it as **clsSupplyOrder**. This
class encapsulates an order for school supplies from the inventory. Add the
following code to the General Declarations section of the class. The global
members of the class are declared. Note that a global collection,
SalesItems, for the class is declared. This collection will hold all the items
being placed in the order.

```
Option Explicit

Dim m_OrderID As Integer
Dim m_TotalSale As Double
Dim m_SalesId As Integer
Dim m_OrderDate As Date
Dim m_SalesCommission As Double

Dim SalesItems As Collection
```

95. The **OrderID** property sets and retrieves the ID for the order.

```
'  Set the order id
Public Property Let OrderID(I As Integer)
    m_OrderID = OrderID
End Property

Public Property Get OrderID() As Integer
    OrderID = m_OrderID
End Property
```

96. The `TotalSale` property handles setting and retrieving the total sale for the order.

```
'  The total sale for the order
Public Property Let TotalSale(D as Double)
    m_TotalSale = D
End Property

Public Property Get TotalSale() As Double
    TotalSale = m_TotalSale
End Property
```

97. The `SalesID` property handles setting and retrieving the ID of the salesperson for the order.

```
'  The sales id
Public Property Let SalesID(I As Integer)
    m_SalesId = I
End Property

Public Property Get SalesID() As Integer
    SalesID = m_SalesId
End Property
```

98. The `OrderDate` property sets and retrieves the date of the order.

```
'  The date of the order
Public Property Let OrderDate(D As Date)
    m_OrderDate = D
End Property

Public Property Get OrderDate() As Date
    OrderDate = m_OrderDate
End Property
```

99. The `SalesCommission` property sets and retrieves the sales commission for the order.

```
'  The sales commission
Public Property Let SalesCommission(D as Double)
    m_SalesCommission = D
End Property

Public Property Get SalesCommission() As Double
    SalesCommission = m_SalesCommission
End Property
```

100. The `AddSaleItem` method of the class adds a new sales item to the order. The ID of the item to be added, quantity, and sale price of the item are passed in. A new `clsOrderItem` class is created, set up, and added to the global `SalesItems` collection.

```
Private Sub AddSaleItem(ItemID, Quantity, SalePrice)

Dim SItem As clsOrderItem
```

continued on next page

continued from previous page

```
'  Create a new order item class
Set SItem = New clsOrderItem

'  Set the item id
SItem.ItemID = ItemID

'  Set the quantity
SItem.Quantity = Quantity

'  Set the sale price
SItem.SalePrice = SalePrice

'  This a customer order versus
'  a re-stock order
SItem.OrderType = 1

'  Add the item to the collection of
'  ordered items
SalesItems.ADD Item:=SItem, Key:=CStr(ItemID)

Set SItem = Nothing

End Sub
```

101. The `UpdateSaleItem` method handles updating the quantity ordered of a sale item.

```
Public Sub UpdateSaleItem(ItemID, Quantity As Integer)

'  Update the item with the new quantity
SalesItems.Item(CStr(ItemID)).Quantity = Quantity

End Sub
```

102. The `GetSaleItemQuantity` method handles returning the quantity ordered of a sale item in the order. Note that this also could be implemented as an indexed property of the class.

```
Public Function GetSaleItemQuantity(ItemID) As Integer

'  Get the quantity of the sale
GetSaleItemQuantity = SalesItems.Item(CStr(ItemID)).Quantity

End Function
```

103. `CalculateTotalOrderPrice` handles looping through the items ordered and getting their total sale price. The total of these is the total order price.

```
Public Function CalculateTotalOrderPrice() As Double

Dim SI As Object
Dim RunningTotal As Double

'  Get the running total
For Each SI In SalesItems
```

```
        RunningTotal = RunningTotal + SI.TotalSale

Next

CalculateTotalOrderPrice = RunningTotal

End Function
```

104. StoreOrder handles storing the order in the database. First, the order is inserted into the database and an Order ID is returned. Then, each ordered item is looped through and added to the database by calling the StoreItem method. Also, the shelf quantity for each ordered stock item is updated.

```
Public Sub StoreOrder()

Dim SI As Object

'  Insert the order
m_OrderID = DS.InsertSupplyOrder(m_TotalSale, m_SalesId, m_OrderDate, ⇐
m_SalesCommission)

For Each SI In SalesItems

    '  Store the ordered item
    If SI.Quantity <> 0 Then
        SI.StoreItem m_OrderID
        DS.UpdateShelfQuantity SI.ItemID, SI.Quantity
    End If

Next

End Sub
```

105. CalculateNetProfit handles calculating the total order price and then calculates the total cost of each item. The net profit is then calculated as the total order price minus the cost of the items minus the sales commission.

```
Public Function CalculateNetProfit() As Double

'  Declare an object for moving
'  through the objects (classes)
'  in our collection
Dim SI As Object
Dim TotalPurchPrice As Double

'  Cacluate the total sale
TotalSale = CalculateTotalOrderPrice

For Each SI In SalesItems

    '  Calculate the total purchase price (cost)
    If SI.Quantity <> 0 Then TotalPurchPrice = TotalPurchPrice +
    (DS.GetPurchPrice(SI.ItemID) * SI.Quantity)
```

continued on next page

continued from previous page

```
Next

'   The net profit is the total sale minus the
'   purchase price minus the sales commission

CalculateNetProfit = TotalSale - TotalPurchPrice - SalesCommission

End Function
```

106. When the class is initialized, the current set of stock items is added to the global **SalesItems** collection.

```
Private Sub Class_Initialize()

Dim RS As rdoResultset

Set SalesItems = New Collection

'   Get all of the stock items
Set RS = DS.GetStockItems

'   Add the items to the list
Do Until RS.EOF

    AddSaleItem RS("itemid") & "", 0, RS("saleprice") & ""

    RS.MoveNext

Loop

End Sub
```

> **NOTE**
>
> The following steps describe how to set up the database if you are unable to utilize the WholeSale.SQL script provided in the Chapter 9 directory on the CD. Note this script does not set up default seed data (see Step 112 later).

107. Add the following stored procedure to the WholeSale SQL Server database. **Insert_Stock_Order** handles building a transaction that will insert a stock order into the database and return the Order ID. By encapsulating the insert into the database in a transaction, we ensure that the correct Order ID is returned in case multiple orders are placed at once.

```
CREATE PROCEDURE Insert_Stock_Order    @TotalPurchasePrice float, ⇐
@OrderDate datetime, @ArrivalDate datetime AS

/*  The Return Value */
declare @OrderID int
```

```
/*  Begin the transaction */
begin transaction

    /*  Insert the order */
    Insert StockOrder (TotalPurchasePrice, OrderDate, ArrivalDate) ⇐
    values(@TotalPurchasePrice, @OrderDate, @ArrivalDate)

    /*  Get back the order ID */
    select @OrderID = max(OrderID) from StockOrder

commit transaction

/*  Return the Order ID in a column calles NewOrderID */
select @OrderID NewOrderID
```

108. The `Insert_Supply_Order` stored procedure handles inserting a supply order into the database. By encapsulating the insert into the database in a transaction, we ensure that the correct Order ID is returned in case multiple orders are placed simultaneously.

```
CREATE PROCEDURE Insert_Supply_Order  @TotalSale float, @SalesID int, ⇐
@OrderDate datetime, @SalesCommission float AS

/*  the return value */
declare @OrderID int

/*  begin the transaction of inserting
    a new order */
begin transaction

    /*  Insert the order */
    Insert SupplyOrder (TotalSale, SalesID, OrderDate, SalesCommission) ⇐
    values(@TotalSale, @SalesID, @OrderDate, @SalesCommission)

    /* get the order id */
    select @OrderID = max(OrderID) from SupplyOrder

/*  commit the order transaction */
commit transaction

/*  Return the new order ID in a column named NewOrderID */
select @OrderID NewOrderID
```

109. The `InsertSaleItem` stored procedure handles inserting an ordered item into the `OrderItems` table.

```
CREATE PROCEDURE InsertSaleItem @OrderId int, @ItemID int, @Quantity int, ⇐
@SalePrice float, @OrderType int AS

/*  Insert the Sale Item */
insert OrderItems values(@OrderID, @ItemID, @Quantity, @OrderType,
@SalePrice)
```

110. The `UpdateBackOrder` procedure handles updating the quantity on back order of an item.

```
CREATE PROCEDURE UpdateBackOrder @ItemID int, @Quantity int AS

/*   update the stock item backorder */
update StockItem set BackOrder = @Quantity where ItemID = @ItemID
```

111. The `UpdateShelfQuantity` procedure handles updating the quantity in inventory of an item.

```
CREATE PROCEDURE UpdateShelfQuantity @ItemID int, @Quantity int AS

/*   Update the ShelfQuantity of the stock Item */
update StockItem set ShelfQuantity = @Quantity where ItemID = @ItemID
```

112. Add the following tables to the WholeSale SQL Server database with the corresponding fields. Note that you will need to insert several seed values in the `StockItem`, `Suppliers`, and `SalesPersons` tables for the How-To example to work. Sample data is provided following each table.

```
OrderItems
    OrderID                 int              NOT NULL
    ItemID                  int              NOT NULL
    Quantity                int              NULL
    OrderType               tinyint          NULL
    SalePrice               float            NULL

    PRIMARY KEY
        ItemID
        OrderID


SalesPerson
    SalesID                 int              NOT NULL
    FirstName               varchar (20)     NULL
    LastName                varchar (20)     NULL
    CommissionRate          float            NULL

    PRIMARY KEY
        SalesID
```

SalesPerson Sample Data (Column Order as Shown Above):

```
1           Wendy          Winner          0.16
2           Tommy          Thumb           0.12
3           Sammy          Sellem          0.09
4           Cindy          Commision       0.17


StockItem
    ItemID                  int              NOT NULL
    ItemName                char (50)        NOT NULL
    ItemDesc                varchar(255)     NULL
    ShelfQuantity           int              NULL
    BackOrder               int              NULL
    PurchPrice              float            NULL
    SalePrice               float            NULL
    SupplierID              int              NULL
```

```
PRIMARY KEY
    ItemID
```

StockItem Sample Data (Column Order as Shown Above):

```
1   Erasers                 Hot Disney Erasers      ⇐
104   200   0.25   0.75   1
2   Yellow Legal Notepads   Lined Yellow Legal Notepad  ⇐
4039  500   0.65   1.23   4
3   Big Blue Note Pads      For Kids 7 and Under    ⇐
22    0     2.23   3.5    4
4   Ticky Tacky Glue        The best kids art glue  ⇐
121   234   0.78   1.22   3
5   Roy Bob's Pencil Box    Multipurpose pencil box ⇐
84    300   1.23   2.24   5
6   Right Angle Protractor  For making the best angles  ⇐
456   0     0.43   0.68   5
7   The Cool Notebook       Stylish for the coolest kid ⇐
57    0     3.5    5.0    2
8   Fruity Crayons          For eating and drawing  ⇐
311   0     1.89   2.76   5
9   El Velcro               The notebook that sticks ⇐
258   0     7.5    9.0    2
```

```
StockOrder
    OrderID             int          NOT NULL
    TotalPurchasePrice  float        NULL
    OrderDate           datetime     NULL
    ArrivalDate         datetime     NULL

    PRIMARY KEY
        OrderID

Suppliers
    SupplierID          int          NOT NULL
    Name                varchar (50) NULL
    Address1            varchar (50) NULL
    Address2            varchar (50) NULL
    City                varchar (50) NULL
    State               varchar (2)  NULL
    Zip                 varchar (10) NULL
    Phone               varchar (20) NULL

    PRIMARY KEY
        SupplierID
```

Suppliers Sample Data (Column Order as Shown Above):

```
1 EraserHeads      100 Rub Out Lane  (null) Child State   ⇐
VA 22601 555-555-5551
2 Notebook Heaven 1100 Spiral Ave.   (null) Three Ringville ⇐
NY 33333 555-555-5552
3 Glue It Inc.     100 Stuck On You  (null) Paste City    ⇐
TX 32332 555-555-5553
```

continued on next page

continued from previous page

```
4 Worthy of Note  34 Write It Down  (null) Jot It        ⇐
MN 87877 555-555-5554
5 Supplies R Us   87 School's In    (null) Studyville    ⇐
TX 87874 555-555-5555

SupplyOrder
     OrderID              int              NOT NULL
     TotalSale            float            NULL
     SalesID              int              NULL
     OrderDate            datetime         NULL
     SalesCommission      float            NULL


     PRIMARY KEY
        OrderID
```

How It Works

This How-To example encompasses many different techniques to pull together this three-tier client/server application. These include a user interface client, a business objects middle layer, and a Data services tier that includes stored procedures. To implement this architecture, we are using remote data objects (RDO) and remote OLE Automation Servers that are part of the Enterprise Edition of Visual Basic 5. And, on the project design side, we are throwing in a little object-oriented design to build the functionality of the application. So, to start let's take a look at the classes and objects built in this application.

Figure 9-5 shows a general relationship diagram between the objects developed in the business objects layer. Table 9-7 following the figure reviews each Visual Basic class.

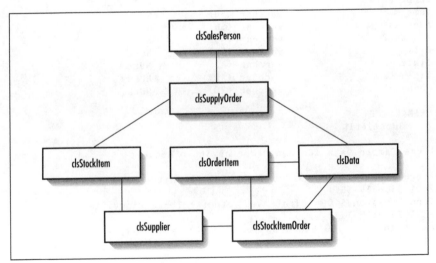

Figure 9-5 The class relationships

Table 9-7 Class descriptions

CLASS	DEFINITION
clsData	Handles all direct interfacing with the Data services layer and uses RDO
clsOrderItem	Encapsulates a stock item that is part of an order
clsSalesPerson	Defines a salesperson
clsStockItem	Defines an item in the stock inventory
clsStockItemOrder	Encapsulates an order for inventory stock and utilizes clsOrderItem
clsSupplier	Defines a supplier of a stock item
clsSupplyOrder	Encapsulates an order for an item from inventory and utilizes clsOrderItem

The classes shown in Table 9-7 work together with the User services and Data services layer to provide the underlying functionality of the application. As we will see in the next How-To, these classes will be reused and utilized as the fundamental building blocks for creating a decision support set of tools.

Note that the **clsData** class utilizes RDO and ODBC to interface with SQL Server. There are a couple of technical programming points to watch out for in utilizing the stored procedures that reside on the Data services layer. Two of the stored procedures, **Insert_Supply_Order** and **Insert_Stock_Order**, return the ID of the inserted row. In order to call these from RDO, we need to use RDO–prepared statements. But stored procedures that do not return data can be executed using the **Execute** method of an RDO connection, which is much simpler. **Insert_Supply_Order** and **Insert_Stock_Order** execute multiple select statements; however, SQL Server cursors cannot handle returning these resultsets, but ODBC cursors can. In order to use ODBC cursor drivers, we need to ensure the **rdoEngine** cursor driver is set to use ODBC. The following statement does this and must be done before the connection is created (**InitConnect** of **clsData**).

```
rdoEngine.rdoDefaultCursorDriver = rdUseOdbc
```

Once this is done, setting up the prepared statement is not difficult. Review the **InsertStockOrder** and **InsertSupplyOrder** methods of **clsData** to see how each is set up.

Three of our classes have built in what is called a meta method. A *meta method* of a class is a method that works on an entire set of objects, instead of just a single instance of an object. In this example these methods include **GetSalesPersons** from **clsSalesPerson**, **GetSuppliers** from **clsSuppliers**, and **GetStockItems** from **clsStockItem**. These methods all handle filling a collection with an instance of each referenced item in the database. These methods are actually building instances for each item in the database which is really just the persistent (or stored) data for these objects. Normally a method in a class only operates on the item represented by the instance of the object.

These business objects are implemented in an ActiveX component. The easiest way to test the server is to simply run two instances of Visual Basic at once. The first instance will run the 9-1-srv.vbp project. Because the settings for the project are as an ActiveX executable, a reference to the project will show up in the system registry. Run the 9-1.vbp User services project and reference the WholeSale Business Objects server and then run the project. In fact, you can run multiple instances of the User services project and utilize the same server object. Review Chapter 7, Business Objects, for further details on how to implement business objects. For large-scale deployment of business objects, consider building a pool manager to manage object availability and connections.

The User services project, 9-1.vbp, contains forms and a module that build the interface to the business objects layer. This layer does not have to be concerned with the underlying implementation of the business objects or the database. It simply relies on passing data to and from the properties and methods of the classes. An MDI form is used to show two order entry forms.

The final tier, Database services, finishes off the three-tier implementation. The database is referenced through ODBC. The Data services tier also encapsulates some implementation logic that is placed at this level. These include stored procedures that make adding orders to the database straightforward and safe. Also, stored procedures are provided for easily updating inventory quantities. The `clsData` class is the business object that *knows* how to work with the database and provides services to the other objects.

Comments

This application builds two order entry screens for our inventory system. By designing the basic set of objects that define the business process, we have encapsulated the business rules in easy-to-use Visual Basic classes. You are then able to deploy these business objects anywhere on your enterprise and scale them appropriately with a pool manager. And, as your transaction load for your database grows or becomes more complex, you may wish to move more of the logic from the `clsData` class to stored procedures on the database. This can all be done without redeploying the User interfaces layer. The next How-To will demonstrate how the business objects and Data services developed in How-To 9.1 can be utilized to develop decision support tools for the inventory system.

COMPLEXITY

ADVANCED

9.2 How do I...
Build a three-tier client/server decision support system?

Problem

I have a set of business objects that encapsulate business rules developed for order entry. How can I take these same business objects and use object-oriented design to make them easily reusable?

Technique

In the last How-To, we developed seven classes that encapsulated various objects in our inventory system. In this How-To we will build three decision support tools. The first will review sales commissions and allow for commission adjustments based on performance. The second will review sales prices and allow for adjustment in the product price. The third will allow a general review of our business order history. These three tools will help the end user, probably a sales manager, review sales trends, how salespeople are doing, how the products are doing, and determine what adjustments to make.

Note that Step 40 will explain how to set up and seed the WholeSale database for this application. Also, you will need to have a 32-bit ODBC data source for the database. In this example, the database was set up in Microsoft SQL Server 6.5 as WholeSale and the ODBC DSN was also set to WholeSale. You may place the database tables and choose a name; just ensure that the ODBC connection is set up properly (refer to Chapter 2, Getting Connected).

Steps

First open and run the 9-2-Srv.VBP project. This project will load the appropriate objects for the user interface project. Next, open the 9-2.VBP project. You will have to delete the current reference to **WholeSaleObjects2** and then add a reference to the currently running **WholeSale Objects2**. Then run 9-2.VBP. The running program appears as shown in Figure 9-6.

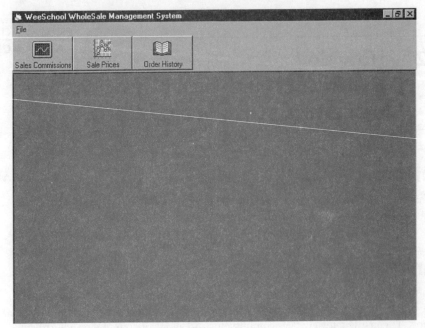

Figure 9-6 The project as it appears at runtime

There are three options available to review the inventory system transactions. The first toolbar button allows the user to review sales commissions for the company's salespersons. The second button reviews the sales history of stock items. The last reviews the inventory order history. Figure 9-7 shows the sales commissions screen.

Select the salesperson from the drop-down listbox. The sales for that salesperson will be displayed in the listbox. These can be sorted by date or commission. The total sales for the person are shown as well as the current commission rate. The commission rate can be updated by entering a new commission rate and selecting the Update button as shown in Figure 9-8.

The sale price of stock items can be reviewed by selecting the stock item from the drop-down listbox. The order history will be shown in the listbox. The sale price for the order is shown along with the quantity. The sales total for the stock item is

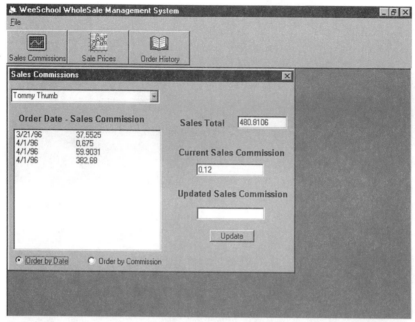

Figure 9-7 The Sales Commission review screen

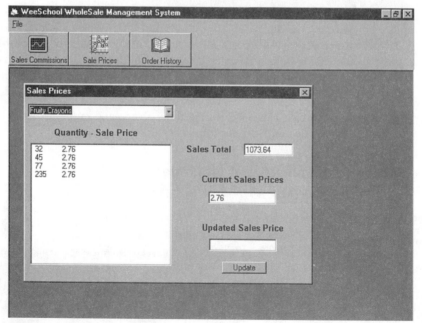

Figure 9-8 The Sales Prices review screen

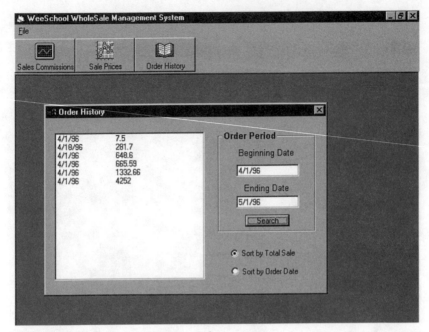

Figure 9-9 The Order History review screen

shown along with the current sale price. A new sales price can be entered and then updated by selecting Update.

Last, the user can review the overall order history of the wholesaler. Figure 9-9 shows the order history screen. A search date range can be entered to review what sales occurred during the specified period. The orders can be sorted by order date and total sale.

1. Create a new project called 9-2.VBP. Add the objects and properties listed in Table 9-8 to Form1 and save the form as 9-2.FRM.

Table 9-8 The form's objects and properties

OBJECT	PROPERTY	SETTING
MDIForm	Name	MDIForm1
	AutoShowChildren	0 'False
	Caption	"WeeSchool WholeSale Management System"
	WindowState	2 'Maximized
ImageList	Name	ImageList1
	ImageWidth	32
	ImageHeight	32

OBJECT	PROPERTY	SETTING
	NumImages	3
	i1	"9-2.frx":0000
	i2	"9-2.frx":04F7
	i3	"9-2.frx":09EE
Toolbar	Name	Toolbar1
	Align	1 'Align Top
	ImageList	"ImageList1"
	ButtonWidth	2540
	ButtonHeight	1376
	NumButtons	3

2. Add the menus in Table 9-9 to the MDI form.

Table 9-9 The ImageTracker form's menus

MENU NAME	CAPTION
mFile	"&File"
mExit	"E&xit"

3. Insert a new form into the project and save it as OrderHist.frm. Add the objects and properties in Table 9-10 to the form.

Table 9-10 The form's objects and properties

OBJECT	PROPERTY	SETTING
Form	Name	OrderHist
	BorderStyle	1 'Fixed Single
	Caption	"Order History"
	MDIChild	-1 'True
OptionButton	Name	OrderSort
	Caption	"Sort by Order Date"
OptionButton	Name	SaleSort
	Caption	"Sort by Total Sale"
	Value	-1 'True
ListBox	Name	OrderList
Frame	Name	Frame1
	Caption	"Order Period"

continued on next page

continued from previous page

OBJECT	PROPERTY	SETTING
	Font	
	name	"Arial"
	weight	700
	size	9.75
CommandButton	Name	Search
	Caption	"Search"
TextBox	Name	EndDate
TextBox	Name	BeginDate
Label	Name	Label2
	AutoSize	-1 'True
	Caption	"Ending Date"
	Font	
	name	"Arial"
	weight	400
	size	9.75
Label	Name	Label1
	AutoSize	-1 'True
	Caption	"Beginning Date"
	Font	
	name	"Arial"
	weight	400
	size	9.75

4. Insert a new form into the project and save it as SalesComm.frm. Add the objects and properties in Table 9-11 to the form.

Table 9-11 The form's objects and properties

OBJECT	PROPERTY	SETTING
Form	Name	SalesComm
	BorderStyle	3 'Fixed Dialog
	Caption	"Sales Commissions"
	MDIChild	-1 'True
OptionButton	Name	CommOrder
	Caption	"Order by Commission"

OBJECT	PROPERTY	SETTING
OptionButton	Name	DateOrder
	Caption	"Order by Date"
	Value	-1 'True
TextBox	Name	TotalSales
CommandButton	Name	Update
	Caption	"Update"
TextBox	Name	NewCommRate
TextBox	Name	SalesCommission
	Locked	-1 'True
ListBox	Name	SalesHistory
ComboBox	Name	SalesList
Label	Name	Label4
	Caption	"Sales Total"
	Font	
	name	"Arial"
	size	9.75
Label	Name	Label3
	AutoSize	-1 'True
	Caption	"Updated Sales Commission"
	Font	
	name	"Arial"
	weight	700
	size	9.75
Label	Name	Label2
	AutoSize	-1 'True
	Caption	"Current Sales Commission"
	Font	
	name	"Arial"
	weight	700
	size	9.75
Label	Name	Label1
	AutoSize	-1 'True
	Caption	"Order Date – Sales Commission"
	Font	
	name	"Arial"
	weight	700
	size	9.75

5. Insert a new form into the project and save it as SalesPrices.frm. Add the objects and properties in Table 9-12 to the form.

Table 9-12 The form's objects and properties

OBJECT	PROPERTY	SETTING
Form	Name	SalesPrices
	BorderStyle	3 'Fixed Dialog
	Caption	"Sales Prices"
	MDIChild	-1 'True
ComboBox	Name	ItemsList
ListBox	Name	SalesHistory
TextBox	Name	CurrentPrice
	Locked	-1 'True
TextBox	Name	NewPrice
CommandButton	Name	Update
	Caption	"Update"
TextBox	Name	TotalSales
Label	Name	Label1
	AutoSize	-1 'True
	Caption	"Quantity - Sale Price"
	Font	
	name	"Arial"
	weight	700
	size	9.75
Label	Name	Label2
	AutoSize	-1 'True
	Caption	"Current Sales Prices"
	Font	
	name	"Arial"
	weight	700
	size	9.75
Label	Name	Label3
	AutoSize	-1 'True
	Caption	"Updated Sales Price"
	Font	
	name	"Arial"
	weight	700
	size	9.75

OBJECT	PROPERTY	SETTING
Label	Name	Label4
	Caption	"Sales Total"
	Font	
	name	"Arial"
	weight	700
	size	9.75

NOTE

The code from this How-To builds on the last How-To. Only changes to the code will be commented. For additional help, refer to the Comments section in the last How-To.

6. Add the following set of code to the MDI form. When the form is loaded, the **LoadStockItems**, **LoadSalesPersons**, and **LoadSuppliers** procedures are called to set up the collection of stock items, salespersons, and suppliers. Note that the first section checks to ensure appropriate seed data has been placed into the database.

```
Private Sub MDIForm_Load()

'   Note the following code checks to ensure that
'   there has been appropriate seed data in
'   the database for salespersons, Stock Items,
'   and Suppliers.  See the book text for example
'   data and how to setup the database.

Dim DS As clsdata

Set DS = New clsdata

DS.initconnect

Dim CheckRS As rdoResultset

'   Check for salespersons
Set CheckRS = DS.getsalespersons

If CheckRS.EOF = True Then
    MsgBox "There are no salespersons in the database"
    End
End If

'   Check for suppliers
Set CheckRS = DS.getsuppliers

If CheckRS.EOF = True Then
    MsgBox "There are no suppliers in the database"
```

continued on next page

continued from previous page

```
        End
End If

'  Check for stock items
Set CheckRS = DS.getstockitems

If CheckRS.EOF = True Then
    MsgBox "There are no stock items in the database"
    End
End If

Set DS = Nothing

'  Load up the collections for each
'  type of object
LoadStockItems
LoadSalesPersons
LoadSuppliers

End Sub
```

7. When the exit menu is selected, the form is unloaded.

```
Private Sub mExit_Click()

'  Unload the project.
Unload Me

End Sub
```

8. The appropriate form is shown when one of the toolbar buttons is selected.

```
Private Sub Toolbar1_ButtonClick(ByVal Button As Button)

Select Case Button.Index

    Case 1
        '  Show the Sales Commission form
        SalesComm.Show

    Case 2
        '  Show the Sales Prices form
        SalesPrices.Show

    Case 3
        '  Show the order history form.
        OrderHist.Show

End Select

End Sub
```

9. Add the following set of code to the OrderHist form. Add the following to the General Declarations section of the form. A collection is declared that will contain a specified set of orders.

```
Option Explicit

'   Declare a collection of orders for
'   the history search
Dim OrderHistory As Collection
```

10. The `order sort` option calls the `Search_Click` procedure to sort the set of orders by date.

```
Private Sub OrderSort_Click()

'   Make sure a begin and end date
'   have been entered.
If (BeginDate.Text <> "") And (EndDate.Text <> "") Then Search_Click

End Sub
```

11. The `sale sort` option calls the `Search_Click` procedure to sort the set of orders by sales total.

```
Private Sub SaleSort_Click()

'   Make sure a begin and end date
'   have been entered.
If (BeginDate.Text <> "") And (EndDate.Text <> "") Then Search_Click

End Sub
```

12. When the Search button is selected, a check is done to ensure two dates have been entered; otherwise the subroutine is exited. Then the order history collection is created. A supply order class is created and the `GetOrderHistory` method is called and the collection passed in. The collection is filled with the supply orders that meet the search criteria. Then the orders are displayed in the listbox.

```
Private Sub Search_Click()

Dim MetaSO As clsSupplyOrder
Dim Order As Object
Dim Sort As Integer
Dim Hist As String

'   Make sure a begin and end date
'   have been entered.
If (BeginDate.Text = "") Or (EndDate.Text = "") Then Exit Sub

'   Create the collection.
Set OrderHistory = New Collection

'   Create a meta class for supply order
Set MetaSO = New clsSupplyOrder

'   Clear the listbox
OrderList.Clear
```

continued on next page

continued from previous page

```
'  Get the type of sort
If SaleSort.Value = True Then Sort = 2 Else Sort = 1

' Get the order history
MetaSO.GetOrderHistory OrderHistory, BeginDate.Text, EndDate.Text, Sort

'  Fill the listbox with each order
For Each Order In OrderHistory

    Hist = Left(Order.OrderDate & "          ", 10)

    OrderList.AddItem Hist & Chr$(9) & Order.TotalSale

Next

End Sub
```

13. Add the following set of code to the `SalesComm.frm`. Add the following to the General Declarations section of the form. The `SalesOrders` collection will hold the list of orders for the specified salesperson.

```
Option Explicit

'  Declare a collection for
'  sales orders
Dim SalesOrders As Collection
```

14. When the CommOrder button is selected, the `SalesList_Click` procedure is called to sort the orders by commission.

```
Private Sub CommOrder_Click()

'  Make sure a salesperson was
'  selected
If SalesList.ListIndex <> -1 Then SalesList_Click

End Sub
```

15. When the DateOrder button is selected, the `SalesList_Click` procedure is called to sort the orders by date.

```
Private Sub DateOrder_Click()

'  Make sure a salesperson was
'  selected
If SalesList.ListIndex <> -1 Then SalesList_Click

End Sub
```

16. When the form is loaded, the drop-down listbox is filled with the list of salespersons.

```
Private Sub Form_Load()

Dim SP As Object
Dim Cnt As Integer
```

```
'   Load the sale persons in the
'   listbox
For Each SP In SalesPersons
    SalesList.AddItem SP.FirstName &  " " & SP.LastName
    SalesList.ItemData(Cnt) = SP.SalesID
    Cnt = Cnt + 1
Next

End Sub
```

17. When an item from the salespersons listbox is selected, the salespersons set of orders will be shown. First, the **SalesOrders** collection is created. Then, the **GetSalesHistory** method of the **clsSalesPerson** class is called and the collection is passed in. The collection is filled with the list of orders. Finally, the listbox is filled with the list of sales orders.

```
Private Sub SalesList_Click()

Dim SO As Object
Dim Hist As String
Dim Sort As Integer
Dim SalesTotal As Double

Set SalesOrders = New Collection

'   Clear the listbox
SalesHistory.Clear

'   Clear out the new commission
'   rate box.
NewCommRate.Text = ""

'   Get the sort option
If DateOrder.Value = True Then Sort = 1 Else Sort = 2

'   Get the sales history for the selected
'   salesperson
SalesPersons.Item(SalesList.ItemData(SalesList.ListIndex)).GetSalesHistory ⇐
SalesOrders, Sort

'   Add the orders to the listbox
For Each SO In SalesOrders

    '   Total the sales
    SalesTotal = SalesTotal + SO.SalesCommission

    '   Get the order date and ensure the string
    '   is 10 characters long.
    Hist = Left(Str$(SO.OrderDate) + "          ", 10)

    '   Add the info. to the listbox
    SalesHistory.AddItem Hist & Chr$(9) & SO.SalesCommission

Next
```

continued on next page

continued from previous page

```
'  Show the total sales
TotalSales.Text = SalesTotal

'  Show the salesperson commission
SalesCommission.Text =
SalesPersons.Item(SalesList.ItemData(SalesList.ListIndex)).CommissionRate

End Sub
```

18. When the Update button is selected, the new commission rate is set in the
`salesperson` class and the `UpdateCommissionRate` method of the class
is called to store the new rate.

```
Private Sub Update_Click()

'  Ensure a new commission rate is entered.
If NewCommRate.Text <> "" Then

    '  Set the new commission rate

SalesPersons.Item(SalesList.ItemData(SalesList.ListIndex)).CommissionRate⟸
    = NewCommRate.Text

    '  Update the commission rate

SalesPersons.Item(SalesList.ItemData(SalesList.ListIndex)).UpdateCommissionR
ate

End If

End Sub
```

19. Add the following the code to the General Declarations section of the
SalesPrices form. Add the following to a new collection, `OrderItems`, is
declared that will hold all the orders for the specified stock item.

```
Option Explicit

Dim OrderItems As Collection
```

20. When the form is loaded, the drop-down listbox is filled with the list of
stock items.

```
Private Sub Form_Load()

Dim SI As Object
Dim Cnt As Integer

'  Load the stock items into the
'  listbox.  The ItemData property
'  will contain the Item ID
For Each SI In StockItems
    ItemsList.AddItem SI.ItemName
    ItemsList.ItemData(Cnt) = SI.ItemID
```

```
    Cnt = Cnt + 1
Next

End Sub
```

21. When an item in the list is selected, the collection of `OrderItems` is created and filled by calling the `GetSalesHistory` method of the `clsStockItem` class. Once the collection is retrieved, the list of orders is displayed in the listbox.

```
Private Sub ItemsList_Click()

Dim OI As Object
Dim Hist As String
Dim Sort As Integer
Dim SalesTotal As Double

Set OrderItems = New Collection

'  Clear listbox
SalesHistory.Clear

'  Clear the new price text box
NewPrice.Text = ""

'  Get the sales history for the item
StockItems.Item(ItemsList.ItemData(ItemsList.ListIndex)).GetSalesHistory ⇐
OrderItems

'  Show the orders
For Each OI In OrderItems

    '  Calculate the sales total
    SalesTotal = SalesTotal + OI.Quantity * OI.SalePrice

    '  Get the quantity and pad out to 10 spaces
    Hist = Left(Str$(OI.Quantity) + "          ", 10)

    '  Add to the listbox
    SalesHistory.AddItem Hist & Chr$(9) & OI.SalePrice

Next

'  Show the total sales
TotalSales.Text = SalesTotal

'  Show the current price of the item
CurrentPrice.Text =
StockItems.Item(ItemsList.ItemData(ItemsList.ListIndex)).SalePrice

End Sub
```

22. When the Update button is selected, the new sale price is set in the class and then the `UpdateSalePrice` method of the class is called to store the new sale price.

```
Private Sub Update_Click()

' Ensure a price is entered
If NewPrice.Text <> "" Then

    ' Set the sale price
    StockItems.Item(ItemsList.ItemData(ItemsList.ListIndex)).SalePrice ⇐
    = NewPrice.Text

    ' Update the sale price
    StockItems.Item(ItemsList.ItemData(ItemsList.ListIndex)).UpdateSalePrice

End If

End Sub
```

23. Insert a new module into the project and save it as global.bas.

```
Option Explicit

Global StockItems As Collection
Global SalesPersons As Collection
Global Suppliers As Collection

Global SupplyOrder As clsSupplyOrder
Global StockOrder As clsStockItemOrder

Public Sub main()

' Create the stock items collection
Set StockItems = New Collection

' Create the salespersons collection
Set SalesPersons = New Collection

' Create the suppliers collection
Set Suppliers = New Collection

' Show the form
MDIForm1.Show

End Sub

Public Sub LoadStockItems()

' Create a meta stock class
Dim MetaSI As clsStockItem

Set MetaSI = New clsStockItem

' Build the items in the class
MetaSI.GetStockItems StockItems

Set MetaSI = Nothing

End Sub
```

```
Public Sub LoadSalesPersons()

'   Create a meta salespersons class
Dim MetaSP As clsSalesPerson

Set MetaSP = New clsSalesPerson

'   Get the salespersons
MetaSP.GetSalesPersons SalesPersons

Set MetaSP = Nothing

End Sub

Public Sub LoadSuppliers()

'   Create a meta supplier class
Dim MetaSI As clsSupplier

Set MetaSI = New clsSupplier

'   Get the suppliers
MetaSI.GetSuppliers Suppliers

Set MetaSI = Nothing

End Sub
```

24. Start a new project and save it as 9-1-srv.vbp. Insert a new module into the project and save it as 9-2-srv.bas.

```
Option Explicit

'   Declare the data class
Global DS As clsData

Public Sub Main()

'   Create the data class
Set DS = New clsData

End Sub
```

25. Insert a new class into the project and save it as **clsData**.

```
Option Explicit

'   Dim a remote data environment
Dim Env As rdoEnvironment

'   Dim a remote data connection
Dim Con As rdoConnection

'   Declare a remote data record set
Dim RS As rdoResultset
```

continued on next page

continued from previous page

```
Public Sub InitConnect()

'   Set the default engine cursor driver
'   to ODBC.  This is needed to support calling
'   stored procedures that use multiple select
'   statments.
rdoEngine.rdoDefaultCursorDriver = rdUseOdbc

'   Set the remote data environment
Set Env = rdoEnvironments(0)

'   Open the ODBC connection
Set Con = Env.OpenConnection(dsName:="WholeSale", Prompt:=rdDriverNoPrompt)

End Sub

Private Sub DBExec(Cmd$)

'   Execute the specified SQL Command
Con.Execute Cmd$

End Sub

Private Sub DBOpenRec(Cmd$)

'   Open a resultset based on the
'   SQL query.  rdOpenKeySet indicates
'   that the rows can be updated.
Set RS = Con.OpenResultset(Cmd$, rdOpenKeyset, rdConcurRowver)

End Sub
```

26. The `GetStockHistory` method returns the inventory order history for the specified stock item.

```
Public Function GetStockHistory(ItemID) As rdoResultset

'   Get the list of suppliers
DBOpenRec "Select * from OrderItems where OrderType = 1 and ItemID = " & ⟸
ItemID & " order by Quantity"

Set GetStockHistory = RS

End Function
```

27. The `GetSupplyOrderHistory` method handles retrieving the set of inventory orders that fall within the specified date range. The `Sort` parameter indicates how the resultset should be ordered.

```
Public Function GetSupplyOrderHistory(BeginDate, EndDate, Sort) As
rdoResultset

'   Get the supply order records
'   that fit into the date period.
'   The record set is ordered by
```

```
'    date or sale.
If Sort = 1 Then DBOpenRec "Select * from SupplyOrder where OrderDate >= ⇐
'" & BeginDate & "' and OrderDate <= '" & EndDate & "' order by OrderDate"

If Sort = 2 Then DBOpenRec "Select * from SupplyOrder where OrderDate >= ⇐
'" & BeginDate & "' and OrderDate <= '" & EndDate & "' order by TotalSale"

Set GetSupplyOrderHistory = RS

End Function
```

28. The `GetSalesHistory` method of the class returns the set of orders for the specified salesperson. The `Sort` parameter indicates how the resultset should be ordered.

```
Public Function GetSalesHistory(SalesID, Sort) As rdoResultset

'    Get the sales order records
'    The record set is ordered by
'    date or commission.
If Sort = 1 Then DBOpenRec "Select orderid, SalesCommission, OrderDate ⇐
from SupplyOrder where SalesID = " & SalesID & " order by OrderDate"

If Sort = 2 Then DBOpenRec "Select orderid, SalesCommission, OrderDate ⇐
from SupplyOrder where SalesID = " & SalesID & " order by SalesCommission"

Set GetSalesHistory = RS

End Function

Public Function GetSuppliers() As rdoResultset

'    Get the list of suppliers
DBOpenRec "Select * from Suppliers"

Set GetSuppliers = RS

End Function

Public Function GetStockItems() As rdoResultset

'    Get the list of stock items
DBOpenRec "Select * from StockItem"

Set GetStockItems = RS

End Function

Public Function GetBackOrder(ItemID) As Long

'    Get the back order quantity for the item
DBOpenRec "Select backorder from StockItem where itemid = " & ItemID

GetBackOrder = RS("backorder") & ""
```

continued on next page

continued from previous page

```
End Function

Public Function GetSalesPersons() As rdoResultset

'  Get the list of salespersons
DBOpenRec "Select * from SalesPerson"

Set GetSalesPersons = RS

End Function

Public Function InsertSupplyOrder(TotalSale, SalesID, OrderDate, ⇐
SalesCommission) As Integer

Dim InsertSupplyOrderPS As rdoPreparedStatement

'  Create an RDO prepared statement for calling
'  the stored procedure
Set InsertSupplyOrderPS = Con.CreatePreparedStatement⇐
("INSERT_SUPPLY_ORDER", "{ ? = call INSERT_SUPPLY_ORDER (?, ?, ?, ?) }")

'  The first parameter is the return value which
'  will be the order id
InsertSupplyOrderPS.rdoParameters(0).Direction = rdParamReturnValue

'  Set the four input parameters
InsertSupplyOrderPS.rdoParameters(1) = TotalSale
InsertSupplyOrderPS.rdoParameters(2) = SalesID
InsertSupplyOrderPS.rdoParameters(3) = OrderDate
InsertSupplyOrderPS.rdoParameters(4) = SalesCommission

'  Open the result set for the return
'  value from the stored procedure
Set RS = InsertSupplyOrderPS.OpenResultset(rdOpenStatic, rdConcurReadOnly)

'  Return the new order id
InsertSupplyOrder = RS(0)

'  Close the prepared statement
InsertSupplyOrderPS.Close

End Function

Public Function InsertStockOrder(TotalPurchasePrice, OrderDate, ⇐
ArrivalDate) As Integer

Dim InsertStockOrderPS As rdoPreparedStatement

'  Create an RDO prepared statement for calling
'  the stored procedure
Set InsertStockOrderPS = Con.CreatePreparedStatement⇐
("INSERT_STOCK_ORDER", "{ ? = call INSERT_STOCK_ORDER (?, ?, ?) }")

'  The first parameter is the return value which
'  will be the order id
```

```
InsertStockOrderPS.rdoParameters(0).Direction = rdParamReturnValue

'   Set the three input parameters
InsertStockOrderPS.rdoParameters(1) = TotalPurchasePrice
InsertStockOrderPS.rdoParameters(2) = OrderDate
InsertStockOrderPS.rdoParameters(3) = ArrivalDate

'   Open the result set for the return
'   value from the stored procedure
Set RS = InsertStockOrderPS.OpenResultset(rdOpenStatic, rdConcurReadOnly)

'   return the order id
InsertStockOrder = RS(0)

'   Close the prepared statement
InsertStockOrderPS.Close

End Function

Public Sub InsertSaleItem(OrderID, ItemID, Quantity, SalePrice, OrderType)

'   Execute the stored procedure to
'   insert an ordered sale item
DBExec "exec insertsaleitem " & OrderID & ", " & ItemID & ", " & ⇐
Quantity & ", " & SalePrice & ", " & OrderType

End Sub

Public Function GetShelfQuantity(ItemID) As Long

'   Get the shelf quantity
'   for the product.
DBOpenRec "Select shelfquantity from StockItem where itemid = " & ItemID

GetShelfQuantity = RS("shelfquantity") & ""

End Function

Public Sub UpdateSalePrice(ItemID, SalePrice)

'   Update the sale price for the
'   stock item
DBExec "Update StockItem set SalePrice = " & SalePrice & " ⇐
where ItemId = " & ItemID

End Sub

Public Sub UpdateCommissionRate(SalesID, CommissionRate)

'   Update the commission rate for
'   the salesperson
DBExec "Update SalesPerson set CommissionRate = " & CommissionRate ⇐
& " where SalesId = " & SalesID

End Sub
```

continued on next page

continued from previous page

```
Public Sub UpdateShelfQuantity(ItemID, UpdateQuantity)

Dim CurrentQuantity

'  Get the current quantity
CurrentQuantity = GetShelfQuantity(ItemID)

'  Update the shelf quantity
DBExec "exec updateshelfquantity " & ItemID & ", " & (CurrentQuantity ⇐
- UpdateQuantity)

End Sub

Public Sub UpdateBackOrder(ItemID, UpdateQuantity)

Dim CurrentQuantity

'  Get the current back order
'  quantity
CurrentQuantity = GetBackOrder(ItemID)

'  Update the back order quantity
DBExec "exec updatebackorder " & ItemID & ", " & (CurrentQuantity ⇐
+ UpdateQuantity)

End Sub

Public Function GetPurchPrice(ItemID) As Double

'  Get the pruchase price for the item
DBOpenRec "Select PurchPrice from StockItem where ItemID = " & ItemID

GetPurchPrice = RS("PurchPrice") & ""

End Function

Private Sub Class_Initialize()

'  Initialize the connection
InitConnect

End Sub
```

29. Insert a new class into the project and save it as `clsSupplyOrder`.

```
Option Explicit

Dim m_OrderID As Integer
Dim m_TotalSale As Double
Dim m_SalesId As Integer
Dim m_OrderDate As Date
Dim m_SalesCommission As Double

Dim SalesItems As Collection

'  Set the order id
```

```
Public Property Let OrderID(I As Integer)
    m_OrderID = I
End Property

Public Property Get OrderID() As Integer
    OrderID = m_OrderID
End Property

'   The total sale for the order
Public Property Let TotalSale(D as Double)
    m_TotalSale = D
End Property

Public Property Get TotalSale() As Double
    TotalSale = m_TotalSale
End Property

'   The sales id
Public Property Let SalesID(I As Integer)
    m_SalesId = I
End Property

Public Property Get SalesID() As Integer
    SalesID = m_SalesId
End Property

'   The date of the order
Public Property Let OrderDate(D As Date)
    m_OrderDate = D
End Property

Public Property Get OrderDate() As Date
    OrderDate = m_OrderDate
End Property

'   The sales commission
Public Property Let SalesCommission(D as Double)
    m_SalesCommission = D
End Property

Public Property Get SalesCommission() As Double
    SalesCommission = m_SalesCommission
End Property

Private Sub AddSaleItem(ItemID, Quantity, SalePrice)

Dim SItem As clsOrderItem

'   Create a new order item clas
Set SItem = New clsOrderItem

'   Set the item id
SItem.ItemID = ItemID

'   Set the quantity
```

continued on next page

continued from previous page

```
SItem.Quantity = Quantity

'  Set the sale price
SItem.SalePrice = SalePrice

'  This a customer order versus
'  a re-stock order
SItem.OrderType = 1

'  Add the item to the collection of
'  ordered items
SalesItems.ADD Item:=SItem, Key:=CStr(ItemID)

Set SItem = Nothing

End Sub

Public Sub UpdateSaleItem(ItemID, Quantity As Integer)

'  Update the item with the new quantity
SalesItems.Item(CStr(ItemID)).Quantity = Quantity

End Sub

Public Function GetSaleItemQuantity(ItemID) As Integer

'  Get the quantity of the sale
GetSaleItemQuantity = SalesItems.Item(CStr(ItemID)).Quantity

End Function

Public Function CalculateTotalOrderPrice() As Double

Dim SI As Object
Dim RunningTotal As Double

'  Get the running total
For Each SI In SalesItems

    RunningTotal = RunningTotal + SI.TotalSale

Next

CalculateTotalOrderPrice = RunningTotal

End Function

Public Sub StoreOrder()

Dim SI As Object

'  Insert the order
m_OrderID = DS.InsertSupplyOrder(m_TotalSale, m_SalesId, m_OrderDate, ⇐
m_SalesCommission)
```

```
For Each SI In SalesItems

    ' Store the ordered item
    If SI.Quantity <> 0 Then
        SI.StoreItem m_OrderID
        DS.UpdateShelfQuantity SI.ItemID, SI.Quantity
    End If

Next

End Sub

Public Function CalculateNetProfit() As Double

Dim SI As Object
Dim TotalPurchPrice As Double

' Cacluate the total sale
TotalSale = CalculateTotalOrderPrice

For Each SI In SalesItems

    ' Calculate the total purchase price (cost)
    If SI.Quantity <> 0 Then TotalPurchPrice = TotalPurchPrice ⇐
    + (DS.GetPurchPrice(SI.ItemID) * SI.Quantity)

Next

' The net profit is the total sale minus the
' purchase price minus the sales commission

CalculateNetProfit = TotalSale - TotalPurchPrice - SalesCommission

End Function
```

30. The `GetOrderHistory` method of the class handles retrieving the set of school supply orders that fits with the specified date and which is sorted as indicated by the **sort** parameter. A collection is sent into the subroutine, which will be filled with a set of supply order classes that fit the search criteria.

```
Public Sub GetOrderHistory(OrderHistory As Object, BeginDate As String, ⇐
EndDate As String, Sort As Integer)

Dim SO As clsSupplyOrder
Dim RS As rdoResultset

' Get the order history by begin and end date
Set RS = DS.GetSupplyOrderHistory(BeginDate, EndDate, Sort)

Do Until RS.EOF

    ' Create the new class
    Set SO = New clsSupplyOrder
```

continued on next page

continued from previous page

```
    ' set the order id
    SO.OrderID = RS("orderid")

    ' Set the total sale
    SO.TotalSale = RS("TotalSale")

    ' set the order date
    SO.OrderDate = RS("orderdate")

    ' add the class to the collection
    OrderHistory.ADD Item:=SO, Key:=CStr(RS("orderid") & "")

    ' move to the next record
    RS.MoveNext

Loop

Set SO = Nothing

End Sub

Private Sub Class_Initialize()

Dim RS As rdoResultset

Set SalesItems = New Collection

' Get all of the stock items
Set RS = DS.GetStockItems

' Add the items to the list
Do Until RS.EOF

    AddSaleItem RS("itemid") & "", 0, RS("saleprice") & ""

    RS.MoveNext

Loop

End Sub
```

31. Insert a new class into the project and save it as **clsSupplier**.

```
Option Explicit

Dim m_SupplierID As Integer
Dim m_Name As String
Dim m_Address1 As String
Dim m_Address2 As String
Dim m_City As String
Dim m_State As String
Dim m_Zip As String
Dim m_Phone As String

' The supplier id
```

```
Public Property Let SupplierID(I As Integer)
    m_SupplierID = I
End Property

Public Property Get SupplierID() As Integer
    SupplierID = m_SupplierID
End Property

'   The supplier name
Public Property Let Name(S As String)
    m_Name = S
End Property

Public Property Get Name() As String
    Name = m_Name
End Property

'   The supplier address1
Public Property Let Address1(S As String)
    m_Address1 = S
End Property

Public Property Get Address1() As String
    Address1 = m_Address1
End Property

'   The supplier address2
Public Property Let Address2(S As String)
    m_Address2 = S
End Property

Public Property Get Address2() As String
    Address2 = m_Address2
End Property

'   The supplier city
Public Property Let City(S As String)
    m_City = S
End Property

Public Property Get City() As String
    City = m_City
End Property

'   The supplier state
Public Property Let State(S As String)
    m_State = S
End Property

Public Property Get State() As String
    State = m_State
End Property

'   The supplier zip
Public Property Let Zip(S As String)
```

continued on next page

continued from previous page

```
    m_Zip = S
End Property

Public Property Get Zip() As String
    Zip = m_Zip
End Property

' The supplier phone
Public Property Let Phone(S As String)
    m_Phone = S
End Property

Public Property Get Phone() As String
    Phone = m_Phone
End Property

' Meta function to get the suppliers
Public Sub GetSuppliers(Suppliers As Object)

Dim RS As rdoResultset
Dim SI As clsSupplier

' Get the record set of suppliers
Set RS = DS.GetSuppliers

Do Until RS.EOF

    ' Create the class
    Set SI = New clsSupplier

    ' Set the supplier id
    SI.SupplierID = RS("supplierid") & ""

    ' Set the supplier name
    SI.Name = Trim(RS("name") & "")

    ' Set the supplier address
    SI.Address1 = Trim(RS("address1") & "")

    ' Set the supplier address
    SI.Address2 = Trim(RS("address2") & "")

    ' Set the supplier city
    SI.City = RS("city") & ""

    ' Set the supplier state
    SI.State = RS("State") & ""

    ' Set the supplier zip
    SI.Zip = RS("zip") & ""

    ' Set the supplier phone
    SI.Phone = RS("phone") & ""

    ' Add the supplier to the collection
```

```
        Suppliers.ADD Item:=SI, Key:=CStr(RS("supplierid") & "")

        RS.MoveNext

    Loop

    Set SI = Nothing

    End Sub
```

32. Insert a new class into the project and save it as clsStockOrder.

```
Option Explicit

Dim m_OrderID As Integer
Dim m_TotalPurchase As Double
Dim m_OrderDate As Date
Dim m_ArrivalDate As Date
Dim SI As clsOrderItem

'  The order id
Public Property Let OrderID(I As Integer)
    m_OrderID = OrderID
End Property

Public Property Get OrderID() As Integer
    OrderID = m_OrderID
End Property

'  The total purchase price
Public Property Get TotalPurchase() As Double

    '  Calculate the total purchase
    TotalPurchase = DS.GetPurchPrice(SI.ItemID) * SI.Quantity

End Property

'  The order date
Public Property Let OrderDate(D As Date)
    m_OrderDate = D
End Property

Public Property Get OrderDate() As Date
    OrderDate = m_OrderDate
End Property

'  The arrival date
Public Property Let ArrivalDate(D As Date)
    m_ArrivalDate = D
End Property

Public Property Get ArrivalDate() As Date
    ArrivalDate = m_ArrivalDate
End Property

'  The ID of the item to purchase
```

continued on next page

continued from previous page

```
Public Property Get PurchaseItem() As Integer
    PurchaseItem = SI.ItemID
End Property

Public Property Let PurchaseItem(I As Integer)
    SI.ItemID = I
End Property

'   The quantity sold
Public Property Let Quantity(L As Long)
    SI.Quantity = L
End Property

Public Property Get Quantity() As Long
    Quantity = SI.Quantity
End Property

Public Sub StoreOrder()

'   Insert the order
m_OrderID = DS.InsertStockOrder(Me.TotalPurchase, m_OrderDate,
m_ArrivalDate)

'   Store the ordered item
SI.StoreItem m_OrderID

'   Update the back order quantity
DS.UpdateBackOrder SI.ItemID, SI.Quantity

End Sub

Private Sub Class_Initialize()

Set SI = New clsOrderItem

'   Set the order type to 2 for a stock order
SI.OrderType = 2

End Sub
```

33. Insert a new class into the project and save it as `clsStockItem`.

```
Option Explicit

Dim m_ItemID As Integer
Dim m_ItemName As String
Dim m_ItemDesc As String
Dim m_ShelfQuantity As Long
Dim m_SalePrice As Double
Dim m_PurchasePrice As Double
Dim m_BackOrder As Long
Dim m_SupplierID As Integer


'   The stock item id
Public Property Get ItemID() As Integer
    ItemID = m_ItemID
```

```
End Property

Public Property Let ItemID(I As Integer)
    m_ItemID = I
End Property

'   The item name
Public Property Get ItemName() As String
    ItemName = m_ItemName
End Property

Public Property Let ItemName(S As String)
    m_ItemName = S
End Property

'   The item description
Public Property Get ItemDesc() As String
    ItemDesc = m_ItemDesc
End Property

Public Property Let ItemDesc(S As String)
    m_ItemDesc = S
End Property

'   The shelf quantity
Public Property Get ShelfQuantity() As Long
    m_ShelfQuantity = DS.GetShelfQuantity(m_ItemID)
    ShelfQuantity = m_ShelfQuantity
End Property

Public Property Let ShelfQuantity(L As Long)
    m_ShelfQuantity = L
End Property

'   The supplier id
Public Property Let SupplierID(I As Integer)
    m_SupplierID = I
End Property

Public Property Get SupplierID() As Integer
    SupplierID = m_SupplierID
End Property

'   The back order quantity
Public Property Get BackOrder() As Long
    '   Get the latest back order quantity
    m_BackOrder = DS.GetBackOrder(m_ItemID)
    BackOrder = m_BackOrder
End Property

Public Property Let BackOrder(L As Long)
    m_BackOrder = L
End Property

'   The purchase price
```

continued on next page

continued from previous page

```
Public Property Get PurchasePrice() As Double
    PurchasePrice = m_PurchasePrice
End Property

Public Property Let PurchasePrice(D as Double)
    m_PurchasePrice = D
End Property


'  The sale price
Public Property Get SalePrice() As Double
    SalePrice = m_SalePrice
End Property

Public Property Let SalePrice(D as Double)
    m_SalePrice = D
End Property


Public Property Get ProfitPercentage() As Double

Dim CommissionAvg As Double
Dim Costs As Double
Dim OverHeadAdd As Double

'  Calculate the average commission
CommissionAvg = m_SalePrice * 0.1

'  Calculate the overhead addition
'  Note see the chapter discussion
'  about decision support and business
'  objects for how this can be handled
OverHeadAdd = m_SalePrice * 0.08

'  Total the costs
Costs = m_PurchasePrice + OverHeadAdd + CommissionAvg

'  Calculate the profit percentage
ProfitPercentage = ((m_SalePrice - Costs) / m_SalePrice) * 100

End Property

'  Meta function to retrieve the
'  the stock items
Public Sub GetStockItems(Stock As Object)

Dim RS As rdoResultset
Dim SI As clsStockItem

'  Get the items
Set RS = DS.GetStockItems

Do Until RS.EOF

    '  Create a new class
    Set SI = New clsStockItem
```

```
'  Set the id
SI.ItemID = RS("itemid") & ""

'  Set the name
SI.ItemName = Trim(RS("itemname") & "")

'  Set the description
SI.ItemDesc = Trim(RS("itemdesc") & "")

'  Set the purchase price
SI.PurchasePrice = RS("purchprice") & ""

'  Set the sale price
SI.SalePrice = RS("saleprice") & ""

'  Set the supplier id
SI.SupplierID = RS("supplierid") & ""

'  add the class to the collection
Stock.ADD Item:=SI, Key:=CStr(RS("itemid") & "")

'  Move to the next record
RS.MoveNext

Loop

Set SI = Nothing

End Sub
```

34. The `GetSalesHistory` method of the class handles retrieving the sales history for the stock item. A collection is passed into the subroutine, which is filled with the set of order item classes that represent the sales history.

```
Public Sub GetSalesHistory(StockHistory As Object)

Dim OI As clsOrderItem
Dim RS As rdoResultset

'  Get the sale history for the stock item
Set RS = DS.GetStockHistory(m_ItemID)

Do Until RS.EOF

    '  Create the new class
    Set OI = New clsOrderItem

    '  set the item id
    OI.ItemID = m_ItemID

    '  Set the quantity
    OI.Quantity = RS("quantity") & ""

    '  set the sale price
    OI.SalePrice = RS("saleprice")
```

continued on next page

continued from previous page

```
            '   add the class to the collection
            StockHistory.ADD Item:=OI, Key:=CStr(RS("orderid") & "")

            '   move to the next record
            RS.MoveNext

Loop

Set OI = Nothing

End Sub
```

35. `UpdateSalePrice` handles storing the new item sale price in the database.

```
Public Sub UpdateSalePrice()

'   Update the price of the item
DS.UpdateSalePrice m_ItemID, m_SalePrice

End Sub
```

36. Insert a new class into the project and save it as `clsSalesPerson`.

```
Option Explicit

Dim m_SalesId As Integer
Dim m_FirstName As String
Dim m_LastName As String
Dim m_CommissionRate As Double

'   salesperson ID
Public Property Get SalesID() As Integer
    SalesID = m_SalesId
End Property

Public Property Let SalesID(I As Integer)
    m_SalesId = I
End Property

'   First name of the salesperson
Public Property Get FirstName() As String
    FirstName = m_FirstName
End Property

Public Property Let FirstName(S As String)
    m_FirstName = S
End Property

'   Last name of the salesperson
Public Property Get LastName() As String
    LastName = m_LastName
End Property

Public Property Let LastName(S As String)
    m_LastName = S
```

```
End Property

'   The commission rate for the
'   salesperson
Public Property Get CommissionRate() As Double
    CommissionRate = m_CommissionRate
End Property

Public Property Let CommissionRate(D as Double)
    m_CommissionRate = D
End Property

'   Meta function that gets all the
'   salespersons
Public Sub GetSalesPersons(SalesPersons As Object)

Dim RS As rdoResultset
Dim SP As clsSalesPerson

'   Get the record set of salespersons
Set RS = DS.GetSalesPersons

Do Until RS.EOF

    '   Create the new class
    Set SP = New clsSalesPerson

    '   set the sales id
    SP.SalesID = RS("salesid") & ""

    '   set the first name
    SP.FirstName = Trim(RS("firstname") & "")

    '   set the last name
    SP.LastName = Trim(RS("lastname") & "")

    '   set the commission rate
    SP.CommissionRate = Trim(RS("commissionrate") & "")

    '   add the class to the collection
    SalesPersons.ADD Item:=SP, Key:=CStr(RS("salesid") & "")

    '   move to the next record
    RS.MoveNext

Loop

Set SP = Nothing

End Sub
```

37. The `GetSalesHistory` procedure handles retrieving and sorting the sales history for the salesperson. A collection and the desired sort order are passed in as arguments to the subroutine. The collection is filled with classes representing each order for the salesperson.

```
Public Sub GetSalesHistory(SalesHistory As Object, Sort)

Dim SO As clsSupplyOrder
Dim RS As rdoResultset

' Get the sales history
Set RS = DS.GetSalesHistory(m_SalesId, Sort)

Do Until RS.EOF

    ' Create the new class
    Set SO = New clsSupplyOrder

    ' set the order date
    SO.OrderDate = RS("orderdate") & ""

    ' set the sales commission
    SO.SalesCommission = RS("salescommission") & ""

    ' add the class to the collection
    SalesHistory.ADD Item:=SO, Key:=CStr(RS("orderid") & "")

    ' move to the next record
    RS.MoveNext

Loop

Set SO = Nothing

End Sub

' Calculates the commission for the sale
Public Function CalculateCommission(Sale) As Double
    CalculateCommission = CommissionRate * Sale
End Function
```

38. The `UpdateCommissionRate` procedure is called to store the new commission rate for the salesperson.

```
Public Sub UpdateCommissionRate()

' Update the salespersons
' commission rate
DS.UpdateCommissionRate m_SalesId, m_CommissionRate

End Sub
```

39. Insert a new class into the project and save it as `clsOrderItem.cls`.

```
Option Explicit

Dim m_OrderID As Integer
Dim m_ItemID As Integer
Dim m_Quantity As Long
Dim m_SalePrice As Double
Dim m_OrderType As Integer
```

```
'  The ID of the order for
'  the stock item
Public Property Let OrderID(I As Integer)
    m_OrderID = I
End Property

Public Property Get OrderID() As Integer
    OrderID = m_OrderID
End Property

'  The ID of the ordered item
Public Property Let ItemID(I As Integer)
    m_ItemID = I
End Property

Public Property Get ItemID() As Integer
    ItemID = m_ItemID
End Property

'  The quantity ordered
Public Property Let Quantity(L As Long)
    m_Quantity = L
End Property

Public Property Get Quantity() As Long
    Quantity = m_Quantity
End Property

'  The type of order.  1 is a supply order
'  2 is a restock order
Public Property Let OrderType(I As Integer)
    m_OrderType = I
End Property

Public Property Get OrderType() As Integer
    OrderType = m_OrderType
End Property

'  The sale price of the item
Public Property Let SalePrice(D as Double)
    m_SalePrice = D
End Property

Public Property Get SalePrice() As Double
    SalePrice = m_SalePrice
End Property

'  Calculates the total sale price for
'  the ordered quantity
Public Function TotalSale() As Double
    TotalSale = m_SalePrice * m_Quantity
End Function

Public Sub StoreItem(OrderID)
```

continued on next page

continued from previous page

```
'   Save the ordered item
DS.InsertSaleItem OrderID, m_ItemID, m_Quantity, m_SalePrice, m_OrderType

End Sub
```

> **NOTE**
>
> The following steps describe how to set up the database if you are
> unable to utilize the WholeSale.SQL script provided in the Chapter
> 9 directory on the CD. Note that this script does not set up default
> seed data (see Step 40 below).

40. Add the following stored procedures and tables to the WholeSale SQL
Server database. Note, you will need to seed the StockItem and Suppliers
tables with data in order for the application to work.

```
CREATE PROCEDURE Insert_Stock_Order  @TotalPurchasePrice float, ⇐
@OrderDate datetime, @ArrivalDate datetime AS

/*  The Return Value */
declare @OrderID int

/*  Begin the transaction */
begin transaction

    /*  Insert the order */
    Insert StockOrder (TotalPurchasePrice, OrderDate, ArrivalDate) ⇐
    values(@TotalPurchasePrice, @OrderDate, @ArrivalDate)

    /*  Get back the order ID */
    select @OrderID = max(OrderID) from StockOrder

commit transaction

/*  Return the Order ID in a column called NewOrderID */
select @OrderID NewOrderID


CREATE PROCEDURE Insert_Supply_Order  @TotalSale float, @SalesID int, ⇐
@OrderDate datetime, @SalesCommission float AS

/*  the return value */
declare @OrderID int

/*  begin the transaction of inserting
    a new order */
begin transaction

    /*  Insert the order */
    Insert SupplyOrder (TotalSale, SalesID, OrderDate, SalesCommission) ⇐
    values(@TotalSale, @SalesID, @OrderDate, @SalesCommission)

    /* get the order id */
```

```
      select @OrderID = max(OrderID) from SupplyOrder

/*   commit the order transaction */
commit transaction

/*   Return the new order ID in a column named NewOrderID */
select @OrderID NewOrderID



CREATE PROCEDURE InsertSaleItem @OrderId int, @ItemID int, @Quantity int, ⇐
@SalePrice float, @OrderType int AS

/*   Insert the Sale Item */
insert OrderItems values(@OrderID, @ItemID, @Quantity, @OrderType,
@SalePrice)



CREATE PROCEDURE UpdateBackOrder @ItemID int, @Quantity int AS

/*   update the stock item backorder */
update StockItem set BackOrder = @Quantity where ItemID = @ItemID



CREATE PROCEDURE UpdateShelfQuantity @ItemID int, @Quantity int AS

/*   Update the ShelfQuantity of the stock Item */
update StockItem set ShelfQuantity = @Quantity where ItemID = @ItemID
```

TABLES:
OrderItems

OrderID	int	NOT NULL
ItemID	int	NOT NULL
Quantity	int	NULL
OrderType	tinyint	NULL
SalePrice	float	NULL

        PRIMARY KEY
            ItemID
            OrderID

SalesPerson

SalesID	int	NOT NULL
FirstName	varchar (20)	NULL
LastName	varchar (20)	NULL
CommissionRate	float	NULL

        PRIMARY KEY
            SalesID

SalesPerson Sample Data (Column Order as Shown Above):

1	Wendy	Winner	0.16

continued on next page

continued from previous page

```
2          Tommy          Thumb              0.12
3          Sammy          Sellem             0.09
4          Cindy          Commision          0.17


StockItem
    ItemID                int              NOT NULL
    ItemName              char (50)        NOT NULL
    ItemDesc              varchar(255)     NULL
    ShelfQuantity         int              NULL
    BackOrder             int              NULL
    PurchPrice            float            NULL
    SalePrice             float            NULL
    SupplierID            int              NULL

    PRIMARY KEY
        ItemID
```

StockItem Sample Data (Column Order as Shown Above):

```
1  Erasers                 Hot Disney Erasers         104    200
0.25  0.75  1
2  Yellow Legal Notepads   Lined Yellow Legal Notepad 4039   500
0.65  1.23  4
3  Big Blue Note Pads      For Kids 7 and Under       22     0
2.23  3.5  4
4  Ticky Tacky Glue        The best kids art glue     121    234
0.78  1.22  3
5  Roy Bob's Pencil Box    Multipurpose pencil box    84     300
1.23  2.24  5
6  Right Angle Protractor  For making the best angles 456    0
0.43  0.68  5
7  The Cool Notebook       Stylish for the coolest kid 57    0
3.5   5.0   2
8  Fruity Crayons          For eating and drawing     311    0
1.89  2.76  5
9  El Velcro               The notebook that sticks   258    0
7.5   9.0   2


StockOrder
    OrderID               int              NOT NULL
    TotalPurchasePrice    float            NULL
    OrderDate             datetime         NULL
    ArrivalDate           datetime         NULL

    PRIMARY KEY
        OrderID


Suppliers
    SupplierID            int              NOT NULL
    Name                  varchar (50)     NULL
    Address1              varchar (50)     NULL
    Address2              varchar (50)     NULL
    City                  varchar (50)     NULL
    State                 varchar (2)      NULL
```

```
    Zip                      varchar (10)      NULL
    Phone                    varchar (20)      NULL

    PRIMARY KEY
        SupplierID
```

Suppliers Sample Data (Column Order as Shown Above):

```
1 EraserHeads      100 Rub Out Lane  (null) Child State    VA 22601 555-
555-5551
2 Notebook Heaven 1100 Spiral Ave.   (null) Three Ringville NY 33333 555-
555-5552
3 Glue It Inc.     100 Stuck On You  (null) Paste City     TX 32332 555-
555-5553
4 Worthy of Note    34 Write It Down  (null) Jot It         MN 87877 555-
555-5554
5 Supplies R Us     87 School's In    (null) Studyville     TX 87874 555-
555-5555
```

```
SupplyOrder
    OrderID                  int               NOT NULL
    TotalSale                float             NULL
    SalesID                  int               NULL
    OrderDate                datetime          NULL
    SalesCommission          float             NULL

    PRIMARY KEY
        OrderID
```

How It Works

This example provides three straightforward methods for providing decision support to the user. The key to making this example work is utilizing the business objects and Data services tiers of our three-tier model built in the last How-To. Of course, a new User services tier needs to be developed to deliver the new functionality.

Let's briefly review the business objects layer developed in the last How-To. This is where we will need to develop the new functionality to provide the decision support utilities. Figure 9-10 shows the class relationships of the projects. Table 9-13, which follows, defines each class.

Table 9-13 Class descriptions

CLASS	DEFINITION
clsData	Handles all direct interfacing with the Data services layer and uses RDO
clsOrderItem	Encapsulates a stock item that is part of an order
clsSalesPerson	Defines a salesperson
clsStockItem	Defines an item in the stock inventory
clsStockItemOrder	Encapsulates an order for inventory stock and utilizes clsOrderItem
clsSupplier	Defines a supplier of a stock item
clsSupplyOrder	Encapsulates an order for an item from inventory and utilizes clsOrderItem

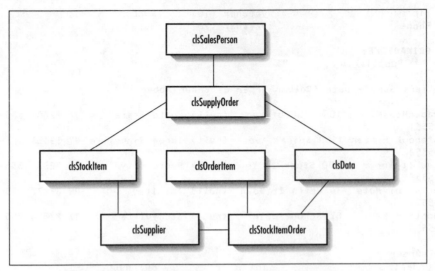

Figure 9-10 The class relationships

To implement the sales commission review, the `clsSalesPerson` class needs to have two new methods added to provide the needed functionality. The first, `GetSalesHistory`, will fill a collection with all the orders for the salesperson represented by the class. This collection can then be utilized by the User services layer to display the sales history as appropriate. The second method to be added is `UpdateSalesCommission`. This will handle storing the new sales commission for the salesperson.

For the inventory stock items, we also need a way to get the sales history for the sale item. So, for the `clsStockItem` class, we will need to add two methods to provide the needed functionality: `GetSalesHistory`, which will return the order history in a collection for the stock item, and `UpdateSalePrice`, to update the sales price for the item.

Finally, we need to add functionality to review orders based on specified search parameters. This means updating the `clsSupplyOrder` with a new method (you guessed it), `GetOrderHistory`, which will retrieve all the orders for the specified search parameters.

Note that the `GetOrderHistory` methods are actually meta methods for their classes. This means that the method works on all the class objects, not just the object represented by the current instance of the class.

Finally, the User interface tier must be built to appropriately represent the decision support capabilities to the user. The sample here provides straightforward methods for updating sales commission rates, stock sale prices, and reviewing order history. A simple MDI application is built with toolbar functionality provided for accessing the different functions.

Note that the Data services layer does not change to support this new functionality and, in fact, the business objects change very little. The User interface tier built in the last How-To would not have to be updated at all to run with this new set of classes. If these business objects were implemented as ActiveX components, potentially only one machine would need to be updated to provide the new functionality. Also note that the underlying object model fits our new requirements because the up-front design closely represented the objects involved in our business environment. Because this is the case, we achieve one of the promises of object technology, code reuse. For example, the **Stock Item** class gets its sales history by utilizing the **clsSupplyOrder** class, not by building new functionality.

Comments

Consider updating the user interface of the application to be more robust, as demonstrated in Chapter 4, User Interface Design. Also, keep in mind that this application can be scaled to fit different size enterprises by utilizing a pool manager and playing with the partitioning of the data interface between the **clsData** class and SQL Server stored procedures.

COMPLEXITY
ADVANCED

9.3 How do I...
Build a three-tier client/server image tracking system?

Problem

In Chapter 4, User Interface Design, we developed an interface for an Image Tracking system. But, that example was distinctly two-tier in design and did not take advantage of many of the new features of Visual Basic 5. How can this application be converted into a three-tier client/server application?

Technique

Primarily what we are changing in this example over the final How-To in Chapter 4 is the underlying architecture. We are keeping the same user interface, but implementing a true three-tier model. To accomplish the basic task of tracking images on a system, it is important to abstract away the primary objects used in the system as we did in the last two examples. The difference between this new image tracking system and the previous examples is that this is more of a processing (images) system rather than a business system. But, that does not mean that there are not important abstractions to make. Table 9-14 overviews three classes we will build into the system.

Table 9-14 Second-tier business objects

BUSINESS OBJECT	DESCRIPTION
IData	Encapsulates the interface to the Data services layer
DiskFile	Encapsulates a single disk file
Bitmap	Encapsulates a bitmap image

Since the Image Tracker works on a set of bitmap objects, we will utilize a collection to browse the bitmaps With the encapsulation of the bitmaps and the **IData** class, the User interface tier will not have any code that directly relates to the data storage for the program. There is also one stored procedure used in the data tier as outlined in Table 9-15.

Table 9-15 Third-tier SQL Server stored procedures

STORED PROCEDURE	DESCRIPTION
Insert_Image	Inserts a new image into the database and returns the Image ID.

By building these second- and third-tier objects, we can successfully divide the application in Chapter 4 into three tiers. By doing this, we will have a new application that will be easier to maintain, easier to implement, and easier to modify.

Note, Step 53 will explain how to set up the **IData** database for this application. Also, you will need to have a 32-bit ODBC data source for the database. In this example, the database was set up in Microsoft SQL Server 6.5 as **IData** and the ODBC DSN was set to ImageData. You will want to install the ImageData table in a different database than the one utilized in the previous two How-To's. You may place the database tables in with a name of your choosing; just ensure the ODBC connection is set up properly (refer to Chapter 2, Getting Conncted).

Steps

Open and run 9-3.VBP. The running program appears as shown in Figure 9-11.

To load the image database, click on the Open Folder toolbar button. The Image and Data View forms are shown. To browse the database, utilize the arrow buttons on the toolbar or the corresponding menu selections. A new image can be added to the database by selecting the new document toolbar button. The image can be stretched and flipped by selecting the appropriate toolbar buttons or the view menu options. Figure 9-12 shows the MDI form with Data and Image View forms visible.

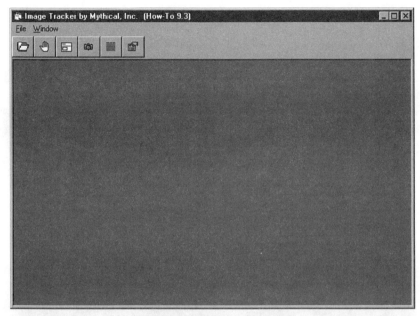

Figure 9-11 The form as it appears at runtime

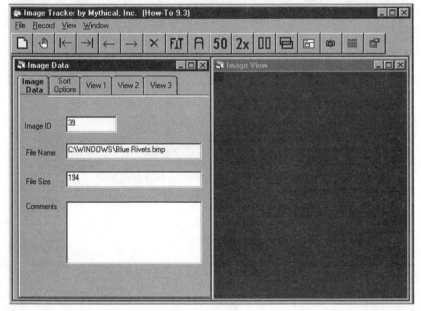

Figure 9-12 The MDI form with the Data and Image View forms

Figure 9-13 shows the Windows 95 Explorer along with the Image Tracking application. Bitmap image files can be dragged from Explorer to the Image View window. The images will be automatically be added to the database.

The program also implements a preview option to view images before they are added to the database. Drag an image from the Windows Explorer to the Preview window. If you wish to add the Image to the database, drag the bitmap from the Preview window to the Image window in the ImageTracker. Figure 9-14 shows the Image Tracker program with the Preview window.

1. Create a new project called 9-3.VBP. Add the objects and properties listed in Table 9-16 to Form1 and save the form as 9-3.FRM.

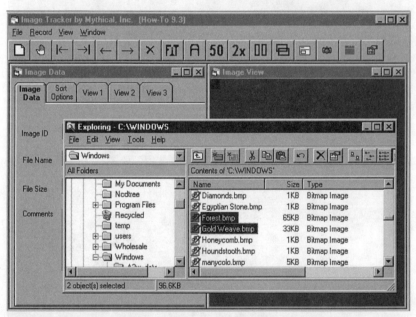

Figure 9-13 The Image Tracker program with the Windows Explorer

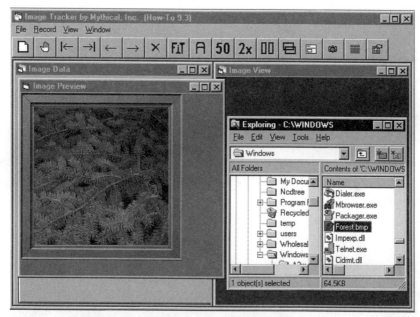

Figure 9-14 The Image Tracker program with the Preview window

Table 9-16 The MDI form's objects and properties

OBJECT	PROPERTY	SETTING
MDIForm	Name	ImageTracker
	AutoShowChildren	0 'False
	Caption	"Image Tracker by Mythical, Inc.
		(How-To 9.3)"
Toolbar	Name	ImageTool
	Align	1 'Align Top
	Negotiate	-1 'True
	ImageList	"MDIButtons"
	ButtonWidth	926
	ButtonHeight	847
	AllowCustomize	0 'False
	NumButtons	18
	AlignSet	-1 'True
	Wrappable	0 'False

continued on next page

continued from previous page

OBJECT	PROPERTY	SETTING
ImageList	Name	MDIButtons
	ImageWidth	28
	ImageHeight	26
	MaskColor	12632256
	NumImages	18
	i1	open.bmp
	i2	new.bmp
	i3	hand.bmp
	i4	first.bmp
	i5	last.bmp
	i6	prev.bmp
	i7	next.bmp
	i8	delete.bmp
	i9	fit.bmp
	i10	actual.bmp
	i11	50.bmp
	i12	2x.bmp
	i13	tile.bmp
	i14	cascade.bmp
	i15	data.bmp
	i16	camera.bmp
	i17	menu.bmp
	i18	prop.bmp

2. Add the menus shown in Table 9-17 to the Image Tracker form.

Table 9-17 The Image Tracker form's menus

CONTROL NAME	CAPTION	INDEX	CHECKED	SHORTCUT KEY
mFile	"&File"			
mOpenImage	"&Open Image Database"			
mBar	"-"			
mExit	"E&xit"			
mWindow	"&Window"			
mImageData	"Image &Data"			
mImageView	"Image &View"			

CONTROL NAME	CAPTION	INDEX	CHECKED	SHORTCUT KEY
mBar3	"-"			
mShowToo	"Show Toolbar"	-1	'True	
mShowMenu	"Show Menu"	-1	'True	

3. Insert a new form into the project and save it as IView.frm. Add the following objects and properties to the form.

Table 9-18 The Image View form's objects and properties

OBJECT	PROPERTY	SETTING
Form	Name	ImageView
	Caption	"Image View"
	MDIChild	1 'True
PictureBox	Name	DispPict
	BackColor	H00C00000&
	BorderStyle	'None
	Picture	"pastel.bmp"
	ScaleMode	'Pixel
PictureBox	Name	BackPict
	AutoRedraw	1 'True
	AutoSize	1 'True
	BackColor	H000000FF&
	BorderStyle	0 'None
	Picture	"pastel.bmp"
	ScaleMode	'Pixel
	Visible	'False
Msghook	Name	Msghook

4. Add the menus shown in Table 9-19 to the Image View form.

Table 9-19 The Image View form's menus

CONTROL NAME	CAPTION	INDEX	CHECKED	SHORTCUT KEY
mFile	"&File"			
mNewImage	&New Image"			
mBar	"-"			
mExit	"E&xit"			

continued on next page

continued from previous page

CONTROL NAME	CAPTION	INDEX	CHECKED	SHORTCUT KEY
mRecord	"&Record"			
mBrowse	"&First"	0		F1
mBrowse	"&Last"	1		F2
mBrowse	"&Back"	2		F3
mBrowse	"or&ward"	3		F4
mBar2	"-"			
mDelete	"&Delete Record"			
mView	"&View"			
mSize	"&Fit in Window"	0		
mSize	"&Actual Size"	1	-1 'True	
mSize	"&50 Percent"	2		
mSize	"&200 Percent"	3		
mViewSet	"Viewer Settings"			
Flip	"Flip &Horizontal"	0"		
Flip	"Flip &Vertical"	1		
mWindow	"&Window"			
mTile	"&Tile"			
mCascade	"&Cascade"			
mBar1	"-"			
mShowWindow	"Image &Data"	0		
mShowWindow	"Image &View"	1		
mPreview	"Image &Preview"			
mBar3	"-"			
mShowTool	"Show Tool&Bar"		-1 'True	
mShowMenu	"Show &Menu"		-1 'True	

5. Insert a new form into the project and save it as IData.frm. Add the objects and properties shown in Table 9-20 to the form.

Table 9-20 The Image Data form's objects and properties

OBJECT	PROPERTY	SETTING
Form	Name	ImageData
	Caption	"Image Data"
	MDIChild	-1 'True
	Visible	0 'False

OBJECT	PROPERTY	SETTING
SSTab	Name	SSTab1
	Caption	"View 3"
	TabsPerRow	5
	Tab	4
	TabOrientation	0
	Tabs	5
	Style	0
	TabMaxWidth	1323
	TabHeight	794
	TabCaption(0)	"Image Data"
	Tab(0).ControlCount	10
	Tab(0).ControlEnabled	0 'False
	Tab(0).Control(0)	"ImageInfo(0)"
	Tab(0).Control(1)	"ImageInfo(1)"
	Tab(0).Control(2)	"ImageInfo(2)"
	Tab(0).Control(3)	"ImageInfo(3)"
	Tab(0).Control(4)	"ImageInfo(4)"
	Tab(0).Control(5)	"ImageLabel(0)"
	Tab(0).Control(6)	"ImageLabel(1)"
	Tab(0).Control(7)	"ImageLabel(2)"
	Tab(0).Control(8)	"ImageLabel(3)"
	Tab(0).Control(9)	"ImageLabel(4)"
	TabCaption(1)	"Sort Options"
	Tab(1).ControlCount	4
	Tab(1).ControlEnabled	0 'False
	Tab(1).Control(0)	"Option1(0)"
	Tab(1).Control(1)	"Option1(1)"
	Tab(1).Control(2)	"Option1(2)"
	Tab(1).Control(3)	"Option1(3)"
	TabCaption(2)	"View 1"
	Tab(2).ControlCount	2
	Tab(2).ControlEnabled	0 'False
	Tab(2).Control(0)	"View(0)"
	Tab(2).Control(1)	"Thumb(0)"
	TabCaption(3)	"View 2"
	Tab(3).ControlCount	2

continued on next page

continued from previous page

OBJECT	PROPERTY	SETTING
	Tab(3).ControlEnabled	0 'False
	Tab(3).Control(0)	"View(1)"
	Tab(3).Control(1)	"Thumb(1)"
	TabCaption(4)	"View 3"
	Tab(4).ControlCount	2
	Tab(4).ControlEnabled	-1 'True
	Tab(4).Control(0)	"View(2)"
	Tab(4).Control(1)	"Thumb(2)"
ListBox	Name	Thumb
	Index	2
ListBox	Name	Thumb
	Index	1
ListBox	Name	Thumb
	Index	0
OptionButton	Name	SortOpts
	Caption	"Sort by Image ID"
	Index	0
OptionButton	Name	SortOpts
	Caption	"Sort by File Name"
	Index	1
OptionButton	Name	SortOpts
	Caption	"Sort by File Size"
	Index	2
OptionButton	Name	SortOpts
	Caption	"Sort by File Format"
	Index	3
TextBox	Name	ImageInfo
	DataField	"ImageID"
	DataSource	"MSRDC1"
	Index	0
	Locked	-1 'True
TextBox	Name	ImageInfo
	DataField	"FileName"
	DataSource	"MSRDC1"
	Index	1

OBJECT	PROPERTY	SETTING
TextBox	Name	ImageInfo
	DataField	"FileSize"
	DataSource	"MSRDC1"
	Index	2
	Locked	-1 'True
TextBox	Name	ImageInfo
	DataField	"FileFormat"
	DataSource	"MSRDC1"
	Index	3
TextBox	Name	ImageInfo
	DataField	"Comments"
	DataSource	"MSRDC1"
	Index	4
	MultiLine	-1 'True
Image	Name	View
	Index	
	Stretch	1 'True
Image	Name	View
	Index	1
	Stretch	-1 'True
Image	Name	View
	Index	0
	Stretch	-1 'True
Label	Name	ImageLabel
	AutoSize	-1 'True
	Caption	"Image ID"
	Index	0
Label	Name	ImageLabel
	AutoSize	-1 'True
	Caption	"File Name"
	Index	1
Label	Name	ImageLabel
	AutoSize	-1 'True
	Caption	"File Size"
	Index	2

continued on next page

continued from previous page

OBJECT	PROPERTY	SETTING
Label	Name	ImageLabel
	AutoSize	-1 'True
	Caption	"File Format"
	Index	3
Label	Name	ImageLabel
	AutoSize	-1 'True
	Caption	"Comments"
	Index	4
CommonDialog	Name	CommonDialog1
	DefaultExt	".bmp"
	DialogTitle	"Find Image File"
	Filter	"*.bmp; *.wmf"
	FilterIndex	1
	InitDir	"c:\windows"
MSRDC	Name	MSRDC1
	Visible	0 'False
	DataSourceName	"Image Database"
	RecordSource	"select * from ImageData order by ImageID"
	RecordsetType	1
	KeysetSize	0
	ReadOnly	0 'False
	UserName	""
	Password	""
	CursorDriver	2
	EOFAction	1
	BOFAction	1
	Prompt	3
	LockType	3

6. Add the menus shown in Table 9-21 to the Image Data form.

Table 9-21 The Image Data form's menus

CONTROL NAME	CAPTION	INDEX	CHECKED	SHORTCUT KEY
mFile	"&File"			
mNewImage	"&New Image"			

CONTROL NAME	CAPTION	INDEX	CHECKED	SHORTCUT KEY
mBar	"-"			
mExit	"E&xit"			
mRecord	"&Record"			
mBrowse	"&First"	0		F1
mBrowse	"&Last"	1		F2
mBrowse	"&Back"	2		F3
mBrowse	"For&ward"	3		F4
mBar2	"-"			
mDelete	"&Delete Record"			
mView	"&View"			
mSize	"&Fit in Window"	0		
mSize	"&Actual Size"	1	-1 'True	
mSize	"&50 Percent"	2		
mSize	"&200 Percent"	3		
mWindow	"&Window"			
mTile	"&Tile"			
mCascade	"&Cascade"			
mBar1	"-"			
mShowWindow	"Image &Data"	0		
mShowWindow	"Image &View"	1		
mPreview	"Image &Preview"			
mBar3	"-"			
mShowTool	"Show Tool&Bar"		-1 'True	
mShowMenu	"Show &Menu"		-1 'True	

7. Insert a new form into the project and save it as Preview.frm. Add the objects and properties shown in Table 9-22 to the form.

Table 9-22 The Preview form's objects and properties

OBJECT	PROPERTY	SETTING
Form	Name	Preview
	Caption	"Image Preview"
PictureBox	Name	PrevPict
	Appearance	0 'Flat
	BackColor	&H00808080&
	BorderStyle	0 'None

continued on next page

continued from previous page

OBJECT	PROPERTY	SETTING
	DragIcon	"pastel.bmp"
	DragMode	1 'Automatic
	ForeColor	H80000008&
Msghook	Name	Msghook

NOTE

Only the routines that have changed from those presented in Chapter 4 will be commented. For additional help, please refer to How-To 4.5.

8. Add the following code to the MDI form.

```
Option Explicit

Private Sub ImageTool_ButtonClick(ByVal Button As Button)

Select Case Button.Index

    Case 1
        '   Open the Image Database
        MenuOpenData

    Case 2
        '   Call the MenuNewImage function to get
        '   a new image
        MenuNewImage SaveData

    Case 3
        '   Exit the program
        MenuExit

    Case 4
        '   Move to the first record
        MenuBrowse 0, SaveData

    Case 5
        '   Move to the last record
        MenuBrowse 1, SaveData

    Case 6
        '   Move back a record
        MenuBrowse 2, SaveData

    Case 7
        '   Move forward a record
        MenuBrowse 3, SaveData

    Case 8
        '   Delete the current bitmap
```

```
        MenuDelete

    Case 9
        '  Set the View to fit in the Window
        SetView 0

    Case 10
        '  Set the View to actual size
        SetView 1

    Case 11
        '  Set the View to 50 %
        SetView 2

    Case 12
        '  Set the View to 200 %
        SetView 3

    Case 13
        '  Tile the windows
        MenuTile

    Case 14
        '  Cascade the Windows
        MenuCascade

    Case 15
        '  If the ImageData form is not
        '  visible then call the
        '  MenuOpenData function to open
        '  the database.  Otherwise, show
        '  the ImageData Window (0)
        If ImageData.Visible = False Then
            MenuOpenData
        Else
            MenuShowWindow 0
        End If

    Case 16
        '  If the ImageData form is not
        '  visible then call the
        '  MenuOpenData function to open
        '  the database.  Otherwise, show
        '  the ImageView Window (1)
        If ImageData.Visible = False Then
            MenuOpenData
        Else
            MenuShowWindow 1
        End If

    Case 17
        '  Show or hide the Menu depending
        '  on the current setting.
        MenuShowMenu
```

continued on next page

continued from previous page

```
        Case 18
            ' Start the drag process for the
            ' toolbar.
            ImageTool.Drag

End Select

End Sub

Private Sub ImageTool_MouseDown(Button As Integer, Shift As Integer, X ⇐
As Single, Y As Single)

' Check for the right mouse
' button click
If Button = vbPopupMenuRightButton Then

        ' If the ImageData form is not visible then
        ' show the popup menu for ImageTracker form.
        ' Otherwise show the pop up menu for the
        ' ImageData form.
        If ImageData.Visible = False Then
            Me.PopupMenu mWindow, vbPopupMenuCenterAlign, , , mShowTool
        Else
            ImageData.PopupMenu ImageData.mWindow, vbPopupMenuCenterAlign, , ⇐
        , ImageData.mShowTool
        End If

End If

End Sub

Private Sub MDIForm_DragDrop(Source As Control, X As Single, Y As Single)

' Check to see if the drop was on
' the top or bottom half of the
' MDI form
If (Y - (ImageTool.Height / 2)) > (ImageTracker.Height / 2) Then
    ImageTool.Align = 2
Else
    ImageTool.Align = 1
End If

End Sub
```

9. When the MDI form is loaded, the collection of bitmap images is loaded into a collection object by calling the **LoadCollection** subroutine. Also, note that the **BmpIndex** is set to 1 to reference the first object in the Bitmaps collection. A check is done first to ensure that appropriate seed data has been entered into the database (see Step 53).

```
Private Sub MDIForm_Load()

' Note the following code checks to ensure that
' there has been appropriate seed data in
' the database for salespersons, Stock Items,
```

```
'   and Suppliers.  See the book text for example
'   data and how to setup the database.

Dim DS As clsdata

Set DS = New clsdata

DS.initconnect

Dim CheckRS As rdoResultset

'   Check for salespersons
Set CheckRS = DS.getsalespersons

If CheckRS.EOF = True Then
    MsgBox "There are no salespersons in the database"
    End
End If

'   Check for suppliers
Set CheckRS = DS.getsuppliers

If CheckRS.EOF = True Then
    MsgBox "There are no suppliers in the database"
    End
End If

'   Check for stock items
Set CheckRS = DS.getstockitems

If CheckRS.EOF = True Then
    MsgBox "There are no stock items in the database"
    End
End If

Set DS = Nothing

'   Load the bitmap collection with the images
'   sorted by ID
LoadCollection ImageIDSort

'   Hide the ImageData form when
'   the MDI form is first loaded
ImageData.Hide

'   Set the index to the first bitmap
BmpIndex = 1

End Sub

Private Sub MDIForm_MouseDown(Button As Integer, Shift As Integer, X As ⇐
Single, Y As Single)

'   If the ImageData form is not visible,
'   then show the File menu from the
```

continued on next page

continued from previous page

```
'    ImageTracker form
If (Button = vbPopupMenuRightButton) And (ImageData.Visible <> True) Then
    Me.PopupMenu mFile, vbPopupMenuCenterAlign, , , mOpenImage
    Exit Sub
End If

'    If the ImageData form is visible,
'    then show the Window menu from the
'    ImageData form
If (Button = vbPopupMenuRightButton) And (ImageData.Visible = True) Then
    ImageData.PopupMenu ImageData.mWindow, vbPopupMenuCenterAlign ', , ⇐
, ImageData.mImageData
End If

End Sub

Private Sub MDIForm_QueryUnload(Cancel As Integer, UnloadMode As Integer)

'    Call the MenuExit program to
'    end the program
MenuExit

End Sub

Private Sub MDIForm_Unload(Cancel As Integer)

'    Call the MenuExit program to
'    end the program
MenuExit

End Sub

Private Sub mExit_Click()

'    Call the MenuExit program to
'    end the program
MenuExit

End Sub

Private Sub mImageData_Click()

'    Call the MenuOpenData method to open the
'    Image database
MenuOpenData

End Sub

Private Sub mImageView_Click()

'    Call the MenuOpenData method to open the
'    Image database
MenuOpenData

End Sub
```

```
Private Sub mOpenImage_Click()

'   Call the MenuOpenData method to open the
'   Image database
MenuOpenData

End Sub

Private Sub mShowMenu_Click()

'   Show or hide the Menu
MenuShowMenu

End Sub

Private Sub mShowTool_Click()

'   Show or hide the Toolbar
MenuShowTool

End Sub
```

10. Add the following code to the Image Data form. Add the **PopulateLists** method to the General Declarations section of the form. First, the listboxes of images to select thumbnail views are cleared. Then we loop through each bitmap object in the Bitmaps collection and show the image filename.

```
Public Sub PopulateLists()

Dim Bmp As Object

'   Clear the three thumb nail lists
Thumb(0).Clear
Thumb(1).Clear
Thumb(2).Clear

'   Loop through the bitmaps in the collection
'   and add them the listbox
For Each Bmp In Bitmaps
    Thumb(0).AddItem Bmp.FileInfo.FileName
    Thumb(1).AddItem Bmp.FileInfo.FileName
    Thumb(2).AddItem Bmp.FileInfo.FileName
Next

End Sub

Private Sub Form_Load()

'   Populate the list boxes
PopulateLists

End Sub
```

continued on next page

continued from previous page

```
Private Sub Form_MouseDown(Button As Integer, Shift As Integer, ⇐
X As Single, Y As Single)

If Button = vbPopupMenuRightButton Then
    '   Show the Record menu for moving
    '   through the image records in the
    '   database
    Me.PopupMenu mRecord, vbPopupMenuCenterAlign, , , mBrowse(3)

End If

End Sub

Private Sub Form_Resize()

Dim N As Integer

'   Size the tab control to fit in
'   the form.
SSTab1.Width = ImageData.Width - 110
If Me.WindowState <> vbMinimized Then SSTab1.Height = ImageData.Height - ⇐
500

'   Resize the other controls on the tab
For N = 1 To 3
    '   Resize the image info text
    '   boxes
    ImageData.ImageInfo(N).Width = SSTab1.Width - 1400

    '   Resize the thumb nail lists
    '   and the view image controls
    If N < 4 Then
        Thumb(N - 1).Width = SSTab1.Width - 450
        View(N - 1).Width = SSTab1.Width - 450
        View(N - 1).Height = SSTab1.Height - View(N - 1).Top - 750
    End If
Next N

End Sub

Private Sub Form_Unload(Cancel As Integer)

'   We don't want the form to be unloaded so that
'   it will not have to be re-initialized
Cancel = -1

'   Instead minimize the form
Me.WindowState = 1

End Sub


Private Sub mBrowse_Click(Index As Integer)

'   Browse the bitmaps depending
```

```
'   on the menu selected
MenuBrowse Index, SaveData

End Sub

Private Sub mCascade_Click()

'   Cascade the windows
MenuCascade

End Sub

Private Sub mDelete_Click()

'   Delete the current bitmap
MenuDelete

End Sub

Private Sub mExit_Click()

'   Call the MenuExit method to
'   exit the program
MenuExit

End Sub

Private Sub mNewImage_Click()

'   Cal the MenuNewImage function to allow
'   the user to select a new image to add to the
'   database
MenuNewImage SaveData

End Sub

Private Sub mPreview_Click()

'   Show the Preview form
Preview.Show

End Sub

Private Sub mShowMenu_Click()

'   Show or hide the Menu
MenuShowMenu

End Sub

Private Sub mShowTool_Click()

'   Show or hide the toolbar
MenuShowTool
```

continued on next page

continued from previous page

```
End Sub

Private Sub mShowWindow_Click(Index As Integer)

'  Call the MenuShowWindow function to show
'  the window selected
MenuShowWindow Index

End Sub

Private Sub mSize_Click(Index As Integer)

'  Set the View based on the menu
'  selection
SetView Index

End Sub

Private Sub mTile_Click()

'  Tile the windows
MenuTile

End Sub
```

11. When the different image sort options are selected from the second tab, the collection of bitmaps is re-created to be ordered appropriately. The sort option constants, **ImageIDSort**, **FileNameSort**, and **FileSizeSort**, are used to indicate the type of sort to be done. Then, the thumbnail listboxes are repopulated and we move to the beginning of the set of images.

```
Private Sub SortOpts_Click(Index As Integer)

'  Depending on the sort option, reload
'  the collection with the appropriate sort
Select Case Index

    Case 0
        '  Sort by Image ID
        LoadCollection ImageIDSort

    Case 1
        '  Sort by File Name
        LoadCollection FileNameSort

    Case 2
        '  Sort by File Size
        LoadCollection FileSizeSort

End Select

'  Show the new lists
PopulateLists
```

```
'   Move to the first record and
'   save
MenuBrowse 0, SaveData

End Sub

Private Sub Thumb_Click(Index As Integer)

    '   When the lists are clicked on
    '   load the files into the image
    '   controls
    View(Index).Picture =
LoadPicture(Thumb(Index).List(Thumb(Index).ListIndex))

End Sub
```

12. Add the following code to the Image View form.

```
Option Explicit

Private Sub disppict_DragDrop(Source As Control, X As Single, Y As Single)

'   If the dropped control is the
'   toolbar then we need to do the
'   necessary checking to see if the
'   toolbar should be re-aligned
If Source.Name = "ImageTool" Then

    '   Check to see if the toolbar drop
    '   was on the top or bottom half of the
    '   picture box.  Note that the picture
    '   box is in pixel mode so we need to
    '   convert the coordinates to twips.
    If ((Y * Screen.TwipsPerPixelY) - ⇐
    (ImageTracker.ImageTool.Height / 2)) ⇐
  > (ImageTracker.Height / 2) Then
        ImageTracker.ImageTool.Align = 2
    Else
        ImageTracker.ImageTool.Align = 1
    End If

    Exit Sub

End If

'   Otherwise a new file should have
'   been dropped on the picture box
'   from the preview window.  We need
'   to check to ensure that there is
'   a picture file associated with the
'   preview.  If so then add the image to
'   the database.
If Preview.PreviewFileName <> "" Then
    DropNewImage Preview.PreviewFileName
End If
```

continued on next page

continued from previous page

```
End Sub

Private Sub mPreview_Click()

'  Show the preview window
Preview.Show

End Sub

Private Sub Msghook_Message(ByVal msg As Long, ByVal wp As Long, ByVal lp ⇐
As Long, result As Long)

Dim NumFiles As Integer
Dim Buffer As String 'Byte
Dim N As Integer
Dim NameLen As Integer

'  Set the buffer up to recieve the
'   filename
Buffer = Space$(256)

'  See if the drop file message was
'   sent
If msg = WM_DROPFILES Then

    '  Retrieve the number of files
    '   dropped.
    NumFiles = DragQueryFile(wp, -1&, Buffer, Len(Buffer))

    '  Loop through the files and add them to
    '   the image database.
    For N = 0 To (NumFiles - 1)

        '  Get the filename of the file and
        '   retrieve the length of the
        '   filename
        NameLen = DragQueryFile(wp, N, Buffer, 128)

        '  Check to see if the file is a
        '   bitmap or icon.
        If (UCase(Right((Left(Buffer, NameLen)), 3)) = "BMP") Or ⇐
(UCase(Right((Left(Buffer, NameLen)), 3)) = "ICO") Then

            '  Add the image to the database
            DropNewImage Left(Buffer, NameLen)

        End If

    Next N

    ' Tell the system the drag is done
    Call DragFinish(wp)

    '  Set the result
```

```
        result = 0

    End If

End Sub

Public Sub SizeViewPict()

'   Allow for a small border
'   around the display picture
DispPict.Top = 5
DispPict.Left = 5
DispPict.Width = Me.Width - 5
DispPict.Height = Me.Height - 5

'   Set the view to the current
'   view option
SetView Iview

End Sub

Private Sub DispPict_MouseDown(Button As Integer, Shift As Integer, X As ⇐
Single, Y As Single)

'   If the right mouse button is selected, then
'   the different image size options are shown.  If
'   it is a left mouse click then the flip options
'   are shown
If Button = vbPopupMenuRightButton Then
    Me.PopupMenu mView, vbPopupMenuCenterAlign, , , mSize(0)
Else
    Me.PopupMenu mViewSet, vbPopupMenuCenterAlign
End If

End Sub

Private Sub Flip_Click(Index As Integer)

'   When the flip menu is clicked, the
'   check on the menu is set appropriately
If Flip(Index).Checked = False Then
    Flip(Index).Checked = True
Else
    Flip(Index).Checked = False
End If

'   It is important to ensure that only
'   a vertical or horizotal flip can be
'   performed.  This, the menu item that
'   was not clicked is unchecked.
If Index = 1 Then
    Flip(0).Checked = False
Else
    Flip(1).Checked = False
End If
```

continued on next page

continued from previous page

```
'  Based on the selection,
'  the image is redisplayed.
SizeViewPict

End Sub
```

13. Add the following code to the MDI form. Note that when the Image View form is loaded, we will be ready to move to the first image in the database. But, we have to be careful not to save the data since no changes have taken place yet. So, we will call the **MenuBrowse** function and indicate that no changes will be saved by using the **NoSaveData** constant.

```
Private Sub Form_Load()

'  Enable the form to accept
'  file drops
EnableFileDrop Me.hwnd

'  Setup MsgHook control
Msghook.HwndHook = Me.hwnd
Msghook.Message(WM_DROPFILES) = True

'  Intially set IView to 0.
Iview = 1

'  Call the MenuBrowse function
'  to show the first record
MenuBrowse 1, NoSaveData

End Sub

Private Sub DispPict_Paint()

'  Size the view picture
SizeViewPict

End Sub

Private Sub Form_Unload(Cancel As Integer)

'  Cancel the unload.  We don't want the
'  form to be unloaded while the program is
'  running so that it does not have to be
'  re-initialized.  Instead, the form will be
'  minimized.
Cancel = -1
Me.WindowState = 1

End Sub

Private Sub mBrowse_Click(Index As Integer)

'  Browse the record set depending on the
'  menu option chosen.
```

```
MenuBrowse Index, SaveData

End Sub

Private Sub mCascade_Click()

'  Cascade the windows
MenuCascade

'  Size the view picture after the cascade
SizeViewPict

End Sub

Private Sub mDelete_Click()

'  Call the MenuDelete function to
'  delete the selected record.
MenuDelete

End Sub

Private Sub mExit_Click()

'  Call the MenuExit function to
'  exit the program.
MenuExit

End Sub

Private Sub mNewImage_Click()

'  Call the MenuNewImage function to get
'  a new image
MenuNewImage SaveData

End Sub

Private Sub mShowMenu_Click()

'  Show or hide the Menu
MenuShowMenu

End Sub

Private Sub mShowTool_Click()

'  Show or hide the toolbar
MenuShowTool

End Sub

Private Sub mShowWindow_Click(Index As Integer)

'  Call the MenuShowWindow function to show
```

continued on next page

continued from previous page

```
'   the selected window.
MenuShowWindow Index

End Sub

Private Sub mTile_Click()

'   Call the menu tile function to
'   tile the windows
MenuTile

End Sub

Private Sub mSize_Click(Index As Integer)

'   Set the view depending on the menu option
'   selected
SetView Index

End Sub
```

14. Add the following code to the Preview form. Note that the
PreviewFileName variable is globally accessible so that when an image is
dragged from the Preview window to the Image window, the image
filename can be accessed.

```
'   Public property that will indicate
'   what filename is associated with
'   the preview
Public PreviewFileName As String

Private Sub Form_Load()

'   Enable the preview to accept
'   file drag and drop
EnableFileDrop Me.hwnd

'   Setup the MsgHook control
Msghook.HwndHook = Me.hwnd
Msghook.Message(WM_DROPFILES) = True

'   Move the preview picture to the
'   top left
PrevPict.Top = 0
PrevPict.Left = 0

'   Set the preview picture width
'   and height
PrevPict.Width = Preview.Width
PrevPict.Height = Preview.Height

End Sub

Private Sub Form_Resize()
```

```vb
'  When the form is resized,
'  resize the picture
PrevPict.Width = Preview.Width
PrevPict.Height = Preview.Height

End Sub

Private Sub Form_Unload(Cancel As Integer)

'  When the preview is unloaded,
'  make sure the ImageTracker form
'  is visible
ImageTracker.Show

End Sub

Private Sub Msghook_Message(ByVal msg As Long, ByVal wp As Long, ByVal lp ⇐
As Long, result As Long)

Dim NumFiles As Integer
Dim Buffer As String 'Byte
Dim N As Integer
Dim NameLen As Integer

'  Set the buffer up to receive the
'  filename
Buffer = Space$(256)

'  See if the drop file message was
'  sent
If msg = WM_DROPFILES Then

    '  Retrieve the number of files
    '  dropped.
    NumFiles = DragQueryFile(wp, -1&, Buffer, Len(Buffer))

    '  Get the filename of the file and
    '  retrieve the length of the
    '  filename
    NameLen = DragQueryFile(wp, N, Buffer, 128)

    '  Check to see if the file is a
    '  bitmap or icon.
    If (UCase(Right((Left(Buffer, NameLen)), 3)) = "BMP") Or ⇐
    (UCase(Right((Left(Buffer, NameLen)), 3)) = "ICO") Then

        '  Load the picture into the preview
        PrevPict.Picture = LoadPicture(Left(Buffer, NameLen))

        '  Set the filename of the form
        PreviewFileName = Left(Buffer, NameLen)

    End If

    '  Tell the system the drag done.
```

continued on next page

continued from previous page

```
    Call DragFinish(wp)

    ' Set the result
    result = 0

End If

End Sub
```

15. Insert a new class into the project and save it as `Bitmap.cls`. Add the following code to the General Declarations section of the form. First, a global reference, `FileInfo`, is created to the `DiskFile` class. The `Bitmap` class will inherit the properties and methods of the `DiskFile` class. Also declared are the global members of the class.

```
Option Explicit

'   A Bitmap is a type of DiskFile
'   So, the Bitmap class will use
'   the properties and methods of
'   the DiskFile class for its
'   functionality
Public FileInfo As DiskFile

'   Declare the global properties of the
'   class.  m_DispPict is the standard
'   display picture.  m_BackPict is the
'   background picture that will be used
'   for the image flipping.
Private m_DispPict As Control
Private m_BackPict As Control
Private m_ID As Integer
```

16. The `ID` property of the class can be both set and retrieved. This is the ID of the image in the database.

```
'   Provide a unique ID to reference the bitmap
Public Property Let ID(I As Integer)
    m_ID = I
End Property

Public Property Get ID() As Integer
    ID = m_ID
End Property
```

17. The `DispPict` property of the class will reference the display picture for the image.

```
'  Get the Display picture control
Public Property Set DispPict(AControl As Control)
    Set m_DispPict = AControl
    m_DispPict.AutoSize = True
End Property
```

18. The `BackPict` property references a working back picture box for displaying the image. This picture will be used for building the image flips and other graphics effects. Note that the picture box is set up as a memory device context by setting its `AutoRedraw` property to `True` and its `Visible` property to `False`.

```
'  Get the Back ground picture control
'  It is important to ensure that this
'  picture is invisible and that the
'  AutoRedraw property is true so that it
'  will act as a memory device context and
'  hold its image for later work
Public Property Set BackPict(AControl As Control)
    Set m_BackPict = AControl
    m_BackPict.AutoRedraw = True
    m_BackPict.Visible = False
    m_BackPict.AutoSize = True
End Property
```

19. The `Loadback` function loads the image into the `BackPict` picture box.

```
'  Loads the back picture with the image
Public Sub LoadBack()
    m_BackPict.Picture = LoadPicture(FileInfo.FileName)
End Sub
```

20. The `Load` method will load the picture into both the `BackPict` and `DispPict` picture boxes.

```
'  The load method of the class loads
'  the image into the two display pictures
Public Sub Load()
    m_DispPict.Picture = LoadPicture(FileInfo.FileName)
    m_BackPict.Picture = LoadPicture(FileInfo.FileName)
    m_DispPict.Visible = True
End Sub
```

21. The `Flip` method of the class will flip the image based upon the passed parameter. To rotate the image, the `PaintPicture` method of the picture box is used.

```
'  The Flip method of the class will rotate
'  the picture accordingly
Public Sub Flip(Rotate)

'  Depending on the rotation selected, the
'  original image will be copied to the
'  display picture appropriately
Select Case Rotate

'  Note that for the vertical and
'  horizontal flips, the height or
'  width is set to a negative value
'  and the starting point is set to
'  the height or width for the image
```

continued on next page

continued from previous page

```
'   to be displayed.   The PaintPicture
'   method of the picture box is used
'   to do the rotation
    Case 1  'Actual Size
             '  Flip Horizontal
      m_DispPict.PaintPicture m_BackPict.Picture, ⇐
      m_BackPict.ScaleWidth, 0, -1 * m_BackPict.ScaleWidth, ⇐
      m_BackPict.ScaleHeight, 0, 0, m_BackPict.ScaleWidth, ⇐
      m_BackPict.ScaleHeight

    Case 2
             '  Flip Vertical
      m_DispPict.PaintPicture m_BackPict.Picture, 0, ⇐
      m_BackPict.ScaleHeight, m_BackPict.ScaleWidth, -1 * ⇐
      m_BackPict.ScaleHeight, 0, 0, m_BackPict.ScaleWidth, ⇐
      m_BackPict.ScaleHeight

End Select

End Sub
```

22. The `GetBitmaps` method is a meta method of the class. This method will build bitmap objects for each image in the database. Note that a collection, Bitmaps, is sent into the class to add the bitmap objects to. Also, the `sort` option for the images is passed into the function. The `GetIDSort` method of the `IData` class is called to get the resultset of images. These records are then looped through and bitmap objects are created for each image and added to the collection.

```
Public Sub GetBitmaps(Bitmaps As Object, Sort)

Dim N As Integer
Dim Bmp As Bitmap
Dim ID As Integer

'  Get the ID set
DS.GetIDSet Sort

'  Intially set ID to true
ID = True

'  Loop through the images in the
'  database until all are added to
'  our bitmaps collection
Do Until ID = False

    '  Create an instance of the bitmap
    Set Bmp = New Bitmap

    '  Set the display picture
    '  properties
    Set Bmp.BackPict = m_BackPict
    Set Bmp.DispPict = m_DispPict
```

```
    ' Get the next image ID
    ID = DS.GetNextID

    ' Check to see if False was returned
    ' if so then end the loop
    If ID = False Then Exit Do

    ' Set the bitmap filename
    Bmp.FileInfo.FileName = DS.GetFileName(ID)

    ' Set the bitmap description
    Bmp.FileInfo.FileDesc = DS.GetComments(ID)

    ' Set the bitmaps ID
    Bmp.ID = ID

    ' Add the Bitmap class to the
    ' collection of bitmaps and set
    ' the key as the count
    Bitmaps.Add Item:=Bmp, Key:=CStr(ID)

Loop

End Sub
```

23. The **SaveBmp** method of the class handles storing the changes to the bitmap image. Note the two fields that can be updated are the file size and comments. Thus, the **UpdateFileSize** and **UpdateComments** methods of the **IData** class are called to store the new values.

```
Public Sub SaveBmp()

' Save the file size.  This could
' have been updated
DS.UpdateFileSize FileInfo.FileSize, m_ID

' Save the file comments
DS.UpdateComments FileInfo.FileDesc, m_ID

End Sub
```

24. The **SetView** routine handles setting the view indicated by the index. The current picture is cleared and, depending on the index, the image is copied from the **BackPict** picture box to the **DispPict** picture box. **StretchBlt** is used to perform the image stretching or the **PaintPicture** method of the **Picture** object is used to perform the horizontal and vertical flips of the image. Finally, the palette from the **BackPict** is copied to the display picture to ensure that the image colors are correct.

```
Public Sub SetView(Iview)

' Copy the palette
m_DispPict.Picture.hPal = m_BackPict.Picture.hPal
```

continued on next page

continued from previous page

```
' Clear the displayed picture
m_DispPict.Cls

' Depending on the view selected, the
' original image will be copied to the
' display picture appropriately
Select Case Iview

' Note that for the vertical and
' horizontal flips, the height or
' width is set to a negative value
' and the starting point is set to
' the height or width for the image
' to be displayed.

    Case 0  'Fit in the Window
        If ImageView.Flip(0).Checked = True Then
            ' Flip Horizontal
            m_DispPict.PaintPicture m_BackPict.Picture, ⇐
            m_DispPict.ScaleWidth,  0, -1 * m_DispPict.ScaleWidth, ⇐
        m_DispPict.ScaleHeight, 0, 0, m_BackPict.ScaleWidth, ⇐
        m_BackPict.ScaleHeight
        Else

            If ImageView.Flip(1).Checked = True Then
                ' Flip Vertical
                m_DispPict.PaintPicture m_BackPict.Picture, 0, ⇐
            m_DispPict.ScaleHeight, m_DispPict.ScaleWidth, -1 * ⇐
            m_DispPict.ScaleHeight, 0, 0, m_BackPict.ScaleWidth, ⇐

            Else
                ' Normal Display
                Call StretchBlt(m_DispPict.hdc, 0, 0, ⇐
            m_DispPict.ScaleWidth, m_DispPict.ScaleHeight, ⇐
            m_BackPict.hdc, 0, 0, m_BackPict.ScaleWidth, ⇐
            m_BackPict.ScaleHeight, SRCCOPY)
            End If
        End If

    Case 1  'Actual Size
        If ImageView.Flip(0).Checked = True Then
            ' Flip Horizontal
            m_DispPict.PaintPicture m_BackPict.Picture, ⇐
        m_BackPict.ScaleWidth, 0, -1 * m_BackPict.ScaleWidth, ⇐
        m_BackPict.ScaleHeight, 0, 0, m_BackPict.ScaleWidth, ⇐
        m_BackPict.ScaleHeight
        Else
            If ImageView.Flip(1).Checked = True Then
                ' Flip Vertical
                m_DispPict.PaintPicture m_BackPict.Picture, 0, ⇐
            m_BackPict.ScaleHeight, m_BackPict.ScaleWidth, -1 * ⇐
            m_BackPict.ScaleHeight, 0, 0, m_BackPict.ScaleWidth, ⇐
            m_BackPict.ScaleHeight
            Else
                ' Normal Display
```

```
                    Call StretchBlt(m_DispPict.hdc, 0, 0, ⇐
            m_BackPict.ScaleWidth, ⇐
            m_BackPict.ScaleHeight, m_BackPict.hdc, 0, 0, ⇐
            m_BackPict.ScaleWidth, m_BackPict.ScaleHeight, SRCCOPY)
                End If
        End If

    Case 2 '50%
        If ImageView.Flip(0).Checked = True Then
            '  Flip Horizontal
            m_DispPict.PaintPicture m_BackPict.Picture, ⇐
m_BackPict.ScaleWidth ⇐
        * 0.5, 0, -1 * m_BackPict.ScaleWidth * 0.5, ⇐
m_BackPict.ScaleHeight⇐
        * 0.5, 0, 0, m_BackPict.ScaleWidth, m_BackPict.ScaleHeight
        Else
            If ImageView.Flip(1).Checked = True Then
                '  Flip Vertical
                m_DispPict.PaintPicture m_BackPict.Picture, 0, ⇐
            m_BackPict.ScaleHeight * 0.5, m_BackPict.ScaleWidth * 0.5, ⇐
            -1 * m_BackPict.ScaleHeight * 0.5, 0, 0, ⇐
            m_BackPict.ScaleWidth,  m_BackPict.ScaleHeight
            Else
                '  Normal Display
                Call StretchBlt(m_DispPict.hdc, 0, 0, ⇐
            m_BackPict.ScaleWidth *⇐
            0.5, m_BackPict.ScaleHeight * 0.5, m_BackPict.hdc, 0, 0, ⇐
            m_BackPict.ScaleWidth, m_BackPict.ScaleHeight, SRCCOPY)
            End If
        End If

    Case 3 '200%
        If ImageView.Flip(0).Checked = True Then
            '  Flip Horizontal
            m_DispPict.PaintPicture m_BackPict.Picture, ⇐
        m_BackPict.ScaleWidth * 2, 0, -1 * m_BackPict.ScaleWidth * 2, ⇐
        m_BackPict.ScaleHeight * 2, 0, 0, m_BackPict.ScaleWidth, ⇐
        m_BackPict.ScaleHeight
        Else
            If ImageView.Flip(1).Checked = True Then
                '  Flip Vertical
                m_DispPict.PaintPicture m_BackPict.Picture, 0, ⇐
            m_BackPict.ScaleHeight * 2, m_BackPict.ScaleWidth * 2, ⇐
            -1 * m_BackPict.ScaleHeight * 2, 0, 0, m_BackPict.ScaleWidth, ⇐
            m_BackPict.ScaleHeight
            Else
                '  Normal Display
                Call StretchBlt(m_DispPict.hdc, 0, 0, ⇐
            m_BackPict.ScaleWidth * ⇐
            2, m_BackPict.ScaleHeight * 2, m_BackPict.hdc, 0, 0, ⇐
            m_BackPict.ScaleWidth, m_BackPict.ScaleHeight, SRCCOPY)
            End If
        End If

End Select
```

continued on next page

continued from previous page

```
' Copy the palette from the holding picture
' to the displayed picture.  This ensures that
' the images colors are displayed correctly.
m_DispPict.Picture.hPal = m_BackPict.Picture.hPal

End Sub
```

25. The `InsertNewBitmap` method handles inserting this bitmap into the database. This includes setting the `FileName`, `FileSize`, `FileExt`, and the `File Description` (comments).

```
Public Sub InsertNewBitmap()

'  Insert the new image into
'  the database.  The File Id
'  is returned
m_ID = DS.InsertImage(FileInfo.FileName, FileInfo.FileSize, ⇐
FileInfo.FileExt, FileInfo.FileDesc)

End Sub
```

26. The `DeleteBitmap` method of the class handles calling the `DeleteImage` method of the `IData` class to delete the current image.

```
Public Sub DeleteBitmap()

'  Delete the image from
'  the database
DS.DeleteImage (m_ID)

End Sub
```

27. When the class is initialized, the `DiskFile` class is created.

```
Private Sub Class_Initialize()
    '  When the class is intialized,
    '  the DiskFile class is created
    Set FileInfo = New DiskFile
End Sub
```

28. When the class is terminated, the `DiskFile` class instance is deleted.

```
Private Sub Class_Terminate()
    '  When the class is terminated
    '  the DiskFile class is destroyed
    Set FileInfo = Nothing
End Sub
```

29. Insert a new class into the project and save it as `IData.cls`. Add the following code to the General Declarations section of the form. The `m_IDResultSet rdoResultSet` will hold the set of image IDs from the `GetIDSet` method of the class. An RDO environment, connection, result-set, and prepared statement are globally declared.

```
Option Explicit

'  Declare a global result set which
'  can be used to retrieve all of
'  the image IDs in the database
Dim m_IDResultSet As rdoResultset

'  Dim a remote data environment
Dim Env As rdoEnvironment

'  Dim a remote data connection
Dim Con As rdoConnection

'  Declare a remote data record set
Dim RS As rdoResultset

'  Globally declare the prepared
'  statement
Dim PS As rdoPreparedStatement
```

30. The `InitConnect` method of the class handles initializing the `rdoEnvironment` and `rdoConnection` to the database. Note that in order to be able to use stored procedures with multiple selects, the `rdoEngine` default cursor must be set to use ODBC and not server-side cursors. Also, an RDO-prepared statement is created for calling the `INSERT_IMAGE` stored procedure.

```
Public Sub InitConnect()

'  Set the default engine cursor driver
'  to ODBC.  This is needed to support calling
'  stored procedures that use multiple select
'  statements.
rdoEngine.rdoDefaultCursorDriver = rdUseOdbc

'  Set the remote data environment
Set Env = rdoEnvironments(0)

'  Open the ODBC connection
'  Be sure to use an appropriate User ID (UID), password (pwd),
'  and database name for your database setup.
Set Con = Env.OpenConnection(dsName:="Image Data", Prompt:=rdDriverNoPrompt)

'  Create an RDO prepared statement for calling
'  the INSERT_IMAGE stored procedure
Set PS = Con.CreatePreparedStatement("INSERT_IMAGE", "{ ? = call ⇐
INSERT_IMAGE (?, ?, ?, ?) }")

End Sub
```

31. The `DBExec` method handles executing the specified SQL command on the database.

```
Private Sub DBExec(cmd$)

'  Execute the specified SQL Command
Con.Execute cmd$

End Sub
```

32. The `DBOpenRec` method of the class handles opening an `rdoResultSet` on the database utilizing the specified SQL statement.

```
Private Sub DBOpenRec(cmd$)

'  Open a resulset based on the
'  SQL query.  rdOpenKeySet indicates
'  that the rows can be updated.
Set RS = Con.OpenResultset(cmd$, rdOpenKeyset, rdConcurRowver)

End Sub
```

33. The `GetComments` method of the class handles retrieving the comments of an image specified by the image ID.

```
Public Function GetComments(ImageID As Integer) As String

'  Get the comments field for the specified
'  image
DBOpenRec "Select Comments from ImageData Where ImageID = " & ⇐
Trim(Str$(ImageID))

'  Return the value
GetComments = RS("Comments") & ""

End Function
```

34. The `GetFileSize` method of the class handles returning the file size of an image specified by the image ID.

```
Public Function GetFileSize(ImageID As Integer) As Long

'  Get the file name for the specified
'  image
DBOpenRec "Select FileSize from ImageData Where ImageID = " & ⇐
Trim(Str$(ImageID))

'  Return the file name
GetFileName = RS("FileSize")

End Function
```

35. The `GetFileName` method of the class handles returning the filename of an image specified by the image ID.

```
Public Function GetFileName(ImageID As Integer) As String

'  Get the file name for the specified
'  image
DBOpenRec "Select FileName from ImageData Where ImageID = " & ⇐
```

```
Trim(Str$(ImageID))

'   Return the file name
GetFileName = RS("FileName")

End Function
```

36. The `GetFileFormat` method of the class handles returning the file format of an image specified by the image ID.

```
Public Function GetFileFormat(ImageID As Integer) As String

'   Get the file format for the specified
'   image
DBOpenRec "Select FileFormat from ImageData Where ImageID = " & ⇐
Trim(Str$(ImageID))

'   Return the file format
GetFileFormat = RS("FileFormat")

End Function
```

37. The `GetIDSet` method of the class handles retrieving a resultset, `m_IDResultSet`, of all the images in the database. Note that a **sort** option is sent into the method to indicate how the images should be ordered.

```
Public Sub GetIDSet(Sort)

'   Select all of the images
'   in the database
Select Case Sort

    Case 1
        '   Sort by the image id
        DBOpenRec "Select * from ImageData order by ImageId"

    Case 2
        '   Sort by the file name
        DBOpenRec "Select * from ImageData order by FileName"

    Case 3
        '   Sort by the file size
        DBOpenRec "Select * from ImageData order by FileSize"

End Select

'   Set the global IDResultSet class
'   member to have the list of images
Set m_IDResultSet = RS

End Sub
```

38. The `GetNextID` method works in conjunction with the `GetIDSet` method. Each time this method is called, the next image ID in the `m_IDResultSet` RDO resultset is returned.

```
Public Function GetNextID() As Integer

'  Check to see if the end of the
'  result set has been reached
If m_IDResultSet.EOF <> True Then
    '  Get the next Image ID and
    '  return the value
    GetNextID = m_IDResultSet("ImageID")

    '  Move to the next record
    m_IDResultSet.MoveNext
Else
    '  Close the result set if the
    '  end of the result set was reached.
    m_IDResultSet.Close

    '  Return False as the value
    GetNextID = False
End If

End Function
```

39. The `DeleteImage` method of the class handles deleting the specified image from the database.

```
Public Sub DeleteImage(ID)

'  Delete the image from the database
DBExec "delete imagedata where imageid = " & LTrim(Str$(ID))

End Sub
```

40. `InsertImage` handles inserting a new image into the database. This is done by calling the **INSERT_IMAGE** SQL stored procedure. We do this by using **rdoPreparedStatements**. The first parameter of the prepared statement is the return value, which will be the image ID. The next four parameters are the image variables passed into the stored procedure. The function returns the new image ID.

```
Public Function InsertImage(FileName, FileSize, FileFormat, Comments) As
Integer

'  The first parameter is the return value which
'  will be the order id
PS.rdoParameters(0).Direction = rdParamReturnValue

'  Set the three input parameters
PS.rdoParameters(1) = FileName
PS.rdoParameters(2) = FileSize
PS.rdoParameters(3) = FileFormat
PS.rdoParameters(4) = Comments

'  Open the result set for the return
'  value from the stored procedure
Set RS = PS.OpenResultset(rdOpenStatic, rdConcurReadOnly)
```

```
'   return the order id
InsertImage = RS(0)

End Function
```

41. The `UpdateFileSize` method handles updating an image's file size for the specified image ID.

```
Public Sub UpdateFileSize(NewFileSize As String, ID As Integer)

'   Update the comments for the
'   specified Image
DBExec "Update imageData set FileSize = " & NewFileSize & " ⇐
where ImageID = " & LTrim(Str$(ID))

End Sub
```

42. The `UpdateComments` method handles updating an image's comments for the specified image ID.

```
Public Sub UpdateComments(NewComments As String, ID As Integer)

'   Update the comments for the
'   specified Image
DBExec "Update ImageData set Comments = '" + NewComments + "' ⇐
where ImageID = " & LTrim(Str$(ID))

End Sub
```

43. Insert a new class into the project and save it as `DiskFile.cls`. Refer to Chapter 4, User Interface Design, for detailed comments on utilizing this class.

```
Option Explicit

'   Member property of the class that
'   stores the filename
Private m_FileName As String

'   Member property of the class that
'   stores the file description
Private m_FileDesc As String

'   The get and set properties of the class
'   for the file description
Public Property Let FileDesc(s As String)
    m_FileDesc = s
End Property

Public Property Get FileDesc() As String
    FileDesc = m_FileDesc
End Property

'   Get the file name by itself.
'   I.E.   c:\windows\cloulds.bmp is clouds.bmp
```

continued on next page

continued from previous page

```vb
Public Property Get File() As String
    File = ParseFile()
End Property


'  Set and get the filename property for the
'  the class
Public Property Let FileName(s As String)
    m_FileName = s
End Property


Public Property Get FileName() As String
    FileName = m_FileName
End Property


'  Get the file size
Public Property Get FileSize() As Long
    FileSize = FileLen(m_FileName)
End Property


'  Get the file extension
Public Property Get FileExt() As String
    FileExt = ParseExt()
End Property


'  Get the directory of the file
Public Property Get Directory() As String
    Directory = ParseDir()
End Property


'  Get the date of the file
Public Property Get FileDate() As Date
    FileDate = FileDateTime(m_FileName)
End Property


'  Parse out the file name.  Note that this is
'  a private method.  It is only utilized in the
'   File property
Private Function ParseFile() As String

Dim N As Integer

ParseFile = ""

'  Start from the end of the file name
'  and look for the '\' character.  Thus the
'  file part of the file name will be known
For N = Len(m_FileName) To 1 Step -1

    If Mid(m_FileName, N, 1) = "\" Then
        ParseFile = Right(m_FileName, Len(m_FileName) - N)
        N = -1
    End If

Next N
```

```
End Function

'   Parse out the file directory.  Note that
'   this is a private class method and is only
'   utilized by the Directory property
Private Function ParseDir() As String

Dim N As Integer

ParseDir = ""

'   Start from the end of the file name
'   and look for the first '\' character.  Thus
'   the location of the file name will be known
'   and the rest is the directory location
For N = Len(m_FileName) To 1 Step -1

    If Mid(m_FileName, N, 1) = "\" Then
        ParseDir = Left(m_FileName, N)
        N = -1
    End If

Next N

End Function

'   GetExt retrieves the file extension if
'   there is one.  This is only used by the
'   FileExt property
Private Function ParseExt() As String

Dim N As Integer

ParseExt = "(N/A)"

'   Start from the end of the file name
'   and look for the '.' character.  Thus
'   the location of the extension will be known
'   in the file name string
For N = Len(m_FileName) To 1 Step -1

    If Mid(m_FileName, N, 1) = "." Then
        ParseExt = Right(m_FileName, Len(m_FileName) - N)
        N = -1
    End If

Next N

End Function

'   Public method of the class to
'   copy the file to a new location
Public Sub CopyFile(NewLocation)
    FileCopy m_FileName, NewLocation & ParseFile
End Sub
```

continued on next page

continued from previous page

```
'   Public method of the class to
'   delete the file
Public Sub DeleteFile()
    Kill m_FileName
End Sub


'   When the class is initialized
'   the filename, description and
'   extension will be set to
'   N/A.
Private Sub Class_Initialize()

m_FileName = "Uninitialized"
m_FileDesc = "N/A"

End Sub
```

44. Insert a new module into the project and save it as `MenuLogic.bas`. Add the following set of code to the General Declarations section of the form. Also, the global constants for the project are declared. The `IData` class is globally declared for accessing the SQL database. The Bitmaps collection is also globally declared for the collection of bitmap objects. `BmpIndex` will hold the index into the Bitmaps collection for the currently displayed image.

```
Option Explicit

'   Sort Constants
Global Const ImageIDSort = 1
Global Const FileNameSort = 2
Global Const FileSizeSort = 3
Global Const NoSaveData = 1
Global Const SaveData = 0

'   IView globally stores the current view for
'   the image I.E.  Fit in Window, 50%
Public Iview As Integer

'   Globally declare the IData class
Global DS As IData

'   Globally declare the bitmaps collection
Global Bitmaps As Collection

'   BmpIndex will track the current bitmap
'   shown in the collection
Global BmpIndex As Integer


'   Handles ending the program when
'   users select exit from the menu
Public Sub MenuExit()
    End
End Sub
```

```
'   Handles tiling the windows
'   on the MDI form
Public Sub MenuTile()

'   Do a vertical tile
ImageTracker.Arrange vbTileVertical

End Sub

Public Sub MenuCascade()

'   Cascade the child forms
ImageTracker.Arrange vbCascade

End Sub
```

45. This routine handles setting up the Image View picture box and then the `SetView` method of the bitmap class is called to display the image with the appropriate display option.

```
Public Sub SetView(Index)

'   Size the display picture
ImageView.DispPict.Top = 5
ImageView.DispPict.Left = 5
ImageView.DispPict.Width = ImageView.Width - 5
ImageView.DispPict.Height = ImageView.Height - 5

'   When a new image view is selected,
'   the original menu selection is
'   unchecked
ImageView.mSize(Iview).Checked = False
ImageData.mSize(Iview).Checked = False

'   Set the new view to the index
'   parameter
Iview = Index

'   Set the view for the current bitmap
Bitmaps.Item(BmpIndex).SetView Iview

'   Check the new menu option for the
'   selected view.
ImageData.mSize(Iview).Checked = True
ImageView.mSize(Iview).Checked = True

End Sub

Public Sub MenuShowWindow(Index)

'   Check to see which Windows (Form)
'   is to be displayed.
Select Case Index

    Case 0  'Show ImageData
        ImageData.Show
```

continued on next page

continued from previous page

```
            ImageData.WindowState = 0

    Case 1  'Show ImageView
        ImageView.Show
        ImageView.WindowState = 0

End Select

End Sub

Public Sub MenuOpenData()

Dim msg As String
Dim Style As Integer
Dim Title As String
Dim Response As Integer
Dim N As Integer

'  Set the Message, Style and Title
'  of the message box
msg = "Do you want to open the Image Database ?"
Style = vbYesNo + vbCritical + vbDefaultButton1
Title = "Open Image Database"

'  Retrieve the user's response
Response = MsgBox(msg, Style, Title)

'  If it was a yes, then show the ImageData
'  and ImageView forms.  Also start the view
'  in Tiled mode.
If Response = vbYes Then

    '  Check to see if there are no images
    '  in the database.  If so then prompt the
    '  user to add an image
    If Bitmaps.Count = 0 Then
        MsgBox "You must have at least one image in the database."
        MenuNewImage NoSaveData
    End If

    '  Show the forms
    ImageView.Show
    ImageData.Show

    '  Tile the forms
    MenuTile

    '  Make the open data button
    '  invisible
    ImageTracker.ImageTool.Buttons(1).Visible = False

    '  Make the rest of the toolbar buttons visible
    For N = 2 To ImageTracker.ImageTool.Buttons.Count
        ImageTracker.ImageTool.Buttons(N).Visible = True
    Next N
```

```
'  Ensure that the menu items the same
'  for the ImageData and ImageView forms
ImageView.mShowMenu.Checked = ImageTracker.mShowMenu.Checked
ImageData.mShowMenu.Checked = ImageTracker.mShowMenu.Checked
ImageView.mShowTool.Checked = ImageTracker.mShowTool.Checked
ImageData.mShowTool.Checked = ImageTracker.mShowTool.Checked

'  Move to the first record, but do not
'  save the record data
MenuBrowse 0, NoSaveData

End If

End Sub
```

46. The `MenuBrowse` subroutine handles moving through the Bitmaps collection. The `BmpIndex` is incremented or decremented appropriately depending on the browse selection. Then the image is shown by loading the image in the `BackPict` picture box and calling the `SetView` method of the Bitmap class. Finally, the image values are shown in the appropriate text boxes on the `ImageData` form.

```
Public Sub MenuBrowse(MoveType, Save)

Dim ImageName As String

'  If there are no records then we can
'  not browse
If BmpIndex = 0 Then Exit Sub

'  If we are to save then
'  store the new data
If Save = SaveData Then
    Bitmaps.Item(BmpIndex).FileInfo.FileDesc = ImageData.ImageInfo(3).Text
    Bitmaps.Item(BmpIndex).SaveBmp
End If

'  Check the RowCount.  If it is 0
'  then there are no images in the
'  database.  We then need to show the New Image
'  dialog to add the first image.
If Bitmaps.Count = 0 Then Exit Sub

'  Depending on the type of move
'  selected by the user, the index into
'  the collection is updated appropriately
Select Case MoveType

    Case 0   'Move to First Record
        BmpIndex = 1

    Case 1   'Move to Last Record
        BmpIndex = Bitmaps.Count
```

continued on next page

continued from previous page

```
      Case 2  'Move to Previous Record
          BmpIndex = BmpIndex - 1

      Case 3   'Move to Next Record
          BmpIndex = BmpIndex + 1

End Select

'  Check to see if we have moved past
'  the first or last record
If BmpIndex < 1 Then BmpIndex = 1
If BmpIndex > Bitmaps.Count Then BmpIndex = Bitmaps.Count

'  Get the Image file
Bitmaps.Item(BmpIndex).LoadBack

'  Set the view
SetView Iview

'  Display the image id, name, size and description
ImageData.ImageInfo(0).Text = Bitmaps.Item(BmpIndex).ID
ImageData.ImageInfo(1).Text = Bitmaps.Item(BmpIndex).FileInfo.FileName
ImageData.ImageInfo(2).Text = Bitmaps.Item(BmpIndex).FileInfo.FileSize
ImageData.ImageInfo(3).Text = Bitmaps.Item(BmpIndex).FileInfo.FileDesc

End Sub
```

47. The `MenuNewImage` method of the class handles adding a new image to the database. Once the filename is retrieved, a new bitmap class is created, the values for the bitmap are set up, and then the `InsertNewBitmap` method of the class is called to add the image to the database. Finally, the bitmap is added to the Bitmaps collection, the `PopulateLists` method of the `Idata` form is called, and we move to the last record, which is now the new image.

```
Public Sub MenuNewImage(Save)

Dim ImageID As Integer
Dim ImageType As String

If Save = SaveData Then
    '  Save the current data
    Bitmaps.Item(BmpIndex).FileInfo.FileDesc = ImageData.ImageInfo(3).Text
    Bitmaps.Item(BmpIndex).SaveBmp
End If

'  Set the filter type of the dialog
'  box
ImageData.commondialog1.Filter = "Bitmaps (*.bmp)|*.bmp|Icons ⇐
(*.ico)|*.ico|All Files (*.*)|*.*"

'  Set the title of the dialog
ImageData.commondialog1.DialogTitle = "New Image File"

'  Set the filter index to that of the
```

```
'   bitmap
ImageData.commondialog1.FilterIndex = 1

'   Set the flags to ensure that the
'   file must exist
ImageData.commondialog1.Flags = cdlOFNFileMustExist

'   Show the dialog box
ImageData.commondialog1.ShowOpen

'   Check to see if the filename was set
If ImageData.commondialog1.FileName <> "" Then

    '   Create the new bitmap class
    Dim NewBitmap As Bitmap

    '   Create the new bitmap
    Set NewBitmap = New Bitmap

    '   Set the description
    NewBitmap.FileInfo.FileDesc = ""

    '   Set the file name
    NewBitmap.FileInfo.FileName = ImageData.commondialog1.FileName

    '   Set the display pictures
    Set NewBitmap.DispPict = ImageView.DispPict
    Set NewBitmap.BackPict = ImageView.BackPict

    '   Insert the bitmap into the database
    NewBitmap.InsertNewBitmap

    '   Add the bitmap to the collection
    Bitmaps.Add Item:=NewBitmap, Key:=CStr(NewBitmap.ID)

    '   Since we have changed the record set
    '   the image lists need to be updated
    ImageData.PopulateLists

    '   Move to the last record which was
    '   just added.
    MenuBrowse 1, SaveData

End If

End Sub
```

48. The **MenuDelete** subroutine handles calling the **DeleteBitmap** method of
the Bitmap class to delete the image from the database. Then, that bitmap
object is removed from the **Bitmaps** collection and the thumbnail listboxes are updated. Finally, we will move to the next record in the database.
Note that when we make this move, we cannot save the changes for the
current image since it has just been deleted.

```
Public Sub MenuDelete()

If Bitmaps.Count = 0 Then Exit Sub

' Delete the bitmap from the database
Bitmaps.Item(BmpIndex).DeleteBitmap

' Remove from the collection
Bitmaps.Remove BmpIndex

' Since we have changed the record set
' the image lists need to be updated
ImageData.PopulateLists

' Move to the next record.
MenuBrowse 2, NoSaveData

End Sub

Public Sub MenuShowTool()

' If the toolbar is checked then
' do the logic to hide the toolbar
If ImageTracker.mShowTool.Checked = True Then

        ' If the menu is not shown, then don't
        ' hide the toolbar.
        If ImageTracker.mShowMenu.Checked = False Then Exit Sub

        ' Hide the toolbar
        ImageTracker.ImageTool.Visible = False

        ' Change the menu check
        ImageTracker.mShowTool.Checked = False

        ' If the ImageData and ImageView forms
        ' are visible then handle setting their
        ' menu check marks.  If they are not
        ' visible, they are not loaded.
        If ImageData.Visible = True Then
            ImageData.mShowTool.Checked = False
            ImageView.mShowTool.Checked = False
        End If

Else

        ' Make the toolbar visible
        ImageTracker.ImageTool.Visible = True

        ' Change the menu check
        ImageTracker.mShowTool.Checked = True

        ' If the ImageData and ImageView forms
        ' are visible then handle setting their
        ' menu check marks.  If they are not
        ' visible, they are not loaded.
```

```
        If ImageData.Visible = True Then
            ImageData.mShowTool.Checked = True
            ImageView.mShowTool.Checked = True
        End If

    End If

End Sub

Public Sub MenuShowMenu()

'   Check to see If the menu is already visible
If ImageTracker.mShowMenu.Checked = True Then

    '   If the toolbar is not visible,
    '   we do not want to also make the
    '   menu invisible
    If ImageTracker.ImageTool.Visible = False Then Exit Sub

    '   Make the ImageTracker menus
    '   invisible and set the menu
    '   check mark appropriately
    ImageTracker.mFile.Visible = False
    ImageTracker.mShowMenu.Checked = False
    ImageTracker.mWindow.Visible = False

    '   If the ImageData and ImageView forms
    '   are visible then handle setting their
    '   menu check marks and visible properties.
    '   If they are not visible, they are not
    '   loaded.
    If ImageData.Visible = True Then
        ImageData.mShowMenu.Checked = False
        ImageView.mShowMenu.Checked = False
        ImageView.mFile.Visible = False
        ImageData.mFile.Visible = False
        ImageData.mWindow.Visible = False
        ImageView.mWindow.Visible = False
        ImageData.mRecord.Visible = False
        ImageView.mRecord.Visible = False
        ImageData.mView.Visible = False
        ImageView.mView.Visible = False
        ImageView.mViewSet.Visible = False
    End If

Else

    '   Make the ImageTracker menus
    '   visible and set the menu
    '   check mark appropriately
    ImageTracker.mFile.Visible = True
    ImageTracker.mShowMenu.Checked = True
    ImageTracker.mWindow.Visible = True

    '   If the ImageData and ImageView forms
```

continued on next page

continued from previous page

```
'   are visible then handle setting their
'   menu check marks and visible properties.
'   If they are not visible, they are not
'   loaded.
If ImageData.Visible = True Then
    ImageData.mShowMenu.Checked = True
    ImageView.mShowMenu.Checked = True
    ImageData.mFile.Visible = True
    ImageView.mFile.Visible = True
    ImageData.mWindow.Visible = True
    ImageView.mWindow.Visible = True
    ImageData.mRecord.Visible = True
    ImageView.mRecord.Visible = True
    ImageView.mView.Visible = True
    ImageData.mView.Visible = True
    ImageView.mViewSet.Visible = True
End If

End If

End Sub
```

49. The `DropNewImage` method of the class handles adding a new image to the database. A new bitmap class is created and the values for the bitmap set up. Then the `InsertNewBitmap` method of the class is called to add the image to the database. Finally, the bitmap is added to the **Bitmaps** collection, the `PopulateLists` method of the `Idata` form is called, and we move to the last record, which is now the new image.

```
Public Sub DropNewImage(FileName)

Dim ImageID As Integer
Dim ImageType As String
Dim NewBitmap As Bitmap

'   Set the description
Bitmaps.Item(BmpIndex).FileInfo.FileDesc = ImageData.ImageInfo(3).Text

'   Save the bitmap
Bitmaps.Item(BmpIndex).SaveBmp

'   Create the new bitmap
Set NewBitmap = New Bitmap

'   Set the file description
NewBitmap.FileInfo.FileDesc = ""

'   Set the file name
NewBitmap.FileInfo.FileName = FileName

'   Set the display and back picture
Set NewBitmap.DispPict = ImageView.DispPict
Set NewBitmap.BackPict = ImageView.BackPict
```

```
'   Insert the image into the database
NewBitmap.InsertNewBitmap

'   Add the bitmap to the collection
Bitmaps.Add Item:=NewBitmap, Key:=CStr(NewBitmap.ID)

'   Since we have changed the record set
'   the image lists need to be updated
ImageData.PopulateLists

'   Move to the last record which was
'   just added.
MenuBrowse 1, SaveData

End Sub
```

50. The `LoadCollection` subroutine handles setting up the `Bitmaps` collection. A temporary meta bitmap is set up so we can call the `GetBitmaps` method of the Bitmap class. Note that we need to set up the `BackPict` and `DispPict` method of the meta class since these will be used by the `GetBitmaps` method.

```
Public Sub LoadCollection(Sort)

'   Declare the meta bitmap
Dim MetaBMP As Bitmap

'   Declare the IData class
Set DS = New IData

'   Create the collection
Set Bitmaps = New Collection

'   Initialize the collection
DS.InitConnect

'   Create the meta bitmap
Set MetaBMP = New Bitmap

'   Set the display picture
'   properties
Set MetaBMP.BackPict = ImageView.BackPict
Set MetaBMP.DispPict = ImageView.DispPict

'   Get the list of bitmaps
MetaBMP.GetBitmaps Bitmaps, Sort

'   Delete the meta bitmap
Set MetaBMP = Nothing

End Sub
```

51. Insert a new module into the project and save it as `DropFile.bas`. This module handles setting up the drop file capability of the project.

```
'  Declare the API file functions
'  and constants for the file drag
'  and drop
Declare Function GetWindowLong Lib "user32" Alias "GetWindowLongA" (ByVal ⇐
hwnd As Long, ByVal nIndex As Long) As Long

Declare Function SetWindowLong Lib "user32" Alias "SetWindowLongA" (ByVal ⇐
hwnd As Long, ByVal nIndex As Long, ByVal dwNewLong As Long) As Long

Declare Sub DragAcceptFiles Lib "shell32.dll" (ByVal hwnd As Long, ByVal ⇐
fAccept As Long)

Declare Sub DragFinish Lib "shell32.dll" (ByVal HDROP As Long)

Declare Function DragQueryFile Lib "shell32.dll" Alias "DragQueryFileA" ⇐
(ByVal HDROP As Long, ByVal UINT As Long, ByVal lpStr As String, ⇐
ByVal ch As Long) As Long

Public Const GWL_EXSTYLE = (-20)
Public Const WS_EX_ACCEPTFILES = &H10&
Public Const WM_DROPFILES = &H233

Sub EnableFileDrop(hwnd As Long)

Dim Style As Long

'  Get the Window style
Style = GetWindowLong(hwnd, GWL_EXSTYLE)

'  Set to the form to accept
'  dropped files
Style = SetWindowLong(hwnd, GWL_EXSTYLE, Style Or WS_EX_ACCEPTFILES)

'  Indicate to the system that
'  dragged files will be accepted
'  by the form
DragAcceptFiles hwnd, True

End Sub
```

NOTE
The following steps describe how to set up the database if you are unable to utilize the IData.SQL script provided in the Chapter 9 directory on the CD.

52. Add the following stored procedure to the IData SQL database. It handles beginning an insert transaction to place the new image in the database. Once the image is inserted, the new image ID is returned.

```
CREATE PROCEDURE Insert_Image  @FileName VarChar(255), @FileSize int,
@FileFormat VarChar(255), @Comments VarChar(255) AS

/*  The Return Value */
declare @ImageID int
```

```
/*  Begin the transaction */
begin transaction

    /*  Insert the order */
    Insert ImageData (FileName, FileSize, FileFormat, Comments)
values(@FileName, @FileSize, @FileFormat, @Comments)

    /*  Get back the order ID */
    select @ImageID = max(ImageID) from ImageData

commit transaction

/*  Return the Order ID in a column calles NewOrderID */
select @ImageID NewImageID
```

53. Add the following tables to the IData SQL database.

```
ImageData
    ImageID             int             NOT NULL
    FileName            varchar (255)   NULL
    FileSize            int             NULL
    FileFormat          varchar (255)   NULL
    Comments            varchar (255)   NULL

    PRIMARY KEY
        ImageID
```

How It Works

Comparing this How-To to How-To 4.5 will show the distinct structural differences between a two-tier and three-tier application. In How-To 4.5, the database interface was handled by the remote data control. The logic for manipulating the database was scattered throughout the routines in the entire project. Any changes to the database would not have been easy to update, whereas in this example, the primary database interface is handled by the **IData** class. The **Bitmap** class which encapsulates a bitmap image, does work with resultsets returned by **IData**, but it has no code that interfaces with the database directly. The **IData** class handles interfacing with SQL Server, the Data tier of the project.

In How-To 4.5 we did not have any second tier business objects. Indeed we had not defined any of the objects utilized in the project. In this example, we have abstracted away two primary objects. First, a bitmap image is primarily defined as a file on a disk. So, we *reuse* the **DiskFile** class created in Chapter 4, User Interface Design, to define the file for the image. The other primary object we are working with in the project is that of a bitmap image. Thus, a new class, **Bitmap**, is created to encapsulate and abstract away from the user interface the idea of a bitmap image. The application works on a set of images by allowing the user to browse, add, and delete images from the database. Instead of working directly on the database, the user interface will work with the **Bitmap** class and use its method and properties. The **Bitmap** class will inherit the capabilities of the **DiskFile** class. Note that this is not true inheritance, but is enforced through code by declaring the **Bitmap** class as containing a **DiskFile** class. And the **Bitmap** class and **IData** class will collaborate to work with the third tier.

By dividing the application into these logical elements, we have many new opportunities for deploying the application, implementing changes, and scaling for the enterprise. For example, if we were to scale this application to be an image tracking system for an entire company, we would have to consider which user's machine the image resided on and the URL location. By having the application logically divided, we have many more options for implementing and deploying these changes.

Comments

In this example, the application was not divided into a user interface project and ActiveX components. The **Bitmap** and **DiskFile** classes could be placed in an ActiveX executable and partitioned across the enterprise. Note that in order to do this, you cannot pass user interface objects into the **Bitmap** class (i.e., **DispPict** and **BackPict**). You would have to take out the methods of the **Bitmap** class that work on the user interface directly (i.e., **SetView**) and move these into either a BAS module or another class.

BASIC SQL SERVER MANAGEMENT

10

by David Jung

BASIC SQL SERVER MANAGEMENT

How do I...

In the process of building the three-tiered client/server model, the last tier consists of the data and its services. Data services manages the information of your enterprise. Business objects interact with it directly to make decisions and enforce business rules.

The Data services layer supports data definitions, data management, and transactions. *Data definitions* specify the logical design of your information and the Data Definition Language (DDL) used to control the information. *Data management* is the use of the Database Manipulation Language (DML) to perform operations on the data. *Transactions* consist of updating the data and ensuring referential integrity.

This chapter focuses on the basics of building a database using Microsoft SQL Server 6.5 and optimizing tips and tricks. This chapter assumes you already have installed SQL Server 6.5 on a system and you have System Administrator rights to the server. Also, this chapter assumes that you have installed Microsoft SQL Server 6.5 Utilities on your client workstation (see Figure 10-1). All the steps in this chapter's How-To's will step through the graphical user interface portion of the SQL Enterprise Manager. In the How It Works sections, the Data Definition Language (DDL) equivalents will be discussed because the DDL is what the graphical interface is executing. SQL Server refers to these components as Transact-SQL.

This chapter's How-To's include the following:

10.1 Create a Device

As you start designing your Data services tier, you need to define a disk file to store your databases and transaction logs. This How-To describes what they are and how to create them.

10.2 Create a Database

The database is an organized collection of data, logically structured and maintained. This How-To offers some techniques for designing your databases and explains how to create them.

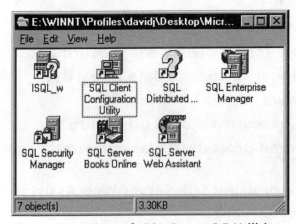

Figure 10-1 Microsoft SQL Server 6.5 Utilities folder

10.3   Create a Table

The most important function of a database is its tables because that is where the information is stored. This How-To shows you how to create tables and fields using the SQL Enterprise Manager

10.4   Define Primary and Foreign Keys

A *relational database* implies the presence of relationships between the tables. To have a relationship, you first define a primary key. The elements that make up a table's primary key can be part of another table. These become foreign keys in the table, thus creating the primary key/foreign key relationship. This How-To explores this relationship further and shows you how to define the primary key/foreign key relationship.

10.5   Index a Table for Efficiency and Performance

The use of indexes is a way to increase performance when retrieving information from the tables. This How-To shows you how to create indexes on your tables.

10.6   Create a Trigger to Control Data Integrity

Triggers are a special kind of stored procedure that is executed automatically when a user attempts data modification on a specific table. This How-To shows you how to create them.

10.7   Create a View

A view is a virtual table derived from one or more base tables in the database. Views provide a different look at the data in your tables, improve performance, and add another layer of security. This How-To shows you how to implement them.

10.8   Create and Execute a Stored Procedure

A stored procedure is a precompiled collection of Data Manipulation Language statements that can accept and return one or more user-supplied parameters. This How-To shows you how to create and use them.

10.9   Create a Stored Procedure That Performs a Transaction

Stored procedures are often designed to handle a unit of work, such as inserting or updating data in a database table. This How-To shows you how to create a stored procedure that performs a transaction process and returns information back to the calling procedure.

10.10   Create a Query Using SQL Server Web Assistant

This How-To shows you how to use the Web Assistant to create an HTML document, which will be generated every time a new reservation is made to an Intranet.

10.11 Optimize My Server

There is no magic wand that one can wave over the SQL Server to make it run optimally. There are techniques and pitfalls to look out for that help tune your server. This How-To provides some common things that go wrong when trying to tune your server.

COMPLEXITY
BEGINNING

10.1 How do I...
Create a device?

Problem

I've finished the database design that I'm going to use for my application. I've been told that I need to create a device for my database. What's a device and how do I create one?

Technique

A general definition of a device is that it's a physical disk file where all SQL Server databases and transaction logs reside. A device consists of two names, a logical and a physical name. The logical name is used by SQL Server to identify the device and is used in most **SQL** statements. It can be up to 30 characters in length. The physical name is an operating system file that specifies the full path where the device is physically located on the server's disk drive. The naming convention follows the rules for filenames in the operating system.

Two types of devices can be defined. They are the database device and the backup device. A *database device* stores databases and transaction logs. This device requires preallocating storage space on your server's disk drive and has to reside on the server's local hard drive. A *backup device* stores backups of the database and transaction logs. Unlike a database device, a backup device can reside on both local and network storage media. If the backup device is on network media, it needs to be on a shared network directory. See Table 10-1 for an example of what logical and physical devices will look like.

Table 10-1 Example of a logical and physical device

TYPE OF DEVICE	EXAMPLE
Logical	`dv_Hotels`
Physical database	`C:\MSSQL\DATA\DVHOTELS.DAT`
Physical backup device	`C:\MSSQL\BACKUP\DVDHOTEL.DAT`
Physical network backup device	`\\SQLSERVR\BACKUP\DVDHOTEL.DAT`

Steps

This example is in two parts. The first part will illustrate how to create a database device and the other part will illustrate how to create a backup device.

Creating the Database Device

A database device is a file on the physical hard drive on the SQL Server used to allocate space to store a database and its transaction log.

1. Open the SQL Enterprise Manager from your Microsoft SQL Server 6.5 Utilities group.

2. In the Server Manager window, select the server on which you want to create the device. In this example we chose to use the server GOTHAM_CITY.

3. Either click the Manage Database Device button from the toolbar or select the **Manage** menu item and select the **Database Devices** item. The Manage Database Devices window, shown in Figure 10-2, will appear.

4. To create a device on the Manage Database Devices window's toolbar select the New Device button, which is the first button on the toolbar. The New Database Device window will appear, similar to Figure 10-3, except the text fields will be blank. The graph at the bottom of this window illustrates how much used/free space is available. By placing the mouse pointer over one of the bars in the graph, the amount of drive space available and used by that database device will be displayed in the status bar of the Manage Database Devices window.

5. Assign the values listed in Table 10-2 to the New Database Device window. When you are finished, the window should resemble Figure 10-3.

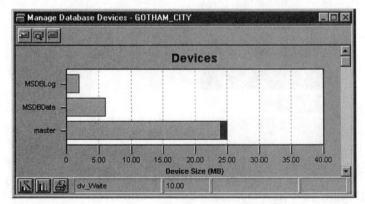

Figure 10-2 Manage Database Devices window

Table 10-2 Properties for New Database Device

FIELD	PROPERTY	DESCRIPTION
Name	dv_Waite	Logical database device name
Drive	C:	Disk drive the database will reside on
Path	\MSSQL\DATA\dv_Waite.DAT	Physical database device name
Size (MB):	10	Size of the device in megabytes

6. For this How-To, do not check the **Default Device** check box. If you check this option on a device, it would become part of the pool of default devices. If a database is designed without a device specified, a default device is used. Default devices are used in alphabetical order and once one is filled up, SQL Server uses the next one. It is a good practice not to create default devices because databases and transaction logs are placed in database devices. If you build a database in a default device, you will not know which device it is placed in, which will make server maintenance more difficult.

7. To add the new device, press the Create Now button.

8. If the device is successfully added, a dialog will appear notifying you.

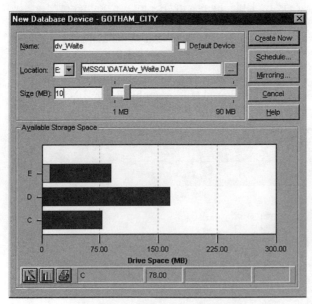

Figure 10-3 New Database Device window

Creating the Backup Device

A backup device is used to back up and restore a database and transaction log. In previous versions of SQL Server, this was known as a dump device. A backup device is different from a database device in that a backup device does not have to reside solely on the SQL Server's physical hard drive. It can be stored on storage media like floppy drives, hard drives, tape, or other servers on the network.

1. From the Server Manager window, select the `Backup Devices` folder and click the folder with the right mouse button. Your screen will look like Figure 10-4.

2. Select the `New Backup Device` menu item from the pop-up menu. The New Backup Device window will appear, similar to Figure 10-5.

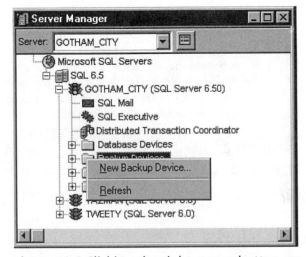

Figure 10-4 Clicking the right mouse button on the Backup Devices folder

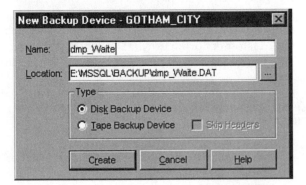

Figure 10-5 Create Backup Device window

3. In the `Name` text box, type in the logical backup device name of `dmp_Waite`.

4. In this example, the backup device will be stored on the same physical drive of SQL Server that contains the database device created earlier. If you want the backup device to be located on a network drive, you would type in a value similar to this:

`\\SQLSRVR\BACKUP\dmp_Waite`

5. In the `Type` frame, the Disk Backup Device radio button is marked (default) and for this example, we will leave it marked. If you want the backup device to be stored on a tape, select the Tape Backup device radio button. By selecting the Tape radio button, you will need to mark or clear the `Skip Headers` check box. The Skip Headers radio button is used to determine whether or not the ANSI tape labels are read. If the option is clear, SQL Server will recognize any existing ANSI tape labels on the tape you are writing to. This can be important because if there is any ANSI tape label on the tape you are writing to and the radio button is clear, SQL Server will notify you as to the contents of the ANSI label. If the radio button is marked, SQL Server will ignore the ANSI label and perform its task of writing to the tape. The ANSI label could have been a notification that the information on the tape is still valid and your write sequence just overwrote current data with your data.

6. Select the `Create` command button to create the backup device.

7. If the device is successfully added, a dialog will appear notifying you.

How It Works

All the steps you are doing through the SQL Enterprise Manager graphical interface perform the Data Definition Language (DDL) equivalents that you would issue through the Query Manager interface which is also part of the SQL Enterprise Manager. The Query Manager is an interface that allows you to enter in DDL or Data Manipulation Language (DML) calls directly against every database object you specify. In creating a database device through the SQL Enterprise Manager, you are issuing the `DISK INIT` command. From the Query Manager, you would issue the following command:

```
DISK INIT
NAME = dv_WaiteSQL
PHYSNAME = C:\MSSQL\DATA\dv_WaiteSQL.DAT
VDEVNO = 5
SIZE =   1024
```

The `VDEVNO` property is the number of the new device and is a number between 1-255. The number zero is reserved for the master device, and therefore, cannot be used. The master device is a device that SQL Server creates when it is installed on the server. It stores the master, model, and tempdb system databases and transaction logs. All SQL Server objects created are based from model database objects. Once a device number is used, it cannot be used again until the device has been dropped. By using the SQL Enterprise Manager, you do not have to know what device number to assign the device you are creating because the application figures it out for you.

The **SIZE** property at the command line is different from that used with the SQL Enterprise Manager. Rather than megabytes, the **SIZE** property is in 2K pages (2048 bytes); therefore, 2MB is equal to 1024 2K pages.

Creating a backup device through the SQL Enterprise Manager is the same as executing the system stored procedure, **sp_addumpdevice** through ISQL. From the ISQL prompt, you would type the following:

```
sp_addumpdevice 'disk', 'dmp_Waite', 'C:\MSSQL\BACKUP\DMPWAITE.dat'
```

The first parameter after the **sp_addumpdevice** indicates whether the device is going to be created on a disk or tape. The next parameter is the logical name of the backup device. The last parameter in the example is the physical name and path of the backup device. If the backup device is to be created on a tape, an additional parameter would be included:

```
@devstatus = noskip or skip
```

The **@devstatus** property is the equivalent of the **Skip Header** check box. If the property is set to **no skip**, SQL Server will read the ANSI label of the tape before performing a backup. If the ANSI label on the tape warns SQL Server that you do not have permission to write the tape, you as the SQL Administrator will be notified. Setting the property to **skip**, SQL Server will not read the ANSI label, therefore, ignoring such a warning.

Comments

When creating a backup device on a network, make sure that the account that SQL Server runs has the appropriate rights capabilities to the network server.

There is a limit of 256 devices per SQL Server. Since device 0 is already used by SQL Server, you really only have 255 devices you can define.

COMPLEXITY
BEGINNING

10.2 How do I...
Create a database?

Problem

Now that I've created my devices, I'm supposed to create a database. How do I do this?

Technique

A database is an organized, logical unit of storage and work within SQL Server. Each database defined is different and separate from other databases. A database can reside on one or more database devices that have been previously defined. Within a database, there are a number of associated database objects. Database objects consist of the following:

- Tables and indexes
- Derived tables (Views)
- User-defined datatypes
- Defaults
- Rules
- Stored procedures
- Triggers

The usage of tables, derived tables, stored procedures, and triggers will be discussed later in this chapter. For more information on user-defined datatypes, defaults, and rules, you should refer to the SQL Server Books Online.

Before you can create a database, you must first have created a database device for it. As stated earlier, a database can be located on one device or across multiple database devices. See Figure 10-6.

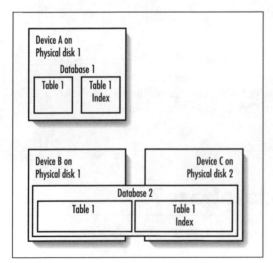

Figure 10-6 Devices and database structure

Each database has a transaction log associated with it. A *transaction log* is a storage area reserved by SQL Server that tracks all transactions—updates, inserts, and deletions—made to the database. By default, the transaction log is written to the same device that you assign your database to. When any change to the database is issued, the process is written to the transaction log before any physical changes are performed. As a general rule, your database device and transaction log should always be on a separate device. This will help improve your performance and will allow you to keep a backup. Since the transaction log records every transaction, it competes for disk space and processing I/O with database data. By not having the transaction log on a separate device, you lose the ability to back up the transaction log. This can be important in an environment that has a high transaction traffic, like an order entry system for a telemarketing company.

When allocating space for the transaction log, you should allocate roughly 10 to 30 percent of your database size. The size will vary based on the database usage so it is a good idea to monitor the size of the log to determine how much space you really need.

If you find your database is running out of storage space or you want to reclaim unused storage space, you can resize the database. This is accomplished by using either the SQL Enterprise Manager or the **ALTER DATABASE** statement through the Query Analyzer. For information on the **ALTER DATABASE** syntax, refer to SQL Server 6.5 Books Online. If you need to increase the size of the database's transaction log, you would use either the SQL Enterprise Manager or the **ALTER DATABASE** statement. The size of a transaction log can only be increased.

For data recovery purposes, you should back up the transaction log on a regular basis. To dynamically back up your transaction log, you can either write an **ISQL** file that performs the **DUMP TRANSACTION** statement or use the SQL Enterprise Manager to schedule the backup. If the transaction log is located on the same device as the database, this cannot be done.

Steps

This example will illustrate how to create a database and create a separate transaction log.

1. Open the SQL Enterprise Manager from your Microsoft SQL Server 6.5 Utilities group.

2. In the Server Manager window, select the server in which you wish to create the database. In this example we chose to use the server **GOTHAM_CITY**.

3. Either click the Manage Database button from the toolbar or select the **Manage** menu item and select the **Databases** item. The Manage Databases window, shown in Figure 10-7, will appear. The graph shows you a list of all the databases defined on the server and their storage usage. The light blue segment of the bar represents the used space that your database is occupying with actual information. The dark red signifies the available free space of the database.

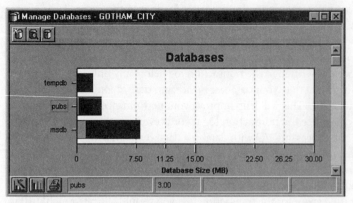

Figure 10-7 Manage Databases window

4. To create a database in the Manage Databases window's toolbar, select the New Database button, which is the first button on the toolbar. The New Database window will appear. The graph at the bottom of this window shows the devices on the server and their used/free space usage.

5. Assign the values listed in Table 10-3 in the New Database window.

Table 10-3 First three properties for New Database

FIELD	PROPERTY	DESCRIPTION
Name	db_HotelSystem	Logical database name
Data Device	dv_Waite	Logical database device name
Size (MB)	5	The amount of space to allocate for the database

6. In the Log Device combo box, we are going to create a new device to store the transaction log. Select <new> from the list and the New Database Device window will appear, similar to Figure 10-8. Assign the values listed in Table 10-4 in the New Database Device window to create the new device.

Table 10-4 Properties for the transaction log device

FIELD	PROPERTY	DESCRIPTION
Name	dvl_Waite	Logical database device name
Drive	C:	Disk drive the device will reside on
Path	\MSSQL\DATA\dvl_Waite.DAT	Physical database device name
Size (MB)	10	Size of the device in megabytes

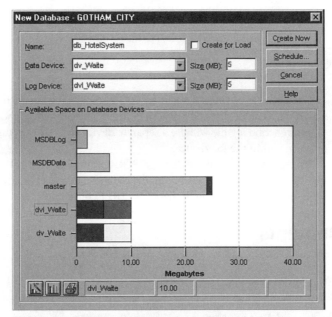

Figure 10-8 New Database window

7. Do not mark the **Default Device** check box. By marking this option, this device would become part of the pool of default devices. This is generally undesirable, for reasons given earlier in Step 6 of How-To 10.1.

8. After the New Database Device window closes, assign 5MB to the **Log Device**.

9. Press the Create Now button to add the database. Now that the database has been defined, you can start creating database objects like tables and stored procedures.

How It Works

Each database is created in the image of the Model database. The Model database is created when SQL Server is first installed. If we did not specify a database device, the database would be created on the default device, assuming it has space available. If no size is specified, the database is created either with the size of the Model database or the database size value in the system stored procedure, **sp_configure**. Whichever value is larger is the value that will be used.

All the steps you are doing through the SQL Enterprise Manager perform the Data Definition Language (DDL) equivalents that you would issue through the Query Analyzer. In creating a database through the SQL Enterprise Manager, you are issuing the

CREATE DATABASE statement. From an ISQL prompt, you issue the following command to create this database:

```
CREATE DATABASE db_HotelSystem
ON dv_Waite = 5
LOG ON dvl_Waite = 5
```

The CREATE DATABASE statement creates the database named db_HotelSystem within the database device dv_Waite utilizing 5 megabytes of space within the device. The transaction log file will use a separate device dvl_Waite utilizing 5 megabytes of space within the log device.

By creating the database through SQL commands, you will need to make sure that the devices you are assigning the database to already exist. If they don't, you have to create them through the DISK INIT command.

Comments

The maximum number of databases per SQL Server installation is 32,767.

COMPLEXITY
BEGINNING

10.3 How do I...
Create a table?

Problem

I've finished the database design that I'm going to use for my application. I've created the database and backup device, and the database object. How do I create a table to store the actual data?

Technique

A table is a database object that is a logical, two-dimensional data structure organized into rows and columns that data is stored in. Tables can be created through either the SQL Enterprise Manager or by using Data Definition Language scripts (SQL statements).

Steps

In this example, you are going to use the SQL Enterprise Manager to create the table in the database that was created in the last How-To.

1. Open the SQL Enterprise Manager from your Microsoft SQL Server 6.5 Utilities group.

2. In order to create a table, you need to tell SQL Server which database it belongs to. From the Server Manager window, select the server that contains the database that you wish to create the table in. In the previous example, we created the database on the server called **GOTHAM_CITY** and the database was called **db_HotelSystem**. Click on the plus sign next to the database name, **db_HotelSystem**. The Server Manager explorer will expand the database and show the components of the database, **Groups/Users** and **Objects**.

3. Click on the plus sign next to the **Objects** item. The Server Manager explorer will expand the **Objects** item and show all the database objects that you can work with: **Tables**, **Views**, **Stored Procedures**, **Rules**, **Defaults**, and **User Defined Datatypes**.

4. Select the **Table** object. Then click the **Manage** menu item and choose the **Tables** item.

5. The window Manage Tables will appear. For now, leave the Table combo box set to <new>. Assign the values listed in Table 10-5 to the Manage Table window. When you are finished, the window should resemble Figure 10-9. Note that when defining an Integer data type, you cannot assign the size. A size of 4 is automatically filled in.

Table 10-5 Properties for the Hotel Table

COLUMN NAME	DATATYPE	SIZE	NULLS
Hotel	int		No
Name	varchar	50	Yes

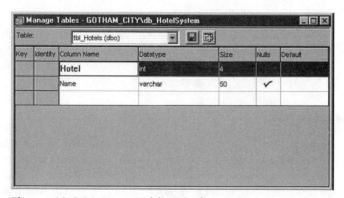

Figure 10-9 Manage Table window

6. This table is designed for basic hotel information: a hotel number and the name of the hotel. The column, Hotel, has been designed not to allow for nulls. Whenever a record in this table is inserted or updated, a non-null value must be provided in the Hotel column. If the user attempts to assign a null value to a field that has the **Nulls** column not marked, an error will occur. You do not want a null value in the Hotel column because the Hotel column is required to have a legitimate row in the table.

7. To save the table, select the Save button, which is the button with diskette on it on the Manage Tables toolbar. A dialog window will appear. Enter the name of the table, **tbl_Hotels**, into the text box and press the OK button.

8. The table you have just created is empty. To populate it, run the SQL script, **FILHOTEL.SQL**, found in the chapter's subdirectory on the CD-ROM through **ISQL** or the SQL Enterprise Manager's Query Analyzer.

9. Run the SQL script, **HTL10A.SQL** found in this chapter's subdirectory on the CD-ROM to build the rest of the tables in this database and **HTL10B.SQL** to populate the tables.

How It Works

All the steps you are doing through the SQL Enterprise Manager graphics interface perform the Data Definition Language (DDL) equivalents that you would issue through the Query Analyzer. In creating a table through the SQL Enterprise Manager, you are issuing the **CREATE TABLE** command. From an **ISQL** prompt, you would issue the following command:

```
CREATE TABLE tbl_Hotels
    (Hotel          Int                NOT NULL,
     Name           VarChar(50)        NULL)
```

When creating a table, there are a few rules you should keep in mind. A table name can be up to 30 characters long. The maximum number of columns you can define for a table is 250 columns. Not including text and image fields, the number of bytes per row should not exceed 1,962 bytes.

Comments

Through the SQL Enterprise Manager, you can change a column name or add more columns. You cannot modify the **Data** type, **Size**, **Nulls**, and **Default** columns. If you need to modify or remove a column, you will have to create a new table with the new or removed column, copy the data into it from the old table to the new table, then drop the old table.

Using the Query Analyzer to add a column to a table that already exists, you will use the **ALTER TABLE** statement. For further information on the **ALTER TABLE** syntax, refer to the SQL Server Book Online.

COMPLEXITY
BEGINNING

10.4 How do I...
Define primary and foreign keys?

Problem

I've created my tables, but how do I ensure the integrity of my data? I've heard of referential integrity but what does it mean and how does it apply to my tables?

Technique

Data integrity is an important part of database design. Data integrity schemes prevent users from entering incorrect or invalid data into the database tables. With the previous version of SQL Server, enforcing data integrity was not easily implemented. Unique indexes and triggers had to be used to enforce integrity. SQL Server now supports data integrity with the use of primary and foreign key relationships, also known as referential integrity.

Primary and foreign key relationships are constraints placed on tables that define conditions the data must meet in order to be entered into a database table. A *primary key* is used to ensure that no duplicate values are entered into the table, that null values are not allowed, and whether a clustered or non-clustered index is created to enhance performance. It is a good practice to make a database table's primary key a non-clustered index. Indexes are discussed in greater depth in the next section. Only one primary key may be defined for a given table. Sixteen columns is the maximum number of columns that can make up a primary key, with a total byte length of less than or equal to 254 bytes.

A *foreign key* is one or more columns that reference a primary key in a different table. It does not have to be unique. An unlimited number of foreign keys can be defined for a table. Like the primary key, 16 columns is the maximum number of columns that can make up a foreign key, and its total byte length must be less than or equal to 254 bytes. The columns must match one for one the order of the columns and data type of the columns the primary key is referencing. When designing queries, primary and foreign keys are what you use to join two tables together. This also enforces referential integrity.

To create the primary key to foreign key relationships, you can either use the SQL Enterprise Manager or the Data Definition Language scripts (SQL statements) through the ISQL prompt.

Steps

This example is going to use the SQL Enterprise Manager to create the primary and foreign key relationship between the Hotels and Rooms tables. If you did not go through the previous How-To, run the SQL script, `CMPLTHTL.SQL`, found in this chapter's subdirectory on the CD-ROM, in the SQL Enterprise Manager's Query Analyzer or ISQL to build and populate the tables you will use in this example.

The tables you will be working with are based on the Hotel Reservation tables used in Chapter 5, Presenting Data to the User. To understand the relationship of the tables, see Figure 10-10 for the Entity-relationship diagram. As a rule of thumb, you should create all the primary key information for the tables first before creating the foreign key relations.

Create Primary Key for `tbl_Hotels` Table

1. Open the SQL Enterprise Manager from your Microsoft SQL Server 6.5 Utilities group.

2. In the Server Manager window, select the server that contains the database you wish to create the table in. Using the information from the previous example, use the server called `GOTHAM_CITY` and the database called `db_HotelSystem`.

3. Click on the plus sign next to the database name. The Server Manager explorer will expand the database and show the components of the database.

4. Click on the plus sign next to the item called Objects. The Server Manager explorer will expand the Objects item and show all the database objects that you can work with.

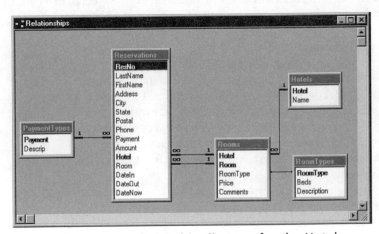

Figure 10-10 Entity-relationship diagram for the Hotel database (`db_HotelSystem`)

5. Click on the plus sign next to the Tables folder. Select the Table object **Hotels** with the right mouse button and select **Edit** for the pop-up menu. The Manage Tables window will appear.

6. Click on the Advanced Features button on the Manage Tables toolbar. This will bring up more detailed information about the table. If you can't see all the fields, maximize the Manage Tables window. Your screen should look similar to Figure 10-11.

7. On the first tab, Primary Key/Identify, you will be setting up the primary key for the Hotels table. Click on the Column Names combo box in the Primary Key frame. A list of column names that do not have the Null column marked will be displayed. Select the Hotel column name to be the primary key.

8. The type of index should be defined as non-clustered. Clustered and non-clustered indexes will be discussed later in this chapter.

9. Click the Add button to add the primary key information to the table. In the Key column in the table grid, a key icon will appear to illustrate that the column has been designated as the primary key.

10. The Identity Column information is only relevant when you are creating a table. An Identity column is an auto-incrementing column, similar to the **Counter** field in Microsoft Access.

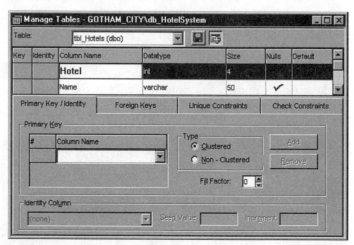

Figure 10-11 Manage Tables with the Advanced Features selected

Create Primary and Foreign Keys for the tbl_Rooms Table

1. Click on the Tables combo box and select the table, tbl_Rooms.

2. In the Primary Key frame, the column names that can be used for the primary key are those columns that have the Nulls column not marked. Select the values listed in Table 10-6 to define the primary key for the Rooms table.

Table 10-6 Primary key columns for the Rooms table

COLUMN	SELECTION
1	Hotel
2	Room

3. The type of Index should be defined as non-clustered; therefore, select the non-clustered radio button. Non-clustered indexes are discussed in greater detail in the next section.

4. Click the Add button to add the primary information to the table.

5. In order to create the foreign key relations, you need to click the Foreign Key tab. Your screen should look similar to Figure 10-12.

6. The tbl_Rooms table is dependent on the tbl_Hotels table; therefore, choose the tbl_Hotels table primary key in the Referenced Table combo box. The list item will look similar to this:

```
dbo.tbl_Hotels - PK_tbl_Hotels_2__10
```

> **NOTE**
> Because the primary key name was built by the SQL Enterprise Manager, the exact primary key name may vary.

Figure 10-12 The Additional Features tab showing Foreign Key information

7. The foreign key of the **tbl_Rooms** table is Hotel. It relates to the primary key of the **tbl_Hotels** table, which is Hotel. In the Foreign Keys grid, select the Hotel column under the Foreign Key columns. This means that a room record cannot exist in the **tbl_Rooms** table without a valid hotel number referenced in the **tbl_Hotels** table. For example, you want to enter a new room number to the **tbl_Rooms** table, one of the requirements is that you entered a valid Hotel number that resides in the **tbl_Hotels** table. Why is this important? This is to ensure that you don't end up with a room that does not exist in a hotel.

8. The Add button will be enabled if the criteria selected are valid. Click on the Add button and the SQL Enterprise Manager dynamically builds a foreign key name and displays it in the Foreign Keys combo box. The foreign key's name will look similar to this:

```
FK_tbl_Rooms_2__10
```

9. To save the information, select the Save button.

How It Works

All of the steps performed through the SQL Enterprise Manager perform the Data Definition Language (DDL) equivalents via Transact-SQL, which you would issue through the **ISQL** prompt. Adding a primary and a foreign key to a table, you are issuing the **ALTER TABLE** statement and adding constraints to the table. The **ALTER TABLE** statement for the **Hotels** table will look like this:

```
ALTER TABLE tbl_Hotels
    ADD
    CONSTRAINT PK_hotel PRIMARY KEY NONCLUSTERED
        (Hotel)
```

The **ALTER TABLE** is used to either add a new column or data integrity constraint to a database table. This **ALTER TABLE** statement is adding a primary key constraint and non-clustered index to the **tbl_Hotels** database table using the column **Hotel** as the primary key. The non-clustered index is called **PK_hotel**.

Creating the primary and foreign keys of the **Rooms** table will look like this:

```
ALTER TABLE tbl_Rooms
    ADD
    CONSTRAINT PK_Rooms PRIMARY KEY NONCLUSTERED
        (Hotel, Room),
    CONSTRAINT FK_Hotels FOREIGN KEY
        (Hotel)
        REFERENCES dbo.tbl_Hotels (Hotel)
```

The **ALTER TABLE** statement first adds a primary key constraint and non-clustered index to the tbl_Rooms database table using the columns Hotel and Room as the primary key. The second half of the **ALTER TABLE** statement adds a foreign key constraint to the tbl_Rooms database table using the **tbl_Hotels** database table as the reference table. The column used to list the reference is the Hotel column. The non-clustered index based on the columns Hotel and Room is called `PK_Rooms`. The foreign key constraint name is called `FK_Hotels`.

Comments

You may have noticed that by using ISQL, you need to supply the constraint names. Actually, if you do not provide a constraint name, SQL Server will generate a name and assign it to the constraint.

COMPLEXITY
BEGINNING

10.5 How do I...
Index a table for efficiency and performance?

Problem

My tables have been created and they all have their primary and foreign keys defined. I know that our developers are not going to write queries that solely go against the primary keys of a table. I have been told that I should have created indexes for my tables so these auxiliary queries will run at a decent speed. How do I create indexes on my tables?

Technique

Indexes are used to speed access to data and to enforce uniqueness within a table. Indexes offer a good method for increasing data storage performance because they keep track of key information and where it is located in the tables.

Before you start defining indexes on your tables, you should be aware that there are two types of indexes you can use, clustered and non-clustered. In a *clustered index*, the data is physically sorted and stored in the index order. For example, before a clustered index is applied to the customer database table, the physical order of the data in the database is in the order in which it was entered. For reporting purposes, you base a lot of reports on customer's First and Last Name (last name first), so you create a clustered index on the database table based on the last and first name columns. The data will now be physically sorted by the customer's last and first name. Now when you do a report, you do not need to add an Order By in your query because the data is retrieved alphabetized by the customer's last and first name.

A *non-clustered index* maintains an index file that contains pointers that reference where data is located in the table based on how the clustered index organized the data. When a query is performed and it uses a non-clustered index, a minimum of two disk reads is required. The first read scans the index for the indexed field and the second read retrieves the actual data from the table.

Since the non-clustered index bases the location of the data on how the clustered index organizes it, it is a good practice to define your clustered index first, before you create a lot of non-clustered indexes. If you create a lot of non-clustered indexes, then you create your clustered index, all the non-clustered indexes are going to get rebuilt because the locations of the data are going to get reorganized. If you have a lot of non-clustered indexes when this happens, the rebuild can take a long time.

Using a clustered index over non-clustered indexes for data retrieval is almost always faster. When a query is performed and it uses a clustered index, since the data is already in index order, another read is not required since we are already positioned on the rows we need. In Figure 10-13, the clustered index is based on the guest's last name. The guest's information has been rearranged based on the index, regardless of when the information was entered. When information needs to be retrieved from this index, only one read from the index is necessary because the data is already in last name order. In the non-clustered index, the index is also based on the guest's last name, but the guest's information stays in the order in which it was entered into the system. When information needs to be retrieved from this index, two processes need to be performed; the first process reads the index to find out where the data is stored, and the second process retrieves the data.

When you create the primary key for your tables, you can create it as either a clustered or non-clustered index to the table. It is not a good idea to create the clustered index against the primary key of the table because that is not how the information

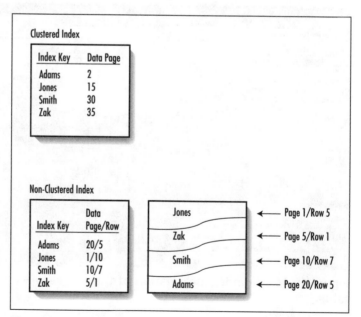

Figure 10-13 Clustered vs. non-clustered indexes

is always grouped or displayed in a report or a customer look-up chart. For example, you rarely want to look up a chart by the customer number. The most common look-up would be the customer's last name or their company name. When you perform a look-up on a customer's number, you are usually interested in one record; therefore, you are using the overhead of a clustered index just to find one record.

Steps

This example is going to use the SQL Enterprise Manager to create a clustered index in the Reservations database table using the guest's last and first name as the index.

1. Open the SQL Enterprise Manager from your Microsoft SQL Server 6.5 Utilities group.

2. In the Server Manager window, select the server that contains the database in which you wish to create the table. Using the information from the previous example, use the server called **GOTHAM_CITY** and the database called **db_HotelSystem**.

3. Select the **Indexes** item from the Manage menu. The Manage Indexes window will be displayed.

4. In the **Table** combo box, select the **tbl_Reservations** table. Your Manage Indexes window should look similar to Figure 10-14.

5. In the **Index** combo box, select <New> so we can create a new index.

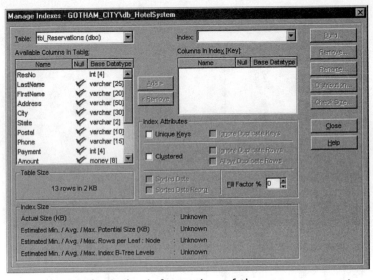

Figure 10-14 The index information of the **tbl_Reservations** table

6. The text field of the combo box will clear and you can type in the name of the new index, `idx_LastFirst`.

7. From the Available Columns In Table listbox, select the LastName column and press Add. This will move the column name to the Columns In Index (Key) listbox.

8. Select the FirstName column and press the Add button.

9. In the `Index Attribute` frame, mark the Clustered check box. A check mark will appear.

10. The two radio buttons next to Clustered should become enabled so you can modify them. Select the Allow Duplicate Rows radio button. You are allowing duplicate rows because a person with the same last name can make more than one reservation. Also, since this is not a primary key, duplicate rows do not matter as much.

11. Press the Build button to create the index.

12. A dialog window will appear, like the one in Figure 10-15, asking you if you wish to execute this process now or at a scheduled time. Since we don't have a lot of data or non-clustered indexes defined, press the Execute Now button.

13. The index is created and a row is placed in the sysindexes database system table. Sysindexes is a system table defined in each database that contains a record of all the clustered and non-clustered indexes. It also contains a record of all tables that have no indexes.

How It Works

The Data Definition Language (DDL) statement that the SQL Enterprise Manager performed is the `CREATE INDEX` statement. The statement in ISQL would look something like this:

```
CREATE CLUSTERED INDEX idx_LastFirst
ON Reservations (LastName, FirstName)
WITH ALLOW_DUP_ROW
```

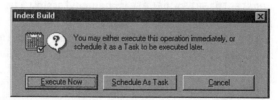

Figure 10-15 Execute Now or schedule the Task Later dialog window

Comments

In an online transaction processing system, defining clustered indexes can slow your system down. This is due to the data reorganization that occurs after each transaction, whether it is a single transaction or batch transactions. It is better to define clustered indexes on systems like decision support system or systems that have very little data input, or on tables that are used primarily for querying information.

When defining a clustered index, it is better to assign it before the tables get too much information or too many non-clustered indexes. When a clustered index is defined, all non-clustered indexes are rebuilt to reflect the clustered index. Depending on how much data or how many non-clustered indexes exist, this can be a very slow process.

COMPLEXITY
BEGINNING

10.6 How do I...
Create a trigger to control data integrity?

Problem

In previous versions of SQL Server, triggers have been used to enforce complex business rules and integrity of the data enforcing the primary and foreign key relationship. If I do not need triggers to enforce the primary and foreign key relationships any more, what else can I use triggers for?

Technique

A trigger is a special kind of stored procedure of Data Manipulation Language statements that is automatically executed when an INSERT, DELETE, or UPDATE is performed. It is executed automatically whenever an application makes a specified change to the database. Triggers are executed based on events that occur within the database. In most DBMSs, triggers can be defined that will execute when an UPDATE, INSERT, or DELETE is attempted against a table. Triggers get activated once per query and are treated as one transaction that can be rolled back if an error is detected during their execution. Each trigger can perform any number of functions and can call up to 16 stored procedures. The stored procedures can be either system stored procedures or user-defined stored procedures, like the ones illustrated in How-To's 10.8 and 10.9 of this chapter. A trigger cannot be created against a view or temporary table although it can reference them.

As mentioned earlier, previous versions of SQL Server relied on triggers to maintain data consistency. They would enforce business rules about the relationships between tables. In a traditional two-tier client/server model, enforcement of business rules could be handled on either tier. In a three-tier model, business rules are handled in the middle tier, the Business services layer. Triggers should only be used to handle data operations. For further explanation of what makes up the Business services layer, refer to Chapter 1, Client/Server Basics and Chapter 7, Business Objects.

Steps

This example will be applied to the **tbl_Rooms** database table. It is going to cascade a change throughout related tables in the database. Suppose you're changing all the room numbers for all the rooms in all the hotels in the system. Without the use of triggers, you could not update the room numbers without affecting the **tbl_Reservations** database table. The room numbers in the **tbl_Reservations** database table are related to the room numbers in the **tbl_Rooms** database table. The primary and foreign key relationship would not allow this to happen because the foreign key cannot exist without a primary key value. By using an update trigger, the change of the room number in the **tbl_Rooms** database table will also update the room number in the **tbl_Reservations** database table, thus maintaining referential integrity.

1. Open the SQL Enterprise Manager from your Microsoft SQL Server 6.5 Utilities group.

2. In the Server Manager window, select the server that contains the database in which you wish to create the table. Using the information from the previous example, use the server called **GOTHAM_CITY** and the database called **db_HotelSystem**.

3. Select the **Manage** menu item and click on the **Triggers** item. The Manage Triggers window will appear, as shown in Figure 10-16.

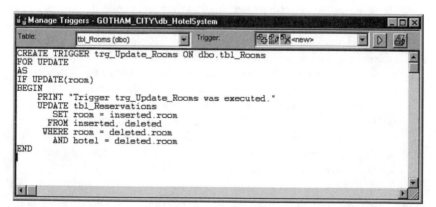

Figure 10-16 Manage Triggers window with default information

4. Any triggers in the database will be listed in the triggers combo box.

5. Choose the database table that the trigger will be designed for. In this example, choose `tbl_Rooms` (dbo). Since there are no triggers for this table defined yet, choose <New> from the Triggers combo box to create a new trigger. The window will display what you need to start creating a trigger.

```
CREATE TRIGGER <TRIGGER NAME> ON dbo.tbl_Rooms
FOR INSERT,UPDATE,DELETE
AS
```

6. Enter the following code in the Manage Triggers window. Change the `<TRIGGER NAME>` to `trg_Update_Rooms`. Remove the `INSERT` and `DELETE` options from the `FOR` definition because this trigger only applies to update actions against this table. The `IF UPDATE` keyword tests for an `INSERT` or `UPDATE` action against a specific column or columns in the database table. You did not leave `INSERT` in because SQL Server treats updates as a `DELETE` and `INSERT` process. In this example, you are checking to see if the column `room` is being updated.

```
CREATE TRIGGER trg_Update_Rooms ON DBO.tbl_Rooms
FOR UPDATE

AS
IF UPDATE(room)
```

7. Continue to enter the following code in the Manage Trigger window. The `BEGIN` statement marks the beginning of the transaction. The `PRINT` statement will print a message to the test environment, either the Query Analyzer or ISQL. The `UPDATE` statement is going to update the room value in the `tbl_Reservations` database table. The `SET` keyword is used to specify which column is going to be updated. In this example, the value the room is going to be updated to comes from the inserted table. The `WHERE` clause is used to perform a search to find the row or rows that are going to be affected by the `UPDATE`. The values it is trying to match against are the room and hotel values from the deleted table. The inserted and deleted tables are special system tables. They are temporary tables that triggers use to store information about the transaction. During a `DELETE`, SQL Server stores a copy of the deleted rows in the deleted table. During an `INSERT`, SQL Server stores a copy of the new rows being inserted in the inserted table. To SQL Server, an `UPDATE` is both a `DELETE` and an `INSERT`; therefore, the old rows being updated are copied in the deleted table, while the new, updated rows are copied in the inserted table. The `END` statement notifies SQL Server that the transaction is completed.

```
BEGIN
     PRINT "Trigger trg_Update_Rooms was executed."
     UPDATE tbl_Reservations
     SET tbl_Rooms.room = inserted.room
     FROM inserted, deleted
     WHERE tbl_Rooms_room = deleted.room
```

```
     AND tbl_Rooms.hotel = deleted.hotel

END
```

8. Press the Execute button next to the Trigger combo box. If the editor does not encounter any errors, the trigger will be saved.

9. To test the trigger, load the Query Analyzer. In the Query tab, type in the **UPDATE** statement. You are going to update the room number 2980 in hotel number 1 to 2780 in the **tbl_Rooms** database table. After you have typed it in, press the Execute button.

```
UPDATE tbl_Rooms
SET Room = 2780
WHERE Room = 2980
AND Hotel = 1
```

How It Works

When an update transaction is performed against the room column in the **tbl_Rooms** database table, this trigger is executed. Since the **tbl_Reservations** database table has a primary and foreign key relationship on the Room column with the **tbl_Rooms** database table, the room value in **tbl_Reservations** needs to be updated as well. A reservation cannot exist without a valid room assigned to it. If you only update the room column in the **tbl_Rooms** database table without the corresponding room column in the **tbl_Reservations** database table, you violate this relationship rule. It is possible that the room you are updating does not have a reservation assigned to it, but you would never know that unless you had a report of all the rooms that did not have an assigned reservation.

As mentioned earlier, an **UPDATE** first performs a **DELETE** then an **INSERT**. The **UPDATE** statement issued in Step 9 deletes the row from the **tbl_Rooms** database table and copies the deleted row into the deleted table. Then it adds the new row with new information into the **tbl_Rooms** database table and copies the inserted row in the inserted table. The trigger gets executed and performs an **UPDATE** on the **tbl_Reservations** database table. The criteria the **UPDATE** statement is going to use come from the inserted and deleted table. The **UPDATE** statement is going to update the room value in the **tbl_Reservations** database table with a value of 2780 where the old room number used to be 2980 and the old hotel value was 1.

Comments

As you can see from this example, certain data integrity rules are handled through the use of the primary and foreign key constraints; therefore, there is little reason to use triggers to enforce that relationship as long as the table relationship is within the same database. As we have shown here, triggers are generally used not to implement referential integrity but to keep tables in synch with one another. SQL Server still does not perform cross database data integrity. Triggers would need to be used for this type of data integrity.

10.7 How do I...
Create a view?

Problem

This system is going to be available to a lot of people and I'm afraid it is going to become a security nightmare. I've been told that I can create view tables and base my security on these tables rather than the actual database tables. What are view tables and how can I implement them?

Technique

A good method to restrict access to information is called a derived table, or view. A *view* is a virtual table that looks and feels like a real table. Views limit the amount of data a user can see and modify. They can range from a single column of a table to the entire table, or even a combination of several tables. Views are not tables; therefore, they store no data so any actual modifications to the real table will be under your control. But to the user or application developer, a view looks and acts like a table. Views may be used to control user access to data and to simplify data presentation.

Since views are derived from tables, data access can be improved. Complex queries often join against a lot of tables; therefore, they take a long time to process. By defining views based on the query, the view has already arranged the information it is ultimately going to display or use. An example of a view might be one based on an employee table. The base table might contain the employee's salary, Social Security Number, and other items of information that only someone in human resources should see. By using a view table, you can filter out all the private information and only display the public information. If you did not define a view table, you would have built some data security around the base table. Figure 10-17 illustrates how views interact with base tables.

View Table 1 is a derived table based on Base Table 1. The actual view table can be one column from Base Table 1, several columns, or a mirror of Base Table 1. View Table 2 is derived from Base Table 2. In this instance, it probably consists of several columns from Base Table 2. View Table 3 is derived from View Table 2, Base Table 3 and Base Table 4. This type of view table probably derived from a query that needed to retrieve information from all three tables. Rather than have the query go against three physical database tables to make up the resultset, the query goes after one virtual table that is based on the three tables. View Table 4 is derived from Base Table 4.

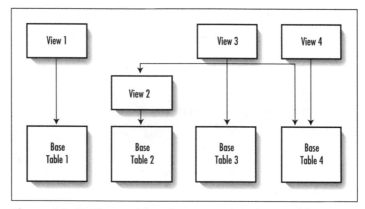

Figure 10-17 View table schema against base tables

Views provide an additional layer of security because they can limit the visible rows based on specified criteria without changing permission to the underlying table or tables. A view is created by using a standard SQL statement, so any selection that can be done with a DML statement can also be done from a view table.

Steps

This example will create a view table to show specific data from the Reservations, Rooms, RoomTypes, and PaymentTypes tables. This view table will consist of a guest's registration number, their last and first name, the name of the hotel the reservation is made for, the room number they will be staying in, the number of beds in the room, and a description of the room. Without this view table, the programmer would have to create a query that retrieves this information from four tables. By using the view, the programmer only has to search one table for the information. As a database administrator (DBA), without the view table, you would need to define security access for the programmer to all four tables. With the view, you only need to define security for the view table.

1. Open the SQL Enterprise Manager from your Microsoft SQL Server 6.5 Utilities group.

2. In the Server Manager window, select the server that contains the database that you wish to create the table in. Using the information from the previous example, use the server called **GOTHAM_CITY** and the database called **db_HotelSystem**.

3. Select the **Manage** menu item and click on the **Views** item. The Manage Views window will appear, as shown in Figure 10-18.

4. Any views in the database will be listed in the Views combo box.

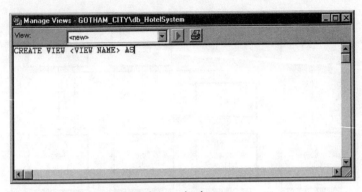

Figure 10-18 Manage View window

5. Choose <New> from the View combo box to create a new view. The window will display what you need to start creating a view:

```
CREATE VIEW <VIEW NAME> AS
```

6. Enter the following code into the Manage View window to create the view to display certain aspects of a guest's reservation. The view table is called **vr_Reservations**. The column names that are going to make up this table are **ResNo**, **LastName**, **FirstName**, **PaymentDesc**, **Room**, **Beds**, and **RoomDesc**. As you can see, since a view is a virtual table, you can make column names a bit more meaningful than how they were originally designed. In this example, there are two description fields, one from the **tbl_PaymentTypes** tables and the other from the **tbl_RoomTypes** table. Rather than have two columns with Description as their column name, we are going to name them **PaymentDesc** and **RoomDesc** to distinguish the differences. The **Select** statement defines the view table. The view is the set of rows and columns that result when the **Select** statement is executed. The **Select** statement is based on joining information from four tables with equal key values: Payment in **tbl_PaymentTypes** is equal to Payment in **tbl_Reservations**, Room in **tbl_Rooms** is equal to Room in **tbl_Reservations**, Hotel in **tbl_Rooms** is equal to Hotel in **tbl_Reservations**, and RoomType in **tbl_RoomTypes** is equal to RoomType in **tbl_Rooms**.

```
CREATE VIEW vr_Reservations
(ResNo, LastName, FirstName, PaymentDesc, Room, Beds, RoomDesc)
AS
SELECT a.ResNo, a.LastName, a.FirstName
     , b.Description
     , c.Room
     , d.Beds, d.Description
  FROM tbl_Reservations a, tbl_PaymentTypes b
     , tbl_Rooms c, tbl_RoomTypes d
 WHERE b.Payment = a.Payment
   AND c.Room = a.Room
```

```
AND c.Hotel = a.Hotel
AND d.RoomType = c.RoomType
```

> **NOTE**
>
> Rather than typing in the table name before each column name,
> you can use aliases to reduce your amount of typing when you
> have to fully qualify each column. For example, had you not used
> aliases, you would have to type: Select tbl_Reservations.ResNo,
> tbl_Reservations.LastName, and so on.

7. Press the Execute button to save the view. SQL Server will scan the view for errors and if none are found, the view will be saved.

8. To retrieve information for the newly created view table, start the Query Analyzer and enter the following statement:

```
select * from vr_Reservations
```

The resulting data should look similar to Figure 10-19.

How It Works

This is a simple view statement. When this view table is queried against, the query will perform as if it was going against the base tables. The difference is that the join will have already been preprocessed and simply executed. Had this join been written into your application, the engine would first check to see if all the elements in the query exist, process the query, then execute.

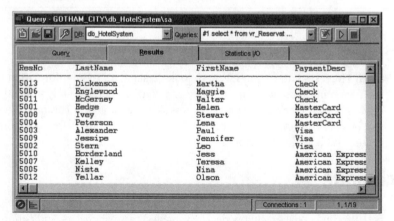

Figure 10-19 Resulting data from querying the
vr_Reservations view table

When you press the Execute button in Step 7, the editor scans the view statement for errors. Also, SQL Server inserts the following lines before your procedure:

```
if exists (select * from sysobjects where id =
object_id('dbo.vr_Reservations') and sysstat & 0xf = 2)
drop view dbo.vr_Reservations
GO
```

This statement checks to see if there is a view procedure in your database with
the same name. This statement is necessary when you make changes to the view procedure because when you make changes to a view procedure, you actually drop the
original procedure and replace it with the new one.

Comments

When naming your views, there are different naming strategies that are used.
Because views have to be used for read-only access or controlled update access, you
might want to note that in your naming convention. For example, if the view we
just created was to be an update view, we would have named it **vu_Reservations**
rather than **vr_Reservations**. By no means is this a standard, but it does help developers and DBAs distinguish what type of views they are.

COMPLEXITY
INTERMEDIATE

10.8 How do I...
Create and execute a stored procedure?

Problem

In my Hotel system, I always want to look up standard room information that the
users are going to use when making a reservation. The query is fairly straightforward,
but I do not want the query replicated across all our applications. This probably belongs
in a business object, but I want it to be a stored procedure. What is a stored procedure and how do I write one?

Technique

A stored procedure is a compiled SQL program. Within a stored procedure you can
perform conditional execution, declare variables, pass parameters, and perform other
programming tasks. Stored procedures are reusable but not reentrant. If two users
execute the same procedure simultaneously, two copies of the plan are loaded into
memory. Since procedure query plans are built and optimized the first time they are
read from disk, there's no guarantee that the plan is optimal every time the

procedure is invoked. If your stored procedure accepts parameter lists that may require different forms of optimization, using exec with the recompile clause will cause SQL Server not to cache the query plan. It will rebuild the plan each time the stored procedure is called.

The advantages of using stored procedures include:

- Better performance and reduced server load because SQL is precompiled

- Easier change management

- Better control over database access because only approved SQL is permitted to run against the server

- Easier and tighter security administration, because the only entry point to the database is through stored procedures

- Less network chat, because fewer calls are made by the client and any required cursor processing takes place on the server exclusively

- More opportunity for asynchronous server processing because the client does not need to be involved in complicated transactions

- A solid foundation for migration to emerging three-tier client/server products

In a two-tiered model, business logic would be part of the stored procedure. In a distributed environment, stored procedures should be used to handle the basic data manipulation tasks needed by the business layer.

Steps

1. Open the SQL Enterprise Manager from your Microsoft SQL Server 6.5 Utilities group.

2. In the Server Manager window, select the server that contains the database in which you wish to create the stored procedure. Using the information from the previous example, use the server called **GOTHAM_CITY** and the database called **db_HotelSystem**.

3. Select the Manage menu item and click on the **Stored Procedures** item. The Manage Stored Procedures window will appear, as shown in Figure 10-20.

4. Any stored procedures in the database will be listed in the **Procedures** combo box.

5. Choose <New> from the **Procedure** combo box to create a new stored procedure. The window will display what you need to start creating a stored procedure:

```
CREATE PROCEDURE <PROCEDURE NAME> AS
```

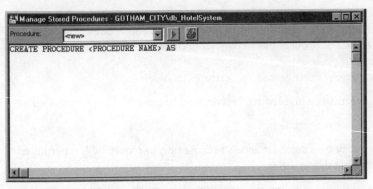

Figure 10-20 Manage Stored Procedures window

6. Replace the `<PROCEDURE NAME>` with `proc_RoomDesc`.

7. Since we do not want all the rooms in all the hotels to be displayed, you are going to add the following argument variable to the first line of the procedure. This goes after the procedure name and before the AS.

`@Hotel int`

8. Your first line should look like the following:

`CREATE PROCEDURE proc_RoomDesc @Hotel int AS`

The name of the stored procedure is `proc_RoomDesc`. The argument variable, `@Hotel`, is defined as a integer datatype to match the datatype of Hotel within the `tbl_Rooms` and `tbl_RoomTypes` tables. This means that the Visual Basic code that is using this stored procedure will pass the Hotel number in from an integer value. This argument will be used as part of the query's `Where` clause to retrieve only the rooms for a given hotel.

9. For readability, enter the following on the next line as illustrated below. At this point, you are simply entering a standard SQL query statement to retrieve the desired information.

```
SELECT a.room, b.beds, b.description, a.price
  FROM tbl_Rooms a, tbl_RoomTypes b
 WHERE a.hotel = @Hotel
   AND a.roomtype = b.roomtype
```

10. Press the Execute button next to the `Procedures` combo box. This will scan the procedure for errors. If no errors are found, then the procedure is stored in the database on the server.

How It Works

The syntax for creating a stored procedure is as follows:

```
CREATE PROCEDURE procedure_name [parameter1, ...]
AS SELECT select_criteria
FROM table_name
```

The `procedure_name` is the name of the stored procedure, which we called `sp_RoomDesc`. We used a parameter that is used as part of the **WHERE** criteria in our SQL query. A procedure can have up to 255 parameters defined. When placing a parameter in your stored procedure, the first character needs to be the at symbol (@) and needs to be the same datatype it is requesting. In this example, the **Hotel** datatype is an integer in the database; therefore, the parameter argument also needs to be an integer datatype. When this stored procedure is called, a parameter must be supplied; otherwise an error will occur. If you would like the user to execute the stored procedure whether a parameter is supplied or not, you can provide a default value. For example, if you wanted the stored procedure to use hotel number 1 as the default value, the code in Step 7 would look like this:

```
@Hotel int = 1
```

The **Select** statement returns the room number from the Rooms table and returns the beds, description, and price data from the RoomTypes table that have corresponding room numbers in the Rooms table.

The **Where** clause checks to make sure the room number returned from the Rooms table belongs to the hotel number that was requested.

When you press the Execute button in Step 10, the editor scans the procedure for errors. Also, SQL Server inserts the following lines before your procedure:

```
if exists (select * from sysobjects where id =
object_id('dbo.proc_RoomDesc') and sysstat & 0xf = 4)
drop procedure dbo.proc_RoomDesc
GO
```

This statement checks to see if there is a stored procedure in your database with the same name. This statement is necessary when you make changes to the stored procedure, because when you make changes to a stored procedure, you actually drop the original procedure and replace it with the new one.

When this procedure is called from either your program or from within ISQL, it will perform the query and retrieve the information requested about the **Rooms** and **RoomTypes**.

Comments

When creating a stored procedure, almost everyone uses the editor that comes with the SQL Enterprise Manager, like you did in this example. There is nothing wrong with working on the procedures this way, but you need to be aware that by using this editor, you have no way to "version control" your changes to a procedure. In other words, once you have made a change and pressed the Save Object button, there is no way for you to go back to a previous version of the procedure. Once you have created your stored procedures, it is a good practice to create SQL scripts for them and store them on a drive that routinely gets backed up.

It also might be a good idea to use a tool like Microsoft Visual SourceSafe to handle version control of the SQL scripts. Using a version control tool for your SQL scripts offers the same advantages of using it for your source code. Refer to Chapter 1, Client/Server Basics, for more information on using Visual SourceSafe.

There are quite a few third party tools available to create, manage, and maintain stored procedures. For an idea of what is available, see Appendix B, Client/Server Database Resources, for more information.

COMPLEXITY
INTERMEDIATE

10.9 How do I...
Create a stored procedure that performs a transaction?

Problem

Now that I know how to make simple stored procedures that replace my SQL queries in my code, I would like to know how to make more sophisticated stored procedures which perform updating of a database table and contain error handling. What do I need for my stored procedure to do that?

Technique

For more information on how to call a stored procedure, refer to Chapter 3, Remote Data Objects.

Steps

1. Open the SQL Enterprise Manager from your Microsoft SQL Server 6.5 Utilities group.

2. In the Server Manager window, select the server that contains the database in which you wish to create the stored procedure. Using the information from the previous example, use the server called **GOTHAM_CITY** and the database called **db_HotelSystem**.

3. Select the Manage menu item and click on the **Stored Procedures** item. The Manage Stored Procedures window will appear.

4. Any stored procedures in the database will be listed in the **Procedures** combo box.

5. Choose <New> from the **Procedure** combo box to create a new stored procedure. The window will display what you need to start creating a stored procedure:

```
CREATE PROCEDURE <PROCEDURE NAME> AS
```

6. Replace the **<PROCEDURE NAME>** with the **proc_Submit_Resv**. The first line of the procedure should look like this:

```
CREATE PROCEDURE proc_submit_resv
```

7. This stored procedure is going to insert a reservation for a guest into the **tbl_Reservation** database table. In order to insert a guest, the **Insert** statement needs some information about the guest: the hotel they wish to stay at, the guest's first and last name, his address, phone number, method of payment, the cost of the room, and the date range the guest is staying in. Also, the type of room the guest would like to stay in is passed. Insert the following argument parameters into the stored procedure to define the argument parameters and their datatypes.

```
@Hotel          int,
@LastName       varchar (25),
@FirstName      varchar (20),
@Address        varchar (50),
@City           varchar (30),
@State          varchar (2),
@Postal         varchar (10),
@Phone          varchar (15),
@Payment        int,
@Amount         Money,
@DateIn         DateTime,
@DateOut        DateTime,
@RoomType       int,

AS
```

8. Insert the following code into the stored procedure to define some variables that are going to be used within this procedure. The declare statement defines the name and datatype of a local variable that can be used within the procedure. The text between /* and */ are comments. They are not considered executable code, simply comments to help document the procedure.

```
/* Use this variable to hold our transaction return status */
declare @tran_status    int

/* Use this variable to hold the room number */
declare @RoomNbr        smallint

/* this will store the new reservation number after we create */
/* a reservation */
declare @resv_nbr       int
```

9. Insert the following code into the stored procedure to mark the starting point of a transaction.

```
BEGIN TRAN
```

10. Insert the following code into the stored procedure. Within the If statement, a query checks to make sure that the desired room type is available at the time this process was performed. It's a good practice to check this because during the time you were on the phone with customers, you were only looking at an image of the data. Someone could have updated the room status after you performed your initial lookup. If a room exists, the process continues; otherwise, a negative value will be moved to the `trans_status` local variable and the `abort_trans_exit` routine is performed.

```
/* make sure rooms are available */

if not exists(select * from tbl_Rooms where roomtype = @RoomType
and Hotel = @hotel and RoomStatus = "0")
begin
select @tran_status = -10000
        goto abort_trans_exit
end
```

11. Add the following code to the stored procedure. The last statement will perform the insertion of the reservation into the `tbl_Reservations` database table. If an error occurs during the insertion transaction, a -10001 is passed to the `@trans_error` local variable and the `abort_trans_exit` routine is performed.

```
/* create a reservation */

select @resv_nbr = max(resno) + 1 from tbl_Reservations
where hotel = @hotel

select @RoomNbr = min(room) from tbl_Rooms where Hotel = @hotel
    and roomtype = @RoomType

insert into tbl_Reservations
(ResNo, LastName, FirstName, Address, City, State, Postal, Phone, Payment,
 Amount, Hotel, Room, DateIn, DateOut, DateNow)
values(@resv_nbr, @lastname, @firstname, @address, @city, @state, @postal,
 @phone, @payment, @amount, @hotel, @roomnbr, @datein, @dateout, getdate())
if (@@error <> 0) /* something went wrong */
begin
select @tran_status = -10001
goto abort_trans_exit
end
```

12. Insert the following code into the stored procedure. This section handles the transaction when no errors occur. The `Commit Tran` statement completes the transaction. The `Print` statement is used only during the debugging process. When this stored procedure is compiled and executed through a program, SQL Server does not perform this statement. On successful processing, the return code of 0 is returned back to the program that called this stored procedure and the procedure will terminate.

```
/* complete a normal transaction */
normal_exit:
commit tran
print 'tran completed'
return 0
```

13. Insert the following code into the stored procedure. This routine is performed whenever an error occurs during the course of this transaction. The **Rollback Tran** statement rolls you back to the beginning of the transaction and undoes everything up to that point. Any inserts, updates, or deletions to any table during the course of a transaction is cleared out as if the statements were never performed. A message of **Trans Abort** is displayed for debugging purposes. When this stored procedure is compiled and executed through a program, SQL Server does not perform this statement. The return code of whatever was passed to the local variable, **@trans_status**, is returned back to the program that called this stored procedure and the procedure will terminate.

```
/* something went wrong and the transaction needs to be undone */
abort_trans_exit:

rollback tran
print 'tran aborted'
return @tran_status
```

14. After you have entered all the code, press the Execute button. If no errors are found, the stored procedure will be saved.

15. To test the stored procedure, open the Query Analyzer. On the Query tab, enter the following code and press the Execute Query button. The **Declare** statement defines **@ret_code** as a local variable within the Query Analyzer environment. The **Exec** statement will execute the stored procedure, **proc_submit_resv**. By assigning the stored procedure to the local variable, **@ret_code**, any return code returned by the procedure will be passed to the variable. The information after **proc_submit_resv** is the information the procedure needs to complete the insert transactions. After the procedure has completed execution, the select statement displays the value the local variable, **@ret_code**, contains. Your Query Analyzer should look similar to Figure 10-21.

```
DECLARE @ret_code int
EXEC @ret_code = proc_submit_resv 1, "Smith", "Ben", "153 N. Main St.",
"Irvine", "CA", "92714", "(714)555-1212", 1, 75.00, "08/07/96", "08/08/96",
31
SELECT @ret_code
```

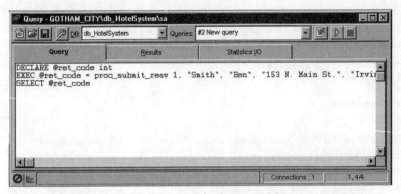

Figure 10-21 Query Analyzer with the test SQL statement

How It Works

When this stored procedure is executed, it needs to receive argument values from the Visual Basic procedure that is calling it. In Step 15, you are simulating a call to the stored procedure. First, you define a variable, **@ret_code**, that will receive a return code from the stored procedure when it finishes executing. Next, the stored procedure is executed with all the necessary argument values. The arguments get loaded into argument variables that are defined in Step 7. The local variables defined in Step 8 will be used within this procedure. The **Begin Tran** statement marks the beginning of a transaction; this notifies SQL Server that a unit of work is about to be performed. At this time, a transaction has been recorded in the database's transaction log as an open transaction.

The first condition criteria, found in Step 10, checks the **tbl_Rooms** database table to ensure that the room the customer is requesting is still available. If the query returns no information, it means that no rooms that match the customer's request are available. If this happens, -10000 is assigned to the **@tran_status** variable and the **abort_trans_exit** subroutine will be performed.

Why is this check so important? Before a reservation is actually processed, your users are looking at a snapshot, or static picture, of the data. When the user wants to modify the data, such as to make or update a reservation, you want to make sure that the picture has not been changed while you were looking at it. In this example, you want to make sure there are still rooms available to make a reservation with.

In Step 11, a query is performed to get a new reservation number to assign to this reservation. The query retrieves the largest reservation number found in the **tbl_Reservations** database table and increments that number by one. Then the new number is assigned to the local variable, **@resv_nbr**.

Next, a room number is retrieved from the **tbl_Rooms** database table. The room number will be assigned to the reservation. The query retrieves the first room number that is available based on the customer's request. The room number received from the query is assigned to the local variable, **@roomnbr**.

Now that all the necessary components needed to make a reservation have been collected, an insert statement is issued to save the reservation information into the **tbl_Reservations** database table. The **@@error** variable is a global variable in SQL Server. Global variables are defined with the prefix of **@@**. The **@@error** variable is used to store the status of the last SQL statement performed. If it is equal to zero, then the SQL statement executed was successful. In this example, if the global variable does not equal zero, -10001 is assigned to the **@tran_status** variable and the **abort_trans_exit** subroutine is performed.

The procedure now passes the **normal_exit** label, described in Step 12. If there were no errors along the way, the **Commit Tran** statement is issued. This notifies SQL Server that the unit of work has been completed successfully and the transaction record in the database's transaction log is marked as complete. In the **Results** tab of the Query Analyzer, the message **tran completed** will be displayed. When this stored procedure is called from Visual Basic, a return code value of zero will be passed back to the calling procedure. In this example, the return code value of zero is passed to the **@ret_code** variable defined in the Query Analyzer's Query tab.

Had any errors occurred, the procedure would have performed the subroutine, **abort_trans_exit**. The **Rollback Tran** statement ends the transaction by updating any database tables. It will be as if the transaction never took place. The database's transaction log will be updated to show that the transaction was completed, even though no data was written to any database table. In the **Results** tab of the Query Analyzer, the message **tran aborted** will be displayed. When this stored procedure is called from a Visual Basic program, the value in the local variable, **@tran_status**, will be passed back to the calling procedure. In this example, the value in the local variable, **@tran_status**, is passed to the **@ret_code** variable defined in the Query Analyzer's Query tab.

The Select **@ret_code** is used to display the return code that is passed back from the stored procedure. Figure 10-22 illustrates a successful transaction. Except for a return code of zero, the negative values do not mean anything unless you define them in your application.

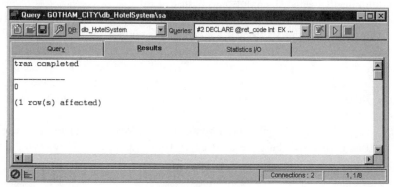

Figure 10-22 Query Analyzer displaying a successful transaction

Comments

As you might have noticed, the stored procedure has one entry point at the top, and then a standard exit and error exit subroutine, much like a Visual Basic function. It is recommended that you always try to handle the rollback of your transaction and exit of the stored procedure in one location, as illustrated in Steps 12 and 13.

COMPLEXITY

BEGINNING

10.10 How do I...
Create a query using SQL Server Web Assistant?

Problem

I would like to post the most current reservation list on our Intranet. How can I create an HTML document that updates every time a new reservation is made?

Technique

Client/server development has expanded due to the popularity of the Internet. Through the use of browser technology and HTML (Hypertext Markup Language), the Internet, which gives companies the freedom to communicate with their customers on an international scale, is being used to communicate with employees as well. An internal version of the Internet is called an Intranet. HTML documents are created to contain internal information like stock and financial reports, company announcements, and policy manuals. Employees are able to obtain more up-to-date information about their company without printing a lot of manuals, leaflets, and memorandums that get shelved, misplaced, or discarded.

SQL Server 6.5 introduced a new tool that makes it easy to generate an HTML document based on data from SQL Server. This tool is called the SQL Server Web Assistant and acts like any other Wizard tool. It prompts you with a variety of questions and creates an HTML document. This document can be used once or set up to run as a scheduled SQL Server task. By setting the document up as a scheduled task, it can be created at designated times—for example, every hour—or whenever a table is updated.

In the following example, you are going to use the Web Assistant to create an HTML document that will be generated every time the `tbl_Reservation` table is updated.

Steps

1. From the SQL Server Utilities folder, double-click on the SQL Server Web Assistant icon. This will launch the wizard. Figure 10-23 illustrates the opening screen of the SQL Server Web Assistant.

2. The first dialog to appear establishes SQL Server login information. Within the Login Information frame, enter the information in Table 10-7:

Table 10-7 Login information for Web Assistant login screen

TEXT BOX	VALUE	DESCRIPTION
SQL Server Name	GOTHAM_CITY	Name of the Register Server the data resides on
Login ID:	sa	Login ID of the user who has the privilege to create procedures and access to the tables being queried

3. The registered server is **GOTHAM_CITY**; make appropriate changes for your system. Since this HTML document is the result of a query, it would be a good idea to use a login ID that only has query access but privileges to issue the **CREATE PROCEDURE** command. By marking the "Use Windows NT security to log in instead of entering a login ID and/or a password" check box, the trigger will rely on Windows NT's security to determine if you have the appropriate database privileges.

4. Press the Next button to navigate to the next screen. Figure 10-24 portrays the SQL Server Web Assistant Query screen.

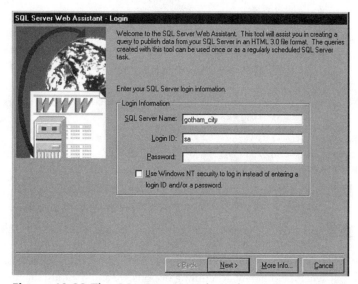

Figure 10-23 The SQL Server Web Assistant–Login screen

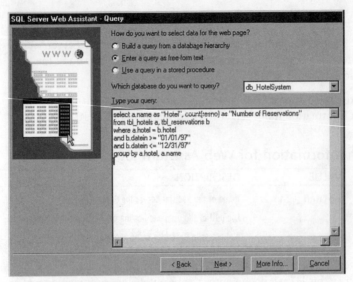

Figure 10-24 SQL Server Web Assistant–Query screen

5. This screen is used to build that query for the HTML document. Select the radio button Enter a query as free-form text. By selecting this option, the form will change so you can enter the Transact-SQL statement that you will associate with this HTML document.

6. Select the database **db_HotelSystem** from the combo box labeled, Which database do you want to query? This tells the Web Assistant which database you plan to use.

7. We want to generate an HTML document that displays the name of the hotel and the number of reservations that have been made this year, 1997. Enter the following Transact-SQL statement in the Type your query text box.

```
select a.name as "Hotel", count(resno) as "Number of Reservations"
from tbl_hotels a, tbl_reservations b
where a.hotel = b.hotel
and b.datein >= "01/01/97"
and b.datein <= "12/31/97"
group by a.name
```

8. Press the Next button to navigate to the next screen. See Figure 10-25 for the SQL Server Web Assistant Scheduling screen.

9. This screen is used to schedule when the query for the HTML document will be executed. In this example, we want the most up-to-date information. Select **When Data Changes** in the combo box. Table 10-8 explains what the different scheduling options are and their arguments.

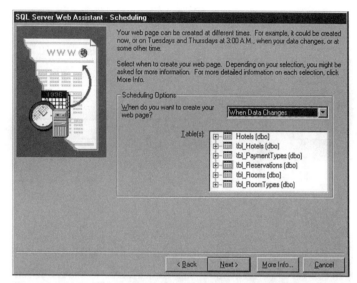

Figure 10-25 SQL Server Web Assistant–Scheduling screen

Table 10-8 Scheduling time options

OPTION	ARGUMENT	DESCRIPTION
Now	None	Performs the query and creates HTML document immediately
Later	Date and Time	Performs the query and creates HTML document at a selected time
When Data Changes	Table(s) and/or column(s)	Creates a trigger for a table base to perform the query and create the HTML document
On Certain Days of the Week	Days and time	Executes the query and creates the HTML document on a select day and time of the week
On a Regular Basis	Every n hours, minutes, days, or weeks	Executes the query and creates the HTML document at a recurring time

10. We are tracking data that is being entered into the table, `tbl_Reservations`. Select that table in the Table(s) listbox. A border will appear around the table icon letting you know that the column has been selected.

11. Press the Next button to navigate to the next screen. The File Options screen of the SQL Server Web Assistant is illustrated in Figure 10-26.

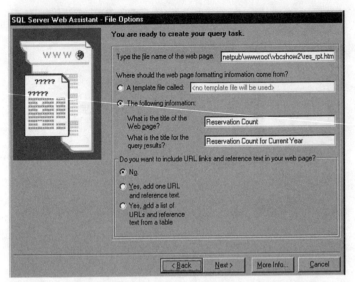

Figure 10-26 SQL Server Web Assistant–File Options
screen

12. This screen is used to set up file information about the HTML document
that is to be generated. In the first text box, "Type the file name of the web
page," enter in the following information:

```
e:\InetPub\wwwroot\vbcshow2\resv_rpt.htm
```

> **NOTE**
>
> You should place this document whatever path is appropriate for
> your system.

13. Select the radio button, The following information, if it isn't already
marked.

14. In the "What is the title of the Web page?" text box, enter `Reservation`
`Count`. This will be the title that appears in the title bar of your HTML
browser.

15. In the "What is the title for the query results?" text box, enter
`Reservation Court for Current Year`. This will be the name of the
report as it appears within the HTML document.

16. For this example, leave the radio button, No, selected. Since this HTML
document is not going to be part of a larger Web page, we are not going to
refer the viewers of the document to any other document or URL (Uniform
Resource Locator).

17. Press the Next button to navigate to the next screen. Figure 10-27 shows
what the SQL Server Web Assistant–Formatting looks like.

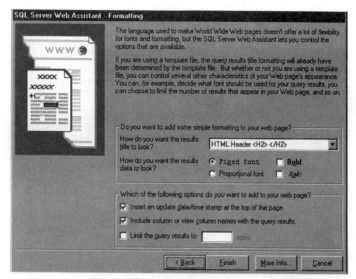

Figure 10-27 SQL Server Web Assistant–Formatting screen

18. This screen is used to format the HTML document that is going to be generated. The combo box labeled, "How do you want the results title to look?", leaving the selected, **HTML Header <H2> </H2>**, is sufficient. HTML Header tags 1 through 6 are allowed.

19. Use **Fixed font** as the font format to display the query result in the HTML document.

20. Within the second frame, mark the Insert an update date/time stamp at the top of the page and Include column or view column names with the query results. By marking the first check box, the date and time the document was created will appear on the report. This will let the viewer know when the report was last updated. The next check box will display the column name of each column within the query.

21. This is the last screen of the Web Assistant. Press Finish to continue. To go back and look over what you have entered, you can press the Back command button to review any entry.

22. Once the Web Assistant has completed its task, a Done dialog is displayed, as shown in Figure 10-28.

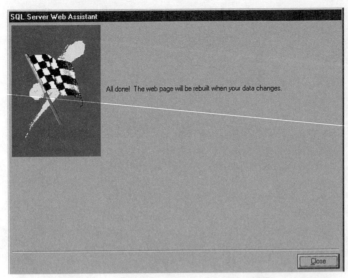

Figure 10-28 The final screen of the SQL Server Web Assistant displaying the completion message

23. To test the trigger created by the Web Assistant, open the Query Analyzer. On the **Query** tab, enter the following **Transact-SQL** statement and press the Execute Query button. The **Declare** statement defines **@ret_code** as a local variable within the Query Analyzer environment. The **Exec** statement will execute the stored procedure, **proc_submit_resv**. By assigning the stored procedure to the local variable, **@ret_code**, any return code returned by the procedure will be passed to the variable. The information after **proc_submit_resv** is the information the procedure needs to complete the insert transactions. After the procedure has completed execution, the **Select** statement displays the value the local variable, **@ret_code**, contains.

```
DECLARE @ret_code int
EXEC @ret_code = proc_submit_resv 1, "Dela Rental", "Oscar", "486 N. Ocean
Place", "Atlanta", "GA", "30339", "(703)853-1212", 1, 125.00, "9/23/97",
"9/25/97", 31
SELECT @ret_code
```

How It Works

Like all the other graphical user interface components within SQL Server, the Web Assistant is an interface to Transact-SQL. The HTML document will be generated based on your scheduling option. In Step 2, you are specifying which registered server you wish to log on to. When you enter in the user ID and password, the Assistant is logging you into SQL Server. By having the check box marked, you're telling SQL Server to use Windows NT security levels to determine if you have access to SQL Server or not.

The `Transact-SQL` statement you entered into the query text box in Step 3 is the same as typing it into ISQL. This join query is going to retrieve information based on the contents of the `tbl_Hotels` and `tbl_Reservations` tables. The first part of the selection criteria retrieves the hotel names from the `Name` column of the `tbl_Hotel` table. The aggregate function, Count, will return the number of rows within the `tbl_Reservations` table. The `As` parameter and the following quoted text replace the default column name. In the `Where` clause, to avoid a Cartesian product, we match the hotel number from the `tbl_Hotels` table with the hotel number from the `tbl_Reservations` table. A *Cartesian* product is a result query that contains the number of rows in the first table times the number of rows in the second table. If this occurs, the result of your query will be meaningless because you would have received all the possible combinations of the rows in every table in your query. For example, you have 4 hotels and 16 reservations. The result of the query will be 64 rows. Basically multiply 4 by 16. If your tables had more information, a query like this could really slow down your server. Since we are interested only in the reservations made in 1997, we are checking the values in the `datain` column of the `tbl_Reservations` table. The `Group By` clause will group the output by the hotel names.

When you press the Next command button in Step 8, the Web Assistant checks to make sure you entered a valid `Transact-SQL` statement. However, it does not ensure that the query works. Therefore, it's best to try out your query within ISQL or the Query Analyzer before continuing to the next step.

In Steps 9 and 10, we selected `When Data Changes` and the table, `tbl_Reservations`. This means when the data in the table changes, whether it is an update, insert, or delete, the `Transact-SQL` query and HTML document will be generated. This will be performed by the means of a trigger. Refer to How-To 10.6 for information on how to use triggers.

In Step 12 you determine where the HTML document will be created. It should be placed with other related HTML documents. The title, `Reservation Count`, will be placed with the `<TITLE> </TITLE>` tags within the HTML document. It will appear in the title bar of your browser. `Reservation Count for the Current Year` will appear in the body of the HTML document and be the page header over the report columns. Since we specified No, no other URL (Uniform Resource Locator) address will be added to the HTML document.

Steps 18 and 19 are for formatting the contents within the HTML document. In Step 18 we are telling the document to size the report title with the Header 2 tags. In Step 19, the actual contents of the report will be printed in a fixed font rather than a proportional font.

When the Done button is pressed in Step 22, it will generate the `Insert`, `Update`, and `Delete` triggers for the table, `tbl_Reservations`, based on the criteria we selected. The triggers use the store procedure, `sp_makewebtask`, and use all the data we inputted through the Web Assistant as arguments.

After you execute the query in Step 23, a new reservation will be added to `tbl_Reservation`, assuming you created the stored procedure in How-To 10.9. To find out the results of the transaction and view the HTML document generated by the trigger, open your Internet browser. Then select the `File|Open` file from the menu bar. Go to the directory you specified in Step 12, select the file, and click OK. The HTML document should look similar to Figure 10-29.

Comments

As the Internet and Intranet continue to grow, the need for real-time data retrieval with a method to deliver the information quickly and easily will continue to increase. The use of the Web Assistant will become an invaluable tool.

COMPLEXITY
INTERMEDIATE

10.11 How do I...
Optimize my server?

Problem

I've installed an SQL Server based on what I've read in the manuals, but I know that a generic installation is not optimized for a production environment. What are some things I can do to increase performance?

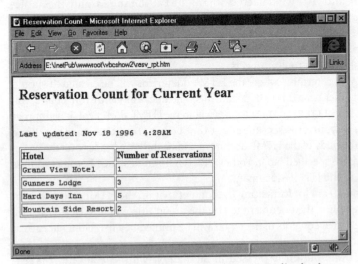

Figure 10-29 Microsoft Internet Explorer 3.0 displaying the results of the HTML document

Technique

Unlike a musical instrument, you cannot use a tuning fork to optimize a SQL Server. There are, however, some other techniques you can apply to your SQL Server to help performance.

Steps

1. *Add More Memory*. With any windows applications, the more physical memory available the better. The minimum memory requirement for an Intel-based Windows NT Server with SQL Server is 16MB. Configuring your system like this would be considered a bare bones system and should not be used unless you are the only person using the server and do not expect lightning fast response time from SQL Server. Windows NT Server alone requires that you have at least 16-20MB. In general, you should not configure a Windows NT Server with SQL Server with less than 32MB.

You need to be careful though. Surprisingly, it is possible to allocate too much memory. If this happens, you can actually decrease performance by causing excessive paging. Be sure to use the Performance Monitor to watch the counter **PAGE FAULTS/SEC**. If page faults are being generated, then your server has too much memory allocated to it.

2. *Choose a Fast Microprocessor*. Since a lot of processing is done through the use of memory, it is a good idea to have a fast microprocessor in your server. Increasing your CPU power is considered one of the most effective ways to improve performance on the hardware level, next to increasing memory. Faster CPUs provide additional processing power to the operating system, SQL Server, and any other applications a server can use.

Windows NT Workstation 3.51 and Windows NT Server 3.51 support symmetric multiprocessing (SMP). Windows NT Workstation can handle up to two CPUs while Windows NT Server can handle up to four. Since SQL Server is been designed using native Windows NT threads-level multiprocessing, it can take advantage of multiple CPUs; therefore, taking advantage of SMP. *Native thread-level multiprocessing* means that tasks are processed at the thread level rather than the process level. This allows for preemptive operation and dynamic load balancing across multiple CPUs. Threads are a unit of execution within an application. A process is a running instance of an application. SQL Server is a process comprised of multiple threads.

3. *Choose a Fast Disk System*. Not only are SQL Server transactions competing for processor and memory time, they are competing for disk input and output (I/O) as well. Data is constantly being read from and written to the disk drives. The components of a disk system are the drive controllers, I/O bus, and the disk drives. All these components should be some of the latest and greatest technology. For example, a dual-Pentium system with high speed SCSI (small computer small interface) drives will have poor response time if the SCSI controller is based on a 16-bit ISA (industry standard architecture) technology. The power of the system CPU is also a crucial factor in effective I/O processing, of course. You may have the fastest drives money can buy but if they are installed in a system that is running on Intel-based 486DX/2 66 MHz CPU you're going to have a processing bottleneck.

4. *Treat Transaction Log as a Separate Device*. As mentioned earlier in this chapter, it is a good practice to leave the transaction log on a separate database device. In a heavy transaction-based system, the transaction log is going to be busy. If the transaction log is on the same device as the database, transactions will be competing for disk I/O time. A transaction gets recorded as an open transaction in the transaction log first, then it is performed against the database tables, and then the transaction is closed in the transaction log. This might not sound so bad in a small environment, but what if the server is hit with more than 1,000 transactions an hour? By having the two separated, as soon as the first transaction is recorded, the transaction is executed without delay, at which time, the next transaction is recorded, and so on.

More importantly, you should make sure the transaction log is also on a separate *physical* device (disk). This allows for faster writing (depending on the controller).

Disaster recovery is another important reason why you should have the transaction log on a separate device. In a heavy transaction processing environment, like an order entry center, there can be more than 10,000 transactions an hour. In order to back up your data, you would have to take down the SQL Server to back up the database. This can take several hours to do and a lot of companies might not be able to afford that sort of downtime. This is why backups are usually performed at night and during non-peak hours. Since the transaction logs record every transaction that takes place, you have a *picture* of all the transactions taking place. Since transactions are smaller than database tables, it would be good practice to back up the transaction log more frequently, say every hour, every half hour, or even every 15-minutes. If your SQL Server database crashes some time during the day, you will first recover the database from the previous night's backup. Then you apply the transaction logs by performing the restore on the transaction log to the database. The transaction log will apply all the data insertions, deletions, and updates that are recorded in the log. For the specifics on applying the transaction log to a restore, read the section entitled "Restoring a Database or Applying a Transaction Log" in the SQL Server Online Books.

5. *Increase the LOCKS.* Locks are a restriction on access to a resource in a multiuser environment. SQL Server installs with 5,000 maximum locks. In practice, this is never even close to what you will actually need. Try something more like 50,000.

6. *TempDB in RAM.* The tempdb is a database created by SQL Server. It is used by SQL Server to store temporary tables and other temporary working storage information. If at all possible, you should put the `tempdb` in RAM. By setting the configuration option to a positive number, the `tempdb` is in RAM. Be careful not to allocate too large a `tempdb` for the physical memory on the machine. SQL Server behaves rather badly if it is trying to start with more memory than is actually available.

Also note that the TempDB configuration setting is in megabytes (that is 30 == 30 MB), Memory is in 2K pages (that is 30 == 60K (not much memory at all)). Don't get them mixed up.

Normally, a 30–40MB tempdb is more than enough, unless you are doing some intense sorting or grouping. If you exceed the `tempdb` on a regular basis, first try to rethink the queries that are causing the problem before you increase the size of `tempdb`.

7. *Use the `DBCC MEMUSAGE`.* The `DBCC MEMUSAGE` statement has been enhanced in version 6.0, for it displays more detailed output than can be used in tuning memory. This statement is used either through ISQL or the Query Analyzer. It displays information on how memory is being used, provides a snapshot of the procedure and data caches, and it is the way to accurately determine the size of the SQL Server executable code.

The information is broken down into three sections: how much of the server's memory is set aside at startup, how much memory the largest 20 objects in the buffer cache used, and how much memory the largest 12 objects used in the procedure cache. The information that the `DBCC MEMUSAGE` statement returns can be used to assist you in your tuning process. `DBCC MEMUSAGE` is the only tool within SQL Server that can accurately determine the size of the SQL Server executable and how it is taking up resources on your server.

SQL Server reserves two areas for cache: procedure and data. These areas increase as the amount of memory increases. The procedure cache stores the most frequently used stored procedures. It is also used for compiling SQL for ad hoc queries. If SQL Server finds a procedure or a compilation already in the cache, SQL Server does not need to read it from the disk.

The data cache is used to store the most recently used data or index pages. If SQL Server finds a data or index page that has already been called by a user in the cache, SQL Server does not need to read it from the disk.

There is a fixed amount of space that can be used by the procedure cache; therefore, it is possible to run out of space. There is a formula documented in the SQL Server Books Online section "Sizing the Procedure Cache" that states that this is a good starting point for estimating the size of the procedure cache:

procedure cache = (maximum concurrent users) * (size of largest plan) * 1.25

To determine the size of the largest page, use the **DBCC MEMUSAGE** statement. Remember that 1MB is equal to 512 pages.

Comments

Keep in mind, you may turn all the right knobs and flip all the right switches, and you may only get a minor increase in performance. Always remember, when tuning your SQL Server, your mileage may vary.

CHAPTER 11

ACTIVATING CLIENT/SERVER ON THE WEB

*by David Jung and
George Szabo*

11

ACTIVATING CLIENT/SERVER ON THE WEB

How do I...

11.1 Submit a query and populate a listbox using the results from an Internet Database Connector Query?

11.2 Create an ActiveX control to validate credit card information?

11.3 Embed an ActiveX control into an HTML document?

11.4 Use the Setup Wizard to create a CAB file for an ActiveX control?

HTML is the lingua franca of the Internet. While HTML has provided great advantages in the displaying of various types of media—like video, audio, and graphics—it has very little to offer in the way of true programming logic. With the Internet's explosion of popularity, many developers have found themselves in a difficult situation as they seek to implement applications within the browser's domain. Companies like Microsoft, Netscape, and others have rushed to provide solutions and direction to this new technological frontier.

With regard to client/server development, Internet and Intranet solutions provide some very important opportunities. These are

▪ A clear client/server relationship as implemented by the browser as client and Web site as server

▪ Interactive access to database information

▪ Implementation of component based architectures through the creation of Java applets and ActiveX controls that execute within the browser

These are just a few of the additions to the Web toolbox that assist in the development of Web-based solutions.

Web technology today clearly provides a three-tier data access model with the browser as the client and provider of user services, the Web server as the provider of business rules services, and any back-end data source as the provider of data services. Refer to Figure 11-1. For more information on the Service Model of client/server development refer to Chapter 1, Client/Server Basics.

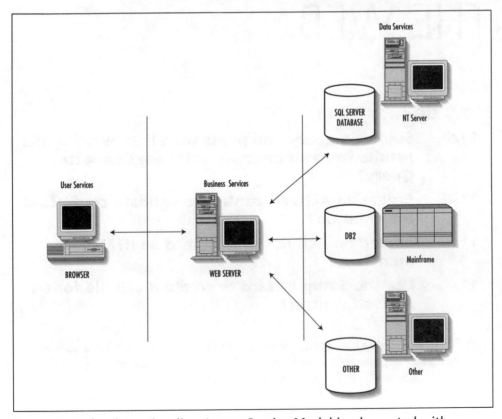

Figure 11-1 The three-tier client/server Service Model implemented with Internet technologies

It is beyond the scope of this chapter to cover all the new technologies and changes that have occurred with regard to Internet development languages and tools. Instead, this chapter seeks to provide you with a few How-To examples to help you become productive today with this new technology.

11.1 Submit a Query and Populate a Listbox Using the Results from an Internet Database Connection Query

One of the most compelling business uses for Intranet and Internet technology is the ability to easily retrieve and display information. A key component to retrieving information is the ability to submit a query against a data source. In this How-To, the Internet Database Connector, which is included with both Internet Information Server and the FrontPage Personal Web Server, is used to submit an SQL query against an ODBC data source and format the results to a Web browser. The results will also be loaded into a listbox to enhance their functionality since manually editing HTML pages and lists is a very time-consuming task. As a site grows in size, maintaining pages manually becomes unmanageable. Where lists of information change on a regular basis, it is critical that an automatic process be implemented that populates lists with current information so that pages always stay relevant. Storing changing information in a database and using a query to retrieve and display information provides a solution.

11.2 Create an ActiveX Control to Validate Credit Card Information

Rather than creating an ActiveX EXE or ActiveX DLL (out-of-process server or in-process server, respectively), you can use ActiveX controls instead within a distributed environment. This How-To explains how to create an ActiveX control to be used as a Business service.

11.3 Embed an ActiveX Control into an HTML Document

The implementation of HMTL 3.2 in the most popular Internet browsers includes the implementation of the **<Object>** tag which allows you to add ActiveX controls. This How-To, with the help of the Microsoft ActiveX Control Pad, will show how you can add ActiveX controls to your HTML documents.

11.4 Use the Setup Wizard to Create a CAB File for an ActiveX Control

With so many Web sites utilizing ActiveX controls, you need a way to deploy the controls that you created and that are part of your HMTL documents. This How-To will show you how to create a distribution file—**CAB** (or cabinet) file—using the Visual Basic Application Setup Wizard.

11.1 How do I...

Submit a query and populate a listbox using the results from an Internet Database Connector Query?

Problem

I am creating a Web page with a list of items that changes on a regular basis. Each time this list changes I must open the HTML and edit the source manually. This is very time consuming and is becoming unmanageable.

Technique

If the information being included in a list is stored in a database, then a Web-based query to the database source can automatically populate a listbox with the current information found in the data source. Use an Internet Database Connector file to submit a query and an **HTX** file to format the results to display within a listbox control.

Steps

Copy all the files from the Web Example directory on the book's CD to a directory available to your Web server. The directory must have read and execute privileges. For information on how to do this please refer to your Web server documentation. Once you copy all files into the Web server directory, open **default.htm** and select Example 2. The HTML page generated by this How-To appears in Figure 11-2.

This example uses the Internet Database Connector. This is a DLL provided with both the Internet Information Server and the FrontPage Personal Web Server. The DLL is **HTTPODBC.DLL** and can be found in the Scripts directory of either server. Since IDC is a feature of Microsoft's Internet Information Server and the FrontPage Personal Web Server, you must be using one of these servers with this How-To. You must also make sure that your Web server machine has a data source name of VB5CS that accesses the PUBS database. For information on creating a data source name refer to Chapter 2, Getting Connected.

1. Create a text file and save it as **Example1.idc**. Make sure you place it in a Web directory that has execution rights.

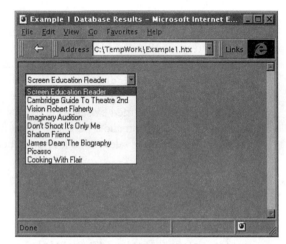

Figure 11-2 Query results formatted in a listbox within a browser

2. Add the following code to the **Example1.idc** file. The file contains a reference to the data source name that is used to submit the query. Only the data source name, template name, and SQL statement are required in an IDC file. If you are using an Access MDB file you may not need the username or password if you have not activated Access security. Refer to the Access online help for more information on security if this is an issue for you. If this is going to an SQL database, then you must provide a valid user name and password. In this case **sa** is used with a blank password. The template that will format the results is also listed along with the query that will be submitted.

```
Datasource: VB5CS
Username: sa
Password:
Template: example1.htx
SQLStatement:
+SELECT title_id, title
+FROM titles
```

3. Create a text file and save it as **Example1.htx**. Make sure you place it in the directory with the IDC file.

4. Add the following code to **Example1.htx**. This provides the header information for the HTML document that will be returned to the browser.

```
<html>
<head>
<title>Example 1 Database Results</title>
</head>
<body>
```

5. Add the following code to `Example1.htx`. This is the key to using the resultset creatively. Standard HTML is used to create a listbox. This is done with the Form tag and the Select tag. Embedded in this, you will find the IDC `BeginDetail` and `EndDetail` tags as well as the title ID and title fields from the resultset. Note that the title ID is placed invisibly as the actual value that is returned by selecting the visible option which is the title. This means you can allow people to select from a list that makes sense but actually sends more relevant codes like `title_id` back to the server for further processing.

```
<form method="POST">
    <p><select name="Example2 Listbox" size="1">

        <%begindetail%>

        <option value="<%title_id%>"><%title%></option>

        <%enddetail%>

    </select></p>
</form>
```

6. Add the following code to `Example1.htx`. This completes the HTX template.

```
</body>
</html>
```

7. To launch the IDC script file and HTX template file that was just created, embed the following line in any HTML document. This code creates a hypertext link that calls the `IDC` file.

```
<a href=/scripts/example1.idc?> Launch IDC query </a>
```

8. You may need to change the IDC file directory reference depending on where you actually created and stored it on your Web site.

How It Works

The Internet Database Connector (IDC) is a dynamic link library (DLL) that uses the Information Server Application Programming Interface (ISAPI) to submit SQL queries to ODBC-compliant data sources as well as format the resultset. Figure 11-3 shows the flow of execution through the various client and server components.

In this example you create three files, two of which are required as part of the IDC design and the third file simply used to demonstrate how to use a hyperlink to activate the submission of a query in an IDC file.

The first file created uses an IDC extension and holds all the information that IDC needs in order to make a valid SQL submission. This information includes, minimally, the data source name (DSN), an SQL query, and the name of the template that

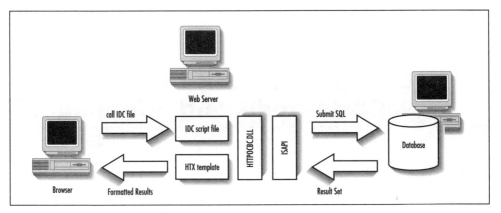

Figure 11-3 Internet Database Connector

will be used to format the results. The IDC script file can also include passed parameters, default parameters, a user name, and a password for security, as well as being able to set a host of ODBC driver options. You can additionally limit the number of rows returned to the browser, a nice feature when you consider that someone could generate a resultset with thousands if not millions of rows depending on your data model and the data available. The IDC script file must be in a directory with execution rights.

The second file created is a template for the query results. This file uses an HTX template. The HTX template is stored in a directory on a Web site with read rights. The template file is simply passed to the browser untouched by the Internet Database Connector program until it encounters the `<%BeginDetail%>` and `<%EndDetail%>` tags. Once these tags are found, IDC replaces any field tags that correlate to fields returned in the resultset with the actual values. In this example, `BeginDetail` and `EndDetail` are located within the HTML that populates the listbox.

Comments

HTML is a mark-up language. It is not a programming language. As the push for relevant content continues to grow, developers will need to consider and resolve the need to keep content fresh. Using databases to store and retrieve information is often the most logical direction. In this example, a query is used to populate a listbox. Perhaps that listbox can be filled with names of employees from a department with e-mail addresses. Take this How-To and try to extend its functionality. Try embedding the resultset in hypertext link tags that pass a resultset field selected to another IDC file that uses it as a parameter for its query. Perhaps the first query returns a list of names. Click on the name and it is passed the name or employee ID as a parameter to another IDC file that retrieves that person's directory information. This type of drill-down querying makes IDC a very powerful tool.

11.2 How do I...
Create an ActiveX control to validate credit card information?

Problem

I would like to create an ActiveX component that will help me validate credit card information.

Technique

In a distributed application environment, ActiveX technology can play a large part within this paradigm. You can use ActiveX components within any Service Model, User Interface, Business, or Data. You can have ActiveX components run locally on your users' workstations, on your servers running remotely, or both. ActiveX components also can be used within your Intranet and Internet solutions.

In previous versions of Visual Basic, the creation of ActiveX components was not possible. These components would have to be created in environments like C/C++, Pascal, or Assembler.

This How-To explains how to create an ActiveX control that will be used as a business component. This control will be used within the user interface. Even though it is part of the user interface, the business logic resides within the ActiveX control. If the business logic needs to be changed or updated, just update the control. You will also need to have installed the add-in, ActiveX Control Interface Wizard, into your development environment. This How-To can also be developed using the Microsoft Visual Basic 5 Custom Control Edition available free from the Microsoft Web site (http://www.microsoft.com/vbasic).

Steps

The following procedure will illustrate how to create the control with two components: the credit card number and the credit card expiration date. It will also show you how to test your control using a test application within the same development environment.

1. Create a new project by selecting New Project from the File menu. From the New Project dialog window, select the Standard EXE icon and press the OK button. Figure 11-4 illustrates what the New Project window will look like. A new project will be created within the Project window. This project will be used as the test application for your control.

2. Add an ActiveX control project to the project group. This project will be used to contain the modules for your ActiveX control. From the File menu, select Add Project.... Select the ActiveX Control icon from the Add Project dialog window, illustrated in Figure 11-5. Save the project as CS5CC.VBP.

3. Working with CS5CC's UserControl1 module, you are going to create the credit card number control. Place a text box on the user interface. Set its properties to those shown in Table 11-1. Notice the left and top position of the text box. They are at the 0 position. Also, you will have made the height and width of the UserControl the same as the text box. The reasons for this will be explained later in this example.

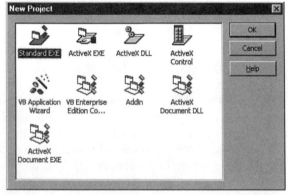

Figure 11-4 Select the Standard EXE icon from the New Project window

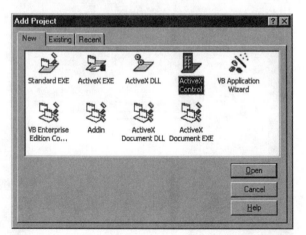

Figure 11-5 Select the ActiveX Control project icon from the Add Project window

Table 11-1 Objects, properties, and settings for `UserControl1`

OBJECT	PROPERTY	SETTING
UserControl	Height	315
	Name	CreditCardNumber
	ToolboxBitmap	creditcard.bmp
	Width	1675
TextBox	Height	315
	Left	0
	MaxLength	16
	Name	txtCCNbr
	Text	""
	ToolTipText	"Credit Card Number"
	Top	0
	Width	1675

4. You will notice that while you have the **CreditCardNumber** UserControl module open, your toolbox's OLE control is disabled. You will find a generic ActiveX Control icon disabled as well. It will be disabled as long as the UserControl object is displayed within the development environment. To illustrate, see Figure 11-6. For every UserControl module you have in your project, there will be a generic ActiveX Control icon in your toolbox.

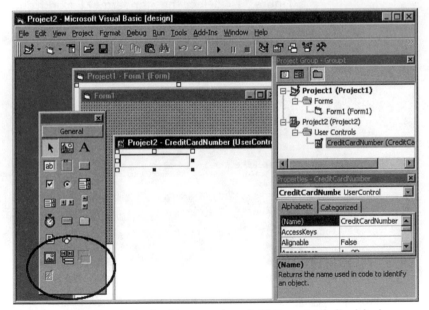

Figure 11-6 Generic ActiveX control and OLE control disabled while the control is being developed

5. Use the Project Add User Control menu item to add a new UserControl to CS5CC.VBP. Place a text box on the user interface. Set its properties to those shown in Table 11-2.

Table 11-2 Objects, properties, and settings for UserControl2

OBJECT	PROPERTY	SETTING
UserControl	Height	315
	Name	CreditCardExpDate
	ToolboxBitmap	date.bmp
	Width	675
TextBox	Height	315
	Left	0
	MaxLength	5
	Name	txtCCNbr
	Text	""
	ToolTipText	"Credit Card Expiration Date"
	Top	0
	Width	675

6. ActiveX controls developed within Visual Basic come with a set of default properties and events. To add some of the more standard properties and events, you should run the ActiveX Control Interface Wizard against each UserControl. If it is not already part of your add-ins, you can add it by selecting the Add-Ins Add-in Manager menu item and marking the ActiveX Control Interface Wizard's check box and pressing the OK button.

7. Select the ActiveX Control Interface Wizard from the Add-Ins menu. Press the Next button to move from the Introduction screen to the Select a Control screen. From this screen, you are going to select the control to which you want to apply properties, methods, and events. Select the **CS5CC:CreditCardExpDate** item and press the Next button.

8. On the Select Interface Members screen, you will select which properties, methods, and events you wish to add to the control. When this screen first appears, the items in the Selected names listbox are the default properties, methods, and events of the control. For this control, you are going to add the **Resize** event and **Text** property. Select them from the Available names listbox and move them to the Selected names listbox. Then press the Next button.

9. On the Create Custom Interface Member screen, you can add your own members to the control. For this control, you are not going to use any. Press the Next button to move to the next screen.

10. On the Set Mapping screen, select all the Public Name items in the listbox. In the Map To Control combo box, select the `txtCCExpDate` control. Then press the Next button. This will create the appropriate class procedures for the properties, methods, and events for the public names.

11. On the Set Attributes screen, you can set default values and attributes for any unmapped members. For this control, you will not need to change anything. Press the Next button to go to the next screen.

12. As with all wizards, there is a Finished screen. From this screen, if you press the Finish button with the View Summary Report marked, all the properties, methods, and events will be applied to the control and you will see a summary of what needs to be done with the control. You can save this information to view at a later time if you like. If you press the Finish button without the View Summary Report marked, all the properties, methods, and events will be applied to the control and you will not see a summary report.

13. Repeat steps 7 through 12 for the `Project2:CreditCardNumber` control using the same options.

14. View the code of the control, `CreditCardNumber`, and enter the following code in the `UserControl_Resize` event. This is to ensure that when you resize the control on a form, the text box will resize as well. Also, it is to ensure that you cannot resize it any smaller than a default size.

```
Private Sub UserControl_Resize()
' Ensure that the Text box is the same
' size as the User Control background
' and that it does not get smaller than
' a default size.
    If Width < 1675 Then
        Width = 1675
    ElseIf Height < 315 Then
        Height = 315
    Else
        txtCCNbr.Move 0, 0, Width, Height
    End If
End Sub
```

15. Add the following business logic to the `txtCCNbr_KeyPress` event. Credit card numbers consist of numbers. This logic ensures that only numbers or the backspace key are used within the control.

```
Private Sub txtCCNbr_KeyPress(KeyAscii As Integer)
' Ensure that only numbers and the backspace
' key are the only valid input
    If KeyAscii = vbKeyBack Then
        Exit Sub
    ElseIf KeyAscii < vbKey0 Or KeyAscii > vbKey9 Then
        KeyAscii = 0
    End If
End Sub
```

16. View the code of the control, `CreditCardExpDate`, and enter the following code in the `UserControl_Resize` event. This is to ensure that when you resize the control on a form, the text box will resize as well. Also, it is to ensure that you cannot resize it any smaller than a default size.

```
Private Sub UserControl_Resize()
' Ensure that the Text box is the same
' size as the User Control background
' and that it does not get smaller than
' a default size.
    If Width < 675 Then
        Width = 675
    ElseIf Height < 315 Then
        Height = 315
    Else
        txtCCExpDate.Move 0, 0, Width, Height
    End If
End Sub
```

17. Add the following business logic to the `txtCCExpDate_KeyPress` event. Credit card expiration dates consist of numbers and a slash dividing the month and the year. This logic ensures that only numbers, the slash, or the backspace key are used within the control.

```
Private Sub txtCCExpDate_KeyPress(KeyAscii As Integer)
' Ensure that only numbers, the slash, and the backspace
' key are the only valid input
    If KeyAscii = vbKeyBack Then
        Exit Sub
    ElseIf KeyAscii = Asc("/") Or KeyAscii = vbKeyDivide Then
        Exit Sub
    ElseIf KeyAscii < vbKey0 Or KeyAscii > vbKey9 Then
        KeyAscii = 0
    End If
End Sub
```

18. Add the following business logic to the `txtCCExpDate_LostFocus` event. This procedure validates that the date entered into the text box is not less than the current date. If so, a message box will notify the user and the cursor will return to the text box.

```
Private Sub txtCCExpDate_LostFocus()
' Ensure that valid Dates are entered into
' this field
    On Error GoTo Err_txtCCExpDate_LostFocus

    If Len(Trim((txtCCExpDate.Text))) = 0 Then
        GoTo Exit_txtCCExpDate_LostFocus
    ElseIf CDate(txtCCExpDate.Text) < Format(Now, "m/yy") Then
        Call MsgBox("Invalid date entered.", vbCritical, _
            "Credit Card Expiration Date Error")
        txtCCExpDate.SetFocus
    End If
```

continued on next page

continued from previous page

```
Exit_txtCCExpDate_LostFocus:
    Exit Sub
Err_txtCCExpDate_LostFocus:
    If Err.Number = 13 Then   ' Type Mismatch
        Call MsgBox("Invalid date entered.", vbCritical, _
            "Credit Card Expiration Date Error")
        txtCCExpDate.SetFocus
    Else
        Call MsgBox("Error: " & Err.Description & " occurred.", vbCritical,
_
            "Credit Card Expiration Date Error")
    End If
    GoTo Exit_txtCCExpDate_LostFocus
End Sub
```

19. You are now at a good point to spot test the controls. To do this, you will use the Project1 project from Step 1. Close any of the UserControl modules that might be open. To Form1, add the objects and properties with the settings as shown in Table 11-3.

Table 11-3 Objects, properties, and settings for Form1

OBJECT	PROPERTY	SETTING
Form	Caption	"Test Container"
	Name	frmTestContainer
Label	Caption	"Credit Card Number""
	Name	lblCCNbr
Label	Caption	"Credit Card Exp Date:"
	Name	lblCCExpDate
CreditCardNumber	Name	txtCCNbr
CreditCardExpDate	Name	txtCCExpDate
Command Button	Name	cmdOK
	Caption	"OK"

20. Add the following code to the command button, **cmdOK_Click**. Every program should have a way to end itself.

```
Private Sub cmdOK_Click()
    End
End Sub
```

21. Press the Start button to test the application with the controls. Enter any values into the CreditCardNumber control up to 16 characters. The control should stop you from entering any number larger than 16 characters and any value that is not numeric. The CreditCardExpDate control should prevent you from entering any invalid date like 00/00 or 06/96 if the system date is 12/96. If the date is invalid, you should see a message box similar to Figure 11-7.

22. After you have tested the control, it is time to make it available to the rest of your developers. In the Project Group window, select CS5CC. Select Project from the main menu and select the CS5CC Properties menu item. Change the following property settings found in Table 11-4.

Table 11-4 Project properties and settings

OBJECT	PROPERTY	SETTING
General	Project Name	"CreditCardControl"
	Project Description	"VBCS5 Credit Card Control"
Make	Auto Increment	Yes
	Application Title	"VBCS5 Credit Card Control"

23. Make sure the CS5CC.VBP project is selected in the Project Group window. Select the Make CS5CC.OCX... menu item from the File menu.

24. Similar to making an application project, the Make Project dialog box appears. Since you already updated the project properties in Step 22, you do not need to update any of the options for the control. Select where you would like the ActiveX control to go and press the OK button to create it.

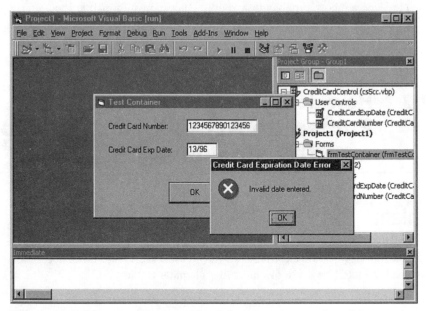

Figure 11-7 Error message received for entering an invalid expiration date

25. After the control has been built, Visual Basic will register the control in your Registry. Distribution of the control and registering it on a user's system will be discussed later in this chapter.

How It Works

The basic premise of this control works a lot like any other Visual Basic application. The CreditCardNumber limits the user input to numbers and the Backspace key. The CreditCardExpDate limits the user input to numbers, a slash, and the Backspace key. When the cursor leaves the expiration date control, the **LostFocus** event is performed. This event checks to make sure that the date entered is a valid date in the format of MM/YY. If the date is not valid, the user is notified with an error message and the cursor is brought back to the control.

When the mouse pointer is placed over either control, a Tooltips pop-up window appears to notify the user what the control is for.

By making these controls into an ActiveX control, they can be used by any development environment (such as Visual Basic, Visual C++, or Internet platforms) that takes advantage of ActiveX technology.

Comments

This is a very basic control. There is a very limited amount of error checking in the control itself. Had this been a control that you would put into production, you would include more robust error handling routines. For more information about creating ActiveX controls with Visual Basic 5, refer to the *Visual Basic 5 SuperBible* (Waite Group Press).

COMPLEXITY
BEGINNING

11.3 How do I...
Embed an ActiveX control into an HTML document?

Problem

Our company is expanding our application development to an Intranet as well as to the Internet. I would like to use ActiveX controls within my HTML document to provide an interface that looks more like a familiar application.

Technique

As mentioned previously within this chapter, an Intranet architecture as well as the Internet is fast becoming a common way of deploying applications throughout an enterprise as well as to your customer. Through the use of ActiveX technology, you can make your applications browser-centric rather than form-centric.

Applications that are developed for the Microsoft Windows operating system are built around the concept of window forms. On the Internet, as well as on Intranets, information is not displayed on window forms, but forms within a browser like Netscape Navigator or Microsoft's Internet Explorer. Through the use of ActiveX technology, you can create HTML documents that have a look and feel like those of Visual Basic applications. This How-To will illustrate how you can add ActiveX controls to your HTML document. Note that there are different HTML editors that you can use like SoftQuad HoTMetaL, Netscape Navigator Gold, or Microsoft FrontPage. For this How-To, the author opted to use the Microsoft ActiveX Control Pad, which can be downloaded from the Microsoft Web site or found on the enclosed CD-ROM.

Steps

The following steps show how to design an HTML document with ActiveX controls.

1. Open an HTML document with the ActiveX Control Pad. The default document has the essential tags for a basic HTML document. Figure 11-8 is an example of the default document. We are including this on the CD-ROM.

2. Between the **<TITLE>** tags, change the New Page caption to "VBCS5 ActiveX Document." This will change the document title that is displayed in the browser's title bar.

3. Change the background of the document to a light gray. This will give the HTML document a Visual Basic look. Add the **BGCOLOR** attribute to the **<BODY>** tag.

```
<BODY BGCOLOR=SILVER>
```

4. Add the following text information to the HTML document to give your user some information about the form. This information goes between the **<BODY>** tags.

```
Please enter the following information:<P>
<HR>
```

5. Add the following text information to the HTML document and press the Enter key. This will create text appearing like a label field for an ActiveX text box.

```
First Name:
```

Figure 11-8 Default document using the Microsoft ActiveX Control Pad

6. With the cursor just below the line you just typed, select Insert ActiveX Control from the Edit menu. The Insert ActiveX Control dialog box will appear. Select the Microsoft Forms 2.0 TextBox control and press OK. Edit ActiveX Control and Properties windows will appear as illustrated in Figure 11-9. You will notice that it bears some resemblance to Visual Basic's development environment.

7. You can resize the text box or change any property within this environment. In the Properties window, select the `ID` property and change it to `txtFirstName`. Then press the Close button on the Edit ActiveX Control window to insert this object into your HTML document. Your HTML document should resemble Figure 11-10. A lot of the popular HTML document editors have the ability to insert objects just like the ActiveX Control Pad. If it weren't for these tools, you would have to go through your system's Registry to find the CLSID (class ID) of the object in order to insert it. It would be a long and tedious process. There would also be a greater chance for a mistake. Also, you would not know right away what property values are available to the object. That would also take a lot of investigation.

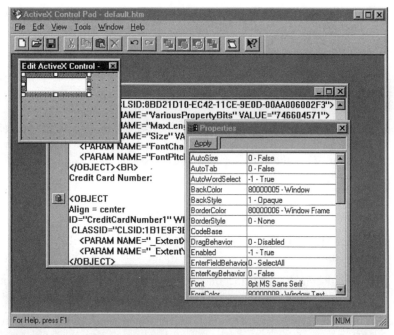

Figure 11-9 Edit ActiveX Control and Properties windows for the TextBox control

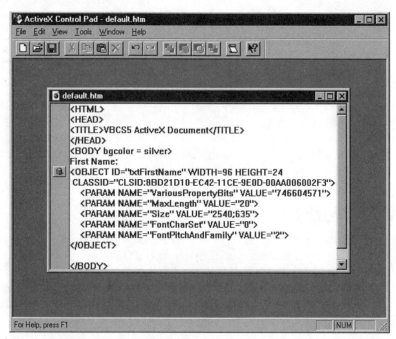

Figure 11-10 HTML document with a TextBox ActiveX control inserted

8. On the line that closes the `<OBJECT>` tag, `</OBJECT>`, place a line break tag, `<BR>`.

9. Add the following text information to the HTML document and press the Enter key. This will create text appearing like a label field for an ActiveX text box.

```
Last Name:
```

10. With the cursor just below the line you just typed, select Insert ActiveX Control from the Edit menu. The Insert ActiveX Control dialog box will appear. Select the Microsoft Forms 2.0 TextBox control and press OK.

11. In the Properties window, select the `ID` property and change it to `txtLastName`. Then press the Close button on the Edit ActiveX Control window to insert this object into your HTML document.

12. On the line that closes the `<OBJECT>` tag, `</OBJECT>`, place a line break tag, `<BR>`.

13. With the cursor just below the line break tag, select Insert ActiveX Control from the Edit menu. Then Select the Microsoft Forms 2.0 CommandButton.

14. In the Properties window, select the `ID` property and change it to `cmdUOK`. Then select the `Caption` property and change it to `OK`. Press the close button on the Edit ActiveX Control window to insert this object into your HTML document.

15. Add the following Visual Basic script to display a message when the command button is pressed in the HTML document.

```
<SCRIPT LANGUAGE="VBScript">
<!--
Sub cmdOK_Click()
    msgbox "Your Information Has Been Processed."
end sub
-->
</SCRIPT>
```

16. Open up your HTML 3.x-compliant browser and load the HTML document. Your result should look similar to Figure 11-11.

How It Works

An HTML document is nothing more than an ASCII file with HTML tags that the browser interprets into formatting systems. HMTL version 3.2 introduced the HTML tag to allow objects, such as ActiveX controls, to be inserted into documents. This allows developers to enhance their documents by making them more interactive through text fields and command buttons without having to implement Java, JavaScript, CGI, or Perl.

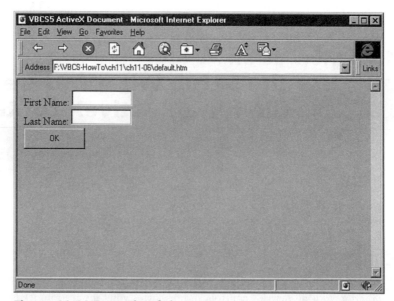

Figure 11-11 Example of the HTML document with ActiveX controls

The object properties used in this How-To are **ID**, **WIDTH**, **HEIGHT**, **CLASSID**, **PARAM NAME**, and **VALUE**. The **ID** is the equivalent of the control's **NAME** property in Visual Basic. The **WIDTH** and **HEIGHT** properties relate to the appearance of the control on the HTML document. The class ID is the CLSID of the ActiveX control found in your Registry. Every control has a unique class ID, or CLSID. This helps with version control on objects. The **PARAM NAME** and **VALUE** relate to the internal properties of the control that would be modified using the Properties window.

In Step 15, Visual Basic Scripting was used to produce a message box to the user. The Script tag is not limited to Visual Basic Scripting. You can also use Netscape JavaScript, which is a scripting subset of Sun's Java language. Through the use of scripts, you can write some procedures and methods for objects by simply referencing their ID names with the procedure calls.

In an HTML document, whether it has embedded ActiveX controls, uses scripting, or both, information is still fairly static. Once an HTML document is unloaded, any information entered into a text box or selected from a list is lost if it's not passed to a holding variable that the next form can pick up.

Comments

For more information on how to transfer information from one HTML document to another, refer to the How-To's earlier in this chapter.

11.4 How do I...
Use the Setup Wizard to create a CAB file for an ActiveX control?

Problem

Within my HTML document, I'm using ActiveX controls that are not on my users' workstations. What do I need to do to deploy the control to them all?

Technique

In a traditional application environment, when deploying an application, you would include all ActiveX controls and resources your application needs within a set of distribution files, or Setup disk. With the Internet, or within an Intranet environment, ActiveX component references and HTML documents are sent to users whenever a request is made through the browser. Users do not want to wait for a set of application disks to download, install, and configure their systems just to view some documents or interact with forms. A quick and efficient method to deploy your components is necessary.

Assume your HTML document has ActiveX components within it. When a user receives your HTML document from a request his browser made, as the HTML is being translated by the browser, the browser checks the user's system to see if he has the ActiveX components your HTML document references. If the browser finds the components on the system, the document is opened and the user can interact with it. If the components are not found, the browser will download and install the components it needs from your server. This How-To will explain how to create a distribution file, or cabinet (.CAB) file, for your ActiveX control, and write a sample HTML document that will download the CAB file to a client's system.

Steps

The following steps will show you how to create a CAB file for your ActiveX control and what entries are necessary within your HTML document to download the ActiveX components.

1. From your Visual Basic 5.0 group, select the Application Setup Wizard. Press the Next button to bypass the Introduction screen.

2. Select the Visual Basic project file from How-To 11-4, CS5CC.VBP.

3. For this How-To, mark the Rebuild the Project check box. This will cause the control to be rebuilt. You do not always have to do this. However, it is a good practice to mark this box every once in a while when developing controls or applications. This way you are assured you will be distributing the latest build of a product.

4. Select the Create Internet Download Setup option button and press the Next button. This tells the Setup Wizard you are building a CAB file for Internet distribution.

5. In the Internet Distribution Location screen, select where you want the distribution files to go. You will probably want them in a central location with other downloadable components on your Web server. For this example, select a project directory like c:\ch11\ch11-06 and press the Next button. If the directory does not exist, you will be asked if you wish to create it. Select the Yes button.

6. In the Internet Package screen, you have two options. You can either have certain dependent resource files downloaded from the Microsoft Web site, or you can reference a location on your Web server or a different server altogether. There are some base Microsoft runtime components that are always being upgraded. By selecting either one, you are telling the CAB file that there are support files somewhere else on the Internet or within your own network. For this example, leave the Download from Microsoft option button marked.

7. On the same screen, select the Safety command button. By selecting this button, the Safety dialog window will appear. This is used to mark that your controls are safe to be loaded into memory or safe to use within an HTML document. Select each control and mark both check boxes, then press OK.

NOTE

Security and safety on the Web are a big issue. There are a lot of hackers out there who can create malicious controls that invoke a virus onto one's system or simply cause your machine to reformat its hard drive. Granted, these are extreme examples, but you should be aware of them. By marking these items as safe, you are guaranteeing the safety of your controls.

8. After marking the controls as safe, press the Next button to bring up the next screen, the ActiveX Server Components. This screen allows you to add additional ActiveX components like Local ActiveX Servers or Remote ActiveX Servers that can be used via DCOM. For this How-To, leave the defaults and press the Next button.

9. The Setup Wizard will start to create the **CAB** file for your ActiveX control. During this process, it will ask you if the ActiveX control is going to be used within a development environment other than Visual Basic. If it is, press Yes to include the Property Page DLL; otherwise press No. For this How-To, press Yes.

10. Like all Microsoft wizards, a file summary report is displayed. It lists all the files that will be included in the CAB. You can read the file properties of a resource file, what the file is a dependent of, and so on. Press the Next button to continue.

11. You have reached the Finished screen. Here, you are given the ability to save all the choices you've made into a template file. It would be a good idea to create one because, if you are going to make any enhancements or modifications to the control, you will have to create a new **CAB** file. Using a template will help reduce a lot of the questions you went through in the previous steps. Now press the Finish button to complete the process. When it is finished, the wizard will notify you with a dialog box that it has completed its work.

12. The Application Setup Wizard provides you with a sample HTML document within the target directory you chose in step 5. It will have the name of the ActiveX control project file. In this example, the file is called **cs5cc.htm**.

13. Copy or move the contents of this directory, the **CAB** file, the **HTM** file, and the support directory to your development or test Web server.

14. From a client machine, request to open the **cs5cc.htm** document.

How It Works

When a browser makes a request for an HTML document, the server sends the requested HTML document to the client. Once the browser receives the HTML documents, it checks to make sure the system contains the files necessary for the document. If the document contains ActiveX controls, it compares the object's class ID from the **<Object>** tag to see if the class ID exists in the Registry. If the system finds the class ID in the Registry, it checks the **CODEBASE** property of the **<OBJECT>** tag to verify that the version needed in the HTML document is the same version that is on the system. If it is, the document will be displayed. If not, the system will download the newer object and register it in the Registry.

If the client machine does not have the component at all, the system will download the object's **CAB** file. The contents of the **CAB** file are then expanded on the system, installed, and registered in the Registry.

Comments

On your Web server, you should have an area designated for testing the development and deployment of ActiveX controls.

by George Szabo

GLOSSARY

Action query

A query that makes changes, either administrative or manipulative, to many records with a single request. Here are some keywords used in action queries: INSERT, UPDATE, and DELETE. Action queries can also use stored procedures.

ActiveX Automation Server

An application (ActiveX EXE or library ActiveX DLL) based on the Component Object Model that provides an ActiveX interface by which clients can access services the server provides. This is also referred to as an ActiveX component.

Application Programming Interface (API)

A set of routines available in an application that can be used by programmers to design application interfaces. Visual Basic allows access to APIs through the `Declare` statement.

Asynchronous

A situation in data access in which a client can make a request of the server and control is returned to the client prior to the completion of the task. Once the query is processed, the client is notified.

Authentication

The process of verifying a user's login ID and password.

Back-end

In a client/server system, the back-end is synonymous with the database engine that resides on the server or host. It is the database engine or back-end that processes SQL requests, as well as stores and retrieves data.

Binding

Associates a default or rule with a column or datatype. The `rdoPreparedStatement` provides object support for the attributes that have been defined for a parameter. Among other things, this includes enforcing the datatype of a parameter.

Buffer

A reserved area in memory, designated to hold the value of a file or variable. One type of buffer is a cache that holds data during input/output (I/O) transfers.

Business rules

An organization's operating procedures that must be followed to ensure a correctly run business. The implementation of business rules is designed to maintain accuracy and integrity of the database from the business perspective. A business rule may be that credit cannot be extended to anyone with a balance due.

Cartesian product

Named after a French mathematician and philosopher, René Descartes. This describes the result of a join that generates all possible combinations of rows and columns from each table referenced in the SQL statement. The number of rows in a Cartesian product of two tables is equal to the number of rows in the first table times the number of rows in the second table, and so on.

Cascading delete

A delete in which all related database rows or columns are deleted. This is often implemented as a trigger in a database.

Case sensitivity

With regard to SQL statement submission, case sensitivity specifies whether the query engine will regard the same table name spelled with a different number of lower- and uppercase letters as matching. Microsoft SQL Server default installation is case-insensitive.

Child

Within the Windows environment, child is a synonym for an MDI child window. With the introduction of class modules to Visual Basic, child can also describe an object related to but lower in the object hierarchy than a parent object.

Class module

A class module is used in Visual Basic to define classes and their properties and methods. A class module defines a single class. You must create a class module for each class you want to define.

Clause

The portion of an SQL statement that begins with a keyword. The keyword names the basic operation that will be performed. WHERE is a common keyword and the WHERE clause contains conditions that restrict the retrieval of records.

Client

The user of a service provided by a server. This is commonly a front-end application. Many refer to the computer hosting the application as the client, but this should actually be referred to as the client computer.

Client/server

An architecture founded on the concept of dividing a process between two separate entities, a client and a server. Most commonly refers to a database system. Within this type of client/server system, the client application presents and manipulates data on the client's workstation while the server services the client, request for storing, deleting, and retrieving data.

CLSID

The unique identification key that is assigned to all class objects when they are created. This value is used to uniquely identify the class through the registry.

Clustered Index

An index type available in SQL Server and other back-end databases. The order of the key values is the same as the physical order of the corresponding rows that exist in the table. Clustered Indexes are associated with high overhead and fast retrieval of data.

Column

The smallest meaningful unit of information within a database when defined as synonymous with field. A column can also represent all values in a table that have a common attribute. An example would be a ZIP code field in a table filled with addresses.

Commit

A process by which data is written to disk. Transaction processing often requires that a variety of changes to data occur as a unit. A commit occurs either under programmer control or database engine control at the successful completion of the specified transaction task.

Component Object Model (COM)

A standard that defines a set of component interfaces that are supported at the system level. This object model is designed to allow complete interoperability between components, regardless of language or vendor.

Concurrency

The ability to allow multiple clients to access the same data—whether that be a table, row, or field—at the same time without causing a collision.

Connection

The channel of communication established between a client and a back-end database engine. A client can have one or more connections. Each connection allows the submission of requests and the retrieval of results. A connection allows sequential execution. A new request cannot be submitted via a connection until the previous request is completely processed or canceled.

Cursor

The pointer to a record in an SQL resultset. The cursor concept was introduced to SQL database engines to mimic record-oriented access methods. Cursors allow the manipulation of data by rows instead of by sets. The use of cursors allows multiple operations to be executed row-by-row on the results of a query. Cursors can be executed on the server side or maintained on the client side of a client/server scenario.

Data Definition Language (DDL)

The portion of the Structured Query Language that allows you to create, manipulate, and delete objects within a database like tables, indexes, and so on.

Database

An organized collection of information. The data is stored in tables; other objects like stored procedures and triggers are also organized within the database. A database provides for a logical as well as physical grouping of related information and allows searching, sorting, and recombination of this data.

Database device

A physical file that can house one or more databases. One database can be stored on several devices.

Database Manipulation Language (DML)

A subset of the SQL language that is used to retrieve and manipulate data stored in a database. The primary DML statement is a SELECT.

Database object

Any one of the components found in a database. These components are tables, indexes, procedures, views, defaults, triggers, constraints, and rules.

Database object owner

The user who creates a database object. The owner of an object has the ability to grant permission to others with regard to the object. Database object ownership cannot be transferred. This is different than the owner of the database, because ownership of the database can be reassigned to a different user.

DBLIB

DB-Library is an Application Programming Interface (API) to Microsoft SQL Server. Transact SQL statements can be transmitted to the SQL Server engine via the `DBLIB.DLL` for execution. Note that the SQL Server ODBC Driver does not use `DBLIB.DLL` to process interations with SQL Server .

DBMS

Database Management System. A computer-maintained repository of data that allows users to insert, update, and delete data, as well as generate reports and perform other data management-related tasks.

Deadlock

A situation that occurs when two users that have a data page locked within a database try simultaneously to lock each other's page of information. A deadlock is created because each user is waiting for the other to release the lock he have on his own page of data. SQL Server detects the occurrence of deadlocks and kills one of the users' processes.

Denormalization

This is the act of combining two or more relational tables into a single flat table comprising data from both. Denormalization of data tables is common when constructing data warehouses.

Dependent object

An object that cannot be instantiated directly by a user. The dependent object exists as part of a larger component object, which is responsible for creating and releasing the dependent object as it is needed to fulfill the greater component's service. An invoice component object may have a dependent detail object that contains detailed information for each line of the invoice object. By itself, the detail line means nothing and therefore has been implemented as a dependent object.

Distributed Component Object Model (DCOM)

Another name for what has previously been referred to as Network OLE. The Distributed Component Object Model (DCOM) is a protocol that allows applications to make object-oriented remote procedure calls (RPCs) in distributed computing environments (DCEs).

DLL

A dynamic link library (DLL) is a collection of executable routines. These routines usually are grouped by the services they provide. DLL is the extension of the physical file name. DLLs load and execute within the same thread of execution as the instantiating client application.

Domain

A domain is a collection of computers grouped together for administrative purposes within the NT environment. A domain shares a single common security database and allows for the centralized control of resources. A single network server is designated as the domain controller and houses the security database.

DSS

A decision support system (DSS) is one that makes use of data and exploits computing resources to provide support for decision analysis and other decision-related activities. A decision support system usually requires just read-only access to data. In many cases, companies are creating separate data warehouses to facilitate this type of analysis without impacting their production database operations.

Encapsulate

This is the ability to contain and hide information about an object's internal implementation. This pertains to data structures as well as code. This allows for the isolation of an object's internal complexity from the object's use and operation within the greater application. As an example, an application asking a business component object to validate a credit card number does not need to know how this was actually accomplished, but only whether the number was approved.

Exclusive lock

A lock applied to a database table during `INSERT`, `UPDATE`, and `DELETE` operations. An exclusive lock prevents any other transaction from getting a lock on that table until the original lock is released.

Fifth normal form

A rule for relational databases which requires that a table which has been divided into multiple tables be capable of being reconstructed, via one or more `JOIN` statements, to its exact original structure.

First normal form

A rule for relational databases which specifies that tables must be flat. Flat tables can contain only one data value set per row. Members of the data value set are called data cells, are contained in one column of the row, and must have only one value. Data cells are often referred to as fields.

Flow control

Conditional expressions that control the flow of execution of statements that exist within the code of an application or procedure.

Foreign key

A column or collection of columns that must match a column or columns designated as a primary key in another table. Unlike primary keys, foreign keys do not need to be unique.

Fourth normal form

A rule for relational databases which requires that only related data entities be included in a single table. Additionally, tables may not contain data related to more than one data entity when many-to-one relationships exist among the entities.

Front-end

An application used by a client to access any database engine or to present information to the user. A Visual Basic application is often a front-end for a database.

Gateway

A software product used on a network to allow networks or computers that are running dissimilar protocols to communicate. A gateway provides transparent access to a variety of foreign database management systems. An SQL Server can be used as a gateway to DB2 database files.

GUID

The Globally Unique Identification Key that is used to identify ActiveX components and their interfaces. GUIDs are a mechanism defined by the Component Object Model.

Handle

A handle is an address system that allows programmers to utilize structures created by the ODBC API. These structures consist of stored parameters, errors, and returned arguments. There are three types of objects that have handles within the ODBC API. These are the environment, the connection, and the statement. These handles are available also when working with the Remote Data Objects layer.

Index

A database object that provides a cross-reference of one or more columns in a table to provide quick access to data.

In-process

This term is used in conjunction with the creation of software components referred to as servers. An in-process server is one whose code executes in the same process space as the client application. Starting with Visual Basic 4, you are able to create in-process servers as ActiveX DLLs.

Instantiate

The act of creating an instance of an object. Instantiation brings an object into existence for use by the instantiating application or component. Once all references to the object are dropped, the object terminates.

Internet database connector

A program distributed with Microsoft's Internet Information Server and Front Page's Personal Web Server that allows for the submission of SQL statements to any ODBC data source. The Internet database connector is found in **HTTPODBC.DLL** and runs as an in-process server, which provides enhanced speed of query submission, as well as formatting of results.

Join

A keyword used in SQL syntax to allow the combination of two or more tables into a resultset.

Keyset

A set of values used to access specific records in a database. A keyset can be maintained by the server or it can be maintained using ODBC–maintained cursors.

Livelock

When a request for an exclusive lock is repeatedly denied because of a several overlapping shared locks that currently exist, a livelock is created. An exclusive lock is a request for read/write access to the data page, while the shared locks are read-only access.

Marshaling

The process of packaging interface parameters and sending them across process boundaries. In the mainframe environment, keystrokes are marshaled from the terminal to the host. With regard to Remote Automation, requests are marshaled to remotely deployed objects.

MDB

The Microsoft Database format used by Microsoft Access and Joint Engine Technology (JET). Unlike dBASE data files, the MDB allows for storage of database-related objects, including queries, reports, forms, macros, and code.

Mission-critical

This is a term referring to specific systems within a business that cannot fail. If they fail, the company cannot conduct any business. An airline reservation system would be such a system, as would an air traffic controller application.

Multiuser

With regards to data, the ability of a front-end application or back-end database engine to allow multiple users to access data stored in a single table or set of tables simultaneously.

Normal forms

A set of five rules that are used to design relational databases; the first three were defined by Dr. E. F. Cobb. Five normal forms are generally accepted in the creation of relational databases.

Normalization

This is the act of removing redundancy within a database design. For rules regarding accepted normal form rules, see normal forms and first through fifth normal forms.

NTFS

A file storage management system available for the NT operating system. NTFS provides a much higher level of security over access to a computer's resources as well as methods for file system recovery. All files are treated as objects with user and system-defined attributes. NTFS also supports long file names.

Null

In SQL terms, null refers to a field with no assigned value. This is not the same as zero for numeric data or an empty string for a character field. When defining the attributes of a field in a table, it is possible to prevent the addition of a new record with a null value.

Object

Within the back-end database, an object refers to any one of the number of database components: table, view, index, trigger, constraint, default, rule, procedure, or user-defined datatype. Within the Component Object Model, an object refers to a component.

OLAP

On-line Analytical Processing. This is a high-end, analysis-oriented DBMS application that allows for process-intensive analysis of data warehouse information.

OLTP

On-line Transaction Processing. This refers to high-end applications that are optimized for transaction-oriented DBMS systems like airplane reservation systems or automatic teller machine (ATM) operations.

Open Database Connectivity (ODBC)

A standard API and protocol that is database independent. Using ODBC allows a programmer to develop applications using a standard set of syntax that can be directed to any ODBC–compliant data source.

Optimizer

This is the component of a database engine that is responsible for finding the optimal plan for processing a query.

Out-of-process

Refers to an ActiveX server that runs in a separate process space from the client requesting services. In Visual Basic, this equates to the ActiveX EXE component and how it operates.

Page

A virtual storage system for data within the database. Within Microsoft Access and Microsoft SQL Server, a page is a fixed length and equal to two kilobytes. It is important to note that, since locking is performed on a page level and not on a row or record level, two or more records could be locked by locking one page. This is because a single record may be less than two kilobytes in length.

Parameter query

A query that requires the client submitting the query to specify values at the time of submission. A parameter is the equivalent of an argument.

Partitioning

A method for encapsulating an application's functionality into components and making it deployable. Once an application is partitioned into components, the components can be deployed across networks on another machine transparent to the client application. This allows the integration of more hardware into the application's execution, which supports the benefits of distributed processing.

Persistent data

Data stored in a database in a physical form rather than just in memory. Data stored in tables within a database system is considered persistent data.

Persistent objects

Objects stored in a database in a physical form, rather than just in memory.

Prepared statement

A precompiled request submitted by a client for temporary storage by a back-end database engine. The ODBC API uses the SQLPrepare function to submit SQL statements to the back-end that will be used over and over during a single session. Allowing the engine to precompile the statement allows for faster execution each time it is called. A prepared statement can accept parameters each time it is called. When the connection is dropped, the statement is released.

Primary key

The column or columns that uniquely identify each row in a table. The primary key may not contain any duplicate values. This key is used when joining to other tables to find additional related data. The primary key field must never be null.

Property

One of the two main characteristics of an object (the other is methods). A property can be read-only, write-only, or read/write. Properties are defined in Visual Basic by creating GET, LET, or SET procedures within a class module. Public variables declared in the declaration section of a class module also become properties of the component object.

Proxy

An object that packages parameters for an interface in preparation for a remote method call. A proxy runs in the address space of the client and communicates with a corresponding stub in the receiver's address space on a remote machine.

Query

A request that can result in either the retrieval or manipulation of records in a database. SQL is the de facto standard as a universal query language, but other proprietary languages do exist.

RDO

Remote Data Objects. A thin layer that sits on top of the ODBC API, providing a simplified object model to assist in programming data access. The objects of RDO closely resemble those of the Data Access Objects found in JET.

Recursion

A situation in which a function or procedure calls itself. This can cause unpredictable results in Visual Basic and is discouraged.

Referential Integrity

A set of rules created to establish and maintain the relationship between related tables. Referential Integrity is enforced whenever records are added, modified, or deleted, to assure that table relations have not been violated.

Registry

A database repository found in Windows NT and Windows 95 that is used to store information relating to system and application configuration. The registry also serves as a warehouse for container and ActiveX server information.

Remote automation

Through the use of remote procedure calls, remote automation allows access to an ActiveX component on a remote machine. This technology employs a technique involving the use of local proxies and an application called the Remote Automation Manager to marshal requests over a network.

Resultset

The rows or return values provided in response to a query submitted against a database.

Rollback

A term used in transaction processing that allows any partial transactions to be returned to their original state. Since a transaction can have many parts, and all parts must succeed in order for the transaction to be valid, rollback provides a way to reverse transactions that do not succeed in their entirety.

Row

Another name for record. Refers to a single entity of a database table that contains each of the columns of data cells defined for the table.

RPC

Remote Procedure Call. The invocation of a stored procedure on a remote server from a procedure on another server. RPCs play an important role in the communication between local and remote ActiveX Automation Servers.

Rule

Used to define what data can be entered into a column. A rule is a database object and is bound to a specific column. The `INSERT` and `UPDATE` statements trigger the execution of the validation information stored in a rule associated with any given column in a table. Limit and list checking are available to a rule implementation.

Second normal form

This is a rule for relational databases which requires columns that are not key fields to be related to the key field. This means that a row cannot contain values in a field that do not pertain to the value of the key field. In an orders table, for instance, the columns of each row must pertain only to the order whose order number is the key field.

SELECT

An SQL statement used to retrieve records from a database. The `SELECT` statement can include one or many tables and is often accompanied by a `WHERE` clause that restricts the resultset.

Server

A machine on a network designated to provide centralized resource services. A server can share files, printers, or house a database management system such as SQL Server. Also refers to an application (such as a database engine) that services requests from other applications.

SQL

A Structured Query Language (SQL) that has become a de facto standard for relational databases. Originally developed by IBM® for use with its mainframe computer systems. There currently exists an ANSI-standard SQL definition for every computer system. SQL can be used to query and manipulate data, as well as manage objects within a relational database.

Stored procedure

A precompiled set of instructions that a database engine can execute. A stored procedure can contain anything from a single action query that returns no records to returning multiple resultsets. In addition to SQL statements, stored procedures can also contain control-of-flow statements.

Stub

An object that unbundles parameters that have been marshaled across processes from a remote machine. Once unbundled, the stub makes the requested method call to the interface. A stub runs in the same address space as the receiver.

Subquery

A `SELECT` statement that is nested inside another SQL statement. Subqueries can be used in `SELECT`, `INSERT`, `UPDATE`, or `DELETE` statements. You can also use a subquery inside another subquery.

Table

Similar to a database file. A table is a unit of data storage in a relational database system. A table is comprised of rows and columns that represent individual data records.

TCP/IP

Transfer Control Protocol/ Internet Protocol. The basic transport mechanism for the Internet. Originally developed by the U.S. military to create a secure network in the case of atomic attack.

Third normal form

The rule for relational databases which imposes the requirement that a column that is not a key column may not be dependent upon another column that is not a key column.

Thread

A thread is the part of a process that can run as an object or an entity. A thread is made up of a stack, the state of the CPU registers, as well as an entry in the system scheduler's execution list. In other words, it executes separately.

Transact-SQL

A standard language for communicating with SQL Server. Transact-SQL is an enhanced version of the Structured Query Language (SQL), complete with syntax to perform data definition as well as manipulation. Stored procedures allow Transact-SQL to implement control-of-flow syntax, as well.

Transaction

A collection of database actions that represents a unit of work. A transaction must either be completed in its entirety or rolled back to its original state.

Trigger

A database object that is much like a stored procedure. Triggers are executed in response to an action like an `INSERT`, an `UPDATE`, or a `DELETE`. It is often the function of a trigger to maintain referential integrity, among other things.

UPDATE

An SQL statement that allows the addition, deletion, or changing of data in one or many tables.

UUID

The Universally Unique Identification Key that is used to identify ActiveX components and their interfaces. A UUID is a mechanism defined by the Distributed Component Object Model.

View

A virtual table. A view or virtual table is created as a collection of columns from one or more tables, referred to as base tables. It is possible to create a view based on another view. A view is referred to as a virtual table because, although you can see the data within the view structure, the data still physically resides within the base table.

WAN

A wide area network system that allows for the connection of multiple computers in geographically disparate locations through the use of leased data lines or switched telephone networks. Optical lines are becoming very popular for this type of network configuration.

by David Jung

CLIENT/SERVER DATABASE RESOURCES

This appendix provides information on various client/server support products and tools, as well as a list of areas of support on various online services and user groups.

ActiveX

The first method of expanding Visual Basic was through the use of custom controls called Visual Basic Extensions or VBXs. As Visual Basic evolved, the controls became more enriched and Visual Basic's usage of controls increased. The use of OLE controls or OCXs started to appear and Microsoft Access 2.0 was the first product to use them. When Visual Basic 4.0 was released in 1995, all VBX controls were migrated into OCX controls in both 16- and 32-bit versions. Early in 1996, Microsoft announced a technology known as ActiveX. Its first associations were related to technologies regarding the Internet and applications that would use the Internet as their connectivity layer. As the specifications became further defined, the inclusion of OCXs was made. Currently, ActiveX technology does not refer to just Internet technology or OLE control technology. It encompasses both technologies as well as OLE Embedding and Automation. For more information on ActiveX technology, refer to the Microsoft ActiveX SDK.

In this section, it would be impossible to list all the ActiveX controls and the independent software vendors who developed them. There are several Web sites and mail order companies you can refer to for this information. Table B-1 lists some of the Internet Web sites you can refer to for more information.

Table B-1 Web sites that reference ActiveX

URL	DESCRIPTION
http://www.activex.com	Sponsored by Cnet. An ActiveX control library
http://www.active-x.com	A site dedicated to providing information about ActiveX for developers
http://www.activex.org	The ActiveX working group that has been formed to provide direction for the ActiveX standard as it is implemented on multiple platforms and operating systems
http://www.microsoft.com/activex	Microsoft site dedicated to ActiveX resources
http://www.vbextra.com	Mail order company that lists and sells thousands of ActiveX controls and development tools

BackOffice Products

This category is for products that will assist you with your development with the Microsoft BackOffice products. Microsoft BackOffice products consist of Microsoft SQL Server, Microsoft Internet Information Server, and Microsoft Exchange.

Asymetrix Corp.

110 110th Ave. NE, #700
Bellevue, WA 98004
   Phone: (206) 462-0501
          (800) 448-6543
     Fax: (206) 637-1504
Internet: http://www.asymetrix.com

InfoModeler

InfoModeler is a visual data modeling tool that allows you to design your data model from business rules defined in regular terms, not programming jargon. It comes in two editions: Designer and Developer. Designer is a data modeling and re-engineering tool. Developer is an application generator that creates client-side and server-side programs based on the data model. The re-engineering component of Designer tracks all changes made to your database and provides tools for reviewing changes and synchronizing design models with your database. Client-side–generated applications are developed in Visual Basic 4.0. This application is available for the Windows operating system.

Brio Technology, Inc.

650 Castro St., Ste. 500
Mountain View, CA 94041
   Phone: (415) 961-4110
          (800) TRY-BRIO
     Fax: (415) 961-4572
Internet: http://www.brio.com

BrioQuery

BrioQuery Enterprise is a graphical analysis tool designed for data warehousing with integrated charting, querying, and reporting capabilities. It is based on three separate tools: BrioQuery Designer, BrioQuery Explorer, and BrioQuery Navigator. BrioQuery Designer is intended for database administrators (DBAs) to design and maintain data models and standard queries. It allows the DBA to establish security restrictions on database tables, views, and other database objects. BrioQuery Explorer is designed for users as a query tool. BrioQuery Navigator is designed for users who will be viewing the reports and queries developed by the BrioQuery Explorer. All three components are sold individually and are available on the Macintosh, Windows, and UNIX operating systems.

DataEdit System

DataEdit System resides in your relational database system. It includes a data entry forms-building program with a built-in SQL generator and uses a centralized data model to ensure data integrity. The DataEdit System is based on three components: DataEdit, DataEdit Designer, and DataEdit Client. DataEdit is the development tool you would use to create forms and applications for your users to interact with. DataEdit Designer is the development tool you would use to create your data model. Database Client is the software you would install on every user's machine to execute the applications developed using DataEdit. DataEdit and DataEdit Designer are sold as a single product. This product is available for both the Macintosh and Windows operating systems.

Chen & Associates

4884 Constitution Ave., Ste. 1-E
Baton Rouge, LA 70808
  Phone: (504) 928-5765
         (800) 448-CHEN
    Fax: (504) 928-9371

ER-Designer

ER-Designer is a tool that lays out user requirements using entity-relationship diagrams (ERDs) and data flow diagrams. It is PC-based and has a repository system. It handles triggers and stored procedures and generates DBMS schemas for more than 30 DBMSs. The reverse-engineering module converts existing file structures and DBMS schemas into ERDs. The normalizer decomposes tables into third normal form.

Logic Works, Inc.

University Square at Princeton
111 Campus Drive
Princeton, NJ 08540
  Phone: (800) 78ERWIN
Internet: http://www.logicworks.com

Erwin/Desktop for Visual Basic

Erwin/Desktop for Visual Basic is a full development life-cycle tool. It handles data modeling through the use of entity-relationship diagrams (ERDs), generates Microsoft Access database structures based on the ERDs, and builds a Visual Basic prototype application based on your ERDs and business rules. It also has the ability to reverse-engineer your existing Microsoft Access databases into data models and then generate your Visual Basic prototype.

Sheridan Software Systems

35 Pinelawn Road
Melville, NY 11747
  Phone: (516) 753-0985
    Fax: (516) 753-3661
Internet: http://www.shersoft.com
CompuServe: GO SHERIDAN

sp_Assist

sp_Assist is a development tool for SQL Server to allow DBAs to quickly create, maintain, and manage database objects such as stored procedures, triggers, tables, indexes, and so on. It also generates Visual Basic code to call queries and stored procedures defined by sp_Assist.

Sylvain Faust, Inc.

880 Boulevard de la Carriere
Hull, Quebec, J8Y 6T5 Canada
  Phone: (800) 567-9127
        (819) 778-5045
    Fax: (819) 778-7943
Internet: http://www.sfi-software.com

SQL-Programmer for Windows

SQL-Programmer is a "test while you edit" development environment featuring a unique virtual editor. It replaces command-line ISQL programming with the live editing, creation, testing, and impact assessment with all database objects, such as stored procedures, triggers, views, and so on. It features multiple SQL Server connections including support for Sybase System 10 & SQL Server 6.0 and team programming. It has an Automatic SQL Server System Documentation generation feature that creates 16 standard reports and full ISQL scripts that can be used by other relational database systems.

Client/Server Development Tools

This category is for products that will allow you to leverage your client/server development.

Asymetrix Corp.

110 110th Ave. NE, #700
Bellevue, WA 98004
  Phone: (800) 448-6543
    (206) 462-0501
  Fax: (206) 637-1504
Internet: http://www.asymetrix.com

InfoAssistant

InfoAssistant is a client/server decision-support tool suite to access, analyze, and report information from a wide variety of database systems. It includes a browser-based query tool that allows nontechnical users to easily obtain accurate, reliable query results. There are also several types of views for analysis and presentation.

CenterView Software, Inc.

1875 Berry Street, Suite 3800
San Francisco, CA 94107
  Phone: (415) 547-7000
    Fax: (415) 547-7070
Internet: http://www.centerview.com

Choreo for Visual Basic

Choreo is an integrated client/server development extension for Visual Basic that enables developers to quickly and visually create high-performance, multiuser applications. It features a drag-and-drop user interface and object-oriented data access engine that integrates into the Visual Basic development environment. It is based on two components: DataLink Manager and DataDirector. The DataLink Manager extends the VB design environment with additional menus and toolboxes that help you manage database objects, like stored procedures and view tables, that your application is going to use. The DataDirector automates all runtime data access operations. It also ships with two custom controls: the Navigation Toolbar and the DataGrid. The Navigation Toolbar helps you move through and display data retrieved from the database. The DataGrid gives you an easy way to modify and view data in a tabular format.

Crescent Software, Division of Progress Software Corporation

14 Oak Park
Bedford, MA 01730
  Phone: (800) 352-2742
Internet: http://www.progress.com/crescent

EnQuiry

EnQuiry is a point-and-click solution to SQL query building and data-bound control layout. As a well-integrated add-in application to Visual Basic, EnQuiry can take you away from the time-consuming tasks of database access and form layout. With EnQuiry, query generation, query preview, and form layout have become a single speedy process.

Integra Technology International

70-15 Austin St., 3rd Floor
Forest Hills, NY 11375
    Tel: (718) 793-7963
         (800) 535-3267
    Fax: (718) 793-9710

Integra VDB for Visual Basic

Integra VDB for Visual Basic is a graphical database builder to help build client/server applications easily, quickly, and often with virtually no code. It consists of database custom controls, a database class library, database functions, a visual query builder, a visual data manager, and an SQL engine based on the ANSI SQL 92 standard. It comes in two editions: Desktop and Client/Server. The Desktop Edition supports Microsoft Access, FoxPro, Btrieve, dBASE, Paradox, and Integra SQL. The Client/Server Edition supports all the Desktop Edition databases, as well as other database systems that support ODBC such as DEC Rdb, SQL 400, DB2, Oracle, Sybase, Microsoft SQL Server, Ingres, Informix, Watcom SQL, and others.

Microsoft Corp.

One Microsoft Way
Redmond, WA 98052
  Phone: (800) 426-9400
Internet: http://www.microsoft.com

Microsoft Visual Basic 5.0, Enterprise Edition

Visual Basic makes it possible to create 32-bit multitiered client/server applications with true distributed processing within the application. The foundation for this distributed process is OLE. OLE already has become the industry standard for application interoperability on the desktop. In Visual Basic 5.0 you can create OLE Automation Servers for application interoperability. Through this capability, you can create OLE-based business objects that can be used across development environments. Remote data access has been enhanced through the use of a remote data control and the remote data object. You can create ActiveX controls that contain business logic for use over the Internet or within your intranet. ActiveX documents can help you develop applications that are browser-centric rather than form-centric. Management of team development can be done directly through the Visual Basic design environment with the integrated Microsoft Visual SourceSafe version control system.

Microsoft Visual C++ 5.0

Visual C++ is a development system that provides tools to help you take advantage of the power of code reuse. Key pieces of the reuse architecture are the Component Gallery, customizable AppWizards, and Microsoft Foundation Class (MFC) extensions. The Component Gallery contains reusable C++ components and OLE controls shareable with other tools. The AppWizard allows you to create and use templates to "jump-start" application development. MFC extensions are dynamic link libraries that extend MFC libraries by deriving new custom classes. Through the use of Visual C++, you can extend your client/server development by using it to build middle-tier components.

Moss Micro, LLC

36 Executive Drive, Suite 260
Irvine, CA 92614
   Phone: (714) 260-0300
           (800) 608-6585
    Fax: (714) 260-0325
Internet: http://www.mossmicro.com

Start Developing for Microsoft Access

Start Developing for Access provides a new method of developing robust applications in Microsoft Access. Start Developing makes solving problems at every step of the application development faster and easier. The Application Wizard within Start Developing splits your application in two, providing you with a number of choices about the application and creates a working application shell. Every project requires error handling, registry/INI manipulation, security, WinAPI calls, and so on. Using the OFX Modules, representing more than 250 functions and procedures, you can immediately begin working your first procedures and designing your first form. The Add-in Assistants automate routine, tedious tasks, and get things done, like creating new procedures with error handling, implementing function headers for code documentation, and gathering project statistics. Every step in the Application Wizard, every line of code in the OFX Modules, and every Add-in Assistant, is there for the singular purpose of building better Access applications faster.

Start Developing for Visual Basic

Start Developing for Visual Basic is a framework for developers on which to build applications with Microsoft Visual Basic. Start Developing takes care of key components such as ActiveX, messaging, database connectivity, and error handling, which are important and necessary tasks in Visual Basic application development. An Application

Wizard within Start Developing for Visual Basic walks you through a set of interactive questions. This allows you to specify the look and feel of the application, as well its key features without having to write strings of code. This process cuts hours off development time and also results in a virtually bullet-proof Visual Basic application. A set of Start Developing Assistants, which are also included, automate the usual manual processes that are performed repeatedly—such as setting up new function/procedure calls or error handling functions—as you write the application. In addition, Office Framework Code (OFX) Modules included in the program offer a wealth of functionality through reusable code, again saving time and ensuring bug-free applications.

Database Connectivity

In a distributed environment, your database connectivity is an important link to a successful project. This category will list components and their manufacturers that provide a connection layer to your database.

Intelligent Objects Corp.

47 Stonewall St.
Cartersville, GA 30120
   Phone: (770) 382-6585
           (800) 876-6585
     Fax: (770) 382-6374
Internet: http://www.intelligent-objects.com

SQL Objects

SQL Objects Database Class Library is an award-winning tool that allows you to fully utilize database independence under OS/2, Windows NT, 95, and many flavors of UNIX by enabling easy cross-platform development. SQL Objects gives you drivers for Oracle, Sybase, SQL Server, SQL Base, Watcom SQL, Informix, DB2/2, NetWare SQL, Btrieve, and many more. Also included is ODBC Objects (this adds a class library to your ODBC development; it also allows you to access any database we don't have native drivers for).

SQL OLE!

SQL OLE! is a complete high-level API that provides DBMS-independent access, query, and data handling methods to rapidly build applications. SQL OLE! provides the database independence your application needs (without having to rely on ODBC). SQL OLE! provides access to Oracle, SQL Server, Sybase, Informix, Watcom SQL, DB2/2, SQL Base, and many more. Also included is ODBC Objects (which allows you to access any database we don't have native drivers for).

ODBC Objects

ODBC Objects is an ODBC class library for any ODBC driver. ODBC Objects will assist you with your development by leveling out the inconsistencies of ODBC as well as using our database classes for your ODBC development.

Intersolv

9420 Key West Ave.
Rockville, MD 20850
    Phone: (301) 838-5000
            (800) 547-7827
      Fax: (301) 838-5064
Internet: http://www.intersolv.com

Intersolv DataDirect ODBC Pack

Intersolv DataDirect ODBC Pack is a comprehensive suite of ODBC drivers that connect ODBC-compliant applications across multiple platforms to all major databases and gateways. These database drivers allow you to seamlessly access information from any ODBC-based application. DataDirect ODBC Pack drivers provide a consistent level of ODBC implementation. All DataDirect ODBC drivers support the ODBC Core, Level 1, and primary Level 2 functions.

Microsoft Corp

One Microsoft Way
Redmond, WA 98052
    Phone: (800) 426-9400
Internet: http://www.microsoft.com

Active Database Connector (ADC)

This is a key piece of Microsoft's Internet client/server technology for building useful Intranet applications that mimic existing client/server systems' ability to handle live data. This software links Microsoft's Internet Explorer Web browser to server databases across the Internet. Current Web-based applications can only present a static view of data retrieved from databases. Through ADC, developers can build applications that cache database information locally on the client machines, thus improving performance of applications by distributing the workload across the application environment.

Internet

The Internet has become a very natural extension to the client/server environment. This category will depict resources that will allow you to leverage your client/server components over the Internet.

Microsoft Corp.

One Microsoft Way
Redmond, WA 98052
    Phone: (800) 426-9400
Internet: http://www.microsoft.com

Microsoft Visual J++

This product is a Java development tool utilizing Microsoft's Developer Studio Integrated Development Environment (IDE). It is optimized for both novice and experienced Java developers. It contains wizards to help developers create applications that take advantage of animation sequences, forms, databases, multiple threads, and more. It includes a Java source compiler that drastically cuts build time with its ability to compile up to 10,000 lines of code per second.

Microsoft Visual Basic 5.0 Custom Control Edition

This product is designed specifically to be the easiest and fastest way to create ActiveX components. Unlike its full version counterparts, the Custom Control Edition can only be used to create ActiveX controls; it cannot be used to create standalone applications. It is free and available for download from the Internet.

Symantec Corp.

10201 Torre Avenue
Cupertino, CA 95014
  Phone: (800) 441-7234
Internet: http://www.symantec.com

Visual Café

Visual Café is a rapid Java development environment. Through the use of drag-and-drop, a comprehensive component library, and extensive Java toolset, application development time is drastically reduced. Visual Café is also available in a Pro version. The Pro version includes all the features of Café, as well as database connectivity through the usage of Symantec dbANYWHERE Workgroup Server, a middleware database server.

TVObjects

29 Emmons Drive
Princeton, NJ 08540
  Phone: (609) 514-1444
    Fax: (609) 514-1004
Internet: http://www.tvobjects.com

Applet Designer

This add-in allows Visual Basic developers to create Java applets from within their VB environment. You create an application through the Visual Basic development environment, and the Applet Designer saves your form and code module with a .JAV extension. Then you click on the Applet Designer's Make Applet button and it converts your VB code into a Java code. At this point, you need to compile the Java-generated code with a Java compiler like Microsoft Visual J++ or Symantec Visual Café. It is available in three versions: Applet Designer, Applet Designer Professional, and Applet Designer Enterprise. The Professional edition does all that was just mentioned and it includes. Java Database Connectivity code based on Visual Basic's Data Access Object. It ships with Sun's Java Developer's Kit. The Enterprise edition will also support industry-standard CORBA.

VBNet

VBNet is an add-in to Visual Basic that will migrate your entire project to the Web. This is accomplished by converting your project to HTML 3.2, VBScript, and JavaScript, as well as integrating any ActiveX controls used in your project into the HTML document. VBNet supports ODBC connectivity and Microsoft's Internet Information Server by using the Internet Server API (ISAPI) extensions.

Internet Servers

With the Internet playing a large role in distributed application development, the need for more robust Internet servers has increased. No longer are Internet servers residing only on UNIX servers, but also on Windows NT and Windows 95 servers.

Microsoft Corp.

One Microsoft Way
Redmond, WA 98052
   Phone: (800) 426-9400
Internet: http://www.microsoft.com/iis

Microsoft Internet Information Server

The Microsoft Internet Information Server (IIS) is an active server fully integrated into Windows NT Server. IIS security is tied into NT Server's, which makes managing users and resources easier. Its toolset includes content creation and management with Microsoft FrontPage, context indexing with Microsoft Index Server, database connectivity through ODBC, CGI support, and integration with Microsoft BackOffice products. It also is capable of server-side scripting, which allows developers to create Web applications that dynamically build HTML documents on the server before they are sent across the wire to the user's browser. These documents are called Active Server pages. A server-side scripted application does not rely on just one language but can be developed using JavaScript, VBScript, HTML, Perl, and CGI.

Netscape Communications

501 E. Middlefield Rd.
Mountain View, CA 94043
   Phone: (415) 937-2555
Internet: http://www.netscape.com

Netscape SuiteSpot

SuiteSpot is a suite of five integrated servers that allows your business and network to communicate using Internet technology. It includes the following servers: Netscape Enterprise Server, Netscape Proxy Server, Netscape Catalog Server, Netscape News Server, and Netscape Mail Server. It also includes the LiveWire Pro development environment. Its integrated management services include SNMP versions 1 and 2, and SSL 3.0-based security. It also provides database support through native drivers for Informix, Oracle, and Sybase, as well as database connectivity through ODBC.

O'Reilly & Associates

101 Morris St.
Sebastopol, CA 95472
  Phone: (800) 998-9938
Internet: http://www.ora.com

WebSite

WebSite is an Internet server that not only works with Windows NT but Windows 95 as well. It's available in two editions, WebSite and WebSite Professional. Both allow you to publish and maintain your HTML documents, control user access, and use CGI to access applications within your HTML documents. The latest version comes with the ability to use Visual Basic to create Web-based applications. WebSite Professional not only has CGI support, but Java and Microsoft ISAPI compatibility as well. It also includes database connectivity through the use of ColdFusion, a powerful application package with templates and a software development kit.

Report Writers

Report writers access data stored in database tables and allow users to manipulate the information into a more useful and informative manner.

Borland International, Inc.

100 Borland Way
Scotts Valley, CA 95066
  Phone: (408) 431-1000
Internet: http://www.borland.com

ReportSmith

ReportSmith is a reporting and query tool that lets you interact with data directly. ReportSmith takes a different approach to reports; it creates reports by allowing you to work with *live* data to give a true WYSIWYG (what you see is what you get) environment.

Concentric Data Systems, Inc.

110 Turnpike Rd.
Westborough, MA 01581
  Phone: (508) 366-1122
       (800) 325-9035
    Fax: (508) 366-2954
Internet: http://www.infointf.com/rrinfo.htm

R&R Report Writer for Windows, SQL Edition

R&R Report Writer lets you select, analyze, summarize, and present data from client/server databases. No knowledge of SQL syntax or programming is necessary. Through the use of menus, data selection automatically generates the SQL statements for you.

Customizable report wizards make creating new reports easy for any user. R&R can be incorporated into almost any application through the use of runtime EXE, DLL, and VBX modules.

Microsoft Corporation

One Microsoft Way
Redmond, WA
Phone: (800) 426-9400
Internet: http://www.microsoft.com

Microsoft Access v7.0 for Windows 95

Microsoft Access on its own can be used to develop multiuser applications. By incorporating it as one of your client/server tools, it can be used as part of your business objects. Microsoft Access now demonstrates its reporting capabilities as an OLE object. As demonstrated in Chapter 8, Reporting and Data Connection Support, you will see how easy it is to incorporate an Access report into your VB applications.

Seagate Software Information Management Group1095

West Pender Street, 4th Floor
Vancouver BC Canada V6E 2M6
   Phone: (604) 681-3435
      Fax: (604) 681-2934
Internet: http://www.img.seagatesoftware.com/

Crystal Reports Professional

Crystal Reports combines the ease-of-use with report design and data analysis features that make reporting tasks really efficient. It has support of Access 2.0 OLE picture fields and version 2.5 of the Microsoft Access engine, the ability to export to Excel 5.0, the ability to save report options with a report (simplifying report distribution), and the ability to drill down on graphs. You can access Crystal Reports directly through the Crystal DLL or through its custom control. It is available for both the 16- and 32-bit Windows operating systems.

Transaction Servers

For years, mainframe applications took advantage of transaction servers to manage the execution of applications and resources across the enterprise. With the reintroduction of distributed processing and applications at the personal computer network level, transaction servers are being introduced to a new generation of application developers.

IBM Corp.

1133 Westchester Avenue
White Plains NY 10604
   Phone: (800) 426-3333
Internet: http://www.ibm.com

Transaction Server for Windows NT

This transaction processing solution provides CICS functionality for business-critical applications that will help leverage client/server applications, and extend application capabilities to meet future business requirements. It's a robust, enterprise-wide process coordinator and integrator of servers across the network. It includes five (5) basic components: CICS for Windows NT Server; CICS clients that support OS/2, DOS, Windows 3.x, Macintosh, Windows 95, and Windows NT operating systems; Encina for Windows NT; Encina Clients for AIX and Windows NT; and CICS Client for AIX.

Microsoft Corp

One Microsoft Way
Redmond, WA
   Phone: (800) 426-9400
Internet: http://www.microsoft.com

Microsoft Transaction Server

Previously referred to as Viper, this Active Server is a key component to Microsoft's Active Server lineup. Applications designed for the Internet using Microsoft Internet Information Server to Visual Basic applications developed for DCOM can take advantage of this server. Its components include transaction process monitoring, transaction resource scalability, component configuration, and security services.

Progress Software Corp.

14 Oak Park
Bedford, MA 01730
   Phone: (800) 477-6473
Internet: http://webspeed.progress.com

WebSpeed Transaction Server

The WebSpeed Transaction Server is a Web-based transaction processing environment that ensures the integrity of your database transaction. It contains three (3) components: Messenger, Transaction Broker, and Transaction Agent. The Messenger is compatible with any common gateway interface (CGI)-compliant Web server. Its purpose is to transfer data directly between the Web server and the Transaction Agent during a single transaction. The Transaction Broker manages the pool of Transaction Agents and maintains the status information of Web requests. This eliminates the overhead of starting a new Agent for each user request, and it dynamically increases the Agent pool size when resources start to get low. The Transaction Agent executes Web objects and database transactions, and dynamically merges data into HTML format to build Web documents real-time.

> **NOTE**
>
> In no way are any of the authors endorsing any of these products, nor is this a complete list of client/server database resources. Many of the vendors' Web sites refer to other client/server products through links. This portion of the appendix is just to give you a good place to start.

CompuServe/Internet/World Wide Web Support

A popular form of getting support from peers is through electronic sources like CompuServe or the Internet. The support areas listed here are a very small representation of what online support is available. To find more online support, go to any of the Web sites listed below and look for links to other Visual Basic Web sites.

Advanced Visual Basic

Internet:
http://www.duke-net.com/vb

California State University, San Marcos
Internet:
http://coyote.csusm.edu/cwis/winworld/
vbasic.html

Codd Multimedia Home Page - Home of VB Online
Internet:
http://www.vbonline.com
CompuServe:
GO BASIC

Fawcette Technical Publishings
Internet:
http://www.windx.com
CompuServe:
GO VBPJ
GO WINCOMPA
GO WINCOMPB
GO WINCOMPC

Gary 'n Carl's Visual Basic Home Page
Internet:
http://www.apexsc.com/vb

Gary Beene's Visual Basic World
Internet:
http://www.iadfw.net/gbeene/visual.html

Microsoft Corporation
Internet:
http://www.microsoft.com/msdn
http://www.microsoft.com/support

VB Tips & Tricks Home Page
Internet:
http://www.apexsc.com/vb/davem/vbtt.html

Visual Basic User Groups

Amateur Computer Group of New Jersey (ACGNJ)
Jim Wong
113 Mt. Arlington Blvd.
Landing, NJ 07850
Phone: (201) 398-2087

Atlanta Visual Basic User's Group
Andy Dean, Paul Goldsman
946 Glen Arden Way, NE
Atlanta, GA 30306
Phone: (404) 874-6938
Fax: (404) 872-1286
CompuServe: 71233,1412
Internet:
http://www.mindspring.com/~andyd/
avbug.html

Australian Visual Basic User's Group
Mark Henry
Information Technology
3/489 Swanston Street
Melbourne, Vic 3000
Australia
Phone: 61-3-9623-3262 (business hrs)
61-3-9877-5969 (after hours)
Fax: 61-3-9894-2738
BBS: 61-3-9761-4043

Bay Area Visual Basic User Group
Gustavo Eydelsteyn
2625 Alcatraz Avenue #271
Berkeley, CA 94705
Phone: (510) 547-7295

Belleville Area Visual Basic UG
Robert Morris
507 North Fourth Street
Mascoutah, IL 62258
Phone: (618) 566-7505

Big Blue and Cousins - Visual Basic
Victoria, BC V8R 6S4
Elliott Building
Phone: (604) 382-3934

Boston Computer Society VB-SIG
John Barrie
30 Clark Street
Holden, MA 01520
Phone: (508) 829-2181
CompuServe: 70373,2241
Internet:
http://www.bcs.org/

Calgary Visual Basic UG
Jean Paradis
3100-150 6th Ave SW
Calgary, Alberta, Canada T2P 4M5
Phone: (403) 234-2929
Internet:
http://www.iadfw.net/gbeene/calgary.html

Capital District User Group
Jeff Polansky, President
420 Sand Creek Road, Suite 132
Albany, NY 12205
Phone: (518) 459-8536 ext. 19
CompuServe: 73114,2754

Capital PC UG
Charles Kelly
3613 Rose Lane
Annandale, VA 20550
Phone: (202) 357-9796
Fax: (703) 642-2329
Internet:
http://cpcug.org/user/windows

Central Florida VB UG
Chris Douglas
Route 3, Box 55W
Aachua, FL 32615

Central Texas PC User's Group
Internet:
http://www.ctpcug.com/newsltr/9506/sigs.htm

Charlotte Area VB Users Group
Gary Baker
102 Higgins Court
Huntersville, NC 28078
CompuServe: 75505,1114
Internet:
http://www.iadfw.net/gbeene/charlott.html

Charlotte Visual Basic Users Group
Tim Booker
One Nations Bank Plaza, Ste. 3710
Charlotte, NC 28280
Phone: (704) 375-5788
Fax: (704) 375-5699

Chicago Computer Society
Allan Wolff
1560 North Sandburg Terrace, Suite 1715
Chicago, IL 60610
Phone: (312) 787-8966

Chicago Corporate Visual Basic User Group
Hoffman Estates, IL 60194
Phone: (708) 952-3687
Internet:
http://www.mossmicro.com/CCVBUG

**Computer Experts of Northern California
- Visual Basic**
1266 Sir Francis Drake
Kentfield, CA 94904-1005
Phone: (415) 925-9880

Computer Language Society
Bill Sharpe
455 Lincoln Blvd
Santa Monica, CA 90402
Phone: (310) 451-9598

Connecticut Visual Basic Special Interest Group
North Haven, CT
Phone: (203) 239-6874
Fax: (203) 239-6874
Internet:
http://www.vb-bootcamp.com/

Danbury Area Computer Society - Visual Basic
Danbury, CT
Phone: (203) 791-2283

Des Moines VB Users Group
Tej Dhawan
5233 Walnut St.
West Des Moines, IA 50265

Diablo Valley PC UG
Steve Israel
3687 Mt. Diablo Blvd. Ste. 350
Layfayette, CA 94549

Edmonton VB/Access Developers SIG
Nisku, Alberta
Phone: (403) 955-3065

Gold Coast User Group
Joe Homnick
Maureen Callery
2300 Glades Road
Suite 150 Tower West
Boca Raton, FL 33431
Phone: (407) 368-0010
Fax: (407) 347-0765

Gotham New York PC Corporation - Visual Basic
New York, NY
Phone: (212) 686-6972

Greater Cleveland PC Users Group - Visual Basic
Cleveland, OH
Phone: (216) 781-4132

Hartford Visual Basic UG
Daniel Mezick
New Technology Solutions
6 Robin Court Suite 720
North Haven, CT 06473
Phone: (203) 239-6874

Heartland Windows PC UG
Ken Neal
10201 W. 89th Terrace
Overland Park, KS 66212
Phone: (913) 541-0591

Houston Area League
Fred Thorlin
10819 Lakeside Forest Lane
Houston, TX 77042-1025
Phone: (713) 784-8906
Internet:
http://www.hal-pc.org/

Houston VB SIG
Robert D. Thompson
3215 Mulberry Hill Lane
Houston, TX 77084
Phone: (713) 398-9042

Indianapolis Computer Society
Bill Seltzer
2064 Emily Dr.
Indianapolis, IN 46260
Internet:
http://www.otisnet.com/ICS/ics.htm

iVBug (The Irish Visual Basic Users Group)
Donal P Higgins
c/o Carmichael House
60 Lower Baggot Street
Dublin 2
Ireland
Phone: 353-1-676-2240
Fax: 353-1-676-2447

Ivy Tech Terre Haute Region 7 VB User Group
7999 US Highway 41
Terre Haute, IN 47802
Internet:
http://www.ivy.tec.in.us/haute/thaute.htm

Kansas City Heartland User's Group VB SIG
Belton, MO
Phone: (816) 322-1845

Kentucky/Indiana PC UG
Tim Landgrave
200 Whittington Parkway, Suite 100A
Louisville, KY 40222

Las Vegas PC Users Group - Visual Basic
3200 E. Cheynne Ave.
Las Vegas, NV 89119
Phone: (702) 736-3788

London Life Visual Basic UG
Stephen Baldock, Consultant
255 Dufferin Avenue
London, Ontario
N6A 4K1 Canada
Phone: (519) 432-2000 x4429
Fax: (519) 432-3862
Internet:
http://www.iadfw.net/gbeene/london.html

Long Island PC Users Group - Visual Basic
235 Pinelawn Road
Baldwin, NY 11510-1031
Phone: (516) 223-1761

Los Angeles Visual Basic Users Group
Covina, CA
Phone: (818) 332-8879

Madison PC UG
Peter Welter
1225 W. Dayton St., Rm. 1229
Madison, WI 53706
Phone: (608)263-3447

Maryland Visual Basic User Group
College Park, MD
Phone: (301) 405-2977
Fax: (301) 314-9198

**Melbourne PC User Group-
Basic Programming**
South Melbourne, VIC
Phone: (613) 699-622
Internet:
http://www.melbpc.org.au/

Memphis PC Users Group, Inc. - Visual Basic
5983 Macon Cove
Memphis, TN 38124-1756
Phone: (901) 375-4316

Mexican VB User Group
Internet:
http://www.iadfw.net/gbeene/mexico.html

Milwaukee Area Visual Basic Users' Group
Arthur Edstrom
P.O. Box 28
Waterford, WI 53815-0028
Phone: (414) 534-5181 (daytime)
        (414) 534-3440 (evening)
CompuServe: 75410,2203

Montreal-Groupe d'entraide Visual Basic
Internet:
http://www.login.net/gvbm/vb.htm

Napa Valley PC UG
Frank Sommer
1253 Monticello Road
Napa, CA 94558
Phone: (707) 258-2509
Internet:
http://community.net/~stevefc/vb.html

North Orange County Computer Club
Bill Hines
712 N. Clinton
Orange, CA 92667
Phone: (714) 633-4874

North Texas PC UG
Woody Pewitt
3200 W. Pleasant Run Road, Suite 328
Lancaster, TX 75146-1046
Phone: (214) 230-3485

North Texas PC UG (Beginners Group)
Jim Carter
1112 Pueblo Drive
Richardson, TX 75080
Phone: (214) 235-5968

NYPC Visual Basic SIG
David Kulick
147 - 51 72nd Road, #3F
Flushing, NY 11367
Phone: (718) 261-0285

Oklahoma City PC Users Group - Visual Basic
1900 Spring Lake Drive
Oklahoma City, OK 73157-2027
Phone: (405) 791-0894

Orange Coast IBM PC UG
Wendy Sarrett
3700 Park View Lane #22D
Irvine, CA 92715
Phone: (714) 966-3925

Orange County Visual Basic UG
Irvine, CA
Phone: (714) 260-0300
Fax: (714) 260-0325
Internet:
http://www.mossmicro.com/moss/dev_res/
    ocvbug/ocvbug.htm

Pacific NorthWest PC UG
Sean Bleichschmidt
9602 NE 35th Place
Bellevue, WA 98004
Phone: (206) 462-8395

Pacific NorthWest PC UG
Richard Buhrer
1202 East Pike Street #665
Seattle, WA 98122
Phone: (206) 324-9024

Pasadena IBM UG
Rod Ream and David Jung
2026 South 6th Street
Alahambra, CA 91830
Phone: (818) 280-6850
Internet:
http://www.socalvillage.com/white_pages/
    vbsig.htm

PC Users' Group Inc. (ACT) - Visual Basic
Belconnen, ACT 2616 Australia
Phone: (616) 239-6511

Philadelphia Area Computer Society
Steve Longo
c/o LaSalle University
1900 West Olney
Philadelphia, PA 19141
Phone: (215) 951-1255

Phoenix PC UG
P.O. Box 35637
Phoenix, AZ 85069-5637
Phone: (602) 222-8511
BBS: (602) 222-5491
Internet:
http://www.phoenixpcug.org/

Pinellas IBM PC UG
Thomas Kiehl
14155 102nd Avenue N
Largo, FL 34644

Portable Computing UG
Virginia Benedict
208 E. 51 St. #366
New York, NY 10022
Phone: (212) 348-0690

Portland Visual Basic User Group
Hillsburo, OR 97123
Phone: (503) 628-0705
Fax: (503) 628-6005
Internet:
http://www.teleport.com/~pdxvbug/

Poughkeepsie IBM Club Microcomputer Club - Basic
Hyde Park, NY
Phone: (914) 229-6551

Queensland VB Group
Internet:
http://www.odyssey.com.au/vb/index.html

Research Triangle Park VB User Group
Bob Canavan
c/o Fonville Morisey Realtors
3600 Glennwood Avenue, Suite 150
Raleigh, NC 27612
Phone: (919) 781-7809

Richmond Access/Visual Basic Developers' Forum
Glen Allen, VA
Phone: (804) 273-6244
Fax: (804) 273-1804

Sacramento PC UG - VB/Access
Larry Clark
345 Prewett Drive
Folsom, CA 95630
Phone: (916) 983-3950
Internet:
http://www.iadfw.net/gbeene/mento.html

St. Louis User Group for the PC - Basic
St. Louis, MO 63169-0099
Phone: (314) 458-9597

St. Louis Visual Basic Users Group
Brian Back
2066 Willow Leaf
St. Louis, MO 63131
Phone: (314) 984-8779
e-mail: brianb@mo.net

San Diego Visual Basic Users Group
7480 Mission Valley Road
La Jolla, CA 92037
Phone: (619) 459-5535
Fax: (619) 459-5535
Internet:
http://www.apexsc.com/vb/davem/sdvbug.html

San Fernando Valley Visual Basic Users Group
Internet:
http://www.instanet.com/~mdorris

San Francisco Software Forum's VB-SIG
Dov Gorman
1164 18th Street
San Francisco, Ca
Phone: (415) 552-3859
Internet:
http://www.softwareforum.org

Santa Clarita Valley PC Group - Visual Basic
Canyon Country, CA
Phone: (805) 252-8852

Silicon Valley Software Forum's VB-SIG
Allan Colby
107 Lake Road
Portola Valley, CA 94028-8116
Phone: (415) 851-4567
Internet:
http://www.softwareforum.org

Software Forum
Barbara Cass
Phone: (415) 854-7219
Internet:
http://www.softwareforum.org/

South Florida Database and Developers Group VB/Access SIG
Coconut Grove, FL
Phone: (305) 858-8200
Fax: (305) 858-3719
Internet:
http://www.shadow.net/~datachem
    /sfddg12.html

Space Coast PC Users Group - Visual Basic
308 Forest Avenue
Cocoa, FL 32923-0369
Phone: (407) 254-1926

State College Area Visual Basic Users Group
c/o Blue Mountain Software
W. David Raike
208 West Hamilton Avenue
State College, PA 16810
Phone: (814) 234-2417

Tampa Bay Computer Society
Clearwater, FL
Phone: (813) 443-4433
Internet:
http://www.iadfw.net/gbeene/tampa.html

TC/PC VB-SIG
Bill Rothermal
3629 Sumter Avenue S.
St. Louis Parl, MN 55426-4007
Phone: (612) 935-0513

Toronto VB Users Group
Dwayne Lamb
3555 Don Mill Rd.
Suite 6-1705
North York, ON, Canada, M2H 3N3
Phone: (416) 499-1978
Fax: (416) 499-1681
e-mail: mrsheep@visualbyte.com

Toronto Windows UG
Don Roy
6327 Atherley Crescent
Mississaugua, ONT, Canada, L5N 2J1
Phone: (416) 826-0320

Tucson Computer Society
Bruce Fulton
516 East Mabel
Tucson, AZ 85705
Phone: (602) 577-7700
CompuServe: 73510,3550
Internet:
http://www.azstarnet.com/public/
  nonprofit/tcs

Tulsa Computer Society - Visual Basic
Tulsa, OK
Phone: (918) 622-3417

**Twin Cities PC UG, Inc. - Access/ Visual
Basic Professional**
Edina, MN 55424
Phone: (612) 229-5850

UK Visual Basic User Group
Jeff Cabrie
15 Mount Way
Chepstow
Gwent
NP6 5NF England
Phone: 44-0291-620720
Fax: 44-0291-627320
Internet:
http://www.exe.co.uk/home/vbug.html

**University of Maryland Visual Basic User
Group**
Internet:
http://wonderland.dial.umd.edu/
  documents/VisualBasic/AboutVBUG.html

Utah Computer Society - Visual Basics
Jim Murtha
P.O. Box 510811
Salt Lake City, UT 84151
Phone: (801) 521-7830
BBS: (801) 521-5009
Internet:
http://www.ucs.org

VB Large Users Group
Englewood, NJ 07631
Phone: (201) 816-8900
Fax: (201) 816-1644

VB Large Users Group-NYC
George Febish
50 East Palisade Ave., Suite 411
Englewood, NJ 07631
Phone: (201) 816-8900
Fax: (201) 816-1644

VBSpecialists
Lewisville, TX 75067
Phone: (214) 315-7528

VB.UG
Louisville, KY 40222
Phone: (502) 327-0333
Fax: (502) 327-7418

VBUG MEXICO
Alberto Curiel
Torres Adalid 707-302
Mexico D.F. 03100
Phone: (608) 742-5373

Visual Basic Developer Network
John Chemla
10300 South Cicero
Oak Lawn, IL 60453
Phone: (708) 430-2819
Fax: (708) 430-3643
CompuServe: 72066,3035
Internet:
http://d_us.pd.mcs.net/vbdn

**Visual Developer's Group (VisDev—an
online user group)**
Internet:
http://www.galstar.com/~qt2/visdev.html

Visual Basic Groep (Dutch)
Internet:
http://www.xs4all.nl/~treffers/vbgg.htm

Visual Basic Milwaukee
Waterford, WI 53185-0028
Phone: (414) 534-4309
Fax: (414) 534-7809

Visual Basic Users of Nova Scotia
Enfield, NS
Phone: (902) 883-1010
Fax: (902) 883-8586

VDUNY - Visual Developer of Upstate New York
Robert H. Mowery III
c/o SofTech Multimedia, Inc.
79 Springfield Avenue
Rochester, NY 14609-3607
Phone: (716) 288-5830
Fax: (716) 482-7105
Internet:
http://www.frontiernet.net/~softech/vduny/

Westchester PC Users Group VB Sig
Michael Lee
Dictaphone Corp.
3191 Broadbridge Rd.
Stratford, CT 06497
WPCUG Hotline: (914) 962-8022 for the
latest on the Sigs.
Phone: (203) 381-7138 (Day)
CompuServe: 75720,1221
Internet:
http://www.wpcug.org/

Winnipeg PC UG
Darryl Draeger
61 Amundsen Bay
Winnipeg, MB, Canada, R3K0V1
Phone: (204) 831-7163

Windows on the Rockies User Group - Visual Basic
Highlands Ranch, CO 80126
Phone: (303) 470-6504
Fax: (303) 449-7525

Windows NT/BackOffice User Groups

Advanced Systems User Group
Annandale, VA 22003
Phone: (703) 642-2329
Internet:
http://cpcug.org/user/ckelly/new_asug.html

Aetna Database User Group
HartFord, CT 06156
Phone: (203) 273-2016
Fax: (203) 273-2016

Anchorage Windows NT Users Group
Internet:
http://www.rmm.com/awntug/

Arizona Society For Computer Information Inc. - DataBases
Phoenix, AZ
Phone: (602) 978-9031

Association of Database Developers
Oakland, CA
Phone: (415) 281-5638

Atlanta BackOffice Users Group
Atlanta, GA
Phone: (404) 233-5500
Fax: (404) 233-9698

Bellevue Database Users
Omaha, NE
Phone: (402) 592-9620
Fax: (402) 593-0886

Boston Computer Society Windows NT Users Group
e-mail: wihl@shore.net
Internet:
http://www.shore.net/~wihl/nentug.html

Brisbane NT User Group
e-mail: dkowald@ozemail.com.au
Internet:
http://www.ozemail.com.au/~dkowald/
bntug.htm

Canberra - Microsoft Systems User Group
e-mail: neil.pinkerton@cao.mts.dec.com

Central Texas PC Users' Group, Inc. Database
26th Red River
Austin, TX 78766
Phone: (512) 343-7258

Champaign-Urbana NT Users Group
e-mail: kashi@uiuc.edu
Internet:
http://www.cofsci.uiuc.edu/~kashi

Chattanooga - River Valley NT Users Group
e-mail: james@press.southern.edu

Chicago Area NT Business Users Group
Oak Brook, IL
Phone: (708) 368-7000
Fax: (708) 368-7090

Chicago, Great Lakes SQL Server User Group
Don_Opperthauser@rdisoft.com

Colorado Springs PC Users Group - Windows NT
Colorado Springs, CO
Phone: (719) 578-2215

Compunet Computer Club - Data Base
Sardinia, OH
Phone: (513) 446-2202

Computer Experts of Northern California - Database
1266 Sir Francis Drake
Kentfield, CA 94904-1005
Phone: (415) 925-9880

Crossroads Computer Club - Database
Alexandria, LA
Phone: (318) 487-4078

Danbury Area Computer Society - Database
Danbury, CT
Phone: (203) 791-2283

Database Developers Group
Peoria, AZ
Phone: (602) 977-2177

Developers' SIG
e-mail: djs@cnj.digex.net

Diablo Valley PC Users Group Windows NT
Walnut Creek, CA
Phone: (510) 943-1367

Dublin Database User Group
Dublin, OH
Phone: (614) 766-9828

French NT Users Group
Internet:
http://fwntug.esf.org/

Golden Gate Computer Society - Database SIG
618 B Street
San Rafael, CA
Phone: (415) 454-5556

Gotham New York PC Corporation - NT Developers
New York, NY
Phone: (212) 686-6972

Great Lakes SQL Server Users Group, The
Buffalo Grove, IL
Phone: (847) 609-8783
Fax: (847) 419-0190
Internet:
http://www.glssug.com/glssug/

Greater Cleveland PC Users Group - Database
Cleveland, OH
Phone: (216) 781-4132

Groupware & Data Bases
100 Mill Plain Rd.
Danbury, CT
Phone: (914) 892-9030
Fax: (914) 892-9068

Huntsville PC User Group, Inc. - Databases
Huntsville, AL
Phone: (205) 883-4154

Indiana University Windows NT Users Group, IUWNTUG
Internet:
http://www.iuinfo.indiana.edu/nt/

Interior Alaska Windows NT Users Group
Internet:
http://www.iawntug.org/iawntug/

The International Windows NT Users Group
Internet:
http://www.iwntug.org/

Kansas City Windows NT Users Group
e-mail: srodgers@kumc.edu

Long Beach IBM Users Group - Database
5155 E. Pacific Coast Hwy
Lakewood, CA
Phone: (310) 420-3670

Los Angeles Windows NT/Microsoft Networking Users Group
Internet:
http://www.bhs.com/lantug/

Madison PC User's Group - Database
5445 Cheryl Parkway
Madison, WI 53701
Phone: (608) 231-2725

Melbourne PC User Group - DBMS
Phone: (613) 699-6222
Internet:
http://www.melbpc.org.au/

Melbourne - Australian NT Users Group
e-mail: rcomg@chudich.cse.rmit.edu.au

Memphis PC Users Group, Inc. Database Users
5983 Macon Cove
Memphis, TN 38124-1756
Phone: (901) 375-4316

Microsoft Databases User Group of San Diego
Oceanside, CA
Phone: (619) 433-7374
Fax: (619) 433-0776

Microsoft Networking SIG
e-mail: deborahl@microsoft.com

Minneapolis - Windows NT Users Group
e-mail: quadling@mnhepo.hep.umn.edu

New York City NT Developers SIG
e-mail: lee_t@access.digex.net
e-mail: iams@smosna.cs.nyu.edu

North Orange County Computer Club - Database
333 N. Glassell Street
Orange, CA 92665
Phone: (714) 645-5950

North Texas SQL Server User Group
Plano, TX
Phone: (214) 509-6137
Fax: (214) 509-3509

NT User's Group St. Louis
St. Louis, MO
Phone: (314) 997-4700
Fax: (314) 997-5426

NW Database Society
James Erickson
10305 SW Denney Rd. #8
Beaverton, OR 97005
Phone: (503) 626-8485

Oklahoma Computer Society - Database
Stillwater, OK
Phone: (405) 372-6800

Ontario NT Users Group
Internet:
http://www.ontug.org/

Orange Coast IBM PC User Group - DataBase Review
Costa Mesa, CA
Phone: (714) 843-2048
Internet:
http://www.wecom.com/~ocipug/

Orange County Computer Society - Windows NT
Anaheim, CA

Orange County SQL Server Developers Group
Taco Bell Office
17901 Von Karman Ave.
Irvine, CA 92614
Phone: (714) 831-6856
Fax: (714) 831-1456

Pacific Northwest IBM PC User Group - Windows NT
Bellevue, WA
Phone: (206) 728-7075

Pacific Northwest SQL Server UG
Bellevue, WA
Phone: (206) 467-5651

PC Users' Group Inc. (ACT) - PC Database Developers
Belconnen, ACT
Phone: (616) 239-6511

PC Users' Group of Jacksonville - Database
2800 North University Blvd.
Jacksonville, FL 32247-7197
Phone: (904) 221-5628

Personal Computer Club of Sun Lakes - Data Base
Banning, CA
Phone: (909) 845-5822

Philadelphia Area Computer Society - SQL
Philadelphia, PA
Phone: (215) 951-1255

Philadelphia NT Users Group
aengel@netaxs.com

Phoenix PCUG Windows NT SIG
Phoenix, AZ
Phone: (602) 222-8511
Internet:
http://www.phoenixpcug.org/

Portland Area Windows NT User Group
e-mail: andreas@mail.inprot.com
Internet:
http://www.inprot.com/NT

Portland Oregon SQL User Group
Hillsburo, OR
Phone: (503) 628-0705
Fax: (503) 628-6005

Portland PC Users Group - Database
1819 NW Everett
Portland, OR 97205
Phone: (503) 226-4143
Internet:
http://odin.cc.pdx.edu/~psu01435/cgi/
ppcug.cgi

Poughkeepsie IBM Club Microcomputer Club -Database
Hyde Park, NY
Phone: (914) 229-6551

Professional DBMS Developers
Hermsillo, Sonora
Phone: (621) 546-8600

Rocky Mountain Windows NT Users Group
Louisville, CO
Phone: (303) 673-2935
Internet:
http://budman.cmdl.noaa.gov/
RMWNTUG/RMWNTUG.HTM

San Diego County Windows NT Users Group
Internet:
http://www.bhs.com/sdug/

Sarasota Personal Computer User Group, Inc. - Database
4826 Ashton Road
Sarasota, FL 34232
Phone: (941) 377-4072

Silicon Northwest Database Professionals
Seattle, WA
Phone: (206) 781-0225

Southeast Florida Database Developer's Group
Internet:
http://www.shadow.net/~datachem/
sfddg12.html

Swiss NT Users Group
e-mail: deffer@eunet.ch

Sydney NT User's Group
e-mail: robg@pactok.peg.apc.org

Triangle NT Users Group
Raleigh, NC
Phone: (919) 510-6970
Fax: (919) 510-6971
e-mail: tntug@networks.com
Internet:
http://www.nando.net/ads/ncs

Tulsa Computer Society - Database
Tulsa, OK
Phone: (918) 622-3417

Twin Cities PC UG, Inc. - Client Server
Edina, MN
Phone: (612) 229-5850

Washington DC Microsoft SQL Server Users Group
Sterling, VA
Phone: (703) 356-1717
Fax: (703) 356-3009

Windows NT User Group of Indianapolis
Internet:
http://www.wintugi.org/

INDEX

ReportSmith, 888

resize
 detailed reports, 579-580
 RDO error forms, 48

resultsets, 143-151, 873
 load balancing, 170-172, 178-179
 multiple, 179-183

RESVINFO.FRM, 358

RETSET.VBP, 170-172

ReturnsRows property, 86

review tools (sales), creating, 679-721

rollback, 873

routines
 DropNewImage, 302-303
 EnableFileDrop, 286-288, 291
 LoadCollection subroutine
  Image Tracker, 773
  three-tier client/server, 736-739
 LoadStoredProcedures, 156-157
 MDI forms, 206-207, 210
 MenuBrowse subroutine, 767-768
 MenuDelete subroutine, 769-772
 MenuShowMenu, 228
 MenuShowTool, 228
 ParseFile, 418
 PopulateLists, 321-324
 SetView
  Image Tracker, 753-756
  mouse pop-up menus, 259-268

Rows (records), 873
 controlling, 170-172, 178-179
 display control, 375-382

RowSetSize property, 170

Royalties class, 22, 540-551

ROYCOLL.VBP, 543

RPCs (remote procedure calls), 17, 537, 874

RTFPRINT.VBP, 576-579

rules, 20, 874; *see also* logic

RunTest procedure, 496-497

S

SalePrice property, 657, 661-662

Sales Commission review tool, creating, 679-721

Sales Prices review screen, 681

SalesComm.frm, 684-685

SalesCommission property, 669

SalesID property, 658, 669

SalesList_Click, 690

SalesPrices.frm, 686-687

Save As command (File menu; Crystal), 563

Save command (File menu; Crystal), 563

SaveBmp method, 753

Search_Click, 689-690

second normal form, 874

second tier business objects, 626

security
 Remote Connection Manager, 33
 transaction server, 29

SELECT, 874

sending multiple queries, 587-606

SERVER.CLS, 485
 business objects, 488-491
 encapsulating logic, 504-505, 510

Servers, 874, 887-888
 ActiveX servers, 23, 863
 granularity, 28
 in-process, 16-17, 23, 869
 out-of-process, 16-17, 23
 remote servers, 530, 537
 SQL, configuring, 830-834
 transaction, 26-29, 889-890

Services Model, 18-23

SetColumnWidths, 601-602

SetPattern property, 448

Setup method, 451-452

Setup Wizard
 CAB files, creating, 858-860
 ODBC connection strings, writing, 52-53

SetupBitmap method, 446

SetupRTB, 581

SetView
 method, 765-767
 routine, 753-756
  MDI forms, 205
  mouse pop-up menus, 259-268

ShelfQuantity property, 661

Show Menu option, 228

ShowPattern method, 448

ShowWindow control array, 207

Single server deployment, 24-25

SIZE property, 787

SizeViewPict , 205-206

SizingmSize menu options, 208

sorting, *see* tab controls

Source code controls, 39-41

SourceSafe, 37-41

spreadsheets, displaying (unbound grids), 357-364

Sp_addumpdevice parameter, 787

Sp_Assist, 880

SP_HELPTEXT, 152-163

SQL (Structured Query Language), 9-10, 135, 874
 asynchronous queries, 183-192
 BuildSQL function, 379
 cursors, 866
 DDLs, 866
 deadlocks, 867
 DMBS (Database Management Systems), 9-10
 Enterprise Manager
  back-up devices, creating, 785-787
  database devices, creating, 783-784
  foreign keys, creating, 798-800
  primary keys, creating, 796-800
 objects, 884
 ODBC functions, 60-61
 OLE!, 884
 passthrough option, 80-86
 queries

ACTIVEX CONTROL PAD

IMPORTANT: PLEASE READ CAREFULLY:

This Microsoft End-User License Agreement (EULA) is a legal agreement between you (either an individual or a single entity) and Microsoft Corporation for the Microsoft software product(s) listed above, which includes computer software and associated media and printed materials (if any), and may include online or electronic documentation and software product (collectively, the "SOFTWARE PRODUCT(s)"). By installing, copying, or otherwise using the SOFTWARE PRODUCT, you agree to be bound by the terms of this EULA. If you do not agree to the terms of this EULA, you are not authorized to use the SOFTWARE PRODUCT. The SOFTWARE PRODUCT is protected by copyright laws and international copyright treaties, as well as other intellectual property laws and treaties. The SOFTWARE PRODUCT is licensed, not sold.

1. GRANT OF LICENSE.

(a) MS grants to Recipient a limited, non-exclusive, nontransferable, royalty-free license to use one copy of the executable code of the Product software on a single CPU residing on Recipient's premises, solely to test the compatibility of Recipient's application or other product(s) which operate in conjunction with the Product and to evaluate the Product for the purpose of providing feedback thereon to MS. Recipient may not redistribute any portion of the Product. All other rights are reserved to MS. Recipient shall not rent, lease, sell, sublicense, assign, or otherwise transfer the Product, including any accompanying printed materials. Recipient may not reverse engineer, decompile or disassemble the Product except to the extent that this restriction is expressly prohibited by applicable law. MS and its suppliers shall retain title and all ownership rights to the Product.

(b) Recipient agrees to provide reasonable feedback to MS, including but not limited to usability, bug reports and test results, with respect to the Product testing. Recipient will use reasonable efforts to review and comment on all documentation supplied. All bug reports, test results and other feedback made by Recipient shall be the property of MS and may be used by MS for any purpose. Due to the nature of the development work, MS is not certain as to when errors or discrepancies in the Products may be corrected.

2. TERM OF AGREEMENT. The term of this Agreement shall commence on the Effective Date and shall continue until terminated by MS in writing at any time, with or without cause. This Agreement will terminate without notice upon the commercial release of the Product. Upon the termination of this Agreement, Recipient shall promptly return to MS, or certify destruction of, all full or partial copies of the Product and related materials provided by MS.

3. PRODUCT MAINTENANCE. MS is not obligated to provide maintenance or updates to Recipient for the Product. However, any maintenance or updates provided by MS shall be covered by this Agreement.

4. DISCLAIMER OF WARRANTY. Product is deemed accepted by Recipient. The Product constitutes pre-release code and may be changed substantially before commercial release. The PRODUCT is provided "AS IS" WITHOUT WARRANTY OF ANY KIND. TO THE MAXIMUM EXTENT PERMITTED BY APPLICABLE LAW, MICROSOFT FURTHER DISCLAIMS ALL WARRANTIES, INCLUDING WITHOUT LIMITATION ANY IMPLIED WARRANTIES OF MERCHANTABILITY, FITNESS FOR A PARTICULAR PURPOSE, AND NONINFRINGEMENT. THE ENTIRE RISK ARISING OUT OF THE USE OR PERFORMANCE OF THE PRODUCT AND DOCUMENTATION REMAINS WITH RECIPIENT. TO THE MAXIMUM EXTENT

PERMITTED BY APPLICABLE LAW, IN NO EVENT SHALL MICROSOFT OR ITS SUPPLIERS BE LIABLE FOR ANY CONSEQUENTIAL, INCIDENTAL, DIRECT, INDIRECT, SPECIAL, PUNITIVE, OR OTHER DAMAGES WHATSOEVER (INCLUDING, WIHOUT LIMITATION, DAMAGES FOR LOSS OF BUSINESS PROFITS, BUSINESS INTERRUPTION, LOSS OF BUSINESS INFORMATION, OR OTHER PECUNIARY LOSS) ARISING OUT OF THIS AGREEMENT OR THE USE OF OR INABILITY TO USE THE PRODUCT, EVEN IF MICROSOFT HAS BEEN ADVISED OF THE POSSIBILITY OF SUCH DAMAGES. BECAUSE SOME STATES/JURISDICTIONS DO NOT ALLOW THE EXCLUSION OR LIMITATION OF LIABILITY FOR CONSEQUENTIAL OR INCIDENTAL DAMAGES, THE ABOVE LIMITATION MAY NOT APPLY TO RECIPIENT.

5. GOVERNING LAW; ATTORNEYS FEES. This Agreement shall be governed by the laws of the State of Washington and Recipient further consents to jurisdiction by the state and federal courts sitting in the State of Washington. If either MS or Recipient employs attorneys to enforce any rights arising out of or relating to this Agreement, the prevailing party shall be entitled to recover reasonable attorneys' fees.

6. U.S. GOVERNMENT RESTRICTED RIGHTS. The Product is provided with RESTRICTED RIGHTS. Use, duplication, or disclosure by the Government is subject to restrictions as set forth in subparagraph (c)(1)(ii) of The Rights in Technical Data and Computer Software clause of DFARS 252.227-7013 or subparagraphs (c)(i) and (2) of the Commercial Computer Software -- Restricted Rights at 48 CFR 52.227-19, as applicable. Manufacturer is Microsoft Corporation, One Microsoft Way, Redmond, WA 98052-6399.

7. EXPORT RESTRICTIONS. Recipient acknowledges that the Product licensed hereunder is subject to the export control laws and regulations of the U.S.A., and any amendments thereof. Recipient confirms that with respect to the Product, it will not export or re-export it, directly or indirectly, either to (i) any countries that are subject to U.S.A. export restrictions (currently including, but not necessarily limited to, Cuba, the Federal Republic of Yugoslavia (Serbia and Montenegro), Haiti, Iran, Iraq, Libya, North Korea, South Africa (military and police entities), and Syria); (ii) any end user who Recipient knows or has reason to know will utilize them in the design, development or production of nuclear, chemical or biological weapons; or (iii) any end user who has been prohibited from participating in the U.S.A. export transactions by any federal agency of the U.S.A. government. Recipient further acknowledges that the Product may include technical data subject to export and re-export restrictions imposed by U.S.A. law.

8. ENTIRE AGREEMENT. This Agreement constitutes the complete and exclusive agreement between MS and Recipient with respect to the subject matter hereof, and supersedes all prior oral or written understandings, communications or agreements not specifically incorporated herein. This Agreement may not be modified except in a writing duly signed by an authorized representative of MS and Recipient.

This program was reproduced by MacMillan Computer Publishing under a special arrangement with Microsoft Corporation. For this reason, MacMillan Computer Publishing is responsible for the product warranty and for support. If your diskette is defective, please return it to MacMillan Computer Publishing, which will arrange for its replacement. PLEASE DO NOT RETURN IT TO MICROSOFT CORPORATION. Any product support will be provided, if at all, by MacMillan Computer Publishing. PLEASE DO NOT CONTACT MICROSOFT CORPORATION FOR PRODUCT SUPPORT. End users of this Microsoft program shall not be considered "registered owners" of a Microsoft product and therefore shall not be eligible for upgrades, promotions or other benefits available to "registered owners" of Microsoft products.

Books have a substantial influence on the destruction of the forests of the Earth. For example, it takes 17 trees to produce one ton of paper. A first printing of 30,000 copies of a typical 480-page book consumes 108,000 pounds of paper, which will require 918 trees!

Waite Group Press™ is against the clear-cutting of forests and supports reforestation of the Pacific Northwest of the United States and Canada, where most of this paper comes from. As a publisher with several hundred thousand books sold each year, we feel an obligation to give back to the planet. We will therefore support organizations that seek to preserve the forests of planet Earth.

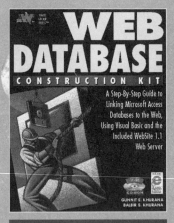

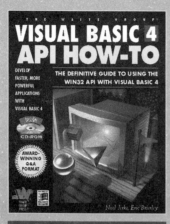

Message from the
Publisher

WELCOME TO OUR NERVOUS SYSTEM

Some people say that the World Wide Web is a graphical extension of the information superhighway, just a network of humans and machines sending each other long lists of the equivalent of digital junk mail.

I think it is much more than that. To me, the Web is nothing less than the nervous system of the entire planet—not just a collection of computer brains connected together, but more like a billion silicon neurons entangled and recirculating electro-chemical signals of information and data, each contributing to the birth of another CPU and another Web site.

Think of each person's hard disk connected at once to every other hard disk on Earth, driven by human navigators searching like Columbus for the New World. Seen this way the Web is more of a super entity, a growing, living thing, controlled by the universal human will to expand, to be more. Yet, unlike a purposeful business plan with rigid rules, the Web expands in a nonlinear, unpredictable, creative way that echoes natural evolution.

We created our Web site not just to extend the reach of our computer book products but to be part of this synaptic neural network, to experience, like a nerve in the body, the flow of ideas and then to pass those ideas up the food chain of the mind. Your mind. Even more, we wanted to pump some of our own creative juices into this rich wine of technology.

TASTE OUR DIGITAL WINE

And so we ask you to taste our wine by visiting the body of our business. Begin by understanding the metaphor we have created for our Web site—a universal learning center, situated in outer space in the form of a space station. A place where you can journey to study any topic from the convenience of your own screen. Right now we are focusing on computer topics, but the stars are the limit on the Web.

If you are interested in discussing this Web site or finding out more about the Waite Group, please send me e-mail with your comments, and I will be happy to respond. Being a programmer myself, I love to talk about technology and find out what our readers are looking for.

Sincerely,

Mitchell Waite

Mitchell Waite, C.E.O. and Publisher

200 Tamal Plaza
Corte Madera, CA 94925
415-924-2575
415-924-2576 fax

Website:
http://www.waite.com/wa
ite

CREATING THE HIGHEST QUALITY COMPUTER BOOKS IN THE INDUSTRY

Waite Group Press

Come Visit
WAITE.COM
Waite Group Press World Wide Web Site

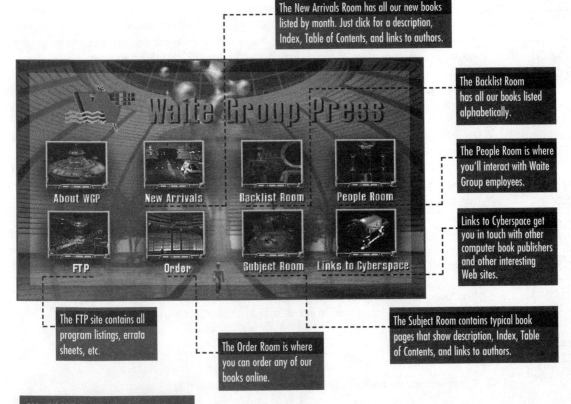

Now find all the latest information on Waite Group books at our new Web site, **http://www.waite.com/waite**. You'll find an online catalog where you can examine and order any title, review upcoming books, and send e-mail to our authors and editors. Our FTP site has all you need to update your book: the latest program listings, errata sheets, most recent versions of Fractint, POV Ray, Polyray, DMorph, and all the programs featured in our books. So download, talk to us, ask questions, on **http://www.waite.com/waite**.

The New Arrivals Room has all our new books listed by month. Just click for a description, Index, Table of Contents, and links to authors.

The Backlist Room has all our books listed alphabetically.

The People Room is where you'll interact with Waite Group employees.

Links to Cyberspace get you in touch with other computer book publishers and other interesting Web sites.

About WGP

New Arrivals

Backlist Room

People Room

FTP

Order

Subject Room

Links to Cyberspace

The FTP site contains all program listings, errata sheets, etc.

The Order Room is where you can order any of our books online.

The Subject Room contains typical book pages that show description, Index, Table of Contents, and links to authors.

World Wide Web:

COME SURF OUR TURF—THE WAITE GROUP WEB

http://www.waite.com/waite
Gopher: gopher.waite.com
FTP: ftp.waite.com

This is a legal agreement between you, the end user and purchaser, and The Waite Group®, Inc., and the authors of the programs contained in the disc. By opening the sealed disc package, you are agreeing to be bound by the terms of this Agreement. If you do not agree with the terms of this Agreement, promptly return the unopened disc package and the accompanying items (including the related book and other written material) to the place you obtained them for a refund.

SOFTWARE LICENSE

1. The Waite Group, Inc. grants you the right to use one copy of the enclosed software programs (the programs) on a single computer system (whether a single CPU, part of a licensed network, or a terminal connected to a single CPU). Each concurrent user of the program must have exclusive use of the related Waite Group, Inc. written materials.

2. The program, including the copyrights in each program, is owned by the respective author and the copyright in the entire work is owned by The Waite Group, Inc., and they are therefore protected under the copyright laws of the United States and other nations, under international treaties. You may make only one copy of the disc containing the programs exclusively for backup or archival purposes, or you may transfer the programs to one hard disk drive, using the original for backup or archival purposes. You may make no other copies of the programs, and you may make no copies of all or any part of the related Waite Group, Inc. written materials.

3. You may not rent or lease the programs, but you may transfer ownership of the programs and related written materials (including any and all updates and earlier versions) if you keep no copies of either, and if you make sure the transferee agrees to the terms of this license.

4. You may not decompile, reverse engineer, disassemble, copy, create a derivative work, or otherwise use the programs except as stated in this Agreement.

GOVERNING LAW

This Agreement is governed by the laws of the State of California.

LIMITED WARRANTY

The following warranties shall be effective for 90 days from the date of purchase: (i) The Waite Group, Inc. warrants the enclosed disc to be free of defects in materials and workmanship under normal use; and (ii) The Waite Group, Inc. warrants that the programs, unless modified by the purchaser, will substantially perform the functions described in the documentation provided by The Waite Group, Inc. when operated on the designated hardware and operating system. The Waite Group, Inc. does not warrant that the programs will meet purchaser's requirements or that operation of a program will be uninterrupted or error-free. The program warranty does not cover any program that has been altered or changed in any way by anyone other than The Waite Group, Inc. The Waite Group, Inc. is not responsible for problems caused by changes in the operating characteristics of computer hardware or computer operating systems that are made after the release of the programs, nor for problems in the interaction of the programs with each other or other software.

THESE WARRANTIES ARE EXCLUSIVE AND IN LIEU OF ALL OTHER WARRANTIES OF MERCHANTABILITY OR FITNESS FOR A PARTICULAR PURPOSE OR OF ANY OTHER WARRANTY, WHETHER EXPRESSED OR IMPLIED.

EXCLUSIVE REMEDY

The Waite Group, Inc. will replace any defective disc without charge if the defective disc is returned to The Waite Group, Inc. within 90 days from date of purchase.

This is the Purchaser's sole and exclusive remedy for any breach of warranty or claim for contract, tort, or damages.

LIMITATION OF LIABILITY

THE WAITE GROUP, INC. AND THE AUTHORS OF THE PROGRAMS SHALL NOT IN ANY CASE BE LIABLE FOR SPECIAL, INCIDENTAL, CONSEQUENTIAL, INDIRECT, OR OTHER SIMILAR DAMAGES ARISING FROM ANY BREACH OF THESE WARRANTIES EVEN IF THE WAITE GROUP, INC. OR ITS AGENT HAS BEEN ADVISED OF THE POSSIBILITY OF SUCH DAMAGES.

THE LIABILITY FOR DAMAGES OF THE WAITE GROUP, INC. AND THE AUTHORS OF THE PROGRAMS UNDER THIS AGREEMENT SHALL IN NO EVENT EXCEED THE PURCHASE PRICE PAID.

COMPLETE AGREEMENT

This Agreement constitutes the complete agreement between The Waite Group, Inc. and the authors of the programs, and you, the purchaser.

Some states do not allow the exclusion or limitation of implied warranties or liability for incidental or consequential damages, so the above exclusions or limitations may not apply to you. This limited warranty gives you specific legal rights; you may have others, which vary from state to state.

MACMILLAN COMPUTER PUBLISHING USA
A VIACOM COMPANY

Technical ----
---- ## Support:

If you need assistance with the information in this book or with a CD/Disk accompanying the book, please access the Knowledge Base on our Web site at **http://www.superlibrary.com/general/support**. Our most Frequently Asked Questions are answered there. If you do not find the answer to your questions on our Web site, you may contact Macmillan Technical Support **(317) 581-3833** or e-mail us at **support@mcp.com**.

SATISFACTION REPORT CARD

Please fill out this card if you wish to know of future updates to *Visual Basic 5 Client/Server How-To,* or to receive our catalog.

SATISFACTION CARD

First Name: _____ **Last Name:** _____

Street Address: _____

City: _____ **State:** _____ **Zip:** _____

E-Mail Address _____

Daytime Telephone: (_____) _____

Date product was acquired: Month _____ **Day** _____ **Year** _____ **Your Occupation:** _____

Overall, how would you rate *Visual Basic 5 Client/Server How-To?*

☐ Excellent ☐ Very Good ☐ Good
☐ Fair ☐ Below Average ☐ Poor

What did you like MOST about this book? _____
_____
_____

What did you like LEAST about this book? _____
_____
_____

Please describe any problems you may have encountered with installing or using the disc: _____
_____

How did you use this book (problem-solver, tutorial, reference...)?
_____

What is your level of computer expertise?
☐ New ☐ Dabbler ☐ Hacker
☐ Power User ☐ Programmer ☐ Experienced Professional

What computer languages are you familiar with? _____
_____

Please describe your computer hardware:
Computer _____ Hard disk _____
5.25" disk drives _____ 3.5" disk drives _____
Video card _____ Monitor _____
Printer _____ Peripherals _____
Sound Board _____ CD-ROM _____

Where did you buy this book?
☐ Bookstore (name): _____
☐ Discount store (name): _____
☐ Computer store (name): _____
☐ Catalog (name): _____
☐ Direct from WGP ☐ Other _____

What price did you pay for this book? _____

What influenced your purchase of this book?
☐ Recommendation ☐ Advertisement
☐ Magazine review ☐ Store display
☐ Mailing ☐ Book's format
☐ Reputation of Waite Group Press ☐ Other

How many computer books do you buy each year? _____

How many other Waite Group books do you own? _____

What is your favorite Waite Group book? _____
_____

Is there any program or subject you would like to see Waite Group Press cover in a similar approach? _____
_____

Additional comments? _____
_____
_____

Please send to: Waite Group Press
200 Tamal Plaza
Corte Madera, CA 94925

☐ **Check here for a free Waite Group catalog**

BEFORE YOU OPEN THE DISK OR CD-ROM PACKAGE ON THE FACING PAGE, CAREFULLY READ THE LICENSE AGREEMENT.

Opening this package indicates that you agree to abide by the license agreement found in the back of this book. If you do not agree with it, promptly return the unopened disk package (including the related book) to the place you obtained them for a refund.

The ActiveX Control Pad is covered by Microsoft's End User License Agreement (EULA). You must agree to the EULA before opening this disk package.